AUDIT & ACCOUNTING GUIDE

Investment Companies

MAY 1, 2012

is edition of the AICPA Audit and Accounting Guide *Investment Companies*, which was originally issued 1981, has been modified by the AICPA staff to include certain changes necessary because of the issuance authoritative pronouncements since the guide was originally issued and other changes necessary to keep e guide current on industry and regulatory matters. The appendix "Schedule of Changes Made to the Text om the Previous Edition" identifies all changes made in this edition of the guide. The changes do *not* include those that might be considered necessary if the guide was subjected to a comprehensive review and revision.

Copyright © 2012 by

American Institute of Certified Public Accountants, Inc. New York, NY 10036-8775

All rights reserved. For information about the procedure for requesting permission to make copies of any part of this work, please e-mail copyright@aicpa.org with your request. Otherwise, requests should be written and mailed to the Permissions Department, AICPA, 220 Leigh Farm Road, Durham, NC 27707-8110.

2 3 4 5 6 7 8 9 0 AAP 1 9 8 7 6 5 4 3 2

ISN 978-1-93735-103-8

Preface

About AICPA Audit and Accounting Guides

This AICPA Audit and Accounting Guide has been developed by the AICPA Investment Companies Guide Task Force to assist management in the preparation of their financial statements in conformity with U.S. generally accepted accounting principles (GAAP) and to assist practitioners in performing and reporting on their audit and attestation engagements.

This guide describes operating conditions and auditing procedures unique to the investment company industry and illustrates the form and content of investment company financial statements and related disclosures.

Because many investment companies are subject to regulation under the Investment Company Act of 1940, rules under that act are discussed extensively in this guide. However, the rules, regulations, practices, and procedures of the investment company industry have changed frequently and extensively in recent years. The independent practitioner should keep abreast of those changes as they occur.

The financial accounting and reporting guidance contained in this guide, when developed by the original task force, was approved by the affirmative vote of at least two-thirds of the members of the Accounting Standards Executive Committee, now the Financial Reporting Executive Committee (FinREC). FinREC is the designated senior committee of the AICPA authorized to speak for the AICPA in the areas of financial accounting and reporting. Conforming updates made to the financial accounting and reporting guidance contained in this guide in years subsequent to the original development are reviewed by select FinREC members, among other reviewers, when applicable.

This guide does the following:

- Identifies certain requirements set forth in the Financial Accounting Standards Board (FASB) *Accounting Standards Codification*™ (ASC).
- Describes FinREC's understanding of prevalent or sole industry practice concerning certain issues. In addition, this guide may indicate that FinREC expresses a preference for the prevalent or sole industry practice, or it may indicate that FinREC expresses a preference for another practice that is not the prevalent or sole industry practice; alternatively, FinREC may express no view on the matter.
- Identifies certain other, but not necessarily all, industry practices concerning certain accounting issues without expressing FinREC's views on them.
- Provides guidance that has been supported by FinREC on the accounting, reporting, or disclosure treatment of transactions or events that are not set forth in FASB ASC.

Accounting guidance for nongovernmental entities included in an AICPA Audit and Accounting Guide is a source of nonauthoritative accounting guidance. As discussed later in this preface, FASB ASC is the authoritative source of U.S. accounting and reporting standards for nongovernmental entities, in addition to guidance issued by the Securities and Exchange Commission (SEC).

AAG-INV

Accounting guidance for governmental entities included in an AICPA Audit and Accounting Guide is a source of authoritative accounting guidance described in category (b) of the hierarchy of GAAP for state and local governmental entities and has been cleared by the Governmental Accounting Standards Board (GASB). AICPA members should be prepared to justify departures from GAAP as discussed in Rule 203, *Accounting Principles* (AICPA, *Professional Standards*, ET sec. 203 par. .01).

AICPA Audit and Accounting Guides also include guidance from the questions and answers section of AICPA *Technical Practice Aids*. These questions and answers are not sources of established authoritative accounting principles as described in FASB ASC, the authoritative source of GAAP for nongovernmental entities. This material is based on selected practice matters identified by the staff of the AICPA's technical hotline and various other bodies within the AICPA and has not been approved, disapproved, or otherwise acted upon by any senior technical committee of the AICPA.

Auditing guidance included in an AICPA Audit and Accounting Guide is recognized as an interpretive publication pursuant to AU section 150, *Generally Accepted Auditing Standards* (AICPA, *Professional Standards*). Interpretive publications are recommendations on the application of Statements on Auditing Standards (SASs) in specific circumstances, including engagements for entities in specialized industries. An interpretive publication is issued under the authority of the Auditing Standards Board (ASB) after all ASB members have been provided an opportunity to consider and comment on whether the proposed interpretive publication is consistent with the SASs. The members of the ASB have found this guide to be consistent with existing SASs.

The auditor should be aware of and consider interpretive publications applicable to his or her audit. If an auditor does not apply the auditing guidance included in an applicable interpretive publication, the auditor should be prepared to explain how he or she complied with the SAS provisions addressed by such auditing guidance.

Attestation guidance included in an AICPA Audit and Accounting Guide is recognized as an attestations interpretive publication as defined in AT section 50, *SSAE Hierarchy* (AICPA, *Professional Standards*). Attestation interpretations are recommendations on the application of Statements on Standards for Attestation Engagements (SSAEs) in specific circumstances, including engagements for entities in specialized industries. Attestation interpretations are issued under the authority of the ASB. The members of the ASB have found the attestation guidance in this guide to be consistent with existing SSAEs.

A practitioner should be aware of and consider attestation interpretations applicable to his or her attestation engagement. If the practitioner does not apply the guidance included in an applicable AICPA Audit and Accounting Guide, the practitioner should be prepared to explain how he or she complied with the SSAE provisions addressed by such attestation guidance.

Purpose and Applicability

Limitations

This guide does not discuss the application of all GAAP, generally accepted auditing standards (GAAS), and Public Company Accounting Oversight Board (PCAOB) standards that are relevant to the preparation and audit of financial statements of investment companies. This guide is directed primarily to those aspects of the preparation and audit of financial statements that are unique to investment companies or those aspects that are considered particularly significant to them.

Recognition

Richard C. Paul, *Chair*
Financial Reporting Executive Committee

Darrel R. Shubert, *Chair*
Auditing Standards Board

Investment Companies Expert Panel (2011–2012)

Robert Fabio, *Chair*
Amy Edwards
Nancy Grimaldi
John T. Hague
John R. Hildebrand
Adeel H. Jivraj
Quintin I. Kevin
Joseph O'Donnell
Brent D. Oswald
Paul Ricci
Paul A. Roselli
Jessica Seidlitz
Winston W. Wilson
Brian Wixted

In addition to the 2011–2012 expert panel listed previously, the AICPA gratefully acknowledges those who reviewed and otherwise contributed to the development of this guide: Jennifer Austin, Michael Barkman, Joe D'Introno, Chad B. Gazzillo, Richard H. Grueter, Mathew Maulbeck, Robert Moynihan, Steve Recor, Krysten Schieltz, John Stomper, Maryna Tully, Kristy Von Ohlen, and Irina Portnoy.

The following AICPA Investment Companies Guide Task Force (1996–2000) originally developed this guide to assist management in the preparation of their financial statements in conformity with GAAP and to assist auditors in auditing and reporting on such financial statements.

Investment Companies Guide Task Force (1999–2000); Investment Companies Committee (1998–1999)

Alan R. Latshaw, *Chair*
Howard Altman
Brian J. Gallagher
Steven Goodbarn
Joseph Grainger, Jr.
Timothy Jacoby
Marie Karpinski
James Francis Mahoney

B. Robert Rubin
David Seymour
Kenneth Stoll
James Yost

Investment Companies Committee (1997–1998)

Alan R. Latshaw, *Chair*
Howard Altman
Brian J. Gallagher
Steven Goodbarn
Joseph Grainger, Jr.
Timothy Jacoby
Marie Karpinski
Steven D. Krichmar
James Francis Mahoney
B. Robert Rubin
David Seymour
Kenneth Stoll
James Yost

Investment Companies Committee (1996–1997)

Steven E. Buller, *Chair*
Joseph A. Carrier
Jerome L. Duffy
Mari B. Ferris
Scott Gilman
Steven N. Kearsley
Alan R. Latshaw
B. Robert Rubin
Andrew B. Shoup
Kevin L. Smith
Dennis F. Wasniewski
John Woodcock, Jr.

AICPA Staff

Teresa Brenan
Technical Manager,
Accounting and Auditing Publications

Keira A. Kraft
Technical Manager,
Accounting and Auditing Publications

Guidance Considered in This Edition

This edition of the guide has been modified by the AICPA staff to include certain changes necessary due to the issuance of authoritative guidance since the guide was originally issued, and other revisions as deemed appropriate. Authoritative guidance issued through May 1, 2012, has been considered in the development of this edition of the guide.

Authoritative guidance that is issued and effective for entities with fiscal years ending on or before May 1, 2012, is incorporated directly in the text of this guide. The presentation of authoritative guidance issued but not yet effective as of May 1, 2012, for entities with fiscal years ending after that same date is being presented differently than in past editions of this guide. This information is being presented as a guidance update, which is a shaded area that contains information on the new guidance and a reference to appendix A, "Guidance Updates," where appropriate. The distinct presentation of this content is intended to aid the reader in differentiating content that may not be effective for the reader's purposes.

This includes relevant guidance issued up to and including the following:

- FASB Accounting Standards Update (ASU) No. 2012-12, *Comprehensive Income (Topic 220): Deferral of the Effective Date for Amendments to the Presentation of Reclassification of Items Out of Accumulated Other Comprehensive Income in ASU No. 2011-05*

- SAS No. 125, *Alert That Restricts the Use of the Auditor's Written Communication*, (AICPA, *Professional Standards*, AU-C sec. 905)

- Interpretation No. 1, "Dating the Auditor's Report on Supplementary Information," of AU section 551, *Supplementary Information in Relation to the Financial Statements as a Whole* (AICPA, *Professional Standards*, AU sec. 9551 par. .01–.04)

- Revised interpretations issued through May 1, 2012, including Interpretation No. 1 of AU section 551

- Statement of Position 09-1, *Performing Agreed-Upon Procedures Engagements That Address the Completeness, Accuracy, or Consistency of XBRL-Tagged Data* (AICPA, *Technical Practice Aids*, AUD sec. 14,440)

- SSAE No. 17, *Reporting on Compiled Prospective Financial Statements When the Practitioner's Independence Is Impaired* (AICPA, *Professional Standards*, AT sec. 301)

- Interpretation No. 1, "Reporting Under Section 112 of the Federal Deposit Insurance Corporation Improvement Act," of AT section 501, *An Examination of an Entity's Internal Control Over Financial Reporting That Is Integrated With an Audit of Its Financial Statements* (AICPA, *Professional Standards*, AT sec. 9501 par. .01–.07)

- PCAOB Auditing Standard No. 15, *Audit Evidence* (AICPA, *PCAOB Standards and Related Rules*, Auditing Standards)

Users of this guide should consider guidance issued subsequent to those items listed previously to determine their effect on entities covered by this guide. In determining the applicability of recently issued guidance, its effective date should also be considered.

The changes made to this edition of the guide are identified in appendix J, "Schedule of Changes Made to the Text From the Previous Edition." The changes do not include all those that might be considered necessary if the guide were subjected to a comprehensive review and revision.

AAG-INV

Applicability of GAAS, the Requirements of the Sarbanes-Oxley Act of 2002, and PCAOB Standards

Audits of the financial statements of *nonissuers* (those entities not subject to the Sarbanes-Oxley Act of 2002 or the rules of the SEC—that is, private entities, generally speaking) are conducted in accordance with GAAS as issued by the ASB, the designated senior committee of the AICPA with the authority to promulgate auditing standards for nonissuers. The ASB develops and issues standards in the form of SASs through a due process that includes deliberation in meetings open to the public, public exposure of proposed SASs, and a formal vote. The SASs and their related interpretations are codified in the AICPA's *Professional Standards*. Paragraph .03 of AU section 150 establishes that an AICPA member's failure to follow ASB standards for audits of nonissuers is a violation of Rule 202, *Compliance With Standards* (AICPA, *Professional Standards*, ET sec. 202 par. .01), of the AICPA Code of Professional Conduct.

For audits of a nonissuer, in accordance with both GAAS and PCAOB standards, Interpretation No. 18, "Reference to PCAOB Standards in an Audit Report on a Nonissuer," of AU section 508, *Reports on Auditing Financial Statements* (AICPA, *Professional Standards*, AU sec. 9508 par. .89–.92), provides reporting guidance applicable to such engagements.

Definition of an *Issuer*

The Sarbanes-Oxley Act of 2002 states that the term *issuer* means an issuer as defined in Section 3 of the Securities Exchange Act of 1934 (Commerce and Trade, U.S. Code [USC] 15, Section 78c) (the 1934 Act), the securities of which are registered under Section 12 of that act (15 USC 78l), or that is required to file reports under Section 15(d) (15 USC 78o[d]), or that files or has filed a registration statement that has not yet become effective under the Securities Act of 1933 (15 USC 77a et seq.), and that it has not withdrawn.

Issuers and other entities, when prescribed by the rules of the SEC (collectively referred to in this guide as *issuers* or *issuer*), and their public accounting firms that must be registered with the PCAOB are subject to the provisions of the Sarbanes-Oxley Act of 2002, implementing SEC regulations, and the rules and standards of the PCAOB, as appropriate. The provisions of the Sarbanes-Oxley Act of 2002, the regulations of the SEC, and the rules and standards of the PCAOB are numerous and not all addressed in this section or guide. The SEC has oversight authority over the PCAOB, including the approval of its rules, standards, and budget.

This guide primarily discusses auditing guidance issued by the ASB that applies to nonissuers. Issuers include registered investment companies and audits of issuers are required to be performed under PCAOB standards. Users should evaluate their audit engagements to determine which auditing standards are applicable.

Guidance for Issuers

Management Assessment of Internal Control

As directed by Section 404 of the Sarbanes-Oxley Act of 2002, the SEC adopted final rules requiring companies subject to the reporting requirements of the 1934 Act, other than registered investment companies and certain other entities, to include in their annual reports a report from management on the company's internal control over financial reporting. Business development companies, however, do not fall within the scope exception contained in Section 405 and are required to include a report from management on the company's internal control over financial reporting. The SEC rules clarify that management's assessment and report is limited to internal control over financial reporting. The SEC's definition of *internal control* encompasses the Committee of Sponsoring Organizations of the Treadway Commission (COSO) definition, but the SEC does not mandate that the entity use COSO as its criteria for judging effectiveness.

As established by Rule 12b-2 of the 1934 Act, the auditor's attestation for large accelerated and accelerated filers is currently effective. However, Section 404(c) of the Sarbanes-Oxley Act of 2002 provides that an attestation report of a registered public accounting firm on internal control over financial reporting is not required for an issuer that is neither an accelerated filer nor a large accelerated filer.

Guidance for Auditors

The Sarbanes-Oxley Act of 2002 mandates a number of requirements concerning auditors of issuers, including mandatory registration with the PCAOB, and the setting of auditing standards, inspections, investigations, disciplinary proceedings, prohibited activities, partner rotation, and reports to audit committees, among others. The PCAOB continues to establish rules and standards implementing provisions of the Sarbanes-Oxley Act of 2002 concerning the auditors of issuers.

Applicability of GAAS and PCAOB Standards

Subject to SEC oversight, Section 103 of the Sarbanes-Oxley Act of 2002 authorizes the PCAOB to establish auditing and related attestation, quality control, ethics, and independence standards to be used by registered public accounting firms in the preparation and issuance of audit reports for entities subject to the Sarbanes-Oxley Act of 2002 or the rules of the SEC. Accordingly, public accounting firms registered with the PCAOB are required to adhere to all PCAOB standards in the audits of issuers and other entities when prescribed by the rules of the SEC.

For those entities not subject to the Sarbanes-Oxley Act of 2002 or the rules of the SEC, the preparation and issuance of audit reports remain governed by GAAS, as issued by the ASB.

References to Professional Standards

In citing GAAS and their related interpretations, references use section numbers within the codification of currently effective SASs and not the original statement number, as appropriate. For example, SAS No. 54, *Illegal Acts by Clients*, is referred to as AU section 317, *Illegal Acts by Clients* (AICPA, *Professional Standards*). In those sections of the guides that refer to specific auditing standards of the PCAOB, references are made to the AICPA's *PCAOB Standards and Related Rules* publication.

AICPA.org Website

The AICPA encourages you to visit the new website at www.aicpa.org and the new Financial Reporting Center at www.aicpa.org/frc. The Financial

AAG-INV

Reporting Center was created to support members in the execution of high quality financial reporting. Whether you are a financial statement preparer or a member in public practice, this center provides exclusive member-only resources for the entire financial reporting process, and provides timely and relevant news, guidance and examples supporting the financial reporting process, including accounting, preparing financial statements and performing compilation, review, audit, attest or assurance and advisory engagements. Certain content on the AICPA's websites referenced in this guide may be restricted to AICPA members only.

Select Recent Developments Significant to This Guide

ASB's Clarity Project

To address concerns about the clarity, length, and complexity of its standards, the ASB has made a significant effort to clarify the SASs. The ASB established clarity drafting conventions and undertook to redraft all of its SASs in accordance with those conventions, which include the following:

- Establishing objectives for each clarified SAS
- Including a definitions section, where relevant, in each clarified SAS
- Separating requirements from application and other explanatory material
- Numbering application and other explanatory material paragraphs using an A- prefix and presenting them in a separate section that follows the requirements section
- Using formatting techniques, such as bulleted lists, to enhance readability
- Including, when appropriate, special considerations relevant to audits of smaller, less complex entities within the text of the clarified SAS
- Including, when appropriate, special considerations relevant to audits of governmental entities within the text of the clarified SAS

In addition, as the ASB redrafted standards for clarity, it also converged the standards with the International Standards on Auditing (ISAs), issued by the International Auditing and Assurance Standards Board. Among other improvements, the clarified auditing standards specify more clearly the objectives of the auditor and the requirements with which the auditor has to comply when conducting an audit in accordance with GAAS.

With the release of SAS Nos. 117–120 and Nos. 122–125, the project is near completion. As of the date of this guide, the only SASs remaining to be clarified are the following:

- SAS No. 59, *The Auditor's Consideration of an Entity's Ability to Continue as a Going Concern,* as amended (AICPA, *Professional Standards*, AU sec. 341)
- SAS No. 65, *The Auditor's Consideration of the Internal Audit Function in an Audit of Financial Statements* (AICPA, *Professional Standards*, AU sec. 322)

Note that SAS No. 122, *Statements on Auditing Standards: Clarification and Recodification* (AICPA, *Professional Standards*), withdraws SAS No. 26, *Association With Financial Statements*, as amended, from *Professional Standards*.

SAS Nos. 122–125 will be effective for audits of financial statements for periods ending on or after December 15, 2012. Refer to the individual AU-C sections in the codification of the SASs for specific effective date language. Early adoption is not permitted.

As part of the clarity project, the resulting clarified auditing standards are numbered based on equivalent ISAs and are located in "AU-C" sections within AICPA *Professional Standards*. This is a change from the "AU" section numbers where the extant standards are located. "AU-C" is a temporary identifier being used to avoid confusion with references to existing "AU" sections, which remain effective through 2013. The "AU-C" identifier will revert to "AU" in 2014, by which time the clarified auditing standards become fully effective for all engagements. Note that AU-C section numbers for clarified SASs with no equivalent ISAs have been assigned new numbers. The ASB believes that this recodification structure will aid firms and practitioners that use both ISAs and GAAS.

All auditing interpretations corresponding to a SAS have been considered in the development of a clarified SAS and incorporated accordingly and have been withdrawn by the ASB except for certain interpretations that the ASB has retained and revised to reflect the issuance of SAS No. 122. A listing of the retained interpretations can be found in AU-C exhibit B, *Retained Interpretations* (AICPA, *Professional Standards*). The effective date of the revised interpretations aligns with the effective date of the corresponding clarified SAS.

This AICPA Audit and Accounting Guide will be fully conformed to the clarified auditing standards in a subsequent edition. In the interim, readers are encouraged to refer to appendix B, "Guidance Updates—Clarified Auditing Standards," in this guide for information on the changes to the extant auditing standards found to be substantive (that is, likely to affect the firms' audit methodology and engagements because they contain substantive or other changes) or primarily clarifying (that is, intended to explicitly state what may have been implicit in the extant standards).

Summary of Significant Differences Between PCAOB and AICPA Risk Assessment Standards

On August 5, 2010, the PCAOB issued Release No. 2010-004, *Auditing Standards Related to the Auditor's Assessment of and Response to Risk and Related Amendments to PCAOB Standards* (AICPA, *PCAOB Standards and Related Rules*, Select PCAOB Releases). This release includes eight auditing standards (collectively referred to as the PCAOB risk assessment standards), as adopted by the PCAOB. The eight standards, which were approved by the SEC on December 23, 2010, are as follows:

1. Auditing Standard No. 8, *Audit Risk* (AICPA, *PCAOB Standards and Related Rules*, Auditing Standards)

2. Auditing Standard No. 9, *Audit Planning* (AICPA, *PCAOB Standards and Related Rules*, Auditing Standards)

3. Auditing Standard No. 10, *Supervision of the Audit Engagement* (AICPA, *PCAOB Standards and Related Rules*, Auditing Standards)
4. Auditing Standard No. 11, *Consideration of Materiality in Planning and Performing an Audit* (AICPA, *PCAOB Standards and Related Rules*, Auditing Standards)
5. Auditing Standard No. 12, *Identifying and Assessing Risks of Material Misstatement* (AICPA, *PCAOB Standards and Related Rules*, Auditing Standards)
6. Auditing Standard No. 13, *The Auditor's Responses to the Risks of Material Misstatement* (AICPA, *PCAOB Standards and Related Rules*, Auditing Standards)
7. Auditing Standard No. 14, *Evaluating Audit Results* (AICPA, *PCAOB Standards and Related Rules*, Auditing Standards)
8. Auditing Standard No. 15

The release also includes conforming amendments to other interim standards related to the PCAOB risk assessment standards. The effective date of the PCAOB risk assessment standards is for audits of financial statements of issuers with fiscal periods beginning on or after December 15, 2010.

In general, the PCAOB risk assessment standards are consistent with the AICPA SASs related to risk assessment (the AICPA risk assessment standards). Where differences exist, they are primarily due to the PCAOB

    a. addressing audits of financial statements in conjunction with audits of effectiveness of internal control (often referred to as integrated audits). The AICPA risk assessment standards only address audits of financial statements.

    b. presenting content in standards different than the AICPA risk assessment standards. For example, the PCAOB

        i. incorporated fraud risk assessment procedures into the PCAOB risk assessment standards,

        ii. created Auditing Standard No. 10 to separately address supervision of the audit engagement,

        iii. created Auditing Standard No. 14 to separately address the evaluation of audit results, and

        iv. moved content related to other audit areas such as analytical review procedures and audits of group financial statements.

The PCAOB risk assessment standards are not as voluminous as the AICPA risk assessment standards because the PCAOB standards do not contain as much application guidance as do the AICPA risk assessment standards. Appendix 11, "Comparison of the Objectives and Requirements of the Accompanying PCAOB Auditing Standards with the Analogous Standards of the International Auditing and Assurance Standards Board and the Auditing Standards Board of the American Institute of Certified Public Accountants," of the release contains a more detailed comparison of the differences between the PCAOB risk assessment standards and the AICPA risk assessment standards.

International Financial Reporting Standards

The AICPA governing council voted in May 2008 to recognize the International Accounting Standards Board (IASB) as an accounting body for purposes of establishing international financial accounting and reporting principles. This amendment to ET appendix A, *Council Resolution Designating Bodies to Promulgate Technical Standards* (AICPA, *Professional Standards*), of the AICPA's Code of Professional Conduct gives AICPA members the option to use International Financial Reporting Standards (IFRS) as an alternative to GAAP. As a result, private entities in the United States can prepare their financial statements in accordance with GAAP as promulgated by FASB; an other comprehensive basis of accounting, such as cash- or tax-basis; or IFRS, among others. However, domestic issuers are currently required to follow GAAP and rules and regulations of the SEC. In contrast, foreign private issuers may present their financial statements in accordance with IFRS as issued by the IASB without a reconciliation to GAAP, or in accordance with non-IFRS home-country GAAP reconciled to GAAP as permitted by Form 20-F.

The growing acceptance of IFRSs as a basis for U.S. financial reporting could represent a fundamental change for the U.S. accounting profession. Acceptance of a single set of high quality accounting standards for worldwide use by public companies has been gaining momentum around the globe for the past few years. See appendix I, "International Financial Reporting Standards," of this guide for a discerning look at the status of convergence with IFRS in the United States and the important issues that accounting professionals need to consider now.

TABLE OF CONTENTS

Chapter		Paragraph
1	The Investment Company Industry	.01-.41
	Kinds of Investment Companies	.03-.08
	History	.09-.10
	Definition and Classification	.11-.16
	Organizations Providing Services to Investment Companies	.17-.24
	The Investment Adviser	.18-.19
	The Distributor	.20-.21
	The Custodian	.22
	The Transfer Agent	.23
	The Administrator	.24
	Regulation	.25-.32
	Financial Reporting to Shareholders	.33-.34
	Accounting Rules and Policies	.35-.36
	Effective Date of Transactions	.37-.38
	Other Rules	.39-.41
2	Investment Accounts	.01-.258
	Investment Objectives and Policies	.02-.03
	Operations and Controls	.04-.18
	Recordkeeping Requirements	.04-.05
	Custody of Securities	.06-.08
	Accounting for Segregated Accounts	.09-.11
	Routine Investment Procedures	.12-.18
	Accounting	.19-.163
	Net Asset Value Per Share	.19-.24
	Basis of Recording Securities Transactions	.25-.31
	Valuing Investments	.32-.43
	Fair Value Determination When the Volume or Level of Activity Has Significantly Decreased	.44-.49
	Valuation Techniques	.50-.58
	Present Value Techniques	.59-.61
	The Fair Value Hierarchy	.62-.66
	Application of Fair Value Measurements to Assets	.67-.68
	Application of Fair Value Measurements to Liabilities	.69-.74
	Investments in Entities That Calculate Net Asset Value per Share	.75-.89
	Determining Costs and Realized Gains and Losses	.90-.98
	Accounting for Investment Income	.99-.117
	Defaulted Debt Securities	.118-.119
	Accounting for Expenditures in Support of Defaulted Debt Securities	.120-.123
	Lending of Portfolio Securities	.124-.126

Chapter		Paragraph
2	Investment Accounts—continued	
	Accounting for Derivatives	.127-.129
	Accounting for Foreign Investments	.130-.163
	Understanding the Entity and Its Environment and Assessing the Risks of Material Misstatement	.164-.165
	Auditing Procedures	.166-.214
	Principal Audit Objectives	.174
	Obtaining an Understanding of the Entity and Its Environment, Including Internal Control	.175-.180
	Examination of Transactions and Detail Records	.181-.214
	Consideration of Fraud in a Financial Statement Audit	.215-.258
	The Importance of Exercising Professional Skepticism	.217
	Discussion Among Engagement Personnel Regarding the Risks of Material Misstatement Due to Fraud	.218-.219
	Examples of Fraud Risk Factors	.220
	Obtaining the Information Needed to Identify the Risks of Material Misstatement Due to Fraud	.221-.225
	Identifying Risks That May Result in a Material Misstatement Due to Fraud	.226-.242
	Assessing the Identified Risks After Taking Into Account an Evaluation of the Entity's Programs and Controls That Address the Risks	.243-.248
	Responding to the Results of the Assessment	.249-.250
	Evaluating Audit Evidence	.251-.252
	Responding to Misstatements That May Be the Result of Fraud	.253-.256
	Communicating About Possible Fraud to Management, the Audit Committee, and Others	.257
	Documenting the Auditor's Consideration of Fraud	.258
3	Financial Instruments	.01-.67
	Money Market Investments	.02-.03
	Repurchase Agreements	.04-.05
	Reverse Repurchase Agreements	.06
	U.S. Government Securities (Treasury Bills, Notes, and Bonds)	.07
	Municipal Notes and Bonds	.08-.11
	Insured Portfolios	.12
	To Be Announced Securities	.13-.17
	When-Issued Securities	.18-.19
	Synthetic Floaters	.20-.21
	Mortgage-Backed Securities	.22-.24
	Adjustable Rate Mortgages	.25
	Collateralized Mortgage Obligations	.26
	Real Estate Mortgage Investment Conduits	.27

Table of Contents

Chapter		Paragraph
3	**Financial Instruments—continued**	
	High-Yield Securities	.28-.29
	Payment-in-Kind Bonds	.30-.31
	Step Bonds	.32-.33
	Put and Call Options	.34-.37
	Warrants	.38-.39
	Loan Commitments	.40-.41
	Standby Commitments	.42
	Commodity and Financial Futures Contracts	.43-.47
	Forward Contracts	.48
	Forward Exchange Contracts	.49-.50
	Interest Rate, Currency, and Equity Swaps and Swaptions	.51-.55
	Credit Derivatives	.56-.57
	Structured Notes or Indexed Securities	.58-.61
	Short Positions	.62
	Mortgage Dollar Rolls	.63-.67
4	**Capital Accounts**	.01-.62
	Operations and Controls	.02-.21
	Distributors	.02-.07
	Orders to Purchase or Redeem	.08-.12
	Cancellation of Orders	.13
	Shareholder Transactions	.14-.21
	Accounting for Capital Share Transactions and Distributions	.22-.30
	Equalization	.28-.30
	Auditing Procedures	.31-.62
	Principal Audit Objectives	.31
	Obtaining an Understanding of the Entity and Its Environment, Including Internal Control	.32-.38
	Examination of Transactions and Detail Records	.39-.49
	Other Auditing Matters	.50-.54
	Reports on Controls at Outside Service Organizations	.55-.62
5	**Complex Capital Structures**	.01-.94
	Operational and Accounting Issues	.02-.29
	Multiple-Class Funds	.02-.17
	Master-Feeder Funds	.18-.21
	Funds of Funds	.22-.25
	Other Considerations for Investments in Nonpublicly Traded Investees	.26-.29
	Financial Statement Presentation	.30-.61
	Multiple-Class Funds	.31-.38

Chapter		Paragraph
5	**Complex Capital Structures**—continued	
	Master-Feeder Funds	.39-.52
	Funds of Funds	.53-.61
	Audit Considerations	.62-.88
	Planning	.66-.68
	Control Environment	.69-.72
	Investment in Master Fund and Income-Gain Allocations	.73-.76
	Other Transactions	.77
	Prospectus Restrictions and Compliance	.78-.81
	Tax Qualifications and Compliance	.82-.85
	Financial Statements	.86-.88
	Funds of Funds	.89-.94
	Control Environment	.91-.94
6	**Taxes**	.01-.130
	Overview	.01-.02
	Financial Statements and Other Matters	.03-.15
	Income Tax Expense	.03-.11
	Federal Income Tax Provisions Affecting Investment Accounts	.12
	Foreign Withholding Taxes	.13
	Financial Statement Presentation	.14
	Diversification of Assets	.15
	Taxation of RICs	.16-.130
	General Discussion of the Taxation of RICs	.16
	Taxation of a RIC's Taxable Income and Net Capital Gains	.17-.23
	Taxation of Shareholder Distributions	.24-.42
	Excess Reported Amounts	.43
	Qualification Tests	.44-.56
	Variable Contracts	.57-.62
	Distribution Test	.63-.78
	Excise Tax on Undistributed Income	.79-.91
	Computation of Taxable Income and Gains	.92-.121
	Offshore Funds	.122-.126
	Small Business Investment Companies	.127-.130
7	**Financial Statements of Investment Companies**	.01-.194
	Comparative Financial Statements	.05-.07
	Consolidation	.08-.20
	Reporting Financial Position	.21-.95
	Reporting of Fully Benefit-Responsive Investment Contracts	.26-.28
	Schedule of Investments	.29-.44
	Assets	.45-.66

Chapter		Paragraph
7	**Financial Statements of Investment Companies—continued**	
	Liabilities	.67-.79
	Fair Value Disclosures	.80-.84
	Fair Value Option	.85-.87
	Net Assets	.88-.95
	Statement of Operations	.96-.129
	Investment Income	.97-.100
	Expenses	.101-.113
	Net Investment Income	.114
	Net Realized Gain or Loss From Investments and Foreign Currency Transactions	.115-.118
	Net Increase (Decrease) in Unrealized Appreciation or Depreciation on Investments and Translation of Assets and Liabilities in Foreign Currencies	.119-.120
	Net Increase From Payments by Affiliates and Net Gains (Losses) Realized on the Disposal of Investments in Violation of Restrictions	.121-.126
	Net Realized and Unrealized Gain or Loss From Investments and Foreign Currency	.127
	Net Increase or Decrease in Net Assets From Operations	.128
	Reporting of Fully Benefit-Responsive Investment Contracts	.129
	Statement of Changes in Net Assets	.130-.134
	Subsequent Events	.135-.140
	Statement of Cash Flows	.141-.152
	Financial Highlights	.153-.166
	Other Disclosure Requirements	.167-.169
	Fully Benefit-Responsive Investment Contract Disclosures	.169
	Interim Financial Statements	.170-.173
	Illustrative Financial Statements of Investment Companies	.174-.185
	Illustrations of Calculations and Disclosures When Reporting Expense and Net Investment Income Ratios	.186
	Illustration of Calculation and Disclosure When Reporting the Internal Rate of Return	.187
	Illustration of Calculation and Disclosure When Reporting the Total Return Ratio	.188
	Condensed Schedule of Investments	.189
	Illustrations of Nonregistered Investment Partnerships Schedule of Investments	.190
	Presentation of Fully Benefit-Responsive Investment Contracts	.191
	Illustration of Deferred Fees	.192
	Disclosure—Fair Value Measurements of Investments in Certain Entities That Calculate Net Asset Value per Share (or its Equivalent)	.193

Chapter		Paragraph
7	**Financial Statements of Investment Companies—continued**	
	Illustration of Reporting Financial Highlights, Net Asset Value Per Share, Shares Outstanding, and Share Transactions When Investors in Unitized Nonregistered Funds Are Issued Individual Classes or Series of Shares	.194
8	**Other Accounts and Considerations**	.01-.58
	Investment Advisory (Management) Fee	.01-.03
	Expenses	.04-.10
	Distribution Expenses	.11-.21
	Minutes	.22
	Organization and Offering Costs	.23-.36
	Unusual Income Items	.37
	Form N-SAR	.38-.42
	Business Combinations	.43-.53
	Diversification of Assets	.54
	Auditor's Responsibility for Other Information in Documents Containing Audited Financial Statements	.55-.58
9	**Unit Investment Trusts**	.01-.22
	Fixed-Income and Equity UITs	.05-.13
	Taxes	.14-.15
	Illustrative Financial Statements	.16-.22
10	**Variable Contracts—Insurance Entities**	.01-.64
	Separate Accounts	.01-.06
	History	.07-.10
	Product Design	.11-.22
	Contracts in the Payout (Annuitization) Period	.23-.25
	SEC Registration	.26-.31
	Auditing Considerations	.32-.38
	Taxation of Variable Contracts	.39-.56
	Illustrative Financial Statements	.57-.64
11	**Independent Auditor's Reports and Client Representations**	.01-.42
	Reports on Financial Statements of Nonregistered Investment Companies	.02-.12
	Report Prepared in Accordance With Standards Established by the American Institute of Certified Public Accountants	.12
	Reports on Financial Statements of Registered Investment Companies	.13-.21

Contents

Table of Contents

Chapter		Paragraph
11	**Independent Auditor's Reports and Client Representations—continued**	
	Reports for a Registered Investment Company That Issues a Condensed Schedule of Investments in the Financial Statements Provided to Shareholders	.20-.21
	Report Prepared in Accordance With PCAOB Standards	.21
	Report on Examinations of Securities Pursuant to Rules 17f-1 and 17f-2 Under the 1940 Act	.22
	Report on Examinations of Securities Pursuant to Rule 206(4)-2 Under the Investment Advisers Act of 1940	.23-.31
	Report on Internal Control Required by the SEC Under Form N-SAR	.32
	Report for a Closed-End Fund Security Agency Rating	.33
	Reports on Processing of Transactions by a Transfer Agent	.34-.36
	Reporting Pursuant to the Global Investment Performance Standards	.37-.40
	Illustrative Representation Letter—XYZ Investment Company	.41-.42

Appendix

A	Guidance Updates
B	Guidance Updates—Clarified Auditing Standards
C	Mapping and Summarization of Changes—Clarified Auditing Standards
D	Venture Capital, Business Development Companies, and Small Business Investment Companies
E	Computation of Tax Amortization of Original Issue Discount, Market Discount, and Premium
F	Illustrative Financial Statement Presentation for Tax-Free Business Combinations of Investment Companies
G	Illustrations for Separately Calculating and Disclosing the Foreign Currency Element of Realized and Unrealized Gains and Losses
H	References to AICPA *Technical Practice Aids*
I	International Financial Reporting Standards
J	Schedule of Changes Made to the Text From the Previous Edition
Glossary	

Chapter 1

The Investment Company Industry

1.01 An *investment company*,[1] as described in Financial Accounting Standards Board (FASB) *Accounting Standards Codification* (ASC) 946-10-05-2 and as used in this guide, generally is an entity that pools shareholders' funds to provide the shareholders with professional investment management.[2] This term does not match the legal definition of an investment company in the federal securities laws. Typically, an investment company sells its capital shares to investors; invests the proceeds, mostly in securities, to achieve its investment objectives; and distributes to its shareholders the net income earned on its investments and net gains realized on the sale of its investments.

1.02 The investment company industry is highly specialized; intensely competitive; and subject to specific governmental regulation, special tax treatment, and public scrutiny. Accordingly, before starting an engagement to audit an investment company's financial statements, an auditor should become familiar with the entity's business, its organization, and operating characteristics

---

[1] The Financial Accounting Standards Board (FASB) and the International Accounting Standards Board (IASB) have a joint project on their agenda with the objective of providing comprehensive guidance for addressing whether an entity is an investment company and providing measurement requirements for an investment company's investments. Both boards released exposure drafts in the second half of 2011. In addition to entities regulated under the Investment Company Act of 1940 (the 1940 Act), the boards decided an investment company is an entity which meets the following criteria:

    a. The only substantive activities are investing in multiple investments for returns from capital appreciation, investment income (such as dividends or interest), or both.

    b. The express business purpose of the entity is investing to provide returns from capital appreciation, investment income (such as dividends or interest), or both.

    c. Unit ownership.

    d. Pooling of funds.

    e. The investments are managed, and their performance is evaluated on a fair value basis.

    f. The entity is a reporting entity. The entity can be, but does not need to be a legal entity.

Further, FASB would require an investment company to consolidate its controlling financial interest in another investment company as well as controlling interests in an investment property entity. FASB has decided that an investment company must measure all other investments, including interests in investment companies and investment property entities that the investment company can significantly influence, at fair value with changes recognized in net income. The IASB decided that an investment entity must measure all investments in entities that it controls (including other investment companies) at fair value through profit or loss and that investment entities would be exempt from consolidation requirements. Readers should remain alert for updates on this joint project, which can be accessed from the Technical Plan and Project Updates page at www.fasb.org.

[2] On June 11, 2007, Statement of Position (SOP) 07-1, *Clarification of the Scope of the Audit and Accounting Guide* Investment Companies *and Accounting by Parent Companies and Equity Method Investors for Investments in Investment Companies*, was issued. The intent of SOP 07-1 was to provide guidance for determining whether an entity was within the scope of this guide. The SOP also addressed specific accounting issues as they relate to entities referred to in this guide. In response to the SOP, FASB issued FASB Staff Position (FSP) SOP 07-1-1, *Effective Date of AICPA Statement of Position 07-1*, which delays the effective date of SOP 07-1 indefinitely. FSP SOP 07-1-1 amends paragraph 56 of SOP 07-1 to (*a*) delay the effective date of the SOP and (*b*) prohibit adoption of the SOP for an entity that has not early adopted the SOP before issuance of the final FSP, which occurred on February 14, 2008. An entity that early adopted SOP 07-1 before issuance of the final FSP would be permitted but not required to continue to apply the provisions of the SOP. An entity that did not early adopt SOP 07-1 would not be permitted to adopt the SOP. The effective date of FSP SOP 07-1-1 is December 15, 2007.

    Given the possibility of early adopters continuing to follow the guidance provided in SOP 07-1, SOP 07-1 was included in FASB *Accounting Standards Codification* (ASC) 946, *Financial Services—Investment Companies*, but has been labeled as indefinitely delayed "Pending Content." FASB ASC 946-10-65-1 explains the circumstances and all indefinitely delayed pending content from SOP 07-1 is linked to this paragraph.

AAG-INV 1.02

and the industry's terminology; legislation; and, if applicable, the securities and income tax rules and regulations.

Kinds of Investment Companies

1.03 Several kinds of investment companies exist. FASB ASC 946-10-05-3 identifies management investment companies, unit investment trusts (UITs), common (collective) trust funds, investment partnerships, certain separate accounts of life insurance companies, and offshore funds. Management investment companies may be open-end funds, usually known as mutual funds; closed-end funds; special purpose funds; venture capital investment companies; small business investment companies (SBICs); and business development companies (BDCs). Investment companies are organized as corporations (in the case of mutual funds, under the laws of certain states that authorize the issuance of common shares redeemable on demand of individual shareholders), common law trusts (sometimes called business trusts), limited partnerships, limited liability investment partnerships and companies, and other more specialized entities such as separate accounts of insurance companies that are not in themselves entities at all except in the technical definition of the Investment Company Act of 1940 (the 1940 Act).

1.04 The auditing procedures discussed in this guide apply to most investment companies.[3] As stated by FASB ASC 946-10-15-2, the accounting principles discussed in this guide and in FASB ASC 946, *Financial Services—Investment Companies*, apply to all investment companies. Consistent with FASB ASC 946-10-15-3, this guide does not apply to real estate investment trusts, which have some of the attributes of investment companies but are covered by other U.S. generally accepted accounting principles (GAAP).[4]

1.05 Mutual funds and closed-end companies registered with the Securities and Exchange Commission (SEC) under the 1940 Act are common forms of investment companies and are required to follow many rules and regulations prescribed by the SEC.

1.06 As explained by FASB ASC 946-10-15-2, an investment company (other than a separate account of an insurance company, as defined in the 1940

---

[3] This guide primarily discusses auditing guidance issued by the Auditing Standards Board that applies to nonissuers. Issuers are defined by Section 3 of the Securities Exchange Act of 1934 (the 1934 Act) and include registered investment companies. Audits of issuers are required to be performed under Public Company Accounting Oversight Board standards. Users should evaluate their audit engagements to determine which auditing standards are applicable.

[4] In October 2011, FASB released the proposed Accounting Standards Update (ASU) *Real Estate—Investment Property Entities (Topic 973)*, which defines an *investment property entity* and includes only those entities within its scope. An investment property entity is one which (*a*) has substantially all of its business activities comprised of investing in a real estate property or properties; (*b*) has an express business purpose to invest in a real estate property or properties for total return, including an objective to realize capital appreciation (for example, through disposal of its real estate property or properties); (*c*) has unit ownership; (*d*) pools investors funds and has investors that are not related to the parent (if there is a parent) and those investors, in aggregate, hold a significant ownership interest in the entity; and (*e*) is a reporting entity though it does not need to be a legal entity. Investment properties acquired by an investment property entity would initially be measured at transaction price, including transaction costs, and subsequently measured at fair value with all changes in fair value recognized in net income. An investor in an investment property entity would be permitted to use the net asset value (NAV) practical expedient in FASB ASC 820, *Fair Value Measurement*, to estimate the fair value of its investment if investors in the investment property entity would transact at NAV per share. Readers should remain alert for updates on this project, which can be accessed from the Technical Plan and Project Updates page at www.fasb.org.

AAG-INV 1.03

Act) must be a separate legal entity to be within the scope of the guide and FASB ASC 946. Though many aspects of venture capital investment companies, including SBICs and BDCs, differ from aspects of other types of investment companies, the provisions of this guide and FASB ASC 946 generally apply. (Venture capital investment companies are discussed in appendix D, "Venture Capital, Business Development Companies, and Small Business Investment Companies," of this guide.)

1.07 The specialized accounting principles in this guide should be applied to an investment made after March 27, 2002, only if the investment is held by an investment company that is a separate legal entity. Investments acquired prior to March 28, 2002, or those acquired after March 27, 2002, pursuant to an irrevocable binding commitment that existed prior to March 28, 2002, should continue to be accounted for in accordance with the entity's existing policy for such investments.

1.08 As explained by FASB ASC 946-10-15-2, investment companies discussed in FASB ASC 946 and this guide are required to report their investment assets at fair value, as defined by FASB ASC 820, *Fair Value Measurement*, and have the following attributes:

   a. *Investment activity*. The investment company's primary business activity involves investing its assets, usually in the securities of other entities not under common management, for current income, appreciation, or both.
   b. *Unit ownership*. Ownership in the investment company is represented by units of investments, such as shares of stock or partnership interests, to which proportionate shares of net assets can be attributed.
   c. *Pooling of funds*. The funds of the investment company's owners are pooled to avail owners of professional investment management.
   d. *Reporting entity*. The investment company is the primary reporting entity.

History

1.09 The concept of investment companies originated in England in 1868 with the formation of the Foreign & Colonial Government Trust. Its purpose was to provide investors of moderate means with the same advantages as those of more affluent investors (that is, to diminish risk by spreading investments over many different securities). Massachusetts Investors Trust, the first mutual fund, was organized in 1924.

1.10 The investment company industry has changed considerably since its origin and has attracted insurance companies, brokerage firms, conglomerates, banks, and others as sponsors to perform advisory or distribution services. Initially, the industry was characterized by one- or two-person managements, relatively simple investment techniques, and rudimentary sales practices. Today, investment techniques are more sophisticated, and selling practices are more creative and aggressive. For example, in the 1970s, tax-exempt and money market funds came into use; in the 1980s, funds entered foreign markets; in the 1990s, funds entered the derivative security markets, which necessitated new investment expertise and increasingly sophisticated data processing capability; and in the 2000s, funds expanded their derivative activity investing in asset-backed securities and the like, which can be difficult to value. Fund organization structures have become more complex in recent years with the introduction of multiple class funds, series funds and master-feeder funds. These funds potentially provide greater flexibility to multiple markets such as retail customers (who may be charged a front-end load, level load, or contingent deferred sales load) and institutions.

Definition and Classification

1.11 The term *mutual fund* is the popular name for an open-end management investment company (open-end company) as defined in the 1940 Act. An open-end company stands ready to redeem its outstanding shares, based on net asset value, at any time. Shares of an open-end company routinely are not traded. Most open-end companies offer their shares for sale to the public continuously, although they are not required to do so. The price at which the shares of mutual funds are sold is determined by dividing each fund's net assets, stated at fair value, by the number of its shares outstanding; the resulting net asset value per share may be increased by a sales charge, called a *load*, that provides commissions to the underwriter and dealer. Funds whose shares are sold at net asset value without a sales charge or that have a 12b-1 plan (see paragraph 8.11 of this guide) that charges not more than 0.25 percent of average net assets per year (that is, 25 basis points) are known as no-load funds. Some funds or classes of shares of funds may charge contingent deferred sales loads or fees when shares are redeemed.

1.12 Unlike an open-end company, a closed-end management investment company generally does not offer to redeem its outstanding capital shares on a daily basis. However, some closed-end funds do make periodic repurchase offers for their outstanding shares. Those closed-end funds that repurchase their shares on a periodic basis at stated intervals are commonly known as interval funds. The outstanding shares of closed-end funds that are not considered to be interval funds are usually exchange listed and traded on the open market at prices that generally differ from net asset value per share, although market prices are influenced by net asset value per share reported regularly in financial publications. Most closed-end companies offer their shares to the public in discrete offerings, although some closed-end funds offer their shares on a continuous basis. Closed-end investment companies may offer their shareholders a dividend reinvestment plan. Investments are valued, and net asset value per share is calculated, using the same method as mutual funds.

1.13 Investment companies are grouped according to their primary investment objectives (for example, income, growth, balanced, money market, or tax exempt or combinations of those groups). The kinds of investments made by those funds reflect their stated objectives. For example, growth funds invest almost exclusively in securities with appreciation potential, whereas money market funds invest solely in short-term debt instruments.

1.14 Investment companies registered with the SEC under the 1940 Act are classified as diversified investment companies or nondiversified investment companies.[5] According to the 1940 Act, shareholder approval is required for an investment company registered as diversified to become nondiversified but not

---

[5] Section 5(b) of the 1940 Act.

for a company registered as nondiversified to become diversified. If a nondiversified company operates as a diversified company, it may change back to a nondiversified company within three years of the change to a diversified company without shareholder approval, provided that its registration statement has not been amended.

1.15 Closed-end investment companies include venture capital investment companies, SBICs and BDCs. A venture capital investment company is a closed-end company whose primary investment objective is capital growth and whose capital is invested at above-average risk to form or develop companies with new ideas, products, or processes. An SBIC is an entity that provides equity capital, long-term loans, or both to small businesses; is licensed by the Small Business Administration (SBA) under the Small Business Investment Act of 1958; and may also be registered under the 1940 Act or be a subsidiary of another company. It may obtain financing from the federal government in the form of subordinated debentures based on the amount of its equity capital and the amount of its funds invested in venture-type investments. A BDC is a form of a publicly traded vehicle registered under the 1940 Act.

1.16 A UIT is an investment company organized under a trust indenture or similar instrument and registered under the 1940 Act. A UIT has no board of directors or trustees and issues only redeemable units, each representing an undivided interest in a group of securities (such as corporate debentures or municipal debt) or a unit of specified securities or securities of a single issuer (such as shares of a particular mutual fund). UITs that provide a formal method of accumulating mutual fund shares under a periodic payment plan or a single payment plan are commonly known as contractual plans.

Organizations Providing Services to Investment Companies

1.17 Most mutual funds and many closed-end investment companies have no employees; however, registered investment companies are required to have a chief compliance officer who may or may not be compensated wholly or partially by the investment company. Portfolio management, recording of shares, administration, recordkeeping, distribution, and custodianship are examples of significant activities that are performed for such funds and companies. These activities generally are performed by organizations other than the investment company (for example, an investment adviser [manager or general partner], a transfer agent, an administrator, a recordkeeping agent, a principal underwriter [distributor], and a custodian). The distributor is often a separate division or subsidiary company of the investment adviser or administrator. The use of agents to perform accounting or other administrative functions does not relieve the investment company's officers and directors or trustees of the responsibility for overseeing the maintenance and reliability of accounting records and the fairness of financial reports. Mutual funds are governed by a board of directors or trustees that has certain responsibilities, as dictated by the 1940 Act. The board's responsibilities are highlighted throughout this guide.

The Investment Adviser

1.18 The investment adviser or manager generally provides investment advice, research services, and certain administrative services under a contract, commonly referred to as the investment advisory agreement, that provides for an annual fee, which is often based on a specified percentage of average net assets. The fee schedules of many contracts provide for reduced percentage rates on net assets in excess of specified amounts (break points). Other contracts have performance fee schedules that provide for a basic fee percentage plus a bonus, or less a penalty, based on a comparison of the fund's performance to a market index specified in the investment advisory agreement. If a performance fee schedule is used, the potential bonus for performance better than the index must be matched by an equivalent potential penalty for poor performance.[6] Such incentive fee arrangements need not be symmetrical if a fund is not registered with the SEC for sale to the general public. Occasionally, the investment advisory fee may be based wholly or partly on the investment income earned by the fund. Administrative services may be provided by an entity other than the investment adviser under a separate administrative agreement.

1.19 The investment advisory agreement for a registered investment company generally should be approved by the initial shareholder (usually the investment adviser) and thereafter by a majority of the directors or trustees who are not interested persons, as defined by the 1940 Act. Continuation of the contract beyond two years requires annual approval by a vote, cast in person (usually construed to mean face to face, not by telephone), of (*a*) the board of directors or trustees or a majority of the outstanding shares and (*b*) directors or trustees who are not interested persons.[7] Significant modifications to the investment advisory agreement after a registered investment company begins its operations would be subject to approval by the board of directors or trustees and often are also subject to approval by a vote of a majority of the fund's outstanding shares.

The Distributor

1.20 The distributor, also known as an underwriter of the fund's shares, acts as an agent or a principal and sells the fund's shares as a wholesaler through independent dealers or as a retailer through its own sales network. Shares are sold at net asset value, and often a sales charge is added for the underwriter's and dealers' commissions. Other common commission structures use Rule 12b-1 fees or contingent deferred sales loads. The amount of sales charges, including asset-based sales charges (that is, Rule 12b-1 fees) and contingent deferred sales loads, is regulated by the Financial Industry Regulatory Authority. Additionally, Rule 22d-1 of the 1940 Act permits funds to set variable sales charges. A no-load fund may or may not have a distributor.[8]

---

[6] Securities and Exchange Commission (SEC) Final Rule Release No. 7484 under the 1940 Act.

[7] Sections 2(a)(19), 15(a), and 15(c) of the 1940 Act.

[8] The SEC's proposed rule Release No. IC-29367, *Mutual Fund Distribution Fees; Confirmations*, was issued in July 2010 and would replace Rule 12b-1 with Rule 12b-2 under the 1940 Act. The proposed framework would continue to allow funds to give investors choices regarding how and when to pay for sales charges, improve disclosure designed to enhance investor understanding of those charges, limit the cumulative sales charges that each investor pays (no matter how they are imposed), and eliminate uncertainties associated with current requirements while providing a more appropriate role for fund directors. Under the proposal, funds would be required to comply with the amendments for all shares issued after the compliance date of the new rules. However, a five year grandfathering period would exist after the compliance date for share classes issued prior to the compliance date and would deduct fees pursuant to the existing Rule 12b-1, after which those shares would be required to be converted or exchanged into a class that does not deduct an ongoing sales charge. Readers are encouraged to remain alert for developments.

The Investment Company Industry 7

1.21 Requirements for approval of a distributor's contract by the registered investment company's board of directors or trustees are similar to those described for the investment adviser. If the distributor's contract is approved by the board, shareholder approval is not necessary. Many registered investment companies adopt distribution plans under Rule 12b-1 permitting the use of fund assets to pay for distribution expenses. One special requirement of Rule 12b-1 is that members of the board of directors or trustees who are not interested persons, as defined, must approve the plan each year, and the plan can be terminated with 60 days' notice.

The Custodian

1.22 Custody of the fund's cash and portfolio securities is usually entrusted to a bank or, less frequently, a member of a national securities exchange that is responsible for their receipt, delivery, and safekeeping. Custody arrangements and the auditor's responsibilities are discussed in detail in chapters 2, "Investment Accounts," and 11, "Independent Auditor's Reports and Client Representations," of this guide.

The Transfer Agent

1.23 The fund's transfer agent, which may be a bank or a private company, issues, transfers, redeems, and accounts for the fund's capital shares. Sometimes the investment adviser, distributor, or another related party performs those functions. Section 17A of the Securities Exchange Act of 1934 (the 1934 Act) requires certain transfer agents to register with the SEC and prescribes standards of performance concerning their duties.

The Administrator

1.24 The fund may engage an administrator that may or may not be independent of the investment adviser. Occasionally, if the investment adviser is engaged as the administrator, the investment adviser will engage an independent subadministrator. In all of these instances, the administrator would be responsible for performing or overseeing administrative tasks such as the filing of reports with the SEC and the IRS, the registering of fund shares, corresponding with shareholders, and the determination of the fund's compliance with various restrictions. The administrator may also maintain the fund's books and records, assist with calculating the net asset value on a periodic basis, and assist with certain aspects of investment valuation, among other tasks.

Regulation

1.25 Generally, an investment company is required to register with the SEC under the 1940 Act if one of the following is true:[9]

   a. Its outstanding securities, other than short-term paper, are beneficially owned by more than 100 persons (including the number of beneficial security holders of a company owning 10 percent or more of the voting securities of the investment company).[10]

   b. It is offering or proposing to offer its securities to the public.

---

[9] Otherwise, the company is exempted from registration by Section 3(c)(1) of the 1940 Act.
[10] Section 3(c)(7) of the 1940 Act allows certain companies to have an unlimited number of qualified investors.

AAG-INV 1.25

1.26 The Division of Investment Management of the SEC is responsible for reviewing such registrations. The investment company's shares are also registered under the Securities Act of 1933 (the 1933 Act) and with various state securities commissions before being offered for sale to the public. After registering with the SEC under the 1940 Act or both acts, the company must report periodically to its shareholders and the SEC. Accordingly, auditors of investment companies should be familiar with the following acts:

   a. The 1933 Act, often referred to as the disclosure act, regulates the contents of prospectuses and similar documents and is intended to assure that potential investors receive adequate information to make reasonably informed investment decisions.

   b. The 1934 Act regulates securities brokers and dealers, stock exchanges, and the trading of securities in the securities markets. The distributor must register as a broker-dealer under the act. The act also governs disclosures in proxy materials used to solicit the votes of shareholders of an investment company, as does the 1940 Act. According to Section 17(A)(c) of the 1934 Act, if the fund's transfer agent is not a bank, it should be registered under the 1934 Act.

   c. The 1940 Act regulates the investment company industry and provides rules and regulations that govern the fiduciary duties and other responsibilities of an investment company's management. BDCs elect to be regulated under certain sections of this act.

   d. The Investment Advisers Act of 1940 requires persons paid to render investment advice to individuals or institutions, including investment companies, to register and regulates their conduct and contracts.

   e. The Small Business Investment Act of 1958 authorizes the SBA to provide government funds under regulated conditions to SBICs licensed under this act.

   f. The Small Business Investment Incentive Act of 1980 amended the 1940 Act by, among other things, allowing certain closed-end companies to elect to be regulated as BDCs under less rigorous Sections 54–65 of the 1940 Act.

1.27 The federal securities laws are supplemented by formal rules and regulations; the SEC also issues a variety of other releases and statements, including its financial reporting releases and releases under the 1933 Act, the 1934 Act, the 1940 Act, and the Investment Advisers Act of 1940. Many of these rules and regulations apply to the investment company industry. The auditor must be familiar with them and the SEC registration and reporting forms. The forms illustrate the kind of information that generally should be made available to the public, the restrictions imposed on operations, the most applicable statutory provisions, and the statistics that generally should be accumulated and maintained. The forms include the following:

   a. Form N-8A, the notification of registration under the 1940 Act, discloses the company's name and address and certain other general information. An investment company is registered under the act after it has filed the form, which is brief, and it is then subject to all the act's requirements and standards. The information in the form need not be audited.

The Investment Company Industry

b. Form N-1A, the registration statement of open-end companies under the 1940 Act and the 1933 Act, describes in detail the company's objectives, policies, management, investment restrictions, and similar matters. The initial filing of Form N-1A generally requires audited financial statements, which typically are limited to a "seed capital" statement of assets and liabilities. (Form N-2 is the comparable registration statement for closed-end management investment companies.) Part A of Form N-1A includes the information required in a fund's prospectus and states that the prospectus should clearly disclose the fundamental characteristics and investment risks of the fund using concise, straightforward, and easy to understand language. When an investment company incurs organization costs that are not paid for and assumed by the fund sponsor, a "seed statement of operations" for the period from the organization date to the date of the statement of assets and liabilities for seed capital is also required (see chapter 8, "Other Accounts and Considerations," of this guide). The subsequent filing of posteffective amendments to the registration statement on Form N-1A is discussed in paragraph 1.28.

c. Form N-SAR, a reporting form used for semiannual and annual reports by all registered investment companies (other than BDCs) registered under the 1940 Act, is divided into four sections, and only certain investment companies need to complete each section. The sections pertain to open-end and closed-end management investment companies, SBICs, or UITs. The report provides current information and demonstrates compliance with the 1940 Act. The annual report filed by a management investment company must be accompanied by a report on the company's internal control over financial reporting from a registered public accounting firm (see paragraph 11.32 of this guide for an example of that report).

d. Form N-CSR, under which a registered investment company files its annual and semiannual shareholder reports together with the certifications of principal executive and financial officers required by Rule 30a-2 of the 1940 Act. The form also provides for disclosure of other information relating to the investment company's code of ethics, audit committee financial expert, principal accountant fees and services, internal control over financial reporting, evaluation of disclosure controls and procedures, and (for closed-end funds) proxy-voting policies. Registered investment companies that include a summary portfolio schedule of investments in reports to shareholders file complete portfolio schedules for the second and fourth fiscal quarters on Form N-CSR. SBICs registered on Form N-5 and UITs are not required to file Form N-CSR.

e. Form N-Q, under which a registered investment company, other than an SBIC registered on Form N-5, files its complete portfolio schedules (the same schedules of investments that are required in Form N-CSR) for the first and third fiscal quarters under the 1934 Act and the 1940 Act. According to the acts, the form must be signed and certified by the principal executive and financial officers and also provides for disclosure of information relating to the investment company's evaluation of disclosure controls and procedures, and internal control over financial reporting. According

AAG-INV 1.27

to Sections 4 and 26 of the 1940 Act, UITs are not required to file Form N-Q.

f. Form N-MFP is filed by money market funds subject to Rule 2a-7 of the 1940 Act and reports the following items with respect to each portfolio security held on the last business day of the prior month:

   i. The name of the issuer
   ii. The title of the issue, including the coupon or yield designated by the fund; the credit ratings given by each nationally rated statistical rating organization (NRSRO); and whether each security is first tier, second tier, unrated, or no longer eligible
   iii. The Committee on Uniform Securities Identification Procedures, or CUSIP, number
   iv. The category of investment (for example, Treasury debt, government agency debt, asset backed commercial paper, structured investment vehicle note, repurchase agreement)
   v. The NRSROs that are utilized
   vi. The maturity date as determined under Rule 2a-7 of the 1940 Act, taking into account the maturity shortening provisions of Rule 2a-7(d) of the 1940 Act
   vii. The final legal maturity date, taking into account any maturity date extensions that may be effected at the option of the issuer
   viii. Whether the instrument has certain enhancement features
   ix. The principal amount
   x. The current amortized cost value
   xi. The percentage of the money market fund's assets invested in the security
   xii. Whether the security is an illiquid security (as defined in amended Rule 2a-7[a][19] of the 1940 Act)

   Form N-MFP also requires funds to report information about the fund, including information about the fund's risk characteristics such as the dollar-weighted average maturity of the fund's portfolio and its seven-day gross yield. Money market funds also must report on Form N-MFP the market-based values of each portfolio security and the fund's market-based net asset value per share, with separate entries for values that do and do not take into account any capital support agreements into which the fund may have entered.

g. Form N-PX, reports the investment company's proxy voting record for each matter relating to a portfolio security considered at a shareholder meeting held during the 12-month period ending June 30.

h. Form 13F, a quarterly securities inventory of an institutional investment manager (including an investment company) that has either investment discretion or voting power over more than $100 million in securities that are admitted to trading on a national securities exchange or the automated quotation system of a registered

The Investment Company Industry 11

securities association. This form is usually filed in composite for an investment adviser of multiple clients, including the combined holdings of investment companies and other clients.

i. Schedule 13G and annual amendments, each as of December 31 to be filed by the following February 14, concern possession of either investment discretion or voting power over more than 5 percent of a class of equity securities of a publicly owned company, provided that the interests were acquired in the ordinary course of business and not with the purpose or effect of influencing control; if the provision is not applicable, disclosures of changes in holdings must be made promptly on Schedule 13D. Such reports are usually filed in composite form for an investment adviser of multiple clients, including the combined holdings of investment companies and other clients.

j. Form N-3 is the registration statement for variable annuity separate accounts registered as management investment companies under the 1940 Act and the 1933 Act. The form contains information and financial statements similar to the kind found in Form N-1A and information about the insurance contract and sponsoring insurance company, including financial statements of the sponsor.

k. Form N-4 is the registration statement for variable annuity separate accounts registered as UITs under the 1940 Act and the 1933 Act. Information supplied in Form N-4 is similar to the information presented in Form N-1A.

l. Form N-1 is the registration statement for variable life insurance separate accounts registered as management investment companies under the 1940 Act and the 1933 Act.

m. Form N-6 is the form for insurance company separate accounts that are registered as UITs and that offer variable life insurance policies.

n. Forms N-8B-2 and S-6 are the forms for all UITs except those variable annuity and variable life separate accounts registered on Forms N-4 and N-6, respectively, under the 1940 Act and the 1933 Act.

o. Form N-5, the registration statement for SBICs, which are also licensed under the Small Business Investment Act of 1958, is a dual-purpose form registering SBICs under both the 1933 Act and the 1940 Act. The form contains the same kind of information and audited financial statements as required by Forms N-1A and N-2 for management investment companies.

p. Form N-14 is the statement for registration of securities issued by investment companies and BDCs in business combination transactions under the 1933 Act. The form contains information about the companies involved in the transaction, historical financial statements, and pro forma financial statements.

1.28 Information in a currently effective prospectus generally should be updated for significant events that have occurred since the effective date. Prospectuses of mutual funds offering their shares for sale are updated at least annually. Posteffective amendments on Form N-1A, including updated audited financial statements and a complete schedule of investments (if not

AAG-INV 1.28

included within the financial statements), must be filed and become effective under the 1933 Act and the 1940 Act within 16 months after the end of the period covered by the previous audited financial statements if the fund is to continue offering its shares.

1.29 Registration statements and reports filed by open-end and closed-end companies (other than SBICs) on various forms include financial highlights, usually for the preceding 5 years, as described in the instructions to Form N-1A (see footnote 27 to paragraph 11.14 regarding auditing of financial highlights on Form N-1A), and for the preceding 10 years as described in the instructions to Form N-2 (with at least the most recent 5 years audited).

1.30 The form and content of financial statements required in registration statements are governed by Regulation S-X. Articles 6 and 12 of Regulation S-X deal specifically with registered investment companies. (SBICs are covered in Article 5, but they follow the same fair value accounting model as do other investment companies.) Registration statements and Forms N-SAR and N-CSR are filed using the SEC's Electronic Data Gathering Analysis and Retrieval, or EDGAR, System.

1.31 In January 2009, the SEC issued Final Rule Release No. 33-9002, *Interactive Data to Improve Financial Reporting*, which became effective in April 2009 and requires entities to file financial statement information in an interactive data format using eXtensible Business Reporting Language (XBRL). However, the new rules did not include any investment company that is registered under the 1940 Act or any BDC (as defined in Section 2[a][48] of that act) because the standard list of tags for investment companies is under development. Additionally, the implementation of this rule allows registered investment companies to participate under the voluntary program of filing in XBRL.

1.32 In February 2009, the SEC issued Final Release No. IC-28617, *Interactive Data for Mutual Fund Risk/Return Summary*, which requires open-end companies (mutual funds) to provide the "Risk and Return Summary" section of their prospectuses (to the SEC and on their websites) in interactive data format using XBRL. This rule has a compliance date of January 1, 2011.[11,12] The existing voluntary program is being modified to only allow for voluntary participation by mutual funds with respect to financial statement information. Therefore, the voluntary program will continue after the compliance date for the financial statements of investment companies that are registered under the 1940 Act, BDCs, and other entities that report under the 1934 Act and prepare their financial statements under Article 6 of Regulation S-X.

Financial Reporting to Shareholders

1.33 The 1940 Act and the related rules and regulations specify the financial statements and the timing of reports required to be submitted to shareholders and the SEC.[13] According to the act and the related rules, reports

---

[11] SEC Regulation S-T addresses the liability for an interactive data file; however, these liability provisions are only applicable through October 31, 2014. At that point an interactive data file will be subject to the same liability provisions as the related official filing.

[12] The SEC published a preparer's guide to assist in using the eXtensible Business Reporting Language (XBRL) US Mutual Fund Risk/Return Summary Taxonomy and another document that explains how the SEC's rendering engine transforms XBRL instances into HTML output for display in a Web browser. Both documents can be accessed from http://xbrl.sec.gov.

[13] Rules under Section 30(d) of the 1940 Act.

containing those financial statements must be submitted to shareholders and the SEC at least semiannually; annual reports must contain audited financial statements. Financial statements included in such reports contain

- a statement of assets and liabilities and a detailed schedule of investments or a statement of net assets. The SEC, under Regulation S-X, permits a registered investment company to include in its reports to shareholders a summary portfolio schedule of investments, provided that the complete portfolio schedule is filed with the SEC on Form N-CSR semiannually and provided to shareholders free of charge. Regulation S-X also exempts money market funds from including a portfolio schedule in reports to shareholders provided that information is filed with the SEC on Form N-CSR semiannually and provided to shareholders upon request free of charge. (Despite this exemption, GAAP does require a condensed portfolio. See paragraphs 7.29–.30 of this guide for further guidance.)
- a statement of operations.
- a statement of changes in net assets.

In addition to the basic financial statements, financial highlights (see paragraph 7.153 of this guide) should be presented either as a separate schedule or within the notes to the financial statements. For an investment company that issues multiple classes of shares, the schedule of financial highlights would need to reflect, at a minimum, the performance of the class of shares that is addressed in the auditor's report. Financial statements for investment companies are discussed and illustrated in chapter 7, "Financial Statements of Investment Companies," of this guide.

1.34 Funds also may be required to present a statement of cash flows if they do not meet the conditions specified in FASB ASC 230-10-15-4.[14]

Accounting Rules and Policies

1.35 Rules under Section 31 of the 1940 Act prescribe the accounting records that an investment company must maintain and the periods for which they must be retained. Those rules require maintenance of journals, general and subsidiary ledgers, and memorandum records that are subject to examination by representatives of the SEC during periodic and special examinations.

1.36 The accounting policies followed by investment companies result from the companies' role as conduits for the funds of investors interested in investing as a group. Furthermore, the investment company policies are supplemented by the rules and regulations issued under the various acts administered by the SEC and the SBA. Some unique policies are described in more detail in the following chapters.

---

[14] In October 2011, FASB issued a proposed ASU, *Technical Corrections*, which would change the conditions for an investment company to be exempted from providing a statement of cash flows. The proposed ASU deleted the conditions for substantially all of the entity's investments to be highly liquid and carried at market value; these were replaced with the conditions for substantially all of the entity's investments to be carried at fair value and classified as level 1 or level 2 measurements in accordance with FASB ASC 820. Readers should remain alert for developments on this topic, which can be accessed from the Technical Plan and Project Updates page at www.fasb.org.

Effective Date of Transactions

1.37 FASB ASC 946-320-25 explains that when accounting for security purchases and sales, for financial reporting purposes, an investment company is to record transactions as of the trade date (the date on which the company agrees to purchase or sell the securities), so that the effects of all securities trades entered into by or for the account of the investment company to the date of a financial report are included in the financial report. Investment companies record dividend income on the ex-dividend date, not the declaration, record, or payable date, because on the ex-dividend date, the quoted market price of listed securities and other market-traded securities tends to be affected by the exclusion of the dividend declared. Also, investment companies record liabilities for dividends to shareholders on the ex-dividend or ex-distribution date, not the declaration date as other corporations do, because mutual fund shares are purchased and redeemed at prices equal to or based on net asset value. Investors purchasing shares between the declaration and ex-dividend dates are entitled to receive the dividend, whereas investors purchasing shares on or after the ex-dividend date are not entitled to the dividend.

1.38 However, Rule 2a-4 of the 1940 Act permits registered investment companies to record security transactions as of one day after the trade date for purposes of determining net asset value.

Other Rules

1.39 The 1934 Act specifies the records that must be maintained by the principal underwriter for the fund, the period for which the records must be preserved, and the reports that the principal underwriter must file with the SEC. The records are subject to examination by representatives of the SEC.[15] Once during each calendar year, each principal underwriter is required by Section 17 of the 1934 Act (as are other brokers and dealers) to file audited financial statements. The AICPA Audit and Accounting Guide *Brokers and Dealers in Securities* provides additional discussion.

1.40 Section 19 and Rule 19a of the 1940 Act specify the kind of notice to shareholders that should accompany distributions from sources other than accumulated undistributed income determined in accordance with good accounting practice (or net income for the current or preceding fiscal year), describing the source of such distributions. That notice must indicate clearly the portion of the payment (per share of outstanding capital stock) made from net investment income or accumulated undistributed net investment income, realized gains, and accumulated undistributed net realized gains on the sales of securities and capital. Rule 19a-1(e) further requires that "the source or sources from which a dividend is paid shall be determined (or reasonably estimated) to the close of the period as of which it is paid without giving effect to such payment."

1.41 Section 32(a) of the 1940 Act requires that the independent auditor reporting on financial statements of an investment company be selected annually by a majority of directors or trustees who are not interested persons at a meeting held no more than 30 days before or after the commencement of the investment company's fiscal year or before the annual meeting of stockholders

---

[15] Rules 17a-4 and 17a-5 of the 1934 Act.

in that year. Additionally, if the investment company is organized in a jurisdiction that does not require annual shareholder meetings and the investment company does not hold a meeting in a given year and is part of a complex of related investment companies that do not share a common fiscal year, the independent auditor may be selected by the directors or trustees at a meeting held either within 30 days before or within the first 90 days after the commencement of that company's fiscal year. The directors' or trustees' selection must be submitted to the stockholders for ratification during any year in which an annual meeting of stockholders is held, unless the appointment of the auditors is approved by an audit committee solely comprising independent directors or trustees, and the audit committee maintains a charter in an easily accessible place. The employment of the accountant is conditioned upon the right of the investment company to terminate such employment without any penalty by a vote of the outstanding shares of the investment company. If the independent auditor resigns or is unable to carry out the engagement, the disinterested directors or trustees may appoint a successor.[16]

---

[16] Section 32(a), Rule 32a-3, and Rule 32a-4 of the 1940 Act.

Chapter 2

Investment Accounts

2.01 As stated by Financial Accounting Standards Board (FASB) *Accounting Standards Codification* (ASC) 946-320-05-2, an investment company's securities portfolio typically comprises substantially all its net assets. Portfolio securities produce income and expense from dividends and interest, and changes in fair values of securities while they are owned or held short by the fund.

Investment Objectives and Policies

2.02 The composition of an investment company's portfolio is primarily a function of the company's investment objectives and strategy to achieve them. An investment company discloses the investment objectives adopted by its management and the strategies adopted to achieve them in its charter or partnership agreement and documents such as registration statements, prospectuses, or offering circulars. Restrictions, statutory or otherwise, are also disclosed. Those restrictions may include specific limitations or outright prohibitions of transactions in real estate, commodities or commodity contracts, and property other than securities. Other restrictions may include limitations on investing in unregistered securities; making short sales of securities; underwriting securities of other issuers; acquiring securities of other investment companies; or using leveraging techniques, such as margin accounts, bank borrowing, and transactions in options and futures.

2.03 An investment company may also specify the kinds of investments, such as bonds, preferred stocks, convertible securities, common stocks, warrants, or options, in which it may invest and the proportion of its total assets that may be invested in each kind of security. Specific limitations relate to the following:

- The percentage of the investment company's assets that it may invest in the securities of an issuer or in issuers of a specific country, geographic region, or industry
- The percentage of voting securities of an issuer that it may acquire
- Investments in companies for the purpose of control
- The risk profile of the portfolio (for example, restrictions on the allocation of assets between domestic and foreign securities, the percentage of assets invested in illiquid or emerging market securities, or the level of investment in derivative instruments)

Operations and Controls

Recordkeeping Requirements

2.04 The Investment Company Act of 1940 (the 1940 Act) prescribes minimum accounting records for registered investment companies.[1] Section 31 of the 1940 Act and rules under that section require investment records for all registered investment companies to include the following:

---

[1] Section 31 of the Investment Company Act of 1940 (the 1940 Act) and rules under that section.

- Journals or other records of original entry that show all securities purchases and sales, receipts and deliveries of securities, and collections and payments of cash for securities transactions
- A securities record or ledger showing the unit, quantity, price, and aggregate cost separately for each portfolio item and transaction as of the trade date
- A record for each portfolio item of all trading orders for purchase, sale, sell short or cover short by, or on behalf of, the investment company and the action on each order

The books and records of registered investment companies are subject to the retention and inspection requirements set forth in rules under the 1940 Act.[2]

2.05 If any records required by the rules are maintained by an agent, such as a custodian or transfer agent, the registered investment company should obtain the agent's written agreement to make the records available on request and to preserve them for the required periods.

Custody of Securities

2.06 An investment company's securities are usually held in the custody of a bank, which, for registered investment companies, must have prescribed minimum aggregate capital, surplus, and undivided profits.[3] A member firm of a national securities exchange or a central securities system registered with the Securities and Exchange Commission (SEC) also may serve as custodian. To use a member of a national securities exchange as custodian, a registered investment company must initially obtain the approval of a majority of its board of directors or trustees. The 1940 Act and the related rules require that securities held in custody by a member of a national securities exchange be inspected at various times by the registered investment company's auditor and that the auditor issue a report thereon to the SEC.[4] Investment companies may also enter into subcustodial agreements, usually to provide a local custody function for investment in foreign securities. The nature of these agreements can vary regarding whether the principal custodian does or does not assume responsibility for the subcustodian's actions. (See also the discussion in paragraph 2.163 relating to foreign custodian arrangements and in paragraphs 2.177–.182 relating to the auditor's procedures with respect to custodians.)

2.07 Registered investment companies are required to file copies of their custodial agreements with the SEC. Significant provisions of such agreements deal with the following:

- Physical and book segregation of securities in custody
- Denying custodians the power to assign, hypothecate, pledge, or otherwise encumber or dispose of any securities except in acting at the direction and for the account of the registered investment company
- Immunity of such securities to liens asserted by a custodian
- The right of the SEC and the company's independent auditor to inspect the securities at any time[5]

---

[2] Section 31b of the 1940 Act.
[3] Sections 2(a)(5), 17(f), and 26(a) of the 1940 Act.
[4] Rule 17f-1 of the 1940 Act.
[5] Rule 17f-1 of the 1940 Act.

2.08 An investment company may retain custody of its securities by depositing them for safekeeping in a vault or other depository maintained by a bank or company whose functions and physical facilities are supervised by federal or state authorities. The 1940 Act and the related rules require all securities determined to be held in safekeeping, either by a registered investment company or an affiliated bank as a custodian, to be inspected at various times by the registered investment company's independent auditor.[6] The deposited securities are required to be physically segregated and are subject to withdrawal only by duly authorized persons under specified conditions.

Accounting for Segregated Accounts

2.09 Certain investment transactions may involve a registered investment company's issuance of a *senior security*, as defined under Section 18 of the 1940 Act. Section 18 also contains restrictions on the issuance of senior securities. Generally, a senior security represents an indebtedness of the investment company (for example, leverage), including certain transactions under which the investment company enters into a contractual purchase or delivery obligation (for example, futures and written options on securities). The SEC does not raise the issue of compliance with Section 18 with respect to certain transactions if a registered investment company designates certain assets in a segregated account, either with the custodian or in its accounting records, as "cover" for indebtedness. Such assets consist of cash or securities, as permitted by the SEC (that is, that meet the liquidity guidelines specified by the SEC), and they may be replaced only by other similar assets.[7] According to SEC Release No. 10666 under the 1940 Act, securities maintained in such segregated accounts should be valued using an appropriate methodology for those securities. The determination of whether a senior security has been issued or adequately covered is, at times, complex and may require the involvement of legal counsel.

2.10 An investment company using a bank or member of a national securities exchange as custodian of its securities may agree to have qualifying securities deposited in a clearing agency, such as a central securities system, that is registered with the SEC. Clearing agencies use the book entry shares method of accounting for securities transfers rather than methods based on the physical movement of the securities. Most investment companies' portfolio securities that qualify are now held by clearing agencies (for example, The Depository Trust Company) through arrangements with the investment companies' custodians instead of being held by the custodians in a physically issued form. Investment companies or their custodians may also use the Federal Reserve's book entry system as a depository for U.S. and federal agency securities. Special rules apply to the use of central securities systems and book entry systems.[8]

2.11 If a registered investment company uses a bank as custodian for its securities, the proceeds from sales of such securities and other cash assets, except for minor amounts in checking or petty cash accounts approved by the

---

[6] Rule 17f-2 of the 1940 Act.

[7] Securities and Exchange Commission (SEC) Release No. 10666 under the 1940 Act, as modified by a no-action letter to Merrill Lynch Asset Management, L.P., on July 2, 1996, and a letter from the SEC Division of Investment Management Chief Accountant to Investment Company Chief Financial Officers on November 7, 1997.

[8] Rule 17f-4 of the 1940 Act.

AAG-INV 2.11

board of directors or trustees, are required to be kept in the bank's custody.[9] SEC regulations also permit the maintenance of cash balances with futures commission merchants solely for the purpose of clearing daily activity in futures contracts and related options.[10]

Routine Investment Procedures

2.12 Although the overall direction of the investment activities of an investment company is the responsibility of its board of directors or trustees or general partner, the board typically delegates the routine operating and investment decisions to an investment committee; a portfolio manager; or, as occurs in most situations, an investment adviser. Investment decisions are communicated by the investment company's adviser or the adviser's employees who place orders with brokers. An investment company's registration statement or offering circular indicates its policies on selecting brokers and using affiliates to execute trades. A well-designed system of controls for investment transactions generally shall include the procedures described in the following paragraphs.

2.13 A registered investment company is required by Rule 31a-1 of the 1940 Act to document, among other things, the placement of a securities order in an internal record that shows the person who authorized and placed the order, the security, the number of shares or the principal amount ordered, the price or price range, the date and time that the order was entered and executed, the commission rate or amount (or other compensation paid), the broker selected, and the reason for the selection. Executed transactions are routinely confirmed electronically or by telephone, and confirmations are followed by electronic or written advices containing all information pertinent to the trades. The advices for money market instruments ordered through a bank often consist of bank debit or credit memorandums.

2.14 An investment company generally should notify the custodian promptly of each securities transaction and issue detailed instructions to receive or deliver securities and collect or disburse cash. Those instructions ordinarily should include the name of the broker, the description and quantity of the security, the trade and settlement dates, and the net amount of cash to be collected or disbursed. New York Stock Exchange (NYSE) Rule 387 requires the electronic depository confirmation-affirmation system (also known as Broker ID System) to be used to effect securities transactions on a cash-on-delivery or delivery-versus-payment (DVP) basis. The instructions ordinarily should be signed by one or more authorized representatives of the investment company whose signatures are on file with the custodian; if instructions are given by telephone or electronically, procedures should be established to ensure proper authorization.

2.15 As advices confirming trades are received, they should be reviewed promptly for conformity of terms; clerical accuracy; and proper application of commission rates, including volume discounts or negotiated rates, as applicable, and should be compared with the internal records established when the orders were placed.

2.16 Investment companies almost always require receipt of cash for securities delivered by the custodian to settle sales of portfolio investments.

---

[9] Final Rule Release Nos. 6863 and 7164 under the 1940 Act.
[10] Rule 17f-6 under the 1940 Act.

Similarly, the custodian pays on a DVP basis. In certain countries, however, there is no DVP standard. Unless otherwise instructed, the custodian rejects a transaction if either the number of shares or settlement amount determined by the broker does not agree exactly with the written instructions previously authorized by the investment company.

2.17 The custodian notifies the investment company promptly of cash settlements and receipts or deliveries of securities. Settlement dates vary based on the kind of security traded, from same-day settlement to four weeks or more. On receipt of such notifications, the investment company ordinarily should compare them against its records to identify discrepancies. Fails to receive or fails to deliver generally should be identified on the settlement date and followed up promptly.

2.18 The custodian issues periodic statements listing all receipts and deliveries of securities and related collections and disbursements of cash. Securities on hand and the cash balance at the end of the period may also be provided. An investment company generally should reconcile promptly the custodian's statements with its books and records and ordinarily should initiate timely follow-up procedures on reconciling items. The investment company generally should be satisfied with the adequacy of the custodian's procedures and controls that relate to functions carried out on its behalf, especially procedures and controls for receipt, delivery, and safekeeping of securities.

Accounting

Net Asset Value Per Share

2.19 Virtually all open-end investment companies and many closed-end investment companies prepare daily price make-up sheets computing net asset value per share[11] each day that the NYSE conducts trading activity. Rule 22c-1(b) of the 1940 Act establishes customary U.S. business days as the days on which an open-end investment company, at a minimum, must price its redeemable securities, provided that customer orders have been received, and significant price changes in the fund's portfolio securities or other activities or transactions affecting the per share net asset value of the fund exist. Closed-end investment companies may compute net asset value per share less frequently, such as weekly or semimonthly.

2.20 Net asset values per share should reflect portfolio securities at *fair value*, as defined in FASB ASC 946-10-20. Securities should be valued at least as often as net asset value per share is computed or shares are issued or redeemed. Registered investment companies value their portfolios at such time of day and at such frequency as is determined by their boards of directors or trustees or the general partner.[12]

2.21 Rule 2a-4(a) of the 1940 Act requires that changes in security positions be reflected in the net asset value per share computations no later than

---

[11] The Financial Accounting Standards Board (FASB) *Accounting Standards Codification* (ASC) glossary defines *net asset value per share* as the amount of net assets attributable to each share of capital stock (other than senior equity securities [that is, preferred stock]) outstanding at the close of the period. It excludes the effects of assuming conversion of outstanding convertible securities, regardless of whether their conversion would have a diluting effect.

[12] Rule 22c-1(b) of the 1940 Act.

the first calculation following the trade date.[13] Similarly, changes in the number of the investment company's outstanding shares from sales, distributions, and repurchases should be reflected in the computations no later than the first calculation following such changes.

2.22 Because of the importance of net asset value per share, many investment companies perform additional procedures to ensure the accuracy of security valuations. The fair value assigned to each security position may be compared with the fair value used on the preceding valuation date to detect increases or decreases in specific security values that are unusual or that exceed predetermined thresholds for change in fair value amounts or percentages. In addition, unchanged security values may be reviewed to determine whether the valuation continues to be appropriate. It is advisable to review and explain unusual increases, decreases, or unchanged prices.

2.23 Net asset value per share should also reflect expenses, interest, dividends, and other income through the date of the calculation.[14] The 1940 Act does not require expenses, income items, or both to be accrued daily if their net cumulative amount is less than one cent per outstanding share.[15] Other aspects of accrual accounting specific to investment companies, discussed in this chapter and other chapters of the guide, could also be considered.

2.24 Mutual funds with multiple classes of stock must determine the net assets and net asset value per share for each class in accordance with the procedures enumerated by Rule 18f-3 of the 1940 Act (or in accordance with an exemptive order issued by the SEC). See chapter 5, "Complex Capital Structures," of this guide for additional information on multiple-class funds.

Basis of Recording Securities Transactions

2.25 FASB ASC 946-320-25-1 states that an investment company should record security purchases and sales as of the trade date.

2.26 Because securities transactions are recorded as of the trade date rather than the settlement date, the statement of assets and liabilities of most investment companies at the end of an accounting period includes receivables from brokers for securities sold but not delivered and payables to brokers for securities purchased but not received.

2.27 As noted in FASB ASC 946-320-25-2, a securities transaction outside conventional channels, such as through a private placement or by submitting shares in a tender offer, should be recorded as of the date that the investment company obtained a right to demand the securities purchased or to collect the proceeds of sale and incurred an obligation to pay the price of the securities purchased or to deliver the securities sold, respectively. Determining the recording date may sometimes require an interpretation by legal counsel.

2.28 This topic of a securities transaction occurring outside of conventional channels is also discussed in section 404.03.a of the SEC's *Codification of Financial Reporting Policies*.

---

[13] Rule 2a-4(a) of the 1940 Act permits registered investment companies to record security transactions as of one day after the trade date for purposes of determining net asset value. However, as noted by FASB ASC 946-320-25-1, for financial reporting purposes, security transactions should be recorded on the trade date.

[14] See footnote 13.

[15] Rule 2a-4(b) of the 1940 Act.

2.29 FASB ASC 860, *Transfers and Servicing*, provides accounting and reporting standards that are applicable to investment companies' transactions, such as repurchase and reverse repurchase agreements, dollar rolls, and securities borrowed and loaned.

2.30 Paragraphs 42–47 of FASB ASC 860-10-40 specifically discuss the accounting for a *repurchase financing*, which is defined by the FASB ASC glossary as a repurchase agreement[16] that relates to a previously transferred financial asset between the same counterparties (or consolidated affiliates of either counterparty) that is entered into contemporaneously with, or in contemplation of, the initial transfer. FASB ASC 860-10-05-21B explains that if a transferor transfers a financial asset and also enters into a repurchase financing with the transferee, there are typically three transfers of the financial asset:

- *Initial transfer.* The initial transferor transfers a financial asset to an initial transferee.
- *Execution of a repurchase financing.* The initial transferee (the borrower) transfers the previously transferred financial asset back to the initial transferor (the lender) as collateral for a financing between the initial transferor and initial transferee.
- *Settlement of the repurchase financing.* The initial transferor (the lender) returns the financial asset (or substantially the same asset) to the initial transferee (the borrower) upon receipt of payment from the initial transferee.

2.31 FASB ASC 860-10-40-42 states that a transferor and transferee should not separately account for a transfer of a financial asset and a related repurchase financing unless both of the following conditions are met: the two transactions have a valid and distinct business or economic purpose for being entered into separately, and the repurchase financing does not result in the initial transferor regaining control over the financial asset. Paragraphs 44–47 of FASB ASC 860-10-40 discuss the qualifications to categorize the transactions as linked and the resulting applicable accounting guidance to follow. Paragraphs 17A–17C of FASB ASC 860-10-55 provide implementation guidance related to repurchase financings.

Valuing Investments

> **© Update 2-1 *Accounting and Reporting:* Fair Value**
>
> FASB Accounting Standards Update (ASU) No. 2011-04, *Fair Value Measurement (Topic 820): Amendments to Achieve Common Fair Value Measurement and Disclosure Requirements in U.S. GAAP and IFRSs*, issued in May 2011, is effective for public entities during interim and annual periods beginning after December 15, 2011. It is effective for nonpublic entities for annual periods beginning after December 15, 2011. Early application is not permitted for public entities. Nonpublic entities may early implement during interim

---

[16] The FASB ASC glossary definition of a *repurchase agreement* notes that, in certain industries, the terminology is reversed (that is, entities in those industries refer to this type of agreement as a reverse repurchase agreement). Investment companies may fall into this category of reverse terminology.

> periods beginning after December 15, 2011. The guidance should be applied prospectively.
>
> Refer to section A.02 in appendix A, "Guidance Updates," for more information on this ASU if applicable to your reporting period.

2.32 Values and changes in values of investments held by investment companies are as important to investors as the investment income earned. FASB ASC 946-10-15-2 states that investment companies are required to report their investment assets (for example, securities and derivatives) at *fair value*, which is defined by the FASB ASC glossary as the price that would be received to sell an asset or paid to transfer a liability in an orderly transaction between market participants at the measurement date.[17] As discussed in FASB ASC 820-10-35-41, quoted market prices in active markets are the best evidence of the fair value of a financial instrument, except as explained in paragraphs 16D and 42–43 of FASB ASC 820-10-35.[18] An *active market* is defined by the FASB ASC glossary as a market in which transactions for the asset or liability occur with sufficient frequency and volume to provide pricing information on an ongoing basis.

2.33 Registered investment companies are also governed by the definition of *value* found in Section 2(a)(41) of the 1940 Act and further interpreted in section 404.03 of the SEC's *Codification of Financial Reporting Policies*. Section 2(a)(41) states that value is defined, with respect to securities for which market quotations are readily available, the market value of such securities and, with respect to other securities and assets, fair value, as determined in good faith by the board of directors. This is also described in Accounting Series Release No. 118.[19]

2.34 Many financial instruments are traded publicly in active markets; therefore, end-of-day market quotations are readily available. However, if quoted market prices in active markets are not available, fair value may be estimated in a variety of ways, depending on the nature of the instrument and the manner in which it is traded.[20] Management's best estimate in good faith (under the oversight of the board of directors or trustees) of fair value should be based on the consistent application of a variety of factors, in accordance with the valuation policy followed by the fund, with the objective being to determine the exit price or amount at which the investment could be exchanged in a current transaction between willing parties, other than in a forced or liquidation

---

[17] In May 2010, FASB issued the proposed Accounting Standards Update (ASU) *Accounting for Financial Instruments and Revisions to the Accounting for Derivative Instruments and Hedging Activities—Financial Instruments (Topic 825) and Derivatives and Hedging (Topic 815)*. Entities that follow specialized industry guidance in FASB ASC 946, *Financial Services—Investment Companies*, would continue to initially measure their financial instruments at transaction price. Readers should remain alert for developments on this topic, which can be accessed from the Technical Plan and Project Updates page at www.fasb.org.

[18] FASB's Valuation Resource Group provides FASB and FASB staff with information on existing implementation issues related to fair value measurements used for financial statement reporting purposes and the alternative viewpoints associated with those implementation issues. Readers should remain aware of developments from this group and use the information and minutes posted from these meetings under the Advisory Groups tab on the FASB website as a resource.

[19] The SEC has established a bibliography of regulatory guidance relating to the valuation of investments in accordance with the 1940 Act, including references to applicable laws, regulations, releases, selected staff guidance, and enforcement actions. The bibliography is accessible in the Division of Investment Management section of the SEC website.

[20] Section 2(a)(41) of the 1940 Act.

Investment Accounts

sale. The fair value reported for investments is not reduced by transaction costs such as estimated brokerage commissions and other costs that would be incurred in selling the investments.

2.35 FASB ASC 820-10-35 establishes a fair value hierarchy that prioritizes the inputs to valuation techniques used to measure fair value into three broad levels. The fair value hierarchy gives the highest priority to quoted prices (unadjusted) in active markets for identical assets or liabilities (level 1) and the lowest priority to unobservable inputs (level 3). FASB ASC 820, *Fair Value Measurement*, also clarifies that fair value is market based, as opposed to an entity-specific measure.

2.36 An investment company's registration statement or offering circular describes the methods used to value its investments.[21] Section 404.03 of the SEC's *Codification of Financial Reporting Policies* describes various methods for estimating fair value.

2.37 *Valuing market-traded securities.* As discussed in paragraphs 2–3 of FASB ASC 946-320-35, valuing securities listed and traded on one or more securities exchanges or unlisted securities traded regularly in over-the-counter (OTC) markets (for example, U.S. Treasury bonds, notes, and bills or stocks quoted on the OTC Bulletin Board or Pink OTC Markets) ordinarily is not difficult because quotations of completed transactions are published daily, or price quotations are readily obtainable from financial reporting services or individual broker-dealers. A security traded in an active market on the valuation date is valued at the last quoted sales price.

2.38 A security listed on more than one national securities exchange should be valued at the last quoted sales price at the time of valuation on the exchange on which the security is principally traded; securities traded on both a national exchange and in the OTC market should be valued based on the price in the market in which the security is principally traded. If the security was not traded in the principal market on the valuation date, the security should be valued at the last quoted sales price on the next most active market if management determines that price to be representative of fair value. If the price is determined not to be representative of fair value, the security should be valued based on quotations readily available from principal-to-principal markets, financial publications, or recognized pricing services, or a good-faith estimate of fair value should be made.

2.39 FASB ASC 820-10-35-3 and 820-10-30-2 provide that the hypothetical transaction to sell the asset or transfer the liability is considered from the perspective of a market participant that holds the asset or owes the liability. Therefore, the objective of a fair value measurement focuses on the price that would be received to sell the asset or paid to transfer the liability (an *exit price*), not the price that would be paid to acquire the asset or received to assume the liability in an exchange transaction (an *entry price*). Conceptually, entry prices and exit prices are different. However, FASB ASC 820-10-30-3 explains that, in many cases, at initial recognition, a transaction price (entry price) will equal the exit price and, therefore, will represent the fair value of the asset or liability. In determining whether a transaction price represents the fair value of the asset or liability at initial recognition, the reporting entity should consider factors specific to the transaction and the asset or liability.

---

[21] Items 11 and 23 of Form N-1A.

AAG-INV 2.39

2.40 Paragraphs 5–6 of FASB ASC 820-10-35 state that the transaction to sell the asset or transfer the liability occurs in the principal market for the asset or liability or, in the absence of a principal market, the most advantageous market for the asset or liability. As defined by the FASB ASC glossary, the *principal market* is the market in which the reporting entity would sell the asset or transfer the liability with the greatest volume and level of activity for the asset or liability. Also, as defined by the FASB ASC glossary, the *most advantageous market* is the market in which the reporting entity would sell the asset or transfer the liability with the price that maximizes the amount that would be received for the asset or minimizes the amount that would be paid to transfer the liability, considering transaction costs in the respective market(s). In either case, the principal (or most advantageous) market (and, thus, market participants) should be considered from the perspective of the reporting entity, thereby allowing for differences between and among entities with different activities. If there is a principal market for the asset or liability, the fair value measurement should represent the price in that market (whether that price is directly observable or otherwise determined using a valuation technique), even if the price in a different market is potentially more advantageous at the measurement date.

2.41 As explained in FASB ASC 820-10-35-7, the price in the principal (or most advantageous) market used to measure the fair value of the asset or liability should not be adjusted for transaction costs, which should be accounted for in accordance with the provisions of other accounting guidance. As defined by the FASB ASC glossary, *transaction costs* represent the incremental direct costs to sell the asset or transfer the liability in the principal (or most advantageous) market for the asset or liability. Transaction costs are not an attribute of the asset or liability; rather, they are specific to the transaction and will differ depending on how the reporting entity transacts. Transaction costs do not include the costs that would be incurred to transport the asset or liability to (or from) its principal (or most advantageous) market. As further discussed in FASB ASC 820-10-35-8, if location is an attribute of the asset or liability (as it could be for a commodity), the price in the principal (or most advantageous) market used to measure the fair value of the asset or liability should be adjusted for the costs, if any, that would be incurred to transport the asset or liability to (or from) its principal (or most advantageous) market.

2.42 Securities markets, financial publications, and recognized pricing services frequently provide quotations of bid price and asked price. Those quotations may be used if a principal-to-principal market is the primary market for the security on the valuation date or, in the absence of trading, on the valuation date of the security normally traded primarily on an exchange. Some investment companies use the bid price to value all securities, some use the mean between the bid and asked prices, and some use a valuation within the range between the bid and asked prices that is considered to best represent fair value in the circumstances. If price quotations are obtained from individual broker-dealers making a market in the security, some investment companies will estimate fair value as the mean of the quoted prices obtained. Each of those policies is acceptable if applied consistently and in accordance with the investment company's established pricing policy. Neither use of the asked price alone to value investments nor use of the bid price alone to value short sales or short positions is acceptable. If only a bid price or an asked price is available for a security on the valuation date, or the spread between the bid and asked price on that date is substantial, quotations for several days could be, for example, reviewed in determining whether the last quoted price is representative of fair value.

2.43 Many funds utilize pricing services to obtain security valuations. Thee pricing services may include quotations on listed securities and OTC securities, as described in the preceding paragraphs. Also, particularly for debt securities, pricing services may provide valuations determined by other pricing techniques. Methods generally recognized in the valuation of financial instruments include comparison to reliable quotations of similar financial instruments, pricing models, matrix pricing, or other formula-based pricing methods. Those methodologies incorporate factors for which published market data may be available. For instance, the mathematical technique known as matrix pricing may be used to determine fair value based on market data available with respect to the issue and similar issues without exclusive reliance on issuer-specific quoted market prices.

Fair Value Determination When the Volume or Level of Activity Has Significantly Decreased

2.44 Situations may arise when quoted market prices are not readily available or when market quotations are available, but it is questionable whether they represent fair value. Examples include the following instances:

- Market quotations and transactions are infrequent, and the most recent quotations and transactions occurred substantially prior to the valuation date.
- The market for the security is "thin" (that is, there are few transactions or market-makers in the security, the spread between the bid and asked prices is large, and price quotations vary substantially either over time or among individual market-makers).
- The last quoted market prices for foreign securities are as of the close of a market that precedes the fund's normal time for valuation, and certain events have taken place since the close of that foreign market that provide evidence that the market prices of those securities would be substantially different at the fund's normal time for valuation if such foreign market were open at that time. Such matters are referred to by the SEC staff as an example of a significant event.[22]
- Trading in a market or for a specific security had been suspended during a trading day and had not reopened by the fund's normal time for valuation for such reasons as the declaration of a market emergency by a regulatory body, the imposition of daily price change limits or "circuit-breakers," or the intended release of information by an issuer was expected to have a material effect on a security's value.

Similar circumstances may also affect the appropriateness of valuations supplied by pricing services. Situations such as the preceding are expected to be rare but may occur. In those cases, an investment company may establish a policy to substitute a good-faith estimate of fair value for the quoted market

---

[22] April 30, 2001, letter from the SEC Division of Investment Management to the Investment Company Institute regarding valuation issues. The letter further states that significant fluctuations in domestic markets may constitute a significant event.

price or pricing service valuation. Any policy adopted should be consistently applied in all situations when significant pricing differences are determined to exist.

2.45 Paragraphs 51A–51H of FASB ASC 820-10-35 clarify the application of FASB ASC 820 in determining fair value when the volume and level of activity for the asset or liability has significantly decreased. Guidance is also included in identifying transactions that are not orderly. In addition, paragraphs 59A–59I of FASB ASC 820-10-55 include illustrations on the application of this guidance. This guidance does not apply to quoted prices for an identical asset or liability in an active market (level 1 inputs). For example, although the volume and level of activity for an asset or a liability may significantly decrease, transactions for the asset or liability may still occur with sufficient frequency and volume to provide pricing information on an ongoing basis.

2.46 The definition of *fair value* states that it is the price obtained in an orderly transaction. The FASB ASC glossary defines an *orderly transaction* as a transaction that assumes exposure to the market for a period prior to the measurement date to allow for marketing activities that are usual and customary for transactions involving such assets and liabilities; it is not a forced transaction (for example, a forced liquidation or distress sale).

2.47 Consistent with FASB ASC 820-10-35-51D, in determining fair value when the volume and level of activity for the asset or liability has significantly decreased, the objective of a fair value measurement remains the same. FASB ASC 820-10-35-51A lists a number of factors that may be evaluated to determine whether there has been a significant decrease in the volume and level of activity for the asset or liability (or similar assets or liabilities) when compared with normal market activity. According to FASB ASC 820-10-35-51B, if, after evaluating the factors, the conclusion is reached that there has been a significant decrease in the volume and level of activity for the asset or liability in relation to normal market conditions, transactions or quoted prices may not be determinative of fair value. Further analysis of the transactions or quoted prices is needed, and a significant adjustment to the transactions or quoted prices may be necessary to estimate fair value in accordance with FASB ASC 820-10. According to FASB ASC 820-10-35-51C, the objective is to determine the point within the range of fair value estimates that is most representative of fair value under the current market conditions. A wide range of fair value estimates may be an indication that further analysis is needed.

2.48 FASB ASC 820-10-35-51D states that determining the price at which willing market participants would transact at the measurement date under current market conditions if there has been a significant decrease in the volume and level of activity for the asset or liability depends on the facts and circumstances and requires the use of significant judgment. The reporting entity's intention to hold the asset or liability is not relevant, however, because fair value is a market-based measurement, not an entity-specific measurement.

2.49 According to FASB ASC 820-10-35-51E, an entity should evaluate the circumstances to determine whether the transaction is orderly based on the weight of the evidence. Even if there has been a significant decrease in the volume and level of activity for the asset or liability, it is not appropriate to conclude that all transactions are not orderly (that is, distressed or forced). Circumstances that may indicate that a transaction is not orderly include, but are not limited to, the following:

- There was not adequate exposure to the market for a period before the measurement date to allow for marketing activities that are usual and customary for transactions involving such assets or liabilities under current market conditions.
- There was a usual and customary marketing period, but the seller marketed the asset or liability to a single market participant.
- The seller is in or near bankruptcy or receivership (that is, distressed).
- The seller was required to sell to meet regulatory or legal requirements (that is, forced).
- The transaction price is an outlier when compared with other recent transactions for the same or similar asset or liability.

The determination of whether a transaction is orderly or not orderly is more difficult if there has been a significant decrease in the volume and level of activity for the asset or liability. Accordingly, the entity should consider the following guidance:

- If the weight of the evidence indicates that the transaction is not orderly, the reporting entity should place little, if any, weight (compared with other indications of fair value) on that transaction price when estimating fair value or market risk premiums.
- If the weight of the evidence indicates that the transaction is orderly, the reporting entity should consider the transaction price when estimating fair value or market risk premiums. The amount of weight placed on that transaction price when compared with other indications of fair value will depend on the facts and circumstances, such as the volume of the transaction, the comparability of the transaction to the asset or liability being measured at fair value, and the proximity of the transaction to the measurement date.
- If the reporting entity does not have sufficient information to conclude that the transaction is orderly or not orderly, it should consider that transaction price when estimating fair value or market risk premiums. However, that transaction price may not be determinative of fair value (that is, it may not be the sole or primary basis for estimating fair value or market risk premiums). The reporting entity should place less weight on transactions on which the reporting entity does not have sufficient information to conclude whether the transaction is orderly when compared with other transactions that are known to be orderly.

In making the determination regarding whether a transaction is orderly, an entity does not need to undertake all possible efforts but should not ignore information that is available without undue cost and effort. The reporting entity would be expected to have sufficient information to conclude whether a transaction is orderly when it is party to the transaction. Refer to FASB ASC 820 for more information.

Valuation Techniques

2.50 Rule 38a-1 under the 1940 Act requires registered investment companies and business development companies (referred to in the adopting release as funds) to adopt policies and procedures reasonably designed to prevent the violation of federal securities laws. In the adopting release, the SEC stated that Rule 38a-1

> requires funds to adopt policies and procedures that require the fund to monitor for circumstances that may necessitate the use of fair value prices; establish criteria for determining when market quotations are no longer reliable for a particular portfolio security; provide a methodology or methodologies by which the fund determines the current fair value of the portfolio security; and regularly review the appropriateness and accuracy of the method used in valuing securities, and make any necessary adjustments. [footnotes omitted][23]

Investment companies offering their shares on Forms N-1A and N-3 are also required by the SEC to provide a brief explanation in their prospectuses of the circumstances under which they will use fair value prices and the effects of using fair value pricing.[24]

2.51 *Estimating fair values of investments.* The SEC's *Codification of Financial Reporting Policies* provides guidance on the factors to be considered in, and the responsibilities for and methods used for, the valuation of securities for which market quotations are not readily available.[25] The following paragraphs regarding securities valued in good faith are consistent with those SEC policies and are intended to summarize and provide guidance on this topic.

2.52 The objective of the estimating procedures is to state the securities at the amount at which they could be exchanged in a current transaction between willing parties, other than in a forced or liquidation sale. The term *current transaction* means realization in an orderly disposition over a reasonable period. All relevant factors generally should be considered in selecting the method of estimating in good faith the fair value of each kind of security.

2.53 In estimating in good faith the fair value of a particular financial instrument, the board or its designee (the valuation committee) generally should, to the extent necessary, take into consideration all indications of fair value that are available. This guide does not purport to delineate all factors that may be considered; however, the following is a list of some of the factors to be considered:[26]

- Financial standing of the issuer
- Business and financial plan of the issuer and comparison of actual results with the plan
- Cost at the date of purchase
- Size of the position held and the liquidity of the market
- Contractual restrictions on the disposition
- Pending public offering with respect to the financial instrument

---

[23] SEC Final Rule Release No. IC-26299, *Compliance Programs of Investment Companies and Investment Advisers*, under the 1940 Act.

[24] SEC Final Rule Release No. IC-26418, *Disclosure Regarding Market Timing and Selective Disclosure of Portfolio Holdings*, under the 1940 Act.

[25] Sections 404.03–.94 of the SEC's *Codification of Financial Reporting Policies*.

[26] The SEC's *Codification of Financial Reporting Policies* provides guidance on the factors to be considered and the methods used to value securities for which market quotations are not readily available.

Investment Accounts

- Pending reorganization activity affecting the financial instrument (such as merger proposals, tender offers, debt restructurings, and conversions)
- Reported prices and the extent of public trading in similar financial instruments of the issuer or comparable entities
- Ability of the issuer to obtain the needed financing
- Changes in the economic conditions affecting the issuer
- A recent purchase or sale of a security of the entity
- Pricing by other dealers in similar securities
- Financial statements of the investees

2.54 No single method exists for estimating fair value in good faith because fair value depends on the facts and circumstances of each individual case. Valuation methods may be based on a multiple of earnings or a discount or premium from a market of a similar, freely traded security of the same issuer; on a yield to maturity with respect to debt issues; or on a combination of these and other methods. In addition, with respect to derivative products, other factors (such as volatility, interest and foreign exchange rates, and term to maturity) should be considered. The board of directors or trustees should be satisfied, however, that the method used to estimate fair value in good faith is reasonable and appropriate and that the resulting valuation is representative of fair value.

2.55 According to sections 404.03–.04 of the SEC's Codification of Financial Reporting Policies, the information considered and the basis for the valuation decision should be documented, and the supporting data should be retained. The board may appoint individuals to assist it in the estimation process and to make the necessary calculations. The rationale for the use of a good-faith estimate of fair value that is different from market quotations or pricing service valuations ordinarily should be documented. If material, the circumstances surrounding the substitution of good-faith estimates of fair value for market quotations or pricing service valuations should be disclosed in the notes to the financial statements.

2.56 Paragraphs 24–35 of FASB ASC 820-10-35 describe the valuation techniques that should be used to measure fair value. Valuation techniques consistent with the market approach, income approach, or cost approach should be used to measure fair value. These approaches are described, as follows:

- The market approach uses prices and other relevant information generated by market transactions involving identical or comparable assets or liabilities. Valuation techniques consistent with the market approach include matrix pricing and often use market multiples derived from a set of comparables.
- The income approach uses valuation techniques to convert future amounts (for example, cash flows or earnings) to a single present amount (discounted). The measurement is based on the value indicated by current market expectations about those future amounts. Valuation techniques consistent with the income approach include present value techniques, option-pricing models, and the multiperiod excess earnings method.
- The cost approach is based on the amount that currently would be required to replace the service capacity of an asset (often referred

to as current replacement cost). Fair value is determined based on the cost to a market participant (buyer) to acquire or construct a substitute asset of comparable utility, adjusted for obsolescence.

2.57 FASB ASC 820-10-35-24 states that valuation techniques that are appropriate in the circumstances and for which sufficient data are available should be used to measure fair value. In some cases, a single valuation technique will be appropriate (for example, when valuing an asset or a liability using quoted prices in an active market for identical assets or liabilities). In other cases, multiple valuation techniques will be appropriate (for example, as could be the case when valuing a reporting unit), and the respective indications of fair value should be evaluated and weighted, as appropriate, considering the reasonableness of the range indicated by those results. Paragraphs 35–41 (example 3) of FASB ASC 820-10-55 illustrate the use of multiple valuation techniques. A fair value measurement is the point within that range that is most representative of fair value in the circumstances.

2.58 As explained in paragraphs 25–26 of FASB ASC 820-10-35, valuation techniques used to measure fair value should be consistently applied. However, a change in a valuation technique or its application is appropriate if the change results in a measurement that is equally or more representative of fair value in the circumstances. Such a change would be accounted for as a change in accounting estimate, in accordance with the provisions of FASB ASC 250, *Accounting Changes and Error Corrections*.

Present Value Techniques

2.59 Paragraphs 4–20 of FASB ASC 820-10-55 provide guidance on present value techniques. Those paragraphs neither prescribe the use of one specific present value technique nor limit the use of present value techniques to the three techniques discussed therein. They indicate that a fair value measurement of an asset or a liability using present value techniques should capture the following elements from the perspective of market participants as of the measurement date: an estimate of future cash flows; expectations about possible variations in the amount or timing (or both) of the cash flows; the time value of money; the price for bearing the uncertainty inherent in the cash flows (risk premium); other case-specific factors that would be considered by market participants; and, in the case of a liability, the nonperformance risk relating to that liability, including the reporting entity's (obligor's) own credit risk.

2.60 FASB ASC 820-10-55-6 provides the general principles that govern any present value technique, as follows:

- Cash flows and discount rates should reflect assumptions that market participants would use in pricing the asset or liability.
- Cash flows and discount rates should consider only factors attributed to the asset (or liability) being measured.
- To avoid double counting or omitting the effects of risk factors, discount rates should reflect assumptions that are consistent with those inherent in the cash flows. For example, a discount rate that reflects expectations about future defaults is appropriate if using the contractual cash flows of a loan but is not appropriate if the cash flows themselves are adjusted to reflect possible defaults.
- Assumptions about cash flows and discount rates should be internally consistent. For example, nominal cash flows (that include

Investment Accounts

the effects of inflation) should be discounted at a rate that includes the effects of inflation.
- Discount rates should be consistent with the underlying economic factors of the currency in which the cash flows are denominated.

2.61 FASB ASC 820-10-55-9 describes how present value techniques differ in how they adjust for risk and in the type of cash flows they use. For example, the discount rate adjustment technique (also called the traditional present value technique) uses a risk-adjusted discount rate and contractual, promised, or most likely cash flows. In contrast, method 1 of the expected present value technique uses a risk-free rate and risk-adjusted expected cash flows. Method 2 of the expected present value technique uses a risk-adjusted discount rate (which is different from the rate used in the discount rate adjustment technique) and expected cash flows. FASB ASC 820-10-55-13 notes that, in the expected present value technique, the probability-weighted average of all possible cash flows is referred to as the expected cash flows. The traditional present value technique and two methods of expected present value techniques are discussed more fully in FASB ASC 820-10-55.

The Fair Value Hierarchy

2.62 Because fair value is a market-based measurement, as stated in FASB ASC 820-10-35-9, a fair value measurement should be determined based on the assumptions that market participants would use in pricing the asset or liability (referred to as inputs). The FASB ASC glossary defines *inputs* as assumptions that market participants would use in pricing the asset or liability, including assumptions about risk, for example the risk inherent in a particular valuation technique used to measure fair value (such as a pricing model) or the risk inherent in the inputs to the valuation technique. Inputs may be observable or unobservable (both as defined by the FASB ASC glossary):

- *Observable inputs* reflect the assumptions that market participants would use in pricing the asset or liability. These inputs are developed based on market data obtained from sources independent of the reporting entity.
- *Unobservable inputs* reflect the reporting entity's own assumptions about the assumptions that market participants would use in pricing the asset or liability, developed based on the best information available in the circumstances.

2.63 Paragraphs 37–58 of FASB ASC 820-10-35 establish a fair value hierarchy that distinguishes between observable and unobservable inputs. Valuation techniques used to measure fair value should maximize the use of observable inputs and minimize the use of unobservable inputs.

2.64 The fair value hierarchy in FASB ASC 820-10-35 prioritizes the inputs to valuation techniques used to measure fair value into three broad levels. The three levels are discussed in

- FASB ASC 820-10-35-40, which states that level 1 inputs are quoted prices (unadjusted) in active markets for identical assets or liabilities that the reporting entity has the ability to access at the measurement date. FASB ASC 820-10-35-44 affirms the requirement that the fair value of a position in a single financial instrument (including a block) that trades in an active market should be measured as the product of the quoted price for the individual instrument multiplied by the quantity held (within level 1 of the fair value hierarchy). The quoted price should not be adjusted because of the size of the position relative to trading volume (blockage factor). The use of a blockage factor is prohibited, even if a market's normal daily trading volume is not sufficient to absorb the quantity held, and placing orders to sell the position in a single transaction could affect the quoted price.

- paragraphs 47–51 of FASB ASC 820-10-35, which state that level 2 inputs are inputs other than quoted prices included within level 1 that are observable for the asset or liability, either directly or indirectly. If the asset or liability has a specified (contractual) term, a level 2 input must be observable for substantially the full term of the asset or liability. Adjustments to level 2 inputs will vary depending on factors specific to the asset or liability. Those factors include the condition and location of the asset or liability, the extent to which the inputs relate to items that are comparable to the asset or liability (including those factors discussed in FASB ASC 820-10-35-16D), and the volume and level of activity in the markets within which the inputs are observed. An adjustment that is significant to the fair value measurement in its entirety could render the measurement a level 3 measurement, depending on the level in the fair value hierarchy within which the inputs used to determine the adjustment fall. As discussed in FASB ASC 820-10-35-48, level 2 inputs include the following:

  — Quoted prices for similar assets or liabilities in active markets

  — Quoted prices for identical or similar assets or liabilities in markets that are not active

  — Inputs other than quoted prices that are observable for the asset or liability (for example, interest rates and yield curves observable at commonly quoted intervals, volatilities, prepayment speeds, loss severities, credit risks, and default rates)

  — Inputs that are derived principally from, or corroborated by, observable market data by correlation or other means (market-corroborated inputs)

- paragraphs 52–55 of FASB ASC 820-10-35, which state that level 3 inputs are unobservable inputs for the asset or liability. Unobservable inputs should be used to measure fair value to the extent that relevant observable inputs are not available, thereby allowing for situations in which there is little, if any, market activity for the asset or liability at the measurement date. Unobservable inputs should be developed based on the best information available in the circumstances, which could include the entity's own data. In developing unobservable inputs, the reporting entity need not undertake all possible efforts to obtain information about market participant assumptions. Unobservable inputs should reflect the reporting entity's own assumptions about the assumptions that market participants would use in pricing the asset or liability (including assumptions about risk). Assumptions about risk include the risk inherent in the inputs to the valuation technique. A measurement (for example, a mark-to-model measurement) that does not include an adjustment for risk would not represent a fair value measurement if market participants would include one in pricing the related asset or liability. The reporting entity should not ignore information about market participant assumptions that is reasonably available without undue cost and effort. Therefore, the entity's own data used to develop unobservable inputs should be adjusted if information is readily available without undue cost and effort that indicates that market participants would use different assumptions. FASB ASC 820-10-55-22 discusses level 3 inputs for particular assets and liabilities.

As explained in FASB ASC 820-10-35-37, in some cases, the inputs used to measure fair value could fall in different levels of the fair value hierarchy. The level in the fair value hierarchy within which the fair value measurement falls in its entirety should be determined based on the lowest level input that is significant to the fair value measurement in its entirety.

2.65 As discussed in FASB ASC 820-10-35-38, the availability of inputs relevant to the asset or liability and the relative reliability of the inputs could affect the selection of appropriate valuation techniques. However, the fair value hierarchy prioritizes the inputs to valuation techniques, not the valuation techniques. For example, a fair value measurement using a present value technique could fall within level 2 or level 3, depending on the inputs that are significant to the measurement in its entirety and the level in the fair value hierarchy within which those inputs fall.

2.66 As stated in FASB ASC 820-10-35-15, the effect on a fair value measurement of a restriction on the sale or use of an asset will differ depending on whether market participants would consider the restriction in pricing the asset. Paragraphs 51–55 (example 6) of FASB ASC 820-10-55 explain that restrictions that are an attribute of an asset and, therefore, would transfer to a market participant are the only restrictions reflected in fair value.

Application of Fair Value Measurements to Assets

2.67 FASB ASC 820-10-35-10 provides that a fair value measurement of an asset assumes the highest and best use of the asset by market participants, considering the use of the asset that is physically possible, legally permissible, and financially feasible at the measurement date. Highest and best use is determined based on the use of the asset by market participants, even if the intended use of the asset by the reporting entity is different.

2.68 FASB ASC 820-10-35-10 further notes that the highest and best use for an asset is established by one of two valuation premises: value in use or value in exchange. The highest and best use of the asset is in use if the asset would provide maximum value to market participants principally through its use in combination with other assets as a group (as installed or otherwise configured for use). For example, value in use could be appropriate for certain nonfinancial assets. The highest and best use of the asset is in exchange if the asset would provide maximum value to market participants principally on a stand-alone basis. For example, value in exchange could be appropriate for a financial asset. According to paragraphs 12–13 of FASB ASC 820-10-35, an asset's value in use should be based on the price that would be received in a current transaction to sell the asset, assuming that the asset would be used

Application of Fair Value Measurements to Liabilities

2.69 According to paragraphs 16–16A of FASB ASC 820-10-35, a fair value measurement assumes that both (*a*) the liability is transferred to a market participant at the measurement date (the liability to the counterparty continues; it is not settled), and (*b*) the nonperformance risk relating to that liability is the same before and after its transfer. Further, it is also assumed that a liability is exchanged in an orderly transaction between market participants. Certain liabilities, such as debt obligations, are traded in the marketplace as assets. However, many liabilities are rarely transferred in the marketplace due to contractual or other legal restrictions.

2.70 FASB ASC 820-10-35-16B states that if a quoted price in an active market for an identical liability is available, it represents a level 1 measurement. If that is not available, a reporting entity should measure fair value using one or more of the following techniques:

- A valuation technique that uses
  - the quoted price of the identical liability when traded as an asset
  - quoted prices for similar liabilities or similar liabilities when traded as assets
- Another valuation technique that is consistent with the principles of FASB ASC 820, such as an income or a market approach

2.71 According to FASB ASC 820-10-35-16D, when measuring the fair value of a liability using the quoted price of the liability when traded as an asset, the reporting entity should adjust the quoted price for factors specific to the asset that are not applicable to the fair value measurement of the liability. For example, the quoted price for the asset may relate to a similar, but not identical, liability traded as an asset, or the unit of account for the asset may not be the same as for the liability.

2.72 FASB ASC 820-10-35-16G explains that when measuring the fair value of a liability using a valuation technique, the reporting entity should ensure that the fair value measurement is consistent with FASB ASC 820. For example, when using a technique based on the amount at the measurement date that the reporting entity would receive to enter into the identical liability, the inputs should reflect the assumptions that market participants would use (or the reporting entity's own assumption about the assumptions that market participants would use) in the principal or most advantageous market for the issuance of a liability with the same contractual terms.

2.73 When estimating the fair value of a liability, FASB ASC 820-10-35-16E states that the reporting entity should not include a separate input or adjustment to other inputs relating to the existence of a restriction that prevents the transfer of the liability because the effect of that restriction is already either implicitly or explicitly included in the other inputs to the fair value measurement.

2.74 Paragraphs 17–18 of FASB ASC 820-10-35 provide that a fair value measurement of a liability should reflect its nonperformance risk (the risk that the obligation will not be fulfilled). Because nonperformance risk includes the reporting entity's credit risk, the reporting entity should consider the effect of its credit risk (credit standing) on the fair value of the liability in all periods in which the liability is measured at fair value.

Investments in Entities That Calculate Net Asset Value per Share

2.75 Paragraphs 58–62 of FASB ASC 820-10-35 contain guidance intended to improve financial reporting by permitting the use of a practical expedient, with appropriate disclosures, when measuring the fair value of an alternative investment that does not have a readily determinable fair value if certain criteria are met. According to FASB ASC 820-10-15-4, this guidance only applies to an investment that meets both of the following criteria:

 a. The investment does not have a readily determinable fair value.[27]

 b. The investment is in an entity that has all the attributes specified in FASB ASC 946-10-15-2 (investment activity, unit ownership, pooling of funds, and reporting entity) or, if one or more of the attributes specified in FASB ASC 946-10-15-2 are not present, is in an entity for which it is industry practice to issue financial statements using guidance that is consistent with the measurement principles in FASB ASC 946, *Financial Services—Investment Companies*.

2.76 FASB ASC 820-10-35-59 states that a reporting entity may adopt a practical expedient to estimate the fair value of an alternative investment within the scope of paragraphs 4–5 of FASB ASC 820-10-15 using the net asset value per share (or its equivalent, such as member units or an ownership interest in partners' capital to which a proportionate share of net assets is attributed) of the investment if the net asset value per share of the investment (or its equivalent) is calculated in a manner consistent with the measurement principles of FASB ASC 946 as of the reporting entity's measurement date.

2.77 Therefore, certain attributes of the investment (such as restrictions on redemption) and transaction prices from principal-to-principal or brokered transactions will not be considered in measuring the fair value of the investment if the practical expedient is used. The practical expedient reduces complexity and improves consistency and comparability in the application of FASB ASC 820 while reducing the costs of applying FASB ASC 820. This guidance also improves transparency by requiring additional disclosures about investments within its scope to enable users of financial statements to understand the nature and risks of investments and whether the sale of the investments is probable at amounts different from net asset value per share.

---

[27] FASB ASC 820-10-15-5 notes that the FASB ASC glossary definition of *readily determinable fair value* indicates that an equity security would have a readily determinable fair value if any one of three conditions is met. One of those conditions is that sales prices or bid-and-asked quotations are currently available on a securities exchange registered with the SEC or in the over-the-counter (OTC) market, provided that those prices or quotations for the OTC market are publicly reported by the National Association of Securities Dealers Automated Quotations System or Pink Sheets LLC. The definition notes that restricted stock meets that definition if the restriction terminates within one year. If an investment otherwise would have a readily determinable fair value, except that the investment has a restriction expiring in more than one year, the reporting entity should not apply the guidance in paragraphs 59–62 of FASB ASC 820-10-35 and FASB ASC 820-10-50-6A to the investment.

2.78 As discussed in Technical Questions and Answers (TIS) section 2220.18, "Applicability of Practical Expedient" (AICPA, *Technical Practice Aids*), these investments, typically referred to as alternative investments, include interests in hedge funds, private equity funds, real estate funds, venture capital funds, offshore fund vehicles, commodity funds, and funds of funds. Further, TIS section 2220.19, "Unit of Account" (AICPA, *Technical Practice Aids*), states that, for interests in alternative investments, the appropriate unit of account is the interest in the investee fund itself, not the underlying investments within the investee fund; this is because the reporting entity owns an undivided interest in the whole of the investee fund portfolio and typically lacks the ability to dispose of individual assets and liabilities in the investee fund portfolio.

2.79 FASB ASC 820-10-35-60 notes that, if the net asset value obtained from the investee is not as of the reporting entity's measurement date or is not calculated in a manner consistent with the measurement principles of FASB ASC 946, the reporting entity should consider whether an adjustment to the most recent net asset value is necessary. The objective of this adjustment would be to estimate a net asset value per share that is consistent with the aforementioned measurement principles.

2.80 TIS section 2220.20, "Determining Whether NAV Is Calculated Consistent With FASB ASC 946, *Financial Services—Investment Companies*" (AICPA, *Technical Practice Aids*), provides guidance to assist management of the reporting entity in determining whether net asset value is calculated consistent with FASB ASC 946. As part of this determination, a reporting entity should independently evaluate the fair value measurement process utilized by the investee fund manager to calculate the net asset value. This evaluation is a matter of professional judgment and includes determining that the investee fund manager has an effective process and related internal controls in place to estimate the fair value of its investments that are included in the net asset value calculation. The reporting entity's controls used to evaluate the process of the investee fund manager may include initial due diligence, ongoing monitoring, and financial reporting controls. Only after considering all relevant factors can the reporting entity reach a conclusion about whether the reported net asset value is calculated consistent with the measurement principles of FASB ASC 946. The reporting entity may consider the following key factors relating to the valuation received from the investee fund manager:

- The investee fund's fair value estimation processes and control environment and any changes to those processes or control environment
- The investee's fund policies and procedures for estimating fair value of the underlying investments and any changes to those policies or procedures
- The use of independent third-party valuation experts to augment and validate the investee fund's procedures for estimating fair value
- The portion of the underlying securities held by the investee fund that are traded on active markets
- The professional reputation and standing of the investee fund's auditor (this is not intended to suggest that the auditor is an element of the investee fund's internal control system but as a

Investment Accounts

general risk factor in evaluating the integrity of the data obtained from the investee fund manager)

- Qualifications, if any, of the auditor's report on the investee fund's financial statements
- Whether there is a history of significant adjustments to the net asset value reported by the investee fund manager as a result of the annual financial statement audit or otherwise
- Findings in the investee fund's adviser or administrator's type 2 Service Organization Control (SOC) 1 report, if any
- Whether net asset value has been appropriately adjusted for items such as carried interest and clawbacks
- Comparison of historical realizations to the last reported fair value

2.81 TIS section 2220.20 goes on to discuss the scenario in which a reporting entity invests in a fund of funds. That reporting entity could conclude on the consistency of the net asset value calculation with FASB ASC 946 by assessing (*a*) whether the fund-of-funds manager has a process that considers the aforementioned key factors in the calculation of the net asset value reported by the fund of funds and (*b*) if the fund-of-funds manager has obtained or estimated the net asset value from underlying fund managers in a manner consistent with paragraphs 59–62 of FASB ASC 820-10-35 as of the measurement date. The reporting entity is not required to look through the fund-of-funds interest to underlying fund investments if the reporting entity has concluded that the fund-of-funds manager reports net asset value consistent with FASB ASC 946 for the fund-of-funds interest.

2.82 TIS section 2220.22, "Adjusting NAV When It Is Not as of the Reporting Entity's Measurement Date" (AICPA, *Technical Practice Aids*), illustrates how the reporting entity should estimate an adjustment when net asset value is calculated consistently with FASB ASC 946 but not as of the reporting entity's measurement date. One option is for the reporting entity to request the investee fund manager to provide a supplemental net asset value calculation consistent with the measurement principles of FASB ASC 946 as of the reporting entity's measurement date. Alternatively, it may be necessary to adjust or roll forward (or roll back) the reported net asset value for factors that could cause it to differ from the net asset value at the measurement date. When the reporting entity's measurement date is prior to the net asset value calculation date, it may be more appropriate to use that net asset value and perform a rollback, rather than using a reported net asset value calculated prior to the entity's measurement date. TIS section 2220.22 lists factors that may necessitate an adjustment to the reported net asset value when it is not calculated as of the reporting entity's measurement date and contains an example rollforward net asset value calculation.

2.83 TIS section 2220.23, "Adjusting NAV When It Is Not Calculated Consistent With FASB ASC 946" (AICPA, *Technical Practice Aids*), illustrates how a reporting entity may estimate the adjustment when a reported net asset value is not calculated consistently with the measurement principles of FASB ASC 946. In this situation, the reporting entity should consider and understand the reasons why net asset value has not been based upon fair value, whether a fair value based net asset value can be obtained from the investee manager, and whether the specific data needed to adjust the reported net asset value can be

AAG-INV 2.83

obtained and properly utilized to estimate a fair value based net asset value. Some examples of circumstances in which the reporting entity may be able to obtain data to estimate an adjustment include, but are not limited to, the reported net asset value is on a cash basis, the reported net asset value utilizes blockage discounts taken on securities valued using level 1 inputs (which is inconsistent with FASB ASC 820), and the reported net asset value has not been adjusted for the impact of unrealized carried interest or incentive fees. Consequently, if the reporting entity finds that it is not practicable to calculate an adjusted net asset value, then the practical expedient is not available. The reporting entity may also elect not to utilize the practical expedient. In those cases, the reporting entity should apply the general measurement principles of FASB ASC 820 instead.

2.84 FASB ASC 820-10-35-61 states that the decision about whether to apply the practical expedient should be made on an investment-by-investment basis and applied consistently to the fair value measurement of a reporting entity's entire position in a particular investment, unless it is probable at the measurement date that a reporting entity will sell a portion of an investment at an amount different from net asset value per share (or its equivalent), as described in FASB ASC 820-10-35-62. In those situations, the reporting entity should account for the portion of the investment that is being sold in accordance with other provisions in FASB ASC 820-10 and should not apply the practical expedient discussed in FASB ASC 820-10-35-59.

2.85 According to FASB ASC 820-10-35-62, a reporting entity is not permitted to estimate the fair value of an investment within the scope of paragraphs 4–5 of FASB ASC 820-10-15 using the net asset value per share of the investment (or its equivalent) as a practical expedient if it is probable at the measurement date that a reporting entity will sell a portion of the investment at an amount different from the net asset value per share (or its equivalent). A sale is considered probable only if all of the following criteria are met as of the reporting entity's measurement date:

- Management, having the authority to approve the action, commits to a plan to sell the investment.
- An active program to locate a buyer and other actions required to complete the plan to sell the investment have been initiated.
- The investment is available for immediate sale subject only to terms that are usual and customary for sales of such investments.
- Actions required to complete the plan indicate that it is unlikely that significant changes to the plan will be made or that the plan will be withdrawn.

2.86 TIS section 2220.27, "Determining Fair Value of Investments When the Practical Expedient Is Not Used or Is Not Available" (AICPA, *Technical Practice Aids*), discusses what inputs or investment features should be considered in estimating fair value for entities that do not elect to use net asset value as a practical expedient or are unable to adjust the most recently reported net asset value to estimate a net asset value that is calculated in a manner consistent with the measurement principles of FASB ASC 946 as of the reporting entity's measurement date. In this situation, examples of factors that could be used when estimating fair value (depending on the valuation technique[s] and facts and circumstances) are as follows:

- Net asset value (as one valuation factor)

Investment Accounts

- Transactions in principal-to-principal or brokered markets (external markets) and overall market conditions
- Features of the alternative investment
- Expected future cash flows appropriately discounted
- Factors used to determine whether there has been a significant decrease in the volume and level of activity for the asset when compared with normal market activity for the asset (FASB ASC 820-10-35-51A)

TIS section 2220.27 also discusses investment features of alternative investments, such as lockup periods and the ability of the fund to identify and make acceptable investments, which a reporting entity may consider in determining fair value when the practical expedient is unavailable or not elected.

2.87 FASB ASC 820-10-35-58 states that classification within the fair value hierarchy of a fair value measurement of an investment that is measured at net asset value per share requires judgment. This guidance provides the following considerations:

- If a reporting entity has the ability to redeem its investment with the investee at net asset value per share (or its equivalent) at the measurement date, the fair value measurement of the investment should be categorized as a level 2 fair value measurement.
- If a reporting entity will never have the ability to redeem its investment with the investee at net asset value per share (or its equivalent), the fair value measurement of the investment should be categorized as a level 3 fair value measurement.
- If a reporting entity cannot redeem its investment with the investee at net asset value per share (or its equivalent) at the measurement date, but the investment may be redeemable with the investee at a future date (for example, investments subject to a lockup or gate or investments whose redemption period does not coincide with the measurement date), the reporting entity should consider the length of time until the investment will become redeemable in determining whether the fair value measurement of the investment should be categorized as a level 2 or level 3 fair value measurement. For example, if the reporting entity does not know when it will have the ability to redeem the investment, or it does not have the ability to redeem the investment in the near term at net asset value per share (or its equivalent), the fair value measurement should be categorized as a level 3 fair value measurement.[28]

---

[28] Refer to the May 12, 2011, AICPA Expert Panel Meeting Highlights. Expert panel (EP) members discussed situations where an investment company holds investments in multiple classes of an investee fund. For instance, a fund of funds holds $3,000,000 in Class A of the investee, and $500,000 in Class S (a side pocket class) of the investee. For the purposes of leveling in the FASB ASC 820 hierarchy, a question arises whether the investment should be bifurcated if the investment into Class A meets the criteria for level 2, but the investment into Class S is illiquid, and, therefore, a level 3 investment. The EP discussed industry practice in leveling such investments and noted that the EP members generally believe that in the situation of a unitized fund as described above, there could be multiple units of account for an interest in an investee fund, and that a similar analogy would apply to investments in partnerships where a portion of the investment is locked up or has other varying liquidity characteristics.

AAG-INV 2.87

2.88 TIS section 2220.24, "Disclosures—Ability to Redeem Versus Actual Redemption Request" (AICPA, *Technical Practice Aids*), discusses redemptions from alternative funds. In most cases, redemptions at net asset value are only permitted with advance notice, ranging from 30 to 120 days. Even if the reporting entity has not submitted a redemption request effective on the measurement date, as long as the reporting entity has the ability to redeem at net asset value in the near term (for example, it has the contractual and practical ability to redeem) at the measurement date, then, consistent with FASB ASC 820-10-35-58(a), the investment may be classified as level 2. TIS section 2220.25, "Impact of 'Near Term' on Classification Within Fair Value Hierarchy" (AICPA, *Technical Practice Aids*), explains that what is viewed as near term is a matter of professional judgment and depends on the specific facts and circumstances. A redemption period of 90 days or less generally would be considered near term because any potential discount relative to the time value of money to the next redemption date would be unlikely to be considered a significant unobservable input, in accordance with FASB ASC 820. However, other factors, such as the likelihood or actual imposition of gates, may influence the determination of whether the investment will be redeemable in the near term.

2.89 *Money market funds.*[29] As set forth in Rule 2a-7 under the 1940 Act, a money market fund may value securities using the amortized cost or penny-rounding method,[30] subject to certain determinations by its board of directors or trustees. Rule 2a-7 requires, among other things, in the case of a money market fund using the amortized cost method, that the fund's board of directors or trustees "establish written procedures reasonably designed ... to stabilize the money market fund's net asset value per share, as computed for the purpose of distribution, redemption and repurchase at a single value." Rule 2a-7 sets forth procedures that must be adopted by the board of directors or trustees when using the amortized cost or penny-rounding method of valuation. Additionally, for funds using the amortized cost method, the board of directors or trustees should perform a periodic review of both the monitoring of and the extent of any deviation from fair value and the methods used to calculate the deviations.

Determining Costs and Realized Gains and Losses

2.90 As stated in FASB ASC 946-320-40-1, the cost of investment securities held in the portfolio of a registered investment company and the net realized gains or losses thereon should be determined, for financial accounting purposes, on the specific identification or average-cost methods. An investment company should use only one method for all securities. Cost includes commissions and other charges that are a part of securities purchase transactions.

2.91 Rule 2a-2 of the 1940 Act is consistent with FASB ASC in stating that the cost of investment securities held in the portfolio of a registered investment company and the net realized gains or losses thereon are determined, for financial accounting purposes, on the specific certificate, first in first out, last in first out, or average-value methods. The average-value method of computing gains and losses may not presently be used for federal income tax purposes.

---

[29] See footnote 17.

[30] A money market fund using either method (*a*) may not acquire any instrument with a remaining maturity (as the term is defined in Rule 2a-7) of greater than 397 calendar days; (*b*) must maintain a dollar-weighted average portfolio maturity of 60 days or less; or (*c*) must maintain a dollar-weighted average portfolio maturity of 120 calendar days, determined without reference to the exceptions regarding interest rate readjustments.

2.92 An investment company occasionally may be entitled to receive award proceeds from litigation relating to an investment security. Awards should be recorded in accordance with the gain contingency provisions of FASB ASC 450, *Contingencies*, considering such factors as the enforceability of the right to settlement and the ability to determine the amount receivable.

2.93 As explained in FASB ASC 946-320-35-21, if the investment company holds the securities, the proceeds are accounted for as a reduction of cost. If the investment company no longer holds the securities, the proceeds should be accounted for as realized gains on security transactions.

2.94 As described in paragraphs 2–3 of FASB ASC 946-320-30, an investment company may receive securities in a spin-off wherein the entity in which the investment company has invested spins off a portion of its operations. A portion of the cost of the securities held should be allocated to the securities received in the spin-off. That amount is based on the ratio of the fair value of the securities received to the sum of the fair value of such securities and the fair value of the original securities held by the investment company of the entity affecting the spin-off.

2.95 Spin-offs are usually tax-free reorganizations, and no gain or loss is recognized for income tax or financial reporting purposes.[31]

2.96 From time to time, tender offers may be received for securities held by an investment company. The terms of the offer may be for cash, debentures of the acquiring entity, stock of the acquiring entity, or a combination thereof.

2.97 As explained in FASB ASC 946-320-25-3, even if the investment company tenders its securities, it should continue to value the shares tendered until the number of shares accepted in the tender is known. Thereafter, the investment company should value the assets to be received for the shares tendered.

2.98 Accrued interest on bonds bought between interest dates should be accounted for as accrued interest receivable. Accrued interest on bonds sold should be accounted for as a reduction of accrued interest receivable and is not a factor in determining gain or loss on a sale.

Accounting for Investment Income

2.99 An investment company's investment income consists primarily of dividends and interest.

2.100 *Dividends.* As stated in FASB ASC 946-320-35-5, dividends on investment securities should be recorded on the ex-dividend date. Distributions that represent returns of capital should be credited to investment cost rather than investment income. The FASB ASC glossary defines *return of capital* as distributions by investment companies in excess of tax-basis earnings and profits.

2.101 As described in FASB ASC 946-320-35-6, stock splits and stock dividends in shares of the same class as the shares owned are not income to the investment company. However, dividends for which the recipient has the choice to receive cash or stock are usually recognized as investment income in

---

[31] For further information related to spinoffs, see FASB ASC 845, *Nonmonetary Transactions*, and 810, *Consolidation*.

the amount of the cash option because, in such cases, cash is usually the best evidence of fair value of the stock.

2.102 As noted in FASB ASC 946-320-35-7, other noncash dividends should be recognized as investment income at the fair value of the property received.

2.103 FASB ASC 946-320-35-8 states that stock rights (that is, subscription rights) received should be allocated a prorated portion of the cost basis of the related investment; however, allocation is not required if the fair value of the rights is 15 percent or less of the fair value of the investment company's holdings.

2.104 Investment companies usually follow tax accounting from Internal Revenue Code Section 307 that, consistent with the guidance of the prior paragraph, does not require allocation if the fair value of the stock rights is 15 percent or less of the fair value of the investment company's holdings.

2.105 FASB ASC 946-320-35-9 explains that cash dividends declared on stocks for which the securities portfolio reflects a short position as of the record date should be recognized as an expense on the ex-dividend date.

2.106 As a routine operating policy, investment companies should consult reliable published or other sources for daily dividend declarations and other corporate actions to be sure that they obtain and record relevant dividend information in a timely manner. Investment companies should have procedures that provide for follow up and disposition of dividends not collected in the regular course of business because of delays in settling securities transactions or completing transfer procedures.

2.107 *Interest.* As stated in FASB ASC 946-320-35-20, premiums and discounts should be amortized using the interest method. As explained in FASB ASC 310-20-35-18, the objective of the interest method is to arrive at periodic interest income (including recognition of fees and costs) at a constant effective yield on the net investment (that is, the principal amount of the investment adjusted by unamortized fees or costs and purchase premium or discount). FASB ASC 835-30-35-2 states that the difference between the present value and the face amount of the net investment should be treated as a discount or premium and amortized as interest expense or income over the life of the note in such a way as to result in a constant rate of interest when applied to the amount outstanding at the beginning of any given period.

2.108 The economic substance of an investment in a debt security is that the discount or premium paid is an adjustment of the stated interest rate to a current market rate. Amortizing premiums and accreting discounts, as an adjustment to interest income, is consistent with the economic substance of the transaction.

2.109 Paydown gains and losses on mortgage- and asset-backed securities should also be presented as an adjustment to interest income. Amortization of bond premiums and accretion of bond discounts for federal income tax purposes is discussed in chapter 6, "Taxes," of this guide. Original issue discount on bonds and other debt securities is required to be amortized for tax and financial reporting purposes. Discounts on the purchase of bonds that do not provide for periodic interest payments, sometimes called zero coupon bonds, should be amortized to income by the interest method.

Investment Accounts

2.110 FASB ASC 325-40-15-7 states that for income recognition purposes, beneficial interests classified as trading are included in the scope of FASB ASC 325-40 because it is practice for certain industries (such as investment companies) to report interest income as a separate item in their income statements, even though the investments are accounted for at fair value. The FASB ASC glossary defines *beneficial interests* as rights to receive all or portions of specified cash inflows received by a trust or other entity, including, but not limited to, all of the following: senior and subordinated shares of interest, principal, or other cash inflows to be passed through or paid through; premiums due to guarantors; commercial paper obligations; and residual interests, whether in the form of debt or equity.

2.111 FASB ASC 325-40-35-1 explains that the holder of a beneficial interest should recognize accretable yield as interest income over the life of the beneficial interest using the effective yield method. The holder of a beneficial interest should continue to update, over the life of the beneficial interest, the expectation of cash flows to be collected. FASB ASC 325-40-35-3 goes on to explain that after the transaction date, *cash flows expected to be collected* are defined as the holder's estimate of the amount and timing of estimated principal and interest cash flows based on the holder's best estimate of current information and events. In FASB ASC 325-40, a change in cash flows expected to be collected is considered in the context of both the timing and amount of the cash flows expected to be collected.

2.112 FASB ASC 325-40-35-4 notes that, if based on current information and events, there is a favorable (or an adverse) change in cash flows expected to be collected from the cash flows previously projected, then the investor should recalculate the amount of accretable yield for the beneficial interest on the date of evaluation as the excess of cash flows expected to be collected over the beneficial interest's reference amount. The reference amount equals the initial investment minus cash received to date plus the yield accreted to date. Based on cash flows expected to be collected, interest income may be recognized on a beneficial interest even if the net investment in the beneficial interest is accreted to an amount greater than the amount at which the beneficial interest could be settled if prepaid immediately in its entirety. The adjustment should be accounted for prospectively as a change in estimate, in conformity with FASB ASC 250, with the amount of periodic accretion adjusted over the remaining life of the beneficial interest.

2.113 Paragraphs 5–6 of FASB ASC 325-40-35 explain that determining whether there has been a favorable (or an adverse) change in cash flows expected to be collected from the cash flows previously projected (taking into consideration both the timing and amount of the cash flows expected to be collected) involves comparing the present value of the remaining cash flows expected to be collected at the initial transaction date (or at the last date previously revised) against the present value of the cash flows expected to be collected at the current financial reporting date. The cash flows should be discounted at a rate equal to the current yield used to accrete the beneficial interest.

2.114 According to TIS section 6910.21, "Recognition of Premium/Discount on Short Positions in Fixed-Income Securities" (AICPA, *Technical Practice Aids*), when recognizing interest income on long positions or when recognizing interest expense on short positions on fixed-income securities, all economic elements of interest should be recognized, including premium and discount to the par value of the bond.

2.115 Interest income on debt securities, such as corporate bonds, municipal bonds, or treasury bonds, is accrued daily. An investment company should also consider collectability of interest when making accruals.

2.116 Interest received on bonds that were in default or that were delinquent in the payment of interest when acquired should be accounted for as follows: (*a*) the amount of interest earned from the date of acquisition of the bond through the current period should be recorded as interest income, and (*b*) the amount of interest in arrears at the date of acquisition of the bond should be recorded as a reduction of the cost of the investment.[32]

2.117 The accrued interest receivable account should be analyzed at regular intervals to make sure that interest payments due are received promptly and in the correct amount. Similarly, the disposition of purchased interest receivable and interest accruals on debt securities sold between interest dates should be analyzed periodically.

Defaulted Debt Securities

2.118 In accordance with the guidance provided by FASB ASC 450-20-25-2, accrued interest should be written off when it becomes probable that the interest will not be collected, and the amount of uncollectible interest can be reasonably estimated.

2.119 As explained in paragraphs 17–18 of FASB ASC 946-320-35, the portion of interest receivable on defaulted debt securities written off that was recognized as interest income should be treated as a reduction of interest income. Write-offs of purchased interest should be reported as increases to the cost basis of the security, which will result in an unrealized loss until the security is sold.

Accounting for Expenditures in Support of Defaulted Debt Securities

2.120 As noted in FASB ASC 946-320-05-9, when issuers of debt securities default, the bondholders often become active in any negotiations and the workout process. This process often results in new terms that restructure the obligations to allow the issuer to continue to meet its ongoing interest obligations and maintain some, if not all, of the principal value to the holders of the obligations.

2.121 As explained in FASB ASC 946-320-05-10, adverse economic developments often lead to increases in the default rates of debt securities. In addition to occasional capital infusions, professional fees to legally restructure the investments are frequently incurred by the bondholders.

2.122 *Capital infusions.* The nature of capital infusions is to enhance or prevent substantial diminution in the fair value of the investment. According to the FASB ASC glossary, *capital infusions* are expenditures made directly to the issuer to ensure that operations are completed, thereby allowing the issuer to generate cash flows to service the debt. Such expenditures are usually

---

[32] Section 404.02 of the SEC's *Codification of Financial Reporting Policies.*

nonrecurring. In certain cases, bondholders may receive additional promissory notes, or the original bond instrument may be amended to provide for repayment of the capital infusions. As further noted in FASB ASC 946-320-35-14, all capital infusions in support of defaulted securities should be recorded as an addition to the cost basis of the related security.

2.123 *Workout expenditures.* According to the FASB ASC glossary, *workout expenditures* consist of professional fees (legal, accounting, appraisal) paid to entities unaffiliated with the investment company's adviser or sponsor in connection with (*a*) capital infusions, (*b*) restructurings or plans of reorganization, (*c*) ongoing efforts to protect or enhance an investment, or (*d*) the pursuit of other claims or legal actions. Paragraphs 15–16 of FASB ASC 946-320-35 further explain that workout expenditures that are incurred as part of negotiations of the terms and requirements of capital infusions or that are expected to result in the restructuring of, or a plan of reorganization for, an investment should be recorded as realized losses. Ongoing expenditures to protect or enhance an investment or expenditures incurred to pursue other claims or legal actions should be treated as operating expenses.

Lending of Portfolio Securities

> ©Update 2-2 *Accounting and Reporting:* **Reconsideration of Effective Control**
>
> FASB ASU No. 2011-03, *Transfers and Servicing (Topic 860): Reconsideration of Effective Control for Repurchase Agreements*, issued in April 2011, is effective for the first interim or annual period beginning on or after December 15, 2011, and should be applied prospectively to transactions or modifications of existing transactions that occur on or after that date. Early adoption is not permitted.
>
> Refer to section A.01 in appendix A for more information on this ASU if applicable to your reporting period.

2.124 Investment companies may lend securities (principally to broker-dealers). Such transactions are documented as loans of securities in which the borrower of securities generally is required to provide collateral to the lender, commonly cash but sometimes other securities or standby letters of credit, with a value slightly higher than that of the securities borrowed. If the collateral is cash, the lender of securities normally earns a return by investing that cash, typically in short-term, high-quality debt instruments, at rates higher than the rate paid or rebated to the borrower. Investment of cash collateral is subject to the investment company's investment restrictions. If the collateral is other than cash, the lender of securities typically receives a fee. The investment company, as lender, receives amounts from the borrower equivalent to dividends and interest on the securities loaned. As with other extensions of credit, there are risks of delay in recovery or even loss of rights in the collateral should the borrower of the securities fail financially.

2.125 As discussed in FASB ASC 860-30-25-7, many securities lending transactions are accompanied by an agreement that both entitles and obligates the transferor to repurchase or redeem the transferred financial assets before their maturity. FASB ASC 860-10-40-24 states that an agreement that both entitles and obligates the transferor to repurchase or redeem transferred financial assets from the transferee maintains the transferor's effective control over those assets, as described in FASB ASC 860-10-40-5(c)(1), if all of the conditions in FASB ASC 860-10-40-24 are met. Those transactions should be accounted for as secured borrowings in which either cash or securities that the holder is permitted by contract or custom to sell or repledge received as collateral are considered the amount borrowed, the securities loaned are considered pledged as collateral against the cash borrowed and reclassified as set forth in FASB ASC 860-30-25-5(a), and any rebate paid to the transferee of securities is interest on the cash that the transferor is considered to have borrowed.

2.126 Paragraphs 4–5 of FASB ASC 860-30-25 explain that the accounting for noncash collateral by the debtor (or obligor) and the secured party depends on whether the secured party has the right to sell or repledge the collateral and whether the debtor has defaulted. Cash collateral should be derecognized by the payer and recognized by the recipient not as collateral but, rather, as proceeds of either a sale or borrowing.

Accounting for Derivatives

2.127 FASB ASC 815, *Derivatives and Hedging*, establishes accounting and reporting standards for derivative instruments, including certain derivative instruments embedded in other contracts (referred to collectively as derivatives), and hedging activities. FASB ASC 815-10-15-83 defines a derivative instrument as a financial instrument or other contract with all of the following characteristics:

    a. It has (1) one or more underlying instruments and (2) one or more notional amounts or payment provisions or both. Those terms determine the amount of the settlement or settlements, and, in some cases, whether or not a settlement is required.

    b. It requires no initial net investment or an initial net investment that is smaller than would be required for other types of contracts that would be expected to have a similar response to changes in market factors.

    c. Its terms implicitly or explicitly require or permit net settlement, it can readily be settled net by a means outside the contract, or it provides for delivery of an asset that puts the recipient in a position not substantially different from net settlement.

FASB ASC 815 requires that an entity recognize all derivatives as either assets or liabilities in the statement of financial position and measure those instruments at fair value, and recognize changes to fair value in the statement of operations for those not designated as hedging instruments. FASB ASC 815-10-50 contains extensive disclosure requirements for derivatives. Refer to the full text of FASB ASC 815 when testing accounting and reporting issues related to derivative instruments.[33]

---

[33] In May 2010, FASB issued the proposed ASU *Accounting for Financial Instruments and Revisions to the Accounting for Derivative Instruments and Hedging Activities—Financial Instruments (Topic 825) and Derivatives and Hedging (Topic 815)*. This was followed up with a discussion paper in February 2011 intended to solicit input on how to improve, simplify, and converge the financial reporting requirements for hedging activities. Specifically, it requests stakeholders to comment on whether the IASB's exposure draft *Hedge Accounting* (issued in December 2010) is a better starting point for any changes to U.S. generally accepted accounting principles as it relates to derivatives and hedging activities. Readers should remain alert for developments on this topic, which can be accessed from the Technical Plan and Project Updates page at www.fasb.org.

Investment Accounts

2.128 The following transactions may meet the definition of a derivative, and therefore require certain additional disclosures:

- swaps (credit default, interest rate, total return, and currency),
- future contracts (eurodollar, treasuries, municipal bond indexes, equity indexes, commodities, individual stocks, foreign bonds),
- forward currency contracts, interest rate caps and floors,
- purchased and written options (equities, indices, futures, currencies, treasuries, and the like),
- swaptions (total return, credit default and interest rate swaps),
- certain capital support arrangements (for example, money market fund support agreements to maintain a $1.00 net asset value), and
- certain warrants (refer to chapter 3, "Financial Instruments," of this guide for further discussion relating to when a warrant could be considered a derivative).

2.129 AU section 332, *Auditing Derivative Instruments, Hedging Activities, and Investments in Securities* (AICPA, *Professional Standards*), provides guidance to auditors in planning and performing auditing procedures for assertions about derivative instruments; hedging activities; investments in debt and equity securities; and certain investments accounted for under FASB ASC 323, *Investments—Equity Method and Joint Ventures*, or 325, *Investments—Other*. In addition, the AICPA Audit Guide *Auditing Derivative Instruments, Hedging Activities, and Investments in Securities* provides practical guidance for implementing the related audit requirements.

Accounting for Foreign Investments

2.130 Investments in securities of foreign issuers involve considerations not typically associated with domestic investments. Foreign securities are denominated and pay distributions in foreign currencies, exposing investment companies to changes in foreign currency exchange rates. Investments in certain foreign countries may include the risk of expropriation or confiscatory taxation, limitations on the removal of funds or other assets, political or social instability, or adverse diplomatic developments. Individual foreign economies may differ from the economy of the United States in growth of gross domestic product, rates of inflation, capital reinvestments, resource self-sufficiency, and balance of payments positions. Securities of many foreign entities may be less liquid and their prices more volatile.

2.131 Because most foreign securities are not registered with the SEC, most of the issuers of foreign securities are not subject to the SEC's reporting requirements. Usually, there is less government supervision and regulation of stock exchanges, brokers, and entities in foreign countries than in the United States. As a result, financial or regulatory information concerning certain foreign issuers of securities may not be as readily available. Also, foreign entities may not be subject to uniform accounting, auditing, and financial reporting standards or practices and requirements comparable to those that apply to domestic entities. Further, many foreign stock markets are not as developed or efficient as those in the United States. Fixed commissions on transactions on foreign stock exchanges usually are higher than negotiated commissions on U.S. exchanges. The time between the trade and settlement dates of securities transactions on foreign exchanges ranges from one day to four weeks or longer.

AAG-INV 2.131

2.132 Foreign exchange transactions may be conducted on a cash basis at the prevailing spot rate for buying or selling the currency. Under normal market conditions, the spot rate differs from the published exchange rate because of the costs of converting from one currency to another. Some funds use forward foreign exchange contracts as hedges against possible changes in foreign exchange rates. These funds contract to buy or sell specified currencies at specified future dates and prices that are established when the contract is initiated. Dealings in forward foreign exchange contracts may relate to specific receivables or payables occurring in connection with the purchase or sale of portfolio securities, hedging all or a portion of a portfolio or the payment of dividends and other distributions.[34]

2.133 The cost of foreign currency transactions varies with such factors as the currency involved, the length of the contract period, and prevailing market conditions. Because exchanges in foreign currencies are usually transacted by principals, most often, there are no fees or commissions.

2.134 As an alternative to buying shares of foreign-based entities in overseas markets, investment companies can buy shares in the United States, denominated in U.S. dollars (for example, American depository receipts [ADRs]). These receipts are for shares of a foreign-based corporation that are held by a U.S. bank as trustee. The trustee bank collects dividends and makes payments to the holders of the ADR.

2.135 *Valuation of foreign securities.* FASB ASC 946-320-35-4 states that, in general, the discussion of valuation of securities in the related subtopic of FASB ASC 946-320 (and in this chapter) also applies to foreign securities. Portfolio securities that are traded primarily on foreign securities exchanges should be valued at the functional currency (usually the U.S. dollar equivalent) values for such securities on their exchanges.

2.136 *Other matters.* In addition to the foreign currency risk associated with investing in foreign securities, such investments present the following additional risks that need to be assessed continuously by management and considered for financial statement disclosure, as stated in paragraphs 2–3 of FASB ASC 946-830-50:

- *Liquidity.* Because certain foreign markets are illiquid, market prices may not necessarily represent realizable value.
- *Size.* When market capitalization is low, a fund's share in the entire market (particularly when single-country funds are involved) or specific securities may be proportionately very large, and the quoted market price would not necessarily reflect realizable value.
- *Valuation.* Because of liquidity and size problems, as well as other factors, such as securities that are unlisted or thinly traded, funds would have to adopt specific fair valuation procedures for determining the values of such securities. Doing so may be difficult in a foreign environment; although others may perform the research and provide supporting documentation for fair values, the ultimate responsibility for determining the fair values of securities rests with the directors.

---

[34] Registered investment companies investing in forward foreign exchange contracts are subject to limitations under Section 18 of the 1940 Act.

Investment Accounts

The disclosures suggested previously are no different from those that could be required for domestic securities with the same attributes. The preceding risks shall be disclosed in the notes to the financial statements if such factors exist in the markets in which the fund has material investments.

2.137 Management should also make sure that prices provided by local sources (such as the last sale price, bid or ask, mean of bid and ask, closing price, and so on) do represent the fair value of the securities. This is especially important for open-end funds or closed-end funds that allow limited redemption.

2.138 *Gains and losses from foreign investment holdings and transactions.* As stated in paragraphs 2–4 of FASB ASC 946-830-45, the differences between originally recorded amounts and currently consummated or measured amounts in the reporting currency are a function of changes in two factors: foreign exchange rates and changes in market prices. Those effects should be identified, computed, and reported other than for gains and losses on investments. The practice of not disclosing separately the portion of the changes in market values of investments and realized gains and losses thereon that result from foreign currency rate changes is permitted. However, separate reporting of such gains and losses is allowable and, if adopted by the reporting entity, should conform to the guidance in FASB ASC 946-830. Refer to appendix G, "Illustrations for Separately Calculating and Disclosing the Foreign Currency Element of Realized and Unrealized Gains and Losses," of this guide for illustrations of separately calculating and disclosing the foreign currency element of realized and unrealized gains and losses.

2.139 As explained in FASB ASC 946-830-45-15, a fund investing in foreign securities generally invests in such securities to reap the potential benefits offered by the local capital market. It may also invest in such securities as a means of investing in the foreign currency market or benefiting from the foreign currency rate fluctuation. The extent to which separate information regarding foreign currency gains or losses will be meaningful will vary, depending on the circumstances, and separate information may not measure with precision foreign exchange gains or losses associated with the economic risks of foreign currency exposures. A foreign currency rate fluctuation, however, may be an important consideration in the case of foreign investments, and a reporting entity may choose to identify and report separately any resulting foreign currency gains or losses as a component of unrealized market gain or loss on investments.

2.140 *Bifurcation.* As noted in FASB ASC 946-830-45-16, the market value of securities should be determined initially in the foreign currency and translated at the spot rate on the purchase trade date. The unrealized gain or loss between the original cost (translated on the trade date) and the market value (translated on the valuation date) comprises both of the following elements:

    a. Movement in market price
    b. Movement in foreign currency exchange rate

2.141 FASB ASC 946-830-45-17 states that such movements may be combined or bifurcated (that is, separate disclosure of the foreign currency gains and losses). If bifurcation is chosen, the movement in market prices should be measured as the difference between the market value in foreign currency and the original cost in foreign currency translated at the spot rate on the valuation date. The effect of the movement in the foreign exchange rate should

AAG-INV 2.141

be measured as the difference between the original cost in foreign currency translated at the current spot rate and the historical functional currency cost. These values can be computed as follows:

    a. (Market value in foreign currency − original cost in foreign currency) × valuation date spot rate = unrealized market value appreciation or depreciation

    b. (Cost in foreign currency × valuation date spot rate) − cost in functional currency = the unrealized foreign currency gain or loss

    2.142 FASB ASC 946-830-45-19 notes that, for short-term securities held by a fund that uses the amortized cost method of valuation, the amortized cost value should be substituted for market value in the preceding formulas if separate reporting is chosen by the reporting entity.

    2.143 *Sales of securities.* FASB ASC 946-830-45-20 explains that if bifurcation is chosen by the reporting entity, the computation of the effects of market change and the foreign currency rate change is similar to that described in paragraph 2.141. Market value in the formula given in paragraph 2.141 should be replaced with sale proceeds, and the valuation date should be replaced with the sale trade date, as follows:

    a. (Sale proceeds in foreign currency − original cost in foreign currency) × sale trade date spot rate = realized market gain or loss on sale of security

    b. (Cost in foreign currency × sale trade date spot rate) − cost in functional currency = realized foreign currency gain or loss

    2.144 As discussed in FASB ASC 946-830-45-21, the sale of a security results in a receivable for the security sold. That receivable should be recorded on the trade date at the spot rate. On the settlement date, the difference between the recorded receivable amount and the actual foreign currency received converted into the functional currency at the spot rate is recognized as a realized foreign currency gain or loss.

    2.145 *Purchased interest and sale of interest.* FASB ASC 946-830-45-14 explains that purchased interest represents the interest accrued between the last coupon date and the settlement date of the purchase. It should be recorded in the functional currency as accrued interest receivable at the spot rate on the purchase trade date and marked to market using each valuation date's spot rate. After the settlement date, daily interest income should be accrued at the daily spot rate. It may be impractical to prepare the foregoing calculations daily; therefore, the use of a weekly or monthly average rate may be appropriate in many cases, especially if the exchange rate does not fluctuate significantly. However, if the exchange rate fluctuation is significant, the calculation should be made daily.

    2.146 As stated by FASB ASC 946-830-45-22, interest sold represents the accrued interest receivable between the last coupon date and the settlement date of sale of the security. The difference between the recognized interest receivable amount and the actual foreign currency received (converted into the functional currency at the spot rate) should be recognized as a realized foreign currency gain or loss.

    2.147 *Receivables and payables.* As explained in FASB ASC 946-830-45-23, all receivables and payables that are denominated in a foreign currency relating to income or expense or securities sold or purchased should be translated into the functional currency at each valuation date at the spot rate on that date. The difference between that amount and the functional currency amount that was recorded at various spot rates for income and expense items and at the trade date spot rate, in the case of sales and purchases of securities, is unrealized foreign currency gain or loss. Upon liquidation of the receivable or payable balance in a foreign currency, the difference should be reclassified as realized foreign currency gain or loss.

2.148 *Cash.* As explained in FASB ASC 946-830-45-7, foreign currency cash balances and movements should be accounted for in the same manner as foreign currency-denominated securities. Every receipt of a foreign currency should be treated as a purchase of a security and recorded in the functional currency at the spot rate on the cash receipt date. Similarly, every disbursement of a foreign currency should be treated as a sale of a security, and the appropriate functional currency cost should be released, depending on whether a specific identified cost, first-in first-out method, or average cost method is used.

2.149 Paragraphs 8–9 of FASB ASC 946-830-45 state that the acquisition of foreign currency does not result in any foreign currency gain or loss. However, the disbursement of foreign currency results in a realized foreign currency gain or loss that is the difference between the functional currency equivalent of the foreign currency when it was acquired and the foreign currency disbursement translated at the spot rate on the disbursement date. Also, as is the case with all other assets and liabilities denominated in foreign currency, foreign currency cash balances should be translated on each valuation date at the spot rate on that date, resulting in unrealized foreign currency gain or loss.

2.150 *Dividends and interest.* As noted in FASB ASC 946-830-45-31, dividend income on securities denominated in a foreign currency should be recorded on the ex-dividend date using the spot exchange rate to translate the foreign currency amount into the functional currency on that date. The related dividend receivable should be translated into the functional currency daily at the spot rate, and the difference between the dividend accrued in the functional currency and the foreign currency receivable at the valuation date spot rate is unrealized foreign currency gain or loss. When the dividend is received, the unrealized foreign currency gain or loss should be reclassified as realized foreign currency gain or loss.

2.151 Further, FASB ASC 946-830-45-32 notes that the preceding approach to measuring investment income ensures that investment income accrued on foreign securities reflects the investment transaction without regard to the foreign currency gain or loss created in the time between the accrual and collection of the income.

2.152 FASB ASC 946-830-45-25 explains that interest on securities denominated in a foreign currency should be calculated at the stated rate of interest in the foreign currency. Interest on these securities should be accrued daily in the foreign currency at the stated interest rate and translated into the functional currency at the daily spot rate. Preparing such a calculation daily may be impractical; therefore, the use of a weekly or monthly average rate may be appropriate in many cases, especially if the exchange rate does not fluctuate significantly. However, if the exchange rate fluctuation is significant, the calculation should be made daily.

2.153 As noted in FASB ASC 946-830-45-26, the related receivable balance along with purchased interest, if any, should be accumulated in the foreign currency and translated into the functional currency daily using the spot rate for that date. The difference between the income accrued in the functional currency and the foreign currency receivable at the valuation date spot rate is unrealized foreign currency gain or loss.

2.154 As further stated in FASB ASC 946-830-45-27, when the interest is received and recorded in the functional currency at the spot rate on that date, the unrealized foreign currency gain or loss should be reclassified as realized foreign currency gain or loss.

2.155 FASB ASC 946-830-45-30 states that recording dividends on foreign securities is often difficult because, in certain countries, entities customarily declare dividends retroactively, or there is a lack of timely information. Additionally, in some countries, the sequencing of the declaration date and ex-dividend date may be different from the sequencing of these dates in the United States, thus necessitating a modification of the practice of recording dividends on the ex-dividend date (see paragraph 2.100). Also, foreign entities often declare stock dividends instead of cash dividends or take other corporate actions, such as issuing rights or warrants.

2.156 The SEC staff has stated that delayed recording of foreign corporate actions may be acceptable for registered investment companies if the investment company, exercising reasonable diligence, did not know that the corporate action had occurred; in such event, the investment company should record the action promptly after receipt of the information.[35]

2.157 *Amortization.* FASB ASC 946-830-45-28 states that amortization of premiums and accretion of discounts on bonds should be calculated daily in the foreign currency. The resulting amount of income or offset to income should be translated into the functional currency using that day's spot rate. The same foreign currency amount should be recorded as an addition to cost for accretion of discounts and a reduction to cost for amortization of premiums. Accordingly, cost consists of the original cost, translated at the spot rate in effect on the trade date that the bond was bought, adjusted for discount accretion or premium amortization at the spot rate on the date of adjustment. As stated in paragraph 2.152, use of a weekly or monthly average rate may be appropriate in certain circumstances.

2.158 As discussed in FASB ASC 946-830-45-29, on maturity, the carrying cost (including accretion or amortization) of the security in the foreign currency equals the proceeds. However, this will not be the case in the functional currency. The original cost should be translated into the functional currency at the spot rate on the trade purchase date, and the accretion or amortization is translated at periodic spot rates. The proceeds should be translated into the functional currency at the spot rate on the maturity date. The difference between the proceeds and the accumulated cost in the functional currency is realized foreign currency gain or loss.

2.159 *Withholding tax.* As FASB ASC 946-830-05-3 explains, dividends and interest received from foreign investments may result in withholding taxes and other taxes imposed by foreign countries, usually at rates from 10 percent

---

[35] November 1, 1996, Letter of SEC Division of Investment Management Chief Accountant to Investment Company Chief Financial Officers.

to 35 percent. Tax treaties between certain countries and the United States may reduce or eliminate such taxes. According to FASB ASC 946-830-45-33, many foreign countries do not tax capital gains on investments by foreign investors; however, if such gains are taxable, an accrual for capital gains taxes payable on both realized and unrealized gains should be included in the net asset value per share calculation.

2.160 The auditor should review the collectability of recorded receivables if withholding taxes have been reclaimed. FASB ASC 946-830-45-34 explains that whenever tax is to be withheld from investment income at the source, the amounts to be withheld that are not reclaimable should be accrued at the same time as the related income on each income recognition date if the tax rate is fixed and known. If a tax withheld is reclaimable from the local tax authorities, the tax should be recorded as a receivable, not an expense. When the investment income is received net of the tax withheld, a separate realized foreign currency gain or loss should be computed on the gross income receivable and the accrued tax expense. If the tax rate is not known or estimable, such expense or receivable should be recorded on the date that the net amount is received; accordingly, there would be no foreign currency gain or loss. However, if a receivable is recorded, there may be a foreign currency gain or loss through the date such receivable is collected.

2.161 FASB ASC 946-830-45-39 notes that taxes withheld that are not reclaimable on foreign source income should be deducted from the relevant income item and shown either parenthetically or as a separate contra item in the "Income" section of the statement of operations. Taxes levied on the aggregate income or capital gains of the investment company itself should be presented in a manner that is similar to that used for income taxes. The normal withholding taxes should be presented as follows.

Interest or dividend income (net of withholding taxes of $X)	$XXX
Or	
Interest or dividend income	$XXX
Less withholding tax	(XXX)

See paragraph 7.181 of this guide for an illustrative disclosure of the first method.

2.162 *Expenses.* FASB ASC 946-830-45-35 states that the accounting for expenses payable in a foreign currency is analogous to that for investment income receivable in a foreign currency. An expense should be accrued as incurred and translated into the functional currency at the spot rate each day. The use of an average weekly or monthly foreign currency rate would be acceptable if the foreign currency rate does not fluctuate significantly. The related accrued expense balance should be accumulated in the foreign currency and translated into the functional currency daily, using the spot rate for that date. The difference between the expense accrued in the functional currency and the related foreign currency accrued expense balance translated into the functional currency at the valuation date spot rate is unrealized foreign currency gain or loss. When the expense is paid, the unrealized foreign currency gain or loss should be reclassified as realized foreign currency gain or loss.

2.163 *Safekeeping of foreign assets.* Investing in foreign securities often involves custodial or subcustodial agreements with U.S. banks and their foreign branches, as well as foreign banks and trust entities, for the safekeeping of fund assets held outside the United States. Rule 17f-5 of the 1940 Act permits registered investment companies to maintain their foreign securities with eligible foreign custodians (for example, foreign banks and trust entities that meet certain requirements, securities depositories, and clearing agencies). Rule 17f-5 sets forth the conditions that must be included in the foreign custody agreement, as well as the specific responsibilities of the investment company's board of directors or trustees in reviewing and approving the arrangements. Additionally, Rule 17f-7 establishes conditions under which an investment company may place its assets in the custody of a foreign central securities depository.

Understanding the Entity and Its Environment and Assessing the Risks of Material Misstatement [36, 37]

2.164 Paragraph .01 of AU section 314, *Understanding the Entity and Its Environment and Assessing the Risks of Material Misstatement* (AICPA, *Professional Standards*), establishes requirements and provides guidance about implementing the second standard of field work, as follows: the auditor must obtain a sufficient understanding of the entity and its environment, including its internal control, to assess the risks of material misstatement of the financial statements whether due to error or fraud, and to design the nature, timing, and extent of further audit procedures. The importance of the auditor's risk assessment as a basis for further audit procedures is discussed in the explanation of audit risk in AU section 312, *Audit Risk and Materiality in Conducting an Audit* (AICPA, *Professional Standards*). At the account balance, class of transactions, relevant assertion, or disclosure level, audit risk consists of (*a*) the risks of material misstatement (consisting of inherent risk and control risk) and (*b*) detection risk. Paragraph .23 of AU section 312 states that auditors should assess the risks of material misstatement at the relevant assertion level as a basis for further audit procedures (tests of controls or substantive procedures). It is not acceptable to simply deem risk to be at the maximum. This assessment may be in qualitative terms, such as high, medium, and low, or in quantitative terms, such as percentages. See AU section 326, *Audit Evidence* (AICPA, *Professional Standards*), for guidance on how the auditor uses relevant assertions to form a basis for the assessment of risks of material misstatement and to design and perform further audit procedures. The auditor should assess risk at the financial statement and relevant assertion levels based on an appropriate understanding of the entity and its environment, including its internal control. AU section 318, *Performing Audit Procedures in Response to Assessed Risks and Evaluating the Audit Evidence Obtained* (AICPA, *Professional Standards*), discusses the auditor's responsibility to determine overall responses and to design and perform further audit procedures whose nature, timing, and extent are responsive to those risk assessments. Obtaining an understanding of the entity and its environment, including its internal control, is a continuous, dynamic

---

[36] This guide primarily discusses auditing guidance issued by the Auditing Standards Board (ASB) that applies to nonissuers. Issuers are defined by Section 3 of the Securities Exchange Act of 1934 and include registered investment companies. Audits of issuers are required to be performed under Public Company Accounting Oversight Board (PCAOB) standards. Users should evaluate their audit engagements to determine which auditing standards are applicable.

[37] For additional nonauthoritative guidance pertaining to internal control and the risk assessment standards (Statement on Auditing Standards Nos. 104–111 [AICPA, *Professional Standards*]), refer to Technical Questions and Answers sections 8200.05–.16 (AICPA, *Technical Practice Aids*), issued in March and April 2008.

process of gathering, updating, and analyzing information throughout the audit. Throughout this process, the auditor must refer to the guidance in AU section 316, *Consideration of Fraud in a Financial Statement Audit* (AICPA, *Professional Standards*), as discussed subsequently.

2.165
Considerations for Audits Performed in Accordance With Public Company Accounting Oversight Board (PCAOB) Standards

The PCAOB's suite of risk assessment standards (Auditing Standard Nos. 8–15 [(AICPA, *PCAOB Standards and Related Rules*, Auditing Standards]) set forth requirements that are intended to enhance the effectiveness of the auditor's assessment of, and response to, the risks of material misstatement in the financial statements. The risk assessment standards address audit procedures performed throughout the audit, from the initial planning stages to the evaluation of the audit results. Appendix 11, "Comparison of the Objectives and Requirements of the Accompanying PCAOB Auditing Standards with the Analogous Standards of the International Auditing and Assurance Standards Board and the Auditing Standards Board of the American Institute of Certified Public Accountants," of PCAOB Release No. 2010-004, *Auditing Standards Related to the Auditor's Assessment of and Response to Risk and Related Amendments to PCAOB Standards*, discusses certain differences between the objectives and requirements of the PCAOB risk assessment standards and the analogous standards of the International Auditing and Assurance Standards Board and Auditing Standards Board (ASB). Auditing Standard No. 12, *Identifying and Assessing Risks of Material Misstatement* (AICPA, *PCAOB Standards and Related Rules*, Auditing Standards), includes a requirement to evaluate, while obtaining an understanding of the company, whether significant changes in the company from prior periods, including changes in its internal control over financial reporting, affect the risks of material misstatement. The auditor is also required to consider performing certain procedures as part of obtaining an understanding of the company, including observing or reading transcripts of earnings calls, obtaining an understanding of compensation arrangements with senior management, and obtaining information about trading activity in the company's securities and holdings in the company's securities by significant holders.

Auditing Procedures

2.166 AU section 332[38] provides guidance on auditing investments in debt and equity securities, investments accounted for under FASB ASC 323 and 325, and derivative instruments and hedging activities. Refer to the auditing considerations and requirements of AU section 332, as applicable, for the guidance. AU section 328, *Auditing Fair Value Measurements and Disclosures* (AICPA, *Professional Standards*), contains expanded guidance on the audit procedures for fair value measurements and disclosures. Under AU section 328, the auditor's substantive tests of fair value measurements involve (*a*) testing

---

[38] For guidance on implementing the audit requirements regarding securities and derivative instruments, the reader should refer to the AICPA Audit Guide *Auditing Derivative Instruments, Hedging Activities, and Investments in Securities*.

management's significant assumptions, the valuation model, and the underlying data; (*b*) developing independent fair value estimates for corroborative purposes; or (*c*) examining subsequent events and transactions that confirm or disconfirm the estimate. The audit of an investment company's investment accounts is a significant portion of the overall audit because of the relative significance of those accounts and the related income accounts. In auditing the investment accounts, the auditor could test various aspects of the investment company's transactions with brokers, custodians, and pricing services.

2.167 Economic conditions in the jurisdictions in which funds invest may affect the auditor's assessment of inherent risks for relevant assertions in investment companies' financial statements. Factors that the auditor could evaluate include local rates of inflation, government stability, and local tax rules. An auditor could consider whether such indicators create, intensify, or mitigate inherent risk.

2.168 An auditor ordinarily does not have a sufficient basis for recognizing possible violations of security regulations or laws concerning compliance with investment restrictions because they relate more to the entity's operating aspects than its financial and accounting aspects. Even when violations of such laws can have consequences material to the financial statements, the auditor may not become aware of the existence of these illegal acts unless the auditor is informed by the client, or there is evidence of a governmental agency investigation or enforcement proceeding in the records, documents, or other information inspected in an audit of financial statements.

2.169 The auditor may review such relevant investment company documents as the latest prospectus, statement of additional information, certificate of incorporation, bylaws, and minutes of the board of directors' or trustees' and shareholders' meetings to gain an understanding of the investment company's investment restrictions and consider whether management has a program to prevent, deter, or detect noncompliance with the investment company's investment restrictions. As part of that consideration, the auditor could also obtain the written compliance policies and procedures designed to prevent the violation of federal securities laws and could meet with the designated chief compliance officer responsible for administering those policies and procedures (see paragraphs 2.50 and 2.247). The auditor could also consider whether the program has identified noncompliance with the stated investment restrictions and test the operation of the program to the extent considered necessary. An investment company's failure to comply with its stated investment restrictions may be considered a possible illegal act that may have an indirect effect on the financial statements of the fund. When an auditor becomes aware of the possibility of an illegal act, he or she must refer to AU section 317, *Illegal Acts by Clients* (AICPA, *Professional Standards*). Auditors may also be required, under certain circumstances, pursuant to the Private Securities Litigation Reform Act of 1995 (codified in section 10A(b)1 of the Securities Exchange Act of 1934) to make a report to the SEC relating to an illegal act that has a material effect on the financial statements.

2.170 As part of the certification of financial statements required by the Sarbanes-Oxley Act of 2002, the principal executive officer and principal financial officer of an investment company filing financial statements on Form N-CSR are required to disclose to the investment company's audit committee and independent auditors all significant deficiencies and material weaknesses in the design or operation of internal control over financial reporting that are

Investment Accounts

reasonably likely to adversely affect the investment company's ability to record, process, summarize, and report financial information. Further, they are to disclose to the audit committee and auditors any fraud, regardless of whether it is material, that involves management or other employees who have a significant role in the investment company's internal control over financial reporting.

2.171 AU section 339, *Audit Documentation* (AICPA, *Professional Standards*), provides guidance regarding the content, ownership, and confidentiality of audit documentation.

Considerations for Audits Performed in Accordance With PCAOB Standards

Auditing Standard No. 3, *Audit Documentation* (AICPA, *PCAOB Standards and Related Rules*, Auditing Standards), establishes general requirements for documentation that the auditor should prepare and retain in connection with engagements conducted pursuant to PCAOB standards. Auditing Standard No. 5, *An Audit of Internal Control Over Financial Reporting That Is Integrated with An Audit of Financial Statements* (AICPA, *PCAOB Standards and Related Rules*, Auditing Standards), requires that, in addition to the documentation requirements of Auditing Standard No. 5, auditors should document certain items related to their audits of internal control over financial reporting.

2.172 AU section 380, *The Auditor's Communication With Those Charged With Governance* (AICPA, *Professional Standards*), establishes standards and provides guidance on the auditor's communication with those charged with governance in relation to an audit of financial statements. Although this section applies regardless of an entity's governance structure or size, particular considerations apply when all those charged with governance are involved in managing an entity. This section does not establish requirements regarding the auditor's communication with an entity's management or owners, unless they are also charged with a governance role.

© Update 2-3 *Audit*: Clarified Auditing Standards

When effective, the clarified auditing standard AU-C section 265, *Communicating Internal Control Related Matters Identified in an Audit* (AICPA, *Professional Standards*), will supersede AU section 325, *Communicating Internal Control Related Matters Identified in an Audit* (AICPA, *Professional Standards*). AU-C section 265 contains substantive changes from the extant section. The term *extant* is used throughout this guide in reference to the standards that are superseded by the clarified standards.

For audits of financial statements for periods ending on or after December 15, 2012, refer to section B.02 in appendix B, "Guidance Updates—Clarified Auditing Standards," which summarizes these substantive changes that may affect an auditor's practice or methodology.

2.173 AU section 325 establishes standards and provides guidance on communicating matters related to an entity's internal control over financial reporting identified in an audit of financial statements. It is applicable whenever an auditor expresses or disclaims an opinion on financial statements. Among other things, AU section 325 requires the auditor to communicate in writing to management and those charged with governance significant deficiencies and material weaknesses identified in an audit. AU section 325 is not applicable if the auditor is engaged to examine the design and operating effectiveness of an entity's internal control over financial reporting that is integrated with an audit of the entity's financial statements.

Principal Audit Objectives

2.174 The principal objectives in auditing the investment accounts are to provide reasonable assurance of the following:

- The investment company has ownership of, and accounting control over, all its portfolio investments.
- All transactions are authorized and recorded in the accounting records in the proper account, amount, and period.
- Portfolio investments are valued properly, and their costs are recorded properly.
- Income from investments and realized gains and losses from securities transactions are accounted for properly.
- Investments are free of liens, pledges, or other security interests, or if not, such matters are identified properly and disclosed in the financial statements.

Obtaining an Understanding of the Entity and Its Environment, Including Internal Control

2.175 Establishing and maintaining internal control over financial reporting is an important management responsibility. In establishing specific controls that will enable an investment company to record, process, summarize, and report financial data that is consistent with management's assertions in the financial statements, management may wish to consider the following specific objectives:

- Transactions are executed in accordance with management's general or specific authorization.
- Transactions are recorded as necessary to permit the preparation of financial statements in conformity with U.S. generally accepted accounting principles (GAAP) or other criteria applicable to such statements and to maintain accountability for assets.
- Transactions are valued in a manner that permits recording their proper monetary value in the financial statements.
- Access to assets is permitted only in accordance with management's authorization.
- The recorded accountability for assets is compared with the existing assets at reasonable intervals, and appropriate action is taken with respect to any differences.

2.176 The second standard of fieldwork states, "The auditor must obtain a sufficient understanding of the entity and its environment, including its internal control, to assess the risk of material misstatement of the financial statements whether due to error or fraud, and to design the nature, timing, and extent of further audit procedures." Furthermore, AU section 314 states that the auditor should obtain a sufficient understanding of internal control by performing risk assessment procedures to (*a*) evaluate the design of controls relevant to an audit of financial statements and (*b*) determine whether they have been implemented. Refer to paragraphs .40–.101 of AU section 314 for a detailed discussion of internal control. Form N-SAR requires auditors of registered investment companies to report on an investment company's internal control over financial reporting, including those controls exercised on behalf of the company by agents. The report, which is filed with the fiscal year-end Form N-SAR, is based solely on the procedures performed as part of the audit. See paragraph 11.32 of this guide for an example of that report.

2.177 Under AU section 332, if the auditor plans to assess control risk for assertions related to derivatives and securities transactions below the maximum, the auditor should identify specific controls relevant to assertions that are likely to prevent or detect material misstatements and that have been placed in operation by either the entity or a service organization and should gather audit evidence about their effectiveness. Additionally, as noted in the prior paragraph, the second standard of fieldwork states that a sufficient understanding of internal control is to be obtained to plan the audit and determine the nature, timing, and extent of tests to be performed. Accordingly, the auditor may decide to obtain information about controls maintained by a custodian acting as a service organization to an investment company. This information may include whether and to what extent management and the board of directors or trustees have evaluated the investment company's relationship with the securities' custodian in terms of significant recordkeeping responsibilities, financial stability, operational capabilities, and other matters pertaining to the relationship. A custodian's controls that may be relevant to an audit of an investment company's financial statements could include, among others, the following:

- Controls covering the receipt of, and payment for, securities, the delivery of securities, and control over cash received
- Controls for physically segregating and satisfactorily safeguarding the company's securities in the custodian's vaults
- Physical counts of securities and other procedures performed by the custodian's internal auditors
- Controls over securities held in central depositories
- Controls over receipts of cash, including dividend and interest payments

---

© Update 2-4 *Audit*: Clarified Auditing Standards

When effective, the clarified auditing standard AU-C section 402, *Audit Considerations Relating to an Entity Using a Service Organization* (AICPA, *Professional Standards*), will supersede AU section 324, *Service Organizations* (AICPA, *Professional Standards*). AU-C section 402 contains primarily clarifying changes from the extant section.

For audits of financial statements for periods ending on or after December 15, 2012, refer to section B.08 in appendix B, which summarizes these clarifying changes that may affect an auditor's practice or methodology.

2.178 If the custodian has engaged a service auditor to examine the custodian's description of controls over custodial functions, the fund's auditor should consider obtaining a copy of the service auditor's report. The auditor's use of service auditors' reports is discussed in paragraphs 4.55–.62 of this guide. Further guidance for user auditors is provided in AU section 324[39] and for service auditors in SSAE No. 16, *Reporting on Controls at a Service Organization* (AICPA, *Professional Standards*, AT sec. 801). Auditing Standard No. 5 provides further guidance regarding the use of service organizations for an integrated audit. Paragraph .42 of AT section 801 requires a service auditor to inquire whether management is aware of any events subsequent to the period covered by management's description of the service organization's system up to the date of the service auditor's report that could have a significant effect on management's assertion.

2.179 An investment company may enter into subcustodial arrangements for investments in securities with institutions both inside and outside the United States.[40] The auditor should obtain an understanding of the extent of intercustodial responsibilities and rights under subcustodial agreements. For arrangements with foreign subcustodians, the auditor could consider inquiring about the procedures undertaken by the fund's directors or trustees in evaluating the subcustodial arrangement. Additionally, the principal custodian may perform oversight procedures, particularly over foreign subcustodians, that are relevant to the auditor when determining the extent of audit procedures to be applied to subcustodians. The auditor may apply audit procedures to each subcustodial arrangement that is similar to those for principal custodians if the existence assertion is not supported satisfactorily through the other procedures listed previously.

2.180 If an investment company enters into repurchase or securities lending agreements, the auditor may obtain an understanding of whether the investment company's controls include the following:

- A review of the creditworthiness of the issuers of repurchase agreements or counterparties for stock-lending arrangements

- A requirement that actual or constructive possession of the collateral be taken by the investment company, its custodian, or a custodian qualified under the 1940 Act who verifies that the collateral is being held for the investment company

- A requirement to mark the collateral to market daily during the entire period of the agreement

- A requirement that such agreements provide that additional collateral be deposited by the issuer if the fair value of the collateral falls below the repurchase price or stock loan value[41]

The auditor could inspect the terms of the agreements and assess the related accounting and disclosure, in accordance with the criteria of FASB ASC 860.

---

[39] The AICPA Guide *Service Organizations: Applying Service Organizations: Applying SSAE No. 16, Reporting on Controls at a Service Organization Guide (SOC 1*[SM]*)* contains information for CPAs reporting on controls at a service organization that affect user entities' internal control over financial reporting. Also, the AICPA Guide *Reporting on Controls at a Service Organization Relevant to Security, Availability, Processing Integrity, Confidentiality, or Privacy (SOC 2*[SM]*)* summarizes the three new service organization controls (SOC) engagements and provides detailed guidance on planning, performing, and reporting on SOC 2 engagements.

[40] SEC Final Rule Release No. 12354 under the 1940 Act.

[41] SEC Final Rule Release No. 13005 under the 1940 Act.

Examination of Transactions and Detail Records[42]

2.181 *Custody of securities.* For a registered investment company, the auditor should confirm all securities with the custodian, including securities held by the custodian on behalf of the investment company in a central securities system or similar omnibus account, or physically examine the securities, as applicable under the circumstances. Additionally, the SEC requires the auditor to confirm all unsettled securities purchased with the party responsible for delivery.[43] For those confirmations not received, the auditor should perform alternative procedures deemed appropriate in the circumstances.[44] For nonregistered investment companies, the timing and extent of testing custody is a matter of the auditor's professional judgment.

2.182 Other procedures the auditor implements typically include the following:

- Confirmation of when-issued transactions with the underwriter, including the value of such transactions as of the valuation date.

- Confirmation of commodity futures contracts, put or call options, financial futures contracts, swaps, and similar exchange-traded or directly-negotiated (OTC) derivative contracts with the clearing broker or counterparty.

- Confirmation of forward contracts, standby commitment contracts, and repurchase agreements (with the counterparty). For forward contracts, standby commitments, and reverse repurchase agreements, the auditor may review the contracts or agreements and consult with the investment company's legal counsel to determine if a *senior security*, as defined in Section 18(g) of the 1940 Act, exists.

- Confirmation of short securities positions with the broker.

- Confirmation of borrowed or loaned securities and related collateral with the broker or counterparty.

Also refer to paragraph .21 of AU section 332 for examples of substantive procedures relating to the existence and occurrence assertions about derivatives and securities.

---

[42] AU section 318, *Performing Audit Procedures in Response to Assessed Risks and Evaluating Audit Evidence Obtained* (AICPA, *Professional Standards*), states that to reduce audit risks to an acceptably low level, the auditor should (a) determine overall responses to address the assessed risks of material misstatement at the financial statement level and (b) design and perform further audit procedures whose nature, timing, and extent are responsive to the assessed risks of material misstatement at the relevant assertion level. The purpose is to provide a clear linkage between the nature, timing, and extent of the auditor's further audit procedures and the assessed risks. Refer to AU section 318 for additional guidance.

[43] Refer to the SEC Division of Investment Management Staff Issues of Interest Release titled "Business Development Companies—Auditor Verification of Securities Owned" at www.sec.gov. The SEC staff believes that it is a best practice for a BDC to have its auditor verify all of the securities owned by the BDC, either by actual examination or by receipt of a certificate from the custodian, and affirmatively state in the audit opinion whether the auditor has confirmed the existence of all such securities.

[44] Section 404.03 of the SEC's *Codification of Financial Reporting Policies.*

> **◎ Update 2-5 *Audit:* Clarified Auditing Standards**
>
> When effective, the clarified auditing standard AU-C section 505, *External Confirmations* (AICPA, *Professional Standards*), will supersede AU section 330, *The Confirmation Process* (AICPA, *Professional Standards*). AU-C section 505 contains primarily clarifying changes from the extant section.
>
> For audits of financial statements for periods ending on or after December 15, 2012, refer to section B.10 in appendix B, which summarizes these clarifying changes that may affect an auditor's practice or methodology.
>
> Additionally, all auditing interpretations corresponding to an AU section have been considered in the development of the clarified auditing standard and have either been incorporated accordingly and withdrawn by the ASB, or retained and revised to reflect the issuance of the AU-C section. Interpretation No. 1, "Use of Electronic Confirmations," of AU section 330 (AICPA, *Professional Standards*, AU sec. 9330 par. .01–.08), has been incorporated directly into AU-C section 505.

2.183 Interpretation No. 1 of AU section 330 clarifies, among other matters, that the use of an electronic confirmation process is not precluded by AU section 330.[45] Although no confirmation process with a third party is without some risk of interception or alteration, including the risk that the confirmation respondent will not be the intended respondent, paragraph .05 of Interpretation No. 1 states that confirmations obtained electronically can be considered to be reliable audit evidence if the auditor is satisfied that (*a*) the electronic confirmation process is secure and properly controlled, (*b*) the information obtained is a direct communication in response to a request, and (*c*) the information is obtained from a third party who is the intended respondent. The interpretation also provides guidance to assist the auditor in assessing the confirmation process.

2.184 Under certain conditions, Section 17 of the 1940 Act and rules promulgated thereunder, principally Rules 17f-1 and 17f-2, require additional examinations of securities. When possible, in carrying out the examination, the auditor is to make a physical examination of the securities themselves. The auditor is also required to confirm securities not held in physical form or in transit at the examination date.[46,47] In all cases, the auditor is also required to reconcile the physical count or confirmation with the fund's accounting records.

2.185 The exact requirements for the frequency and timing of examinations depend on the kind of custodial arrangement.[48] The kind of custodial arrangements and requirements include the following:

---

[45] In 2010, the PCAOB issued a proposed auditing standard, *Confirmations*, for public comment that would supersede its interim standard: AU section 330, *The Confirmation Process* (AICPA, *PCAOB Standards and Related Rules*, Interim Standards). Readers may access the proposed standard from the Standards' Current Activities page on the PCAOB website. Readers should remain alert for the issuance of this auditing guidance.

[46] Section 404.01.a of the SEC's *Codification of Financial Reporting Policies*.

[47] Because custodians no longer hold most securities in physical form, and custody relationships may extend through two or more levels of subcustodians (especially when funds invest in non-U.S. markets), the confirmation requirements of Rule 17f-2 are fulfilled when the auditor confirms security holdings with the highest-level unaffiliated subcustodian.

[48] See footnote 44.

Investment Accounts

- An investment company maintaining a custodial relationship with a member of a national securities exchange should follow Rule 17f-1 of the 1940 Act. That rule requires the investment company's auditor to examine all securities at the end of each annual and semiannual fiscal period and at least one additional time during the fiscal year chosen by the auditor, without advance notification to the custodian.

- An investment company that retains possession of its securities or maintains its securities in the custody of an affiliated bank should follow Rule 17f-2 of the 1940 Act. That rule requires the company's auditor to examine the securities at least three times in each fiscal year, at least two of which should be chosen by the auditor without prior notice to such company. A certificate of the auditor stating that an examination of such securities and investments has been made and describing the nature and extent of the examination should be attached to a completed Form N-17f-2 and transmitted to the commission promptly after each examination.

After each examination, the auditor should address a report to the investment company's board of directors or trustees. The auditor is required to submit promptly a copy of that report to the SEC stating that such an examination was performed and describing the work done and the results. An illustration of such a report is provided in chapter 11, "Independent Auditor's Reports and Client Representations," of this guide.

2.186 Under Rule 206(4)-2 of the Investment Advisers Act of 1940, all registered investment advisers (or an investment adviser required to register) who have custody of client funds or securities, as defined, must have an independent public accountant conduct an examination on a surprise basis once every calendar year. Advisers to pooled investment vehicles may be deemed to comply with the surprise examination requirements of the rule by obtaining an audit of the pool and delivering the audited financial statements to pool investors within 120 days of the pool's fiscal year-end.[49] That audit must be conducted by an accounting firm registered with, and subject to regular inspection by, the PCAOB. See paragraphs 11.23–.30 of this guide for further information.

2.187 *Tests of portfolio transactions.* The auditor rarely examines all transactions during the period under audit, unless specifically requested to do so, and selects a sample of portfolio transactions for testing. Brokers' advice or other documents may be examined to ascertain that they agree with the entries recorded in the purchase, sales, or general journals or other books of original entry. The auditor may test for proper authorizations, extensions, trade dates, and reasonableness of the transaction prices. The auditor may test whether sales have been properly accounted for during the period and that an acceptable method of costing sales (specific identification or average cost) has been applied consistently and that gains or losses have been calculated properly.

---

[49] In 2006, the SEC issued a letter indicating that it would not recommend enforcement action under this rule against an adviser of a fund of funds relying on the annual audit provision of Rule 206(4)-2 if the audited financial statements of the fund of funds are distributed to investors in the fund of funds within 180 days of the end of its fiscal year. See the August 10, 2006, SEC Staff Letter *ABA Committee on Private Investment Entities*. The amendments to the custody rule in 2009 do not affect the views of the staff expressed in that letter.

2.188 The auditor may test the classification of gains and losses for tax purposes and the adjustments to the bases of investments resulting from stock dividends, splits, rights, recapitalizations, and liquidating dividends.

2.189 *Portfolio transactions with affiliates.* Section 17 of the 1940 Act and related rules impose significant restrictions and, in some cases, prohibitions on transactions with affiliates. The terms *affiliate* and *control* in the 1940 Act have different meanings from their definitions in the FASB ASC glossary. Specifically, the term *affiliate* means an affiliated person, as defined in Section 2(a)(3) of the 1940 Act, and the term *control* has the meaning given in Section 2(a)(9) of the 1940 Act. The term *affiliated person*, as defined in Section 2(a)(3) of the 1940 Act, encompasses control relationships and the direct or indirect ownership of 5 percent or more of the outstanding voting securities of any issuer. An *affiliated person*, as defined in that section, includes officers, directors, partners, employees, investment advisers, and members of the investment adviser's advisory board.

2.190 Regulation S-X requires disclosure of more information about transactions with affiliates in prospectuses and annual reports to the SEC than is required under GAAP. Various rules of Regulation S-X require the financial statements of an investment company to state separately investments in affiliates, investment income from affiliates, gain or loss on sales of securities of affiliates, and management fees or other service fees payable to controlled entities and other affiliates.

2.191 In auditing a registered investment company, the auditor should be familiar with Section 17 of the 1940 Act and related rules. The guidance for auditing related party transactions in AU section 334, *Related Parties* (AICPA, *Professional Standards*), may be applied equally in ascertaining the existence of the 1940 Act *affiliates*, as defined under the 1940 Act, and auditing transactions with them. Further, in addition to the recommended written representation about the existence of related party transactions, in the audit of a registered investment company, the auditor could obtain written representations from management that, except to the extent indicated, the company

- does not own any securities either of directly affiliated or, to the best information and belief of management, indirectly affiliated entities.
- has not received income from, or realized gain or loss on sales of, investments in, or indebtedness of, such affiliated entities.
- has not incurred expenses for management or other service fees payable to such affiliated entities.
- has not otherwise engaged in transactions with such affiliated entities.

Paragraph 11.41 of this guide presents an illustrative management representation letter. If a question arises regarding whether a relationship represents an affiliation, the auditor may request that the investment company's management obtain a written opinion from legal counsel.

2.192 If affiliated entities exist, such as an underwriter or investment adviser, such auditing procedures as confirmation of transactions, examination of supporting documents, and written representations from the management of affiliated entities may be required. These procedures are necessary because the fund is required, by rules under the 1940 Act, to disclose amounts paid to affiliates in connection with their services to the investment company, such as commissions for sales of its shares and brokerage commissions for its portfolio transactions.

2.193 *Income from securities.* The auditor could test investment income, which may include testing a sample of dividends and interest earned during the period, applying analytical procedures, or a combination of both. For example, in the auditor's tests of purchases and sales, the auditor may test the income for the entire year from the securities selected or, in conjunction with other procedures, may select an interim period and test the income earned during that period from a representative sample of securities. In testing a sample of dividends for publicly traded securities, the auditor may consult independent financial reporting services to determine the ex-dividend and payable dates and the rates for the securities selected for testing. Interest payment dates and rates are also available from such services.

2.194 In connection with detailed testing, the auditor could consider unusual amounts of dividends (such as dividends in arrears) or interest (such as defaulted interest) received during the period under audit that may necessitate special disclosure. The auditor should be satisfied that the accounting is proper for significant income from noncash dividends. The auditor should test the investment company's determination of the tax status of dividend income.

2.195 The nature and significance of investment income from sources other than dividends or interest determine the extent of necessary auditing procedures.

2.196 *Net asset value.* The auditor may include among the tests of net asset value per share at the financial statement date and on selected interim dates tests that

- compare with the investment ledger the quantities and descriptions of portfolio securities owned.
- agree the fair value of investments to independent sources and supporting documentation for investments stated at fair value, as determined in good faith by the board of directors or trustees (or by management under procedures approved by the board of directors or trustees).
- test the clerical accuracy of valuation extensions and totals.
- reconcile amounts of assets and liabilities to the general ledger accounts. (If it is impractical to post daily in the general ledger, a company may use worksheets instead and, accordingly, should reconcile the worksheets to the general ledger at the nearest month end or other closing date.)
- review the reasonableness of income and expense accruals.
- reconcile the number of shares outstanding to the capital stock accounts in the general ledger or substitute worksheet.
- calculate the net asset value per share by dividing the difference between total assets and total liabilities by the number of shares outstanding.

2.197 The extent of the auditor's tests of net asset value per share computations depends on, among other factors, the auditor's assessment of control risk.

2.198 *Valuation of investments.*[50] For registered investment companies, the auditor could test all portfolio valuations as of the date of the financial statements. (For nonregistered investment companies, the timing and extent of testing portfolio valuations is a matter of the auditor's judgment.) In addition, because periodic computations of net asset value are based on the fair value of investments, the auditor may wish to evaluate the systems and procedures used by the fund during the period under audit in determining the fair value of investments. The auditor could test transactions on dates selected from the period under audit for agreement with the values computed by the investment company. The extent of those tests should be based on the auditor's judgment after considering tolerable misstatement, the assessed risk of material misstatement, and the degree of assurance that the auditor plans to obtain.

2.199 The fund's board of directors or trustees is responsible for approving and overseeing policies that ensure that its investments are calculated at fair value. The methods used to value investment securities are usually stated in the bylaws or by action of the board of directors or trustees. The methods used by registered investment companies should conform with the 1940 Act. The auditor should determine whether the valuation method used conforms to the company's stated policy and, if applicable, with the rules of regulatory authorities.

2.200 Quoted market prices for investments listed on national exchanges or OTC markets are available from sources such as financial publications, the exchanges, or the National Association of Securities Dealers Automated Quotations (NASDAQ). For certain other investments, quoted market prices may be obtained from broker-dealers. If quoted market prices are not available, estimates of fair value frequently can be obtained from third-party sources based on proprietary models or from the investment company based on internally developed or acquired models.

2.201 Quoted market prices obtained from financial publications or national exchanges and NASDAQ are considered to provide sufficient evidence of the fair value of investments. For certain investments, such as securities that do not trade regularly, the auditor could obtain estimates of fair value from broker-dealers or other third-party sources. In some situations, the auditor may determine that it is necessary to obtain an estimate of fair value from more than one pricing source. For example, this may be appropriate if a pricing source has a relationship with an entity that could impair its objectivity. The auditor should consider the guidance provided in AU sections 332[51] and 328 when auditing the fair value of investments.

---

[50] AU section 328, *Auditing Fair Value Measurements and Disclosures* (AICPA, *Professional Standards*), contains expanded guidance on the audit procedures for fair value measurements and disclosures. Under AU section 328, the auditor's substantive tests of fair value measurements involve (*a*) testing management's significant assumptions, the valuation model, and the underlying data; (*b*) developing independent fair value estimates for corroborative purposes; or (*c*) examining subsequent events and transactions that confirm or disconfirm the estimate. Portions of AU section 328 have been incorporated into the guidance contained in paragraphs 2.205–.214.

[51] For guidance on implementing the audit requirements for securities and derivative instruments, the reader should refer to the AICPA Audit Guide *Auditing Derivative Instruments, Hedging Activities, and Investments in Securities.*

Investment Accounts

> **⊙ Update 2-6 *Audit*: Clarified Auditing Standards**
>
> When effective, the clarified auditing standards AU-C section 402 and AU-C section 620, *Using the Work of an Auditor's Specialist* (AICPA, *Professional Standards*), will supersede the user auditor guidance within AU section 324 and AU section 336, *Using the Work of a Specialist* (AICPA, *Professional Standards*), respectively. AU-C sections 402 and 620 contain primarily clarifying changes from the extant sections.
>
> For audits of financial statements for periods ending on or after December 15, 2012, refer to sections B.08 and B.12 in appendix B, which summarizes these clarifying changes that may affect an auditor's practice or methodology.
>
> Additionally, all auditing interpretations corresponding to an AU section have been considered in the development of the clarified auditing standard and have either been incorporated accordingly and withdrawn by the ASB, or retained and revised to reflect the issuance of the AU-C section. Interpretation No. 1, "Auditing Investments in Securities Where a Readily Determinable Fair Value Does Not Exist," of AU section 332 (AICPA, *Professional Standards*, AU sec. 9332 par. .01–.04) has been incorporated directly into the AU-C section 501, *Audit Evidence—Specific Considerations for Selected Items* (AICPA, *Professional Standards*).

2.202 For estimates of fair value obtained from broker-dealers and other third-party sources, the auditor could consider the applicability of the guidance in AU section 324 or AU section 336. The auditor's decisions about whether such guidance is applicable and which guidance is applicable will depend on the circumstances. The guidance in AU section 336 may be applicable if the third-party source derives the fair value of a security by using modeling or similar techniques. If an entity uses a pricing service to obtain prices of listed securities in the entity's portfolio, the guidance in AU section 324 may be appropriate. Auditing Standard No. 5 provides further guidance regarding the use of service organizations for an integrated audit.

2.203 Interpretation No. 1 of AU section 332 provides guidance for auditors of nonissuers regarding the adequacy of audit evidence, with respect to the existence and valuation assertions in AU section 332, in confirmations received from third parties when a readily determinable fair value does not exist, and the auditor determines that auditing procedures could include verifying the existence and testing the measurement of the investments. For example, an entity may have an investment in a hedge fund that is reported at fair value but for which a readily determinable fair value does not exist. Further, the hedge fund may own interests in investments in limited partnership interests or other private equity securities for which a readily determinable fair value does not exist. As part of the auditor's procedures, in accordance with AU section 332, an auditor typically would satisfy the existence assertion through confirmation with the hedge fund, examination of legal documents, or other means. In confirming existence, the auditor may request the hedge fund to indicate or confirm the fair value of the entity's investment in the hedge fund, including the fair value of investments held by the hedge fund. In some circumstances, the hedge fund will not provide detailed information about the basis and method for measuring the entity's investment in the hedge fund nor will it provide information about specific investments held by the hedge fund. Interpretation No. 1 of AU section 332 illustrates examples of information that

AAG-INV 2.203

2.204 Most fixed income funds use bond dealers or other pricing services to value their portfolios. If such agents are used, the auditor should consider whether controls maintained by the fund or pricing service provide reasonable assurance that material pricing errors would be prevented or detected. Such controls may include the following:

- Testing methods used by the pricing service to obtain daily quotations
- Verifying daily changes of each security's fair value in excess of a stipulated percentage
- Verifying dealer quotations with other dealers on a test basis
- Maintaining a comparison of actual sales prices with the fair value assigned for the preceding day
- Consideration of fair value that has not changed for a stipulated period
- Periodic review of pricing information by portfolio managers and other knowledgeable officials

2.205 When investments are valued by the investment company using a valuation model (including an internally developed matrix pricing model), the auditor should obtain an understanding of the entity's process for determining fair value, including the following:

- Controls over the process used to determine fair value measurements, including, for example, controls over data and the segregation of duties between investment management functions and those responsible for undertaking the valuations
- The expertise and experience of those determining fair value measurements
- The role of IT in the valuation process, including the integrity of change controls and security procedures for valuation models and information systems
- Significant assumptions used in determining fair value, as well as the process used to develop and apply management's assumptions, including whether management used available market information to develop the assumptions
- Documentation supporting management's assumptions

---

[52] The Alternative Investments Task Force of the ASB has developed and issued a practice aid for auditors, *Alternative Investments—Audit Considerations*, which includes guidance on the following:
    a. General considerations pertaining to auditing alternative investments
    b. Addressing management's financial statement existence assertion
    c. Addressing management's financial statement valuation assertion
    d. Management representations
    e. Disclosure of certain significant risks and uncertainties
    f. Reporting

The practice aid also includes an example confirmation for alternative investments and illustrative examples of due diligence, ongoing monitoring, and financial reporting controls.

Investment Accounts

- Controls over the consistency, timeliness, and reliability of data used in valuation models

The role of the investment company's board of directors or trustees in establishing valuation policies and the conformity of the model with those policies and the rules or regulatory authorities should be considered.

2.206 It may be possible to test the validity of the model by comparing fair values with values obtained from a second pricing matrix or quotations obtained from market makers. However, as noted in paragraph 2.37, the use of model valuations may not be necessary when market quotations are available.

2.207 When no market prices are observable, the auditor could evaluate whether the entity's method of measurement is appropriate in the circumstances. An auditor uses professional judgment when making that evaluation. It also involves obtaining an understanding of management's rationale for selecting a particular valuation method by discussing with management its reasons for selecting that method. The auditor should determine whether

- management has sufficiently evaluated and appropriately applied the criteria, if any, provided by GAAP to support the selected method;
- the valuation method is appropriate in the circumstances, given the nature of the item being valued; and
- the valuation method is appropriate in relation to the environment in which the entity operates.

Management may have determined that different valuation methods result in a range of significantly different fair value measurements. In such cases, the auditor could evaluate how the entity has investigated the reasons for these differences in establishing its fair value measurements.

2.208 The auditor should evaluate whether the entity's method for determining fair value measurements is applied consistently and, if so, whether the consistency is appropriate, considering possible changes in the environment or circumstances affecting the entity. For example, the introduction of an active market for an equity security may indicate that use of a discounted cash flow method to estimate the security's fair value is no longer appropriate. If management has changed the valuation method, the auditor should determine whether management can adequately demonstrate that the method to which it has changed provides a more appropriate basis of measurement.

2.209 The auditor should test the data used to develop the fair value measurements and disclosures and evaluate whether the fair value measurements have been properly determined from such data and management's assumptions. Specifically, the auditor should evaluate whether the data on which the fair value measurements are based, including the data used in the work of a specialist, is accurate, complete, and relevant and whether fair value measurements have been properly determined using such data and management's assumptions. The auditor's tests also may include, for example, procedures such as verifying the source of the data and mathematical recomputation of inputs and reviewing information for internal consistency.

2.210 For items valued using a valuation model, the auditor does not function as an appraiser and is not expected to substitute his or her judgment

AAG-INV 2.210

for that of the investment company's management. Rather, the auditor may assess the reasonableness and appropriateness of the model, including whether management has identified the significant assumptions and factors influencing the measurement of fair value and whether the significant assumptions used are reasonable, and the model is appropriate, considering the entity's circumstances. (Significant assumptions cover matters that materially affect the fair value measurement and may include those that are sensitive to variation or uncertainty in amount or nature and are susceptible to misapplication or bias.) Further, the auditor should determine whether the investment company has made appropriate disclosures about the method(s) and significant assumptions used to estimate the fair values of such investments. The auditor should also become familiar with the provisions of the SEC's financial reporting releases on this subject, with emphasis on section 404.03 of the SEC's *Codification of Financial Reporting Policies*.

2.211 Specific assumptions used in determining fair value will vary with the characteristics of the item being valued and the valuation approach being used. For example, when an item is valued using discounted cash flows, there will be assumptions about the level of cash flows, the period of time used in the analysis, and the discount rate. Assumptions ordinarily are supported by differing types of evidence from internal and external sources that provide objective support for the assumptions used. The auditor should evaluate the source and reliability of evidence supporting management's assumptions, including consideration of the assumptions in light of historical and market information. The evaluation of the assumptions relates to the whole set of assumptions, as well as each assumption individually. Assumptions are frequently interdependent and, therefore, need to be internally consistent. A particular assumption that may appear reasonable when taken in isolation may not be reasonable when used in conjunction with other assumptions. Audit procedures dealing with management's assumptions are performed in the context of the audit of the entity's financial statements. The objective of the audit procedures with respect to management's assumptions is therefore not intended to obtain sufficient competent audit evidence to provide an opinion on the assumptions themselves. Rather, the auditor performs procedures to evaluate whether the assumptions provide a reasonable basis for measuring fair values in the context of an audit of the financial statements as a whole.

2.212 Events and transactions that occur after the financial reporting date but before the completion of fieldwork (for example, a sale of an investment shortly after the financial reporting date) may provide audit evidence regarding management's fair value estimates as of the financial reporting date. In such circumstances, it may become unnecessary to test the fair values determined through a valuation model because the subsequent event or transaction can be used to substantiate the fair value measurement. However, some subsequent events or transactions may reflect changes in circumstances occurring after the financial reporting date and, thus, do not constitute competent evidence of the fair value measurement at the financial reporting date. The auditor uses professional judgment in ensuring that only those events or transactions that reflect circumstances existing at the financial reporting date are considered.

2.213 Collateral often is assigned for certain types of investments in debt instruments that are measured at fair value. If the collateral is an important factor in measuring the fair value of the investment, the auditor should obtain sufficient competent audit evidence regarding the existence; value; rights;

and access to, or transferability of, such collateral, including consideration of whether all appropriate liens have been filed, and should consider whether appropriate disclosures about the collateral have been made.

2.214 *Money market funds.* For investment companies registered as *money market funds*, as defined in Rule 2a-7 of the 1940 Act, the auditor should consider reviewing and performing tests of the following:

- The fund's procedures under Rule 2a-7 and the monitoring of those procedures
- Monitoring of the extent of deviation between net asset value per share calculated using amortized cost and net asset value per share calculated using fair value
- Monitoring the portfolio maturity, credit quality, and diversification requirements of Rule 2a-7
- Compliance with the recordkeeping requirements of Rule 2a-7

Consideration of Fraud in a Financial Statement Audit

2.215 AU section 316 is the primary source of authoritative guidance about an auditor's responsibilities concerning the consideration of fraud in a financial statement audit. AU section 316 establishes standards and provides guidance to auditors in fulfilling their responsibility to plan and perform the audit to obtain reasonable assurance about whether the financial statements are free of material misstatement, whether caused by error or fraud, as stated in paragraph .02 of AU section 110, *Responsibilities and Functions of the Independent Auditor* (AICPA, *Professional Standards*).

> *Considerations for Audits Performed in Accordance With PCAOB Standards*
>
> Paragraphs 14–15 in Auditing Standard No. 5 provide additional fraud considerations when performing an integrated audit of financial statements and internal control over financial reporting.

2.216 The two types of misstatements relevant to the auditor's consideration of fraud in a financial statement audit are misstatements arising from fraudulent financial reporting and misstatements arising from misappropriation of assets. Three conditions generally are present when fraud occurs. First, management or other employees have an incentive or are experiencing perceived pressure, which provides a reason to commit fraud. Second, circumstances exist (for example, the absence of controls, ineffective controls, or the ability of management to override controls) that provide an opportunity for management or other employees to perpetuate fraud. Third, those involved must be able to rationalize or justify committing a fraudulent act.

The Importance of Exercising Professional Skepticism

2.217 Because of the characteristics of fraud, the auditor's exercise of professional skepticism is crucial when considering the risks of material misstatement due to fraud. Professional skepticism is an attitude that includes a questioning mind and a critical assessment of audit evidence. Regardless of any past experience with the entity and regardless of the auditor's belief about management's honesty and integrity, paragraph .13 of AU section 316 states that the auditor should conduct the engagement with a mindset that recognizes the possibility that a material misstatement due to fraud could be present. Further, professional skepticism requires an ongoing questioning of whether the information and evidence obtained suggests that a material misstatement due to fraud has occurred.

Discussion Among Engagement Personnel Regarding the Risks of Material Misstatement Due to Fraud[53]

2.218 Members of the audit team should discuss the potential for material misstatement due to fraud, in accordance with the requirements of paragraphs .14–.18 of AU section 316. The discussion among the audit team members about the susceptibility of the entity's financial statements to material misstatement due to fraud should include a consideration of the known external and internal factors affecting the entity that could (*a*) create incentives or pressures for management and others to commit fraud, (*b*) provide the opportunity for fraud to be perpetrated, and (*c*) indicate a culture or an environment that enables management to rationalize committing fraud. Communication among the audit team members about the risks of material misstatement due to fraud also should continue throughout the audit.

2.219

>*Considerations for Audits Performed in Accordance With PCAOB Standards*
>
>Auditing Standard No. 12 requires a discussion among the key engagement team members of specified matters regarding fraud, including how and where the company's financial statements might be susceptible to material misstatement due to fraud, known fraud risk factors, the risk of management override of controls, and possible responses to fraud risks. Certain matters are also required to be emphasized to all engagement team members, including the need to maintain a questioning mind throughout the audit and to exercise professional skepticism in gathering and evaluating evidence, to be alert for information or other conditions that might affect the assessment of fraud risks, and actions to be taken if information or other conditions indicate that a material misstatement due to fraud might have occurred.

Examples of Fraud Risk Factors

2.220 The following are examples of conditions that may indicate the presence of fraud in investment companies. Although the risk factors cover a broad range of situations, they are only examples; accordingly, the auditor may wish to consider additional or different risk factors. Also, the order of the examples of risk factors provided is not intended to reflect any relative importance or frequency of occurrence.

Part 1: Fraudulent Financial Reporting

A. *Opportunities*

  1. The nature of the industry or the entity's operations provides opportunities to engage in fraudulent financial reporting that can arise from the following:

---

[53] The brainstorming session to discuss the entity's susceptibility to material misstatements due to fraud could be held concurrently with the brainstorming session required under AU section 314, *Understanding the Entity and Its Environment and Assessing the Risks of Material Misstatement* (AICPA, *Professional Standards*), to discuss the potential of the risk of material misstatement.

AAG-INV 2.218

Investment Accounts

    a. Significant related party transactions not in the ordinary course of business or with related entities not audited or audited by another firm, such as

        i. significant transactions with affiliates that are not approved by the board of directors or trustees, in accordance with Section 17 of the 1940 Act, and

        ii. transactions involving affiliates that are not readily apparent in the circumstances or are apparent but not properly disclosed.

    b. Significant investments for which readily available market quotes are not available and inadequate procedures for estimating these values

    c. Significant investments in derivative financial instruments for which value is very difficult to estimate

2. Components of internal control may be deficient as a result of the following:

    a. Management's failure to display and communicate an appropriate attitude regarding internal control and the financial reporting process

    b. Unusual and considerable influence of the portfolio manager over the pricing sources and fair valuation methodology used to value securities

    c. Lack of board of directors' or trustees' involvement in the establishment of the fair valuation policies and procedures or lack of oversight over those policies and procedures

    d. Management's ability to unilaterally override internal controls, particularly security valuations

    e. Lack of adviser's supervisory or oversight procedures over its own employees or the subadviser, or both

    f. Inadequate controls around the calculation of the daily net asset value

    g. Reconciliation of security holdings with the custodian that is infrequent and incomplete

    h. Inadequate monitoring of the fund's tax status as a regulated investment company (RIC)

    i. Inadequate monitoring of the fund's compliance with its prospectus requirements

    j. Ineffective transfer agency controls or ineffective implementation of user controls

    k. Lack of an appropriate policy regarding corrections of net asset value errors or failure to comply with the policy

    l. Board of directors' or trustees' limited or lacking understanding of how portfolio management intends to implement the fund's investment restrictions, thereby creating a situation in which management can aggressively interpret or disregard adopted policies

    m. Board of directors' or trustees' limited or lacking understanding of derivatives used by portfolio managers and involvement in approving or disapproving the use of specific

AAG-INV 2.220

strategies, such as embedded leverage, thereby creating a situation in which management can aggressively interpret or disregard adopted policies

n. Incomplete or insufficient description of portfolio positions in accounting records to permit adequate monitoring of prospectus requirements

o. Inadequate segregation of duties between operating (for example, portfolio management, fund distribution) and compliance monitoring functions

p. Inadequate monitoring of compliance by subservicing agents and intermediaries with prospectus requirements regarding transactions in fund shares

B. *Attitudes and Rationalizations*

The auditor may not be able to observe risk factors reflective of attitudes and rationalizations by members of the board of directors or trustees, general partner, management, or employees that allow them to engage in, rationalize, or justify fraudulent financial reporting. Nevertheless, the auditor who becomes aware of the existence of such information should consider that information in identifying the risks of material misstatement arising from fraudulent financial reporting. For example, auditors may become aware of the following:

1. Nonfinancial management's excessive participation in, or preoccupation with, the selection of accounting principles or the determination of significant estimates, such as the following:

    a. An excessive focus on maintaining a high rate of dividend payments, regardless of the fund's actual investment income

    b. A significant number of investments are valued by management, either judgmentally or through valuation models

2. A known history of violations of securities laws or other laws and regulations or claims against the entity, its senior management, or members of the board of directors or trustees alleging fraud or violations of laws and regulations, such as the following:

    a. Past suspensions of the ability to act as an investment adviser or a requirement that the adviser be supervised by others

    b. Significant deficiencies cited in inspection letters by the SEC or other regulatory bodies, with a heightened emphasis on deficiencies cited in prior inspections that management has not remedied

3. A practice by management of committing to creditors and other third parties to achieve aggressive or unrealistic forecasts, such as the following:

    a. Commitment to preserve principal or maintain a certain income or distribution yield

    b. Commitment to achieve a targeted level of assets under management by a specified date

    c. Commitment to achieve a targeted level of gross or net fund share sales during a defined period

Investment Accounts

4. Adviser's fee revenues (including performance incentives) directly related to either the value of fund assets or performance, if the adviser has substantial discretion in valuing portfolio investments, and changes in fee revenues may be significant to the adviser
5. Undisclosed use of soft-dollar credits and other items (for example, to reduce a gross ratio below a cap, so the adviser does not have to reimburse the fund for excess expenses)

Part 2: Misappropriation of Assets

Some of the risk factors related to misstatements arising from fraudulent financial reporting also may be present when misstatements arising from misappropriation of assets exist. For example, ineffective monitoring of management and weakness in internal control may be present when misstatements due to either fraudulent financial reporting or misappropriation of assets exist. The following are examples of risk factors related to misstatements arising from misappropriation of assets.

A. *Opportunities*

1. Certain characteristics or circumstances may increase the susceptibility of assets to misappropriation. For example, opportunities to misappropriate assets increase with the use of soft dollar arrangements for the benefit of the adviser without client consent (including the existence of undocumented or ill-defined arrangements).
2. Inadequate internal control over assets may increase the susceptibility of misappropriation of those assets. For example, misappropriation of assets may occur because of the following:
    a. Access to funds and securities, and accounting for them is directly controlled by the adviser, with inadequate segregation of duties (or no direct communication between the custodian and accounting personnel)
    b. Lack of any periodic review of a transfer agency's control design and operation by an independent auditor knowledgeable in the area (such as a SOC 1 report)
    c. Infrequent and incomplete reconciliation of security holdings with the custodian
    d. Lack of a clearly defined policy with respect to personal investing activities (for example, front-running fund trades or taking investment opportunities for personal use)
    e. Ineffective transfer agency controls or ineffective implementation of user controls in a service center environment, particularly inadequate controls over uncashed dividend or redemption check listings that are returned by the post office and other inactive shareholder accounts; and reconciliations of transfer agency bank accounts
    f. Lack of segregation of duties between portfolio management and trading or an absence of an independent review of trading executions (for example, unexpected concentrations of trading with counterparties, poor trade executions, or higher-than-normal commissions that may indicate the existence of collusion between portfolio personnel and counterparties)

AAG-INV 2.220

Obtaining the Information Needed to Identify the Risks of Material Misstatement Due to Fraud

2.221 AU section 314 establishes requirements and provides guidance about how the auditor obtains an understanding of the entity and its environment, including its internal control, for the purpose of assessing the risks of material misstatement. In performing that work, information may come to the auditor's attention that should be considered in identifying risks of material misstatement due to fraud. As part of this work, the auditor should perform the following procedures to obtain information that is used (as described in paragraphs .35–.42 of AU section 316) to identify the risks of material misstatement due to fraud:

 a. Make inquiries of management and others within the entity to obtain their views about the risks of fraud and how they are addressed (see paragraphs .20–.27 of AU section 316).

 b. Consider any unusual or unexpected relationships that have been identified in performing analytical procedures in planning the audit (see paragraphs .28–.30 of AU section 316).

 c. Consider whether one or more fraud risk factors exist (see paragraphs .31–.33 and the appendix in AU section 316 and paragraph 2.170).

 d. Consider other information that may be helpful in the identification of risks of material misstatement due to fraud (see paragraph .34 of AU section 316).

2.222

Considerations for Audits Performed in Accordance With PCAOB Standards

Auditing Standard No. 12 requires the auditor to make specified inquiries of management and the audit committee regarding tips or complaints about the company's financial reporting. The auditor is required to use his or her knowledge of the company and its environment, as well as information from other risk assessment procedures, to determine the nature of inquiries about risks of material misstatement. The auditor must take into account the fact that management is often in the best position to commit fraud when evaluating management's responses to inquiries about fraud risks.

2.223 In planning the audit, the auditor should also perform analytical procedures relating to revenue, with the objective of identifying unusual or unexpected relationships involving revenue accounts that may indicate a material misstatement due to fraudulent financial reporting. For example, in the investment company industry, the following unusual or unexpected relationships may indicate a material misstatement due to fraud:

 a. Investment performance substantially higher (or lower) when compared with industry peers or other relevant benchmarks, which cannot be readily attributed to the performance of specific securities when prices are readily available in an active market. Particular considerations include the following:

    i. Significant gains (or losses) from securities held for extremely short periods of time

Investment Accounts

      ii. Significant gains (or losses) from instruments not typically acquired by the fund

  b. Unusually high levels of investment purchases and sales in relation to total fund net assets without apparent economic purpose.

  c. A net investment income ratio substantially higher than the industry peers or other relevant benchmarks, particularly in a fund marketed with the objective of making current income distributions.

  d. Expense ratios that change significantly from year to year with inadequate explanation.

  e. Expense ratios and transaction costs exceed industry norms.

  f. Significant differences between the prices at which securities are sold to third parties from the values reflected in the fund's net asset value in the days prior to the sale.

  g. Unusually high volumes of gross fund share sales and redemptions in relation to total shares outstanding.

2.224 As indicated in paragraph 2.218, the auditor may identify events or conditions that indicate incentives or pressures, or both, to perpetrate fraud; opportunities to carry out the fraud; or attitudes or rationalizations, or both, to justify a fraudulent action. Such events or conditions are referred to as fraud risk factors. Fraud risk factors do not necessarily indicate the existence of fraud; however, they often are present in circumstances in which fraud exists.

2.225 AU section 316 provides fraud risk factors that apply to most enterprises. Paragraph 2.220 contains a list of fraud risk factors specific to the investment company industry. Remember that fraud risk factors are only one of several sources of information that an auditor considers when identifying and assessing risks of material misstatement due to fraud.

Identifying Risks That May Result in a Material Misstatement Due to Fraud[54]

2.226 In identifying risks of material misstatement due to fraud, the auditor's consideration of the information that has been gathered in accordance with the requirements of paragraphs .19–.34 of AU section 316 is helpful. The auditor's identification of fraud risks may be influenced by characteristics such as the entity's size, complexity, and ownership attributes. In addition, paragraph .51 of AU section 316 states that the auditing procedures performed in response to identified risks of material misstatement due to fraud will vary depending upon the types of risks identified and the account balances, classes of transactions, and related assertions that may be affected. Certain accounts, classes of transactions, and assertions that have high inherent risk because they involve a high degree of management judgment and subjectivity also may present risks of material misstatement due to fraud because they are susceptible to manipulation by management.

---

[54] Paragraph .102 of AU section 314 states that the auditor should identify and assess the risks of material misstatement at the financial statement level and at the relevant assertion level related to classes of transactions, account balances, and disclosures. This requirement provides a link between the auditor's consideration of fraud and assessment of risk and the auditor's procedures in response to those assessed risks.

2.227

Considerations for Audits Performed in Accordance With PCAOB Standards

Paragraph 4 of Auditing Standard No. 12 states that the auditor should perform risk assessment procedures that are sufficient to provide a reasonable basis for identifying and assessing the risks of material misstatement, whether due to error or fraud, and designing further audit procedures (as described in Auditing Standard No. 15, *Audit Evidence* [AICPA, *PCAOB Standards and Related Rules*, Auditing Standards]). Audit procedures that are necessary to identify and appropriately assess the risks of material misstatement include consideration of both external factors and company-specific factors and are further discussed in Auditing Standard No. 12.

2.228 Due to daily valuation requirements, only a few areas in investment companies' financial statements necessitate significant judgment. The fact that significant amounts of investments are valued by management, either judgmentally or through valuation models, presents a number of risks that the auditor should address. The following are illustrative risk factors related to the fair valuation of investments that the auditor could consider:

a. Lack of approval or oversight, or both, of a fair valuation policy by the board of directors or trustees

b. Lack of specificity in a fair valuation policy and procedures

c. Lack of consistency in the application of valuation procedures

d. Inordinate influence of portfolio management personnel over fair valuation decisions

e. Fair valuation by management when market values appear to be reasonably available

f. Lack of monitoring or follow up, or both, of fair valuation actions taken

g. Lack of evidence for fair valuation decisions made

h. Significant amounts of investments traded in "thin" markets, particularly through one market maker (either exclusively or primarily)

i. For securities not traded in organized markets (in particular, private placements) a determination of whether a purchase of investments has occurred, requiring the initiation of valuation procedures, or whether a sale has occurred for recognition of realized gain or loss, or both

j. Increases in the value of investments valued by management shortly after their acquisition without adequate explanation of the circumstances

2.229 In addition to fair valuation, risks are present in daily market valuation, as well. Risks that the auditor could consider include the following:

a. Use of a pricing service with inadequate capabilities or controls

b. Ability of portfolio management or other unauthorized individuals to override prices

c. Lack of consideration or availability of secondary or comparative, or both, pricing sources

Investment Accounts

    d. Significant levels of pricing from brokers

    e. Manual entry or override of prices

2.230 Derivative instruments are another class of transactions characterized by high inherent risk. The auditor could consider the following risk factors associated with derivatives:

    a. Lack of a policy governing derivative investments, including a clear definition of derivatives

    b. Lack of oversight over the use of derivative investments, including an ongoing risk assessment of derivative instruments

    c. Lack of adequate procedures to value derivatives

    d. Lack of an awareness or understanding of derivative transactions on the part of senior management or the board of directors or trustees

2.231 Trading of investment securities also poses some risks that could include the following factors:

    a. Lack of segregation of duties between portfolio management and trading functions

    b. Lack of a developed and consistently applied and enforced trade allocation policy

    c. Trading through unapproved counterparties

    d. Lack of enforcement of a personal trading (code of ethics) policy

    e. Lack of monitoring of commission levels and volume of trading by a broker

2.232 The auditor could consider the following factors for transfer agency or capital, or both, stock activity:

    a. High volume of cancel, rebook, or "as-of" activity

    b. Credible shareholder complaints

    c. Activity on dormant accounts

    d. Inadequate segregation of duties among mail processing, transaction processing, and reconciliation functions

    e. Inadequate segregation of duties within transaction processing, such as allowing processors to change an address or banking instructions and initiate a redemption

2.233 Other areas that the auditor should consider because they involve a high degree of management judgment and subjectivity and are susceptible to manipulation by management include the following:

    a. Income recognition on high-yield debt instruments when collectability is in question or on asset-backed securities requiring significant estimates regarding the timing of expected cash flows

    b. Major judgments made in determining that a RIC has qualified for pass-through status under IRC Subchapter M, which may include determining issuers for diversification status, major determinations of classification of revenue items as ordinary income or (long-term) realized gain, and satisfaction of the minimum distribution requirement

c. Significant elements of incentive fee computations (including the computation of any benchmarks against which performance is to be measured)

A Presumption That Improper Revenue Recognition Is a Fraud Risk

2.234 Material misstatements due to fraudulent financial reporting often result from an overstatement of revenues (for example, through premature revenue recognition or recording fictitious revenues) or an understatement of revenues (for example, through improperly shifting revenues to a later period). Therefore, the auditor should ordinarily presume that a risk of material misstatement due to fraud relating to revenue recognition exists (see paragraph .41 of AU section 316).

2.235 The risks of material misstatement of an investment company's financial statements due to improper revenue recognition will generally be considered inherently low. Valuations can be readily established for securities traded on active markets; interest on fixed-income securities can be readily computed as the product of coupon rate and par value, and dividend income can be readily determined through the use of widely-available reporting sources. The more that a particular fund departs from this model, the greater the risks of material misstatement due to fraud relating to revenue recognition. For example, as discussed previously, revenue recognition on certain asset-backed securities depends heavily on management's estimation of future cash flows, and management must estimate the collectability of interest (including unamortized discount) on high-yield securities when the underlying issuer is experiencing financial difficulty.

2.236 Various risks exist to the extent that securities cannot be valued on the basis of prices determined on an active market. To the extent that management is estimating the value of portfolio investments, the risk of fraudulent misstatement from systematic bias ordinarily exists, even when using generally recognized models. If an investment is valued through a single market maker (often the counterparty that sold the investment to the investment company), there is a risk that collusion occurred between that market maker and management in establishing a valuation for the investment. In many cases, independent valuation services provide estimates of value for fixed-income securities based on observable market transactions and financial information (including security ratings) available publicly. In some cases, however, the independent valuation service estimates value for securities that are not traded in the market, and for which the investment company may be the predominant or sole holder of the securities, based predominantly or solely on information that is provided by the investment company. In these infrequent cases, there is a risk that the information provided by management to the service is incomplete or otherwise biased. If the market for a security is "thin," there is a risk that the investment company (or related investment companies) may be able to manipulate the quoted price by systematic purchases of the security in the market. An auditor would not ordinarily be expected to identify price manipulation but may be able to identify a "thin" market in which trades are typically sporadic, so that small changes in supply or demand can have a significant effect on quoted prices. Usually, such securities only have an extremely small "float" (that is, freely tradable amounts owned by the public).

2.237 The auditor could consider the following factors related to the recognition of interest and dividend revenues:

- Cash receipts for interest or dividend payments are significantly different from accrued amounts.
- Receivable balances include potentially uncollectible interest or dividends, such as significantly overdue amounts.
- Interest or dividend accrual policies do not comply with GAAP or are not enforced.
- Daily interest income is erratic, rather than reasonably consistent.
- Procedures in place to identify dividends earned are lax.
- Interest or dividends receivable may be written off without independent approval.

2.238 Factors that the auditor could consider with respect to revenue recognition for realized and unrealized gains include the following:

- The stated policy for purchase lot selection on security sales is not followed.
- Realized gains are not properly calculated on sales.

2.239 The auditor also should ensure that an investment company does not record capital contributions from affiliates as revenues (see paragraphs 7.121–.126 of this guide for guidance on accounting for payments by affiliates and corrections of investment restriction violations).

A Consideration of the Risk of Management Override of Controls

2.240 Even if the auditor does not identify specific risks of material misstatement due to fraud, the possibility exists that management override of controls could occur; accordingly, the auditor should address that risk (see paragraph .57 of AU section 316) apart from any conclusions regarding the existence of more specifically identifiable risks. Specifically, the procedures described in paragraphs .58–.67 of AU section 316 should be performed to further address the risk of management override of controls. These procedures include (a) examining journal entries and other adjustments for evidence of possible material misstatement due to fraud, (b) reviewing accounting estimates for biases that could result in material misstatement due to fraud, and (c) evaluating the business rationale for significant unusual transactions.

Key Estimates

2.241 The financial statements of investment companies are typically less complicated than those of other enterprises and have relatively few estimates. Most key estimates relate to revenue recognition, including portfolio valuation, as well as interest recognition on high-yield and asset-backed securities, which are discussed in paragraphs 2.234–.239. Material expense accruals (in particular, performance fees) and the effect of shareholder activity not yet fully processed by the transfer agent on shares outstanding ordinarily require significant estimation procedures.

2.242 Often, nonaccounting estimates are integral to measuring a portfolio's compliance with its investment restrictions and characteristics (for example, the duration of a fixed-income portfolio often is a key characteristic, and estimates are required to measure the duration of asset-backed and other securities subject to prepayment). Although these nonaccounting measures typically are not explicitly tested in an audit of financial statements, the auditor could become aware of their existence and consider how management controls their use. However, the auditor is not responsible for assessing whether the fund is meeting its investment objectives or strategies.

Assessing the Identified Risks After Taking Into Account an Evaluation of the Entity's Programs and Controls That Address the Risks

2.243 The auditor should comply with the requirements of paragraphs .43–.45 of AU section 316 concerning an entity's programs and controls that address identified risks of material misstatement due to fraud.

2.244 Most investment advisers maintain extensive portfolio management controls, including the following:

- Separation of portfolio management and trading functions
- Attribution analysis, which is an explanation of portfolio performance against a stated benchmark, identifying industry or security exposures that caused the performance difference, to assist management in identifying abnormal items for their own follow up
- Dispersion analysis, which is comparing the performance of similar portfolios managed by the same individual or group with an analysis of any outlying performance, to assist management in identifying abnormal items for their own follow up
- Frequent reconciliation of cash and portfolio holdings to custodian records
- Comparison of trade terms to broker confirmation prior to recording the transaction
- Extra level of approval is necessary for nonstandard wire transfers
- Monitoring of activity on dormant shareholder accounts
- Review of nonstandard journal entries

2.245 Many investment companies also maintain extensive controls over the valuation of securities not traded on active markets, including the following:

- Written valuation policies and procedures.
- Valuation committees comprising accounting, portfolio management, and administrative or legal personnel to assess valuation procedures and significant valuation estimates. Some registered investment companies place such committees under the oversight of the board of directors or trustees, or both, and occasionally, board members will participate in committee deliberations on significant matters.
- Tracking of actual sale prices against valuations as determined by management or market makers.
- Use of secondary pricing services for comparison with the primary source.
- "Stale price" and "large price change" reports to identify securities for which prices may not have been updated on a timely basis or that have experienced unusual or abnormal changes.

Investment Accounts

- Segregation of portfolio management from valuation functions.

2.246 Examples of broader programs designed to prevent, deter, and detect fraud include the following:

- Code of conduct regarding ethical behavior, compliance with which is typically documented
- Code of ethics regarding personal trading, compliance with which is typically documented
- Compliance programs
- Periodic documentation of compliance of an investment company with its investment objectives and restrictions
- Systems controls, such as security access
- Channels available for employees to report any fraud concerns

2.247 The SEC requires both registered investment companies and registered investment advisers to adopt and implement written policies and procedures reasonably designed to prevent the violation of federal securities laws.[55] Both funds and advisers are required to appoint chief compliance officers responsible for administering these policies and procedures and to review the policies and procedures annually for adequacy and effectiveness of implementation. Among other things, the designation of a chief compliance officer of a registered investment company is required to be approved by the investment company's board of directors or trustees, and the chief compliance officer is to report directly to the board of directors or trustees and meet in an executive session with independent directors or trustees at least annually.

2.248 The auditor could evaluate whether such programs and controls mitigate the identified risks of material misstatement due to fraud or whether specific control deficiencies exacerbate the risks. After the auditor has evaluated whether the entity's programs and controls have been suitably designed and placed in operation, the auditor could assess these risks, taking into account that evaluation. This assessment could be considered when developing the auditor's response to the identified risks of material misstatement due to fraud.

Responding to the Results of the Assessment[56]

2.249 Paragraphs .46–.67 of AU section 316 provide requirements and guidance about the auditor's response to the results of the assessment of risks of material misstatement due to fraud. The auditor responds to risks of material misstatement due to fraud in the following three ways:

---

[55] Rule 38a-1 under the 1940 Act and Rule 206(4)-7 under the Investment Advisers Act of 1940. See SEC Final Rule Release No. IC-26299 under the 1940 Act (Release No. IA-2204 under the Investment Advisers Act of 1940). The adopting release discusses issues that the SEC expects to see addressed in an adviser's or fund's policies and procedures, to the extent that they are relevant, and reviews the application of certain other critical areas that policies and procedures of investment companies should address, including the pricing of portfolio securities and fund shares, as discussed in paragraph 2.42.

[56] Paragraph .03 of AU section 318 states that to reduce audit risk to an acceptably low level, the auditor should determine overall responses to address the assessed risks of material misstatement at the financial statement level and should design and perform further audit procedures whose nature, timing, and extent are responsive to the assessed risks of material misstatement at the relevant assertion level (see paragraphs .04–.07 of AU section 318). This requirement provides a link between the auditor's consideration of fraud and assessment of risk and the auditor's procedures in response to those assessed risks.

AAG-INV 2.249

a. A response that has an overall effect on how the audit is conducted (that is, a response involving more general considerations apart from the specific procedures otherwise planned) (see paragraph .50 of AU section 316).

b. A response to identified risks involving the nature, timing, and extent of the auditing procedures to be performed (see paragraphs .51–.56 of AU section 316). Investment company audit procedures that may be considered include the following:

  i. Analytical procedures, such as comparing fund performance to benchmark indexes and net investment income ratios to yield indexes for comparable securities or investment funds

  ii. Reading compliance summaries for individual funds and testing compliance determinations contained therein

  iii. Comparisons of valuations of securities determined by management or a single market maker during the year with prices received on actual sales

  iv. Attempting to obtain market quotations for certain securities from broker-dealers or recognized pricing sources other than the primary pricing source (however, this may not always be possible, and even when received, the quotations may be of lesser quality because the secondary source may not have the same access to information about the security as the primary source)

  v. Testing inputs to valuation models for reasonableness in relation to published data or financial information services

  vi. Reviewing minutes of board valuation committee meetings and considering whether the minutes adequately support the valuations determined or the procedures used to reach them

  vii. Testing management's assumptions regarding the collectability of interest or projected cash flows for asset-backed securities by reference to issuer data available from public sources or financial information services

c. A response involving the performance of certain procedures to further address the risk of material misstatement due to fraud involving management override of controls, given the unpredictable ways in which such override could occur (see paragraphs .57–.67 of AU section 316 and paragraph 2.188).

2.250

Considerations for Audits Performed in Accordance With PCAOB Standards

Auditing Standard No. 13, *The Auditor's Responses to the Risks of Material Misstatement* (AICPA, *PCAOB Standards and Related Rules*, Auditing Standards), requires the auditor to design and implement audit responses that address the risks of material misstatement that are identified and assessed in accordance with Auditing Standard No. 12. These audit responses include those that have an overall effect on how the audit is conducted; and those involving the nature, timing, and extent of the audit procedures to be performed. The auditor is required

Evaluating Audit Evidence

2.251 Paragraphs .68–.78 of AU section 316 provide requirements and guidance for evaluating audit evidence. The auditor should evaluate whether analytical procedures that were performed as substantive tests or in the overall review stage of the audit indicate a previously unrecognized risk of material misstatement due to fraud. The auditor should also consider whether responses to inquiries throughout the audit about analytical relationships have been vague or implausible or have produced evidence that is inconsistent with other audit evidence accumulated during the audit.

2.252 At or near the completion of fieldwork, the auditor should evaluate whether the accumulated results of auditing procedures and other observations affect the assessment of the risks of material misstatement due to fraud made earlier in the audit. As part of this evaluation, the auditor with final responsibility for the audit should ascertain that there has been appropriate communication with the other audit team members throughout the audit regarding information or conditions indicative of risks of material misstatement due to fraud.

Responding to Misstatements That May Be the Result of Fraud

2.253 When audit test results identify misstatements in the financial statements, the auditor should consider whether such misstatements may be indicative of fraud. See paragraphs .75–.78 of AU section 316 for requirements and guidance about an auditor's response to misstatements that may be the result of fraud. If the auditor believes that misstatements are, or may be, the result of fraud, but the effect of the misstatements is not material to the financial statements, the auditor nevertheless should evaluate the implications, especially those dealing with the organizational position of the person(s) involved.

2.254 If the auditor believes that the misstatement is, or may be, the result of fraud and either has determined that the effect could be material to the financial statements or has been unable to evaluate whether the effect is material, the auditor could

    a. attempt to obtain additional audit evidence to determine whether material fraud has occurred or is likely to have occurred and, if so, its effect on the financial statements and the auditor's report thereon (see AU section 508, *Reports on Audited Financial Statements* [AICPA, *Professional Standards*]).

    b. consider the implications for other aspects of the audit (see paragraph .76 of AU section 316).

    c. discuss the matter and the approach for further investigation with an appropriate level of management that is at least one level above those involved and with senior management and the audit committee.[57]

    d. if appropriate, suggest that the client consult with legal counsel.

---

[57] If the auditor believes that senior management may be involved, discussion of the matter directly with the audit committee may be appropriate.

2.255 The auditor's consideration of the risks of material misstatement and the results of audit tests may indicate such a significant risk of material misstatement due to fraud that the auditor should consider withdrawing from the engagement and communicating the reasons for withdrawal to the audit committee or others with equivalent authority and responsibility. The auditor may wish to consult with legal counsel when considering withdrawal from an engagement.

2.256
> *Considerations for Audits Performed in Accordance With PCAOB Standards*
>
> Auditing Standard No. 14, *Evaluating Audit Results* (AICPA, *PCAOB Standards and Related Rules*, Auditing Standards), requires the auditor to perform procedures to obtain additional audit evidence to determine whether fraud has occurred or is likely to have occurred, and, if so, its effect on the financial statements and the auditor's report if the auditor believes that a misstatement is or might be intentional, and if the effect on the financial statement cannot be readily determined.

Communicating About Possible Fraud to Management, the Audit Committee, and Others

2.257 Whenever the auditor has determined that there is evidence that fraud may exist, that matter should be brought to the attention of an appropriate level of management. See paragraphs .79–.82 of AU section 316 for further requirements and guidance about communications with management, the audit committee, and others.

Documenting the Auditor's Consideration of Fraud

2.258 Paragraph .83 of AU section 316 states that the auditor is required to document certain items and events.

Chapter 3
Financial Instruments[1]

3.01 This chapter provides brief descriptions of certain financial instruments of investment companies. Consideration should be given to Financial Accounting Standards Board (FASB) *Accounting Standards Codification* (ASC) 815, *Derivatives and Hedging*; 820, *Fair Value Measurement*; 460, *Guarantees*; and 860, *Transfers and Servicing*, in connection with accounting and financial statement presentation for these financial instruments.

Money Market Investments

3.02 Short term investments, such as short term government obligations, commercial paper, bankers' acceptances, and certificates of deposit (CDs), may be bought at their face amount or a discount or premium from their face amount.

3.03 The amortized cost of money market investments that mature within a relatively short period (for example, 60 days) usually approximates fair value. However, the impairment of the credit standing of the issuer or unusual changes in interest rates can affect their fair value significantly. In those circumstances, amortized cost may not approximate the fair value of such investments.

Repurchase Agreements

3.04 A *repurchase agreement* (repo) is, in its simplest form, the purchase of a security at a specified price with an agreement to sell the same or substantially the same security to the same counterparty at a fixed or determinable price at a future date with a stipulated interest factor. A repo allows the investment company to transfer uninvested cash to a seller, usually a broker, for a security. The seller agrees to repay cash plus interest to the investment company in exchange for the return of the same or substantially the same security. Because a repo between the two specific parties involved is not transferable, a repo has no ready market.

3.05 Repos are usually entered into with banks, brokers, or dealers. According to Securities and Exchange Commission (SEC) Release No. 10666 under the Investment Company Act of 1940 (the 1940 Act), the investment company should always be sure that the repo, including accrued interest, is fully secured by the fair value of the collateral that it has received.[2] Rule 5b-3 under the 1940 Act states that for purposes of Sections 5 and 12(d)(3) of the 1940 Act,

---

[1] In May 2010, the Financial Accounting Standards Board (FASB) issued the proposed Accounting Standards Update (ASU) *Accounting for Financial Instruments and Revisions to the Accounting for Derivative Instruments and Hedging Activities—Financial Instruments (Topic 825) and Derivatives and Hedging (Topic 815)*. Entities that follow specialized industry guidance in FASB *Accounting Standards Codification* 946 would continue to initially measure their financial instruments at transaction price. Readers should remain alert for developments on this topic, which can be accessed from the Technical Plan and Project Updates page at www.fasb.org.

[2] Securities and Exchange Commission (SEC) Release No. 10666 under the Investment Company Act of 1940 (the 1940 Act) sets forth the SEC's position that repurchase agreements should be fully collateralized (that is, "the value of the transferred security ... is at least equal to the amount of the loan including accrued interest earned thereon").

the acquisition of a repo may be deemed to be an acquisition of the underlying securities, provided that the obligation of the seller to repurchase the securities from the investment company is fully collateralized at all times by cash items, U.S. government securities, or securities rated in the highest rating category or otherwise determined to be of comparable quality.

Reverse Repurchase Agreements

3.06 A *reverse repurchase agreement* (reverse repo or resale) is, in its simplest form, the sale of a security at a specified price and interest factor with an agreement to purchase the same or substantially the same security from the same counterparty at a fixed or determinable price at a future date. A reverse repo allows the investment company to transfer possession of a security to a buyer, usually a broker, for cash. The investment company agrees to repay cash plus interest in exchange for the return of the same securities.[3]

U.S. Government Securities (Treasury Bills, Notes, and Bonds)

3.07 U.S. government negotiable debt obligations, known as Treasuries, are secured by the government's full faith and credit and issued at various schedules and maturities. These securities clear through book entry form at the Federal Reserve Banks. The income from Treasury securities is exempt from state and local, but not federal, taxes. Treasuries include the following:

- *Treasury bills.* Short term securities with maturities of 1 year or less are issued at a discount from face value. Auctions of 4, 13, and 26 week bills take place weekly, and the yields are watched closely in the money markets for signs of interest rate trends. Many floating-rate loans and variable-rate mortgages have interest rates tied to these bills. The Treasury also auctions 52 week bills once every 4 weeks. Treasury bills are issued in minimum denominations of $100. Individual investors who submit a noncompetitive bid are sold bills at the discount rate determined at auction. Treasury bills are the primary instrument used by the Federal Reserve in its regulation of the money supply through open market operations.

- *Treasury notes.* Intermediate securities with original maturities of 2 to 10 years. Denominations start at $100. The notes are sold through a bank or broker or via auction.

- *Treasury bonds.* Long term debt instruments with an original maturity of 30 years issued in minimum denominations of $100.

In addition to these basic security types, the government issues other structures, such as Separate Trading of Registered Interest and Principal of Securities also known as stripped Treasury securities and Treasury Inflation-Protected Securities.

---

[3] For guidance on accounting for reverse repurchase agreements (reverse repos), see paragraph 7.73 of this guide.

Municipal Notes and Bonds

3.08 Municipal securities are issued by states, cities, and other local government authorities to fund public projects. The interest on these bonds is usually exempt from federal taxes and under certain conditions is exempt from state and local taxes. Municipal notes usually mature in less than three years. They are usually designated as tax, revenue, or bond anticipation notes because they are redeemable on the receipt of anticipated taxes or revenues or on financing from the proceeds of municipal bonds. They include short term tax-exempt project notes issued by public housing or urban renewal agencies of local communities with payment of principal and interest guaranteed by the U.S. government. Another common municipal note is a variable rate demand note, which is a floating rate instrument with frequent reset coupon rates and usually a put feature.

3.09 Municipal bonds are principally classified as general obligation bonds and revenue bonds. General obligation bonds represent the issuer's unqualified pledge, based on its full faith, credit, and taxing power, to pay principal and interest when due. Revenue bonds are payable from revenues derived from a particular class of facilities or other specific revenue sources. Tax-exempt industrial development bonds are usually revenue bonds and do not carry the pledge of the issuer's credit. Yields on municipal bonds depend on a variety of factors, including market conditions, maturity date, ratings assigned to the issue, and tax-exempt status. Some municipal bonds may be prerefunded by the issuer whereby the bonds are collateralized by securities or U.S. Treasury obligations. Because many of these are guaranteed by Treasury obligations, they often maintain an AAA rating and may trade at a premium over other municipal bonds. Other common municipal bonds include municipal lease obligations, which represent a certificate of participation in the cash flows for certain projects or services, whose funding must be appropriated annually by the municipality.

3.10 Among investment companies, municipal notes and bonds are held primarily in the portfolios of both tax-exempt money-market and municipal bond funds and generally require special considerations for valuation. They are traded in a dealer market in which little published price information is available. New issues of municipal notes or bonds are usually sold by competitive bidding. Subsequent market quotations may be obtained from dealers in those securities.

3.11 A significant decline in the fair value of a municipal security that appears to relate to the issuer's creditworthiness may indicate the probability of default. Comparisons of the fair value of the security with the fair value of similar securities or a downgrading of the issuer's credit rating may indicate such decline.

Insured Portfolios

3.12 As stated in FASB ASC 946-20-05-12, many municipal bond funds, primarily those organized as unit investment trusts with fixed portfolios, arrange for insurance for the payment of principal and interest when due. The insurance applies to portfolio securities only while they are owned by the fund, and its coverage is not transferable to buyers of the securities. That arrangement differs from those in which the issuer of the securities acquires the insurance, making the insurance feature an element of the securities and transferable on changes in ownership. According to FASB ASC 946-20-25-11, if the insurance applies only to the fund's portfolio, it does not have a measurable fair value in the absence of default of the underlying securities or of indications of the probability of default; accordingly, the cost of the policy should be treated as an operating expense.

To Be Announced Securities

3.13 The term *to be announced* (TBA) is derived from the fact that the actual security that will be delivered to fulfill a TBA trade is not designated at the time the trade is made. The securities that will ultimately be delivered upon settlement are "announced" 48 hours prior to the established trade settlement date. The fund trading TBA securities makes a forward commitment to purchase a preset principal amount at a preset price on a preset date in the future.

3.14 TBA securities resulting from these transactions are generally included in the portfolio of investments. At the time a fund enters into a commitment to purchase or sell a security, the transaction is recorded and the value of the security acquired is reflected in the fund's net asset value. The price of such security and the date that the security will be delivered and paid for at fixed at the time the transaction is negotiated. No interest accrues to the fund until payment takes place. At the time that a fund enters into this type of transaction, the fund is required to have sufficient cash or liquid securities to cover its commitments.

3.15 The value of the security may vary with market fluctuations, and losses may arise due to changes in the value of the underlying securities or if the counterparty does not perform under the contract's terms, or if the issuer does not issue the securities due to political, economic or other factors. Additionally, losses may arise due to declines in the value of the securities prior to settlement date.

3.16 Funds may enter into TBA commitments with the intent to take possession of or deliver the underlying asset, but can extend the settlement or roll the transaction. TBA commitments involve a risk of loss if the value of the security to be purchased or sold declines or increases, respectively, prior to settlement date.

3.17 For long TBA positions, as with other long investments, the security name, par value, coupon rate, maturity date, cost (presented as part of the aggregate cost of investments) and value should be shown in the Schedule of Investments. The TBA security should be designated as having been purchased on a delayed delivery or when-issued basis, if the settlement extends beyond the "normal" settlement period. For short TBA positions, the security name, par value, coupon rate, maturity date proceeds and value should be presented for each position in the securities sold short section of the Schedule of Investments. The TBA security should be designated as having been sold on a delayed delivery or when-issued basis, if the settlement extends beyond the "normal" settlement period.

When-Issued Securities

3.18 Some securities, principally municipal securities, are traded on a when-issued basis. A municipal securities underwriter solicits expressions of

Financial Instruments

interest in a proposed issue and sends a when-issued price confirmation against which securities are delivered later when the terms of the issue are known. The securities usually begin trading on a when-issued basis on the issuance of the confirmation as if they had been issued a few days before the closing date.

3.19 Securities offerings are rarely aborted after when-issued trading begins. A when-issued security and the obligation to pay for the security should be recorded when the commitment becomes fixed, which is the date that the priced transaction confirmation is issued. When-issued securities for which the fund has not taken delivery are required to be identified in a registered investment company's financial statements.[4] Securities may also be bought on a delayed delivery contract under which the underwriter agrees to deliver securities to buyers at later specified dates.

Synthetic Floaters

3.20 Many investment advisers use tax-exempt derivative securities as a way to increase the pool of creditworthy tax-exempt securities. These derivatives include synthetic floaters, under which issuers of such instruments use interest payments from long term municipal bonds, which may be coupled with an interest rate swap and put feature, to pay the floating short term interest rates. The investor receives regular interest payments that are tied to short term municipal rates while the issuer earns the spread between the long term coupon rate and short term floating rate. The investor may either hold the trust certificate representing ownership of the underlying bond to maturity or put it back to the issuer for cash.

3.21 In some instances, these tax exempt derivative securities are created by the deposit of fixed-rate tax-exempt bonds into special purpose trusts against which synthetic floater certificates and inverse floater certificates, representing rights to principal and any interest remaining after interest payments are made on the synthetic floaters, are issued. The inverse floater certificates often allow, upon unanimous consent of the holders of the inverse floater certificates, for the liquidation of the trust, together with full repayment of the synthetic floaters and delivery of the underlying fixed rate bonds to the holders of the inverse floater certificates. If the holders of the inverse floater certificates also participated in the formation of the special purpose trust (that is, the inverse floater certificates were not acquired on the secondary market), FASB ASC 860 should be considered in evaluating the appropriate accounting and whether the initial transfer of the security into the special purpose trust would be considered a secured borrowing or sale.

Mortgage-Backed Securities

3.22 As defined by the FASB ASC glossary, *mortgage-backed securities* (MBSs) are securities issued by a governmental agency or corporation (for example, the Government National Mortgage Association [GNMA] or the Federal Home Loan Mortgage Corporation [FHLMC or Freddie Mac]) or private issuers (for example, the Federal National Mortgage Association [FNMA], banks, and mortgage banking entities). MBSs generally are referred to as mortgage participation certificates or pass-through certificates. A participation certificate

---

[4] SEC Release No. 10666 under the 1940 Act.

AAG-INV 3.22

represents an undivided interest in a pool of specific mortgage loans. Periodic payments on GNMA participation certificates are backed by the U.S. government. Periodic payments on FHLMC and FNMA certificates are guaranteed by those corporations but not backed by the U.S. government.

3.23 An MBS is a pass-through security created by pooling mortgages and selling interests or participations in the MBS. In some instances the mortgage originator will continue to service the underlying mortgage, or the servicing may be sold to a subsidiary or another institution. Mortgage originators will usually pool mortgage loans and sell interests in the pools created. By selling MBSs, originators can obtain funds to issue new mortgages while retaining the servicing rights on the pooled loans. Most MBSs are guaranteed either by federally sponsored agencies or private guarantors. The GNMA is a U.S. government owned corporation that approves the issue of MBSs whose principal and interest are then fully guaranteed by the U.S. Treasury. The FNMA is a publicly owned, U.S. government sponsored entity that purchases mortgages, including mortgages backed by the Federal Housing Administration or guaranteed by the Veterans Administration and other conventional mortgages, and resells them to investors. Freddie Mac is a government sponsored entity that issues MBSs known as participation certificates. Principal and interest payments received from mortgagors are passed on to the MBS holders 45 days later for the GNMA, 55 days later for the FNMA, and 75 days later for Freddie Mac (45 days for gold Freddie Mac).

3.24 Mortgages are not homogeneous, and as a result different pools have different prepayment experience. MBSs are considered seasoned once they have been outstanding from four to five years. Investors are typically willing to pay more for seasoned mortgages than unseasoned mortgages because seasoned mortgages have payment experience, which investors use to make estimates of future prepayments. Unseasoned MBSs possess more unknown variables and, thus, are more sensitive to market volatility.

Adjustable Rate Mortgages

3.25 An *adjustable rate mortgage* (ARM) is a mortgage loan whose interest rate is reset periodically to reflect market rate changes. In addition, ARMs usually have caps that provide borrowers with some protection from rising interest rates. ARMs' interest rates are usually calculated based on one of three indexes: (*a*) U.S. Treasury securities, (*b*) the Cost of Funds Index, or (*c*) average mortgage rates. Typically, ARM rates are reset every six months, one year, three years, or five years. ARMs are usually priced at a spread above the U.S. Treasury yield. In addition, the GNMA, the FNMA, and the FHLMC or private insurance companies guarantee many ARMs.

Collateralized Mortgage Obligations

3.26 Different kinds of collateralized mortgage obligation (CMO) structures exist, each of which has different cash flow characteristics. A security holder may invest in a CMO equity form (for example, trust interests, stock, and partnership interests) or nonequity form (for example, participating debt securities). Some of these structures include the following:

- CMO bonds are bonds collateralized by either a pool of pass-through securities or a pool of mortgage loans and may be issued in several tranches having different maturities and interest rates. The cash flow from the pool of assets is used to pay the principal and interest on the bonds. The sequence of payments is deal specific and is modeled by the issuer.

- CMO residuals represent the excess cash flows from MBSs or a pool of loans used as collateral for a CMO bond and include reinvestment income thereon after paying the debt service on the CMO and related administrative expenses. Cash flows are generated from the interest differential between the collateral for the CMOs and the CMO itself, the interest differential between the various classes of bonds, reinvestment income, and overcollateralization income. Many different kinds of CMO residuals, including floating-rate residuals; inverse floating residuals (inverse floaters [that is, interest rates vary inversely with floating rates]); and principal amortization class residuals, are available.

- Interest-only (IO) and principal-only (PO) securities are created by splitting a traditional MBS or pool of loans into an IO and a PO portion. IO securities may have fixed or variable interest rates. Both IO and PO securities are subject to prepayments and therefore prepayment risk. IO investors are at risk for faster than anticipated prepayments and PO investors for slower than anticipated prepayments. Assumptions regarding the rates of prepayment play a significant role in the price of these securities. Because they may not pay a current coupon, prices of IOs and POs are more sensitive to changing interest rates than coupon bonds. They can be stripped from fixed or adjustable-rate loans or a pool of fixed-rate loans containing a range of different mortgage rates. The individual mortgages are subject to prepayment and default risk. PO securities issued by government sponsored entities (that is, the FNMA, the FHLMC, and so on) are usually fully or partially guaranteed against credit loss.

- An IOette is an IO with a relatively low principal amount and high coupon rate. The principal and interest components of MBSs are sometimes separated and recombined in varying proportions to create synthetic coupon securities.

Real Estate Mortgage Investment Conduits

3.27 The real estate mortgage investment conduit (REMIC) is a form of CMO specially designated for federal income tax purposes so that the related income is taxed only once (to the security holder). A corporation, a partnership, an association, or a trust may elect to be a REMIC and many special purpose entities that issue CMOs, IOs, POs, and MBSs have elected to structure themselves as REMICs.

High-Yield Securities

3.28 As defined by the FASB ASC glossary, *high-yield debt securities* are corporate and municipal debt securities having a lower-than-investment-grade credit rating (BB+ or lower by Standard & Poor's or Ba1 or lower by Moody's). Because high-yield debt securities typically are used when lower-cost capital is not available, they have interest rates several percentage points higher than investment-grade debt and often have shorter maturities. These high-yielding corporate and municipal debt obligations are frequently referred to as junk bonds. As further explained in FASB ASC 946-320-05-4, they are typically unsecured and subordinate to other debt outstanding. Many issuers of high-yield debt securities are highly leveraged with limited equity capital. These inherent differences from investment grade bonds, including a market for such securities that may not always be liquid, may increase the market, liquidity, and credit risks of these securities as follows:

Market risk. In contrast to investment-grade bonds (the market prices of which change primarily as a reaction to changes in interest rates), the market prices of high-yield bonds (which are also affected by changes in interest rates) are influenced much more by credit factors and financial results of the issuer and general economic factors that influence the financial markets as a whole. Such factors often make it difficult to substantiate the market valuation of high-yield bonds.

Liquidity risk. The market risk is often heightened by liquidity risk (that is, the absence of centralized high-yield bond exchanges and relatively thin trading markets, which make it more difficult to liquidate holdings quickly and increase the volatility of the market price). There is generally no centralized or regulated procedure for pricing high-yield debt issues.

Credit risk. Issues of high-yield debt securities are more likely to default on interest or principal than are issues of investment-grade securities.

3.29 SEC yield formula calculations are required to be made using the specific guidelines presented in SEC Final Rule Release No. 33-6753. Yields calculated that way might not be the same as the interest reported in the financial statements. The ultimate realizable value and the potential for early retirement of securities should be considered when computing SEC yields. Management's best estimates of ultimate realizable value should be reasonable. If current values of high-yield debt securities decline significantly from the issue price, computed yields may be higher than rates expected to be ultimately realized. To avoid unsound yield information, consideration should be given to capping yields of individual securities at some reasonable level and examining the underlying economic viability of the issuers.

Payment-in-Kind Bonds

3.30 As defined in the FASB ASC glossary, *payment-in-kind bonds* (PIK) are bonds in which the issuer has the option at each interest payment date of making interest payments in cash or additional debt securities. Those additional debt securities are referred to as baby bonds or bunny bonds. Baby bonds usually have the same terms, including maturity dates and interest rates, as the original bonds (parent PIK bonds). Interest on baby bonds may also be paid in cash or additional like-kind debt securities at the option of the issuer.

3.31 FASB ASC 946-320-35-10 states that the interest method should be used to determine interest income on PIK bonds. The FASB ASC glossary defines the *interest method* as the method used to arrive at a periodic interest cost (including amortization) that will represent a level effective rate on the sum of the face amount of the debt and (plus or minus) the unamortized premium or discount and expense at the beginning of each period. As further explained in FASB ASC 946-320-30-4, PIK bonds typically trade flat (that is, interest receivable is included in the price quotation obtained each day). Accordingly, that portion of the quote representing interest income needs to be identified. The sum of the acquisition amount of the bond and the discount to be amortized should not exceed the undiscounted future cash collections that are both reasonably estimable and probable. Further, FASB ASC 946-320-35-11 notes that, to the extent that interest income to be received in the form of baby bonds is not expected to be realized, a reserve against income should be established (that is, it should be determined periodically that the total amount of interest income recorded as receivable, plus the initial cost of the underlying PIK bond does not exceed the current market value of those assets).

Step Bonds

3.32 As defined by the FASB ASC glossary, *step bonds* are characterized by a combination of deferred-interest payment dates and increasing interest payment amounts over the bond lives. Thus, they bear some similarity to zero-coupon bonds and traditional debentures.

3.33 As noted in paragraphs 12–13 of FASB ASC 946-320-35, income on step bonds should be recognized using the interest method. Additionally, to the extent that interest income is not expected to be realized, a reserve against income should be established. The sum of the acquisition amount of the bond and the discount to be amortized should not exceed the undiscounted future cash collections that are both reasonably estimable and probable.

Put and Call Options

3.34 An *option* is a contract giving its owner the right, but not the obligation, to buy (call) or sell (put) a specified item at a fixed price (exercise or strike price) during a specified period (American option) or on a specified date (European option). Options may be exchange traded or over the counter. Options may be written on a variety of instruments, indexes, or currencies. The buyer pays a nonrefundable fee (the premium) to the seller (the writer). An investment company may buy or write put and call options, if permitted, as disclosed in the prospectus. As consideration for an option, the buyer pays the writer a premium that is the maximum amount that the buyer could lose. That amount is influenced by such factors as the duration of the option, the difference between the exercise price and fair value of the underlying securities, price volatility, and other characteristics of the underlying securities. In return for the premium

- a covered writer of a call option (a writer who owns the underlying securities) gives up the opportunity to profit from an increase in the fair value of the underlying securities to a point higher than the exercise price of the option outstanding but retains the risk of loss if the fair value of the securities declines.
- an uncovered writer of a call option (a naked option) does not own the underlying securities but assumes the obligation to deliver the underlying securities on exercise of the option. An uncovered writer is exposed to the risk of loss if the fair value of the underlying securities increases above the strike price but has no risk of

loss if the fair value of the underlying securities does not exceed the option exercise price.[5]

- a writer of a put option is exposed to the risk of loss if the fair value of the underlying securities declines but profits only to the extent of the premium received if the underlying security increases in value because the holder of the option will not exercise it if the holder can obtain a greater price elsewhere. The writer is covered if a put option is bought on the same underlying securities with an exercise date equal to or earlier than the option that it covers and an exercise price equal to or greater than the option written.

3.35 After an option is written, the writer's obligation may be discharged in one of the following ways:

a. The option expires on its stipulated expiration date.
b. The writer enters into a closing transaction.
c. The option holder exercises the right to call (buy) or put (sell) the security (not applicable for index options).

3.36 The writer or buyer of an option traded on an exchange can liquidate the position before the exercise of the option by entering into a closing transaction. Such a transaction, in effect, cancels the existing position. The cost of a liquidating purchase, however, may be higher than the premium received for the original option. Because the writer or buyer can enter into a closing transaction, the option originally written may never be exercised. An option traded on an exchange is exercised only through the Options Clearing Corporation (OCC), the obligor on every option, by the timely submission of an exercise notice by the clearing broker acting on behalf of the exercising holder. The exercise notice is assigned by the OCC to a clearing broker acting on behalf of a writer of an option of the same series as the exercised option. The clearing broker is obligated to deliver the underlying security against payment of the exercise price. The assigned broker is selected randomly from clearing members having accounts with the OCC with options outstanding of the same series as the option being exercised.

3.37 Freestanding written put options and certain contracts that function as market value guarantees on a financial asset that is owned by the guaranteed party, even when classified as derivatives under FASB ASC 815, are within the scope of the disclosure provisions of FASB ASC 460-10-50. Under those provisions in FASB ASC 460-10-50-4, guarantors are required to disclose the following information about each guarantee or each group of similar guarantees, even if the likelihood of the guarantor's having to make payments under the guarantee is remote:

a. The nature of the guarantee, including its approximate term; how the guarantee arose; the events or circumstances that would require the guarantor to perform under the guarantee; and the current status (that is, as of the date of the statement of financial

---

[5] An investment company may be exposed to additional losses resulting from the price appreciation of the underlying security. For registered investment companies, Section 18 of the 1940 Act provides additional guidance for writers of naked call options. For example, an investment company may mitigate the option's exposure to Section 18 prohibitions by segregating cash or other securities in an amount greater than or equal to the option written or by purchasing a call option on the underlying security for similar terms.

Financial Instruments

position) of the payment or performance risk of the guarantee (for example, the current status of the payment or performance risk of a credit risk-related guarantee could be based on either recently issued external credit ratings or current internal groupings used by the guarantor to manage its risk). An entity that uses internal groupings should disclose how those groupings are determined and used for managing risk.

b. The undiscounted maximum potential amount of future payments that the guarantor would be required to make under the guarantee, which should not be reduced by the effect of any amounts that may possibly be recovered under any recourse or collateralization provisions. If the terms of the guarantee provide for no limitation to the maximum potential future payments under the guarantee, that fact should be disclosed. If the guarantor is unable to develop an estimate of the maximum potential amount of future payments under its guarantee, the reasons why it cannot estimate the maximum potential amount should be disclosed.

c. The current carrying amount of the liability, if any, for the guarantor's obligations under the guarantee (including the amount, if any, recognized under FASB ASC 450-20-30 that deals with loss contingencies), regardless of whether the guarantee is freestanding or embedded in another contract.

d. The nature of any recourse provisions that would enable the guarantor to recover any amounts paid under the guarantee from third parties.

e. The nature of any assets held either as collateral or by third parties that, upon the occurrence of any triggering event or condition under the guarantee, the guarantor can obtain and liquidate to recover all or a portion of the amounts paid under the guarantee.

f. If estimable, the approximate extent to which the proceeds from liquidation of assets held either as collateral or by third parties would be expected to cover the maximum potential amount of future payments under the guarantee.

Warrants

3.38 A warrant is an instrument giving its owner the right, but generally not the obligation, to purchase shares in an issuer at a predefined price, within a specified time period. Unlike a call option (which may exist between two parties unrelated to the issuer of the shares), the warrant exists solely between the issuer (that is, the entity in which additional shares will be issued upon exercise of the warrant) and the owner of the warrant. Warrants can exist either as freestanding contracts or as instruments embedded in convertible debt or convertible preferred equity.

3.39 Determination of whether a warrant is a derivative may include an analysis under FASB ASC 815-10-15-119 whether one of the parties is required to deliver an asset of the type described in FASB ASC 815-10-15-100, but that asset should be readily convertible to cash or is itself a derivative instrument. FASB ASC 815-10-15-131 states that shares of stock in a publicly traded company to be received upon the exercise of a stock purchase warrant do not meet the characteristic of being readily convertible to cash if both of

AAG-INV 3.39

the following conditions exist: (a) the stock purchase warrant is issued by an entity for only its own stock (or stock of its consolidated subsidiaries) and (b) the sale or transfer of the issued shares is restricted (other than in connection with being pledged as collateral) for a period of 32 days or more from the date the stock purchase warrant is exercised. In contrast, FASB ASC 815-10-15-132 states that restrictions imposed by a stock purchase warrant on the sale or transfer of shares of stock that are received from the exercise of that warrant issued by an entity for other than its own stock (whether those restrictions are for more or less than 32 days) do not affect the determination of whether those shares are readily convertible to cash. The accounting for restricted stock to be received upon exercise of a stock purchase warrant should not be analogized to any other type of contract. Refer to FASB ASC 815-10-15-133 through 815-10-15-138 for further guidance on when to consider a warrant a derivative and hence trigger FASB ASC 815 disclosure requirements.

Loan Commitments

3.40 Certain investment companies acquire interests in bank lending facilities, including interests in lines of credit and other commitments to lend. Loan commitments are generally defined as written agreements, signed by the borrower and lender, detailing terms and conditions under which a loan of up to a specified amount will be made. The commitment has an expiration date and typically a fee will be paid for agreeing to make the commitment. A commitment can be irrevocable or, in many instances, conditioned on the maintenance by the borrower of satisfactory financial standing and absence of default in other covenants. Lines of credit are often less detailed than a formal loan commitment, and are often letter expressions of willingness to lend up to a certain amount over a specified time frame, usually one year. Many lines of credit are cancellable if the borrower's financial condition deteriorates; others are subject to cancellation at the bank's option.

3.41 Loan commitments are typically regarded by financial institutions as off-balance-sheet financial instruments but are not within the scope of FASB ASC 815.

Standby Commitments

3.42 A *standby commitment* is an optional delivery forward placement commitment contract. On the sale of a standby commitment, an investment company is contractually bound to accept future delivery of a security at a guaranteed price or fixed yield on the exercise of an option held by the other party to the agreement. In effect, the investment company sells a put option and receives a fee for its commitment to buy the security. The investment company bears the risk of loss if interest rates rise, causing the fair value of the security at the delivery date to be less than the exercise (strike) price of the option less the fee received.[6]

---

[6] The SEC indicated in Release No. 10666 under the 1940 Act that an investment company's participation in a firm commitment agreement (forward placement commitment or agreement to purchase when-issued securities), standby commitment, or reverse repo may involve the issuance of a security by the investment company. The security may be a *senior security* as defined in Section 18(g) of the act, and the investment company entering into the agreement may be in violation of Section 18(f) (1). However, the Division of Investment Management has determined that it will not raise the issue of compliance with Section 18 with the SEC if the investment company covers the senior security by establishing and maintaining certain segregated accounts.

Commodity and Financial Futures Contracts

3.43 Commodity and financial futures contracts are traded on various exchanges and are thus distinguished from forward contracts, which are entered into privately by the parties.[7] A *commodity futures contract* is a firm commitment to buy or sell a specified quantity of a specified grade of a specified commodity or, for financial futures contracts (including index futures contracts), a standardized amount of a deliverable grade security (or a basket[8] for index futures) at a specified price and specified future date unless the contract is closed before the delivery date. For futures contracts, the date is a specified delivery month, and the contract is typically settled by executing an offsetting futures contract before or during the delivery month.

3.44 The quantity and quality provisions of futures contracts are standardized. For example, every cotton futures contract traded on ICE Futures U.S. (formerly the New York Board of Trade) is for 50,000 pounds, and every Treasury bill futures contract traded on the International Money Market of the Chicago Mercantile Exchange is for $1 million notional par value.

3.45 Although a confirmation of the trade is submitted showing the pertinent price, quantity, and commodity data, no amount is usually entered in the general ledger. The ledger reflects only the margin deposit and the daily mark to market for variation margin. Details of open contracts are in memorandum format. Variation margin normally is settled in cash with the broker each morning for the amount of the previous day's mark to market.

3.46 To initiate a futures contract, the investor is required to make an initial margin deposit in an amount established by the various exchanges. This amount varies according to the commodity or security, the prevailing price, whether the investor is speculating or hedging, and market conditions. The initial margin may often be deposited in Treasury bills. In those cases, the restriction of the ability to trade the Treasury bills should be disclosed in the fund's schedule of investments. Brokers sometimes require margins in excess of those set by the exchanges.

3.47 An investment company may deposit initial margin on futures contracts directly with futures commission merchants (FCMs) that are registered under the Commodity Exchange Act and that are not affiliated with the investment company. A registered investment company is generally not permitted to deposit initial margin deposits on futures contracts in three-party special segregated custody accounts. Cash or securities deposited to meet margin requirements should be identified as margin deposits on the investment

---

[7] In February 2012, the Commodity Futures Trading Commission (CFTC) issued a final rule regarding changes to Part 4 of the regulations involving registration and compliance obligations for commodity pool operators (CPOs) and commodity trading advisors (CTAs). The CFTC will reinstate trading criteria for registered investment companies claiming exclusion from the CPO definition under section 4.5 and add an alternative trading threshold based on net notional value of derivative positions; rescind the exemption from CPO registration under section 4.13(a)(4); and include new risk disclosure requirements for CPOs and CTAs regarding swap transactions. Simultaneously, the CFTC released a proposal on reducing compliance burdens associated with registered investment advisors who would be required to register as CPOs under the changes to section 4.5. Readers should be alert for developments.

[8] A group of securities that compose the underlying index.

company's records. Alternatively, the investment company may arrange to put up performance bonds with FCMs.

Forward Contracts

3.48 A *forward contract* is a legal contract between two parties to purchase and sell a specified quantity of a financial instrument or commodity at a price specified now, with delivery and settlement at a specified future date. Forward contracts are similar to futures contracts, except that they are not traded on an exchange. Their terms are not standardized, and they can be terminated only by agreement of both parties to the forward contract. If a forward contract is held until expiration, settlement by delivery is required. Most forwards are settled in cash. Typically, they do not settle on a daily basis by margin settlement as do futures contracts, although contracts may require collateral to be deposited under certain conditions.

Forward Exchange Contracts

3.49 As defined by the FASB ASC glossary, *a forward exchange contract* is an agreement between two parties to exchange different currencies at a specified exchange rate at an agreed-upon future date.

3.50 Although these contracts can be speculative in nature, a fund typically enters a forward exchange contract to hedge overall portfolio currency risk or settle foreign security transactions. If the purpose of the contract is to hedge portfolio risk, the contract is typically closed by entering into an offsetting contract before the settlement date. In this way, on the settlement date the fund is only obligated to deliver or purchase the net amount of foreign currency involved.

Interest Rate, Currency, and Equity Swaps and Swaptions

3.51 Many variations of swaps exist. Swaps can be linked to any number of underlying instruments and indexes, and swap terms can vary greatly. The *trade date* is the date of the commitment to enter into the swap. Interest begins accruing on the effective date and cash flows are exchanged, as defined by the agreement.

3.52 Interest rate swaps represent an agreement between counterparties to exchange cash flows based on the difference between two interest rates applied to a notional principal amount for a specified period. The most common kind of interest rate swap involves the exchange of fixed-rate cash flows for variable-rate cash flows. Interest rate swaps do not involve the exchange of principal between the parties. Interest is paid or received periodically. Swaps range in maturities, usually 1 to 30 years. Market risk and credit risk are two important risks associated with swaps. Credit risk is often minimized by requiring the counterparty to post collateral if any indication of credit risk exists or if the fair value of the swap changes so that a party to the swap becomes significantly "in the money", or by engaging in swaps only with highly rated counterparties. Market risk requires a careful understanding of the effects on the swap's fair value of changing market conditions. Both risks require close monitoring. Swaps may be structured so that the notional principal amount is adjusted up or down during the term of the swap. Floating rate reset periods vary, ranging from daily to yearly.

3.53 A *currency swap* is an agreement between two parties to exchange two different currencies with an agreement to reverse the exchange at a later date at specified exchange rates. The exchange of currencies at the inception date of the contract takes place at the current spot rate. The re-exchange at maturity may take place at the same exchange rate, a specified rate, or the then current spot rate. Interest payments, if applicable, are made between the parties based on interest rates available in the two currencies at the inception of the contract. The term of currency swap contracts may extend for many years. Currency swaps are usually negotiated with commercial and investment banks. Contracts are subject to the risk of default by the counterparty and, depending on their terms, may be subject to exchange rate risk. Some currency swaps may provide only for exchanging interest cash flows, not principal cash flows.

3.54 Some funds may enter into equity swaps to manage their exposure to the equity markets. In an equity swap, cash flows are exchanged based on a commitment by one party to pay interest in exchange for a market-linked return based on a notional amount. The market-linked return may include, among other things, the total return of a security or an index. These agreements involve elements of credit and market risk. Risks include the possibility that no liquid market exists for these obligations, the counterparty may default on its obligation, or unfavorable changes may exist in the security or index underlying the swap.

3.55 A swaption includes any option that gives the buyer the right, but not the obligation, to enter into a swap on a future date. It also includes any option that allows an existing swap to be terminated or extended by one of the counterparties. These structures are also called cancelable, callable, or putable swaps. Swaptions can be American, exercisable at any point during the option term, or European, exercisable only on the last day of the option term. Swaptions that establish swaps when exercised may be puts or calls. In both cases, the fixed rate that will be exchanged is established when the swaption is purchased. The term of the swap is also specified. If a call interest rate swaption is exercised, the option holder will enter a swap to receive the fixed rate and pay a floating rate in exchange. The exercise of a put would entitle the option holder to pay a fixed rate and receive a floating rate. Calls become more valuable when the underlying securities' prices rise and rates fall. The option holder will exercise a call swaption when rates have fallen from the strike level. The put swaption will be exercised when market rates rise above the fixed rate that the option holder can pay (that is, prices have fallen).

Credit Derivatives

3.56 Many funds enter into credit derivatives, including credit default swaps, credit spread options, and credit index products. The FASB ASC glossary defines a *credit derivative* as a derivative instrument for which (*a*) one or more underlyings are related to the credit risk of a specific entity (or group of entities) or, alternatively, an index based on the credit risk of a group of entities, and (*b*) the derivative exposes the seller to potential loss from credit-risk-related events specified in the contract.

3.57 Credit derivatives related to the credit risk of a specific entity are often referred to as *single-name* credit derivatives.

Structured Notes or Indexed Securities

3.58 A *structured note*, as defined by the FASB ASC glossary, is a debt instrument whose cash flows are linked to the movement in one or more indexes, interest rates, equities, foreign exchange rates, commodities prices, prepayment rates, or other market variables. Structured notes are issued by U.S. government sponsored enterprises, multilateral development banks, municipalities, and private entities. The notes typically contain embedded (but not separable or detachable) forward components or option components, such as caps, calls, and floors. Contractual cash flows for principal, interest, or both can vary in amount and timing throughout the life of the note based on nontraditional indexes or nontraditional uses of traditional interest rates or indexes.

3.59 Additionally, structured notes are sometimes called *indexed securities*. These packaged securities have some similar characteristics to a plain debt instrument, such as commercial paper, medium-term notes, or CDs. Instead of paying a fixed interest rate over time and repaying par at maturity, structured notes index the coupon, principal, or both to virtually anything with a trading market. The indexing may be to currencies, interest rate spreads, stock market indexes, or the price of a security or commodity completely unrelated to the transaction. For example, from the standpoint of the holder, many convertible bonds are considered, for accounting purposes, to represent a form of structured note.

3.60 Although structured notes economically represent a debt instrument with an embedded derivative, FASB ASC 815-15-25-1 states that embedded derivatives are only required to be separated from their host contract and accounted for as a derivative instrument if, among other things, the instrument is not remeasured at fair value under otherwise applicable generally accepted accounting principles with changes in fair value reported in earnings as they occur.

3.61 Because investment companies report all their investments at fair value with changes in fair value reported in earnings, derivatives embedded within structured notes owned need not be separated from their host contracts and separately reported.

Short Positions

3.62 A short sale creates a senior security for registered investment companies that is subject to the limitation of Section 18 of the 1940 Act. To comply with the provisions of Section 18, a registered investment company that sells securities short must establish a segregated account, as discussed in the section on accounting for segregated accounts, to account for cash or cash equivalents equal in fair value to the securities sold short or equivalent securities already owned if the sale is against the box.

Mortgage Dollar Rolls

3.63 Mortgage dollar rolls (MDRs) are documented as agreements to sell and repurchase substantially similar but not identical securities.[9] Dollar rolls differ from regular reverse repo agreements in that the securities sold and

---

[9] See SEC Final Rule Release No. IC-22389.

repurchased, which are usually of the same issuer, are represented by different certificates; are collateralized by similar, but not identical, mortgage pools (for example, single-family residential mortgages with the same coupon rate and contractual term to maturity, such as 15 to 30 years). Additionally, the securities returned to close an MDR need not have identical principal amounts from the securities initially sold, but must be within the recognized standards for "good delivery" for trading in MBSs. The most common kinds of dollar rolls are fixed-coupon and yield-maintenance arrangements.

3.64 The investment company and the counterparty may decide to extend the contract and not return the securities involved in the roll. The contract may be extended in this manner over a number of periods with the agreement of both counterparties.

3.65 An MDR can also be executed entirely in the to-be-announced market when the investment company makes a forward commitment to purchase a security, and instead of accepting delivery, the position is offset by a sale of the security with a simultaneous agreement to repurchase in the future.

3.66 Compensation to the investment company for the risks involved in an MDR transaction is in the form of either a fee or a reduction in the repurchase price of the security, referred to as the drop.

3.67 The appropriate accounting treatment for an MDR transaction should be based on FASB ASC 860.

Chapter 4
Capital Accounts

4.01 This chapter deals primarily with operations, controls, and accounting and auditing matters affecting the capital accounts of open-end investment companies (also known as mutual funds). Among the regulations and limitations that affect the accounting for capital stock transactions of open-end investment companies are the following:

- Rules 2a-4 and 12b-1 of the Investment Company Act of 1940 (the 1940 Act)[1]
- Financial Industry Regulatory Authority (FINRA) limits on sales charges
- Load structures and arrangements for reduced sales charges as established in fund prospectuses
- Rule 18f-3 of the 1940 Act and exemptive orders in effect for individual fund complexes relating to multiple classes of shares

Most transactions affecting the capital accounts of closed-end investment companies can be accounted for and audited similarly to other commercial enterprises.

Operations and Controls

Distributors

4.02 As stated in chapter 1, "The Investment Company Industry," of this guide, many open-end investment companies enter into agreements with a separate distributor (also called an underwriter) under which the distributor obtains the exclusive right, as either principal or agent for the fund, to deal in fund shares as a wholesaler, reselling the shares to independent dealers or through its own sales network. Commonly, the distributor is an affiliate of the fund sponsor.

4.03 How distributors are compensated depends on the kind of arrangement that applies to the shares that they are selling. A commission or sales charge may be assessed on mutual fund investments when the shares are purchased (at the front end), when the shares are redeemed (at the back end), or during the period that the shares are held by a shareholder (level load). Fund shares sold through full-service distribution channels, such as brokers or financial planners, typically include a sales charge or fee of some sort in exchange for providing additional investment advice or services.

---

[1] The Securities and Exchange Commission's (SEC) proposed Rule Release No. IC-29367, *Mutual Fund Distribution Fees; Confirmations*, was issued in July 2010 and would replace Rule 12b-1 under the Investment Company Act of 1940 (1940 Act) with Rule 12b-2. The proposed framework would continue to allow funds to give investors choices regarding how and when to pay for sales charges, improve disclosure designed to enhance investor understanding of those charges, limit the cumulative sales charges that each investor pays (no matter how they are imposed), and eliminate uncertainties associated with current requirements while providing a more appropriate role for fund directors. Under the proposal, funds would be required to comply with the amendments for all shares issued after the compliance date of the new rules. However, a five-year grandfathering period would exist after the compliance date for share classes issued prior to the compliance date and would deduct fees pursuant to the existing Rule 12b-1, after which those shares would be required to be converted or exchanged into a class that does not deduct an ongoing sales charge. Readers are encouraged to remain alert for developments.

AAG-INV 4.03

4.04 When shares with a front-end load are distributed through independent dealers, a significant portion of the load (or commission) is retained by the independent dealer for its services (including payment of a commission to the broker actually selling the shares) and the remainder is remitted to the distributor. The distributor retains the full front-end load when its own sales network is responsible for selling shares but pays commissions to its employees out of the load. When shares with a back-end load, typically known as a contingent deferred sales charge (CDSC) or contingent deferred sales load, are sold, no commission is subtracted from the proceeds received from the investor. Instead, the distributor pays the commission to the independent dealer or its employees. Other installment or noncontingent deferred sales loads may be applied that do not decline to zero, as well as loads paid after purchase during the shareholder's time in the fund.[2]

4.05 Sales commission rates on mutual funds with front-end loads typically decline as the amount of the sale increases. Some funds offer various arrangements, including letters of intent and rights of accumulation, entitling individual purchasers to reduced sales charges based on aggregate purchases of shares of either the individual fund or funds within the same mutual fund complex. Also, front-end loads may either be reduced or waived when shares are sold under employee benefit arrangements such as 401(k) plans.

4.06 Rule 12b-1 (under the 1940 Act) fees generated by the sale of level-load shares are typically used to compensate dealers and sales personnel for their selling and servicing efforts. CDSC shares are typically offered in combination with a Rule 12b-1 distribution plan under which the fund makes payments to the distributor for distribution services. The distributor typically uses 12b-1 payments and CDSC receipts to recover the initial commission that it paid for sales of CDSC shares. The amount of payments that a fund may make for this purpose is capped under FINRA rules.[3]

4.07 Some funds offer both front-end and back-end load shares, including shares with different sales charges, to retail and institutional investors by issuing multiple classes of shares, each with different load structures and distribution fees. To issue multiple classes of shares, most fund groups obtained individual exemptive orders from the Securities and Exchange Commission (SEC) until Rule 18f-3, which provides standard conditions under which multiple classes of shares may be offered, was issued in 1995. Some funds with unique variations have elected not to adopt the provisions of Rule 18f-3 and continue to rely on their individual exemptive orders. Because discounts typically are not provided on sales commissions for back-end load shares, multiple class funds often limit the dollar amount that may be invested by a retail investor in back-end load shares and require those orders over a certain amount

---

[2] SEC Final Rule Release No. IC-22202, *Exemption for Certain Open-End Management Investment Companies to Impose Deferred Sales Loads*.

[3] Under the maximum sales charge rule in the Financial Industry Regulatory Authority's Rules of Fair Practice, no member may offer or sell shares of any open-end investment company registered under the 1940 Act if the public offering price includes a sales charge that is excessive. Under existing rules, the maximum front-end sales charge may not exceed 8.5 percent of the offering price of mutual fund shares. The maximum charge is scaled down in steps to 6.25 percent if investors are not offered 1 of 3 additional services or benefits: dividend reinvestment at net asset value, quantity discounts, or rights of accumulation. Further, asset-based sales charges specifically exclude service fees. *Service fees* are defined as payments by an investment company for personal service or the maintenance of shareholder accounts or both.

Capital Accounts

to be treated as orders for front-end load shares. Chapter 5, "Complex Capital Structures," of this guide contains a more comprehensive discussion of multiple classes of shares.

Orders to Purchase or Redeem

4.08 Investors buy at an offering price, which, for front-end load funds, consists of the net asset value received by the fund plus a sales charge received by the principal underwriter and, in some instances, may include a purchase premium, which, to the extent received by the fund, is credited to capital. Investors redeem shares at net asset value, although in some instances, a fund may charge redemption fees, which, to the extent received by the fund, are credited to capital.[4] Orders accepted by the fund or its agent are executed at prices based on the net asset value per share that is first computed after the order is accepted (forward pricing) and time-stamped when received to substantiate the price.[5] Most funds price their shares once per day, but some do so more often. Confirmations of share transactions are sent to investors. Funds have adopted a variety of ways for shareholders to redeem their shares, including the use of debit cards, ATMs, check writing, wire orders, and telephone redemption procedures. Some funds have established websites that permit shareholders to conduct transactions in fund shares electronically. The auditor should become acquainted with the particular redemption methods described in the fund's prospectus.

4.09 Accurate recording of sales and redemptions of fund shares depends on the adequacy of the distributor's, fund's, and transfer agent's controls over order processing. The accuracy of the information on the order tickets about the investor, the number of shares, and dollar amount depends mainly on the reliability of the distributor's information. The processing of sales and redemptions depends on the integration of a variety of systems that gather and disperse information. The key element of control used when capturing such information to be recorded on the fund's books and records is the daily balancing of net dollars received or paid by the fund with net shares issued or redeemed. The daily reconciliation of cash flows, capital stock receivables and payables, and capital shares outstanding between the fund's accounts and those of the transfer agent and subtransfer agent (if applicable) helps the maintenance of accurate capital accounts.

4.10 Certain kinds of funds (such as money market funds) may sell or redeem a large volume of shares in response to market volatility. The transfer agent's controls over such activities as check writing, wire transfers, and telephone redemptions should be adequate to support periods of heavy volume.

---

[4] This is applicable to all investment companies; however, for funds regulated under the 1940 Act, Rule 22c-2 of that act permits fund directors or trustees (including a majority of independent directors or trustees) of registered open-end investment companies to approve a redemption fee on shares redeemed within 7 or more calendar days after the shares were purchased. The redemption fee may not exceed 2 percent of the value of shares redeemed. The fund would retain the fee. The requirements of Rule 22c-2 do not apply to money market funds; funds that issue securities that are listed on a national securities exchange; and funds that affirmatively permit short term trading and prominently disclose in the prospectus that short term trading of fund shares is permitted and may result in additional costs to the fund, unless those funds elect to impose a redemption fee. See SEC Final Rule Release No. IC-26782, *Mutual Fund Redemption Fees*, for more information.

[5] Rules 2a-4 and 22c-1 under the 1940 Act.

4.11 The fund is responsible for establishing criteria for honoring redemptions. For redemptions made within a prescribed number of days of a purchase by personal check, funds usually do not remit redemption proceeds until they can be assured that the purchase check has cleared. This remittance delay generally does not apply to purchases made by wire transfer or federal funds. Control procedures should provide for the identification, for all accounts, of amounts and dates of purchases by personal checks.

4.12 Capital account data are recorded in sales journals, redemption journals, distribution records, and outstanding share records. Also, to meet SEC disclosure requirements and state Blue Sky laws, the sales journal may contain the source of the order by dealer (primarily load funds), sales statistics by geographic area, the size of the order, and other share data.

Cancellation of Orders

4.13 A purchase or redemption may occasionally be canceled by an investor or broker-dealer before the settlement date. A change in net asset value per share between the original sales date and the date of cancellation or correction results in a gain or loss to the fund. If a distributor is involved and cancellation results in a loss, the distributor may bear the loss or collect cash from the broker-dealer in the amount of the loss. If the cancellation results in a gain, the distributor may accumulate the gain to offset losses from future cancellations and periodically settle the net losses with the fund. If no distributor is involved, the fund should consider refusing to accept sales orders not accompanied by payment, unless a responsible person has indemnified the fund for the failure to pay. Except for preauthorized expedited redemption procedures, the fund might accept orders for redemptions only if the stock certificates or written requests for book shares are properly endorsed and the signatures guaranteed by an appropriate organization, unless indemnified by a responsible person against failure to complete the transaction.

Shareholder Transactions

4.14 Because of the continuous sales and redemptions of open-end fund shares, shareholder transactions are an integral part of a mutual fund's operations and more complex than stock transfers of usual commercial entities. The records for total shares outstanding, total shares issued, and detailed shareholder accounts are kept current on a daily basis. According to federal and state regulations, specialized procedures, controls, and systems are required to maintain adequate shareholder records. Although mutual fund shares may be processed by an in-house operation (an affiliated company of the fund's investment adviser or distributor), an independent transfer agent is often employed to perform this function. The basic operations of all funds are the same; however, the methods used by funds to control stock transfers vary depending on the distribution channel, load structure, and role of the transfer agent in distributing the fund.

4.15 The transfer agent maintains a separate account for each shareholder; performs the detailed recordkeeping associated with sales, redemptions, distributions, and reinvestments within the account; and prepares and mails shareholder communications. Accounts may also be maintained on an omnibus level, in which case a separate entity (subtransfer agent, broker-dealer, or plan administrator) performs the detailed subaccounting by shareholder. A fund and its distributor depend on information provided by the transfer agent's daily statement to record sales and redemption orders sent by investors directly to a transfer agent. The transfer agent's daily statements show the day's activity both in shares and dollars and should be reconciled to the fund's records to promptly identify and satisfactorily account for differences. A significant difference in the number of shares outstanding between the transfer agent's and fund's records could affect net asset value per share.

4.16 Cash used to settle transactions received by the fund, its distributor, or its transfer agent is forwarded to the custodian bank. Cash for redemptions is usually disbursed by the transfer agent to the investor or broker-dealer. Under arrangements in which the distributor and fund do not handle cash, the fund depends on the transfer agent to provide information on paid and unpaid sales and redemptions. Sales of stock and redemptions are usually settled within three business days. The transfer agent, distributor, or fund administrator, depending on the arrangement, follows up on delinquent accounts receivable and unpaid redemption orders.

4.17 A shareholder in an investment company usually chooses to receive distributions from net investment income and net realized gains from securities transactions in cash or additional capital shares. Such payments or issuances of shares are usually made by the transfer agent. IRS regulations may require tax withholding on certain distributions. Besides distributing cash or shares, the transfer agent is responsible for preparing and mailing annual tax notices to all shareholders about the amount and character of distributions paid. To be sure that appropriate information is communicated to shareholders, the fund should transmit such information to the transfer agent on a timely basis.

4.18 Money market funds and some fixed income funds declare and accumulate distributions daily for each account and usually distribute them in cash or additional shares monthly. The fund or its transfer agent mails periodic confirmation statements to the shareholders showing the cash distribution or additional shares credited to the account.

4.19 Accounting for treasury stock may be significant for commercial entities and certain closed-end investment companies. It is less important to mutual funds because only the total number of shares outstanding is relevant in their financial statements, and the number of shares previously redeemed by a fund is important only in connection with certain requirements of regulatory authorities. The SEC and state authorities have varying requirements for the registration of shares sold in their respective jurisdictions. Sections 24e–24f of the 1940 Act permit retroactive registration, under the Securities Act of 1933 (the 1933 Act), of shares sold in excess of shares registered and permit registration of an indefinite number of shares. A fund therefore needs to keep adequate records of the number of shares registered and the number and dollar amounts of shares sold in various jurisdictions. The fund also needs to make the mandated filings within the time permitted under regulatory statutes.

4.20 The 1940 Act and the Securities Exchange Act of 1934 (the 1934 Act) specify certain recordkeeping requirements for funds and transfer agents, respectively. The SEC staff periodically inspects the records for compliance.

AAG-INV 4.20

4.21 The fund should determine that the number of outstanding shares shown on the fund's general ledger and the transfer agent's shareholder control ledger and master security holder file[6] agree and that the detailed shareholder accounts are posted currently. Items that require close attention include transactions in the shareholder control ledger and master security holder file not yet applied to the detailed shareholder accounts and errors in posting to individual shareholder accounts, including postings to incorrect accounts. In addition to these and other similar monitoring activities, the fund may find it necessary to periodically review the transfer agency operation on site. The review often includes an inspection of the files containing shareholders' correspondence and inquiries; these files must be maintained by the company or its transfer agent. A significant volume of complaint letters may indicate problems in the detailed shareholder accounts. The fund should also obtain a copy of any service auditor's report on controls at the transfer agent. When a transfer agent is used by a fund, the user auditor should consider the guidance in AU section 324, *Service Organizations*[7] (AICPA, *Professional Standards*).

Considerations for Audits Performed in Accordance With Public Company Accounting Oversight Board (PCAOB) Standards

Paragraph .B17 of appendix B, "Special Topics," of PCAOB Auditing Standard No. 5, *An Audit of Internal Control Over Financial Reporting That Is Integrated with An Audit of Financial Statements* (AICPA, *PCAOB Standards and Related Rules*, Auditing Standards), provides further guidance regarding the use of service organizations when performing an integrated audit of financial statements and internal control over financial reporting. See the preface to this guide for more information about management's assessment of the effectiveness of internal control. As discussed in the preface, Section 405 of the Sarbanes-Oxley Act of 2002 generally exempts registered investment companies from the provisions of Section 404 that require a report of management on internal control over financial reporting. Additionally, Section 404(c) of the Sarbanes-Oxley Act of 2002 provides that an attestation report of a registered public accounting firm on internal control over financial reporting is not required for an issuer that is neither an accelerated filer nor a large accelerated filer. Business development companies, however, do not fall within the scope of the exception contained in Section 405 and are required, by Section 404, to include a report of management on the company's internal control over financial reporting.

---

[6] *Shareholder control ledger* and *master security holder file* are defined in Rule 17Ad-9 of the Securities Exchange Act of 1934 (the 1934 Act). These files are commonly referred to as supersheets for open-end investment companies.

[7] Paragraph 42 of Statement on Standards for Attestation Engagements No. 16, *Reporting on Controls at a Service Organization* (AICPA, *Professional Standards*, AT sec. 801), states that a service auditor should inquire whether management is aware of any events subsequent to the period covered by management's description of the service organization's system up to the date of the service auditor's report that could have a significant effect on management's assertion.

The AICPA Guide *Service Organizations: Applying SSAE No. 16, Reporting on Controls at a Service Organization (SOC 1*[SM]*)* contains information for practitioners reporting on controls at a service organization that affect user entities' internal control over financial reporting. Also, the AICPA Guide *Reporting on Controls at a Service Organization Relevant to Security, Availability, Processing Integrity, Confidentiality, or Privacy (SOC 2*[SM]*)* summarizes the three new service organization controls (SOC) engagements and provides detailed guidance on planning, performing, and reporting on SOC 2[SM] engagements.

Accounting for Capital Share Transactions and Distributions[8]

4.22 As described in paragraphs 7–8 of Financial Accounting Standards Board (FASB) *Accounting Standards Codification* (ASC) 946-20-25, accounting for shareholder transactions of open-end funds differs from the accounting followed by commercial entities in several key aspects. Sales of fund shares are recorded daily by crediting capital stock for the par value of the stock to be issued and additional paid-in capital for the amount paid over the par value; redemptions are recorded daily by debiting those accounts. The offsetting debit (credit), however, is made to an asset (liability) account, typically captioned "Receivable for Fund Shares Sold" ("Payable for Fund Shares Redeemed"). These entries are made on or as of the date that the order to purchase or sell fund shares is received (trade date), not the day that the payment is due (settlement date), as is typical practice for the recording of the issuance of equity shares by commercial entities. Investment partnerships should record a capital subscription as of the effective date stipulated in the partnership agreement. Cash received before this date should be recorded as an advance capital contribution liability. A receivable for the issuance of equity should be accounted for in accordance with FASB ASC 505-10-45.

4.23 Capital redemptions from investment partnerships should be recorded in the manner described in FASB ASC 480-10-25. FASB ASC 480-10-65 describes the related transition guidance.

4.24 For multiple classes of shares, capital accounts are maintained by class and the transfer agent provides separate share activity that is recorded, as previously stated, on a class-specific basis. Feeder funds within a master-feeder structure account for their capital share activity like typical single-tier funds. If the master fund is a partnership, no capital share transactions are recorded at the master level. Instead, contributions and withdrawals of the various feeders are recorded by the master fund.

4.25 Investment income and realized gains on securities transactions and their distributions are usually accumulated in separate accounts. Proper recording of distributions depends on, among other things, proper recording of the number of outstanding shares. Multiple class funds require specialized earnings allocation and distribution practices as described in chapter 5 of this guide.

4.26 As explained in FASB ASC 946-20-25-9, both closed-end and open-end investment companies record distribution liabilities on the ex-dividend date rather than the declaration date. For closed-end companies, a purchaser typically is not entitled to a dividend for shares purchased on the ex-dividend date. Open-end companies record the liability on the ex-dividend date to properly state the net asset value at which sales and redemptions are made. When large (in excess of 15 percent of a closed-end fund's net asset value) dividends or distributions are declared, it is the policy of some exchanges to postpone the ex-dividend date until the dividend has been paid. In such circumstances, the liability for the dividend distribution would be recorded on the books of the fund on the payment date.

---

[8] For guidance on accounting for scenarios in which a nonregistered investment partnership reports capital by investor class and has provisions that delay the recognition of certain events in the capital accounts until certain conditions have been met, see paragraphs 7.109–.112 of this guide.

AAG-INV 4.26

4.27 Shareholders of investment companies that offer the right to reinvest distributions (that is, receive distributions in additional shares) usually notify the company at the time they make their first purchase of shares of their intention to accept cash or reinvest future distributions. An investment company establishes a policy regarding the date for the reinvestment of distributions (the reinvestment date), which is typically the same as, or the day after, the ex-dividend date. For both closed-end and open-end funds issuing shares on reinvestment, the reinvestment date is the date at which the issuance of additional shares must be recognized in the accounts. Although the payment date is significant to those receiving the distribution in cash, the reinvestment date is important to those electing to reinvest the distribution in additional shares. At the reinvestment date, the actual or, if necessary, estimated number of shares to be issued and the price per share for reinvestment are set using the ex-dividend date's net asset value per share. The total net assets reflect the total dollars reinvested and additional shares outstanding resulting from the distribution reinvestment. At the reinvestment date, both shares and dollars show the effect of the reinvested dividends. Pursuant to a dividend reinvestment plan, a closed-end fund may be required to purchase shares in the open market when the fund's market price per share is less than the net asset value per share.

Equalization

4.28 Certain open-end investment companies use the accounting practice of equalization, which is unique to their industry. The practice was adopted in the 1930s to try to keep the continuing shareholders' interest in undistributed income from being affected by changes in the number of shares outstanding by applying a portion of the proceeds from sales and costs of repurchases of capital shares to undistributed income.

4.29 The equalization theory states that the net asset value of each share of capital stock sold or repurchased comprises the par value of the stock, undistributed income, and paid-in and other surplus. When shares are sold or repurchased, the investment company calculates the amount of undistributed income available for distribution to its shareholders and, based on the number of shares outstanding, determines the amount associated with each share. The per share amount so determined is credited to the equalization account when shares are sold and charged to the equalization account when shares are repurchased.

4.30 Registered investment companies using equalization accounting should disclose net equalization debits or credits in the statement of changes in net assets as stated by Rule 6.09.2 of Regulation S-X.

Auditing Procedures[9]

Principal Audit Objectives

4.31 The tests of the capital accounts (shareholder accounting) of a mutual fund cover a broad area encompassing various aspects of transactions with shareholders. The principal audit objectives are to make sure that

---

[9] This guide primarily discusses auditing guidance issued by the Auditing Standards Board (ASB) that applies to nonissuers. *Issuers* are defined by Section 3 of the 1934 Act and include registered investment companies. Audits of issuers are required to be performed under Public Company Accounting Oversight Board (PCAOB) standards. Users should evaluate their audit engagements to determine which auditing standards are applicable.

Capital Accounts

- the number of outstanding shares of capital stock at the audit date is stated properly.
- procedures are satisfactory for determining the number of outstanding shares used to compute daily net asset value per share.
- procedures are satisfactory for determining the number of shares required to be registered under the 1933 Act.
- the receivable for capital stock sold and the payable for capital stock redeemed are stated properly.
- distributions from investment income, net realized gains from securities transactions and capital, and their reinvestments, if any, are computed and accounted for properly.
- procedures are satisfactory for maintaining control over the recordkeeping for individual shareholder accounts.
- the capital stock purchased and sold throughout the period is accounted for properly.

Obtaining an Understanding of the Entity and Its Environment, Including Internal Control[10]

4.32 Paragraph .01 of AU section 314, *Understanding the Entity and Its Environment and Assessing the Risks of Material Misstatement* (AICPA, *Professional Standards*), states that an auditor must obtain a sufficient understanding of the entity and its environment, including its internal control, to assess the risks of material misstatement of the financial statements.[11] Specific to an audit of an investment company, the auditor should obtain an understanding of the following:

- The rules and regulations under the 1940 Act and Section 17 of the 1934 Act that encompass shareholder accounting, including pricing of fund shares, recordkeeping requirements, and applicable exemptive orders
- The fund's current prospectus, which states the fund's policies for accepting sales orders and redemption of fund shares
- The agreement among the fund, its distributor, and those responsible for the stock transfer function as well as agreements with intermediaries for the acceptance and processing of transactions in fund shares
- State Blue Sky laws, FINRA rules, and the fund's procedures for monitoring compliance

Considerations for Audits Performed in Accordance With PCAOB Standards

---

[10] AU section 314, *Understanding the Entity and Its Environment and Assessing the Risks of Material Misstatement* (AICPA, *Professional Standards*), states that the auditor must obtain a sufficient understanding of internal controls by performing risk assessment procedures to evaluate the design of controls relevant to an audit of financial statements and determine whether they have been implemented. Refer to paragraphs .40–.101 of AU section 314 for a detailed discussion of internal control.

[11] For additional nonauthoritative guidance pertaining to internal control and the risk assessment standards (Statement on Auditing Standards [SAS] Nos. 104–111 [AICPA, *Professional Standards*]), refer to Technical Questions and Answers sections 8200.05–.16 (AICPA, *Technical Practice Aids*).

AAG-INV 4.32

Auditing Standard No. 12, *Identifying and Assessing Risks of Material Misstatement* (AICPA, *PCAOB Standards and Related Rules*, Auditing Standard), includes a requirement to evaluate, while obtaining an understanding of the company, whether significant changes in the company from prior periods, including changes in its internal control over financial reporting, affect the risks of material misstatement.

4.33 The auditor also should obtain an understanding of the shareholder accounting and transfer function, whether performed by the fund or outside agents. (See the discussion in paragraphs 4.55–.62 on reports on controls at outside service organizations.) The auditor should obtain an understanding of the controls over the processing of the following:

- Sales
- Redemptions
- Reinvestments
- Cash distributions
- Correspondence
- Stock issuance and stock dividends
- Letters of intent
- Transactions subject to rights of accumulation
- Collections on sales and repayments for redemptions
- Cancellation of sales and redemptions
- Check writing and telephone redemptions
- Account maintenance (address, name, dividend option, and so on) changes
- Inactive accounts (for example, dormant or undeliverable accounts)
- Fees imposed on or other restrictions placed on frequent trading of fund shares

4.34 If the preceding procedures are implemented properly, the fund or its agent would be furnished promptly with the information required to process properly its shareholder records, as stated by the 1940 Act.

4.35 Administrative arrangements providing for such services as sub-transfer agency and recordkeeping may exist among the fund, its custodian, its transfer agent, or its underwriter. The auditor should obtain an understanding of the contractual responsibilities of the various parties to those arrangements to determine whether to

- obtain information about the controls of those parties that may affect the investment company's IT.[12]
- obtain a service auditor's report on controls at service organizations that may affect the investment company's IT.
- perform other procedures.

---

[12] AU section 314 describes the aspects of an entity's IT that are relevant to an audit of financial statements. PCAOB Auditing Standard No. 5, *An Audit of Internal Control Over Financial Reporting That Is Integrated with An Audit of Financial Statements* (AICPA, *PCAOB Standards and Related Rules*, Auditing Standards), describes the aspects of an entity's IT that apply for an integrated audit.

4.36 Based on the understanding of the entity and its environment, including its internal control, the assessed risk of material misstatement, and controls at service organizations, if applicable, the auditor may decide to test the operating effectiveness of controls. Paragraph .23 of AU section 318, *Performing Audit Procedures in Response to Assessed Risks and Evaluating the Audit Evidence Obtained* (AICPA, *Professional Standards*), states that the auditor should perform tests of controls when the auditor's risk assessment includes an expectation of the operating effectiveness of controls or when substantive procedures alone do not provide sufficient appropriate audit evidence at the relevant assertion level. Tests of the operating effectiveness of controls are performed only on those controls that the auditor has determined are suitably designed to prevent or detect a material misstatement in a relevant assertion. Paragraphs .106–.108 of AU section 314 discuss the identification of controls at the relevant assertion level likely to prevent or detect a material misstatement in a class of transactions, account balance, or disclosure.

4.37 The auditor may select transactions throughout the audit period to test controls in some of the following areas:

- Pricing shares at net asset values next computed
- Review and approval of daily transaction totals
- As-of transactions
- Reprocessed transactions

When the auditor obtains audit evidence about the operating effectiveness of controls during an interim period, the auditor should determine what additional audit evidence should be obtained for the remaining period.

4.38 The auditor may wish to review schedules maintained by the fund of sales of shares in each state concerning Blue Sky laws and federal regulations to test compliance with regulatory requirements or determine that management is monitoring such compliance.

Examination of Transactions and Detail Records [13]

4.39 The auditor performs substantive tests of activity and balances in the capital accounts based on many factors, including the assessment of the risk of material misstatement.

4.40 *Sales and redemptions of fund shares.* The auditor may wish to test whether details on the order form or other customer evidence used in processing a sale or redemption agree with the copy of the form ultimately sent to the shareholder to confirm the sale or redemption. Such tests should determine whether the transactions conform with the fund's prospectus (including sales charges) and the reinvestment and redemption options selected by the shareholder in his or her account application.

---

[13] AU section 318, *Performing Audit Procedures in Response to Assessed Risks and Evaluating the Audit Evidence Obtained* (AICPA, *Professional Standards*), states that to reduce audit risk to an acceptably low level, the auditor should determine overall responses to address the assessed risks of material misstatement at the financial statement level and design and perform further audit procedures whose nature, timing, and extent are responsive to the assessed risks of material misstatement at the relevant assertion level. The purpose is to provide a clear linkage between the nature, timing, and extent of the auditor's further audit procedures and assessed risks. Refer to AU section 318 for additional guidance.

118   Investment Companies

4.41 Depending on the method used to redeem shares, the auditor may examine shareholder requests, wire order forms, telephone tape recordings, telephone order forms, and copies of checks remitted to shareholders.

4.42 The auditor may test totals of daily sales and redemptions of capital shares by comparing them with postings in the related journals. Capital stock outstanding for the days tested may be compared against the applicable daily net asset valuation worksheets used as the basis for computing the net asset value per share.

4.43 *Settlement of sales and redemption transactions.* The auditor should obtain an understanding of the internal controls in place to ensure that receivables for shares sold and payables for shares redeemed are priced and settled promptly. Subsidiary trial balances of receivables and payables should be reconciled with general ledger control accounts as of the balance sheet date. The timely cancellation of sales and redemptions not settled within a specified time and the disposition of losses that may result might be determined.

4.44 *Reconciliation of shares outstanding.* The auditor should determine that the fund has reconciled its general ledger account for outstanding shares with reports of the transfer agent throughout the audit period and satisfactorily resolved all reconciling items. The auditor should examine the underlying support for the reconciling items to the extent considered necessary.

4.45 At the balance sheet date, the auditor should confirm shares outstanding directly with the transfer agent as well as determine whether the shares have been reconciled with the shares shown as outstanding in the fund's records. If the auditor concludes that audit risk has not been reduced to an acceptably low level by the combination of obtaining an understanding of the internal controls (including consideration of any related service auditor's report) and confirming shares outstanding in total with the transfer agent, the auditor may confirm outstanding shares directly with shareholders. The auditor may perform the confirmation procedure at a date other than the balance sheet date. For example, the auditor may confirm the shares outstanding at the interim date of the audit.[14,15]

---

[14] Interpretation No. 1, "Use of Electronic Confirmations," of AU section 330, *The Confirmation Process* (AICPA, *Professional Standards*, AU sec. 9330 par. .01–.08), clarifies, among other matters, that the use of an electronic confirmation process is not precluded by AU section 330. Although no confirmation process with a third party is without some risk of interception or alteration, including the risk that the confirmation respondent will not be the intended respondent, paragraph .05 of Interpretation No. 1 states that confirmations obtained electronically can be considered to be reliable audit evidence if the auditor is satisfied that (*a*) the electronic confirmation process is secure and properly controlled, (*b*) the information obtained is a direct communication in response to a request, and (*c*) the information is obtained from a third party who is the intended respondent. The interpretation also provides guidance to assist the auditor in assessing the confirmation process.

All auditing interpretations corresponding to a SAS have been considered in the development of a clarified SAS and incorporated accordingly, and have been withdrawn by the ASB except for certain interpretations that the ASB has retained and revised to reflect the issuance of SAS No. 122, *Statements on Auditing Standards: Clarification and Recodification* (AICPA, *Professional Standards*). This interpretation was incorporated into the clarified SAS, which will become effective for annual periods ending on or after December 15, 2012. See the preface for further information on the clarity project.

[15] In 2010, the PCAOB issued a proposed auditing standard, *Confirmation*, for public comment that would supersede its interim standard: AU section 330, *The Confirmation Process* (AICPA, *PCAOB Standards and Related Rules*, Interim Standards). Readers may access the proposed standard from the Standards' Current Activities page on the PCAOB website. Readers should remain alert for the issuance of this auditing guidance.

AAG-INV 4.41

4.46 *Dividends and distributions to shareholders and reinvestments.* Payments of dividends on capital stock may be tested to determine that payments in cash or additional capital stock have been computed properly. Distributions based on long term realized gains from securities transactions, except for a supplemental distribution of up to 10 percent of the original distribution, may not be paid more than once per year by a registered investment company, except that an additional distribution of long term gains may be made solely to comply with Internal Revenue Code (IRC) distribution requirements under excise tax regulations. However, pursuant to Rule 19b-1(e) of the 1940 Act, a fund may apply to the SEC for permission to make an additional distribution or distributions of long term capital gains.

4.47 The auditor should inspect the board of directors' or trustees' minutes for relevant dates and amounts of dividend declarations and may test whether shares outstanding on that date (ex-dividend date for open-end companies), according to the fund's records, have been reconciled to information reported by the transfer agent. The total dividend may be recomputed (outstanding shares times rate) and compared against a notification from the dividend-paying agent, who is usually also the transfer agent. To test that the liability for a dividend was recorded on the proper date, the dividend should be compared with the general ledger and the applicable daily net asset valuation worksheet. The computation of the number of shares to be reinvested, as reported by the dividend-paying agent, should be tested, and the portion of the dividend taken in shares should be compared against the capital stock accounts for agreement of both number of shares and dollar amounts.

4.48 The computations of daily dividend rates for funds that declare dividends daily may be tested for selected dates throughout the period.

4.49 *Recordkeeping for individual shareholder accounts.* Based on the assessed level of control risk for assertions that relate to the activities of the transfer agent or shareholder servicing agent, the auditor may wish to select some accounts to test the validity and proper documentation of transactions for name and address changes, share transfers to or from individual accounts, and transactions that are not routine. The auditor may find it desirable to confirm some shareholder accounts, such as for a transfer agent that is not independent of the investment company or situations in which the auditor cannot rely on the transfer agent's controls.

Other Auditing Matters

4.50 If equalization accounting is used, the auditor may test the calculation of equalization amounts.

4.51 Auditors might review, on a test basis, correspondence from shareholders received by the fund or transfer agent. A significant volume of complaints relating to pricing or incorrect calculations of shares issued may suggest to the auditor that additional testing may be necessary.

4.52 The auditor may evaluate the volumes of gross fund share sales and redemptions in relation to total shares outstanding for unusual relationships, in particular considering prospectus restrictions on frequent trading of fund shares or requirements to impose redemption fees on such trading.

4.53 The auditor may wish to confirm balances receivable for capital stock and balances payable for capital shares to be redeemed by the fund directly with the investor or dealers who sell the fund's shares. Details of specific capital stock transactions may also be confirmed. Alternative auditing procedures may also be used to satisfy the auditor concerning receivables and payables for fund shares sold and redeemed.

4.54 Management's representation letter should state that fund shares were sold and redeemed in accordance with the fund's prospectus, the SEC's rules and regulations (see item 14[c] in paragraph 11.41 of this guide), and state securities regulations. For funds with multiple classes of shares, the auditor should determine that the fund has allocated its daily activities among each respective class of shares, based upon the method chosen (see chapter 5 of this guide), and properly calculated its net asset values throughout the period. The auditor should examine the allocations and their underlying support, including records of shares outstanding. In addition, the auditor should determine that class-level fee waivers and reimbursements were not in violation of Rule 18f-3 under the 1940 Act or any related SEC exemptive orders. The auditor should also consider the possible implications of any waivers on the fund's distributions under the IRC (see chapter 6, "Taxes," of this guide).

Reports on Controls at Outside Service Organizations [16]

4.55 When a fund uses a service organization, such as an outside transfer agent, subtransfer agent, or recordkeeping agent, transactions that affect the fund's financial statements are subjected to controls that are, at least in part, physically and operationally separate from the fund. The significance of the controls of the service organization to those of the fund depends on the nature of the services provided by the service organization, primarily the nature and materiality of the transactions that it processes for the fund and the degree of interaction between its activities and those of the fund. For example, if the fund initiates transactions and the service organization executes and does the accounting processing of those transactions, there is a high degree of interaction between the activities of the fund and those at the service organization. In these circumstances, it may be practicable for the user organization to implement effective controls over those transactions. However, if the service organization initiates, executes, and does the accounting processing of the user organization's transactions, there is a lower degree of interaction, and it may not be practicable for the fund to implement effective internal controls over those transactions.

4.56 Auditing Standard No. 5 establishes requirements that apply to an integrated audit. Refer to paragraphs .B17–.B27 of appendix B of Auditing Standard No. 5 regarding the use of service organizations.

4.57 AU section 314 states that an auditor should obtain an understanding of the five components of internal control sufficient to assess the risks of material misstatement of the financial statements whether due to error or fraud, and to design the nature, timing, and extent of further audit procedures. The auditor should obtain a sufficient understanding by performing risk assessment procedures to evaluate the design of controls relevant to an audit of financial statements and determine whether they have been implemented. The auditor should use such knowledge to

  a. identify the types of potential misstatements;

  b. consider factors that affect the risks of material misstatement; and

---

[16] See footnote 7.

c. design tests of controls, when applicable, and substantive procedures.

AU section 314 states an entity's use of IT may affect any of the five components of internal control relevant to the achievement of the entity's financial reporting, operations, or compliance objectives, and its operating units or business functions. In obtaining an understanding of the financial reporting process (including the closing process), the auditor should obtain an understanding of the automated and manual procedures that an entity uses to prepare financial statements and related disclosures and how misstatements may occur.[17] Paragraph .102 of AU section 314 states that the auditor should identify and assess the risks of material misstatement at the financial statement and relevant assertion level related to the classes of transactions, account balances, and disclosures. Paragraph .104 of AU section 314 states that the auditor should determine whether the identified risks of material misstatement relate to specific relevant assertions related to classes of transactions, account balances, and disclosures or whether they relate more pervasively to the financial statements as a whole and potentially affect many relevant assertions. Paragraph .51 of AU section 318 states that regardless of the assessed risks of material misstatement, the auditor should design and perform substantive procedures for all relevant assertions related to each material class of transactions, account balance, and disclosure.

> Ⓤ **Update 4-1** *Audit***: Clarified Auditing Standards**
>
> When effective, the clarified auditing standard AU-C section 402, *Audit Considerations Relating to an Entity Using a Service Organization* (AICPA, *Professional Standards*), will supersede AU section 324. AU-C section 402 contains primarily clarifying changes from the extant section. The term *extant* is used throughout this guide in reference to the standards that are superseded by the clarified standards.
>
> For audits of financial statements for periods ending on or after December 15, 2012, refer to sections B.08 and B.12 in appendix B, "Guidance Updates—Clarified Auditing Standards," which summarizes these clarifying changes that may affect an auditor's practice or methodology.

4.58 If a fund uses a service organization, certain controls and records of the service organization may be relevant to the fund's ability to record, process, summarize, and report financial data in a manner consistent with the assertions in the entity's financial statements. Paragraphs .03–.10 of AU section 324 describe factors that an auditor should consider in determining whether to obtain information about controls at a service organization. AU section 324 provides guidance on the auditor's assessment of control risk in such circumstances. Paragraph .14 of AU section 324 states that, if the auditor plans to assess control risk below the maximum for assertions that are affected by activities of the service organization, the auditor should evaluate the operating effectiveness of controls at the service organization relevant to those assertions

---

[17] IT encompasses automated means of originating, processing, storing, and communicating information and includes recording devices, communication systems, computer systems (including hardware and software components and data), and other electronic devices. An entity's use of IT may be extensive; however, the auditor is primarily interested in the entity's use of IT to initiate, record, process, and report transactions or other financial data.

by obtaining a service auditor's report on the controls placed in operation and tests of operating effectiveness, obtaining an agreed-upon procedures report that addresses those controls, or performing tests of controls at the service organization.

4.59 Paragraph .11 of AU section 324 states that the auditor uses his or her understanding of internal control to assess control risk for the assertions embodied in the account balances and classes of transactions, including those that are affected by the activities of the service organization. In doing so, the user auditor may identify certain user organization controls that, if effective, would permit the user auditor to assess control risk as low or moderate for particular assertions. Such controls may be applied at either the user organization or the service organization. Tests of these control procedures could also be considered.

4.60 Although a service auditor's report on controls placed in operation and tests of operating effectiveness may provide a basis for assessing control risk below the maximum, it does not permit the auditor to assess the level of control risk so low to eliminate the need to perform substantive tests for the fund's capital accounts and transactions.

4.61 Paragraph .18 of AU section 324 provides guidance on the auditor's considerations in using a service auditor's report. The auditor may wish to discuss with the service auditor the scope and results of the service auditor's work for a better understanding of the procedures and conclusions.

4.62 Paragraph .21 of AU section 324 states that the auditor should not refer to the report of the service auditor as a basis, in part, for an opinion on the fund's financial statements. The service auditor's report is used in the audit, but the service auditor is not responsible for examining any portion of the financial statements as of any specific date or for any specific period.

Chapter 5
Complex Capital Structures

5.01 Many investment companies adopt complex capital structures to increase flexibility in pricing and access to alternative distribution channels for their shares. Such structures are principally of two kinds: multiple-class funds and master-feeder funds. In addition, many organizations are offering funds of funds. Funds of funds, master-feeder arrangements, and multiple classes of shares are an increasingly significant segment of the investment companies currently in existence. Funds of funds either permit a fund complex to provide asset allocation products using funds in the complex or allow an investment adviser to allocate assets among many unaffiliated investment advisers. Master-feeder and multiple-class structures permit a common investment vehicle to be distributed through different channels or with different distribution charges to the shareholder, or both.

Operational and Accounting Issues
Multiple-Class Funds

5.02 As stated in Financial Accounting Standards Board (FASB) *Accounting Standards Codification* (ASC) 946-10-05-5, multiple-class funds issue more than one class of shares. Each class of shares typically has a different kind of sales charge, such as a front-end load, contingent deferred sales load, 12b-1 fee, or combinations thereof. Multiple-class funds may charge different classes of shares for specific or incremental expenses, such as transfer-agent, registration, and printing expenses related to each class.

5.03 A commonly used multiple-class structure for registered investment companies includes (but is not limited to) the following classes of shares:

- *Class A*. Class A shares are charged primarily a front-end sales load. (The shares might also be assessed a low 12b-1 or service fee.)
- *Class B*. Class B shares bear a contingent deferred sales charge (CDSC) coupled with a 12b-1 distribution or service fee. Class B shares often convert to class A shares at a specified future date to avoid being assessed a higher 12b-1 fee for an extended period.
- *Class C*. Class C shares bear a level sales load, typically a 12b-1 distribution or service fee similar to the level charged in class B. Class C shares usually have a 1 percent CDSC assessed for 1 year. There is usually no conversion to another class.
- *Institutional shares*. Shares typically bear no sales load and usually do not have 12b-1 distribution charges. There may be a service fee depending upon the source of the shares, whether they are sold through wrap programs or trust departments. Such selling agents often have their own structures that charge the fee directly to the investor.

5.04 Although no legal requirements exist regarding specific class designations, many in the industry have voluntarily adopted the previously mentioned nomenclature to avoid shareholder and sales force confusion.

5.05 Multiple-class funds have unique operational and accounting issues. These issues include the methods and procedures to (*a*) allocate income, expenses, and gains or losses to the various classes to determine the net asset value per share for each class; (*b*) calculate dividends and distributions to shareholders for each class; and (*c*) calculate investment performance for each class (such as total return and Securities and Exchange Commission [SEC] yield).

5.06 Rule 18f-3 under the Investment Company Act of 1940 (the 1940 Act) establishes a framework for an open-end fund's issuance of multiple classes of shares representing interests in the same portfolio. The rule permits certain differences in expenses between classes and prescribes how income, expenses, and realized and unrealized gains and losses may be allocated among the classes.

5.07 To calculate the net asset value per share of each class for multiple-class funds, income, expenses, and realized and unrealized gains or losses must be allocated to each class. Fees and expenses of the fund need to be classified as either fund or class-level expenses. Fund-level expenses, such as investment management fees, apply to all classes. Rule 18f-3 identifies certain expenses, such as distribution and servicing fees, as being class-level expenses and requires that they be generally charged directly to the individual classes to which they relate. Under the rule, other expenses, such as transfer-agent and registration fees attributable to individual classes, may be designated as class-level expenses at the discretion of the fund's board of directors or trustees or remain fund-level expenses. All other expenses are allocated among the classes based on a methodology discussed in paragraph 5.10. Rule 18f-3 provides for the exercise of judgment by the fund and its directors or trustees concerning the appropriateness and fairness of the expense allocation methodology. Because certain expenses are charged to the classes of shares differently, net asset value per share and dividends per share must be calculated separately for each class of shares. Class B and class C shareholders will normally receive a smaller dividend per share from net investment income than class A shareholders because of higher distribution and servicing fees. Net asset value per share may differ among classes.

5.08 Each class of shares bears all its identified class-specific expenses. The IRS currently takes the position that funds with multiple classes have only one class of shares for tax purposes. Revenue Procedure 96-47 essentially provides that if a fund pays dividends of differing amounts (differential dividends) to its various classes of shares pursuant to a capital structure allowed by (or similar to that allowed by) Rule 18f-3, the IRS will not consider such dividends to be preferential. This revenue procedure allows differential dividends due to divergent charges for items such as 12b-1 fees, shareholder servicing fees, and any other class-specific expenses. Fund-level expenses, such as management fees, custodian fees, and other expenses related to the management of the company's assets, must be allocated proportionally among all classes using an allocation methodology discussed in paragraph 5.10. For distributions in taxable years beginning after December 22, 2010, the preferential dividend rule in Internal Revenue Code (IRC) Section 562(c) has been repealed for publicly traded regulated investment companies (RICs) by the RIC Modernization Act of 2010. Full details of changes from the RIC Modernization Act of 2010 are discussed in chapter 6, "Taxes," of this guide.

5.09 Class-specific expenses may be waived or reimbursed at different amounts for individual classes. However, Rule 18f-3 requires a fund's board of

Complex Capital Structures

directors or trustees to monitor waivers or reimbursements to guard against cross-subsidization among the classes. Fund management must also ensure that such waivers or reimbursements do not create a preferential dividend to a particular class of shares from a tax perspective. Revenue Procedure 99-40 covers circumstances under which such expenses may be reimbursed for tax purposes. To protect themselves from an inadvertent preferential dividend, a rigorous approach to the documentation of class expense differences (including waivers or reimbursements) and also compliance with any private letter rulings should be followed carefully by multiple-class funds. See paragraphs 6.67–.68 of this guide for more specific guidance regarding preferential dividends, including details of the repeal of this rule for publicly traded RICs.

5.10 The methods for allocating income, fund-level expenses, and realized and unrealized gains or losses set forth in Rule 18f-3 are as follows:

- *Fair value of shares outstanding—relative net assets.* Under this method, each class of shares participates based on the total net asset value of its shares in proportion to the total net assets of the fund. Under Rule 18f-3, it is expected that this method will be the primary method used to allocate income, fund-level expenses, and realized and unrealized gains and losses for calculating the net asset value of nondaily dividend funds.

- *Fair value of settled shares outstanding.* Under this method, earnings are allocated based on the fair value of settled shares. It is typically used to achieve consistency between the allocation method and a fund's dividend policy with respect to the shares eligible to receive dividends. For example, most daily dividend funds pay dividends only to settled shares and; therefore, in a fund that requires settlement of its shares on a trade-date-plus-three basis, the appropriate basis of allocation of income and nonclass-specific expenses would be the fair value of settled shares. Rule 18f-3 permits daily dividend funds to use the settled-shares method for allocating income and expenses and the relative-net-assets method for allocating realized and unrealized gains and losses.

- *Shares outstanding.* This method provides for each share outstanding to participate equally in the nonclass-specific items of income, expense, gains, and losses. Under Rule 18f-3, this method may be used by funds, provided that (*a*) the fund is a daily dividend fund that maintains the same net asset value per share in each class, (*b*) the fund has agreements in place for waivers or reimbursements of expenses to ensure that all classes maintain the same per share net asset value, and (*c*) payments waived or reimbursed under such agreements may not be carried forward or recouped at a future date.

- *Simultaneous equations.* This method ensures that the annualized rate of return of each class will differ from that of the other classes only by the expense differential among the classes.

- *Any appropriate method.* A fund may use any appropriate allocation method so long as a majority of the fund's directors or trustees, including a majority of the directors or trustees who are not interested persons of the fund, determines that the method is fair to the shareholders of each class and that the annualized rate of return of each class will generally differ from that of the other classes only by the expense differentials among the classes.

Whichever method is selected, Rule 18f-3 requires the fund to use that method consistently. Rule 18f-3 does not specify any requirements regarding the distribution calculation methods that a multiple-class fund generally should use. Illustrations using the allocation methods discussed previously are presented in exhibit 5-1.

5.11 The methods, as they are each defined by the FASB ASC glossary, generally used to calculate distributions to shareholders from net investment income are as follows:

- *Record-share method.* The sum of net investment income available for all classes after deducting allocated expenses but before consideration of class-specific expenses is divided by the total outstanding shares on the dividend record date for all classes to arrive at a gross dividend rate for all shares. From this gross rate, an amount per share for each class (the amount of incremental expenses accrued during the period divided by the record date shares outstanding for the class) is subtracted. The result is the per share dividend available for each class.

- *Actual-income-available method.* Actual net investment income that has been allocated to each class (as recorded on the books) is divided by the record date shares for each class to derive the dividend payable per share.

- *Simultaneous-equations method.* This method seeks to ensure, by using simultaneous equations, that the distribution rates will differ among the classes by the anticipated differential in expense ratios.

Illustrations of the distribution calculation methods are presented in exhibit 5-2.

5.12 The record-share method is most commonly used by funds that do not pay dividends daily (nondaily dividend funds). It is also used by daily dividend funds that employ policies to manage their dividend payout levels (such as to distribute stable dividend amounts or to compensate for book-tax differences). The dividend payout level may be managed for only one share class; the dividend rates for the other classes will vary because class-level expenses differ between classes. The record-share method is simple to apply, provides assurance that the annualized distribution rate for the class with higher expenses will be lower than that for the class with lower expenses, and minimizes the likelihood of a preferential dividend being paid. The disadvantage of this method is that the annualized distribution rates of the various classes usually will not reflect the precise expense ratio difference between the classes because the directly related expenses accrued over time on a varying number of shares are reduced to a per share amount on the record date shares. The larger the fluctuation in shares over time, the greater the potential difference.

5.13 The actual-income-available method is used for funds that declare daily dividends per share equal to the amount of net investment income allocated to each class. This results in the same per share net asset value for all classes (except for differences that may result from rounding). The actual-income-available method is not typically used for funds that pay dividends on a periodic basis.

5.14 The simultaneous-equations method is used for periodic dividend funds and is more complex than other methods. This method ensures that the annualized distribution rates will differ among classes by the approximate amount of the expense ratio difference. Per share net asset value will usually converge after the dividend has been recorded.

5.15 Because distribution amounts under both the record-share and simultaneous-equations methods are determined independently of the amount of net investment income allocated to each class, situations can result whereby, after recording the dividends, one class has positive undistributed income whereas the other class is negative.

5.16 As stated in FASB ASC 946-505-50-4, for financial reporting purposes of multiple-class funds, a return of capital is not determined at the class level, and distributable earnings are disclosed only at the fund level.

5.17 Regardless of the frequency of income dividends or the distribution calculation method selected, to avoid paying a preferential dividend for tax purposes (see paragraph 5.08 and chapter 6 for a discussion on the repeal of the preferential dividend rule for publicly traded RICs by the RIC Modernization Act of 2010), multiple-class funds ordinarily should declare long term capital gain distributions at the fund level, rather than at the class level, so that all shares receive the same per share gain distribution.

Master-Feeder Funds

5.18 In master-feeder structures, separate investment companies often perform the investment management and distribution functions. Feeder investment companies, each having similar investment objectives but different distribution channels for their shares, such as retail or institutional customers, invest their assets solely in another investment company known as the master fund. All investment management functions are conducted by a master fund whereas distribution, shareholder-servicing, and transfer agent functions are conducted by the feeders.

5.19 The master fund is generally organized as a trust, with attributes that qualify it as a partnership for tax purposes, and may be registered under the 1940 Act. For nonregistered investment companies, master funds are generally organized as a partnership or offshore corporation. If the master fund is organized outside the United States, it may serve as an investment vehicle for both offshore feeder funds sold solely to foreign investors (or, in certain circumstances, U.S. tax-exempt investors) and domestic feeder funds sold solely to U.S. investors. Feeder funds are generally organized as corporations or trusts, may be taxed under the IRC as RICs, and may be registered as investment companies under the 1940 Act and the Securities Act of 1933 (the 1933 Act) (and the Securities Exchange Act of 1934, as appropriate). Feeder funds may also be organized under a different legal structure if they are not registered products and are being used as vehicles for nonpublic investing. Feeder funds may be organized with a multiple-class structure.

5.20 Master-feeder sponsors sometimes apply to the IRS for a private letter ruling to ensure that the master will be treated as a partnership for federal income tax purposes and that each feeder will be treated as an owner of its proportionate share of the earnings and profits and net assets of the master.

This is to make sure that the feeders maintain their status as RICs and can afford their shareholders the pass-through tax benefits that result from that status.

5.21 Master-feeder accounting involves allocating the master portfolio's income, expenses, and realized and unrealized gains and losses among its feeder funds. Because most master funds are typically structured as partnerships for tax purposes, the allocation of income, expenses, gains, and losses follows partnership tax allocation rules (partner's distributive share rules, as provided for in IRC Section 704[b]). According to the IRC, each feeder must be allocated its share of gain or loss realized by the master when the master disposes of a particular security lot. The tax allocation process is complicated because the relative interest of the feeder funds in the master portfolio changes, usually daily, as feeder fund shares are sold or redeemed. Two allocation methodologies are permitted under the IRC. The first allocation method follows the literal partnership allocation methodology that implies a property-by-property (lot-by-lot) method for investment partnerships. Performing tax allocations under the property-by-property method requires evaluating each feeder's share of the realized gain or loss on the security lot sold. The second method allows allocation based on an aggregate method. Performing tax allocation under the aggregate method requires evaluating each feeder's share of the unrealized gains or losses on its entire (that is, aggregate) interest in the master, rather than each feeder's share of the realized gain or loss on the sold security lot alone. In the absence of a ruling from the IRS, the regulation allowing an aggregate method for allocating gains and losses does not apply to built-in gains and losses from securities contributed by a feeder to a master in a nontaxable event. However, certain qualified master feeders that meet the requirements of Revenue Procedure 2001-36 are permitted to use the aggregate method for contributed property, although other fund groups would still require a private letter ruling from the IRS.

Funds of Funds

5.22 Funds of funds are investment companies that invest in other investment companies. Funds of funds have been popular in the investment partnership market and have become more popular in the registered fund market. Master-feeder structures can be viewed as funds of funds but usually only with 1 top-tier (portfolio) fund; a more typical fund-of-funds structure has more than 1 top-tier fund. Historically, a registered investment company's ability to invest in other investment companies was limited by Section 12(d) of the 1940 Act. Under Section 12(d), an open-end investment company is limited, among other restrictions, to aggregate investments in other investment companies of 10 percent of the acquiring company's total assets. Master-feeder structures, however, are specifically permitted by Section 12(d)-(1)(E)(ii) of the 1940 Act. As a result, except for a limited number of registered funds that received exemptive orders from the SEC, fund-of-funds structures have been limited to unregistered investment companies. In 1996, Section 12(d) was amended to permit registered investment companies to invest in other investment companies provided that both the investor and investee funds were part of the same group of investment companies (affiliated funds). Investments in nonaffiliated funds would continue to be subject to the historical limitations under Section 12(d) unless an exemptive order is obtained from the SEC.

5.23 In 2006, the SEC adopted Rules 12d1-1 through 12d1-3 under the 1940 Act to broaden the ability of a fund to invest in shares of another fund consistent with the public interest and protection of investors. Rule 12d1-1 allows funds to invest in shares of money market funds in excess of the limits of Section 12(d)(1) and is intended to allow funds to utilize money market funds in "cash sweep" arrangements in which available cash is invested in a money market fund in lieu of short term investments. Rule 12d1-2 permits funds structured as funds of affiliated funds to also purchase shares of unaffiliated funds up to the statutory limits of Section 12(d)(1) and to make direct investments in stocks, bonds, and other types of securities. Rule 12d1-3 provides greater flexibility in operating funds of unaffiliated funds.

5.24 Many multitiered structures are U.S. domiciled, but recent trends include the creation of offshore, domestic, and blended structures. A blended structure might include a fund with significant investments in other investment companies and also investments in individual securities. Participants in such structures include both foreign and domestic investors, individually and through funds, commodity pools, retirement accounts, and other sources.

5.25 For many investee funds, fair value is usually readily determinable through observable market quotes (or, for investments in mutual funds, published net asset values that are used as the basis for current transactions). For those investee funds that do not have readily determinable fair values, refer to paragraphs 2.75–.89 of this guide for further guidance on the use of net asset value per share (or its equivalent) as a practical expedient to value an investment in an investee fund that does not have a readily determinable fair value. The valuation of an investee fund by the investor generally should reflect any incentive or performance fee or incentive allocation of earnings to the general partner based on the current performance of the investee fund.

Other Considerations for Investments in Nonpublicly Traded Investees

5.26 Proper execution of the fund-of-funds strategy ordinarily requires management of the investor fund to exercise significant judgment in selecting and monitoring the performance of the investee funds. Occasionally, management may engage an outside consultant to assist in the performance monitoring and selection process. This process may include many procedures, and a review of prior audited financial results generally should be included.

5.27 Monitoring the performance is an essential control in the operation of the fund. Fund management ordinarily should review regular (for example quarterly) investment results and periodically review the trading strategy being followed by the investee fund to make sure that it is consistent with the strategy approved at the time of the initial investment. The results of daily monitoring functions established by management of the investee fund generally should also be reviewed periodically. Discussions with each investee fund to identify any significant changes or problems with systems, illiquid securities, personnel, or trading strategies generally should be held periodically and documented. At times, such as when there are significant changes in market conditions or a particularly risky strategy, monthly or more frequent discussions may be advisable. Another essential control that management of the investor fund normally should exercise is the comparison of preliminary annual results reported by the investee fund with the investee fund's audited financial statements. The audited financial statements should substantiate the reliability of the investee fund's reporting processes.

5.28 As an additional control over the valuation process, management of the investor fund may wait for the receipt of audited financial statements and individual capital account statements from investee funds to make sure that no significant changes in previously reported results have occurred before the investor fund issues its audited financial statements. This approach provides key audit evidence and instills discipline into the investor fund's financial reporting system.

5.29 Refer to paragraphs 2.75–.89 of this guide for further discussion of controls over investments in nonpublicly traded investees, including a discussion of Technical Questions and Answers (TIS) sections 2220.18–.27 (AICPA, *Technical Practice Aids*).

Financial Statement Presentation

5.30 As discussed in FASB ASC 946-210-45, management investment companies that have multiple classes of shares or master-feeder structures follow reporting guidelines discussed in the following paragraphs when preparing financial statements, including financial highlights. Illustrations are presented at the end of this chapter.

Multiple-Class Funds

5.31 *Example financial statements*. Exhibit 5-3 contains illustrations of multiple-class fund financial statements. Items to follow correspond to this exhibit.

5.32 *Statement of Assets and Liabilities*. As noted in FASB ASC 946-210-45-4, the composition of net assets is reported in total, but net asset value per share and shares outstanding should be reported for each class.

5.33 The maximum public offering price per share is often reported for each class.

5.34 *Statement of operations*. FASB ASC 946-225-45-9 explains that class-specific expenses are reported for each class (or disclosed in the notes to the financial statements). Reporting the amount of fund-level expenses allocated to each class is not required, but disclosure of fund-level expenses by class in the statement of operations or notes to the financial statements is permitted.

5.35 *Statement of changes in net assets*. FASB ASC 946-205-45-4 notes that dividends and distributions paid to shareholders and capital share transactions for each class are required to be presented (or disclosed in the notes to the financial statements).

5.36 *Notes to financial statements*. As FASB ASC 946-235-50-2 states, the notes should

- describe each class of shares, including sales charges, shareholder servicing fees, and distribution fees.
- disclose the method used to allocate income and expenses and realized and unrealized capital gains and losses to each class.
- describe fee arrangements for class-specific distribution plans and any other class-level expenses paid to affiliates.

- disclose capital share transactions (if not disclosed separately in the statement of changes in net assets) for each class.
- disclose total sales charges paid to any affiliates for each class.

5.37 *Financial highlights.* As explained in FASB ASC 946-205-50-27, financial highlights, including total return, should be presented by class except for portfolio turnover, which is calculated at the fund level. As stated in paragraph 7.161 of this guide, portfolio turnover is only required for registered investment companies. The financial highlights for any class for which the shareholders are precluded from investing may be omitted.

5.38 Because the financial highlights table is considered to be a financial statement disclosure, not a financial statement, the SEC has accepted the presentation of a financial highlights table only for a specific class or classes of shareholders for whom the financial statements are intended. In such situations, the auditor's report should be addressed to the fund board and the shareholders in the specific class or classes, not all shareholders taken as a whole. If a class terminates during the year, the financial highlights are not required to be presented in the financial statements for that class.

Master-Feeder Funds

5.39 *Example financial statements.* Exhibits 5-4 and 5-5 contain illustrations of relevant feeder fund and master fund financial statements. Items to follow correspond to these exhibits.

5.40 Under current SEC policies, the annual and semiannual reports for feeder funds should contain two sets of financial statements: one for the master fund and the other for the specific feeder fund. When the master and feeder funds have different year-ends, the SEC has indicated[1] that it would not object if, at each feeder investment company year-end, the audited shareholder report of the feeder is accompanied by the latest audited shareholder report of the master as well as an unaudited balance sheet and schedule of investments of the master as of the date of the feeder's financial statements.

5.41 *Statement of assets and liabilities.* As stated in FASB ASC 946-210-45-6, each feeder fund's statement of assets and liabilities should show an investment in the master fund, which is the sole or principal investment of the feeder fund. The total of all feeder funds' investments in the master fund should equal the total net assets of the master fund. A schedule of portfolio investments is not presented at the feeder level, unless the feeder fund also holds direct investments in addition to its investment in the master fund. The net asset value per share, total shares outstanding, and the components of net assets should be reported. Should the feeder fund have a multiple-class structure, it would report the multiple-class information specified in FASB ASC 946-210.

5.42 As explained in paragraph 5.19, master funds are usually organized as trusts, or in the case of nonregistered investment companies, as a partnership or offshore corporation. In accordance with FASB ASC 946-210-45-5, the statement of assets and liabilities of the master fund usually does not report the

---

[1] See the December 30, 1998, "Dear CFO Letter" issued by the Chief Accountant of the Securities and Exchange Commission (SEC) Division of Investment Management.

components of net assets, shares outstanding, or net asset value per share. The portfolio of investments should be included only in the master fund's financial statements.

5.43 *Statement of operations.* As described in paragraphs 11–12 of FASB ASC 946-225-45, the statement of operations reports details of the feeder fund's allocated share of net investment income from the master fund (that is, separate disclosure of allocated interest, dividends, and expenses). The statement also reports separately the feeder's allocated share of the master fund's realized and unrealized gains and losses. The total of all feeders' income, expense, and realized and unrealized gain or loss components should agree to the corresponding totals of the master fund. Feeder funds should disclose their fund-specific expenses, such as transfer agent, distribution, legal and audit expenses, and registration and directors' or trustees' fees. Additionally, any fee waivers or reimbursements at the feeder-fund level should be reported.

5.44 As stated in FASB ASC 946-225-45-10, for master funds, the standard reporting format for investment companies with simple capital structures should be used.

5.45 *Statement of changes in net assets.* FASB ASC 946-205-45-4 states that, for feeder funds, the standard reporting format for investment companies with simple capital structures is used. If the feeder fund is a multiple-class fund, the guidance for multiple-class funds in FASB ASC 946, *Financial Services—Investment Companies*, should be followed.

5.46 FASB ASC 946-205-45-4 also explains that the statement of changes in net assets of a master fund should report capital transactions from or to feeder funds as contributions and withdrawals, respectively. Dividend distributions are normally not made by the master fund when the master fund is treated as a partnership for tax purposes. In those situations when the master fund is treated as a RIC and taxed either as a corporation or trust, there may be distributions to the feeder funds to eliminate any accumulated taxable income at the master fund level.

5.47 *Notes to financial statements.* FASB ASC 946-235-50-3 explains that notes to the financial statements of each feeder fund should include the following:

- A general description of the master and feeder structure
- The feeder's percentage ownership share of the particular master fund at the reporting date
- A statement that the feeder invests all its investable assets in a corresponding open-end management investment company having the same investment objectives as the feeder and a reference to the financial statements of the master fund, including the portfolio of investments
- Disclosure of or reference to the accounting policies of the master fund that affect the feeders (such as valuation of investments of the master fund)

5.48 FASB ASC 946-235-50-3 further explains that information concerning the purchases and sales of investments and gross unrealized appreciation or depreciation of investments on a tax basis (required by Regulation S-X) is not applicable to the feeder's financial statements.

5.49 *Financial highlights.* As FASB ASC 946-205-50-28 notes, the feeder fund's ratios of expenses and net investment income to average net assets should include the expenses of both the feeder and master fund. Balance credits earned by the master fund should be reflected in the feeder fund ratios as if they had been earned by the feeder fund directly.

5.50 Feeder funds need not disclose a portfolio turnover rate because feeders invest substantially all their assets in the master fund. However, to the extent that the financial highlights table conforms to the instructions of Form N-1A, it should report the portfolio turnover rate experienced by the master. The financial highlights of feeder funds that are registered investment companies generally should comply with the same requirements as for registered investment companies not organized in a master-feeder structure (see paragraphs 7.153–.166 of this guide).

5.51 FASB ASC 946-205-50-29 states that the financial highlights section of the master fund organized as a partnership is substantially modified because per share information is not applicable. The master fund financial highlights section should include the total return, ratios of expenses and net investment income to average net assets, and portfolio turnover rate. Master funds not organized as partnerships should report normal per share data in the financial highlights section.

5.52 *Auditor's report.* The auditor's report for the feeder fund is modified to exclude the phrase "including the portfolio of investments" because the portfolio of investments is not part of the feeder fund's financial statements.

Funds of Funds

5.53 *Example financial statements.* Exhibit 5-6 contains illustrations of relevant fund-of-funds financial statements. Items to follow correspond to this exhibit.

5.54 *Statement of assets and liabilities.*[2] FASB ASC 946-210-45-7 explains that the reporting fund may list the investee (portfolio) funds directly on the statement of assets and liabilities. Additional disclosures may be required for those funds that hold a mixture of investments in other investment companies and direct investments in securities. However, there is usually no need for a separate schedule of investments. Fund management should consider whether an investment in a single underlying fund is so significant to the fund of funds

---

[2] Rule 3-09 of Regulation S-X describes the circumstances under which separate financial statements of an unconsolidated majority-owned subsidiary (for example, unconsolidated non-registered investment company) must be filed with the SEC and the circumstances under which those separate financial statements must be audited. It also explains that, insofar as practicable, the subsidiary's separate financial statements must be as of the same dates and for the same periods as the audited financial statements of the registrant. In accordance with Rule 4-01(a)(1) of Regulation S-X, the subsidiary's financial statements that are filed with the SEC must be prepared in accordance with U.S. generally accepted accounting principles and must comply with Regulation S-X.
Rule 4-08(g) of Regulation S-X states that summarized financial information must be presented, in the notes to the financial statements, for unconsolidated subsidiaries. It explains that, insofar as practicable, the summarized financial information must be as of the same dates and for the same periods as the audited financial statements of the registrant. Rule 4-08(g) also explains that the summarized financial information must include the disclosures prescribed by Rule 1-02(bb) of Regulation S-X. Rule 1-02(bb) of Regulation S-X permits registrants in specialized industries to provide summarized balance sheet information as to the nature and amount of the majority components of assets and liabilities. Rule 1-02(bb) of Regulation S-X permits registrants in specialized industries to provide in their summarized income statement other information necessary for a more meaningful presentation in lieu of providing the required disclosures specified by the rule.

to make the presentation of financial statements in a manner similar to a master-feeder fund (exhibits 5-4–5-5) more appropriate.

5.55 For registered investment companies, investments in affiliated funds are considered investments in affiliates subject to Rule 12-14 of Regulation S-X. Such investments may not be reported using the summary portfolio schedules permitted under Rule 12-12C of Regulation S-X. (Refer to chapter 7, "Financial Statements of Investment Companies," of this guide for further discussion of U.S. generally accepted accounting principles applicable for the preparation of financial statements of investment companies.)

5.56 *Statement of operations.* Paragraphs 13–14 of FASB ASC 946-225-45 describe how income reflected on the statement of operations should represent the net earnings received from investee funds. For example, if the investee funds are all registered investment companies (as in the example in the exhibit), then the income would represent the dividends received from such investee funds. The investor fund should not reflect any operating expenses if the investee funds have agreed to assume certain of the investor fund expenses. To the extent that the investor fund has such agreements, they should be disclosed in the notes.

5.57 FASB ASC 946-225-45-15 notes that when investing in registered investment companies, distributions received from long term capital gains should be reported as realized gains together with gains realized on the disposition of shares of investee entities.

5.58 As a result of the enactment of the RIC Modernization Act of 2010, a registered investment company will be considered a qualified fund of funds if, at the end of its taxable year, at least 50 percent of the value of its total assets is represented by interests in other RICs. A qualified fund of funds will be entitled to pass through to its shareholders the tax-exempt interest character of dividends received from municipal bond funds and foreign tax credits received as a result of its investment in funds investing in non-U.S. securities. This provision is effective for fiscal years beginning after December 22, 2010, which is the date of the enactment of the RIC Modernization Act of 2010.

5.59 FASB ASC 946-225-45-16 notes that expenses are those incurred only at the reporting fund level. Expenses of the investee funds are embedded in the net earnings from such funds.

5.60 *Notes to financial statements.* Paragraphs 4–5 of FASB ASC 946-235-50 illustrate that fund management should consider whether, and to what extent, disclosure of the investee funds' investment policies is appropriate. Notes to the financial statements of the reporting fund should include the following:

- A general description of the fund-of-funds structure
- Disclosure of the valuation policy; values are generally based on information reported by investee funds.[3]

5.61 *Financial highlights.* FASB ASC 946-205-50-30 explains that the financial highlights for the reporting fund in a fund-of-funds structure are usually similar to a standalone feeder fund in a master-feeder structure. Net

---

[3] For those investee funds that do not have readily determinable fair values, refer to paragraphs 2.75–.89 of this guide for further guidance on the use of net asset value per share (or its equivalent) as a practical expedient to value an investment in an investee fund that does not have a readily determinable fair value.

Complex Capital Structures

investment income and expense ratios should be computed based upon the amounts reported in the statement of operations, and portfolio turnover should be measured based on the turnover of investments made by the reporting fund in the investee funds, not looking through the investee funds to their portfolio activity.

Audit Considerations[4]

5.62 In some cases, master-feeder structures are capitalized by transferring the investments and related assets and liabilities of an existing fund to a newly organized master fund. In exchange for the assets transferred, the original fund becomes a feeder fund and receives a proportional ownership interest in the master fund. The auditor should be aware that management may obtain a private letter ruling from the IRS or tax opinions from counsel, in certain instances, to ensure treatment as a tax-free contribution. The auditor should also be familiar with the tax rules that may require subsequent tracking and special allocation of the contributed unrealized gain or loss on the investments transferred to the master fund.

5.63 *Multiple-class funds.* In connection with the audit of multiple-class funds, the auditor should consider whether

- class-level and fund-level expenses have been determined, as required by Rule 18f-3.
- income, expenses, and realized and unrealized gains or losses have been allocated among the classes of shares, in accordance with the allocation methods in Rule 18f-3.
- IRS regulations have been considered regarding the maintenance of class-level expense differentials necessary to avoid preferential dividends for income tax purposes.
- differences between expense and net investment income ratios of various share classes appear reasonable when compared with the amount or percentage differences in class-level expenses.

5.64 *Master-feeder funds.* In connection with the audit of master-feeder funds, the auditor should consider whether

- fees and expenses incurred by the master fund or feeder funds are in accordance with contractual agreements, as disclosed in the registration statement. Advisory and custodian fees are normally incurred only at the master fund; fees and expenses relating to distribution and shareholder servicing are normally incurred at the feeder level.
- controls and procedures are adequate to ensure that investment valuation and related income components are allocated properly to feeder funds.
- systems and controls are adequate to record accurately and timely the daily contributions and withdrawals between the feeder funds

---

[4] This guide primarily discusses auditing guidance issued by the Auditing Standards Board (ASB) that applies to nonissuers. Issuers are defined by Section 3 of the Securities Exchange Act of 1934 and include registered investment companies. Audits of issuers are required to be performed under Public Company Accounting Oversight Board standards. Users should evaluate their audit engagements to determine which auditing standards are applicable.

AAG-INV 5.64

and master fund. This is important to determine properly each feeder fund's proportionate ownership interest for purposes of computing daily allocations. All shareholder purchases and redemptions are recorded at the feeder level. Assuming that cash is transferred on the same day, after the total daily net sales or redemptions are known for each feeder, contributions and withdrawals in the master fund are recorded to reflect changes in the feeders' ownership interests (that is, a net redemption at the feeder level will result in a withdrawal from the master fund). All such transactions at the feeder level generally will affect the investment in the master fund. At the master-fund level, the cash movements flow through the partnership equity or net assets account.

- satisfaction has been obtained concerning the accuracy of master fund tax adjustments allocated to the feeder funds.

5.65 A master-feeder structure could consist of a master fund and feeder funds that are not related to each other, except that they are each feeders of the same master fund. Each feeder could have a different auditor who may also differ from the auditor of the master fund. Considering that the portfolio of investments is held by the master fund and the feeder fund audit would typically consist of auditing the internal profit and loss and owner allocations, it is ordinarily more efficient and preferable to have a single audit firm represent the entire master-feeder group. It is also possible that the master and feeder funds could have different year-ends (see paragraph 5.40). In connection with the audit of feeder funds having different auditors or year-ends from those of the master fund, the following audit considerations should be taken into account.

Planning

5.66 The feeder fund auditor should discuss with the master fund's independent auditor the results of the most recent audit of the master fund.

5.67 The feeder fund auditor should inquire of feeder fund and master fund management about any changes in fee structures, affiliated transactions, significant contingencies, results of regulatory reviews, or proposed transactions since the previous feeder fund and master fund audits. Consideration should be given to the implications of such changes on the nature, scope, and timing of audit testing and feeder fund financial statement presentation and disclosure.

5.68 Timing and logistics considerations will make planning and coordination among management and the auditors of the master and feeder funds necessary.

Control Environment

5.69 Feeder fund auditors should obtain sufficient knowledge of the control environment to understand the attitudes, awareness, and actions of those charged with governance concerning the entity's internal control and its importance in achieving reliable financial reporting. The feeder fund auditor may also consider the control and monitoring procedures performed by the feeder fund's management over its investment in the master fund. AU section 316,

Consideration of Fraud in a Financial Statement Audit (AICPA, *Professional Standards*), must also be considered.

5.70 Paragraph .08 of AU section 314, *Understanding the Entity and Its Environment and Assessing the Risks of Material Misstatement* (AICPA, *Professional Standards*), states that although much of the information that the auditor obtains by inquiries can be obtained from management and those responsible for financial reporting, inquiries of others within the entity, such as production and internal audit personnel and other employees with different levels of authority, may be useful in providing the auditor with a different perspective in identifying risks of material misstatement. The feeder fund auditor also may review the master fund auditor's audit documentation related to the evaluation and testing of the master fund's control environment.

5.71 Inquiries should be made of the master fund's management and auditors with respect to changes or issues in the control environment since the last fiscal year-end of the master fund or since the performance of the most recent tests of controls.

5.72 Based upon the results of the feeder fund auditor's evaluation of the control environment at the master fund, the feeder fund auditor should directly perform or consider requesting the master fund auditor to perform additional tests of controls.

Investment in Master Fund and Income-Gain Allocations

5.73 The auditor should obtain, as of the date of the feeder fund's financial statements, an understanding of the nature of the securities held by the master fund and the procedures used to value these securities. Consideration should be given to directly performing or requesting the master fund auditor to perform additional procedures, particularly related to fair valued,[5] illiquid, or difficult-to-price securities. This may be particularly relevant if the feeder fund has a different year-end from the master fund.

5.74 The feeder fund auditor should consider requesting the master fund auditor to review the master fund's reconciliation of portfolio securities with the custodian bank and brokers as of the date of the feeder fund's financial statements. Based upon the results of these procedures, the feeder fund auditor might request the master fund auditor to test the existence of the master fund's investments in securities with the custodian and brokers as of the date of the feeder fund's financial statements.[6]

5.75 The feeder fund auditor might review the master fund auditor's audit documentation related to valuation testing, existence testing, or both types of testing as of the most recent master fund audit.

---

[5] AU section 328, *Auditing Fair Value Measurements and Disclosures* (AICPA, *Professional Standards*), contains expanded guidance on the audit procedures for fair value measurements and disclosures. Under AU section 328, the auditor's substantive tests of fair value measurements involve (*a*) testing management's significant assumptions, the valuation model, and the underlying data; (*b*) developing independent fair value estimates for corroborative purposes; or (*c*) examining subsequent events and transactions that confirm or disconfirm the estimate. Please refer to the preface at the beginning of this guide for a discussion of the ASB's Clarity Project, which will affect all AU sections.

[6] When the feeder fund has a different year-end from the master fund, another consideration is for the master fund auditor to perform an agreed-upon-procedures engagement for the period between the master fund year-end and the feeder fund year-end.

5.76 The auditor may obtain confirmation from master fund management, as of the date of the feeder fund financial statements, of the value of the feeder fund's investment in the master fund, the feeder fund's percentage ownership in the master fund, allocations of income or gain from the master fund to the feeder fund during the period under audit, and capital contributions and withdrawals during the period under audit.

Other Transactions

5.77 Through discussions with feeder fund and master fund management and review of accounting records, the auditor should consider whether significant transactions of the master fund have been accounted for and disclosed properly in the feeder fund's financial statements.

Prospectus Restrictions and Compliance

5.78 The auditor should consider making inquiries of master fund management with respect to the results of investment restrictions compliance monitoring, including any detected compliance violations and related resolutions during the period of the feeder fund financial statements.

5.79 The auditor should consider directly reviewing or requesting the master fund auditor to review the analyses and documentation with respect to the master fund's investment restrictions compliance.

5.80 The feeder fund auditor may review the master fund auditor's related audit documentation. The feeder fund auditor might directly perform or request the master fund auditor to perform additional tests based upon the results and timing of such inquiries.

5.81 Paragraph .01 of AU section 333, *Management Representations* (AICPA, *Professional Standards*), establishes a requirement that the independent auditor obtain written representations from management as a part of an audit of financial statements performed in accordance with generally accepted auditing standards and provides guidance concerning the representations to be obtained. Consideration should be given to obtaining analyses and schedules related to investment compliance from master fund management or obtaining direct representation of investment compliance from master fund management.

Tax Qualifications and Compliance

5.82 The auditor may review analyses and documentation with respect to the master fund's tax compliance. Any tests of compliance with diversification requirements need to be met for both the master's and feeder's fiscal periods.

© **Update 5-1 *Audit*: Clarified Auditing Standards**

All auditing interpretations corresponding to an AU section have been considered in the development of the clarified auditing standard and have either been incorporated accordingly and withdrawn by the Auditing Standards Board (ASB), or retained and revised to reflect the issuance of the AU-C section. When effective (audits of financial statements for periods ending on or after December 15, 2012), Interpretation No. 1, "The Effect of an Inability to Obtain Audit Evidence Relating to Income Tax Accruals," of AU-C section 500, *Audit Evidence* (AICPA, *Professional Standards*, AU-C sec. 9500 par. .01–.22), will supersede Interpretation No. 2, "The Effect of an Inability to

> Obtain Audit Evidence Relating to Income Tax Accruals," of AU section 326, *Audit Evidence* (AICPA, *Professional Standards*, AU sec. 9326 par. .06–.23). Please refer to the preface of this guide for a discussion of the ASB's clarity project.

5.83 The auditor should obtain sufficient appropriate audit evidence of feeder fund tax compliance (for example, sufficiency of distributions) for the period of the financial statements, consistent with the requirements of Interpretation No. 2 of AU section 326.

5.84 The auditor might review the related master fund auditor's audit documentation.

5.85 The auditor should consider obtaining direct representations of tax compliance from master fund management.

Financial Statements

5.86 As noted in paragraph 5.81, the auditor should obtain a management representation letter. According to paragraph .48 of AU section 328, *Auditing Fair Value Measurements and Disclosures* (AICPA, *Professional Standards*), depending on the nature, materiality, and complexity of fair values, representations may be included in regard to the appropriateness of the measurement methods and consistency in the application of these methods, the completeness and adequacy of disclosures related to fair values, and whether subsequent events require adjustment to the fair value measurements and disclosures included in the financial statements.

5.87 The feeder fund auditor should read the most recent financial statements of the master fund.

5.88 Generally, when master and feeder funds share common reporting periods, the feeder fund's auditor's report should not be dated prior to the master fund's auditor's report.

Funds of Funds

5.89 Significant audit risks[7] may exist if management does not use strong procedural controls in selecting and monitoring a fund's investments in investee companies and determining the investments' fair value. The audit approach to an investor fund's investments in investee funds might focus on the following three areas:

    a. Evaluating the investor and investee funds' control environments

    b. Substantiating the existence of and fair value attributed to investments in investee funds[8]

    c. Review of periodic performance reported by each investee that is recorded by the investor fund

---

[7] Refer to paragraphs .110–.116 of AU section 314, *Understanding the Entity and Its Environment and Assessing the Risks of Material Misstatement* (AICPA, *Professional Standards*), for additional guidance pertaining to significant risks.

[8] See the guidance for nonissuers in Interpretation No. 1, "Auditing Investments in Securities Where a Readily Determinable Fair Value Does Not Exist," of AU section 332, *Auditing Derivative Instruments, Hedging Activities, and Investments in Securities* (AICPA, *Professional Standards*, AU sec. 9332 par. .01–.04), discussed in paragraph 2.203 of this guide.

5.90 An investor fund's auditors may receive audited financial statements of an investee and corroborate that the investor's carrying value matches its proportionate ownership based on the year-end audited financial statements of the investee. It is possible, however, that all or most of the adjustment to the investor's accounting records occurred during the last interim period of the reporting period, which could mask misstatements in the earlier periods. Although the year-end net asset value of the investee would be correct, the interim period misstatements could cause an error in periodic allocations of performance among investors. The auditor may consider reviewing the periodic performance reported by each investee that is recorded by the investor fund.

Control Environment

5.91 The primary concern in the control environment relates to the procedures that management of the investor fund uses to monitor its investments in investee funds. Investments in public investee funds may be valued based on reported daily net asset values, and the auditor may rely upon the structure established by the 1940 Act and the 1933 Act to gain comfort that such reported fair values are accurate.

5.92 For investments in nonpublic investee companies for which the practical expedient discussed in paragraph 2.75 of this guide has been adopted, the auditor might consider the process and controls adopted by the investor fund to evaluate whether net asset value has been calculated consistent with FASB ASC 946 (including the controls discussed in paragraphs 2.80–.81 of this guide). Audit tests may include observation of management site visits or telephone calls to investee funds, or inspection of documentation of such visits or calls. Prior experience with the investee funds' management, results of prior-year audits, or the history of adjustments to unaudited results reported by the investee funds, if any, should be considered in determining the extent to which such participation is necessary. For example, observation of management site visits would be more appropriate if the investee funds represented a significant investment by the investor fund or if serious concerns about the management controls at the investee fund existed. The auditor should also review the investor fund's reconciliation of the unaudited financial results received from the investee funds to their audited financial statements for the prior year if the current year's audited financial statements are not available. Any significant variations, their causes, and their effect on the investor fund's financial statements should be identified.[9]

5.93 If significant variations are discovered in the comparison of prior-year audited financial statements with financial information obtained from the investee funds, the auditor should perform additional procedures, such as observing the management site visit; reviewing the investee fund's audited

---

[9] The Alternative Investments Task Force of the ASB has developed and issued a practice aid for auditors, *Alternative Investments—Audit Considerations*, which includes guidance on the following:
    a. General considerations pertaining to auditing alternative investments
    b. Addressing management's financial statement existence assertion
    c. Addressing management's financial statement valuation assertion
    d. Management representations
    e. Disclosure of certain significant risks and uncertainties
    f. Reporting
The practice aid also includes an example confirmation for alternative investments and illustrative examples of due diligence, ongoing monitoring, and financial reporting controls.

financial statements; or vouching withdrawals, if any, made from the investee fund after year-end, as part of the annual audit tests.

5.94 If the investor fund elects not to or is not permitted to utilize the practical expedient, the auditor might consider evaluating the determination of fair value in a manner similar to its evaluation of the fair value of other investments determined by management, including the inputs discussed in paragraph 2.86 of this guide.

Exhibit 5-1

Methods of Allocating Income, Fund-Level Expenses, and Realized and Unrealized Gains (Losses)

	Total	Class A	Class B
Assumptions:			
Total shares outstanding		2,000,000	3,000,000
Settled shares outstanding		1,990,000	2,900,000
Net asset value per share		$10.52	$10.49
Fair Value of Shares Outstanding—Relative Net Assets:			
Total shares outstanding	5,000,000	2,000,000	3,000,000
Net asset value per share		$10.52	$10.49
Net asset value	$52,510,000	$21,040,000	$31,470,000
Allocation percentage		40.0686%	59.9314%
Fair Value of Settled Shares Outstanding:			
Settled shares outstanding	4,890,000	1,990,000	2,900,000
Net asset value per share		$10.52	$10.49
	$51,355,800	$20,934,800	$30,421,000
Allocation percentage		40.7642%	59.2358%
Shares Outstanding:			
Total shares outstanding	5,000,000	2,000,000	3,000,000
Allocation percentage		40.0%	60.0%

Exhibit 5-2

Methods of Computing Income Distributions Per Share

	Total	Class A	Class B
Assumptions:			
Net investment income before class-specific expenses	$1,000,000		
Class-specific expenses:			
Class A		$13,000	
Class B			$59,000
Record date shares outstanding	5,000,000	2,000,000	3,000,000
Record-Share Method			
Net investment income before class-specific expenses	$1,000,000		
Total record date shares outstanding	5,000,000		
Gross dividend rate for all shares	$.2000	$.2000	$.2000
Per share class-specific expenses:			
Class A ($13,000/2,000,000)		(.0065)	
Class B ($59,000/3,000,000)			(.0197)
Per share dividend for each class		$.1935	$.1803
Actual-Income-Available Method			
Actual net investment income recorded on books of each class	$928,000	$417,600	$510,400
Record date shares outstanding for each class		2,000,000	3,000,000
Per share dividend for each class		$.2088	$.1701

AAG-INV 5.94

Exhibit 5-2—continued
Methods of Computing Income Distributions Per Share

Simultaneous-Equations Method

EQUATION #1: A + B = $928,000

When—A and B represent the total dividend amounts to be paid to each class.

EQUATION #2: A/2,000,000 − B/3,000,000 = (0.5% × $10.50)/4

When

    2,000,000 and 3,000,000 represent the record date shares of each class
    0.5% represents the expense differential between class A and class B
    $10.50 represents the average daily net asset value of the fund
    4 refers to the fact that the dividend period is a quarter

Solving the previous simultaneous equations produces the following results:

Total dividends to be paid	$928,000	$386,961	$541,039
Record date shares outstanding for each class		2,000,000	3,000,000
Per share dividend for each class		$.1935	$.1803
Annualized distribution rates to average daily net asset value		7.37%	6.87%
Difference in distribution rates		0.50%	

Note: The illustrative financial statements and note disclosures included in this guide have been updated to reflect FASB ASC. However, FASB's notice to constituents suggests the use of plain English in financial statement note disclosures to describe broad FASB ASC topic references. FASB suggests a reference similar to "as required by the Derivatives and Hedging Topic of the FASB *Accounting Standards Codification*." Entities might consider revising their financial statement references to reflect this plain English referencing, rather than the use of specific FASB ASC references. The AICPA has provided these detailed references as a resource for its users.

Exhibit 5-3

XYZ Multiple-Class Fund
Statement of Assets and Liabilities
December 31, 20X8

Assets

Investments in securities at fair value (cost $18,674,000)	$ 21,101,000
Cash	199,000
Deposits with brokers for securities sold short	1,555,000
Collateral for securities loaned at fair value	620,000
Receivables:	
Dividends and interest	46,000
Investment securities sold	24,000
Capital shares sold	54,000
Other assets	26,000
Total assets	23,625,000

Liabilities

Options written at fair value (premiums received $110,000)	230,000
Securities sold short at fair value (proceeds $1,555,000)	1,673,000
Demand loan payable to bank	2,000,000
Payable upon return of securities loaned	620,000
Due to broker—variation margin	10,000
Payables:	
Investment securities purchased	52,000
Capital shares reacquired	8,000
Other	4,000
Accrued expenses	8,000
Distribution payable	158,000
Total liabilities	4,763,000
Net assets	$18,862,000
Net assets consist of:[10]	
Paid-in capital	$ 15,184,000
Distributable earnings	3,678,000
Total net assets	$18,862,000

Net asset value per share:

Class A—based on net assets of $15,089,600 and 3,375,750 shares outstanding	$4.47
Class A public offering price ($4.47 net asset value divided by 0.95)	$4.71
Class B—based on net assets of $3,772,400 and 845,830 shares outstanding	$4.46

Redemption price per class B share is equal to net asset value less any applicable contingent deferred sales charge

The accompanying notes are an integral part of these financial statements.

---

[10] This breakout of paid-in-capital and distributable earnings is typically not relevant for non-registered investment companies.

Exhibit 5-3—continued

XYZ Multiple-Class Fund
Statement of Operations
Year Ended December 31, 20X8

Investment income:	
Dividends (net of foreign withholding taxes of $20,000)	$ 742,000
Interest	209,000
Income from loaned securities—net	50,000
Total income	1,001,000
Expenses:	
Investment advisory fee	137,400
Service fees—class A	36,600
Distribution and service fees—class B	37,000
Interest	10,000
Professional fees	18,000
Custodian	5,000
Transfer agent fees—class A	10,000
Transfer agent fees—class B	12,000
Directors' fees	10,000
Dividends on securities sold short	3,000
Total gross expenses	279,000
Less waivers:	
Distribution and service fees—class B	(18,500)
Investment advisory fee	(34,500)
Total net expenses	226,000
Investment income—net	775,000
Realized and unrealized gain (loss) on investments:	
Net realized gain (loss) on investments	1,089,000
Net change in unrealized appreciation (depreciation) on investments	(1,649,000)
Net loss on investments	(560,000)
Net increase in net assets resulting from operations	$215,000

The accompanying notes are an integral part of these financial statements.

Exhibit 5-3—continued

XYZ Multiple-Class Fund
Statements of Changes in Net Assets
Years Ended December 31, 20X8 and 20X7

	20X8	20X7
Increase (decrease) in net assets from operations:		
Investment income—net	$ 775,000	$ 724,000
Net realized gain on investments	1,089,000	1,000,000
Net change in unrealized appreciation or depreciation on investments	(1,649,000)	1,319,000
Net increase in net assets resulting from operations	215,000	3,043,000
Distributions to shareholders:		
Class A	(1,505,250)	(1,104,500)
Class B	(360,750)	(239,500)
Tax return of capital:		
Class A	—	(52,800)
Class B	—	(13,200)
Total distributions	(1,866,000)	(1,410,000)
Net increase from capital share transactions	2,721,000	4,700,000
Total increase in net assets	1,070,000	6,333,000
Net assets:		
Beginning of year	17,792,000	11,459,000
End of year	$18,862,000	$17,792,000

The accompanying notes are an integral part of these financial statements.

AAG-INV 5.94

Exhibit 5-3—continued

XYZ Multiple-Class Fund
Notes to Financial Statements

[The following notes are limited to illustrations of disclosures unique to a multiple-class fund structure. In addition to the disclosures provided, notes for a multiple-class fund would include all standard disclosures presented as part of the illustrative financial statements in chapter 7.]

1. Significant Accounting Policies

XYZ Multiple-Class Fund (the fund) is registered under the Investment Company Act of 1940 as a diversified, open-end management investment company. The fund offers 2 classes of shares (class A and class B). Each class of shares has equal rights concerning earnings and assets, except that each class bears different distribution, shareholder service, and transfer agent expenses. Each class of shares has exclusive voting rights with respect to matters that affect just that class. Income, expenses (other than expenses attributable to a specific class), and realized and unrealized gains or losses on investments are allocated to each class of shares based on its relative net assets. Class B shares are subject to a maximum contingent deferred sales charge of 5 percent upon redemption, decreasing to zero over a period of 6 years. Class B shares automatically convert to class A shares at the end of the month following the second anniversary of issuance.

2. Capital Share Transactions

The fund is authorized to issue an unlimited number of shares in an unlimited number of classes.

Transactions in the capital shares of the fund were as follows:

	20X8 Shares	20X8 Amount	20X7 Shares	20X7 Amount
Class A:				
Shares sold	309,000	$1,444,500	690,500	$3,176,000
Shares issued from reinvestments	195,000	1,040,000	171,000	770,000
Shares redeemed	(57,000)	(253,500)	(40,000)	(186,000)
Shares converted from class B to class A	4,790	22,800		
Net increase from capital share transactions	451,790	$2,253,800	821,500	$3,760,000
Class B:				
Shares sold	61,925	$290,100	185,000	$848,000
Shares issued from reinvestments	57,875	270,000	35,000	160,000
Shares redeemed	(15,000)	(70,100)	(15,000)	(68,000)
Shares converted from class B to class A	4,800	22,800		
Net increase from capital share transactions	100,000	$467,200	205,000	$940,000

AAG-INV 5.94

3. Investment Advisory Fees and Other Transactions With Affiliates

The fund has entered into a distribution plan, pursuant to Rule 12b-1 under the Investment Company Act of 1940, with XYZ Distributors (distributors). Under the plan, class A shares pay a monthly shareholder servicing fee at an annual rate of 0.25 percent of class A average daily net assets. Class B shares pay monthly shareholder servicing and distribution fees at the annual rate of 0.25 percent and 0.75 percent, respectively, of class B average daily net assets. These fees compensate distributors for the services they provide and expenses borne by distributors under the agreement. During the year ended December 31, 20X8, distributors waived $18,500 of their distribution fees related to class B shares.

For the year ended December 31, 20X8, distributors received $70,000 in sales commissions from the sale of class A shares. Distributors also received $6,500 of contingent deferred sales charges relating to redemptions of class B shares.

XYZ Service Company provides transfer agent services to the fund. Under the transfer agent agreement with XYZ Service Company, the fund pays a monthly fee equal, on an annual basis, to $15 and $18 per shareholder account for class A and class B shares, respectively.

AAG-INV 5.94

Exhibit 5-3—continued

XYZ Multiple-Class Fund
Financial Highlights

	Class A 20X8	Class A 20X7	Class A 20X6[11]	Class B 20X8	Class B 20X7	Class B 20X6[12]
Per share operating performance:[13]						
Net asset value, beginning of year	$4.88	$4.46	$4.00	$4.88	$4.45	$4.00
Income from investment operations:						
Net investment income	0.21	0.20	0.12	0.19	0.20	0.11
Net realized and unrealized gain (loss) on investment transactions	(0.12)	0.71	0.50	(0.12)	0.71	0.49
Total from investment operations	0.09	0.91	0.62	0.07	0.91	0.60
Less distributions:						
Dividends and distributions	(0.50)	(0.44)	(0.16)	(0.49)	(0.43)	(0.15)
Tax return of capital distributions	0	(0.05)	0	0	(0.05)	0
Total distributions	(0.50)	(0.49)	(0.16)	(0.49)	(0.48)	(0.15)
Net asset value, end of year	$4.47	$4.88	$4.46	$4.46	$4.88	$4.45
Total return[14]	1.84%	20.40%	15.50%	1.43%	19.90%	15.00%
Percentages and supplemental data:						
Net assets, end of year (000s)	$15,090	$14,167	$9,167	$3,772	$3,625	$2,292
Ratios to average net assets:						
Expenses[15]	1.23%	1.30%	1.35%[16]	1.48%	2.05%	2.10%[17]
Net investment income[18]	4.15%	2.82%	4.00%[19]	3.90%	2.07%	3.25%[20]
Portfolio turnover rate	92%	80%	75%	92%	80%	75%

The accompanying notes are an integral part of these financial statements.

---

[11] For the period from June 1, 20X6 (commencement of operations), to December 31, 20X6.
[12] See footnote 11.
[13] Selected data for a share of capital stock outstanding throughout the year.
[14] Total return excludes the effect of sales charges.
[15] During 20X8, 20X7, and 20X6, the adviser and distributor voluntarily waived a portion of their advisory fees and a portion of the class B distribution and service fee (0.50 percent). Absent these waivers, the expense percentages would have been approximately 1.48 percent, 1.55 percent, 1.60 percent, 2.23 percent, 2.80 percent, and 2.85 percent, respectively.
[16] Annualized.
[17] See footnote 16.
[18] See footnote 15.
[19] See footnote 16.
[20] See footnote 16.

Exhibit 5-4

ABC Feeder Fund, Inc.
Statement of Assets and Liabilities
December 31, 20X8

Assets	
Investment in ABC Master Portfolio	$ 15,089,600
Receivable for capital shares sold	110,000
Prepaid expenses and other assets	35,000
Total assets	15,234,600
Liabilities	
Administrative fee payable	20,000
Payable for capital shares redeemed	30,000
Dividends payable	40,000
Other accrued liabilities	25,000
Total liabilities	115,000
Net assets	$15,119,600
Net assets consist of:[21]	
Paid-in capital, 1,250,000 shares outstanding	$12,258,600
Distributable earnings	2,861,000
Total net assets	$15,119,600
Net asset value per share	$12.10
Public offering price ($12.10 net asset value divided by 0.95)	$12.74

The accompanying notes are an integral part of these financial statements.

---

[21] See footnote 10.

Exhibit 5-4—continued

ABC Feeder Fund, Inc.
Statement of Operations[22,23]
Year Ended December 31, 20X8

Net investment income allocated from ABC Master Portfolio:	
Dividends	$ 579,000
Interest	168,200
Income from loaned securities—net	40,000
Expenses[24]	(179,000)
Net investment income from ABC Master Portfolio	608,200
Fund expenses:	
Administrative fees	15,000
Distribution and servicing fees	37,500
Professional fees	12,000
Transfer agent fees	35,000
Directors' fees	10,000
Registration fees	26,000
Other expenses	12,000
Total expenses	147,500
Investment income—net	460,700
Realized and unrealized gain (loss) on investments allocated from ABC Master Portfolio:	
Net realized gain on investments	865,000
Net change in unrealized appreciation (depreciation) on investments	(1,320,000)
Net loss on investments	(455,000)
Net increase in net assets resulting from operations	$5,700

The accompanying notes are an integral part of these financial statements.

---

[22] In the initial year of adopting a master-feeder structure, the feeder's statement of operations may be a combination of (a) direct income, expenses, and realized gains and losses for the period prior to adoption of the master-feeder structure and (b) the allocated amounts from the master portfolio for the period from adoption to fiscal year-end.

[23] In this example, ABC Master Portfolio is a pass-through entity for tax purposes. If the master portfolio was not a pass-through entity, allocations would not be presented but, rather, distributions would be presented, similar to the fund-of-funds example included within exhibit 5-5.

[24] Any expense waivers should be reported in a note to the statement of operations.

AAG-INV 5.94

Exhibit 5-4—continued

ABC Feeder Fund, Inc.
Statements of Changes in Net Assets
Years Ended December 31, 20X8 and 20X7

	20X8	20X7
Increase (decrease) in net assets from operations:		
Investment income—net	$ 460,700	$ 369,000
Net realized gain on investments	865,000	750,000
Net change in unrealized appreciation or depreciation	(1,320,000)	1,178,000
Net increase in net assets resulting from operations	5,700	2,297,000
Distributions to shareholders	(1,178,700)	(1,071,000)
Net increase from capital share transactions:		
Sold 147,000 and 207,000 shares	1,782,600	2,359,000
Distributions reinvested of 72,000 and 73,000 shares	880,000	820,000
Redeemed 20,700 and 13,000 shares	(250,000)	(150,000)
Net increase from capital share transactions	2,412,600	3,029,000
Total increase in net assets	1,239,600	4,255,000
Net assets: Beginning of year	13,880,000	9,625,000
End of year	$15,119,600	$13,880,000

The accompanying notes are an integral part of these financial statements.

Exhibit 5-4—continued

ABC Feeder Fund, Inc.
Notes to Financial Statements

[*The following notes are limited to illustrations of disclosures unique to feeder fund financial statements. Besides the following disclosures, notes for a feeder fund would include all standard disclosures presented as part of the illustrative financial statements in chapter 7. Exceptions to the standard chapter 7 disclosures would be the omission of notes relating to the master fund portfolio activity and expenses, such as the advisory fee incurred, that are disclosed in the master fund financial statements.*]

1. Significant Accounting Policies

ABC Feeder Fund, Inc. (the fund) is registered under the Investment Company Act of 1940 as a diversified, open-end management investment company. The fund invests substantially all of its assets in the ABC Master Portfolio, an open-end investment company that has the same investment objectives as the fund. The financial statements of the ABC Master Portfolio, including the schedule of investments, are included elsewhere in this report and should be read with the fund's financial statements. The percentage of ABC Master Portfolio owned by the fund at December 31, 20X8, was 80 percent.

Valuation of investments. The fund records its investment in ABC Master Portfolio at fair value. The notes to the ABC Master Portfolio financial statements included elsewhere in this report provide information about ABC Master Portfolio's valuation policy and its period-end security valuations.

Investment income and expenses. The fund records daily its proportionate share of the ABC Master Portfolio's income, expenses, and realized and unrealized gains and losses. In addition, the fund accrues its own expenses.

Exhibit 5-4—continued

ABC Feeder Fund, Inc.
Financial Highlights

	20X8	20X7	20X6[25]
Per share operating performance:[26,27]			
Net asset value, beginning of year	$13.11	$11.75	$10.00
Income from investment operations:			
Net investment income	0.40	0.41	0.38
Net realized and unrealized gain (loss) on investment transactions	(0.39)	2.12	2.47
Total from investment operations	0.01	2.53	2.85
Less distributions	(1.02)	(1.17)	(1.10)
Net asset value, end of year	$12.10	$13.11	$11.75
Total return	0.08%	21.53%	28.50%
Percentages and supplemental data:			
Net assets, end of year (000s)	$15,119	$13,880	$9,625
Ratios to average net assets:[28]			
Expenses	2.25%	2.30%	2.32%[29]
Net investment income	3.21%	2.48%	2.58%[30]

The accompanying notes are an integral part of these financial statements.

---

[25] For the period from March 1, 20X6 (the date of commencement of operations), to December 31, 20X6.

[26] Selected data for a share of capital stock outstanding throughout the year.

[27] The per share amounts and percentages reflect income and expenses assuming inclusion of the fund's proportionate share of the income and expenses of ABC Master Portfolio.

[28] See footnote 27.

[29] See footnote 16.

[30] See footnote 16.

AAG-INV 5.94

Exhibit 5-5

ABC Master Portfolio
Statement of Assets and Liabilities
December 31, 20X8

Assets

Investments in securities at fair value (cost $18,674,000)	$ 21,101,000
Cash	199,000
Deposits with brokers for securities sold short	1,555,000
Collateral for securities loaned at fair value	620,000
Receivables:	
Dividends and interest	100,000
Investment securities sold	24,000
Other assets	26,000
Total assets	23,625,000

Liabilities

Options written at fair value (premiums received $110,000)	230,000
Securities sold short at fair value (proceeds $1,555,000)	1,673,000
Demand loan payable to bank	2,000,000
Payable upon return of securities loaned	620,000
Due to broker—variation margin	10,000
Payables:	
Investment securities purchased	210,000
Other	12,000
Accrued expenses	8,000
Total liabilities	4,763,000
Net assets	$18,862,000

The accompanying notes are an integral part of these financial statements.

Exhibit 5-5—continued

ABC Master Portfolio
Statement of Operations
Year Ended December 31, 20X8

Investment income:	
Dividends (net of foreign withholding taxes of $20,000)	$ 742,000
Interest	209,000
Income from loaned securities—net	50,000
Total income	1,001,000
Expenses:	
Investment advisory fee	171,900
Interest	10,000
Professional fees	18,000
Custodian	13,100
Directors' fees	10,000
Dividends on securities sold short	3,000
Total expenses	226,000
Investment income—net	775,000
Realized and unrealized gain (loss) on investments:	
Net realized gain on investments	1,089,000
Net change in unrealized appreciation on investments	(1,649,000)
Net loss on investments	(560,000)
Net increase in net assets resulting from operations	$215,000

The accompanying notes are an integral part of these financial statements.

Exhibit 5-5—continued

ABC Master Portfolio
Statements of Changes in Net Assets
Year Ended December 31, 20X8 and 20X7

	20X8	20X7
Increase (decrease) in net assets from operations:		
Investment income—net	$ 775,000	$ 492,000
Net realized gain on investments	1,089,000	1,000,000
Net change in unrealized appreciation or (depreciation)	(1,649,000)	1,551,000
Net increase in net assets resulting from operations	215,000	3,043,000
Proceeds from contributions	3,000,000	5,000,000
Fair value of withdrawals	(2,145,000)	(2,751,000)
	855,000	2,249,000
Increase in net assets	1,070,000	5,292,000
Net assets:		
Beginning of year	17,792,000	12,500,000
End of year	$18,862,000	$17,792,000

The accompanying notes are an integral part of these financial statements.

Exhibit 5-5—continued

ABC Master Portfolio
Notes to Financial Statements

[The following notes are limited to illustrations of disclosures unique to master-fund financial statements. Besides the following disclosures, notes for a master fund would include all standard disclosures presented as part of the illustrative financial statements in chapter 7. Exceptions to the standard chapter 7 disclosures would be the omission of notes regarding dividend distributions, capital share transactions, and distribution fees, each of which is disclosed in the financial statements of the feeder fund.]

1. Significant Accounting Policies

ABC Master Portfolio (the portfolio) is organized as a trust and registered under the Investment Company Act of 1940 as a diversified, open-end management investment company. The Declaration of Trust permits the trustees to issue nontransferable interests in the portfolio. For federal income tax purposes, the portfolio qualifies as a partnership, and each investor in the portfolio is treated as the owner of its proportionate share of the net assets, income, expenses, and realized and unrealized gains and losses of the portfolio. Accordingly, as a pass-through entity, the portfolio pays no income dividends or capital gain distributions.

2. Federal Income Taxes

The portfolio will be treated as a partnership for federal income tax purposes. As such, each investor in the portfolio will be subject to taxation on its share of the portfolio's ordinary income and capital gains. It is intended that the portfolio's assets will be managed so an investor in the portfolio can satisfy the requirements of Internal Revenue Code Subchapter M.

3. Financial Highlights

Financial highlights for the portfolio for each period were as follows:

	20X8	20X7	20X6[31]
Total return	1.21%	24.34%	31.20%
Ratios to average net assets:			
Expenses	1.23%	1.25%	1.27%[32]
Net investment income	4.23%	3.25%	3.34%[33]
Portfolio turnover rate	92%	80%	102%

---

[31] See footnote 25.
[32] See footnote 16.
[33] See footnote 16.

Exhibit 5-6

FOF Fund, Inc.
Statement of Net Assets
September 30, 20X8

[*The following sample financial statements are limited to matters directly related to funds of funds. The sample financial statements in this chapter and chapter 7 should be referred to for relevant disclosures.*]

Assets:	
204,100 shares of FOF Growth Fund, Inc.	$2,046,762
182,633 shares of FOF International Fund, Inc.	2,224,470
96,152 shares of FOF Income Fund, Inc.	1,046,134
602,908 shares FOF Money Market Fund, Inc.	602,908
Total investments (cost $5,617,279)[34]	5,920,274
Cash	9,000
Receivable for fund shares sold	23,652
Other assets	2,710
Total assets	5,955,636
Liabilities:	
Payable for fund shares repurchased	37,123
Accrued expenses	8,327
Total liabilities	45,450
Net assets (equivalent to $10.73 per share based on 550,810 shares of capital stock issued and outstanding; unlimited shares authorized)	$5,910,186
Components of net assets:	
Paid-in capital	$5,569,426
Distributable earnings	340,760
	$5,910,186

The accompanying notes are an integral part of these financial statements.

---

[34] Investments in investee funds may be presented in a separate schedule of investments rather than on the statement of net assets.

AAG-INV 5.94

Exhibit 5-6—continued

FOF Fund, Inc.
Statement of Operations
Year Ended September 30, 20X8

Investment income:		
Dividends from investment company shares		$201,942
Expenses:		
Custodian and transfer agent fees	$22,560	
Professional fees	8,318	
Registration fees	1,040	
Directors' fees	1,982	
Total expenses		33,900
Net investment income		168,042
Realized and unrealized gain on investments:		
Realized gain on sales of investment company shares	$12,067	
Realized gain distributions from investment company shares	321,939	
Net realized gain		334,006
Net change in unrealized appreciation (depreciation) on investments during the year		219,837
Net realized and unrealized gain		553,843
Net increase in net assets resulting from operations		$721,885

The accompanying notes are an integral part of these financial statements.

AAG-INV 5.94

Exhibit 5-6—continued

FOF Fund, Inc.
Statements of Changes in Net Assets
Years Ended September 30, 20X8 and 20X7[35]

	20X8	20X7
Increase (decrease) in net assets from:		
Net investment income	$168,042	$32,177
Net realized gain on investments	334,006	16,090
Net change in unrealized appreciation	219,837	83,158
	721,885	131,425
Distributions to shareholders	(484,617)	(27,933)
Capital share transactions—net	2,172,589	3,396,837
Net increase in net assets	2,409,857	3,500,329
Net assets:		
Beginning of year	3,500,329	—
End of year	$5,910,186	$3,500,329

The accompanying notes are an integral part of these financial statements.

---

[35] The fund commenced operations on October 1, 20X6.

Exhibit 5-6–continued

FOF Fund, Inc.
Notes to Financial Statements

1. Significant Accounting Policies

FOF Fund, Inc. (the fund) is registered under the Investment Company Act of 1940, as amended, as a diversified, open-end management investment company. The fund invests solely in shares of other funds within the FOF Group of Mutual Funds with the objective of seeking high total return through investments allocated to diverse equity and fixed-income markets.

Security valuation. Investments in funds within the FOF Group of Mutual Funds are valued at fair value based on the net asset values reported by the underlying funds.

Transaction dates. Share transactions are recorded on the trade date. Dividend income and realized gain distributions from other funds are recognized on the ex-dividend date. Distributions to shareholders, which are determined in accordance with income tax regulations, are similarly recorded on the ex-dividend date. In determining the net gain or loss on securities sold, the cost of securities is determined on the identified cost basis.

Federal income taxes. The fund's policy is to comply with the requirements of the Internal Revenue Code applicable to regulated investment companies and to distribute all of its taxable income to its shareholders. Thus, no federal income tax provision is required.

2. Investment Transactions and Valuation

Cost of purchases and proceeds of sales of shares of funds within the FOF Group of Mutual Funds (excluding FOF Money Market Fund, Inc.) for the year ended September 30, 20X8, were $2,482,315 and $336,232, respectively. At September 30, 20X8, the cost of investments for federal income tax purposes was $5,617,279 and gross unrealized appreciation was $302,995; there was no gross unrealized depreciation.

The fund utilizes various methods to measure the fair value of most of its investments on a recurring basis. U.S. GAAP establishes a hierarchy that prioritizes inputs to valuation methods. The three levels of inputs are as follows:

- *Level 1.* Unadjusted quoted prices in active markets for identical assets or liabilities that the fund has the ability to access.

- *Level 2.* Observable inputs other than quoted prices included in level 1 that are observable for the asset or liability, either directly or indirectly. These inputs may include quoted prices for the identical instrument on an inactive market, prices for similar instruments, interest rates, prepayment speeds, credit risk yield curves, default rates, and similar data. For investments in funds, investments that are redeemable at net asset value per share (or its equivalent) in the near-term are included in level 2.

- *Level 3.* Unobservable inputs for the asset or liability to the extent that observable inputs are not available, representing the fund's own assumptions about the assumptions that a market participant would use in valuing the asset or liability; they would be based on the best information available.

AAG-INV 5.94

The following table summarizes the inputs used to value the fund's assets measured at fair value as of September 30, 20X8.[36]

Valuation Inputs	Investments in Mutual Funds
Level 1	$5,920,274
Level 2	—
Level 3	—
Total	$5,920,274

There were no transfers between level 1 and level 2 during the year.

3. Investment Advisory Services and Other Transactions With Affiliates

The fund receives investment management and advisory services, consisting principally of determining the allocation of the assets of the fund among designated underlying funds, under a management agreement with FOF Investment Management, Inc. (the manager). The manager receives no compensation under this agreement; however, the fund pays management fees and expenses to the manager indirectly as a shareholder in funds of the FOF Group of Mutual Funds. Additionally, each fund in which the fund invests (except FOF Money Market Fund, Inc.) pays a distribution fee to FOF Distributors, Inc., the distributor of the fund, in the amount of 0.25 percent of average annual net assets. The fund pays no sales loads or similar compensation to FOF Distributors, Inc., to acquire shares of each fund in which it invests.

Because the underlying funds have varied expense and fee levels and the fund may own different proportions of underlying funds at different times, the amount of fees and expenses incurred indirectly by the fund will vary.

4. Capital Share Transactions

Transactions in capital shares were as follows:

	Years Ended September 30,			
	20X8		20X7	
	Shares	Amount	Shares	Amount
Shares sold	204,017	$2,077,520	354,695	$3,590,241
Shares issued in reinvestment of dividends	41,817	425,255	2,615	27,013
Shares redeemed	(30,948)	(330,186)	(21,386)	(220,417)
Net increase	214,886	$2,172,589	335,924	$3,396,837

---

[36] The classification of various financial instruments in this table is for illustrative purposes only and should not be construed as recommended practice for any particular financial instrument or class of financial instruments.

5. Components of Capital

Components of capital on a federal income tax basis at September 30, 20X8, were as follows:

Paid-in capital	$ 5,569,426
Undistributed ordinary income	11,460
Undistributed net realized gain	26,305
Unrealized appreciation	302,995
	$ 5,910,186

The tax character of distributions paid during the years ended September 30, 20X8, and 20X7, was as follows:

	20X8	*20X7*
Ordinary income	$160,826	$27,933
Long term capital gain	323,791	—
	$484,617	$27,933

Financial Highlights

	Year Ended September 30,	
	20X8	20X7
Per share data (for a share outstanding throughout the period):		
Net investment income[37]	$ .38	$ .20
Net realized and unrealized (gain) loss on investments	1.04	.38
Total from investment operations	1.42	.58
Less: Distributions to shareholders	(1.11)	(.16)
Net increase (decrease)	.31	.42
Net asset value:		
Beginning of year[38]	10.42	10.00
End of year	$10.73	$10.42
Total return	13.59%	5.86%
Net assets, end of year (000s)	$5,910	$3,500
Ratio of expenses to average net assets[39]	0.72%	0.89%[40]
Net investment income as a percentage of average net assets[41]	3.59%	1.96%[42]
Portfolio turnover rate	21%	5%

---

[37] Recognition of net investment income by the fund is affected by the timing of the declaration of dividends by the underlying investment companies in which the fund invests. The ratio does not include net investment income of the investment companies in which the fund invests.

[38] Investment operations commenced on October 1, 20X6.

[39] Does not include expenses of the investment companies in which the fund invests.

[40] See footnote 16.

[41] See footnote 37.

[42] See footnote 16.

Chapter 6

Taxes

Overview

6.01 This chapter provides information on the Internal Revenue Code of 1986, as amended (IRC). Its intended purpose is to provide auditors with background information, not as a detailed explanation of the IRC. Thus, the auditor should consult a tax adviser with respect to tax issues that arise in the course of an audit. Auditors may not be able to resolve tax issues that arise in the course of an audit based solely on the background information provided in this chapter.

6.02 This chapter has been divided into two sections to focus on distinct aspects of taxes for investment companies: "Financial Statements and Other Matters" and "Taxation of RICs." Due to the extensive interrelationships between taxes and the underlying accounts or products, certain tax matters appear in other chapters, as follows:

Topic	Paragraph Reference
Dividends to shareholders and reinvestments	4.46
Characterization of dividends for financial statement purposes	7.88
Financial statement disclosures:	
• Status under IRC Subchapter M	7.168
• Capital loss carryforwards and post-October capital and currency loss deferrals	7.167
Multiple classes of shares:	
• Preferential dividends	5.08–.09, 5.17, 6.67
• Return of capital	5.16
Master-feeder funds:	
• Master tax qualification	5.20
• Master tax earnings allocation	5.21
• Feeder funds	5.19, 5.21
Tax-free business combinations	8.46, 8.49
Unit investment trusts	9.13–.15
Variable contracts	10.39–.56

AAG-INV 6.02

Financial Statements and Other Matters

Income Tax Expense

6.03 Federal income tax expense normally is not paid by investment companies that qualify under IRC Subchapter M,[1] and distribute all their investment company taxable income and taxable realized gains from securities transactions. For investment companies that qualify as regulated investment companies (RICs) under the IRC, federal income taxes payable on security gains that the investment company elects to retain (see paragraph 6.39) are accrued only on the last day of the tax year.[2] Only shareholders of record on the last day of the fiscal year are entitled to the credit for income taxes paid by the fund. Information regarding retained gains and taxes paid is sent to those shareholders to enable them to report their proportionate share of the gains and taxes paid on their individual returns. Also, no expense for federal excise taxes is required if a fund timely distributes substantially all of its taxable ordinary income, calculated on a calendar-year basis, and substantially all its taxable capital gains, calculated generally on the basis of a 12 month period ending October 31 (see paragraph 6.80). Excise taxes imposed on underdistributed income should be recorded when determinable.

6.04 Income tax expense related to net investment income and net realized gains on investments should be recorded when it is probable that an investment company subject to IRC Subchapter M will not qualify under that subchapter. Management should consider the need for recording a deferred tax expense if management concludes that it is probable that the investment company will not meet its qualification requirements for a period longer than one year.

6.05 Some investment companies may be subject to state, local, or foreign taxes on net investment income and realized gains on a recurring basis. State, local, and foreign taxes, if payable, are reported on the accrual basis, including deferred taxes on the unrealized appreciation or depreciation of investments. A valuation allowance should be established for any deferred tax asset resulting from temporary differences related to unrealized depreciation that could result in deductible amounts in future years when the probability of realization of the tax benefit does not meet the more likely than not criterion of Financial Accounting Standards Board (FASB) *Accounting Standards Codification* (ASC) 740-10-25-6.

6.06 FASB ASC 740, *Income Taxes*, clarifies the accounting for uncertainty in income taxes recognized in an enterprise's financial statements and prescribes a recognition threshold and measurement attribute for the financial statement recognition and measurement of a tax position taken or expected to be taken in a tax return. FASB ASC 740 also provides guidance on derecognition, classification, interest and penalties, accounting for interim periods, disclosure, and implementation. The scope of FASB ASC 740 includes domestic and foreign entities preparing financial statements in accordance with U.S. generally accepted accounting principles. FASB ASC 740 also provides guidance on how an entity should determine whether a tax position is effectively

---

[1] Subchapter M consists of Internal Revenue Code (IRC) Sections 851–860G and provides special tax rules for regulated investment companies (RICs), real estate investment trusts, real estate mortgage investment conduits, and financial asset securitization investment trusts. The rules affecting RICs are found in IRC Sections 851–855 and 860.

[2] Section 404.06b of the Securities and Exchange Commission's *Codification of Financial Reporting Policies*.

settled for the purpose of recognizing previously unrecognized tax benefits. It uses the terms *effectively settled* and *settlement* in the context of income taxes.

6.07 FASB ASC 740-10-15-2AA clarifies that the sections of FASB ASC 740-10 relating to accounting for uncertain tax positions are applicable to all entities, including tax-exempt not-for-profit entities, pass-through entities, and entities that are taxed in a manner similar to pass-through entities such as real estate investment trusts and registered investment companies. *Tax position*, as defined by the FASB ASC glossary, is a position in a previously filed tax return or a position expected to be taken in a future tax return that is reflected in measuring current or deferred income tax assets and liabilities for interim or annual periods. A tax position can result in a permanent reduction of income taxes payable, a deferral of income taxes otherwise currently payable to future years, or a change in the expected realizability of deferred tax assets. The term tax position also encompasses, but is not limited to, the following:

- A decision not to file a tax return
- An allocation or a shift of income between jurisdictions
- The characterization of income or a decision to exclude reporting taxable income in a tax return
- A decision to classify a transaction, an entity, or another position in a tax return as tax exempt
- An entity's status, including its status as a pass-through entity or tax-exempt not-for-profit entity

6.08 FASB ASC 740-10-50-15(c)–(e) discusses required disclosures by all entities related to unrecognized tax benefits. At the end of each annual reporting period, an entity is required to disclose the total amounts of interest and penalties recognized in both the statement of operations and statement of financial position; for positions for which it is reasonably possible that the total amounts of unrecognized tax benefits will significantly increase or decrease within 12 months of the reporting date, the nature of the uncertainty, the nature of the event that could occur in the next 12 months that would cause the change, and an estimate of the range of the reasonably possible change or a statement that an estimate of the range cannot be made; and a description of tax years that remain subject to examination by major tax jurisdictions.

6.09 Technical Questions and Answers section 5250.15, "Application of Certain FASB Interpretation No. 48 (codified in FASB ASC 740-10) Disclosure Requirements to Nonpublic Entities That Do Not Have Uncertain Tax Positions" (AICPA, *Technical Practice Aids*), clarifies that the disclosure requirements in paragraph 15(c)–(e) of FASB ASC 740-10-50 remain in effect (if applicable), regardless of whether an entity has any uncertain tax positions.

6.10 As explained in FASB ASC 740-10-50-15A, in addition to the nonpublic entities' disclosure requirements discussed in FASB ASC 740-10-50, public entities should disclose a tabular reconciliation of the total amounts of unrecognized tax benefits at the beginning and end of each period and the total amount of unrecognized tax benefits that, if recognized, would affect the effective tax rate. Example 30 in FASB ASC 740-10-55-217 gives sample disclosures relating to uncertainty in income taxes. Further, paragraphs 223–229 of FASB ASC 740-10-55 include examples of defining a tax position, attributing income taxes to the entity or its owners, and reporting tax positions for a group of related entities. Per FASB ASC 740-10-50-16, a public entity that is not subject to income taxes because its income is taxed directly to its owners should disclose that fact and the net difference between the tax bases and the reported amounts of the entity's assets and liabilities.

6.11 On December 22, 2006, the staff of the Securities and Exchange Commission's (SEC's) Division of Investment Management issued a letter to the Investment Company Institute on the implementation of accounting for uncertainty in income taxes by registered investment companies. In that letter, the staff

- expressed its belief that the guidance "places [no] limits on the type of evidence that an enterprise can look to in making its determination of the technical merits of a tax position" and that a registered investment company may consider "less formal forms of guidance from [a] taxing authority," weighing "all available forms of evidence based on their persuasiveness."
- observed that "the administrative practices and precedents of [a] taxing authority should be considered in fund's analysis" regarding whether a tax position meets the recognition threshold, including any practice, to the extent that such exists, of addressing industry taxation issues on a prospective basis.

Federal Income Tax Provisions Affecting Investment Accounts

6.12 In establishing investment policies, companies intending to qualify as RICs under IRC Subchapter M must comply with the requirements of Subchapter M relating to diversification of assets, sources of income and realized gains, and similar matters. Those requirements are described later in this chapter.

Foreign Withholding Taxes

6.13 As stated in FASB ASC 946-830-45-34, whenever tax is withheld from investment income at the source, the amounts withheld that are not reclaimable should be accrued, along with the related income on each income recognition date if the tax rate is fixed and known. If the tax withheld is reclaimable from the local tax authorities, it should be recorded as a receivable, not an expense. When the investment income is received net of the tax withheld, a separate realized foreign currency gain or loss should be computed on the gross income receivable and accrued tax expense. If the tax rate is not known or estimable, such expense or receivable should be recorded on the date that the net amount is received; accordingly, there would be no foreign currency gain or loss. However, if a receivable is recorded, there may be a foreign currency gain or loss through the date that such receivable is collected.

Financial Statement Presentation

6.14 FASB ASC 946-225-45-4 explains that income tax expense should be presented by investment companies under the separate income categories (such as investment income or realized and unrealized gains) to which it applies. In addition, taxes in certain foreign jurisdictions may be based on the net investment income and realized gains of the fund within that jurisdiction; the guidance in FASB ASC 740 is applicable to such taxes. According to FASB ASC 946-225-45-3(h), other taxes, such as foreign withholding taxes, should be deducted from the relevant income item and disclosed parenthetically or shown as a separate contraitem in the "Income" section. FASB ASC 946-225-45-6(b)(1) states that any provision for deferred taxes should be presented separately.

Diversification of Assets

6.15 As noted in paragraph 8.54 of this guide, the diversification requirements appearing in an investment company's prospectus and specified in various SEC rules and interpretations may differ from those in IRC Subchapter M, discussed later in this chapter.

Taxation of RICs

General Discussion of the Taxation of RICs

6.16 This chapter discusses, in general terms, the requirements for qualification and taxation as a RIC under IRC Subchapter M, as well as the excise tax on certain undistributed taxable income and certain other federal tax matters affecting investment companies. (Although many states and municipalities have adopted provisions similar to Subchapter M, a discussion of state and local taxes is beyond the scope of this chapter, as is discussion of the tax aspects of investment companies formed as partnerships.) In designing the detailed audit plan, the auditor should refer to the latest IRC, Treasury regulations, and IRS rulings and applicable state laws to be certain that all requirements for qualification have been covered and to determine the need for accruing income, excise, or other taxes.

Taxation of a RIC's Taxable Income and Net Capital Gains

6.17 An investment company organized as a corporation or as a business trust is taxable as a corporation and, as such, subject to federal income taxes and certain state and local taxes the same as any other domestic corporation. However, if the investment company is registered under the Investment Company Act of 1940 (the 1940 Act), it may elect to qualify under the IRC for special federal income tax treatment as a RIC, which allows it to deduct dividends paid to shareholders and pass through tax-favored income, such as capital gains and tax-exempt income (see paragraphs 6.24–.42). A *dividend*, for this purpose, is defined as a distribution of current or accumulated earnings and profits (E&P). Thus, an investment company distributing all its taxable income to its shareholders would have no taxable income and, therefore, no tax liability. If an investment company fails to qualify as a RIC, it will be taxed as a regular corporation. The deduction for dividends paid by the investment company will not be available, and all distributions out of E&P will be taxed as ordinary income to shareholders. The effects of the failure to qualify may extend beyond the income tax consequences because net asset values may be improperly stated in such situations.

6.18 Certain investment companies are organized as series funds. Additionally, shareholders of each respective portfolio may have separate rights with respect to each portfolio's net assets. A series fund includes several portfolios, each of which may have a different investment objective. Series funds are required to treat each portfolio as a separate corporation for tax purposes.[3]

---

[3] IRC Section 851(g).

Investment Companies

6.19 To determine if a RIC has a federal income tax liability, the RIC's investment company taxable income and net capital gain must be computed separately. Investment company taxable income is regular taxable income modified by certain adjustments. The following are among those adjustments:

- Net capital gain (that is, net long term capital gain for the taxable year in excess of any net short term capital loss for such year) is excluded.[4]
- Net operating losses are not allowed as a deduction.[5]
- The corporate deduction for dividends received is not allowed.[6]
- The deduction for dividends paid is allowed.[7]
- The tax imposed by subsections (d)(2) and (i) of IRC Section 851 for failures to satisfy the gross income or assets tests, or both, for the taxable year is deducted.[8]

6.20 Note that although investment company taxable income excludes net capital gain, it includes net short term capital gain in excess of net long term capital loss. Subsequent to the enactment of the Regulated Investment Company Modernization Act, a capital loss (called a post-enactment capital loss), incurred by a RIC in taxable years beginning after December 22, 2010, retains its character as short term or long term, and can be carried forward without expiration. Net capital losses incurred by a RIC in taxable years beginning before December 23, 2010 (such as pre-enactment capital losses), continue to be treated as short term and, to the extent not used, expire eight taxable years after the taxable year of their origination. Pre-enactment capital losses may not be used to offset capital gains until all post-enactment capital losses have been utilized. As a result, some capital loss carryovers incurred by a RIC in pre-enactment years that would have been utilized under prior law may expire unused. A RIC is prohibited from claiming a net operating loss deduction. Because net short term capital gains are considered ordinary income for IRC purposes, a net investment loss incurred in the same taxable year may be offset against any net short term capital gains. However, if the net investment loss exceeds net short term gains, such net investment loss may not be carried forward and deducted as a net operating loss if the investment company elects to be a RIC in succeeding taxable years.

6.21 In order for a RIC to eliminate the imposition of any entity-level federal income tax liability, it must distribute ordinary dividends to shareholders sufficient to offset investment company taxable income and capital gain dividends sufficient to offset net capital gain.

6.22 The RIC's investment company taxable income may be reduced to zero by dividends other than capital gain dividends and exempt-interest dividends paid to shareholders from a RIC's E&P. The RIC's net capital gain may be offset by a capital gain dividend paid by the RIC to its shareholders and reported as a capital gain dividend in written statements, such as Form

---

[4] IRC Section 852(b)(2)(A).
[5] IRC Section 852(b)(2)(B).
[6] IRC Section 852(b)(2)(C).
[7] IRC Section 852(b)(2)(D).
[8] IRC Section 852(b)(2)(G).

1099, furnished to its shareholders.[9] The computation of a RIC's required annual distributions to shareholders is discussed in further detail in paragraphs 6.63–.78.

6.23 An investment company that does not meet all the RIC qualification requirements in a taxable year will be taxed as a regular corporation for that year and must comply with provisions in a subsequent year if it elects to be taxed as a RIC, as follows:

   a. A regular corporation that qualifies to elect to be subject to tax as a RIC will be subject to a corporate-level tax on its net unrealized gains as if its assets had been sold on the day before the first day of the taxable year that the corporation qualifies to elect to be taxed as a RIC.[10] This general rule is designed to prevent regular corporations with appreciated assets from qualifying as a RIC, selling the assets at a gain, and eliminating corporate-level tax by distributing all income to the shareholders of the RIC.

   b. From the general rule discussed previously, it might appear that a RIC disqualified in one taxable year but qualifying the next year would owe a corporate-level tax on its net unrealized gains. However, an exception to the general rule is provided stating that a previously qualifying RIC that fails to meet the requirements of the RIC tax provisions for a single taxable year usually will not be required to recognize net unrealized gain if it requalifies in the immediately succeeding tax year.[11]

   c. A corporation that accumulates E&P in a year in which it is not taxed as a RIC is required to distribute such E&P before the end of its RIC year if it wishes to be taxed as a RIC in such year. This also includes non-RIC E&P acquired in a tax-free reorganization occurring before December 22, 1992.[12]

Taxation of Shareholder Distributions

6.24 A *dividend* is a distribution from current year E&P or E&P accumulated in prior taxable years. E&P is generally determined by adjusting taxable income for items that constitute economic income or deductions, although they do not affect taxable income.[13] Examples of these adjustments include tax-exempt income, amortization of organization costs, and federal income taxes. Expenses and premium amortization allocated to tax-exempt income and net capital losses reduce current E&P, and net capital losses are deemed to arise on the first day of the following taxable year, affecting E&P only to the extent that they offset capital gains.[14]

6.25 Distributions from a RIC are reported to shareholders on Form 1099-DIV as

   a. ordinary dividends, to the extent of the RIC's current or accumulated E&P.[15]

---

[9] IRC Section 852(b)(3)(C).
[10] IRS Notice 88-19, 1988-1 C.B. 486.
[11] IRS Notice 88-96, 1988-2 C.B. 420.
[12] Treasury Regulations 1.852-12 and 1.312-6.
[13] IRC Section 312.
[14] IRC Section 852(c).
[15] IRC Sections 301(c)(1) and 316.

b. nontaxable distributions (that is, return of capital), to the extent that distributions paid within a RIC's taxable year exceed the RIC's current and accumulated E&P.[16]
   c. long term capital gains.[17]
   d. IRC Section 1202 gains on certain small business stock.
   e. IRC Section 1250 depreciation recapture, generally from dividends received by the RIC from real estate investment trusts.
   f. collectibles gains, generally from derivatives based on precious metals.
   g. foreign tax credits.

6.26 If a RIC has made distributions during a taxable year in excess of its current and accumulated E&P, it is required to file Form 5452 with its Form 1120-RIC and report the taxable and nontaxable components of such distributions to its shareholders on Form 1099-DIV. For taxable years beginning after December 22, 2010, E&P is allocated first to distributions paid during the portion of the taxable year prior to December 31. For prior years, IRC and Treasury regulations require the pro rata allocation of E&P among all distributions during the taxable year.[18]

6.27 A dividend from investment company taxable income may qualify in whole or part for the dividends-received deduction available to corporate shareholders.

6.28 A dividend does not qualify for the dividends-received deduction if the stock on which the dividend was paid is held for less than 46 days during a 91-day period that begins 45 days before the stock becomes ex-dividend with respect to the dividend (or, for certain preferred stock, less than 91 days during a 181-day period that begins 90 days before the stock becomes ex-dividend). The holding period generally is suspended for this purpose during any time that the RIC has diminished its risk of loss (for example, through hedging).[19]

6.29 The portion of the dividend qualifying for the dividends-received deduction must be reported in a written statement furnished to its shareholders for the RIC's tax year in which the dividend was paid.[20]

6.30 If greater than 50 percent of the fair market value of the RIC's gross assets comprises, at the end of the taxable year, stock or securities of foreign corporations or, at the close of each quarter of a taxable year, shares of other RICs, the RIC may elect to pass through to its shareholders the foreign source character of any investment income earned, as well as foreign income taxes that the RIC paid during such taxable year in respect to such foreign source income.[21] A RIC that makes this election is not entitled to a tax deduction for the expense or a foreign tax credit in respect to such foreign taxes. However, the RIC is entitled to treat such foreign income taxes passed through to its shareholders as part of the RIC's dividends paid deduction.

---

[16] IRC Section 301(c)(2).
[17] IRC Section 301(c)(3).
[18] IRC Section 316(b)(4).
[19] IRC Section 246(c).
[20] IRC Sections 854(b)(1) and 853(e).
[21] IRC Sections 853(a) and 852(g).

6.31 Shareholders must report as taxable income the gross income received from the RIC (increased by any foreign income taxes deemed passed through by the RIC) and are entitled to either a foreign tax credit (subject to certain limitations) or a deduction (subject to other limitations) for their allowable share of foreign taxes paid by the RIC and passed through to them.[22] To claim or pass through a foreign tax credit, a RIC must hold the stock for 16 days within the 31-day period beginning 15 days before the ex-dividend date (45 days within the 91-day period for certain preferred stock).[23] The holding period generally is suspended for this purpose during any time that the RIC has diminished its risk of loss (for example, through hedging). Foreign taxes paid by a RIC that do not qualify for the foreign tax credit do not increase the taxable income reported to the shareholders (that is, the RIC is allowed to deduct such taxes in computing its investment company taxable income).[24]

6.32 The amount of foreign source income and foreign taxes must be reported by a RIC in a written statement furnished to shareholders for the RIC's tax year in which the dividend was paid.[25]

6.33 A RIC that, at the end of each quarter of its taxable year, has at least 50 percent of its assets comprising federally tax-exempt obligations or shares of other RICs is eligible to distribute exempt-interest dividends to its shareholders. Exempt-interest dividends received by a shareholder are treated as federally tax-exempt income.[26]

6.34 The maximum amount reported as exempt-interest dividends may not exceed the net tax-exempt interest earned by a RIC eligible to distribute exempt-interest dividends. *Net tax-exempt interest* is defined as tax-exempt interest income reduced for the amortization of premium on tax-exempt bonds and also for expenses attributable to the production of its tax-exempt interest income.

6.35 Generally, an acceptable basis for allocation of a RIC's expenses allocable to tax-exempt income is the ratio of gross tax-exempt income to gross investment income (tax exempt plus taxable), excluding capital gain.[27] The required amortization of premium on tax-exempt bonds must be allocated to the tax-exempt income.[28]

6.36 Net gain or loss realized on the sale of tax-exempt securities is treated as capital gain or loss, except to the extent of any gain treated as market discount, which is taxable as ordinary income.

6.37 An exempt-interest dividend must be reported by a RIC in a written statement, such as Form 1099-INT, furnished to a shareholder for the RIC's tax year in which the dividend was paid.[29] However, if the aggregate reported amount of a RIC's exempt-interest dividends in respect of the RIC's taxable year exceeds the RIC's net tax-exempt income for such taxable year, the RIC would be eligible to treat as an exempt-interest dividend for such taxable year

---

[22] IRC Section 853(b)(2).
[23] IRC Section 901(k).
[24] IRC Section 853(e).
[25] IRC Section 853(c).
[26] IRC Sections 852(b)(5) and 852(g).
[27] IRC Section 265(a)(3).
[28] IRC Section 171(a)(2).
[29] IRC Section 852(b)(5)(A).

only an amount equal to the RIC's net tax-exempt income for such taxable year.[30]

6.38 A capital gain dividend is any dividend reported as such by a RIC in a written statement furnished to shareholders.[31] A capital gain dividend distributed by a RIC to a shareholder is generally characterized as long term capital gain by the shareholder, regardless of the actual holding period of the shareholder's shares in such RIC.[32]

6.39 A RIC may retain all or any portion of its net capital gain and elect to have shareholders include the gain in their taxable income as though a capital gain dividend had been paid. In such a case, the RIC will pay corporate income tax (currently 35 percent) on the undistributed net capital gain within 30 days of its year-end and notify shareholders within 60 days of the RIC's tax year-end of the allocable retained capital gain and related income tax paid.[33] The gain is treated as long term capital gain, and the tax is treated as a tax payment by the shareholders.[34] Each shareholder is entitled to increase the basis of his or her shares by a percentage (currently 65 percent) of the deemed distribution.[35] Notification must be provided to shareholders on Form 2439.[36]

6.40 A RIC may also retain all or any portion of the net capital gain and pay the income tax thereon without notifying shareholders. In this situation, the shareholders will not include the capital gain as income nor will they receive a credit for the taxes paid by the RIC or an adjustment to the basis of their shares held.

6.41 A noncorporate taxpayer may generally exclude from taxable income 50 percent of capital gains resulting from the sale of certain qualified small business stock held for more than 5 years. Such gains, however, are taxed (before exclusion) at a rate of 28 percent. To qualify for this exclusion, the stock must be acquired directly by the taxpayer (or indirectly, for example, through a RIC) at its original issuance after August 10, 1993; must be held by the RIC for more than 5 years; and the noncorporate taxpayer must hold shares of the RIC on the date that the RIC acquired the qualified small business stock and at all times thereafter until disposition of the stock by the RIC. For stock acquired after February 17, 2009, and on or before September 27, 2010, the exclusion is increased to 75 percent. For stock acquired after September 27, 2010, and before January 1, 2011, the exclusion is 100 percent.

6.42 Certain types of ordinary dividends received by a RIC may be reported as *qualified dividend income* (QDI) and are eligible for individual taxation at capital gains rates.[37] The Tax Relief, Unemployment Insurance Reauthorization, and Job Creation Act of 2010 extends this favorable treatment through 2012. In order for dividends received by a RIC to be considered QDI, a RIC must hold the stock for 60 days within a 121 day period beginning 60 days before the ex-dividend date (90 days within a 181 day period for certain

---

[30] IRC Section 852(b)(5)(A)(ii).
[31] IRC Section 852(b)(3)(C).
[32] IRC Section 852(b)(3)(B).
[33] IRC Sections 852(b)(3)(D)(i) and (iv).
[34] IRC Section 852(b)(3)(D)(ii).
[35] IRC Section 852(b)(3)(D)(iii).
[36] Treasury Regulation 1.852-9.
[37] IRC Section 1(h)(11).

Taxes

preferred stock). The holding period generally is suspended for this purpose during any time that the RIC has diminished its risk of loss (for example, through hedging).[38]

Excess Reported Amounts

6.43 For RICs with taxable years other than the calendar year, the RIC's net capital gain is allocated first to distributions reported to shareholders as capital gain dividends during the portion of the taxable year ending on December 31, so that any excess reported amounts are allocated first to amounts reported as capital gain distributions after December 31. Similar rules apply to other pass-through items, such as QDI, foreign tax credits, tax-exempt interest, dividends eligible for the corporate dividends received deduction, and qualified interest income and short term capital gains distributed to non-U.S. shareholders. For prior years, any excess was allocated pro rata among all distributions designated as capital gain during the taxable year.

Qualification Tests

6.44 *Requirements for qualification.* To qualify as a RIC for tax purposes, an investment company must

a. be a domestic corporation (or a business trust taxable as a corporation) registered for the entire taxable year under the 1940 Act.[39] An investment company is registered upon filing its notification of registration on Form N-8A.[40]

b. elect, if it has not previously done so, to be taxed as a RIC.[41] To elect RIC status, an investment company prepares its tax return and computes taxable income in accordance with the provisions of Subchapter M. Once elected, the company's status is unchanged as long as the company continues to qualify under the IRC.

c. meet the 90 percent gross income test (see paragraphs 6.47–.51.).

d. meet certain requirements concerning diversification of its total assets at the end of each quarter of the taxable year (see paragraphs 6.52–.56.).

6.45 In order for its distributions to be used to offset taxable income, the RIC must distribute at least 90 percent of its investment company taxable income (which includes net short term capital gains, if any) and net tax-exempt income for the taxable year (see paragraphs 6.63–.78).

6.46 A RIC should keep a record of the computations supporting qualification under the foregoing tests.

6.47 *90 Percent gross income test.* A RIC must derive at least 90 percent of its gross income from (*a*) dividends; interest (including tax-exempt interest income); payments with respect to securities loans; and gains (without including losses) from the sale or other disposition of stocks, securities, or foreign currencies or (*b*) other income (including but not limited to gains from options, futures, or forward contracts) derived with respect to the RIC's investing in such stock,

---

[38] IRC Section 1(h)(11)(B).
[39] IRC Section 851(a).
[40] Each series of a series fund will be considered a registrant for this purpose.
[41] IRC Section 851(b)(1).

AAG-INV 6.47

securities, or currencies and net income from an interest in a qualified publicly traded partnership (PTP).[42]

6.48 Although the IRS may issue regulations that would exclude from qualifying income foreign currency gains that are not directly related to the RIC's principal business of investing in stock or securities (or options and futures with respect to stock or securities), no such guidance has been issued.

6.49 Gross income derived from a partnership (distinguished from what is generally reported on the partner's Form K-1 as taxable income or from cash distributions received by the partner during the year) is treated by the RIC in the same manner as if it were realized directly by the RIC for purposes of the 90 percent test.[43] Thus, gross income earned by a partnership other than income described in paragraph 6.47 would be treated by a RIC partner of such partnership as nonqualifying income.

6.50 Other items of gross income, such as redemption fees, expense reimbursements, and lawsuit settlements, may require individual consideration to determine their tax status and effect on the 90 percent test. The IRS has ruled that if in the normal course of its business a RIC receives a reimbursement of investment advisory fees that was not the result of a transaction entered into to artificially inflate the RIC's qualifying gross income, such reimbursement may be considered qualifying income for purposes of the 90 percent test.[44]

6.51 An investment company that fails to meet the gross income test would not lose its RIC status if such failure is due to reasonable cause, not willful neglect, and if the investment company pays a deductible tax equal to the excess of its nonqualifying gross income over 1/9 of the qualifying gross income.[45]

6.52 *50 percent test.* At the end of each quarter of a RIC's taxable year, at least 50 percent of the fair market value of the RIC's total assets must be represented by cash and cash items (including receivables), U.S. government securities, securities of other RICs, and other securities. For this purpose, other securities do not include investments in the securities of any 1 issuer if they represent more than 5 percent of the fair market value of the investment company's total assets or more than 10 percent of the issuer's outstanding voting securities (except as provided in IRC Section 851[e]).[46]

6.53 *25 percent test.* At the end of each quarter of a RIC's taxable year, not more than 25 percent of the RIC's total assets may comprise the securities of any 1 issuer, except for the securities of the U.S. government or other RICs. This requirement also prohibits investing more than 25 percent of the RIC's total assets in 2 or more issuers that are controlled by the RIC and engaged in the same (or similar) or related trades or businesses.[47] For that purpose, the RIC controls the issuers if it has 20 percent or more of the combined voting power of each corporation.[48] This requirement also prohibits investing more

---

[42] IRC Section 851(b)(2).
[43] IRC Section 851(b).
[44] Revenue Ruling 92-56.
[45] IRC Section 851(b)(i).
[46] IRC Section 851(b)(3)(A).
[47] IRC Section 851(b)(3)(B).
[48] IRC Section 851(c)(2).

than 25 percent of the RIC's total assets in 1 or more qualified PTPs, as defined in IRC Section 851(h).[49]

6.54 For purposes of the diversification tests, the issuer of an option or futures contract is the corporation or government that issued the underlying security.[50] For index instruments, the IRS has concluded that the issuers of an option on a stock index are the issuers of the stocks or securities underlying the index, in proportion to the weighting of the stocks or securities in the computation of the index, regardless of whether the index is broad based or narrow based. The IRS has not published guidance on the valuation of derivative instruments for purposes of this test.

6.55 A RIC that meets the asset diversification requirements at the end of the first taxable quarter of its existence will not lose its status as a RIC if it fails to satisfy those requirements in a later taxable quarter, provided that the noncompliance is due neither in whole nor in part to the acquisition of a security or other property. If a RIC fails to meet the diversification requirements because of an acquisition, it may reestablish its status for such taxable quarter end by eliminating the discrepancy between the diversification requirements and its holdings within 30 days after the end of the quarter using the securities' values as of the end of the quarter.[51] A RIC that fails to meet the diversification requirements will not be disqualified

    a. if the failure is due to the ownership of assets with a value less than $10 million and less than 1 percent of total assets of the RIC, and the RIC disposes of assets or otherwise meets the diversification requirements within 6 months after the quarter in which the failure is identified; or

    b. if the failure is due to reasonable cause, not willful neglect, and the RIC notifies the IRS; files a list of the assets that caused the failure; pays a deductible tax equal to the greater of $50,000 or the highest corporate tax rate times the taxable income attributable to the identified assets during the period of failure; and disposes of the identified assets or otherwise complies with the diversification requirements within 6 months after the quarter in which the failure is identified or such other time period as specified in regulations.[52]

6.56 Special rules apply to an investment company that qualifies as a venture capital investment company.[53]

Variable Contracts

6.57 In addition to the diversification requirements applicable to all RICs (discussed in the previous paragraphs), special quarterly asset diversification tests are to be met by RICs used as investment vehicles for variable annuity, endowment, and life insurance contracts. The fund must meet these diversification requirements on a calendar-year basis without regard to the fund's

---

[49] IRC Section 851(b)(3)(B).
[50] Revenue Ruling 83-69, 1983-1 C.B. 126.
[51] IRC Section 851(d)(1).
[52] IRC Section 851(d)(2).
[53] IRC Section 851(e).

Investment Companies

fiscal year. In general, a segregated asset account will be considered adequately diversified if all of the following criteria are met:

    a. No more than 55 percent of total assets are represented by any 1 investment

    b. No more than 70 percent of total assets are represented by any 2 investments

    c. No more than 80 percent of total assets are represented by any 3 investments

    d. No more than 90 percent of total assets are represented by any 4 investments

In general, for a separate account to be permitted to look through to the assets of a RIC, all the interests in the RIC must be held by one or more insurance company separate accounts or other permissible entities identified in the Treasury regulations and other administrative guidance promulgated under IRC Section 817.[54]

6.58 All securities of the same issuer, all interests in the same real property project, and all interests in the same commodity are each treated as a single investment. Each governmental agency or instrumentality is treated as a separate issuer.

6.59 The IRS regulations provide a safe harbor for segregated asset accounts. If the segregated asset account meets the safe harbor test, it will be deemed as being diversified. The safe harbor test is met if a segregated asset account meets the RIC diversification tests, and the segregated asset account has no more than 55 percent of the value of its total assets invested in cash, cash items, government securities, and securities of other RICs.[55]

6.60 Special rules apply to a segregated asset account with respect to variable life insurance contracts.[56]

6.61 If the diversification test is not met on the last day of a particular quarter, the separate account is allowed a 30 day grace period after such quarter-end to meet the diversification requirements.[57] An exception is also available for certain separate accounts that are in the start-up mode, whereby accounts are considered diversified for the first year of their existence.

6.62 Failure of the underlying segregated asset accounts (separate accounts) to qualify will adversely affect the tax treatment of the variable annuity, endowment, or life insurance contracts.[58] It will not directly affect the tax status of the RIC. However, the auditor should consider the account's compliance with the asset diversification requirements and, if the diversification test is not passed, the effect on financial statement disclosure.

Distribution Test

6.63 *90 percent distribution test.* A RIC must pay dividends (exclusive of capital gain dividends) equal to the sum of 90 percent of investment company

---

[54] Treasury Regulation 1.817-5(f)(3) and Revenue Ruling 2007-58, 2007-2 C.B. 562.
[55] IRC Section 817(h)(2).
[56] Treasury Regulation 1.817-5(b)(3).
[57] Treasury Regulation 1.817-5(d).
[58] Treasury Regulation 1.817-5(c)(2).

taxable income and 90 percent of net tax-exempt income for the year. In addition, a corporation that has E&P from non-RIC years must distribute such E&P by the end of its first RIC year.[59]

6.64 For purposes of this distribution test, a RIC may elect to treat as paid on the last day of the fiscal year all or part of any dividends declared after the end of its taxable year. Such dividends must be declared before the later of the 15th day of the 9th month following the close of the taxable year or the extended due date of the return for the taxable year. The dividends must be paid within 12 months after the end of the taxable year and not later than the first dividend payment of the same type of dividend after such declaration.[60]

6.65 If a RIC meets all the qualification tests and the 90 percent distribution test but does not distribute all its investment company taxable income, it must pay corporate income taxes on the undistributed portion.[61] Similarly, if the company fails to distribute its net capital gains it is subject to tax on any such undistributed gains.

6.66 A nondeductible excise tax on undistributed income is imposed on a RIC to the extent that the RIC does not satisfy certain distribution requirements for a calendar year (see paragraphs 6.79–.91).

6.67 *Preferential dividends.* For nonpublicly offered RICs, a dividends paid deduction is allowed only for distributions that are pro rata, with no preference regarding any share of stock compared with any other share of the same class of stock.[62] This rule has been repealed for RICs that are treated as publicly offered. A publicly offered RIC is any RIC, the shares of which are continuously offered pursuant to a public offering within the meaning of the Securities Act of 1933, regularly traded on an established securities market, or held by or for no fewer than 500 persons at all times during the taxable year.[63] For distributions subject to the preferential dividend rule, a RIC is considered to have only 1 class of stock if the only differences among the classes are expense allocations. However, certain class-specific expenses may be allocated to a particular class if the requirements of IRC Revenue Procedure 96-47 are met. Other expenses, such as advisory fees, must be allocated among all shares pro rata. IRC Revenue Procedure 99-40 provides guidance on waivers or reimbursements of expenses in a multiclass context.

6.68 A RIC must allocate the various kinds of dividends it pays (such as tax-exempt interest, net capital gains, or the dividends-received deduction) proportionately among the classes of stock outstanding if more than one class of stock exists.[64]

6.69 *Distributions made after December 31.* For purposes of a dividend deduction for the RIC and income recognition for the shareholder, distributions declared in October, November, or December payable to shareholders of record in such months and actually paid during January of the following year must be

---

[59] IRC Section 852(e)(1).
[60] IRC Section 855(a).
[61] IRC Sections 852(b)(1) and 852(b)(3)(A).
[62] IRC Section 562(c).
[63] IRC Section 67(c)(2)(B).
[64] Revenue Ruling 89-81, 1989-1 C.B. 226.

treated as having been paid on December 31 of the previous year to the extent of E&P.[65] This rule applies for both income and excise tax purposes.

6.70 A RIC may elect to treat as having been paid in the prior fiscal year (spillback or throwback) all or part of any dividends declared after the end of such taxable year (see paragraph 6.64). This election applies to regular dividends, capital gain dividends, and exempt-interest dividends. It affects only the RIC and does not change the year in which distributions are reported by the shareholders.

6.71 *Deficiency dividends.* A RIC may pay a deficiency dividend as a result of an increase in investment company taxable income, net capital gain, or a decrease in the deduction for dividends paid to protect its special status or avoid the imposition of entity-level federal income taxation.[66]

6.72 For taxable years beginning after December 22, 2010, a deficiency dividend is subject to an interest charge for the period from the due date of the return for the year of the deduction to the filing of a claim for the deduction. For prior taxable years, a deficiency dividend is subject to both the interest charge and a penalty equal to the less of 100 percent of the interest charge or 50 percent of the deficiency dividend.[67]

6.73 *Equalization distributions.* An open-end investment company may use equalization accounting to prevent changes in the per share equity in its undistributed net income that may be caused by the continuous issuance and redemption of shares. Equalization for tax purposes differs substantially from book equalization because the calculation ignores the impact of share subscriptions by purchasing shareholders (for example, gross equalization credits).[68]

6.74 If a RIC is not considered a personal holding company, the RIC would be permitted to claim a dividends-paid deduction for the E&P associated with the redemption of shares (gross equalization debits).[69] Shareholders generally treat the entire redemption distribution as sales proceeds.[70]

6.75 The treatment of equalization debits as a component of a RIC's dividends-paid deduction is well established in the income tax rules.[71] However, the precise method of calculating the E&P attributable to the redeemed shares is not particularly clear. Management generally should consider the most recent IRS pronouncements if equalization debits are to be used.

6.76 Equalization debits used as dividends paid by a RIC may be used to satisfy the RIC's regular distribution requirements and, also, the excise tax distribution requirements.

6.77 *Capital gain dividends.* A RIC may defer all or a portion of any post-October capital loss or late-year ordinary loss in determining the amount of the RIC's capital gain dividends subject to reporting.[72]

---

[65] IRC Section 852(b)(7).
[66] IRC Section 860(a).
[67] IRC Section 860(c).
[68] See paragraph 4.30 of this guide.
[69] Revenue Ruling 55-416, 1955-1 C.B. 416.
[70] IRC Section 302(b)(5).
[71] Treasury Regulation 1.562-1(b)(1).
[72] IRC Sections 852(b)(3)(C) and (b)(8).

6.78 *Elective deferral of late year losses.* A RIC may elect to defer any portion of a post-October capital loss or qualified late-year ordinary loss to the first day of the following taxable year. A *post-October capital loss* is the greatest of the net capital loss, net short term capital loss, or net long term capital loss for the portion of the taxable year after October 31. A *qualified late-year ordinary loss* is the net loss comprising net gain or loss from the sale or other disposition of capital assets for the portion of the taxable year after October 31 and other ordinary income or loss for the portion of the taxable year after December 31.[73]

Excise Tax on Undistributed Income

6.79 *Introduction.* A nondeductible 4 percent entity-level excise tax on undistributed income is imposed on a RIC to the extent that the RIC does not satisfy certain distribution requirements for a calendar year (as shown in the following paragraphs).[74]

6.80 *Measurement periods.* To determine the excise tax, a RIC's ordinary income and capital gain net income are measured separately.

6.81 Ordinary income generally equals the RIC's investment company taxable income before the dividends paid deduction, determined using a calendar-year measurement period, excluding any gains or losses from the sale of capital assets. Ordinary gains or losses from the sale of capital assets after October 31 are generally treated as arising on January 1 of the following year.[75]

6.82 A RIC with a taxable year other than the calendar year may elect to treat a net ordinary loss for the portion of a taxable year ending on December 31 as arising on January 1 of the following calendar year for excise tax purposes.[76]

6.83 Capital gain net income is the net of short term and long term gains and losses from sales or exchanges of capital assets generally computed for the one year period ending on October 31. This amount is reduced by net ordinary loss for the calendar year but not below net long term capital gain.[77]

6.84 RICs with fiscal years ending in November or December may elect to determine their capital gain net income as of the end of that fiscal year.[78]

6.85 *Calculation and elections.* No excise tax is imposed if the RIC makes sufficient distributions during each calendar year at least equal to the sum of the following:

    a. Ninety-eight percent of the ordinary income for the calendar year

    b. Ninety-eight and two-tenths percent (that is, 98.2%) of the capital gain net income for the one year period ending on October 31

    c. One hundred percent of the ordinary income or capital gain net income of the prior year that was not previously distributed[79]

---

[73] IRC Sections 4982(e)(5).
[74] IRC Section 4982(a).
[75] IRC Sections 4982(e)(1) and (e)(5).
[76] IRC Section 4982(e)(7).
[77] IRC Section 4982(e)(2).
[78] IRC Section 4982(e)(4).
[79] IRC Section 4982(b).

6.86 Provided that a RIC distributes in the aggregate an amount at least equal to the sum of the amounts listed previously, the excise distribution requirement will be satisfied.

6.87 Any overdistribution (other than that attributable to a return of capital) from the prior year may be applied to the required distribution of the current year.[80]

6.88 If a RIC retains a portion of its taxable income or gains and pays income tax on that amount, the amount will be treated as distributed for excise tax purposes. A RIC may treat payments of estimated income tax as distributed for excise tax purposes. If a RIC distributes less than the minimum excise requirement, the RIC will be subject to a 4 percent excise tax on the difference between the RIC's minimum annual distribution requirement and the amount actually distributed by the RIC and include 100 percent of such amount on which the excise tax was imposed in the calculation of required distributions in the subsequent year.[81]

6.89 RIC feeder funds include their ratable amounts of all items of income, gain, and loss earned by a master fund organized as a partnership in which it invests for the excise tax periods described in paragraphs 6.83–.84.[82] This contrasts with a RIC maintaining an equity interest in a partnership outside the master-feeder structure. In the latter case, partnership income is included in the measurement period that includes the year-end of the partnership.[83]

6.90 In determining a RIC's required excise tax distribution, the mark-to-market rules for Section 1256 contracts and PFIC stock, the wash sale rules, and the straddle loss deferral rules are applied using October 31 as a year-end (or November 30 or December 31 if a fiscal year election is made).[84] Capital loss carryovers computed using the excise tax measuring period may be used to reduce capital gain net income for purposes of the excise tax.[85] Capital gain net income may be reduced (but not below net long term capital gain) by the RIC's ordinary loss for the calendar year.[86]

6.91 *Exemption for certain RICs.* Excise tax rules do not apply to a RIC if, at all times during a calendar year, each shareholder was a qualified pension trust or segregated asset account of a life insurance company held in connection with variable contracts. Shares owned by the investment adviser attributable to the seed money it contributed (up to $250,000) are not counted for this purpose.[87] RICs that are wholly owned by other exempt entities or other RICs that qualify for this exemption are also exempt from the excise tax rules.

Computation of Taxable Income and Gains

6.92 *Dividends and interest.* RICs record dividend income on the ex-dividend date for tax and accounting purposes.[88]

---

[80] IRC Section 4982(c)(2).
[81] IRC Section 4982(c)(1).
[82] Revenue Procedure 94-71, 1994-2 C.B. 810.
[83] Revenue Ruling 94-40, 1994-1 C.B. 274.
[84] Tax Reform Act of 1986.
[85] Tax Reform Act of 1986.
[86] IRC Section 4982(e)(2)(B).
[87] IRC Section 4982(f).
[88] IRC Section 852(b)(9).

Taxes

6.93 If a dividend or other distribution received by a RIC represents a return of capital, the basis of the security from which such distribution is made is reduced for tax purposes. If the distribution exceeds the RIC's tax basis in the security, the excess is treated as capital gain.[89]

6.94 Interest and original issue discount (OID) are accrued on a daily basis for tax and accounting purposes. However, differences in book and tax accounting for interest and OID related to complex securities and troubled debt securities may exist.

6.95 *Sales of securities.* The basis of securities sold or otherwise disposed of may be either identified specifically or determined following a first in first out convention; average cost may not be used for tax purposes. Identification procedures are prescribed in regulations.[90]

6.96 Under the IRC, a wash sale occurs on a sale of securities (including options) if the seller acquires or enters a contract or an option to acquire substantially identical securities within a period beginning 30 days before the date of a sale at a loss and ending 30 days after such date (61-day period).[91] A loss resulting from such a transaction is deferred for tax purposes; the amount of the loss increases the tax basis of the new security purchased, and the holding period of the new position includes the holding period of the original position.[92] However, a gain on the same type of transaction is taxable, and the tax basis of the new security is not affected by the sale of the old security. Wash sale rules also apply to short-sale transactions such that the date that a short sale is made, rather than the date of close, is considered in determining whether a wash sale has occurred.[93]

6.97 *Commissions.* Commissions related to purchases or sales of securities are not deductible but are added to the basis of the securities or offset against the selling price.[94]

6.98 *Bond discount and premium.* Special, detailed rules prescribe the calculation and treatment of discount and premium on taxable and tax-exempt securities. Although a discussion of these rules is beyond the scope of this guide, the auditor should consider the application of these rules and how they affect the recognition and characterization of income and the deductibility of interest expense for tax purposes.

6.99 *Section 1256 contracts.* Certain financial instruments (Section 1256 contracts) held by a RIC may be subject to mark-to-market rules. Section 1256 contracts include any regulated futures contracts, foreign currency contract, nonequity option, dealer equity option, and dealer securities futures contract. Under these detailed rules, a RIC is treated for tax purposes as selling any Section 1256 contract held on the last day of its taxable year for its fair market value. Gain or loss on an actual or deemed disposition of a Section 1256 contract is treated as 40 percent short term capital gain or loss and 60 percent long

---

[89] IRC Section 301(c).
[90] Treasury Regulation 1.1012-1(c)(1).
[91] IRC Section 1091.
[92] IRC Sections 1091(b),(c), and (d) and 1223(3).
[93] Treasury Regulation 1.1091-1(g).
[94] Treasury Regulation 1.263(a)-2(e).

term capital gain or loss, regardless of the holding period for the Section 1256 contract.[95] A detailed discussion of these rules is beyond the scope of this guide.

6.100 *Tax straddles.* The term *straddle* describes offsetting positions in personal property in which the fair market value of each position is expected to fluctuate inversely to that of the other. The term *position* means an interest (including a futures or forward contract or option) in personal property. An offsetting position occurs whenever risk of loss has been substantially diminished by holding one or more other positions.[96]

6.101 The straddle rules provide that a loss from any position should be recognized only to the extent that such loss exceeds the unrecognized gain with respect to one or more offsetting positions or successor positions or positions that are offsetting to successor positions. Although a detailed discussion of the straddle rules is beyond the scope of this guide, it is important to note that funds that engage in hedging may have significant book versus tax differences in capital gains or losses as a result of the straddle rules.

6.102 *Stock issuance costs.* Stock issuance costs paid by an open-end investment company are deductible for tax purposes, except costs incurred during the initial stock offering period. This also applies to 12b-1 fees.[97] Registration fees and expenses, including accounting procedures, are discussed in further detail in chapter 8, "Other Accounts and Considerations," of this guide

6.103 *Stock redemption costs.* Only stock redemption costs of an open-end investment company, not a closed-end investment company, are deductible in computing investment company taxable income.

6.104 *Limitations on tax benefits of losses.* A 50 percent change of ownership, taking into account only 5 percent shareholders, within a 3-year period, whether through a reorganization or in the ordinary course of business, may limit the tax benefits of losses realized or unrealized before the ownership change in periods after the ownership change. The annual limit on such losses is generally the net fair market value of the assets of the RIC that has experienced the ownership change, multiplied by a long term tax-exempt interest rate on the date of the ownership change.[98]

6.105 *Section 988 transactions.* Special rules apply to the treatment of foreign currency gains and losses attributable to Section 988 transactions. Foreign currency gains and losses from such transactions are characterized as U.S.-source ordinary income or loss.[99]

6.106 A foreign currency gain or loss will result from a Section 988 transaction, described as follows, denominated in a currency other than the RIC's functional currency (nonfunctional currency) or the fair value of which is determined by reference to nonfunctional currency:

    a. Acquiring a debt instrument or becoming the obligor under a debt instrument

    b. Accruing any item of expense or gross income or receipt that is to be paid or received at a later date

---

[95] IRC Section 1256.
[96] IRC Section 1092(c).
[97] Revenue Rulings 73-463 and 94-70.
[98] IRC Sections 381–384.
[99] IRC Section 988(a).

Taxes

  c. Entering or acquiring any forward contract, futures contract, option, or similar financial instrument

  d. Disposing of any nonfunctional currency[100]

6.107 The *functional currency* of a RIC is the currency of the economic environment in which the RIC's operations are predominantly conducted and the currency used in keeping its books and records. The functional currency of a RIC is generally the U.S. dollar. Certain single-country funds may have a functional currency other than the dollar.[101]

6.108 Interest income or expense (including OID and discounts on certain short term obligations) on a nonfunctional currency debt instrument is determined in units of nonfunctional currency and translated into functional currency at the average exchange rate for the accrual period for accrual-basis RICs.[102]

6.109 Foreign currency gain realized on the disposition of a Section 988 debt security will be recognized for tax purposes and treated as U.S.-source ordinary income to the extent of the lesser of the foreign currency gain or the overall gain realized. Similarly, if a foreign currency loss is realized in a Section 988 transaction, it will be recognized for tax purposes and treated as a U.S.-source ordinary loss to the extent of the lesser of foreign currency loss or the overall loss realized.[103]

6.110 The acquisition of nonfunctional currency is treated as an acquisition of property[104] with a functional currency tax basis determined with reference to the spot contract exchange rate (spot rate). A spot contract is a contract to buy or sell nonfunctional currency on or before two business days following the date of the execution of the contract.[105] The disposition or other use of nonfunctional currency will result in a Section 988 transaction if it is exchanged for another nonfunctional currency or functional currency.[106]

6.111 Although Section 988 does not apply to transactions involving equity securities, any fluctuation in the exchange rate between the trade date and settlement date of either a purchase or sale of an equity security will result in a foreign currency gain or loss because the payment of the settlement liability constitutes a Section 988 transaction.[107]

6.112 The sale, closing, or settlement (including by taking or making delivery of currency) of any forward contract, futures contract, option, or other similar financial instrument denominated in (or the fair market value of which is determined by reference to) a nonfunctional currency results in ordinary income or loss, unless the contract is a futures or listed option contract traded on a qualified board or exchange.[108] However, certain elections are available

---

[100] IRC Section 988(c)(1).
[101] IRC Section 985(b) and example 2 of Treasury Regulation 1.985-1(f).
[102] Treasury Regulation 1.988-2(b)(1).
[103] IRC Section 988(b).
[104] Treasury Regulation 1.988-1(a).
[105] Treasury Regulation 1.988-1(b).
[106] Treasury Regulation 1.988-2(a).
[107] Treasury Regulation 1.988-2(a)(2).
[108] Treasury Regulation 1.988-2(a).

AAG-INV 6.112

for these kinds of financial instruments that permit income or gain to be characterized differently. A detailed discussion of these rules is beyond the scope of this guide.

6.113 The IRS has provided special rules for certain Section 988(d) hedging transactions. Current regulations cover certain debt instruments, the currency risk (or a portion thereof) of which is entirely eliminated through a qualified hedge; executory contracts that are hedged; and hedges of trade to settlement date receivables and payables arising due to the sale or purchase of stocks or securities traded on an established securities market. These regulations provide integrated treatment for Section 988(d) hedging transactions. The IRS may also issue rulings to taxpayers regarding net hedging and anticipatory hedging methods.[109]

6.114 The timing of the recognition of gain or loss from contracts subject to both Sections 988 and 1256 is governed by the rules of Section 1256.[110] Such contracts, therefore, are marked to market at fiscal year-end. The character of such gain or loss may be either ordinary or capital, depending upon the kind of contract and whether certain elections are made.

6.115 *Passive foreign investment companies.* If a RIC owns equity securities of a corporation that is determined to be a PFIC for U.S. tax purposes, the RIC may be subject to an entity-level interest charge on excess distributions received from the PFIC, including gains realized on the sale or other disposition of such PFIC's shares. This is true even if the RIC has met its distribution requirements for the taxable year in which such excess distribution is deemed to have occurred.

6.116 The intent of the PFIC legislation was to prevent U.S. taxpayers from deferring taxes by acquiring equity securities of foreign investment companies, which are not subject to U.S. income tax and do not pay dividends currently. The PFIC rules effectively result in the recognition of taxable income by U.S. taxpayers that would be consistent with a situation as if the foreign company made a taxable distribution of all its income and appreciation each year.

6.117 A foreign corporation is a PFIC if 75 percent or more of the corporation's gross income is passive income or if 50 percent or more of the foreign corporation's assets produce passive income.[111] Passive income includes dividends, interest, royalties, rents, annuities, and net gains from the sale of securities; foreign currency; and certain commodity transactions that are not realized from an active trade or business engaged in by the PFIC.[112] Examples of passive assets include cash (even if maintained for working capital requirements), stocks, bonds, and other securities held by the PFIC.

6.118 A RIC that owns a PFIC's equity securities may be able to avoid the imposition of a RIC-level interest charge if the RIC elects to treat the PFIC as a qualified electing fund (QEF).[113] The RIC's share of the PFIC's ordinary income and capital gain each year are included as taxable income if

---

[109] Treasury Regulation 1.988-5.
[110] Treasury Regulation 1.988-2(d).
[111] IRC Section 1297(a).
[112] IRC Section 1297(b).
[113] IRC Section 1295.

the election is made.[114] The earnings of the QEF must be determined based on U.S. tax principles making it difficult for many foreign corporations to provide the necessary information.

6.119 A RIC may alternatively elect to mark its PFIC shares to market at the close of the RIC's taxable year, as well as on October 31, and treat increases in unrealized appreciation (and decreases to the extent that increases have been included previously in taxable income) as part of the RIC's taxable income and required excise tax distribution.[115]

6.120 Both the QEF and mark-to-market elections may result in the RIC having to make distributions of income that it has not yet received.

6.121 A failure to make either of these elections may subject the RIC to an entity-level interest charge, in which case the recording of a tax liability generally should be considered.[116] Thus, it is important to determine that RICs holding foreign securities have policies and procedures to identify PFICs timely.

Offshore Funds

6.122 In recent years, the number of funds that are organized outside the United States (offshore funds) has increased substantially. This has occurred as U.S. fund advisers sought to globalize their customer base and as foreign institutions increased their investments in U.S. securities.

6.123 A myriad of U.S. and foreign tax issues are associated with offshore funds. These funds are typically organized in the form that is most suitable for the expected owners. Further, they are located in the jurisdiction that provides the most beneficial taxation and regulation of the entity, taxation of owners, and withholding tax treatment for income earned and distributions made.

6.124 Offshore funds are usually not subject to income taxes imposed by the country in which they are domiciled. However, they are generally subject to U.S. withholding tax on dividends from U.S. stock holdings. They are not generally subject to entity-level U.S. income taxation, provided that they are structured in such a way that they are not considered engaged in a U.S. trade or business for U.S. tax purposes.[117]

6.125 Consideration of both U.S. and local country tax and regulatory regimes is necessary for each offshore fund due to those regimes' often complex nature. Because an investment company must be organized in the United States in order to qualify as a RIC, an offshore fund subject to U.S. tax cannot elect to be treated as a RIC.

6.126 Management of offshore funds generally should have tax policies and procedures addressing the taxation of the fund in the offshore country in which the fund is domiciled, the taxation of the fund's portfolio securities in the country in which the securities are taxed, and the taxation of fund shareholders in the countries in which they reside.

---

[114] IRC Section 1293(a).

[115] IRC Sections 1296 and 4982(e)(6).

[116] Financial Accounting Standards Board *Accounting Standards Codification* 740-10-45-25 discusses income statement classification of interest and penalties.

[117] Treasury Regulation 1.864-2.

Small Business Investment Companies

6.127 Small business investment companies (SBICs) formed as corporations are generally subject to the corporate tax rules, unless they qualify and elect to be treated as RICs. SBICs also may be structured either as partnerships or disregarded as entities separate from their owners.

6.128 An SBIC organized as a corporation and operating under the Small Business Investment Act of 1958 (SBIA), receives special tax treatment. It is allowed a 100 percent deduction for dividends received that qualify for the dividend received deduction, unless it elects to be taxed as a RIC.[118] In addition, the SBIC may be excluded from the definition of a *personal holding company*.[119]

6.129 A shareholder in an SBIC operating under the SBIA may characterize a loss on its stock as an ordinary loss. In computing the net operating loss deduction, such a loss is treated as a loss from a trade or business.[120]

6.130 The tax rules permit special treatment for investors, including investment companies, in SBICs other than those licensed under the SBIA. Investors in small business corporations may qualify for ordinary loss treatment on the sale of their shares.[121] Investors in qualified small business stock may qualify for a 50 percent exclusion from gross income on the sale of small business stock.[122] Investors may also defer recognition of gain on sales of publicly traded securities by rolling over the proceeds into a specialized SBIC.[123]

---

[118] IRC Section 243(a)(2).
[119] IRC Section 542(c)(8).
[120] IRC Section 1242.
[121] IRC Section 1244.
[122] IRC Section 1202.
[123] IRC Section 1044.

Chapter 7

Financial Statements of Investment Companies

7.01 As illustrated in Financial Accounting Standards Board (FASB) *Accounting Standards Codification* (ASC) 946-205-45-1, the overall objective of financial statements, including financial highlights, of investment companies is to present net assets, results of operations, changes in net assets, and financial highlights resulting from investment activities and, if applicable, capital share transactions. In reporting to shareholders, nonregistered investment companies and investment companies registered with the Securities and Exchange Commission (SEC) should present financial statements and financial highlights as follows.

Nonregistered Investment Companies	*Registered Investment Companies*
A statement of assets and liabilities with a schedule of investments or statement of net assets, which includes a schedule of investments therein, as of the close of the latest period. At a minimum, a condensed schedule of investments (as discussed in paragraphs 4–10 of Financial Accounting Standards Board [FASB] *Accounting Standards Codification* [ASC] 946-210-50) should be provided for each statement of assets and liabilities.	A statement of assets and liabilities with a schedule of investments or statement of net assets, which includes a schedule of investments therein (that is, a detailed list of investments in securities, options written, securities sold short, and other investments) as of the close of the latest period.[1] A schedule of investments should be provided for each statement of assets and liabilities in conformity with Rule 12-12 or 12-12C of Regulation S-X.[2]

(continued)

---

[1] If the most current statement of assets and liabilities included in a registration statement is as of a date more than 245 days prior to the date that the filing is expected to become effective, then the financial statements, which may be unaudited, included in such filing are to be updated to a date within 245 days of the expected effective date. A statement of assets and liabilities as of such date must be provided as well as a statement of operations and cash flows (if applicable) and statement of changes in net assets for the interim period from the end of the most recent fiscal year for which a statement of assets and liabilities is presented and the date of the most recent interim statement of assets and liabilities.

[2] In 2004, the Securities and Exchange Commission (SEC) adopted rule and form amendments that, among other matters, amended Articles 6 and 12 of Regulation S-X to permit a registered investment company to include, under Rule 12-12C, a summary schedule of investments in securities of unaffiliated issuers in its reports to shareholders, provided that the complete portfolio schedule required by Rule 12-12 is filed with the SEC semiannually and provided to shareholders upon request free of charge. All other complete portfolio schedules required by Regulation S-X (Rule 12-12A, *Investments—Securities Sold Short*; Rule 12-12B, *Open Option Contracts Written*; Rule 12-13, *Investments Other than Securities*; and Rule 12-14, *Investments In and Advances To Affiliates*) continue to be required in both shareholder reports and Form N-CSR. The amendments also exempt money market funds (which utilize the exemptive requirements of Rule 2a-7 under the Investment Company Act of 1940 [the 1940 Act]) from including a portfolio schedule in reports to shareholders, provided that this information is filed with the SEC on Form N-CSR semiannually and provided to shareholders upon request free of charge. See SEC Release No. IC-26372 under the 1940 Act for additional information.

Although the SEC rule allows a money market fund to exclude its portfolio of investments from its shareholder reports, the U.S. generally accepted accounting principles (GAAP) requirement discussed in this guide that a money market fund present, at a minimum, a condensed schedule of investments for each statement of assets and liabilities (see paragraphs 1–3 of Financial Accounting Standards Board [FASB] *Accounting Standards Codification* [ASC] 946-210-50) has not been modified.

AAG-INV 7.01

Nonregistered Investment Companies	Registered Investment Companies
A statement of operations for the latest period.	A statement of operations for the latest year.[3,4]
A statement of cash flows for the latest period (if not exempted by FASB ASC 230-10).[5]	A statement of cash flows for the latest year (if not exempted by FASB ASC 230-10).[6,7,8]
A statement of changes in net assets for the latest period.	A statement of changes in net assets for the latest two years (for semiannual reports, the most recent semiannual period and preceding fiscal year).[9,10]
Financial highlights for the latest period consisting of per share operating performance, net investment income, and expense ratios and total return for all investment companies organized in a manner using unitized net asset value.[11]	Financial highlights for the latest five fiscal years[12,13,14] (for semiannual reports, the semiannual period and generally the preceding five fiscal years).

7.02 In addition to complying with U.S. generally accepted accounting principles (GAAP), the financial statements of investment companies registered with the SEC should comply with applicable SEC requirements.

7.03 The financial statements illustrated in this chapter are for typical open-end management investment companies and may need to be modified to fit the requirements of other types of investment companies. Financial reporting requirements with respect to unit investment trusts and variable annuity separate accounts are discussed in chapters 9, "Unit Investment Trusts," and 10, "Variable Contracts—Insurance Entities," of this guide. For guidance on financial statement presentation and disclosure of venture capital and small business investment companies, including additional regulatory requirements, refer to appendix D, "Venture Capital, Business Development Companies, and

---

[3] See footnote 1.

[4] The SEC staff currently requires that sufficient fiscal periods be presented to cover at least 12 calendar months' results of operations ending on the most recent fiscal year-end date (24 calendar months' changes in net assets and 60 months' financial highlights).

[5] In October 2011, FASB issued a proposed Accounting Standards Update (ASU), *Technical Corrections*, which would change the conditions for an investment company to be exempted from providing a statement of cash flows. The proposed ASU deleted the conditions for substantially all of the entity's investments to be highly liquid and carried at market value; these were replaced with the conditions for substantially all of the entity's investments to be carried at fair value and classified as level 1 or level 2 measurements in accordance with FASB ASC 820, *Fair Value Measurement*. Readers are encouraged to remain alert for developments on this topic, which can be accessed from the Technical Plan and Project Updates page at www.fasb.org.

[6] See footnote 5.

[7] See footnote 1.

[8] See footnote 4.

[9] See footnote 1.

[10] See footnote 4.

[11] FASB ASC 946-205-45-2 notes that for investment companies not using unitized net asset value, financial highlights should be presented and consist of net investment income and expense ratios and total return, or the internal rate of return since inception if applicable.

[12] See footnote 1.

[13] See footnote 4.

[14] Item 13(a) of Form N-1A requires financial highlights to be presented for the latest 5 years in the fund's prospectus. Item 4 of Form N-2 requires financial highlights to be presented for the latest 10 years in the fund's prospectus.

Small Business Investment Companies," of this guide. Aspects of reporting on interim financial information are discussed in paragraphs 7.170–.173.

7.04 Financial statements and related disclosures should be presented for each series in a series fund although one or more series may be presented in a separate document.[15] For funds with multiple classes of shares, certain information relating to each class is required to be disclosed as discussed in chapter 5, "Complex Capital Structures," of this guide.

Comparative Financial Statements

7.05 FASB ASC 946, *Financial Services—Investment Companies*, does not require comparative financial statements for nonregistered investment partnerships. If an entity elects to prepare comparative financial statements, the general guidance for the presentation of comparative financial statements, as found in paragraphs 2 and 4 of FASB ASC 205-10-45, indicate that (*a*) in any one year it is ordinarily desirable that the statement of financial position, the income statement, and the statement of changes in equity be presented for one or more preceding years, as well as for the current year, and (*b*) notes to financial statements, explanations, and accountants' reports containing qualifications that appeared on the statements for the preceding years should be repeated, or at least referred to, in the comparative statements to the extent that they continue to be of significance.

7.06 According to Technical Questions and Answers (TIS) section 6910.19, "Information Required to Be Disclosed in Financial Statements When Comparative Financial Statements of Nonregistered Investment Partnerships Are Presented" (AICPA, *Technical Practice Aids*), when comparative financial statements of a nonregistered investment partnership are presented, comparative schedules of investments should be presented as of the end of each period presented. Because the schedule of investments would continue to be considered of significance relative to the statement of assets and liabilities for the prior year, the schedule of investments for the prior year should be included as part of the comparative statements.

7.07 TIS section 6910.19 also notes that when comparative financial statements of a nonregistered investment partnership are provided, comparative financial highlights should be presented for each period provided. Consistent with the requirements of FASB ASC 205-10-45, discussed in paragraph 7.05, comparative financial highlights should be presented when comparative statements of operations are provided because they would be considered a significant disclosure for the prior periods of operation included in the financial statements.

Consolidation [16]

7.08 As explained in FASB ASC 946-810-45-2 and 946-323-45-1, except as discussed in paragraph 7.10, consolidation or use of the equity method

---

[15] Rule 6.03(j) of Regulation S-X.
[16] FASB and the International Accounting Standards Board (IASB) have a project on their agenda with the objective of providing comprehensive guidance for addressing whether an entity

(continued)

AAG-INV 7.08

of accounting by an investment company of a noninvestment company investee is not appropriate. As stated in FASB ASC 323-10-15-4, FASB ASC 323, *Investments—Equity Method and Joint Ventures*, does not apply to investments in common stock held by investment companies registered under the Investment Company Act of 1940 (the 1940 Act) or investment companies that would be included under the 1940 Act (including small business investment companies), except that the number of stockholders is limited, and the securities are not offered publicly. Rule 6-03(c)(1) of Regulation S-X also precludes consolidation by a registered investment company of any entity other than another investment company.

7.09 Investments accounted for at fair value, in accordance with the specialized guidance in FASB ASC 946, are not subject to variable interest entity (VIE) guidance.

7.10 FASB ASC 946-810-45-3 and 946-323-45-2 further note that an exception to this general principle occurs if the investment company has an investment in an operating entity that provides services to the investment company (for example, an investment adviser or transfer agent). In those cases, the purpose of the investment is to provide services to the investment company, rather than realize a gain on the sale of the investment. If an individual investment company holds a controlling interest in such an operating entity, consolidation is appropriate. If an investment company holds a noncontrolling ownership interest in such an operating entity that otherwise qualifies for use of the equity method of accounting, the investment company should use the equity method of accounting for that investment, rather than the fair value of the investee's assets and liabilities.

7.11 Accounting Standards Update (ASU) No. 2009-17, *Consolidations (Topic 810): Improvements to Financial Reporting by Enterprises Involved with Variable Interest Entities*, changes how to determine when an entity that is insufficiently capitalized or is not controlled through voting (or similar rights) should be consolidated. The determination of whether a company is required to consolidate an entity is based on, among other things, an entity's purpose and design and a company's ability to direct the activities of the entity that most significantly impact the entity's economic performance. This ASU also amends

---

(footnote continued)

is an investment company and providing measurement requirements for an investment company's investments. Under FASB's exposure document, an investment company would be required to consolidate its controlling financial interest in another investment company as well as controlling interests in an investment property entity, in accordance with FASB ASC 810, *Consolidation*. Also, an investment company must measure all other investments, including interests in investment companies and investment property entities that the investment company can significantly influence, at fair value with changes recognized in net income. Use of the equity method would be prohibited except for an investment in a noninvestment company that provides services to the investment company (for example, an investment adviser or transfer agent). Under the IASB's exposure document, an investment company must measure investments in entities that it controls (including other investment companies) at fair value through profit or loss, and investment entities would be exempt from consolidation requirements.

In its exposure document, FASB explained that consistent with GAAP, a noninvestment company parent would retain the specialized accounting in FASB ASC 946, *Financial Services—Investment Companies*, for an investment company subsidiary in consolidation. Alternatively, the IASB's proposal would not allow a noninvestment company parent to retain the specialized accounting for investment companies when consolidating an investment company subsidiary. However, both boards agree that the specialized accounting would be retained when a noninvestment company entity is accounting for its interest in an investment company over which it has significant influence. Readers should remain alert for updates on this joint project, which can be accessed from the Technical Plan and Project Updates page on www.fasb.org.

AAG-INV 7.09

Financial Statements of Investment Companies

the consolidation of VIE guidance to eliminate the quantitative approach previously required for determining the primary beneficiary of a VIE, which was based on determining which enterprise absorbs the majority of the entity's expected losses, receives a majority of the entity's expected residual returns, or both.

7.12 ASU No. 2010-10, *Consolidation (Topic 810): Amendments for Certain Investment Funds*, defers the application of the guidance in ASU No. 2009-17 for a reporting enterprise's interest in certain entities that have all the attributes of an investment company or for which it is industry practice to apply measurement principles for financial reporting that are consistent with those followed by investment companies.[17] The deferral also applies to a reporting entity's interest in an entity that is required to comply or operate in accordance with requirements similar to those in Rule 2a-7 of the 1940 Act for registered money market funds. The deferral does not apply to situations in which a reporting entity has the explicit or implicit obligation to fund losses of an entity that could potentially be significant to the entity and interests in securitization entities, asset-backed financing entities, or entities formerly considered qualifying special-purpose entities. Any entities qualifying for the deferral will continue to be assessed under the overall guidance on the consolidation of VIEs in FASB ASC 810-10 before it was updated by ASU No. 2009-17.

7.13 The ASU's amendments also clarify that for entities that do not qualify for the deferral, related parties should be considered when an entity evaluates whether the fee of a decision maker or service provider represents a variable interest. In addition, the requirements for evaluating whether such a fee is a variable interest are modified to clarify FASB's intention that a quantitative calculation should not be the sole basis for this evaluation.

7.14 As a result of the deferral, asset managers must consider their involvement with securitization vehicles (for example, collateralized debt obligations), asset-backed funding facilities, or certain entities for which they have provided a guarantee and that are not similar in nature to money market funds. They must then evaluate whether they have the power to direct the economic activities of those structures and whether the fee received from those structures could be potentially significant to the VIE. If so, the asset manager would most likely be considered the primary beneficiary and would be required to consolidate the VIE.

---

[17] In November 2011, FASB issued a proposed ASU in connection with the joint project on consolidation which is the result of the boards' efforts to develop consistent guidance. The amendments in this proposed update would rescind the indefinite deferral in ASU No. 2010-10, *Consolidation (Topic 810): Amendments for Certain Investment Funds*, and would require all variable interest entities (VIEs) to be evaluated for consolidation under the revised guidance. FASB noted in the proposed update that it does not intend the application of the proposed update to result in money market funds being consolidated. The proposed guidance would clarify whether a decision maker is using its power as a principal or an agent, which would affect the determination of whether the entity is a VIE, and if so, whether a reporting entity should consolidate the entity being evaluated. When assessing whether a decision maker is using its power as an agent or a principal, the assessment would focus on the rights held by other parties, the compensation to which the decision maker is entitled, and the decision maker's exposure to variability of returns from other interests that it holds in the entity. The proposed amendments also change the requirements for determining whether a general partner controls a limited partnership to be consistent with the principal versus agent analysis developed for evaluating VIEs. Rather than focusing on whether a simple majority of the limited partners hold substantive kick-out rights or participating rights, the general partner would evaluate whether it uses its decision-making authority in a principal or an agent capacity.

AAG-INV 7.14

7.15 Public investment companies organized pursuant to master-feeder arrangements, as defined by the SEC,[18] must provide master financial statements with each feeder financial statement, pursuant to SEC requirements.[19] Nonpublic investment companies should follow the applicable provisions of subtopics 205, 210, 225, 230, and 235 of FASB ASC 946. (See also footnote 2 to paragraph 5.54 of this guide discussing the SEC's regulations which require public investment companies that are regulated under the 1940 Act meeting certain criteria to file financial statements or include summarized financial information in the notes to the financial statements, as appropriate, for investments in unconsolidated majority-owned subsidiaries or other unconsolidated subsidiaries.)

7.16 FASB ASC 946-205-45-6 notes that nonpublic investment companies may also present a complete set of master financial statements with each feeder financial statement in a manner that is consistent with the requirements for public investment companies.

7.17 The guidance discussed in paragraphs 7.08–.10 is consistent with long-standing industry practice. That practice results in investment company financial statements that focus on a net asset value that reflects the fair value of the underlying investments. The purpose and nature of investment companies makes fair value for their investments the most relevant measure to report to their investors, the principal users of their financial statements who typically evaluate the performance of the investment company based on changes in net asset value. Exchanges of open-end investment company shares are at, or based on, net asset value. Purchasers and sellers of other investment company (for example, closed-end investment company) shares often consider the premium or discount based on net asset value that is present in the exchange price.

7.18 FASB ASC 810-10-40 discusses when deconsolidation of a subsidiary or derecognition of a group of assets is appropriate and the applicable accounting guidance. FASB ASC 810-10-45 provides accounting and reporting guidance related to the consolidated financial statement presentation of parent and subsidiary financial statements and combined financial statements.

7.19 FASB ASC 810-10-45-15 states that the ownership interests in the subsidiary that are held by owners other than the parent are noncontrolling interests. The noncontrolling interest in a subsidiary is part of the equity of the consolidated group. Further, FASB ASC 810-10-45-16 explains that the noncontrolling interest should be reported in the consolidated statement of financial position within equity and separately from the parent's equity. That amount should be clearly identified and labeled (for example, as noncontrolling interest in subsidiaries). An entity with noncontrolling interests in more than one subsidiary may present those interests in aggregate in the consolidated financial statements. FASB ASC 810-10-55-4I illustrates the application of this guidance.

7.20 According to paragraphs 18–21 of FASB ASC 810-10-45, the amount of intraentity income or loss eliminated in the preparation of consolidated financial statements is not affected by the existence of a noncontrolling interest.

---

[18] The SEC defines a *master-feeder arrangement* as a registered investment company that invests in a single investment vehicle. Also see paragraphs 5.18–.21 of this guide.

[19] From the SEC's Annual Industry Comment Letter From the Division of Investment Management dated December 30, 1998. The full text of the letter can be accessed under the Division of Investment Management section of the SEC's website.

Financial Statements of Investment Companies

The complete elimination of the intraentity income or loss is consistent with the underlying assumption that consolidated financial statements represent the financial position and operating results of a single economic entity. The elimination of the intraentity income or loss may be allocated between the parent and noncontrolling interests. Revenues, expenses, gains, losses, and net income or loss should be reported in the consolidated financial statements at the consolidated amounts, which include amounts attributable to the owners of the parent and noncontrolling interest. Net income or loss should be attributed to the parent and noncontrolling interest. Losses attributable to the parent and noncontrolling interest in a subsidiary may exceed their interests in the subsidiary's equity. The excess and any further losses attributable to the parent and noncontrolling interest should be attributed to those interests. That is, the noncontrolling interest should continue to be attributed its share of losses even if that attribution results in a deficit noncontrolling interest balance.

Reporting Financial Position [20]

7.21 As stated in FASB ASC 946-210-45-1, investment companies report financial position by presenting either a statement of assets and liabilities or statement of net assets.

7.22 Rule 6.05 of Regulation S-X provides that a statement of net assets may be presented if the amount of investments in securities of unaffiliated issuers is at least 95 percent of total assets.

7.23 The statement of assets and liabilities presents a list of assets and liabilities and an amount for net assets equal to the difference between the totals. A separate schedule of investments is required, as described in paragraphs 7.29–.44.

7.24 FASB ASC 946-210-45-2 notes that the statement of net assets includes a schedule of investments (disclosure requirements for a schedule of investments can be found in FASB ASC 946-210-50, and are also discussed in paragraphs 7.29–.44). Details of related-party balances and other assets and liabilities should be presented in the statement of net assets or notes to the financial statements.

7.25 Rule 6.05 of Regulation S-X includes additional disclosures for registered investment companies. According to regulations, net asset value per share for each class of shares of capital stock outstanding should be presented as noted in chapter 5.

Reporting of Fully Benefit-Responsive Investment Contracts

7.26 FASB ASC 946-210 describes the limited circumstances in which the net assets of investment companies should reflect their net asset value using the contract value of investments attributable to fully benefit-responsive investment contracts (as defined by the FASB ASC glossary). Specifically, FASB

---

[20] Staff Accounting Bulletin (SAB) No. 108, *Considering the Effects of Prior Year Misstatements when Quantifying Misstatements in Current Year Financial Statements*, points out that some registrants do not consider the effects of prior year errors on current year financial statements. This allows the entity to report unadjusted (and improper) assets and liabilities. SAB No. 108 also notes that an immaterial error on the balance sheet could be material on the income statement. The purpose of SAB No. 108 is to address diversity in practice in quantifying financial statement misstatements and the potential build-up of improper accounts on the balance sheet and to provide illustrative examples. See the SEC website for the full text of this SAB.

AAG-INV 7.26

ASC 946-210-45-11 notes that contract value is the relevant measurement attribute for the portion of net assets attributable to fully benefit-responsive investment contracts, provided that the investment company is established under a trust whereby the trust itself is adopted as part of one or more qualified employer-sponsored defined-contribution plans (including both health and welfare and pension plans). A qualified plan refers to a plan that qualifies under the Internal Revenue Code (IRC) by allowing full or partial tax-deferred contributions and tax-deferred investment gains on those contributions. Further, FASB ASC 946-210-50-14 requires disclosure (among other disclosures) of a reconciliation between the beginning and ending balance of the amount presented on the statement of assets and liabilities that represents the difference between net assets reflecting all investments at fair value and net assets for each period in which a statement of changes in net assets is presented.

7.27 FASB ASC 946-210-45-15 requires that the following line items be separately reported on the statement of assets and liabilities, with a parenthetical reference that such amounts are being reported at fair value:

 a. Investments (including traditional guaranteed investment contracts)
 b. Wrapper contracts

7.28 As further stated in FASB ASC 946-210-45-16, the statement of assets and liabilities should present the following:

 a. Total assets
 b. Total liabilities
 c. Net assets reflecting all investments at fair value
 d. Net assets

The net assets amount represents the amount at which participants can transact with the fund and should be used for purposes of preparing per share disclosures required by FASB ASC 946-205-50 and as the beginning and ending balance in the statement of changes in net assets of the fund. The difference between net assets reflecting all investments at fair value and net assets should be presented as a single amount on the face of the statement of assets and liabilities, calculated as the sum of the amounts necessary to adjust the portion of net assets attributable to each fully benefit-responsive investment contract from fair value to contract value. Additional financial statement presentation and disclosure requirements for fully benefit-responsive investment contracts are discussed in paragraphs 17–18 of FASB ASC 946-210-45 and FASB ASC 946-210-50-14 (see paragraphs 7.32, 7.129, and 7.169).

Schedule of Investments

Investment Companies Other Than Nonregistered Investment Partnerships

7.29 As explained in paragraphs 1–3 of FASB ASC 946-210-50, in the absence of regulatory requirements, investment companies other than nonregistered investment partnerships (see paragraph 7.33) should

 a. disclose the name, share, or principal amount of all of the following:
  i. Each investment (including short sales, written options, futures contracts, forward contracts, and other investment-related liabilities) whose fair value constitutes

Financial Statements of Investment Companies

more than 1 percent of net assets. In applying the 1-percent test, total long and total short positions in any one issuer should be considered separately.

ii. All investments in any one issuer whose fair values aggregate more than 1 percent of net assets. In applying the 1-percent test, total long and total short positions in any one issuer should be considered separately.

iii. At a minimum, the 50 largest investments.

b. categorize investments by both of the following characteristics:

i. The type of investment (such as common stocks, preferred stocks, convertible securities, fixed income securities, government securities, options purchased, options written, warrants, futures contracts, loan participations and assignments, short term securities, repurchase agreements, short sales, forward contracts, other investment companies, and so forth).

ii. The related industry, country, or geographic region of the investment.[21]

c. disclose the aggregate other investments (each of which is not required to be disclosed by [*a*]) without specifically identifying the issuers of such investments and categorize them as required by (*b*). The disclosure should include both of the following:

i. The percent of net assets that each such category represents.

ii. The total value for each category in (*b*)(*i*) and (*b*)(*ii*).

As required by paragraphs 20–21 of FASB ASC 825-10-50, in addition to the categorization chosen from the preceding, any other significant concentration of credit risk should be reported. For example, an international fund that categorizes its investments by industry or geographic region should also report a summary of its investments by country, if such concentration is significant.

Additionally, as contemplated by the requirement to disclose certain significant estimates in paragraphs 6–15 of FASB ASC 275-10-50, the use of estimates by directors or trustees, general partners, or others in an equivalent capacity to value securities should be reported.

7.30 Rules 6.03, 6.04, 6.05, 12-12, 12-12A, 12-12B, 12-12C, 12-13, and 12-14 of Regulation S-X apply to registered investment companies. In 2004, the SEC adopted rule and form amendments that among other matters amended Articles 6 and 12 of Regulation S-X to permit a registered investment company to include, under Rule 12-12C, a summary schedule of investments in securities of unaffiliated issuers in its reports to shareholders. See footnote 2 for more information. That SEC rule also allows a money market fund to exclude its portfolio of investments from its shareholder reports. The GAAP requirement discussed in paragraph 7.29 stating that a money market fund present, at a

---

[21] Refer to the March 1, 2012, AICPA Investment Companies Expert Panel Conference Call Highlights. The Expert Panel members shared that generally geographic classification is based on the concentration of the risk and economic exposure (where the principal business actually takes place).

minimum, a condensed schedule of investments for each statement of assets and liabilities has not been modified.

7.31 For public registrants, disclosure relating to repurchase agreements should include the parties to the agreement, the date of the agreement, the total amount to be received upon repurchase, the repurchase date, and a brief description of the nature and terms of the collateral.[22] For public registrants that prepare a summary schedule of investments, fully collateralized repurchase agreements are aggregated and treated as a single issue, with a footnote that indicates the range of dates of the repurchase agreements, the total purchase price of the securities, the total amount to be received upon repurchase, the range of repurchase dates, and a description of securities subject to the repurchase agreements, without regard to the percentage of net assets or issuer.[23] Public registrants are also required to disclose investments in restricted securities, affiliated companies, securities subject to call options, and when-issued securities in the schedule of investments; disclosure of specific information in the notes to the financial statements may also be required by other authoritative FASB guidance.[24] The SEC also requires that each security that is nonincome-producing should be identified as such.[25] Securities pledged as collateral should be identified.[26] When a detailed list of short term investments is presented, such investments may be summarized by issuer, disclosing their ranges of interest rates and maturity dates. For public registrants that prepare a summary schedule of investments, short term debt instruments of the same issuer are aggregated and treated as a single issue, with disclosure indicating the range of interest rates and maturity dates.[27]

7.32 FASB ASC 946-210-45-18 requires the following information be disclosed as part of the schedule of investments, to the extent that schedule is already required under FASB ASC 946-210-50-1 (in the absence of regulatory requirements, for investment companies other than nonregistered investment partnerships), and reconciled to the corresponding line items on the statement of assets and liabilities:

    a. The fair value of each investment contract (including separate disclosure of the fair value of the wrapper contract and the fair value of each of the corresponding underlying investments, if held by the fund, included in that investment contract)

    b. Adjustment from fair value to contract value for each investment contract (if the investment contract is fully benefit responsive)

    c. Major credit ratings of the issuer or wrapper provider for each investment contract

Paragraph 7.191 from FASB ASC 946-210-55-2 illustrates the application of this guidance.

---

[22] Rule 12.12 of Regulation S-X requires that each issue shall be listed separately.

[23] Rules 12.12 and 12.12C of Regulation S-X.

[24] For specific requirements concerning disclosures of information relating to restricted securities and affiliated companies, see sections 404.03 and 404.04 of the SEC's *Codification of Financial Reporting Policies* and Rule 12-14 of Regulation S-X.

[25] See footnote 23.

[26] Rule 4.08(b) of Regulation S-X.

[27] See Rule 12.12C of Regulation S-X.

Investment Companies That Are Nonregistered Investment Partnerships

7.33 As noted in paragraphs 4–6 of FASB ASC 946-210-50, investment partnerships that are exempt from SEC registration under the 1940 Act include hedge funds, limited liability companies, limited liability partnerships, limited duration companies, offshore investment companies with similar characteristics, and commodity pools subject to regulation under the Commodity Exchange Act of 1974. Except for investment partnerships regulated as brokers and dealers in securities under the Securities Exchange Act of 1934 (the 1934 Act) (registered broker-dealers) that manage funds only for those who are officers, directors or trustees, or employees of the general partner, investment partnerships that are exempt from SEC registration under the 1940 Act should, at a minimum, include a condensed schedule of investments in securities owned (sold short) by the partnership at the close of the most recent period. Such a schedule should

    a. categorize investments by all of the following:

        i. Type (such as common stocks, preferred stocks, convertible securities, fixed-income securities, government securities, options purchased, options written, warrants, futures, loan participations, short sales, other investment companies, and so forth).

        ii. Country or geographic region, except for derivative instruments for which the underlying is not a security (see *a*[iv]).[28]

        iii. Industry, except for derivative instruments for which the underlying is not a security (see *a*[iv]).

        iv. Derivatives for which the underlying is not a security, by broad category of underlying (for example, grains and feeds, fibers and textiles, foreign currency, or equity indexes) in place of categories *a*(ii) and *a*(iii).

    b. report the percentage of net assets that each such category represents and the total value and cost (proceeds of sale) for each category in *a*(i) and *a*(ii).

    c. disclose the name, shares or principal amount, value, and type of both of the following:

        i. Each investment (including short sales), constituting more than 5 percent of net assets, except for derivative instruments, as discussed in items *e*–*f*. In applying the 5 percent test, total long and total short positions in any one issuer should be considered separately.

        ii. All investments in any one issuer aggregating more than 5 percent of net assets, except for derivative instruments as discussed in items *e*–*f*. In applying the 5 percent test, total long and total short positions in any one issuer should be considered separately.

---

[28] Refer to the March 1, 2012, AICPA Investment Companies Expert Panel Conference Call Highlights. The Expert Panel members shared that generally geographic classification is based on the concentration of the risk and economic exposure (where the principal business actually takes place).

Investment Companies

    d. aggregate other investments (each of which is 5 percent or less of net assets) without specifically identifying the issuers of such investments and categorize them in accordance with the guidance in *a*. In applying the 5 percent test, total long and total short positions in any one issuer should be considered separately.

    e. disclose the number of contracts, range of expiration dates, and cumulative appreciation (depreciation) for open futures contracts of a particular underlying (such as wheat, cotton, specified equity index, or U.S. Treasury bonds), regardless of exchange, delivery location, or delivery date, if cumulative appreciation (depreciation) on the open contracts exceeds 5 percent of net assets. In applying the 5 percent test, total long and total short positions in any one issuer should be considered separately.

    f. disclose the range of expiration dates and fair value for all other derivatives (such as forwards, swaps [such as interest rate and currency swaps], and options) of a particular underlying (such as foreign currency, wheat, a specified equity index, or U.S. Treasury bonds), regardless of the counterparty, exchange, or delivery date, if fair value exceeds 5 percent of net assets. In applying the 5 percent test, total long and total short positions in any one issuer should be considered separately.

    g. provide the following additional qualitative description for each investment in another nonregistered investment partnership whose fair value constitutes more than 5 percent of net assets:

        i. The investment objective

        ii. Restrictions on redemption (that is, liquidity provisions).

7.34 As explained in paragraphs 11.03–.08 of this guide, if financial statements of an investment partnership that is exempt from SEC registration do not include the required schedule of investments disclosures that are listed in the previous paragraph, and it is practicable for the auditor to determine them or any portion thereof, the auditor should include the information in his or her report expressing the qualified or adverse opinion.

7.35 According to TIS section 6910.16, "Presentation of Boxed Investment Positions in the Condensed Schedule of Investments of Nonregistered Investment Partnerships" (AICPA, *Technical Practice Aids*), long and short positions in the same security (*boxed positions*) should be disclosed on a gross basis in the schedule of investments. Although there may be a perfect economic hedge in boxed positions, the determination of which components of the boxed position would be required to be presented in the schedule of investments should be evaluated separately on a gross basis for the purposes of the 5 percent of net assets test. To the extent that one (or both) of the components is required to be disclosed, such component should be disclosed on the schedule of investments because there may be market risk if one position is removed before the other or experiences settlement costs or losses upon disposition. In the event that only one of the positions is required to be disclosed, a nonregistered investment partnership is not precluded from disclosing both positions.

7.36 TIS section 6910.17, "Disclosure of Long and Short Positions" (AICPA, *Technical Practice Aids*), further explains that if a nonregistered investment partnership has a long position that exceeds 5 percent of net assets and a short position in the same issuer that is less than 5 percent of net assets,

Financial Statements of Investment Companies

the investment partnership is not required to disclose both the long and short position in the condensed schedule of investments. In applying the 5 percent test to determine the investments to be disclosed in the condensed schedule of investments, total long and total short positions in any one issuer should be considered separately. Because the value of the long position exceeds 5 percent of net assets, disclosure of the long position is required; however, disclosure of the short position is not required because the short position does not exceed 5 percent of net assets.

7.37 According to TIS section 6910.18, "Disclosure of an Investment in an Issuer When One or More Securities or One or More Derivative Contracts Are Held—Nonregistered Investment Partnerships" (AICPA, *Technical Practice Aids*), if a nonregistered investment partnership holds one or more securities of the same issuer and one or more derivative contracts for which the underlying is a security of the same issuer, the disclosure on the condensed schedule of investments should be consistent with the classification of the securities on the statement of assets and liabilities. However, derivative contracts may be netted for statement of assets and liabilities presentation when the right of offset exists under FASB ASC 210-20 and 815-10, although the disclosures in the condensed schedule of investments should reflect all open contracts by their economic exposure (that is, long exposure derivative versus short exposure derivative). The netting concepts allowed by FASB ASC 210-20 and 815-10 are not considered for purposes of presentation in the condensed schedule of investments. Those securities (market value) and derivative contracts (appreciation or fair value) that are classified as period-end assets on a gross basis (for derivative contracts, regardless of whether they represent long or short exposures) should be aggregated. To the extent that the sum constitutes more than 5 percent of net assets, the positions should be disclosed in accordance with FASB ASC 946-210-50-6. The investment company should similarly sum all the positions classified as liabilities on a gross basis and determine whether they exceed 5 percent of net assets. Separate computations should be performed for assets and liabilities. Illustrative examples of how to apply the disclosure guidelines can be found in TIS section 6910.18 and paragraph 7.190.

7.38 According to TIS section 6910.30, "Disclosure Requirements of Investments for Nonregistered Investment Partnerships When Their Interest in an Investee Fund Constitutes Less Than 5 Percent of the Nonregistered Investment Partnership's Net Assets" (AICPA, *Technical Practice Aids*), if a nonregistered investment partnership owns an interest in another investment partnership[29] (investee fund) that constitutes less than 5 percent of the nonregistered investment partnership's net assets, the reporting investment partnership must still apply the guidance discussed in paragraph 7.42. Even though the amount of the investment in the investee fund does not exceed 5 percent of the reporting investment partnership's net assets, the reporting investment partnership's proportional share of the investee fund's investments in an individual issuer may nonetheless exceed 5 percent of the reporting investment partnership's net assets because an investee fund may have issued debt (recourse or nonrecourse) to purchase investments or may have significant short positions or other liabilities.

---

[29] Such investment partnerships include, but are not limited to, investment partnerships, funds of funds, special purpose vehicles, disregarded entities, and limited liability companies.

AAG-INV 7.38

7.39 TIS section 6910.31, "The Nonregistered Investment Partnership's Method for Calculating Its Proportional Share of Any Investments Owned by an Investee Fund in Applying the '5 Percent Test' Described in TIS Section 6910.30" (AICPA, *Technical Practice Aids*), further explains that the reporting investment partnership should calculate its proportional share of any investments owned by the investee fund as its percentage ownership of the investee fund. Additionally, consistent with the provisions related to direct investments, indirect long and short positions of the same issuer held by the investee fund should not be netted. The disclosure of investments in issuers exceeding 5 percent of the reporting investment partnership's net assets should be made either on the face of the (condensed) schedule of investments or within the financial statement footnotes.

7.40 TIS section 6910.32, "Additional Financial Statement Disclosures for Nonregistered Investment Partnerships When the Partnership Has Provided Guarantees Related to the Investee Fund's Debt" (AICPA, *Technical Practice Aids*), further explains that in addition to considering the recognition provisions described in FASB ASC 460-10-50, the reporting investment partnership should further disclose any guarantees that it has provided on investee fund debt even though the risk of loss may be remote.

7.41 These disclosure requirements are described in paragraphs 2–4 of FASB ASC 460-10-50 and include the following:

 a. Loss contingencies, such as guarantees of indebtedness of others, including indirect guarantees of indebtedness of others and the nature and amount of the guarantee

 b. Guarantor's obligation, including the nature of the guarantee, the approximate term of the guarantee, how the guarantee arose, and the events or circumstances that would require the guarantor to perform under the guarantee

Investments in Other Investment Companies

7.42 Paragraphs 8–10 of FASB ASC 946-210-50 explain that investments in other investment companies (investees), such as investment partnerships, limited liability companies, and funds of funds, should be considered investments for purposes of applying FASB ASC 946-210-50-1(a) and (b) and 946-210-50-6. If the reporting investment company's proportional share of any investment owned by any individual investee exceeds 5 percent of the reporting company's net assets at the reporting date, each such investment should be named and categorized as discussed in FASB ASC 946-210-50-6. These investee disclosures should be made either in the condensed schedule of investments (as components of the investment in the investee) or a note to that schedule. If information about the investee's portfolio is not available, that fact should be disclosed.

Credit Enhancements

7.43 FASB ASC 946-210-45-8 states that credit enhancements should be shown as a component of the security description in the schedule of investments. As illustrated in paragraphs 11–13 of FASB ASC 946-210-50, the terms, conditions, and other arrangements relating to the enhancement should be disclosed in the notes to the financial statements. In addition, for a put option provided by an affiliate, the schedule of investments should describe the put as from an affiliate, and the notes to the financial statements should include the name and relationship of the affiliate. For a letter of credit, the name of the entity issuing the letter of credit should be disclosed separately.

7.44 Separate disclosure of a credit enhancement should be provided on the face of the schedule of investments and should comply with Rules 6.04.1 and 6.04.3 of Regulation S-X, when applicable.

Assets

7.45 Following are the major asset categories reported in a statement of assets and liabilities and statement of net assets.

7.46 *Investments in securities.* The general practice in the investment company industry is to report investments in securities as the first asset because of their relative importance to total assets. *Securities*, as used in this guide, include but are not limited to stocks, bonds, debentures, notes, rights, warrants, certificates of interest or participation in equity or debt instruments, U.S. government securities, bank certificates of deposit, banker's acceptances, commercial paper, repurchase agreements, purchased options, and tranches of fixed income securities (such as interest-only and principal-only investments). Rule 6.04 of Regulation S-X contains guidance for balance sheets of registered investment companies regarding how to present different types of investments, including those of unaffiliated issuers, investments in and advances to affiliates, and investments other than in securities.

7.47 The definitions of affiliated person and control in the 1940 Act are different than in the FASB ASC glossary. The 1940 Act defines an *affiliated person* as (*a*) any person directly or indirectly owning, controlling, or holding with power to vote, 5 percent or more of the outstanding voting securities of such other person; (*b*) any person 5 percent or more of whose outstanding voting securities are directly or indirectly owned, controlled, or held with power to vote, by such other person; (*c*) any person directly or indirectly controlling, controlled by, or under common control with such other person; (*d*) any officer, director, partner, copartner, or employee of such other person; (*e*) if such other person is an investment company, any investment adviser thereof or any member of an advisory board thereof; and (*f*) if such other person is an unincorporated investment company not having a board of directors or trustees, the depositor thereof. The 1940 Act defines *control* as the power to exercise a controlling influence over the management or policies of a company, unless such power is solely the result of an official position with such company. Any person who owns beneficially, either directly or through one or more controlled companies, more than 25 percent of the voting securities of a company shall be presumed to control such company. Any person who does not so own more than 25 percent of the voting securities of any company shall be presumed not to control such company. A natural person shall be presumed not to be a controlled person within the meaning of this title. Any such presumption may be rebutted by evidence.

7.48 As discussed in FASB ASC 946-320, investment companies should report their investments in debt and equity securities at fair value. Investments in foreign securities should be reported at fair value by converting their foreign currency-denominated value into the functional currency using current exchange rates.

7.49 *Cash.* As described in paragraphs 1–2 of FASB ASC 946-305-45, cash on hand and demand deposits are included under the general caption "Cash."

Amounts held in foreign currencies should be disclosed separately at value, with acquisition cost shown parenthetically.

7.50 Time deposits and other funds subject to withdrawal or usage restrictions should be presented separately from other cash amounts.[30] Applicable interest rates and maturity dates should be disclosed.

7.51 TIS section 1100.15, "Liquidity Restrictions" (AICPA, *Technical Practice Aids*), addresses the potential accounting and auditing implications when a fund or its trustee imposes restrictions on a nongovernmental entity's ability to withdraw its balance in a money market fund or other short term investment vehicle. The question and answer section discusses some considerations for when these restriction events occur, such as determining (*a*) whether any assets subject to these restrictions qualify as cash equivalents or current assets; (*b*) whether disclosures about the risks and uncertainties resulting from such restrictions should be made; (*c*) whether these restrictions may trigger violations of debt covenants and consequently if that liability should be classified as current; (*d*) if the occurrence of such restriction occurs between the balance sheet date and issuance date and whether the financial statements need to be adjusted; and (*e*) if the restriction events call into question the entity's ability to continue as a going concern.

7.52 *Receivables.* As paragraphs 1–2 of FASB ASC 946-310-45 explain, receivables are listed separately at net realizable value for each of the following categories, among others:

- Dividends and interest
- Investment securities sold
- Capital stock sold
- Other accounts receivable, such as receivables from related parties, including expense reimbursement receivables from affiliates, and variation margin on open futures contracts

Receivables denominated in foreign currencies should be converted into the functional currency at current exchange rates and may be categorized with the corresponding functional currency receivables.

7.53 Rule 6.04 of Regulation S-X also contains guidance related to receivables of investment companies which is consistent with the guidance described in the previous paragraph.

7.54 Deferred offering costs, prepaid taxes, and prepaid insurance are normally included under the "Other Assets" caption. Separate amounts are usually not reported unless significant. For public registrants, amounts held by others in connection with short sales, open option contracts, and collateral received for securities loaned[31] should be stated separately.

7.55 *Derivatives.*[32] As explained in FASB ASC 815-10-25-1, an entity should recognize all its derivative instruments in its statement of financial

---

[30] Rule 5.02.1 of Regulation S-X.

[31] Rule 6.04.7 and 6.04.11 of Regulation S-X.

[32] In May 2010, FASB issued the proposed ASU *Accounting for Financial Instruments and Revisions to the Accounting for Derivative Instruments and Hedging Activities—Financial Instruments (Topic 825) and Derivatives and Hedging (Topic 815)*. This was followed up with a discussion paper in February 2011 intended to solicit input on how to improve, simplify, and converge the financial

(continued)

position as either assets or liabilities, depending on the rights or obligations under the contracts. In accordance with FASB ASC 815-10-50-1, an entity with derivative instruments should disclose information to enable users of the financial statements to understand all of the following:

- How and why an entity uses derivative instruments
- How derivative instruments and related hedged items are accounted for under FASB ASC 815, *Derivatives and Hedging*
- How derivative instruments and related hedged items affect an entity's financial position, financial performance, and cash flows

7.56 Further, as discussed in paragraphs 1A–1B of FASB ASC 815-10-50, an entity with derivative instruments should disclose its objective for holding or issuing those instruments, the context needed to understand those objectives, its strategies for achieving those objectives, and information that would enable users of its financial statements to understand the volume of its activity in those instruments for every annual and interim reporting period for which a statement of financial position and statement of financial performance are presented. Regarding the disclosure that would enable users to understand the volume of the entity's activity in those instruments, an entity should select the format and specifics of disclosures relating to its volume of such activity that are the most relevant and practicable for its individual facts and circumstances. Regarding the disclosures of the entity's objectives, context, and strategies, they should be disclosed in the context of each instrument's primary underlying risk exposure (that is, interest rate, credit, foreign exchange rate, interest rate and foreign exchange rate, or overall price). Moreover, those instruments should be distinguished between those used for risk management purposes and those used for other purposes. FASB ASC 815-10-50-4 adds that for derivative instruments not designated as hedging instruments, the description should indicate the purpose of the derivative activity.

7.57 FASB ASC 815-10-50-4A notes that an entity that holds or issues derivative instruments should disclose all of the following for every annual and interim reporting period for which a statement of financial position and statement of financial performance are presented:

- The location and fair value amounts of derivative instruments reported in the statement of financial position
- The location and amount of the gains and losses on derivative instruments reported in either the statement of financial performance or statement of financial position (note that investment companies generally report all gains and losses in the statement of operations)

Paragraphs 4D–4E of FASB ASC 815-10-50 add that this information should be presented separately by type of contract (for example, interest rate contracts, foreign exchange contracts, equity contracts, commodity contracts, credit contracts, and other contracts). The line item(s) in the statement of financial

---

(footnote continued)
reporting requirements for hedging activities. Specifically, it requests stakeholders to comment on whether the IASB's exposure draft, *Hedge Accounting* (issued in December 2010), is a better starting point for any changes to GAAP as it relates to derivatives and hedging activities. Readers should remain alert for developments on this topic, which can be accessed from the Technical Plan and Project Updates page at www.fasb.org.

performance in which the gains and losses for these categories of derivative instruments are included should also be disclosed. Further, these disclosures should be presented in tabular format.[33]

7.58 FASB ASC 815-10-50-4F discusses the disclosure requirements when the entity's policy is to include derivative instruments not designated or qualifying as hedging instruments under FASB ASC 815-20 in its trading activities (for example, as part of its trading portfolio that includes both derivative instruments and nonderivative or cash instruments). For those derivative instruments, the entity can elect to not separately disclose gains and losses, as required by FASB ASC 815-10-50-4C(e), provided that the entity discloses all of the following:

    a. The gains and losses on its trading activities (including both derivative instruments and nonderivative instruments) recognized in the statement of financial performance separately by major types of items (for example, fixed income interest rates, foreign exchange, equity, commodity, and credit)

    b. The line items in the statement of financial performance in which trading activities gains and losses are included

    c. A description of the nature of its trading activities and related risks and how the entity manages those risks

If this disclosure option is elected, the entity should include a footnote in the required tables referencing the use of alternative disclosures for trading activities. FASB ASC 815-10-55-184 and 815-10-55-182 illustrate a footnote referencing the use of alternative disclosures for trading activities and the disclosure of information required in items *a* and *b*, respectively.

7.59 According to FASB ASC 815-10-50-4H, an entity that holds or issues derivative instruments should make the following disclosures for every annual and interim reporting period for which a statement of financial position is presented:

    a. The existence and nature of credit-risk-related contingent features

    b. The circumstances in which credit-risk-related contingent features could be triggered in derivative instruments (or such nonderivative instruments) that are in a net liability position at the end of the reporting period

    c. The aggregate fair value amounts of derivative instruments (or such nonderivative instruments) that contain credit-risk-related contingent features that are in a net liability position at the end of the reporting period

    d. The aggregate fair value of assets that are already posted as collateral at the end of the reporting period

    e. The aggregate fair value of additional assets that would be required to be posted as collateral if the credit-risk-related contingent features were triggered at the end of the reporting period

    f. The aggregate fair value of assets needed to settle the instrument immediately if the credit-risk-related contingent features were triggered at the end of the reporting period

---

[33] In July 2010, the SEC issued a letter to the Investment Company Institute on the disclosure of derivatives in prospectuses and shareholder reports. This letter can be accessed from the SEC website at www.sec.gov under "Division of Investment Management," "Staff Guidance and Studies."

Financial Statements of Investment Companies

FASB ASC 815-10-55-185 illustrates a credit-risk-related contingent feature disclosure.

7.60 FASB ASC 815-10-50-4I states that if information on derivative instruments is disclosed in more than a single footnote, an entity should cross-reference from the derivative instruments footnote to other footnotes in which derivative-instrument-related information is disclosed. FASB ASC 815-10-55-182 illustrates the disclosure of fair value amounts of derivative instruments and gains and losses on derivative instruments in tabular format.

7.61 The FASB ASC glossary defines a *credit derivative* as a derivative instrument that has both of the following characteristics: one or more of its underlyings are related to the credit risk of a specified entity (or a group of entities) or an index based on the credit risk of a group of entities; and it exposes the seller to potential loss from credit-risk-related events specified in the contract. Examples of credit derivatives include, but are not limited to, credit default swaps, credit spread options, and credit index products.

7.62 Paragraphs 4J–4K of FASB ASC 815-10-50 specify that the use of the term *seller* refers to the party that assumes the credit risk, which could be either a guarantor in a guarantee-type contract or any party that provides the credit protection in an option-type contract, a credit default swap, or any other credit derivative contract. A seller of credit derivatives should disclose information about its credit derivatives and hybrid instruments (for example, a credit-linked note) that have embedded credit derivatives to enable users of financial statements to assess their potential effect on the seller's financial position, financial performance, and cash flows. Paragraphs 4K–4L of FASB ASC 815-10-50 discuss the specific required disclosures and a method of presentation.

7.63 FASB ASC 815-10-45-4 states that, with respect to derivative instruments, unless the specified conditions in FASB ASC 210-20-45-1 for a right to offset are met, the fair value of derivatives in loss positions should not be offset against the fair value of derivatives in gain positions. Similarly, amounts recognized as accrued receivables shall not be offset against amounts recognized as accrued payables unless a right of setoff exists.

7.64 As further discussed in FASB ASC 815-10-45-5, without regard to the condition in FASB ASC 210-20-45-1(c) (when the reporting party intends to set off), a reporting entity may offset fair value amounts recognized for derivative instruments and fair value amounts recognized for the right to reclaim cash collateral (a receivable) or the obligation to return cash collateral (a payable) arising from a derivative instrument or instruments recognized at fair value executed with the same counterparty under a master netting arrangement. Solely as they relate to the right to reclaim cash collateral or the obligation to return cash collateral, fair value amounts include amounts that approximate fair value. The preceding sentence shall not be analogized to for any other asset or liability. The fair value recognized for some contracts may include an accrual component for the periodic unconditional receivables and payables that result from the contract; the accrual component included therein may also be offset for contracts executed with the same counterparty under a master netting arrangement. A master netting arrangement exists if the reporting entity has multiple contracts, whether for the same type of derivative instrument or different types of derivative instruments, with a single counterparty that are subject to a contractual agreement that provides for the net settlement of all contracts through a single payment in a single currency in the event of default on, or termination of, any one contract.

7.65 FASB ASC 815-10-45-6 notes that a reporting entity should make an accounting policy decision to offset fair value amounts, pursuant to the preceding paragraph. The reporting entity's choice to offset must be applied consistently. A reporting entity should not offset fair value amounts recognized for derivative instruments without offsetting fair value amounts recognized for the right to reclaim cash collateral or the obligation to return cash collateral. A reporting entity that makes an accounting policy decision to offset fair value amounts recognized for derivative instruments, pursuant to the preceding paragraph but determines that the amount recognized for the right to reclaim cash collateral or the obligation to return cash collateral is not a fair value amount should continue to offset the derivative instruments.

7.66 FASB ASC 815-10-45-7 explains that a reporting entity that has made an accounting policy decision to offset fair value amounts is not permitted to offset amounts recognized for the right to reclaim cash collateral or the obligation to return cash collateral against net derivative instrument positions if those amounts either were not fair value amounts or arose from instruments in a master netting arrangement that are not eligible to be offset.

> **Update 7-1** *Accounting and Reporting:* **Offsetting**
>
> ASU No. 2011-11, *Balance Sheet (Topic 210): Disclosures about Offsetting Assets and Liabilities,* issued in December 2011, is effective for fiscal years beginning on or after January 1, 2013, and interim periods within those annual periods. ASU No. 2011-11 requires enhanced disclosures about financial instruments and derivative instruments that are either offset in accordance with FASB ASC 210-20-45 or 815-10-45, or subject to an enforceable master netting arrangement or similar agreement (irrespective of whether they are offset in accordance with the aforementioned FASB ASC sections). Readers are encouraged to consult the full text of the ASU on FASB's website at www.fasb.org.

Liabilities[34]

7.67 The following categories of liabilities are reported in the statement of assets and liabilities.

7.68 *Accounts payable.* FASB ASC 946-405-45-1 states that accounts payable should be listed separately for investment securities purchased and capital stock reacquired. As noted in FASB ASC 850-10-50-1, separate disclosure is required for material related-party transactions other than compensation arrangements, expense allowances, and other similar items in the normal course of business. However, disclosure of transactions that are eliminated in the preparation of consolidated or combined financial statements is not required in those statements.

---

[34] As mentioned in footnote 32, FASB issued the proposed ASU *Accounting for Financial Instruments and Revisions to the Accounting for Derivative Instruments and Hedging Activities—Financial Instruments (Topic 825) and Derivatives and Hedging (Topic 815).* Entities that follow specialized industry guidance in FASB ASC 946 would continue to initially measure their financial instruments at transaction price. Readers should remain alert for developments on this topic, which can be accessed from the Technical Plan and Project Updates page at www.fasb.org.

Financial Statements of Investment Companies

7.69 *Call or put options written, futures contracts, and securities sold short.* Call or put options written and securities sold short at the close of the period should be presented separately at fair value in the statement of assets and liabilities, with premiums received on written options and proceeds from short sales disclosed parenthetically. Variation margin due to a broker on futures contracts should be disclosed separately, if significant. Details of the securities sold short, options written, and futures contracts should include information about quantities, fair values, and proceeds and should be presented within the schedule of investments, as discussed in paragraph 7.29. Information presented for options written should include the number of shares or principal amount, the fair value of each option, the strike price, and the exercise date.

7.70 *Accrued liabilities.* Accrued liabilities include liabilities for management fees, performance fees, distribution fees, interest, compensation, taxes, and other expenses incurred in the normal course of operations.

7.71 *Notes payable and other debt.* Notes payable to banks, including bank overdrafts, and other debt should be stated at amounts payable, net of unamortized premium or discount, and reported separately, unless the fair value option that is permitted under FASB ASC 825, *Financial Instruments*, is elected. Information relating to unused lines of credit, conditions of credit agreements, and long term debt maturities should be disclosed in the notes to the financial statements. If the fair value option is not elected, the investment company should also disclose the fair value of liabilities, in accordance with the disclosure requirements of FASB ASC 825-10-50. The fair value option is discussed further in paragraphs 7.85–.87.

7.72 On November 5, 2007, the SEC released Staff Accounting Bulletin (SAB) No. 109, *Written Loan Commitments Recorded at Fair Value Through Earnings*, which expresses the views of the staff regarding written loan commitments that are accounted for at fair value through earnings under GAAP. Previously, SAB No. 105, *Application of Accounting Principles to Loan Commitments*, stated that in measuring the fair value of a derivative loan commitment, it would be inappropriate to incorporate the expected net future cash flows related to the associated servicing of the loan. SAB No. 109 supersedes SAB No. 105 and expresses the current view of the SEC staff that is consistent with the guidance in FASB ASC 860-50 and 825. Both topics express the view that the expected net future cash flows related to the associated servicing of the loan should be included in the measurement of all written loan commitments that are accounted for at fair value through earnings.

7.73 *Reverse repurchase agreements.* According to TIS section 6910.22, "Presentation of Reverse Repurchase Agreements" (AICPA, *Technical Practice Aids*), *reverse repurchases agreements* are defined as the sale of a security at a specified price with an agreement to purchase the same or substantially the same security from the same counterparty at a fixed or determinable price at a future date.[35] Because reverse repurchase agreements represent a fixed, determinable obligation of the investment company, such agreements should also be presented at amounts payable, unless the fair value option that is permitted under FASB ASC 825 is elected. A reverse repurchase agreement

---

[35] The FASB ASC glossary definition of a *repurchase agreement* notes that in certain industries, the terminology is reversed (that is, entities in those industries refer to this type of agreement as a *reverse repurchase agreement*). Investment companies may fall into this category of reverse terminology.

denominated in a currency that differs from the reporting currency should be translated at the current exchange rate.

7.74 *Deferred fees.* According to TIS section 6910.27, "Treatment of Deferred Fees" (AICPA, *Technical Practice Aids*), the governing documents of some offshore funds may provide that the investment adviser may elect to defer payment of its management fee, incentive fee, or both. Based on the documents, the deferred fees that are payable to the investment adviser do not take the form of a legal capital account and are settled exclusively in cash. Under this arrangement, the fund retains the fee amount and is obligated to pay the investment adviser the deferred fees at a later date, adjusted for the fund's rate of return (whether positive or negative). In accordance with guidance from paragraph 35 of FASB Concept Statement No. 6, *Elements of Financial Statements—a replacement of FASB Concepts Statement No. 3 (incorporating an amendment of FASB Concepts Statement No. 2)*, the fund should record the cumulative deferred fees as a liability. The indexing of this liability to the fund's rate of return represents a hybrid instrument that has a host debt instrument with an embedded derivative, which has attributes of a total return contract. Although FASB ASC 815-15-25-1 and 815-15-55-190 require the embedded total return contract to be bifurcated from the host debt instrument, the SEC staff has previously indicated[36] that the bifurcation requirements of FASB ASC 815 do not extend beyond measurement to financial statement presentation if the embedded derivative and host debt instrument, together, represent the principal and interest obligations of a debt instrument. Although the fund should fair value the embedded return component of the deferral arrangement, according to the guidance from FASB ASC 815-10-25-1, 815-10-30-1, and 815-10-35-1, generally, the fair value of such return component would be the same as the appreciated or depreciated return of the fund because (*a*) the fund fair values all its investments, whether assets or liabilities, which generally represent substantially all its net assets, and (*b*) if the deferred fee liability was transferred, the transfer would likely be transacted at the current net asset value.[37] The deferred fees and embedded total return contracts associated with deferred fees that are at an appreciated or depreciated position as of the reporting date may be presented as one amount titled "Deferred incentive fees payable" on the statement of assets and liabilities.

7.75 *Other liabilities.* As stated by FASB ASC 946-405-45-2, other liabilities include amounts due to counterparties for collateral on the return of securities loaned, deferred income, and dividends and distributions payable. Payables denominated in foreign currencies should be converted into the functional currency at current exchange rates and may be categorized within the corresponding functional currency payables.

7.76 Rule 6.04 of Regulation S-X contains guidance for balance sheets of registered investment companies regarding how to present other liabilities. It requires the following items to be stated separately on the balance sheet: amounts payable for investment advisory, management, and service fees and the total amount payable to officers and directors or trustees, controlled companies, and other affiliates, excluding any amounts owing to noncontrolled affiliates that arose in the ordinary course of business and that are subject to usual trade terms.

---

[36] Remarks by E. Michael Pierce at the Twenty-Eighth Annual National Conference on Current SEC Developments held December 4–6, 2000.

[37] All concepts of FASB ASC 820 should be considered.

> **© Update 7-2 *Accounting and Reporting*: Reconsideration of Effective Control**
>
> ASU No. 2011-03, *Transfers and Servicing (Topic 860): Reconsideration of Effective Control for Repurchase Agreements*, issued in April 2011, is effective for the first interim or annual period beginning on or after December 15, 2011, and should be applied prospectively to transactions or modifications of existing transactions that occur on or after that date. Early adoption is not permitted.
>
> Refer to section A.01 in appendix A, "Guidance Updates," for more information on this ASU if applicable to your reporting period.

7.77 FASB ASC 860-30-25-5 describes the accounting for noncash collateral by the debtor (obligor) and secured party, which depends on whether the secured party has the right to sell or repledge the collateral and whether the debtor has defaulted. FASB ASC 860-30-25-4 explains that cash collateral used in securities lending transactions should be derecognized by the debtor and recognized by the secured party, not as collateral, but, rather, as proceeds of either a sale or borrowing. FASB ASC 860-30-25-7 explains that many securities lending transactions (including those of many investment companies) often both entitle and obligate the transferor to repurchase or redeem the transferred financial assets before their maturity, and the transferor, accordingly, maintains effective control over those assets. Those transactions should be accounted for as secured borrowings if all the conditions in FASB ASC 860-10-40-24 are met. Transactions in which (*a*) cash (or other securities that the holder is permitted by contract or custom to sell or repledge) received as collateral is considered the amount borrowed, (*b*) the securities loaned are considered pledged as collateral against the cash borrowed and reclassified as set forth in FASB ASC 860-30-25-5(a), and (*c*) any rebate paid to the transferee of securities is interest on the cash that the transferor is considered to have borrowed should be accounted for as secured borrowings.

7.78 FASB ASC 860-10-50 discusses required disclosures for transfers and servicing for all entities. FASB ASC 860-10-50-3 explains that the principal objectives of these disclosures are to provide financial statement users with an understanding of the following:

- A transferor's continuing involvement, if any, with transferred financial assets
- The nature of any restrictions on assets reported by an entity in its statement of financial position that relate to a transferred financial asset, including the carrying amounts of those assets
- How servicing assets and servicing liabilities are reported under FASB ASC 860-50
- For transfers accounted for as sales, if a transferor has continuing involvement with the transferred financial assets, how the transfer of financial assets affects an entity's financial position, financial performance, and cash flows
- For transfers of financial assets accounted for as secured borrowings, how the transfer of financial assets affects an entity's financial position, financial performance, and cash flows

7.79 Under "Pending Content" in FASB ASC 480-10-25-4,[38] mandatorily redeemable financial instruments, such as mandatorily redeemable preferred stock, should be classified as a liability, unless the redemption is required to occur upon liquidation or termination of the reporting entity. Although mutual fund shares are not mandatorily redeemable, other types of equity instruments should be considered under FASB ASC 480, *Distinguishing Liabilities from Equity*.

Fair Value Disclosures

> © **Update 7-3 *Accounting and Reporting*: Fair Value**
>
> ASU No. 2011-04, *Fair Value Measurement (Topic 820): Amendments to Achieve Common Fair Value Measurement and Disclosure Requirements in U.S. GAAP and IFRSs*, issued in May 2011, is effective for public entities during interim and annual periods beginning after December 15, 2011. It is effective for nonpublic entities for annual periods beginning after December 15, 2011. Early application is not permitted for public entities. Nonpublic entities may early implement during interim periods beginning after December 15, 2011. The guidance should be applied prospectively.
>
> Refer to section A.02 in appendix A for more information on this ASU if applicable to your reporting period.

7.80 FASB ASC 820-10-50 discusses the disclosures required for assets and liabilities measured at fair value. FASB ASC 820-10-50-1 explains that for assets and liabilities that are measured at fair value on a recurring basis in periods subsequent to initial recognition, the guidance requires the reporting entity to disclose certain information that enables users of its financial statements to assess the valuation techniques and inputs used to develop those measurements. For recurring fair value measurements using significant unobservable inputs (level 3), the reporting entity is required to disclose certain information to help users assess the effect of the measurements on earnings (or changes in net assets) for the period.

7.81 To meet that objective, FASB ASC 820-10-50-2 requires a reporting entity to disclose the following information for each interim and annual period separately for each class of assets and liabilities. The entity should provide sufficient information to permit reconciliation of the fair value measurement disclosures for the various classes of assets and liabilities to the line items in the statement of financial position:

   a. The fair value measurement at the reporting date.

   b. The level within the fair value hierarchy in which the fair value measurement in its entirety falls, segregating the fair value measurement using any of the following: quoted prices in active markets for identical assets or liabilities (level 1), significant other observable inputs (level 2), or significant unobservable inputs (level 3).

---

[38] FASB ASC 480-10-65-1 discusses the various effective dates and deferrals related to FASB ASC 480-10 for mandatorily redeemable financial instruments of certain nonpublic entities and certain mandatorily redeemable noncontrolling interests.

Financial Statements of Investment Companies

- c. The amounts of significant transfers between level 1 and level 2 of the fair value hierarchy and the reasons for the transfers. Significant transfers into each level should be disclosed separately from transfers out of each level. For this purpose, significance should be judged with respect to earnings and total assets or total liabilities or, when changes in fair value are recognized in other comprehensive income, with respect to total equity. A reporting entity should disclose and consistently follow its policy for determining when transfers between levels are recognized. The policy about the timing of recognizing transfers should be the same for transfers into the levels as that for transfers out of the levels. Examples of policies for when to recognize the transfers are the actual date of the event or change in circumstances that caused the transfer, the beginning of the reporting period, and the end of the reporting period.
- d. For fair value measurements using significant unobservable inputs (level 3), a reconciliation of the beginning and ending balances, separately presenting changes during the period attributable to any of the following:
    - i. Total gains or losses for the period (realized and unrealized), separately presenting those gains or losses included in earnings (or changes in net assets), and gains or losses recognized in other comprehensive income and a description of where those gains or losses included in earnings (or changes in net assets) are reported in the statement of income (or activities) or other comprehensive income.
    - ii. Purchases, sales, issuances, and settlements (each type disclosed separately).
    - iii. Transfers in or out of level 3 and the reasons for those transfers. Significant transfers into level 3 should be disclosed separately from significant transfers out of level 3. For this purpose, significance should be judged with respect to earnings and total assets or total liabilities or, when changes in fair value are recognized in other comprehensive income, with respect to total equity. A reporting entity should disclose and consistently follow its policy for determining when transfers between levels are recognized. The policy about the timing of recognizing transfers should be the same for transfers into level 3 as that for transfers out of level 3. Examples of policies for when to recognize the transfers are: the actual date of the event or change in circumstances that caused the transfer, the beginning of the reporting period, and the end of the reporting period.
- e. The amount of the total gains or losses for the period in item $d(i)$ included in earnings (or changes in net assets) that are attributable to the change in unrealized gains or losses relating to those assets and liabilities still held at the reporting date and a description of where those unrealized gains or losses are reported in the statement of income (or activities).
- f. For fair value measurements using significant other observable inputs (level 2) and significant unobservable inputs (level 3), a

AAG-INV 7.81

description of the valuation technique (or multiple valuation techniques) used, such as the market approach, income approach, or cost approach, and the inputs used in determining the fair values of each class of assets or liabilities. If there has been a change in the valuation technique(s) (for example, changing from a market approach to an income approach or the use of an additional valuation technique), the reporting entity should disclose that change and the reason for making it. For examples of disclosures that a reporting entity may present to comply with the requirement to disclose the inputs used in measuring fair value in this paragraph, see paragraphs 22A–B of FASB ASC 820-10-55.

7.82 FASB ASC 820-10-50-2A explains that for equity and debt securities, class should be determined on the basis of the nature and risks of the investments in a manner consistent with the guidance in FASB ASC 320-10-50-1B and, if applicable, should be the same as the guidance on major security type, as described in FASB ASC 942-320-50-2, even if the equity securities or debt securities are not within the scope of FASB ASC 320-10-50-1B. For all other assets and liabilities, judgment is needed to determine the appropriate classes of assets and liabilities for which disclosures about fair value measurements should be provided. Fair value measurement disclosures for each class of assets and liabilities often will require greater disaggregation than the reporting entity's line items in the statement of financial position. A reporting entity should determine the appropriate classes for those disclosures on the basis of the nature and risks of the assets and liabilities and their classification in the fair value hierarchy (that is, levels 1, 2, and 3). In determining the appropriate classes for fair value measurement disclosures, the reporting entity should consider the level of disaggregated information required for specific assets and liabilities under other FASB ASC guidance. For example, under FASB ASC 815, disclosures about derivative instruments are presented separately by type of contract such as interest rate contracts, foreign exchange contracts, equity contracts, commodity contracts, and credit contracts. The classification of the asset or liability in the fair value hierarchy also should affect the level of disaggregation because of the different degrees of uncertainty and subjectivity involved in level 1, level 2, and level 3 measurements. For example, the number of classes may need to be greater for fair value measurements using significant unobservable inputs (that is, level 3 measurements) to achieve the disclosure objectives because level 3 measurements have a greater degree of uncertainty and subjectivity. FASB ASC 820-10-50-3 states that for derivative assets and liabilities, the reporting entity should present both the fair value disclosures discussed in paragraph 7.81*a–c* on a gross basis and the reconciliation disclosures discussed in paragraph 7.81*d–e* on a gross or net basis.

7.83 FASB ASC 820-10-50-6A requires disclosures for investments that are within the scope of paragraphs 4–5 of FASB ASC 820-10-15 and measured at fair value on a recurring or nonrecurring basis during the period and that enable users of financial statements to understand the nature and risks of the investments and whether the investments are probable of being sold at amounts different from net asset value per share (or its equivalent). These disclosures are required regardless of whether the practical expedient has been applied. These disclosures, to the extent applicable, are required for each interim and annual period separately for each class of investment (class of investment should be determined on the basis of the nature and risks of the

Financial Statements of Investment Companies

investments in a manner consistent with the guidance for major security types in FASB ASC 320-10-50-1B). The required disclosures are as follows:

   a. The fair value (as determined by applying paragraphs 59–62 of FASB ASC 820-10-35) of the investments in the class and a description of the significant investment strategies of the investee(s) in the class.
   b. For each class of investment that includes investments that can never be redeemed with the investees, but the reporting entity receives distributions through the liquidation of the underlying assets of the investees, the reporting entity's estimate of the period of time over which the underlying assets are expected to be liquidated by the investees.
   c. The amount of the reporting entity's unfunded commitments related to investments in the class.
   d. A general description of the terms and conditions upon which the investor may redeem investments in the class (for example, quarterly redemption with 60 days' notice).
   e. The circumstances in which an otherwise redeemable investment in the class (or a portion thereof) might not be redeemable (for example, investments subject to a lockup or gate). Also, for those otherwise redeemable investments that are restricted from redemption as of the reporting entity's measurement date, the reporting entity should disclose its estimate of when the restriction from redemption might lapse. If an estimate cannot be made, the reporting entity should disclose that fact and how long the restriction has been in effect.
   f. Any other significant restriction on the ability to sell investments in the class at the measurement date.
   g. If a reporting entity determines that it is probable that it will sell an investment or investments for an amount different from net asset value per share (or its equivalent), as described in FASB ASC 820-10-35-62, the reporting entity should disclose the total fair value of all investments that meet the criteria in FASB ASC 820-10-35-62 and any remaining actions required to complete the sale.
   h. If a group of investments would otherwise meet the criteria in FASB ASC 820-10-35-62, but the individual investments to be sold have not been identified (for example, if a reporting entity decides to sell 20 percent of its investments in private equity funds, but the individual investments to be sold have not been identified), so the investments continue to qualify for the practical expedient in FASB ASC 820-10-35-59, the reporting entity should disclose its plans to sell and any remaining actions required to complete the sale(s).

Paragraph 7.193, from FASB ASC 820-10-55-64A, provides an example of the disclosures required in FASB ASC 820-10-50-6A.

7.84 TIS section 2220.26, "Categorization of Investments for Disclosure Purposes" (AICPA, *Technical Practice Aids*), explains that certain entities that specialize in one particular investment category or have a significant investment in one such category should categorize investments and tailor disclosures to address the concentrations of risk that are specifically attributable to the investments. For example, a private equity fund of funds should not simply categorize its investments as private equity" because this categorization is not specific enough to address the nature and risks of the investee funds. More specific categorization, perhaps relating to industry; geography; vintage year; or the strategy of the investees (venture, buyout, mezzanine), may be more appropriate and useful to the reader.

Fair Value Option

7.85 FASB ASC 825 creates a fair value option under which an entity may irrevocably elect fair value as the initial and subsequent measure for many financial instruments and certain other items, with changes in fair value recognized in earnings as those changes occur. FASB ASC 825-10-35-4 explains that a business entity should report unrealized gains and losses on items for which the fair value option has been elected in earnings at each subsequent reporting date. An election is made on an instrument-by-instrument basis (with certain exceptions), generally when an instrument is initially recognized in the financial statements. The fair value option need not be applied to all identical items, except as required by FASB ASC 825-10-25-7. Most financial assets and liabilities are eligible to be recognized using the fair value option, as are firm commitments for financial instruments and certain nonfinancial contracts.

7.86 As explained by FASB ASC 825-10-15-5, specifically excluded from eligibility are an investment in a subsidiary that the entity is required to consolidate; an interest in a VIE that the entity is required to consolidate; an employer's and a plan's obligations for pension benefits, other postretirement benefits (including health care and life insurance benefits), postemployment benefits, employee stock option and stock purchase plans, and other deferred compensation arrangements (or assets representing net overfunded positions in those plans); financial assets and liabilities recognized under leases (this does not apply to a guarantee of a third-party lease obligation or contingent obligation arising from a cancelled lease); deposit liabilities of depository institutions; and financial instruments that are, in whole or in part, classified by the issuer as a component of shareholder's equity (including temporary equity) (for example, a convertible debt security with a noncontingent beneficial conversion feature).

7.87 FASB ASC 825-10-45 and 825-10-50 also include presentation and disclosure requirements designed to facilitate comparisons between entities that choose different measurement attributes for similar types of assets and liabilities. Paragraphs 1–2 of FASB ASC 825-10-45 state that entities should report assets and liabilities that are measured using the fair value option in a manner that separates those reported fair values from the carrying amounts of similar assets and liabilities measured using another measurement attribute. To accomplish that, an entity should either (*a*) report the aggregate of both fair value and nonfair-value items on a single line, with the fair value amount parenthetically disclosed or (*b*) present separate lines for the fair value carrying amounts and the nonfair-value carrying amounts. As discussed in FASB ASC 825-10-25-3, upfront costs and fees, such as debt issue costs, may not be deferred for items for which the fair value option has been elected.

Net Assets

7.88 FASB ASC 946-20-50-11 requires all investment companies to disclose only two components of capital on the balance sheet: shareholder capital

Financial Statements of Investment Companies

and distributable earnings. The components of distributable earnings, on a tax basis, should be disclosed in a note to the financial statements. This information enables investors to determine the amount of accumulated and undistributed earnings that they potentially could receive in the future and on which they could be taxed. Additionally, as stated by FASB 946-20-50-12, the notes should disclose the tax-basis components of distributable earnings as of the most recent tax year-end, including undistributed ordinary income, undistributed long term capital gains, capital loss carryforwards, and unrealized appreciation (depreciation).

7.89 The statement or the notes should also disclose information about the following:[39]

a. Units of capital, including the title of each class of capital shares or other capital units, the number authorized, the number outstanding, and the dollar amount.

b. Paid-in capital, which includes the net proceeds received on the sale of capital shares less the cost of reacquired shares and the return of capital distributions (that is, the tax return of capital distributions [see paragraph 7.130]). In addition, certain differences between GAAP-basis income or gain amounts and tax-basis amounts distributed from income or gain are reclassified to paid-in capital in the period in which such differences become permanent differences (see paragraph 7.130).

7.90 As further explained by FASB ASC 946-20-50-13, if a provision for deferred income taxes on unrealized appreciation exists, it should be charged against the unrealized gains account and disclosed as such in the statement of operations. Explanations should be provided for the differences between the total of these amounts and distributable earnings (accumulated losses). FASB ASC 946-20-50-14 notes that investment partnerships and other pass-through entities should aggregate all elements of equity into partners' capital because the results from operations are deemed distributed to each partner.

7.91 As defined by the FASB ASC glossary, *net asset value per share* is the amount of net assets attributable to each share of capital stock (other than senior equity securities [that is, preferred stock]) outstanding at the close of the period. It excludes the effects of assuming conversion of outstanding convertible securities, regardless of whether their conversion would have a diluting effect. As further explained in FASB ASC 946-505-50-1, net asset value per share should be disclosed for each class of shares.

7.92 Consistent with FASB Emerging Issues Task Force (EITF) Topic No. D-98, SEC Staff Announcement "Classification and Measurement of Redeemable Securities," a registered investment company should not include preferred stock under the caption "Net Assets" if the investment company may be required to redeem all or part of the preferred stock upon failure to

---

[39] Rules 6.04.16 and 604.17 of Regulation S-X require such information to be included on the face of the statement of assets and liabilities, if such statement is presented. In addition, components of distributable earnings are required to be presented separately.

The requirements of SEC Regulation S-X to disclose individual components of distributable earnings (undistributed income, accumulated gains [losses], and unrealized appreciation [depreciation]) under Rules 6.04.16 and 604.17 and distributions (income, gain, and return of capital) under Rule 6-09.3 continue to apply for SEC registrants, and preparers should continue to accumulate and disclose the necessary additional information.

AAG-INV 7.92

satisfy statistical coverage requirements imposed by its governing documents or a rating agency. The Chief Accountant's Office of the Division of Investment Management released more guidance specific to the application of the "Pending Content" guidance in FASB ASC 480-10 to closed-end funds. Of most significance, the staff indicated that distributions to preferred stockholders should be presented below net investment income on the statement of operations, the statement of changes in net assets, and financial highlights as a component of the net increase (decrease) in net assets resulting from investment operations. The staff indicated that the "Pending Content" in FASB ASC 480-10 provides guidance on preferred stock arrangements that are redeemable on a fixed or determinable date.

7.93 FASB ASC 480-10-65-1 describes the effective date and transition information for all "Pending Content" guidance in FASB ASC 480-10 that is linked to that paragraph. For instruments issued by nonpublic entities that are not SEC registrants and that are mandatorily redeemable on fixed dates for amounts that are either fixed or determined by reference to an interest rate index, a currency index, or another external index, the classification, measurement, and disclosure provisions of FASB ASC 480-10 were effective for fiscal years beginning after December 15, 2004. The guidance in FASB ASC 480-10 is indefinitely deferred pending further FASB action for mandatorily redeemable financial instruments issued by nonpublic entities that are not SEC registrants, other than those mandatorily redeemable instruments described previously. During the indefinite deferral, FASB plans to reconsider implementation issues and, perhaps, classification or measurement guidance for those instruments in conjunction with FASB's ongoing project on liabilities and equity. Mandatorily redeemable financial instruments issued by SEC registrants are not eligible for that deferral, even if the entity meets the definition of a nonpublic entity in FASB ASC 480-10. Those entities should follow the effective dates required by FASB ASC 480-10 and related guidance, including the deferral for certain mandatorily redeemable noncontrolling interests, as appropriate. If an entity is a nonpublic entity that is not an SEC registrant and (*a*) has issued shares that are required to be redeemed under related agreements, and (*b*) if the shares are issued with the redemption agreement and the required redemption relates to those specific underlying shares, then the shares are mandatorily redeemable and fall under the deferral stated previously.

7.94 FASB ASC 480-10-65-1 also explains that the effective date of FASB ASC 480-10 is deferred for certain mandatorily redeemable noncontrolling interests (of all entities, public and nonpublic) as follows:

    a. For mandatorily redeemable noncontrolling interests that would not have to be classified as liabilities by the subsidiary under the liquidation exception in paragraphs 4 and 6 of FASB ASC 480-10-25 but would be classified as liabilities by the parent in consolidated financial statements, the classification and measurement provisions of FASB ASC 480-10 are deferred indefinitely pending further FASB action.

    b. For other mandatorily redeemable noncontrolling interests that were issued before November 5, 2003, the measurement provisions of FASB ASC 480-10 are deferred indefinitely, both for the parent in consolidated financial statements and for the subsidiary that issued the instruments that result in the mandatorily redeemable noncontrolling interest, pending further FASB action. For those instruments, the measurement guidance for redeemable shares and noncontrolling interests in other predecessor literature (for example, in EITF Topic No. D-98) continues to apply during the deferral period. However, the classification provisions of FASB ASC 480-10 are not deferred.

FASB plans to reconsider implementation issues and, perhaps, classification or measurement guidance for those noncontrolling interests during the deferral period, in conjunction with FASB's ongoing projects. During the deferral period for certain mandatorily redeemable noncontrolling interests, all public entities as well as nonpublic entities that are SEC registrants are required to follow the disclosure requirements in paragraphs 1–3 of FASB ASC 480-10-50, as well as disclosures required by other applicable guidance. Further, this project is a joint project between FASB and the International Accounting Standards Board.

7.95 Under "Pending Content" in FASB ASC 480-10-25, financial instruments that are mandatorily redeemable on a fixed date or upon the occurrence of an event certain to occur should be classified initially as liabilities. Contingently redeemable securities, such as those described in paragraph 7.92, are not within the scope of FASB ASC 480-10-25 unless and until the contingency occurs, at which time the instruments should be reclassified as liabilities. "Pending Content" in FASB ASC 480-10-25-7 explains that a financial instrument that will be redeemed only upon the occurrence of a conditional event would be assessed at each reporting period to determine whether circumstances have changed such that the instrument now meets the definition of a mandatorily redeemable instrument (that is, the event is no longer conditional). If the event has occurred, the condition is resolved, or the event has become certain to occur, the financial instrument is reclassified as a liability. Therefore, with respect to contingently redeemable securities for which the contingency has not occurred, the guidance discussed in paragraph 7.92 should continue to be followed by registered investment companies.

Statement of Operations

7.96 As described by FASB ASC 946-225-45-1, the objective of the statement of operations is to present the increase or decrease in net assets resulting from all the company's investment activities by reporting investment income from dividends, interest, and other income less expenses, the amounts of realized gains or losses from investment and foreign currency transactions, and changes in unrealized appreciation or depreciation of investments and foreign currency-denominated assets and liabilities for the period. That format helps the user understand the contribution of each aspect of investment activity to the company's overall operations.

Investment Income

7.97 *Dividend income.* FASB ASC 946-320-25-4 states that dividend income is recorded on the ex-dividend date, not the declaration, record, or payable date, because on the ex-dividend date, the quoted market price of listed securities and other market-traded securities tends to be affected by the exclusion of the dividend declared. As noted by FASB ASC 946-20-50-9, dividends from affiliates and controlled companies should be disclosed.

7.98 Rule 6.07.1 of Regulation S-X for SEC registrants also requires that income from affiliates and controlled companies be disclosed. Investment companies are also required to comply with FASB ASC 850, *Related Party Disclosures*. (Chapter 2, "Investment Accounts," of this guide discusses noncash dividends, dividends in arrears on preferred stocks, and dividends from other than distributable earnings.)

7.99 *Interest income.* Interest income (including amortization of premiums and accretion of discounts) is generally accrued on all debt securities. However, chapter 2 discusses special reporting requirements for interest on high-yield debt securities, bonds in default, and other kinds of securities such as payment-in-kind bonds and step bonds. Interest earned on securities of affiliates and controlled companies should be disclosed separately.

7.100 *Other income.* Other income includes fee income from securities loaned and miscellaneous sources. Individual items, if material, should be disclosed separately. Rule 6.07 of Regulation S-X requires the separate disclosure of any category of income that exceeds 5 percent of the total investment income.

Expenses

7.101 As stated in FASB ASC 946-225-45-3, all of the following expenses are commonly reported separately:

- *a.* Investment advisory (management) fees (or compensation).
- *b.* Administration fees payable to an affiliate (if accrued under a separate agreement).
- *c.* Shareholder service costs, including fees and expenses for the transfer agent and dividend disbursing agent.
- *d.* Distribution (12b-1) expenses (discussed in chapter 8, "Other Accounts and Considerations," of this guide).
- *e.* Custodian fees.
- *f.* Cost of reports to shareholders.
- *g.* Federal and state income taxes. These expenses should be shown separately after the income category to which they apply, such as investment income and realized or unrealized gains. (Chapter 6, "Taxes," of this guide discusses the provision for taxes for entities that do not meet the requirements necessary to qualify as a regulated investment company [RIC].)
- *h.* Other taxes. (Foreign withholding taxes should be deducted from the relevant income item and disclosed parenthetically or shown as a separate contraitem in the "Income" section.)
- *i.* Interest (including interest on debt, bank borrowings, and reverse repurchase agreements).
- *j.* Dividends on securities sold short.
- *k.* Professional fees.
- *l.* Directors' or trustees' fees.
- *m.* Registration fees and expenses (discussed in chapter 8).

Regulation S-X requires separate disclosure of each expense exceeding 5 percent of total expenses. Additionally, the notes to the financial statements should

Financial Statements of Investment Companies

include the total amounts by which expenses are increased and list each category that is increased by at least 5 percent of total expenses.[40]

7.102 Amounts paid to affiliates or related parties (such as advisory fees, administration fees, distribution fees, brokerage commissions, and sales charges) should be disclosed, in accordance with FASB ASC 850. Significant provisions of related-party agreements, including the basis for determining management, advisory, administration, or distribution fees, and, also, other amounts paid to affiliates or related parties should be described in a note to the financial statements.

7.103 As explained in FASB ASC 946-20-05-11, an adviser or a third party may voluntarily or involuntarily waive its fee and reimburse expenses (waivers). An example of an involuntary waiver is when the advisory agreement (or other regulation or agreements that are either outside the adviser's control or require shareholder approval) provides that the adviser should reimburse the investment company for expenses in excess of a specified percentage of average net assets. As further described in FASB ASC 946-20-50-7, all voluntary and involuntary waivers should be disclosed on the face of the statement of operations as a reduction of total expenses. The expense ratio in the financial highlights should be shown net of voluntary and involuntary waivers. The effect of only voluntary waivers on the expense ratio should be disclosed (either as the basis point effect on the ratio or as the gross expense ratio) in a note to, or as part of, the financial highlights. In addition, the terms of all voluntary and involuntary waivers should be disclosed in the notes to the financial statements.

7.104 As noted in FASB ASC 946-20-50-4, if a 12b-1 distribution reimbursement plan[41] provides for the carryover of unreimbursed costs to subsequent periods, the terms of reimbursement and the unreimbursed amount should be disclosed.

7.105 The disclosure requirements in Section 30(e)(5) of the 1940 Act address aggregate remuneration to directors or trustees and each company of which any officer or director is an affiliated person. The auditor may conclude that the investment company has complied with the requirements by disclosure in the notes to the financial statements or in another manner that the investment company's management or legal counsel determines to be appropriate.

7.106 As noted in FASB ASC 946-20-05-9, an investment company may have a brokerage service arrangement with a broker-dealer or an affiliate of a broker-dealer under which the broker-dealer (or its affiliate), in connection with the investment company's brokerage transactions directed to the broker-dealer, provides or pays for services to the investment company (other than brokerage and research services as those terms are used in Section 28[e] of the 1934 Act). As further explained in FASB ASC 946-20-45-3, the relevant expense caption on the statement of operations and the expense ratio in the financial highlights should include the amount that would have been incurred by the investment company for such services had it paid for the services directly in an arm's length

---

[40] Rule 6.07(g) of Regulation S-X.
[41] The FASB ASC glossary defines a *reimbursement plan* as a plan that provides for a 12b-1 fee, payable by the fund that may not exceed the lesser of an annual percentage of the fund's average net assets or actual costs incurred by the distributor net of contingent deferred sales load received by the distributor.

transaction. Such amounts should also be shown as a corresponding reduction in total expenses, captioned as "Fees paid indirectly."

7.107 As illustrated in FASB ASC 946-20-45-5, expense offset arrangements under which a third party explicitly reduces its fees by a specified or readily ascertainable amount for services provided to the investment company in exchange for use of the investment company's assets should be presented in the statement of operations, the expense ratio in the financial highlights, and the notes to the financial statements in the same manner as brokerage service arrangements.

7.108 As discussed in FASB ASC 946-20-05-10, investment companies organized as limited partnerships typically receive advisory services from the general partner. Many partnerships pay fees for such services, chargeable as expenses to the partnership; others allocate net income from the limited partners' capital accounts to the general partner's capital account; and still others employ a combination of the two methods. Further, FASB ASC 946-20-45-4 notes that the amounts of any such payments or allocations should be presented in either the statement of operations or the statement of changes in partners' capital in accordance with the partnership agreement. FASB ASC 946-20-50-5 states that the method of computing such payments or allocations should be described in the notes to the financial statements.

7.109 According to TIS section 6910.29, "Allocation of Unrealized Gain (Loss), Recognition of Carried Interest, and Clawback Obligations" (AICPA, *Technical Practice Aids*), the governing documents of some nonregistered investment partnerships may contain provisions that do not allow allocations of unrealized gains or losses or do not require the recognition of carried interest (also referred to as *carry, incentive,* or *performance fees and allocations*) and clawback obligations (also referred to as *lookback, negative carried interest,* or *general partner*[42] *giveback*) until a specified date or time (for example, at the time of the partnership's liquidation or termination) or the occurrence of a specific event (such as the actual disposition of an investment). Often, in these cases, the partnership's investments are either not marketable or of such limited liquidity that interim valuations are highly subjective, and the intent of the provision is to delay the general partner's receipt of incentive allocations in cash until the gains can be measured objectively.

7.110 TIS section 6910.29 also explains that if a nonregistered investment partnership reports capital by investor class, cumulative unrealized gains (losses), carried interest, and clawback provisions should be reflected in the equity balances of each class of shareholder or partner at the balance sheet date as if the investment company had realized all assets and settled all liabilities at the fair values reported in the financial statements and allocated all gains and losses and distributed the net assets to each class of shareholder or partner at the reporting date consistent with the provisions of the partnership's governing documents. Further discussion of each of these items follows:

    a. Cumulative unrealized gains (losses). Cumulative unrealized gains (losses) should be included in the ending balances of each class

---

[42] Various terms may be used by different legal structures as the equivalents of *general partner* and *limited partner* (for example, *managing member* and *member* for limited liability companies). For convenience, the terms *partnership, general partner,* and *limited partner* are used throughout the Technical Questions and Answers (TIS) section 6910.29, "Allocation of Unrealized Gain (Loss), Recognition of Carried Interest, and Clawback Obligations" (AICPA, *Technical Practice Aids*), discussion but are intended to refer to any equivalent structure.

AAG-INV 7.107

Financial Statements of Investment Companies

of shareholders' or partners' interest in the reporting entity at the reporting date, and the changes in such amounts should be reported in the changes in net asset value and partners' capital for the reporting period.

b. *Carried interest.* The carried interest generally is due to the investment manager, an affiliated entity, or both and is either in the form of a fee (usually for offshore funds) or as an allocation from the limited partners' capital accounts, pro rata, to the general partner's capital account (usually for domestic funds). Although many variations exist, the investment manager is often entitled to receive its carry on a deal-by-deal basis. On this basis, as individual investments are sold, the investment proceeds are allocated based on a specific methodology defined in the governing documents to determine the amount of carry, if any, to which the investment manager is entitled. In presenting each class of shareholders' or partners' interest in the net assets as of the reporting date, the financial statements should consider the carry formula as if the investment company had realized all assets and settled all liabilities at their reported fair value and allocated all gains and losses and distributed the net assets to each class of shareholder or partner at the reporting date.

c. *Clawback.* Although all classes of shareholder or partner may be subject to clawback provisions in the governing documents, a clawback most frequently involves an obligation on the part of the investment manager to return previously received incentive allocations to the investment fund due to subsequent losses. Such clawback amounts, when paid, are typically distributed to other investors. The impact of a clawback should be calculated as of each reporting date under the methodology specified in the fund's governing documents.

7.111 TIS section 6910.29 notes that, consistent with FASB ASC 310-10-45-14, such an obligation should not be recognized as an asset (receivable) in the entity's financial statements unless substantial evidence exists of the ability and intent to pay within a reasonably short period of time. Rather, in most instances, the obligation should be reflected as a deduction from the general partner's capital account. The specific circumstances, including whether the clawback represents a legal obligation to return or contribute funds to the reporting entity, require consideration before determining whether a clawback, resulting in a negative general partner capital balance (that is, contraequity), is recognized in the financial statements. Additionally, it may not be appropriate to reflect a negative general partner capital balance (and a corresponding increase to limited partner capital balances) if the general partner does not have the financial resources to make good on its obligation.

7.112 Even if not recognized within the capital accounts, at a minimum, it would be appropriate to disclose the existence of a clawback in the footnotes to the financial statements because in almost all cases, the existence of the clawback would modify the manner in which future distributions are made.

7.113 *Deferred fees.*[43] According to TIS section 6910.27, because the fund directly earns or incurs the income, expenses, net realized gains or losses, and

---

[43] For further discussion of deferred fee arrangements, see paragraph 7.74.

unrealized appreciation or depreciation on the deferred fee retained in the fund, such amounts should be presented within their respective line items in the investment company's statement of operations. The net change in unrealized appreciation or depreciation on the total return contracts associated with the deferred fees should be reported in earnings (that is, reflected as an expense [appreciation of deferred fees] or a negative expense [depreciation of deferred fees] of the fund, rather than an allocation of earnings or losses) and, following the guidance from FASB ASC 850, should be presented separately from the current period management or incentive fee.

Net Investment Income

7.114 As noted in FASB ASC 946-225-45-5, the excess of investment income over total expenses should be shown as net investment income (or loss). Further, as explained in FASB ASC 946-225-50-1, any income tax provision relating to net investment income should be disclosed separately.

Net Realized Gain or Loss From Investments and Foreign Currency Transactions

7.115 *Net realized gain or loss from investments.* As explained in FASB ASC 946-225-45-6 and 946-225-50-2, the statement of operations should disclose net realized gains or losses. Net realized gains or losses resulting from sales or other disposals should be reported net of brokerage commissions. Gains or losses arising from in-kind redemptions should be disclosed. The net realized gains or losses from investments and net realized gains or losses from foreign currency transactions may be reported separately or combined.

7.116 Registered investment companies should disclose in the statement of operations net realized gains or losses by major kinds of investment transactions as required by Rule 6.07.7 of Regulation S-X. An income tax provision charged against realized gains should also be disclosed separately.

7.117 *Net realized gains or losses from foreign currency transactions.* As explained in FASB ASC 946-225-45-6 and 946-225-50-2, net gains or losses from assets or liabilities denominated in foreign currencies during the period should be reported separately. If separate reporting of foreign currency effects on realized gains or losses from investments is elected, those effects should be included in this caption. Guidance for computing such amounts appears in chapter 2. The net realized gains or losses from foreign currency transactions may be reported separately or combined with net realized gains or losses from investments. Notes to the financial statements should state an entity's practice of either including or excluding that portion of realized and unrealized gains and losses from investments that result from foreign currency changes with or from other foreign currency gains and losses.

7.118 The 1940 Act requires the disclosure of proceeds from sales of securities and the cost of securities purchased.[44] The SEC staff permits exclusion of short term securities (those securities with a maturity of one year or less) from this disclosure. Information about common stocks, bonds, and preferred stocks may be combined or disclosed separately.

---

[44] Section 30(e)(6) of the 1940 Act.

Net Increase (Decrease) in Unrealized Appreciation or Depreciation on Investments and Translation of Assets and Liabilities in Foreign Currencies

7.119 *Net increase (decrease) in unrealized appreciation or depreciation on investments.* As discussed in FASB ASC 946-225-45-6, changes in net unrealized appreciation or depreciation during the period should be reported in the statement of operations. The major components of unrealized appreciation or depreciation should be disclosed in a manner that is consistent with the guidance discussed in paragraph 7.115. Either combining the net unrealized gains or losses from investments with net unrealized gains or losses from foreign currency transactions or reporting them separately is permissible. Any provision for deferred taxes should be reported separately.

7.120 *Net increase (decrease) in unrealized appreciation or depreciation on translation of assets and liabilities in foreign currencies.* As stated in FASB ASC 946-225-45-6, the net change during the period from translating assets and liabilities denominated in foreign currencies should be reported under this caption. Guidance for computing such amounts appears in chapter 2.

Net Increase From Payments by Affiliates and Net Gains (Losses) Realized on the Disposal of Investments in Violation of Restrictions

7.121 As illustrated in FASB ASC 946-20-05-2, affiliates may make payments to a fund related to investment losses for either of the following reasons:

a. *Payments by affiliates.* To reimburse the effect of a loss (realized or unrealized) on a portfolio investment, often caused by a situation outside the fund's or its affiliates' direct control, such as an issuer default or a decline in fair value.

b. *Investment restriction violations (investments not meeting investment guidelines).* Occasionally, a fund adviser may purchase an investment for a fund that clearly violates the fund's investment restrictions (investment restrictions are described in the prospectus or statement of additional information for registered funds and in partnership agreements or offering memorandums for nonregistered funds). The investment held in violation of the fund's investment restrictions may appreciate or depreciate in value. In the case in which the investment has depreciated in value and the fund has consequently incurred a loss, the fund adviser may make a payment to the fund in lieu of settlement of a potential claim resulting from the violation of the fund's investment restrictions. This payment, in effect, makes the fund whole relative to the loss that it has incurred. This type of transaction is, in essence, a payment to put the fund's shareholders in the position they would have been in had the violation not occurred.

7.122 As explained in FASB ASC 946-20-45-1, payments made by affiliates for those two reasons should be combined and reported as a separate line item entitled "Net increase from payments by affiliates and net gains (losses) realized on the disposal of investments in violation of restrictions" in the statement of operations as part of net realized and unrealized gains (losses) from investments and foreign currency. That separate line item would comprise amounts related to the following:

AAG-INV 7.122

a. Voluntary reimbursements by the affiliate for investment transaction losses

b. Realized and unrealized losses on investments not meeting the investment guidelines of the fund

c. Reimbursements from the affiliate for losses on investments not meeting the investment guidelines of the fund

d. Realized and unrealized gains on investments not meeting the investment guidelines of the fund

As further discussed in FASB ASC 946-20-50-2, the amounts and circumstances of payments by affiliates to reimburse the fund for losses on investment transactions should be described in the notes to the financial statements. The gains and losses on investments not meeting investment guidelines of the fund should also be disclosed in the notes to the financial statements. In addition, the effect on total return, which is presented in the financial highlights, of the payments, as well as any gains or losses on investments not meeting investment guidelines of the fund, should be quantified and disclosed in the financial highlights in a manner similar to disclosure of the effect of voluntary waivers of fees and expenses on expense ratios. This is disclosed in accordance with FASB ASC 850-10. Total return should be presented in the financial highlights. The following is an example of total return being presented in a footnote to the financial highlights, as shown in FASB ASC 946-20-55-1:

> In 20XX, a.aa% of the fund's total return consists of a voluntary reimbursement by the adviser for a realized investment loss, and another b.bb% consists of a gain on an investment not meeting the fund's investment restrictions. Excluding these items, total return would have been c.cc%. Additionally, the adviser fully reimbursed the fund for a loss on a transaction not meeting the fund's investment guidelines, which otherwise would have reduced total return by d.dd%.

7.123 The Financial Reporting Executive Committee (FinREC) believes that due to the underlying reasons for such payments, the inclusion of the payments in the statement of operations should not be changed if the person making the payment is also a shareholder in the fund. FinREC was able to distinguish these payments from transactions undertaken by an entity's principal shareholder for the benefit of the entity (see SEC Topic 5T, "Accounting for Expenses or Liabilities Paid by Principal Stockholder[s]" of the SEC's *Codification of Staff Accounting Bulletins*), as arising from the person's service relationship to the fund, not its shareholder relationship. FinREC observed that the payments typically do not enhance the value of the person's equity investment in the fund beyond a pro rata interest in the payment itself, because the value of investment company shares either equals or is directly related to net asset value per share. Thus, FinREC believes that the payments ordinarily are intended to maintain a person's service relationship with the fund, rather than enhance or maintain the value of the person's investment in the fund.

7.124 In considering the presentation of the payments within the statement of operations, FinREC considered the guidance in FASB ASC 225-20-45-16. FinREC recognizes that payments of the type specified in paragraph 7.121(*a*) historically have been infrequent, typically occurring when an investment-grade issuer suddenly and unexpectedly defaulted, and that transactions in violation of investment restrictions, whether resulting in gains or losses, and payments of the type described in paragraph 7.121(*b*) are inherently infrequent. Thus, FinREC recommends the presentation of such items within a separate component of the statement of operations, as described in paragraph 7.122. FinREC also believes that the inconsistency between these transactions and the operating practices stated in the fund's governing documents provides further support for such presentation.

7.125 As explained in FASB ASC 946-20-05-3, payments by affiliates may take several forms, such as the following:

- A direct cash contribution to the fund to offset the effect of a realized loss on a portfolio investment
- Purchase of securities from the fund at prices in excess of the securities' current fair value
- Provision of a credit enhancement to maintain the investment's value

Further, FASB ASC 946-20-25-2 notes that a credit enhancement provided by an affiliate to maintain an investment's value should be recognized when the enhancement becomes available to the fund. FASB ASC 946-20-30-1 adds that the amount of the payment is initially measured by the cost of obtaining a similar enhancement in an arm's length transaction. Lastly, FASB ASC 946-20-35-1 states that any subsequent change in the value of the enhancement should be accounted for as unrealized appreciation or depreciation.

7.126 A fund may receive other payments from affiliates for reasons other than those described in FASB ASC 946-20-05-2. An evaluation must be made to determine whether to disclose the payments on the statement of operations or statement of changes in net assets. Regardless of the type of payment received, the fund should separately disclose the payments received in the respective financial statement, show the impact on the total return relating to such items in the financial highlights, and provide a narrative disclosure of the reasons why such payments were made.

Net Realized and Unrealized Gain or Loss From Investments and Foreign Currency

7.127 FASB ASC 946-225-45-6(c) states that the sum of the net realized gain or loss and change in unrealized gain or loss on investments and foreign currency-denominated assets and liabilities should be presented in the statement of operations as a net gain or loss on investments and foreign currency.

Net Increase or Decrease in Net Assets From Operations

7.128 As noted in FASB ASC 946-225-45-7, the sum of net investment income or loss and net realized and unrealized gain or loss on investments and foreign currency should be shown as a net increase or decrease in net assets resulting from operations.

Reporting of Fully Benefit-Responsive Investment Contracts

7.129 FASB ASC 946-210-45-17 requires that the statements of operations and changes in net assets be prepared on a basis that reflects income credited to participants in the fund and realized and unrealized gains and losses only on those investment contracts that are not deemed fully benefit-responsive.

Statement of Changes in Net Assets

7.130 FASB ASC 946-205-45-3 states that the statement of changes in net assets summarizes results from operations, net equalization credits or debits, dividends and distributions to shareholders, capital share transactions, and capital contributions. The increase or decrease in net assets of a registered investment company comprises the following categories:

    a. Operations. Net investment income or loss, net realized gains or losses from investments and foreign currency transactions, and changes in unrealized appreciation or depreciation on investments and translation of assets and liabilities in foreign currencies, as shown in the statement of operations, should be presented separately to arrive at the net change in net assets resulting from operations.

    b. Net equalization debits or credits. If equalization accounting is used, undistributed investment income included in the price of capital shares issued or reacquired should be shown as a separate line item.

    c. Distributions to shareholders. Distributions should be disclosed as a single line item, except for the tax return of capital distributions, which should be disclosed separately. FASB ASC 946-505-50-5 states that the tax-basis components of dividends paid (ordinary income distributions, long term capital gains distributions, and return of capital distributions) should be disclosed in the notes to the financial statements. FASB ASC 946-20-50-8 requires consistent treatment of dividends.

    Disclosing dividends on a tax basis is consistent with how dividends are reported to shareholders during, and at the end of, the calendar year. The financial highlights table would disclose per share information that is consistent with the statement of changes in net assets.

    FASB ASC 946-205-45-3 notes that distributions made by RICs often differ from aggregate GAAP-basis undistributed net investment income (including net equalization credits or debits and undistributed net investment income) and accumulated net realized gains (total GAAP-basis net realized gains). The principal cause is that required minimum fund distributions are based on income and gain amounts determined in accordance with federal income tax regulations, rather than GAAP. The differences created can be temporary, meaning that they will reverse in the future, or they can be permanent. FASB ASC 946-505-50-6 explains that the primary reasons for any significant difference between total GAAP-basis net investment income and net realized gain and actual distributions should be disclosed in the notes to the financial statements. FASB ASC 946-205-45-3(c) notes that if in a subsequent period all or a portion of a temporary difference becomes a permanent difference, the amount of the permanent difference should be reclassified to paid-in capital.

    d. Capital share transactions. FASB ASC 946-505-50-2 illustrates the net change in net assets (excluding amounts shown separately if equalization accounting is used) arising from capital share

Financial Statements of Investment Companies

transactions that should be disclosed for each class of shares. The components of the change should be disclosed on the face of the statement or in the notes to the financial statements for each class of shares, as follows:

    i. The number and value of shares sold

    ii. The number and value of shares issued in the reinvestment of distributions

    iii. The number and cost of shares reacquired

    iv. The net change

  e. *Capital contributions—net assets.* FASB ASC 946-505-50-3 states that net assets at the beginning and end of the year should be disclosed. The balance of net assets at the end of the year should agree with the comparable amount shown in the statement of assets and liabilities or statement of net assets.

7.131 As explained in FASB ASC 946-205-45-5, for investment partnerships, the statement of changes in net assets may be combined with the statement of changes in partners' capital if a statement of changes in net assets is presented.

7.132 According to TIS section 6910.28, "Reporting Financial Highlights, Net Asset Value (NAV) Per Share, Shares Outstanding, and Share Transactions When Investors in Unitized Nonregistered Funds Are Issued Individual Classes or Series of Shares" (AICPA, *Technical Practice Aids*), when a unitized nonregistered fund issues a separate series of shares to each individual investor in the fund, which remains outstanding so long as the investor maintains its investment in the fund and is not closed until the investor fully redeems, the fund should present disclosures of each series of shares outstanding at period-end and share transactions during the period on an aggregate share basis. These series may be issued within multiple classes of shares, with each series within a class bearing the same economic characteristics. The shares are legally issued and outstanding until redemption (that is, they are not notional interests) but will not be converted or otherwise consolidated into an identifiable permanent series of shares in a series roll-up.[45] Essentially, these unitized funds apply partnership accounting. The issuance of a separate series of shares to each individual investor is done for operational purposes because this enables a fund to allocate profit and loss to each investor in the same manner as a limited partnership allocates profit and loss to an individual partner's capital account.

7.133 FASB ASC 946-210-45-4 indicates that net asset value per share and shares outstanding should be reported for each class. FASB ASC 946-505-50-2 requires disclosure of the number and value of shares sold, the number and value of shares issued in reinvestment of distributions, the number and cost of shares reacquired, and the net change in shares.

7.134 TIS section 6910.28 explains that for funds that issue a separate series of shares to each investor, such funds should satisfy the disclosure requirements in FASB ASC 946-210-45-4 and 946-505-50-2 by presenting such disclosures on an aggregate share basis. For funds that issue multiple classes

---

[45] A series roll-up typically occurs at the end of the year when a temporary series of shares has increased above its high watermark (for example, the highest level in value that a series has achieved, adjusted for subscriptions and redemptions), at which time the outstanding shares of a temporary series of shares are converted (or rolled up) into the permanent series of shares.

232 Investment Companies

of shares that contain multiple series of shares, such disclosure requirements should be presented at the aggregate level for each permanent class of shares from which the individual series of shares have been issued.

Subsequent Events

7.135 Investment companies often distribute, after year-end, a portion of undistributed investment income and security gains realized in the preceding year. If declared before the audit opinion date, per share amounts relating to those distributions are frequently disclosed in the notes to the financial statements.

7.136 FASB ASC 855-10-25-1 explains that an entity should recognize in the financial statements the effects of all subsequent events that provide additional evidence about conditions that existed at the date of the balance sheet, including the estimates inherent in the process of preparing financial statements. The FASB ASC glossary defines *subsequent events* as events or transactions that occur after the balance sheet date but before financial statements are issued or available to be issued. There are two types of subsequent events:

- The first type consists of events or transactions that provide additional evidence about conditions that existed at the date of the balance sheet, including the estimates inherent in the process of preparing financial statements (that is, recognized subsequent events).

- The second type consists of events that provide evidence about conditions that did not exist at the date of the balance sheet but arose subsequent to that date (that is, nonrecognized subsequent events).

The FASB ASC glossary defines *financial statements are issued* as when they are widely distributed to shareholders and other financial statements users for general use and reliance in a form and format that complies with GAAP (U.S. SEC registrants are also required to consider applicable SEC guidance). *Financial statements are available to be issued* is defined by the FASB ASC glossary as when they are complete in a form and format that complies with GAAP, and all approvals necessary for issuance have been obtained (for example, from management, the board of directors or trustees, or significant shareholders). The process involved in creating and distributing the financial statements will vary depending on entity's management and corporate governance structure, as well as statutory and regulatory requirements. FASB ASC 855-10-55-1 contains examples of recognized subsequent events.

7.137 As stated in FASB ASC 855-10-25-1A, an entity that is an SEC filer or a conduit bond obligor for conduit debt securities that are traded in a public market should evaluate subsequent events through the date that the financial statements are issued. The FASB ASC glossary defines an *SEC filer* as an entity that is required to file or furnish its financial statements with either of the following:

- The SEC
- With respect to an entity subject to Section 12(i) of the 1934 Act, the appropriate agency under that section

AAG-INV 7.135

Financial statements for other entities that are not otherwise SEC filers whose financial statements are included in a submission by another SEC filer are not included within this definition. FASB ASC 855-10-25-2 states that an entity that does not meet the criterion in FASB ASC 855-10-25-1A should evaluate subsequent events through the date that the financial statements are available to be issued.

7.138 In accordance with FASB ASC 855-10-25-3, an entity should not recognize subsequent events that provide evidence about conditions that did not exist at the date of the balance sheet but arose after the balance sheet date but before financial statements are issued or available to be issued. FASB ASC 855-10-55-2 contains examples of nonrecognized subsequent events, including changes in the fair value of assets or liabilities (financial or nonfinancial) after the balance sheet date but before financial statements are issued or available to be issued.[46] Further, paragraphs 2–3 of FASB ASC 855-10-50 explain that some nonrecognized subsequent events may be of such a nature that they must be disclosed to keep the financial statements from being misleading. For such events, an entity should disclose the nature of the event and the estimate of its financial effect or a statement that such an estimate cannot be made. Occasionally, a nonrecognized subsequent event may be so significant that disclosure can best be made by means of pro forma financial data.

7.139 The FASB ASC glossary defines *revised financial statements* as financial statements revised only for either correction of an error or retrospective application of GAAP. According to paragraphs 4–5 of FASB ASC 855-10-50, unless the entity is an SEC filer, an entity should disclose in the revised financial statements the dates through which subsequent events have been evaluated in both the issued or available-to-be-issued financial statements and the revised financial statements. Further, revised financial statements are considered reissued financial statements. FASB ASC 855-10-25-4 notes that an entity may need to reissue financial statements (for example, in reports filed with the SEC or other regulatory agencies). After the original issuance of the financial statements, events or transactions may have occurred that require disclosure in the reissued financial statements to keep them from being misleading. An entity should not recognize events occurring between the time that the financial statements were issued or available to be issued and the time that the financial statements were reissued, unless the adjustment is required by GAAP or regulatory requirements.

7.140 FASB ASC 855-10-50-1 explains that if an entity is not an SEC filer, then the entity should disclose the date through which subsequent events have been evaluated and whether that date is either the date that the financial statements were issued or the date that the financial statements were available to be issued.

Statement of Cash Flows

7.141 FASB ASC 230-10-15-3 requires entities providing financial statements that report both financial position and results of operations to also provide a statement of cash flows for each period for which results of operations

---

[46] TIS section 9070.06, "Decline in Market Value of Assets Subsequent to the Balance Sheet Date" (AICPA, *Technical Practice Aids*), addresses whether a decline in market value of an asset subsequent to the balance sheet date should result in the adjustment of the financial statements.

are provided. However, FASB ASC 230-10-15-4 exempts investment companies meeting certain conditions from the requirements of FASB ASC 230, *Statement of Cash Flows*.

7.142 FASB ASC 230-10-15-4 exempts from the requirement to provide a statement of cash flows investment companies subject to the registration and regulatory requirements of the 1940 Act and investment companies that have essentially the same characteristics as those subject to the 1940 Act, provided that all the following conditions are met:[47]

    a. During the period, substantially all the entity's investments were highly liquid (for example, marketable securities and other assets for which a market is readily available).

    b. Substantially all the entity's investments are carried at market value. (Securities for which market value is determined using matrix pricing techniques would meet this condition. Other securities for which market value is not readily determinable and for which fair value must be determined in good faith by the board of directors or trustees would not meet this condition.)

    c. The entity had little or no debt, based on average debt outstanding during the period in relation to average total assets. For this purpose, obligations resulting from redemptions of shares by the entity from unsettled purchases of securities or similar assets or from covered options written generally may be excluded from average debt outstanding. However, any extension of credit by the seller that is not in accordance with standard industry practice for redeeming shares or settling purchases of investments should be included in average debt outstanding.

    d. The entity provides a statement of changes in net assets.

7.143 According to TIS section 6910.25, "Considerations in Evaluating Whether Certain Liabilities Constitute 'Debt' for Purposes of Assessing Whether an Investment Company Must Present a Statement of Cash Flows" (AICPA, *Technical Practice Aids*), although presented in the "Liabilities" section of the statement of assets and liabilities, options sold or written (whether covered or uncovered), short sales of securities, and other liabilities recorded as a result of investment practices are not necessarily debt; rather, their classification depends on the nature of the activity. Certain transactions (for example, securities lending, mortgage dollar rolls, or short sale transactions) may have a practice of being entered into solely for operating purposes (similarly to unsettled purchases of securities) or as an investing strategy (similarly to covered options written), and the investment company either retains the proceeds in cash accounts or uses them to invest in securities that are cash equivalents under FASB ASC 230. In such cases, the proceeds from the transaction should not be considered debt for purposes of assessing whether the conditions in the previous paragraph are met.

7.144 FASB ASC 230-10-45 states that a statement of cash flows should explain the change during the period in cash and cash equivalents. The statement classifies cash receipts and cash payments as resulting from operating, investing, and financing activities and includes a reconciliation of net cash

---

[47] See footnote 5.

Financial Statements of Investment Companies

provided by, and used for, operating activities to net increase or decrease in net assets from operating activities.

7.145 When it is necessary to provide a statement of cash flows, the following information should be disclosed for a presentation using the direct method. (The indirect method is more commonly used. This method adjusts net increase or decrease in net assets from operations to arrive at net cash flows from operating activities.) Cash flows from operating activities should include the fund's investing activities, which may include the following:

- *a.* Interest and dividends received
- *b.* Operating expenses paid
- *c.* Purchases of long term investments (at cost)
- *d.* Sales of long term investments (proceeds)
- *e.* Net sales or purchases of short term investments
- *f.* Cash flows for other types of investing activities related to changes in margin accounts and collateral status, such as written options, financial futures contracts, securities lending, and so forth

7.146 According to TIS section 6910.20, "Presentation of Purchases and Sales/Maturities of Investments in the Statement of Cash Flows" (AICPA, *Technical Practice Aids*), a nonregistered investment partnership should present purchases and sales and maturities of long term investments (securities purchased with no stated maturity or with a stated maturity of greater than one year at the date of acquisition) on a gross basis in the statement of cash flows, pursuant to FASB ASC 230, although the nonregistered investment partnership may consider the provisions in FASB ASC 230-10-45-9 in determining whether or not certain purchases and sales/maturities qualify for net reporting. However, purchases and sales and maturities of short term investments (securities purchased with a stated remaining maturity of one year or less at the date of acquisition) may be presented on a net basis, as described in FASB ASC 230-10-45-18. Additionally, proceeds and costs reported for transactions in short positions are reflected separately from proceeds and costs associated with long positions.

7.147 TIS section 6910.26, "Additional Guidance on Determinants of Net Versus Gross Presentation of Security Purchases and Sales/Maturities in the Statement of Cash Flows of a Nonregistered Investment Company" (AICPA, *Technical Practice Aids*), further explains that one of the requirements of FASB ASC 230-10-45-9 is that the original maturity of assets and liabilities qualifying for net reporting is three months or less. However, FASB ASC 230-10-45-18 permits banks, brokers and dealers in securities, and other entities that carry securities and other assets in a trading account to classify cash receipts and cash payments from such activities as operating cash flows, and cash flows from transactions in available-for-sale securities are reported gross as investing activities.[48]

7.148 In other industries, operating cash flows relating to trading account securities typically are reported on a net basis. If a nonregistered investment company presents a statement of cash flows, the investment company's trading style, investment objectives stated in its offering memorandum, and portfolio

---

[48] Refer to paragraphs 11 and 18–20 of FASB ASC 230-10-45 and FASB ASC 310-10-45-11 for additional guidance.

AAG-INV 7.148

turnover should be the primary determinants of net versus gross reporting. Where the investment company's overall activities comport with *trading*, as discussed in FASB ASC 230 and 320, *Investments—Debt and Equity Securities*,[49] netting is permissible; otherwise, gross reporting of purchases and sales and maturities is required. Regardless of whether net or gross reporting is appropriate based on the stated criteria, an entity should separately report its activity related to long positions from activity related to short positions (that is, changes and activity in account balances reported as assets should not be netted against changes and activity in account balances reported as liabilities).

7.149 Cash flows from financing activities include the following:

  a. Issuance and redemption of fund shares, including both common and preferred shares (excluding reinvestment of dividends and distributions)
  b. Proceeds from and repayments of debt
  c. Dividends and distributions to shareholders (not including stock or reinvested dividends and distributions)
  d. Bank overdrafts

7.150 The reconciliation of net cash provided by, or used for, operating activities to net increase or decrease in net assets from operating activities includes the following:

  a. Changes in noninvestment asset and liability accounts (such as interest receivable, accrued expenses, and other liabilities)
  b. Noncash income and expense items (such as amortization of deferred charges, accretion of discount, and amortization of premium)
  c. Realized and unrealized gains and losses on investment and foreign currency transactions

7.151 FASB ASC 830-230-45-1 states that the effect of any foreign exchange fluctuations on cash balances should be disclosed as a separate part of the reconciliation of the change in cash and cash equivalents during the period. FASB ASC 830-230-55-1 provides an illustration of this guidance.

7.152 FASB ASC 946-230-55-1 states that information about noncash investing and financing activities, such as reinvestments of dividends and distributions, should be disclosed.

Financial Highlights

7.153 Paragraphs 1–3 and 7 of FASB ASC 946-205-50 state that financial highlights (see paragraph 7.01) should be presented either as a separate schedule or within the notes to the financial statements for each class of common

---

[49] The FASB ASC glossary defines *trading securities* as securities that are bought and held principally for the purpose of selling them in the near term and therefore held for only a short period of time. Trading generally reflects active and frequent buying and selling, and trading securities are generally used with the objective of generating profits on short term differences in price.

Although investment companies do not apply FASB ASC 320, *Investments—Debt and Equity Securities,* and, therefore, do not normally categorize securities as trading, available for sale, or held to maturity, the concepts of whether the securities are held for trading purposes and whether the related cash flows would be classified as operating cash flows under paragraphs 11 and 18–20 of FASB ASC 230-10-45 and FASB ASC 310-10-45-11 are relevant in determining whether cash flows from purchases and sales of securities should be presented gross or net by investment companies.

Financial Statements of Investment Companies

shares outstanding. Per share amounts presented are based on a share outstanding throughout each period presented. Investment companies with multiple classes of shares may present financial highlights only for those classes of shares that are included in reports to such shareholders. In such cases, the investment company should include appropriate disclosures related to all classes to ensure that the financial statements are complete (for example, detail of capital share activity in the statement of changes in net assets or notes to the financial statements). Nonregistered investment partnerships should disclose all classes of ownership interests in general purpose financial statements.

7.154 Further, FASB ASC 946-205-50-4 notes that only the classes related to the nonmanaging investors (that is, classes of investors that do not consist exclusively of managing investor interests) are considered to be the common interests requiring financial highlight disclosure.

7.155 According to the FASB ASC glossary term *nonregistered investment partnerships—financial highlights*, nonregistered investment partnerships, when disclosing financial highlights, should interpret the terms classes, units, and theoretical investments as follows:

   a. *Classes.* Nonregistered investment funds typically have one of the following two classes of ownership interest: management interest and investment interest. For unitized funds (that is, funds with units specifically called for in the governing underlying legal or offering documents), the management interest usually is a voting class, and the investment interest is a nonvoting class. Temporary series of shares (that is, shares that are intended at the time of issuance to be consolidated at a later date with another specified series of shares that remains outstanding indefinitely) are not considered separate classes. Permanent series of a class of share should be the basis for which that share's financial highlights are determined and presented. For nonunitized funds, the management interest usually is the general partner class, and the investment interest usually is the limited partner class. Generally, a class has certain rights, as governed by underlying legal documents or offering documents and local law. Rights to certain investments that do not otherwise affect the rights available under the underlying legal documents and local law do not ordinarily represent a separate share class. For example, rights to income and gains from a specific investment attributed solely to investors at the date that the investment is made (side-pocket investments) are not considered to give rise to a share class. Similarly, a temporary series of shares is not considered a share class.

   b. *Units.* Only funds with units specifically called for in the governing underlying legal or offering documents should be considered unitized. Some funds may employ units for convenience in making allocations to investors for internal accounting or bookkeeping purposes, but the units are not required or specified by legal or offering documents and, for all other purposes, operate like nonunitized investment partnerships. For per share operating performance, those funds are not considered unitized.

   c. *Theoretical investment.* The term *theoretical investment* in FASB ASC 946-205-50-20 should be considered as the actual aggregate amount of capital invested by each reporting class of investor as of the beginning of the fiscal reporting period, adjusted for cash flows related to capital contributions or withdrawals during the period. As stated in FASB ASC 946-205-50-5, if a fund is not unitized, only investment returns (either total return or internal rate of return) and net investment income and expense ratios are required to be disclosed as indicated in paragraphs 10–25 of FASB ASC 946-205-50.

7.156 As explained in paragraphs 7–8 of FASB ASC 946-205-50, the following per share information should be presented for registered investment companies and investment companies that compute unitized net asset value. Nonregistered investment partnerships that compute unitized net asset value should disclose information for each reporting share class related to nonmanaging investors. The information should be disclosed for each major category affecting net asset value per share (as shown in the statement of operations and statement of changes in net assets of the fund). The caption descriptions in the per share data should be the same captions used in the statement of operations and statement of changes in net assets to allow the reader to determine which components of operations are included in, or excluded from, various per share data:

   a. Net asset value at the beginning of the period.

   b. Per share net investment income or loss. Other methods, such as dividing net investment income by the average or weighted average number of shares outstanding during the period, are acceptable.

   c. Realized and unrealized gains and losses per share, which are balancing amounts necessary to reconcile the change in net asset value per share with the other per share information presented. The amount shown in this caption might not agree with the change in aggregate gains and losses for the period. If such is the case, the reasons should be disclosed.

   d. Total from investment operations, which represents the sum of net investment income or loss and realized and unrealized gain or loss.

   e. Distributions to shareholders should be disclosed as a single line item, except the tax return of capital distributions should be disclosed separately. Details of distributions should conform to those shown in the statement of changes in net assets.

   f. Purchase premiums, redemption fees, or other capital items.

   g. Payments by affiliates (paragraphs 2–3 of FASB ASC 946-20-05).

   h. Net asset value at the end of the period.

The information required in items *b–g* is not required for separate accounts that represent an ownership interest in the underlying separate account portfolios or mutual funds. Refer to paragraphs 10.57–.64 of the guide for information regarding financial highlights for separate accounts and illustrative financial statements.

7.157 Per share net investment income or loss for registered investment companies is calculated in accordance with the requirements of Forms N-1A or N-2. A more detailed discussion of per share calculation methods for registered investment companies may be found in the instructions for the preparation of registration statements on Forms N-1A and N-2. If used by a registered investment company, the method employed must be disclosed in a note to the

Financial Statements of Investment Companies

table in conformity with SEC requirements. For Form N-2 registrants only, market value at the end of the period should also be presented.

7.158 As explained in paragraphs 10–17 and 25 of FASB ASC 946-205-50, ratios of expenses and net investment income to average net assets are generally annualized for periods less than one year. The ratio of expenses to average net assets should be increased by brokerage service and expense offset arrangements (see paragraphs 3 and 5 of FASB ASC 946-20-45), as follows:

    a. When determining expense and net investment income ratios, nonregistered investment partnerships should calculate average net assets by using the fund's (or class's) weighted-average net assets as measured at each accounting period or periodic valuation (for example, daily, weekly, monthly, quarterly), adjusting for capital contributions or withdrawals from the fund occurring between accounting periods or valuations. (This provision is not intended to require any additional interim accounting period or periodic valuation date beyond that which may be provided in offering or organizational documents of the partnership.)

The expense and net investment income ratios should be calculated by nonregistered investment partnerships based on the expenses allocated to each common or investor class (for example, the limited partner class) prior to the effects of any incentive allocation. Adequate disclosure should be made to indicate that the net investment income ratio does not reflect the effects of any incentive allocation. Expenses directly related to the total return of the fund, such as incentive fees, and nonrecurring expenses, such as organizational costs, should not be annualized when determining the expense ratio. Disclosure should be made of the expenses that have not been annualized.

Generally, the determination of expenses for computing those ratios should follow the presentation of expenses in the fund's statement of operations. Accordingly, if the investment adviser's or general partner's incentive is structured as a fee, rather than an allocation of profits, the incentive fee would be factored into the computation of an expense ratio. Because an incentive allocation of profits is not presented as an expense, it should not be considered part of the expense ratio. However, to avoid potentially significant inconsistencies in ratio presentations based solely on the structuring of incentives as fees or allocations, all incentives should be reflected in the disclosure of financial highlights. See paragraph 7.185 for an example of that disclosure.

Additionally, for the expense ratio, disclosure should be made of the effect of any agreement to waive or reimburse fees and expenses to each reporting class as a whole, as described in FASB ASC 946-20-50-7, and of expense offsets, as described in paragraphs 3 and 5 of FASB ASC 946-20-45. Agreements to waive a portion or all of certain fees to a specific investor, which do not relate to the share class as a whole, do not require disclosure in the financial highlights. However, as ratios are calculated for each common class taken as a whole, the financial statements should disclose that an individual investor's ratio may vary from those ratios.

b. Investment companies that obtain capital commitments from investors and periodically call capital under those commitments to make investments (principally limited-life nonregistered investment partnerships) should disclose in the financial highlights or a note to the financial statements the total committed capital of the partnership (including general partner), the year of formation of the entity, and the ratio of total contributed capital to total committed capital.

c. Funds of funds should compute the expense and net investment income ratios using the expenses presented in the fund's statement of operations. Therefore, funds of funds typically should compute these ratios based on the net investment income and expense items at the fund-of-funds level only. Adequate disclosure should be made so that it is clear to users that the ratios do not reflect the funds-of-funds' proportionate share of income and expenses of the underlying investee funds. In a master-feeder structure, the feeder should include its proportionate share of the income and expenses of the master when computing the ratios at the feeder level. If, in a master-feeder structure, an incentive is levied as an allocation at the master level, the feeder should present its share of the incentive allocation as a separate line item in the statement of operations.

7.159 As discussed in paragraphs 18–24 of FASB ASC 946-205-50, total return is required to be presented for all investment companies (for interim periods, the disclosure should include whether total return is annualized) and should be computed as follows:

a. For nonregistered investment companies organized in a manner utilizing unitized net asset value, based on the change in the net asset value per share during the period and assuming that all dividends are reinvested.

b. For investment companies not utilizing unitized net asset value, including investment partnerships, based on the change in value during the period of a theoretical investment made at the beginning of the period. The change in value of a theoretical investment is measured by comparing the aggregate ending value of each class of investor with the aggregate beginning value of each such class, adjusted for cash flows related to capital contributions or withdrawals during the period.

If capital cash flows occur during the reporting period, returns are geometrically linked based on capital cash flow dates. In general, geometrically linking requires the computation of performance for each discrete period within a year in which invested capital is constant (that is, for each period between investor cash flow dates) then multiplying those performance computations together to obtain the total return for a constant investment outstanding for the entire year.

Because incentive allocations or fees may vary among investors within a class, total return for reporting classes subject to an incentive allocation or a fee should report total return before and after the incentive allocation or a fee for each reporting class taken as a whole. The effect of incentive allocations on total return is

Financial Statements of Investment Companies

computed on a weighted-average aggregate capital basis. That results in an incentive computation less than the maximum if, for example, certain partners had loss carryovers at the beginning of the period. See paragraph 7.188 for an example of that total return calculation and related disclosures.

c. Investment companies that, by the terms of their offering documents, (i) have limited lives; (ii) do not continuously raise capital and are not required to redeem their interests upon investor request (obtaining initial capital commitments from investors at the time of organization and subsequently drawing on those commitments to make investments is not considered continuous for this purpose); (iii) have as a predominant operating strategy the return of the proceeds from disposition of investments to investors; (iv) have limited opportunities, if any, for investors to withdraw prior to termination of the entity; and (v) do not routinely acquire (directly or indirectly) as part of their investment strategy market-traded securities and derivatives should, instead of disclosing annual total returns before and after incentive allocations and fees, disclose the internal rate of return since inception (IRR) of the investment company's cash flows and ending net assets at the end of the period (residual values), as presented in the financial statements, net of all incentive allocations or fees, to each investor class, as of the beginning and end of the period. A footnote to the financial highlights should disclose that the IRR is net of all incentives. The IRR should be based on a consistent assumption, no less frequently than quarterly, about the timing of cash inflows and outflows (for example, on actual cash-flow dates or cash inflows at the beginning of each month or quarter and cash outflows at the end of each month or quarter). All significant assumptions should be disclosed in the footnotes to the financial highlights. See paragraph 7.187 for an example of an IRR calculation and related disclosures.

7.160 For Form N-1A registrants, total return should be calculated based on the change in the net asset value per share during the period and the assumption that all dividends are reinvested. For Form N-2 registrants, total investment return should be calculated based on the change in market value of the fund's shares taking into account dividends reinvested in accordance with the terms of the dividend reinvestment plan or, lacking such a plan, at the lesser of net asset value or market price on the dividend distribution date (total return computed based on net asset value per share may also be presented if the difference in results between the two calculations is explained).

7.161 Additional information for investment companies filing on Forms N-1A and N-2 includes the following ratios and supplemental data:

a. Net assets, end of period.

b. Portfolio turnover rate.

c. If an investment company filing on Form N-2 has senior securities, Item 4.3 requires the year of issuance; the total amount outstanding (exclusive of treasury securities), the asset coverage per unit, and involuntary liquidating preference per unit; and the average market value per unit (excluding bank loans) as of the end of the

7.162 The method of computing the portfolio turnover rate is described in the instructions to Forms N-SAR, N-1A, and N-2.

7.163 *Deferred fees.*[51] According to TIS section 6910.27, the per share information, net investment income ratio, and net expense ratio included in the financial highlights should reflect the amounts presented on the statement of operations including the adjustment associated with the deferred fee amount. In order to reflect the effect of the adjustment on the fund's expense ratio, the fund may also present an expense ratio that excludes the amount of deferred fee expense or negative expense reported in the statement of operations. Consistent with guidance in FASB ASC 946, the fund should disclose the nature of the deferred fee arrangement, including the priority of claim in the event of liquidation; the current period and cumulative amounts deferred; the cumulative earnings or losses on the deferral; the terms of payment; the date that the deferral payments commence (or the next payment date); and the manner in which the deferral will be invested.

7.164 According to TIS section 6910.28, when a unitized nonregistered fund issues a separate series of shares to each individual investor in the fund, which remains outstanding so long as the investor maintains its investment in the fund and is not closed until the investor fully redeems, the fund should present financial highlights (per share data, ratios, and total return) similar to that of a partnership (that is, a nonunitized fund). These series may be issued within multiple classes of shares with each series within a class bearing the same economic characteristics. The shares are legally issued and outstanding until redemption (that is, they are not notional interests) but will not be converted or otherwise consolidated into an identifiable permanent series of shares in a series roll-up.[52] Essentially, these unitized funds apply partnership accounting. The issuance of a separate series of shares to each individual investor is done for operational purposes because this enables a fund to allocate profit and loss to each investor in the same manner as a limited partnership allocates profit and loss to an individual partner's capital account.

7.165 TIS section 6910.28 also states that the financial highlights should be presented at the aggregate level for the entire permanent series of shares from which the individual series of shares has been issued. Because the fund operates like a partnership, the financial highlights should include only those financial highlights applicable to a partnership, which are the ratios to average net assets and total return, but not per share data. When a separate series of shares is issued to each individual investor and remains outstanding until the investor fully redeems, the permanent series of shares will be the fund as a whole, excluding managing investor interests, if the shares otherwise have substantially similar terms. There are situations when a fund will issue multiple classes of shares, which contain multiple series of shares, due to differing fee arrangements or restrictions affecting an investor's ability to participate in the profits and losses generated by new-issue securities. When a fund issues

---

[50] The Item 4 instructions in Form N-2 note that business development companies may be omitted from providing financial highlights but do explain that they are required to furnish the financial information required by Items 301, 302, and 303 of Regulation S-K.

[51] See footnote 43.

[52] See footnote 45.

multiple classes of shares, and in each class of shares, a series of shares is issued to each individual investor and remains outstanding until the investor fully redeems, financial highlights should be presented at the aggregate level for each permanent class of shares from which the individual series of shares have been issued. For example, if a fund has outstanding, at year-end, class A shares series 1–40, which have a 1 percent management fee; class B shares series 1–300, which have a 2 percent management fee; and class C shares, which are only held by the managing investor, the fund should present financial highlights information for class A as a whole and class B as a whole. There is no requirement to present financial highlights for class C because FASB ASC 946-205-50-4 requires financial highlights to be presented only for nonmanaging investors.

7.166 TIS section 6910.28 explains that it would be acceptable for a fund to present supplemental financial highlights data for a single series of shares that the fund determines to be representative. Such financial highlights may be labeled as representing supplemental information and may only be presented in addition to those financial highlights that are required. Factors to consider when determining the representative series of shares include the following:

   a. The series of shares was outstanding for the entire fiscal period (or, if all units of a series of shares outstanding at the beginning of the fiscal period were redeemed during the period, the series of shares at period-end outstanding for the longest period of time).
   b. The fees and other offering terms of the series of shares most closely conform to those that may be described in the fund's offering documents.
   c. The series of shares represent the largest ownership interest in the fund.

The basis of presentation of the financial highlights and the criteria used to determine the most representative series of shares should be disclosed in a note to those highlights and consistently applied. If appropriate, a fund may present other supplemental information if determined to be informative and not misleading.

Other Disclosure Requirements

7.167 FASB ASC guidance that usually affects disclosures by investment companies under GAAP includes the following topics in FASB ASC:

- FASB ASC 740, *Income Taxes*. In particular, as explained in FASB ASC 946-740-55, the amounts and expiration dates of capital loss carryforwards and the amounts of any post-October capital and currency loss deferrals should be considered when an entity discloses the approximate tax effect of each type of temporary difference and carryforward that gives rise to a significant portion of deferred tax liabilities and deferred tax assets (before allocation of valuation allowances). RICs may have realized net capital and foreign currency gains during the period from the beginning of their current taxable year to October 31, which they are required to distribute to avoid federal excise tax. If those RICs then incur net capital or currency losses from November 1 to the close of their taxable year, their Form 1120-RIC tax returns would indicate that they had made distributions during the taxable year in excess of taxable gains (that is, returns of capital), even though the distributions were properly paid from gains at the time of the excise-tax distribution. To avoid this result, federal income tax regulations permit such post-October losses to be deferred and recognized on the Form 1120-RIC tax return of the next succeeding taxable year.

- FASB ASC 825. In particular, as noted in FASB ASC 825-10-05-5(b), the fair value option guidance in FASB ASC 825 establishes presentation and disclosure requirements designed to facilitate comparisons between entities that choose different measurement attributes for similar types of assets and liabilities. Paragraphs 1–2 of FASB ASC 825-10-45 explain that entities should report assets and liabilities that are measured using the fair value option in a manner that separates those reported fair values from the carrying amounts of similar assets and liabilities measured using another measurement attribute. To accomplish that, an entity should either (*a*) present the aggregate of fair value and nonfair-value amounts in the same line item in the statement of financial position and parenthetically disclose the amount measured at fair value included in the aggregate amount or (*b*) present two separate line items to display the fair value and nonfair-value carrying amounts.
- FASB ASC 815.
- FASB ASC 860, *Transfers and Servicing.*
- FASB ASC 275, *Risks and Uncertainties.*
- FASB ASC 820, *Fair Value Measurement.*

7.168 When applicable, investment companies should also disclose the fact that the fund is not subject to income taxes. For registered investment companies, disclosing the fact that they are not subject to income taxes is typically addressed by describing the company's status as a registered investment company under IRC Subchapter M and, also, the principal assumptions on which the company relied in making or not making income tax provisions and deferred tax calculations. The auditor might consider assessing the assumptions used by an entity in determining its income tax status under IRC Subchpater M. Additionally, if the fund is not subject to income taxes, the net difference between the tax bases and the reported amounts of the fund's assets and liabilities should be disclosed. See chapter 6 for further discussion on taxes.

Fully Benefit-Responsive Investment Contract Disclosures

7.169 As discussed in FASB ASC 946-210-50-14, investment companies identified in FASB ASC 946-210-45-11 should disclose the following in the aggregate in connection with fully benefit-responsive investment contracts:

   a. A description of the nature of those investment contracts, how they operate, and the methodology for calculating the interest crediting rate, including the key factors that could influence future average interest crediting rates, the basis for and frequency of determining interest crediting rate resets, and any minimum interest crediting rate under the terms of the contracts. This disclosure should explain the relationship between future interest crediting rates and the amount reported on the statement of assets and liabilities representing the adjustment for the portion of net assets attributable

Financial Statements of Investment Companies

to fully benefit-responsive investment contracts from fair value to contract value.

b. A reconciliation between the beginning and ending balance of the amount presented on the statement of assets and liabilities that represents the difference between net assets reflecting all investments at fair value and net assets for each period in which a statement of changes in net assets is presented. This reconciliation should include (i) the change in the difference between the fair value and contract value of all fully benefit-responsive investment contracts and (ii) the increase or decrease due to changes in the fully benefit-responsive status of the fund's investment contracts.

c. The average yield earned by the entire fund (which may differ from the interest rate credited to participants in the fund) for each period for which a statement of assets and liabilities is presented. This average yield should be calculated by dividing the annualized earnings of all investments in the fund (irrespective of the interest rate credited to participants in the fund) by the fair value of all investments in the fund.

d. The average yield earned by the entire fund with an adjustment to reflect the actual interest rate credited to participants in the fund for each period for which a statement of assets and liabilities is presented. This average yield should be calculated by dividing the annualized earnings credited to participants in the fund (irrespective of the actual earnings of the investments in the fund) by the fair value of all investments in the fund.

e. The following two sensitivity analyses:

   i. The weighted average interest crediting rate (that is, the contract value yield) as of the date of the latest statement of assets and liabilities and the effect on this weighted average interest crediting rate, calculated as of the date of the latest statement of assets and liabilities and the end of the next four quarterly periods, under two or more scenarios in which there is an immediate hypothetical increase or decrease in market yields, with no change to the duration of the underlying investment portfolio and no contributions or withdrawals. Those scenarios should include, at a minimum, immediate hypothetical increases and decreases in market yields equal to one-quarter and one-half of the current yield.

   ii. The effect on the weighted average interest crediting rate calculated as of the date of the latest statement of assets and liabilities and the next four quarterly reset dates, under two or more scenarios in which there are the same immediate hypothetical changes in market yields in the first analysis, combined with an immediate, one-time, hypothetical 10 percent decrease in the net assets of the fund due to participant transfers, with no change to the duration of the portfolio.

f. A description of the events that limit the ability of the fund to transact at contract value with the issuer (for example, premature termination of the contracts by the fund, plant closings, layoffs,

AAG-INV 7.169

  plan termination, bankruptcy, mergers, and early retirement incentives), including a statement about whether the occurrence of those events that would limit the fund's ability to transact at contract value with the participants in the fund is probable or not probable.

 g. A description of the events and circumstances that would allow issuers to terminate fully benefit-responsive investment contracts with the fund and settle at an amount different from contract value.

Paragraph 7.191, from FASB ASC 946-210-55-2, illustrates the application of this guidance.

Interim Financial Statements

 7.170 Rule 30d-1 of the 1940 Act requires that registered investment companies send semiannual reports to shareholders that should be complete, based on GAAP, and conform to the principles used in preparing annual financial statements. The statement of changes in net assets for registered investment companies should present information on the latest interim period (from the preceding fiscal year-end to the end of the interim period) and the preceding fiscal year. For semiannual reports, financial highlights should be presented for the semiannual period and generally the preceding five fiscal years.

 7.171 FASB ASC 946-20-50-10 states that if management of a fund determines that a tax return of capital is likely to occur for the fund's fiscal year, although the exact amount may not be estimable, that fact should be disclosed in a note to the interim financial statements.

 7.172 Unaudited interim financial data should be marked accordingly. Data summarized in condensed form should also be labeled. If the auditor is named or identified in interim reports on which he or she has performed no audit or review procedures, the auditor should insist that the reference be deleted or that a notation be included that the auditor does not express an opinion.

© Update 7-4 *Audit*: Interim Financial Information

In February 2011, the Auditing Standards Board issued Statement on Auditing Standards (SAS) No. 121, *Revised Applicability of Statement on Auditing Standards No. 100,* Interim Financial Information (AICPA, *Professional Standards*, AU sec. 722 par. .05). SAS No. 121 amends AU section 722, *Interim Financial Information* (AICPA, *Professional Standards*), such that AU section 722 would be applicable when the accountant audited the entity's latest annual financial statements, and the appointment of another accountant to audit the current year financial statements is not effective prior to the beginning of the period covered by the review. SAS No. 121 is effective for interim reviews of interim financial information for periods beginning after December 15, 2011. Early application is permitted.

Refer to section A.03 in appendix A for more information on this SAS if applicable to your reporting period.

7.173 AU section 722[53] establishes standards and provides guidance on the nature, timing, and extent of the procedures to be performed by an independent accountant when conducting a review of interim financial information if the following conditions are satisfied:

a. The entity's latest annual financial statements have been audited by the accountant or a predecessor.

b. The accountant has been engaged to audit the entity's current year financial statements, or the accountant audited the entity's latest annual financial statements and expects to be engaged to audit the current year financial statements.

c. The client prepares its interim financial information in accordance with the same financial reporting framework as that used to prepare the annual financial statements.

d. If the interim financial information is condensed information, all of the following conditions are met:

  i. The condensed interim financial information purports to conform with an appropriate financial reporting framework, which includes appropriate form and content of interim financial statements (for example, FASB ASC 270, *Interim Reporting*).

  ii. The condensed interim financial information includes a note that the financial information does not represent complete financial statements and should be read in conjunction with the entity's latest annual audited financial statements.

  iii. The condensed interim financial information accompanies the entity's latest audited annual financial statements or such audited annual financial statements are made readily available by the entity. The financial statements are deemed to be readily available if a third-party user can obtain the financial statements without any further action by the entity (for example, financial statements on an entity's website may be considered readily available, but being available upon request is not considered readily available).

The term *interim financial information* means financial information or statements covering a period less than 1 full year or for a 12 month period ending on a date other than the entity's fiscal year-end. Interim financial information may be condensed or in the form of a complete set of financial statements.

Considerations for Audits Performed in Accordance With Public Company Accounting Oversight Board (PCAOB) Standards

Registered public accounting firms must comply with the standards of the PCAOB in connection with the preparation or issuance of any report on reviews of interim financial information of an issuer, as defined by the Sarbanes-Oxley Act of 2002, and other entities, when

---

[53] This guide primarily discusses auditing guidance issued by the ASB that applies to nonissuers. Issuers are defined by Section 3 of the Securities Exchange Act of 1934 and include registered investment companies. Audits of issuers are required to be performed under Public Company Accounting Oversight Board standards. Users should evaluate their audit engagements to determine which auditing standards are applicable.

prescribed by the rules of the SEC (collectively referred to as *issuers*). Auditing Standard No. 5, *An Audit of Internal Control Over Financial Reporting That Is Integrated with An Audit of Financial Statements* (AICPA, *PCAOB Standards and Related Rules*, Auditing Standards), provides direction regarding the auditor's evaluation responsibilities related to (*a*) management's quarterly certifications on internal control over financial reporting when performing an integrated audit of financial statements and (*b*) internal control over financial reporting. (See the preface of this guide for more information about management's assessment of the effectiveness of internal control.)

Illustrative Financial Statements of Investment Companies

7.174 The amounts in the accompanying financial statements, including the financial highlights, are illustrative[54] only and may not indicate relationships among accounts. The financial statements illustrate the presentation of various items, if material. In addition, in some circumstances, information presented in the notes to the financial statements may be better presented within the financial statements.

7.175 To comply with SEC rules and regulations, registered investment companies must make certain disclosures in addition to those required by GAAP. The illustrative financial statements presented are those of a registered investment company. They include certain, but not all, disclosures required by SEC regulation in addition to requirements under GAAP. From time to time, the SEC may administratively require additional disclosures in the financial statements. At the time of this guide's publication, SEC compliance disclosures in the illustrative financial statements that are not required under GAAP include, but are not limited to, the following:[55]

- A requirement to present a statement of assets and liabilities instead of a statement of net assets if the amount of investments in securities of unaffiliated issuers represents less than 95 percent of total assets
- Additional disclosures required by Rules 12-12 and 12-12C (note 1) of Regulation S-X pertaining to collateral for repurchase agreements
- Details with respect to written options activity as required by Rule 6.07.7(c) (note 3) of Regulation S-X
- Gross unrealized appreciation and depreciation, as well as net unrealized appreciation or depreciation, all on a tax basis, in accordance with Rules 12-12 and 12-12C (note 4) of Regulation S-X
- Disclosure of nonincome producing securities as required by Rules 12-12 and 12-12C of Regulation S-X
- Additional disclosures required by Rules 6.04.2(b), 6.07.1, and 6.07.7 of Regulation S-X pertaining to investments in and income

---

[54] The statement of net assets in the illustrative financial statements that follow presents investments in unaffiliated issuers (not excluding securities loaned) that represent only 90 percent of total assets. An investment company registered with the SEC would be required to present a statement of assets and liabilities, including a separate schedule of investments, rather than a statement of net assets.

[55] See footnote 1.

Financial Statements of Investment Companies

- from affiliates and controlled companies, as defined by Section 2 of the 1940 Act to include any investment in which more than 5 percent of the outstanding voting securities is owned by the fund
- The weighted average interest rate and the maximum amount of debt outstanding during the period, in accordance with Rule 6.04.13(b), referring to Rules 5.02.19(b) and 5.02.22(b), of Regulation S-X (note 5)[56]

Significant disclosures for a registered investment company that are required by SEC regulation, in addition to those required by GAAP, but not presented in the illustrative financial statements include the following:

- Additional disclosures required by Rule 4-08(m) of Regulation S-X if the carrying amounts of repurchase or reverse repurchase agreements exceed 10 percent of total assets, or the amount at risk (as defined) under such agreements exceeds 10 percent of net asset value.
- Additional disclosures about restricted securities (acquisition date, unit carrying value, and cost, among others), in accordance with section 404 of the SEC's Codification of Financial Reporting Policies and Rules 12-12 and 12-12C of Regulation S-X.
- The elements of net assets required by Rules 6-04.16–.18 of Regulation S-X as part of the statement of assets and liabilities.
- Additional disclosures about investments in affiliates, as required by Rules 6-04.2 and 12-14 of Regulation S-X.

Disclosures included in the illustrative financial statements presented in the remainder of this chapter are not intended to be comprehensive and are not intended to establish preferences among alternative disclosures.

> **Note:** The illustrative financial statements and note disclosures included in this guide have been updated to reflect FASB ASC. However, in FASB's notice to constituents, it suggests the use of plain English in financial statement note disclosures to describe broad FASB ASC topic references. FASB suggests a reference similar to "as required by the Derivatives and Hedging Topic of the FASB *Accounting Standards Codification*." Entities might consider revising their financial statement references to reflect this plain English referencing, rather than the use of specific FASB ASC references. We have provided these detailed references as a resource for our users.

---

[56] In September 2010, the SEC issued a proposed rule to enhance the disclosure that registrants provide about short term borrowings. The proposals would require a registrant to provide, in a separately captioned subsection of Management's Discussion and Analysis of Financial Condition and Results of Operations, a comprehensive explanation of its short term borrowings, including both quantitative and qualitative information. Readers should remain alert for any final rulemaking.

AAG-INV 7.175

7.176

XYZ Investment Company
Statement of Assets and Liabilities
December 31, 20X8

Assets

Investments in securities, at fair value (cost $19,292,000)—including $570,000 of securities loaned (note 8)[57]	$21,721,000
Cash denominated in foreign currencies (cost $141,000)	139,000
Cash	60,000
Deposits with brokers for securities sold short	1,555,000
Receivables	
Dividends and interest	46,000
Investment securities sold	24,000
Capital shares sold	54,000
Unrealized gain on foreign currency forward exchange contract (note 3)	419,000
Other assets	26,000
Total assets	24,044,000

Liabilities

Call options written, at fair value (premiums received: $110,000)	230,000
Securities sold short, at fair value (proceeds: $1,555,000)	1,673,000
Demand loan payable to bank (note 5)	2,000,000
Payable upon return of securities loaned (note 8)	620,000
Unrealized loss on foreign currency exchange contract (note 3)	108,000
Unrealized loss on swap contract (note 3)	21,000
Due to broker—variation margin (note 3)	10,000
Payables	
Investment securities purchased	52,000
Capital shares reacquired	8,000
Other	4,000
Accrued expenses	8,000
Distribution payable	137,000
Total liabilities	4,871,000
Net assets	**$ 19,173,000**

Analysis of Net Assets:[58]

Net capital paid in on shares of capital stock	$ 15,184,000
Distributable earnings	3,989,000
Net assets (equivalent to $4.55 per share based on 4,216,000 shares of capital stock outstanding) (note 6)	$ 19,173,000

The accompanying notes are an integral part of these financial statements.

---

[57] Investments in securities include securities purchased with cash proceeds from securities loans.

As stated by FASB ASC 860-30-25-3, when cash is received as collateral in secured borrowings, the cash received should be recognized as the investment company's asset along with the obligation to return the cash. Consistent with FASB ASC 860-30-25-8, if the investment company makes investments with the cash, even if made by agents or in pools with other securities lenders, the investment company should reflect the investments as part of its holdings in the schedule of investments and footnote any restrictions associated with the investment because of the collateral arrangements.

With regard to collateral received in the form of securities in secured borrowings, if the securities received may be sold or repledged, the investment company should account for those securities in the same way as it would account for cash received. That is, the investment company should record the securities received as the investment company's asset along with the obligation to return the securities. However, if the investment company does not have the right to sell or repledge the securities received as collateral, then the investment company should not record the securities or related liability on its books.

[58] This breakout of paid-in-capital and distributable earnings is typically not relevant for nonregistered investment companies.

7.177

XYZ Investment Company
Schedule (or Portfolio) of Investments in Securities
December 31, 20X8

[Note: Securities may be arranged by industry groupings or other groupings (showing percentage of total portfolio or net assets invested in each grouping) that the company believes are most meaningful to users. The basis of the computation of percentages shown (which in this illustration is the ratio of the specific category of securities to the total portfolio owned) should be disclosed.]

	Principal Amount or Shares	Fair Value
Common stocks—29%		
Consumer durable goods—5%		
Allied Manufacturing Corporation[59]	25,000	$620,000
Baker Industries, Inc.[60]	15,000	150,000
Consumer Goods Company	8,000	300,000
Other		16,000
		1,086,000
Consumer nondurable goods—16%		
Amalgamated Buggy Whips, Inc.	10,000	3,280,000
American Company	4,000	100,000
Other		55,000
		3,435,000
Service industries—4%		
Service Company, Inc.[61]	10,000	465,000
Cannon Sales[62]	13,000	396,000
Other		4,000
		865,000
Other industry groupings—4%		921,000
[Additional industry groupings and details of the 50 largest holdings are not included in this illustration]		
Total common stocks		6,307,000
Convertible bonds—25%		
American Retailing Inc.—5.5% debenture due 20XX	$ 500,000	525,000
Paper Airplane Corporation—6.25% debenture due 20XX	4,500,000	4,875,000
Total convertible securities		5,400,000

(continued)

---

[59] A portion of the security is pledged as collateral for call options written.
[60] Nonincome-producing security.
[61] A portion of the security is on loan.
[62] See footnote 61.

	Principal Amount or Shares	Fair Value
Indexed securities—10%		
American Trust Co. (principal linked to Euro yield curve)—10% due 20XX	2,000,000	2,100,000
Mortgage-backed securities—12%		
FNMA 8% due 20XX	2,000,000	1,950,000
FNMA strip, principal only, zero coupon, due 20XX	1,000,000	760,000
Total mortgage-backed securities		2,710,000
Warrants—0.02%		
Banking Corp. (Expires 1/16/X9)	100	1,000
Car Motor Co. (Expires 1/01/Y3)	200	3,000
Total Warrants[63]		4,000
U.S. government obligations—16%		
U.S. Treasury 6% notes due 20XX	500,000	490,000
U.S. Treasury 8% notes due 20XX	3,000,000	2,985,000
Total U.S. government obligations		3,475,000
Short term notes—6%		
Commercial Paper, Inc., 5.5% due 2/5/X9	505,000	506,000
U.S. Treasury bills, 5.2% due 1/20/X9[64]	720,000	719,000
Total short term notes		1,225,000
Repurchase agreements—2%		
Money Center Bank of Large City, 4%, dated 12/29/X8, due 1/3/X9, repurchase price $500,274, collateralized by U.S. Treasury bonds	500,000	500,000
Total—100% (cost $19,292,000)		$21,721,000

Note—Aggregate value of segregated securities—$372,000.

The accompanying notes are an integral part of these financial statements.

---

[63] Warrants entitle the company to purchase a predetermined number of shares of common stock, and are non-income producing. The purchase price and number of shares are subject to adjustment under certain conditions until the expiration date, if any. In this example, warrants presented are considered to be derivatives as defined in FASB ASC 815, *Derivatives and Hedging*, and as such, would require derivative disclosures required in FASB ASC 815.

[64] A portion of the security is purchased with the cash proceeds from securities loans. (The investment company should also footnote any restrictions associated with the investment because of the collateral arrangements.)

7.178

XYZ Investment Company
Call Options Written
December 31, 20X8

Common Stocks / Expiration Date / Exercise Price	*Shares Subject to Call*	*Fair Value*
Allied Manufacturing Corporation/July/25	10,000	$50,000
Allied Manufacturing Corporation/October/30	5,000	2,500
Consumer Goods Company/September/45	7,000	177,500
Total (premiums received: $110,000) (note 3)		$230,000

The accompanying notes are an integral part of these financial statements.

7.179

XYZ Investment Company
Securities Sold Short
December 31, 20X8

Common Stocks	*Shares*	*Fair Value*
International Widgets, Inc.	40,000	$425,000
Paper Airplane Corporation	25,000	265,000
Amber Company	100,000	983,000
Total (proceeds: $1,555,000)		$1,673,000

The accompanying notes are an integral part of these financial statements.

7.180

XYZ Investment Company
Statement of Net Assets
December 31, 20X8

[Note: Securities may be arranged by industry or other groupings (showing percentage of total portfolio or net assets invested in each grouping) that the company believes will be most meaningful to users.]

	Shares or Principal Amount	Fair Value
Assets		
Investment in securities—113% of net assets		
Common stocks—33%		
Consumer durable goods—6%		
Allied Manufacturing Corporation[65]	25,000	$620,000
Baker Industries, Inc.[66]	15,000	150,000
Consumer Goods Company[67]	8,000	300,000
Other	600	16,000
		1,086,000
Consumer nondurable goods—18%		
Amalgamated Buggy Whips, Inc.	10,000	3,280,000
American Company	4,000	100,000
Other	2,000	55,000
		3,435,000
Service industries—4%		
Service Company, Inc.[68]	10,000	465,000
Cannon Sales[69]	13,000	396,000
Other	200	4,000
		865,000
Other industry groupings—5%		921,000
[Additional industry groupings and details of the 50 largest holdings are not included in this illustration.]		
Total common stocks		6,307,000
Convertible bonds—28%		
American Retailing Inc.—5.5% debenture due 20XX	$ 500,000	525,000
Paper Airplane Corporation—6.25% debenture due 20XX	4,500,000	4,875,000
Total convertible bonds		5,400,000

(continued)

---

[65] A portion of the security is pledged as collateral for call options written.
[66] Nonincome-producing security.
[67] See footnote 66.
[68] A portion of the security is on loan.
[69] See footnote 68.

Investment Companies

	Shares or Principal Amount	Fair Value
Indexed securities—11%		
American Trust Co. (principal linked to Euro yield curve)—10% due 20XX	2,000,000	2,100,000
Mortgage-backed securities—14%		
FNMA, 8% due 20XX	2,000,000	1,950,000
FNMA strip, principal only, zero coupon, due 20XX	1,000,000	760,000
Total mortgage-backed securities		2,710,000
Warrants—0.02%		
Banking Corp. (Expires 1/16/X9)	100	1,000
Car Motor Co. (Expires 1/01/Y3)	200	3,000
Total warrants[70]		4,000
U.S. government obligations—18%		
U.S. Treasury 6% notes due 20XX	500,000	490,000
U.S. Treasury 8% notes due 20XX	3,000,000	2,985,000
Total U.S. government obligations		3,475,000
Short term notes—6%		
Commercial Paper, Inc., 5.5% due 2/5/X9	505,000	506,000
U.S. Treasury bills, 5.2% due 1/20/X9[71]	720,000	719,000
Total short term notes		1,225,000
Repurchase agreements—3%		
Money Center Bank of Large City, 4%, dated 12/29/X8 due 1/3/X9, repurchase price $500,274, collateralized by U.S. Treasury bonds	500,000	500,000
Total investments in securities (cost $19,292,000)—including $570,000 of securities loaned (note 8)[72]		21,721,000

---

[70] Warrants entitle the company to purchase a predetermined number of shares of common stock, and are non-income producing. The purchase price and number of shares are subject to adjustment under certain conditions until the expiration date, if any. In this example, warrants presented are considered to be derivatives as defined in FASB ASC 815, and as such, would require derivative disclosures required in FASB ASC 815.

[71] A portion of the security is purchased with the cash proceeds from securities loans. (The investment company should also footnote any restrictions associated with the investment because of the collateral arrangements.)

[72] Investments in securities include securities purchased with cash proceeds from securities loans.

As stated in FASB ASC 860-30-25-3, when cash is received as collateral in secured borrowings, the cash received should be recognized as the investment company's asset, along with the obligation to return the cash. Consistent with FASB ASC 860-30-25-8, if the investment company makes investments with the cash, even if made by agents or in pools with other securities lenders, the investment company should reflect the investments as part of its holdings in the schedule of investments and footnote any restrictions associated with the investment because of the collateral arrangements.

With regard to collateral received in the form of securities in secured borrowings, if the securities received may be sold or repledged, the investment company should account for those securities in the same way as it would account for cash received. That is, the investment company should record the securities received as the investment company's asset along with the obligation to return the securities. However, if the investment company does not have the right to sell or repledge the securities received as collateral, then the investment company should not record the securities or related liability on its books.

AAG-INV 7.180

	Shares or Principal Amount	Fair Value
Foreign currency (cost $141,000)		139,000
Cash		60,000
Deposits with brokers for securities sold short		1,555,000
Receivables		
Dividends and interest		46,000
Investment securities sold		24,000
Capital stock sold		54,000
Unrealized gain on foreign currency forward exchange contract (note 3)		419,000
Other assets		26,000
Total assets		24,044,000
Liabilities		
Call options written at fair value (premiums received: $110,000)		230,000
Securities sold short at fair value (proceeds: $1,555,000)		1,673,000
Demand loan payable to bank (note 5)		2,000,000
Payable upon return of securities loaned (note 8)		620,000
Unrealized loss on foreign currency forward exchange contract (note 3)		108,000
Unrealized loss on swap contract (note 3)		21,000
Due to broker—variation margin (note 3)		10,000
Payables		
Investment securities purchased		52,000
Capital stock reacquired		8,000
Other		4,000
Accrued expenses		8,000
Distribution payable		137,000
Total liabilities		4,871,000
Net assets		$19,173,000
Analysis of Net Assets:[73]		
Net capital paid in on shares of capital stock		$15,184,000
Distributable earnings		3,989,000
Net assets (equivalent to $4.55 per share based on 4,216,000 shares of capital stock outstanding) (note 6)		$19,173,000

Note—Aggregate value of segregated securities: $372,000.

The accompanying notes are an integral part of these financial statements.

---

[73] See footnote 58.

7.181

XYZ Investment Company
Statement of Operations
Year Ended December 31, 20X8

Investment income

Dividends (net of foreign withholding taxes of $20,000)	$742,000	
Interest	209,000	
Income from securities loaned—net	50,000	
Total income		$1,001,000

Expenses

Investment advisory fee	135,000	
Interest	55,000	
Professional fees (note 9)	29,000	
Custodian and transfer agent fees	16,000	
Distribution expenses (note 9)	4,000	
State and local taxes other than income taxes	15,000	
Directors' fees	12,000	
Dividends on securities sold short	9,000	
Total expenses		275,000
Fees paid indirectly (note 9)		(4,000)
Fees waived (note 9)		(45,000)
Net expenses		226,000
Net investment income		775,000

Realized and unrealized gain (loss) from investments and foreign currency:

Net realized gain (loss) from—

Investments		1,089,000
Foreign currency transactions[74]		(44,000)
		1,045,000

Net increase (decrease) in unrealized appreciation (depreciation) on—

Investments		(1,647,000)
Translation of assets and liabilities in foreign currencies[75]		353,000
		(1,294,000)
Net realized and unrealized loss from investments and foreign currency		(249,000)
Net increase in net assets resulting from operations		$ 526,000

The accompanying notes are an integral part of these financial statements.

---

[74] If separate reporting is adopted, these captions would also include foreign currency effects of realized and unrealized gains and losses on investments. If separate reporting is not adopted, such foreign currency effects would be included in the investments captions.

[75] See footnote 74.

7.182

XYZ Investment Company
Statements of Changes in Net Assets
Years Ended December 31, 20X8 and 20X7

	20X8	20X7
Increase (decrease) in net assets from operations		
Investment income—net	$775,000	$492,000
Net realized gain from investments and foreign currency[76]	1,045,000	1,000,000
Unrealized appreciation (depreciation) on investments and translation of assets and liabilities in foreign currencies[77]	(1,294,000)	1,551,000
Net increase in net assets resulting from operations	526,000	3,043,000
Distributions to shareholders	(1,875,000)	(1,350,000)
Tax return of capital to shareholders	—	(66,000)
Capital share transactions (note 6)	2,730,000	1,755,000
Total increase	1,381,000	3,382,000
Net assets		
Beginning of year	17,792,000	14,410,000
End of year	$19,173,000	$17,792,000

The accompanying notes are an integral part of these financial statements.

---

[76] It is also acceptable to present each of these items as a separate line item: net realized gains from investments and net realized gains (losses) from foreign currency transactions.

[77] It is also acceptable to present each of these items as a separate line item: unrealized appreciation on investments and unrealized appreciation on the translation of assets and liabilities in foreign currencies.

7.183

XYZ Investment Company
Statement of Cash Flows
Year Ended December 31, 20X8

Increase (decrease) in cash—
Cash flows from operating activities:

Net increase in net assets from operations	$526,000
Adjustments to reconcile net increase in net assets from operations to net cash used in operating activities:	
Purchase of investment securities	(26,797,000)
Proceeds from disposition of investment securities	26,336,000
Sale of short term investment securities, net	(921,000)
Increase in deposits with brokers for short sales	(555,000)
Increase in collateral for securities loaned	(270,000)
Increase in dividends and interest receivable	(18,000)
Increase in equity on foreign currency forward contracts	(363,000)
Increase in other assets	(2,000)
Premiums from call options written	50,000
Proceeds from securities sold short	802,000
Increase in depreciation on swap contracts	21,000
Increase in payable upon return of securities loaned	270,000
Decrease in variation margin payable	(4,000)
Increase in accrued expenses	1,000
Unrealized appreciation on securities	1,647,000
Net realized gain from investments	(1,089,000)
Net cash used in operating activities	(366,000)
Cash flows from financing activities:	
Decrease in loan payable	(400,000)
Proceeds from shares sold	2,143,000
Payment on shares redeemed	(450,000)
Cash distributions paid	(841,000)
Net cash provided by financing activities	452,000
Net increase in cash	86,000
Cash:	
Beginning balance	113,000
Ending balance	$199,000

Supplemental disclosure of cash flow information:

Noncash financing activities not included herein consist of reinvestment of dividends and distributions of $1,000,000.

The accompanying notes are an integral part of these financial statements.

AAG-INV 7.183

> **⊕ Update 7-5 *Accounting and Reporting*: Fair Value**
>
> ASU No. 2011-04, issued in May 2011, is effective for public entities during interim and annual periods beginning after December 15, 2011. It is effective for nonpublic entities for annual periods beginning after December 15, 2011. Early application is not permitted for public entities. Nonpublic entities may early implement during interim periods beginning after December 15, 2011. The guidance should be applied prospectively.
>
> The disclosures included herein do not contain updates for the amendments of ASU No. 2011-04. Refer to section A.02 updates 2-1, 7-3, and 7-6 in appendix A for more information on this ASU if applicable to your reporting period. In addition, readers are encouraged to consult the full text of the ASU on FASB's website at www.fasb.org.

7.184

XYZ Investment Company
Notes to Financial Statements

1. Significant Accounting Policies

XYZ Investment Company (the company) is registered under the Investment Company Act of 1940 as a diversified, open-end management investment company. The investment objective of the company is to seek a high total return consisting of both current income and realized and unrealized gains from equity and debt securities.

Security valuation. All investments in securities are recorded at their estimated fair value, as described in note 2.

Repurchase agreements. In connection with transactions in repurchase agreements, it is the company's policy that its custodian take possession of the underlying collateral securities, the fair value of which exceeds the principal amount of the repurchase transaction, including accrued interest, at all times. If the seller defaults, and the fair value of the collateral declines, realization of the collateral by the company may be delayed or limited.

Foreign currency. Investment securities and other assets and liabilities denominated in foreign currencies are translated into U.S. dollar amounts at the date of valuation. Purchases and sales of investment securities and income and expense items denominated in foreign currencies are translated into U.S. dollar amounts on the respective dates of such transactions.

The company does not isolate that portion of the results of operations resulting from changes in foreign exchange rates on investments from the fluctuations arising from changes in market prices of securities held. Such fluctuations are included with the net realized and unrealized gain or loss from investments.

Reported net realized foreign exchange gains or losses arise from sales of foreign currencies, currency gains or losses realized between the trade and settlement dates on securities transactions, and the difference between the amounts of dividends, interest, and foreign withholding taxes recorded on the company's books and the U.S. dollar equivalent of the amounts actually received or paid. Net unrealized foreign exchange gains and losses arise from changes in the fair values of assets and liabilities, other than investments in securities at fiscal period-end, resulting from changes in exchange rates.

[*The following paragraphs illustrate disclosures for a fund that chooses to report the foreign currency elements of realized and unrealized gains and losses on investments.*]

The company isolates that portion of the results of operations resulting from changes in foreign exchange rates on investments from the fluctuations arising from changes in market prices of securities held.

Reported net realized foreign exchange gains or losses arise from sales of portfolio securities; sales and maturities of short term securities; sales of foreign currencies; currency gains or losses realized between the trade and settlement dates on securities transactions; and the difference between the amounts of dividends, interest, and foreign withholding taxes recorded on the company's books and the U.S. dollar equivalent of the amounts actually received or paid. Net unrealized foreign exchange gains and losses arise from changes in the values of assets and liabilities, including investments in securities at fiscal period-end, resulting from changes in the exchange rate.

Option writing. When the company writes an option, an amount equal to the premium received by the company is recorded as a liability and subsequently adjusted to the current fair value of the option written. Premiums received from writing options that expire unexercised are treated by the company on the expiration date as realized gains from investments. The difference between the premium and amount paid on effecting a closing purchase transaction, including brokerage commissions, is also treated as a realized gain or, if the premium is less than the amount paid for the closing purchase transaction, as a realized loss. If a call option is exercised, the premium is added to the proceeds from the sale of the underlying security or currency in determining whether the company has realized a gain or loss. If a put option is exercised, the premium reduces the cost basis of the securities purchased by the company. The company as writer of an option bears the market risk of an unfavorable change in the price of the security underlying the written option.

Warrants. The company can invest in warrants and stock purchase rights of companies of any market capitalization. A warrant gives the company the right to buy stock. The warrant specifies the amount of underlying stock, the purchase (or "exercise") price, and the date the warrant expires. The company has no obligation to exercise the warrant and buy the stock.

Security loans. The company receives compensation in the form of fees, or it retains a portion of interest on the investment of any cash received as collateral. The company also continues to receive interest or dividends on the securities loaned. The loans are secured by collateral at least equal, at all times, to the fair value of the securities loaned plus accrued interest. Gain or loss in the fair value of the securities loaned that may occur during the term of the loan will be for the account of the company. The company has the right under the lending agreement to recover the securities from the borrower on demand; if the borrower fails to deliver the securities on a timely basis, the company could experience delays or losses on recovery. Additionally, the company is subject to the risk of loss from investments that it makes with the cash received as collateral.

Financial futures contracts. The company invests in financial futures contracts solely for the purpose of hedging its existing portfolio securities, or securities that the company intends to purchase, against fluctuations in fair value caused by changes in prevailing market interest rates. Upon entering into a financial futures contract, the company is required to pledge to the broker an amount of

Financial Statements of Investment Companies

cash, U.S. government securities, or other assets equal to a certain percentage of the contract amount (initial margin deposit). Subsequent payments, known as *variation margin*, are made or received by the company each day, depending on the daily fluctuations in the fair value of the underlying security. The company recognizes a gain or loss equal to the daily variation margin. If market conditions move unexpectedly, the company may not achieve the anticipated benefits of the financial futures contracts and may realize a loss. The use of futures transactions involves the risk of imperfect correlation in movements in the price of futures contracts, interest rates, and the underlying hedged assets.

Short sales. The company may sell a security that it does not own in anticipation of a decline in the fair value of that security. When the company sells a security short, it must borrow the security sold short and deliver it to the broker-dealer through which it made the short sale. A gain, limited to the price at which the company sold the security short, or a loss, unlimited in size, will be recognized upon the termination of a short sale. The company is also subject to the risk that it may be unable to reacquire a security to terminate a short position except at a price substantially in excess of the last quoted price.

Foreign currency forward exchange contracts. The company may enter into foreign currency forward exchange contracts primarily to hedge against foreign currency exchange rate risks on its non-U.S. dollar denominated investment securities. When entering into a forward currency contract, the company agrees to receive or deliver a fixed quantity of foreign currency for an agreed-upon price on an agreed future date. The company's net equity therein, representing unrealized gain or loss on the contracts, as measured by the difference between the forward foreign exchange rates at the dates of entry into the contracts and the forward rates at the reporting date, is included in the statement of assets and liabilities. Realized and unrealized gains and losses are included in the statement of operations. These instruments involve market risk, credit risk, or both kinds of risks in excess of the amount recognized in the statement of assets and liabilities. Risks arise from the possible inability of counterparties to meet the terms of their contracts and movement in currency and securities values and interest rates.

Credit default swaps. The company may enter into credit default swaps to manage its exposure to the market or certain sectors of the market, to reduce its risk exposure to defaults of corporate and sovereign issuers or to create exposure to corporate or sovereign issuers to which it is not otherwise exposed. In a credit default swap, the protection buyer makes a stream of payments based on a fixed percentage applied to the contract notional amount to the protection seller in exchange for the right to receive a specified return upon the occurrence of a defined credit event on the reference obligation that may be either a single security or a basket of securities issued by corporate or sovereign issuers. Although contract specific, *credit events* are generally defined as bankruptcy, failure to pay, restructuring, obligation acceleration, obligation default, or repudiation or moratorium. Upon the occurrence of a defined credit event, the difference between the value of the reference obligation and the swap's notional amount is recorded as realized gain (for protection written) or loss (for protection sold) in the statement of operations.

Federal income taxes. The company's policy is to continue to comply with the requirements of the Internal Revenue Code that are applicable to regulated investment companies and to distribute all its taxable income to its shareholders. The company also intends to distribute sufficient net investment income and net capital gains, if any, so that it will not be subject to excise tax on

AAG-INV 7.184

undistributed income and gains. Therefore, no federal income tax or excise provision is required.

Distributions to shareholders. Dividends to shareholders from net investment income, if any, are paid semiannually. Distributions of capital gains, if any, are made at least annually, and as required to comply with federal excise tax requirements. Distributions to shareholders are determined in accordance with income tax regulations and recorded on the ex-dividend date.

Use of estimates. The preparation of financial statements in conformity with U.S. generally accepted accounting principles (GAAP) requires management to make estimates and assumptions that affect the reported amounts of assets and liabilities and disclosure of contingent assets and liabilities at the date of the financial statements and the reported amounts of increases and decreases in net assets from operations during the reporting period. Actual results could differ from those estimates.

Other. The company records security transactions based on a trade date. Dividend income is recognized on the ex-dividend date, and interest income is recognized on an accrual basis. Discounts and premiums on securities purchased are accreted and amortized over the lives of the respective securities. Withholding taxes on foreign dividends have been provided for in accordance with the company's understanding of the applicable country's tax rules and rates.

2. Securities Valuations

As described in note 1, the company utilizes various methods to measure the fair value of most of its investments on a recurring basis. GAAP establishes a hierarchy that prioritizes inputs to valuation methods. The three levels of inputs are as follows:

- *Level 1.* Unadjusted quoted prices in active markets for identical assets or liabilities that the company has the ability to access.
- *Level 2.* Observable inputs other than quoted prices included in level 1 that are observable for the asset or liability either directly or indirectly. These inputs may include quoted prices for the identical instrument on an inactive market, prices for similar instruments, interest rates, prepayment speeds, credit risk, yield curves, default rates, and similar data.
- *Level 3.* Unobservable inputs for the asset or liability to the extent that relevant observable inputs are not available, representing the company's own assumptions about the assumptions that a market participant would use in valuing the asset or liability, and that would be based on the best information available.

The availability of observable inputs can vary from security to security and is affected by a wide variety of factors, including, for example, the type of security, whether the security is new and not yet established in the marketplace, the liquidity of markets, and other characteristics particular to the security. To the extent that valuation is based on models or inputs that are less observable or unobservable in the market, the determination of fair value requires more judgment. Accordingly, the degree of judgment exercised in determining fair value is greatest for instruments categorized in level 3.

The inputs used to measure fair value may fall into different levels of the fair value hierarchy. In such cases, for disclosure purposes, the level in the fair

Financial Statements of Investment Companies

value hierarchy within which the fair value measurement falls in its entirety is determined based on the lowest level input that is significant to the fair value measurement in its entirety.

Fair Value Measurements

A description of the valuation techniques applied to the company's major categories of assets and liabilities measured at fair value on a recurring basis follows.

Equity securities (common and preferred stock). Securities traded on a national securities exchange (or reported on the NASDAQ national market) are stated at the last reported sales price on the day of valuation. To the extent these securities are actively traded, and valuation adjustments are not applied, they are categorized in level 1 of the fair value hierarchy. Certain foreign securities may be fair valued using a pricing service that considers the correlation of the trading patterns of the foreign security to the intraday trading in the U.S. markets for investments such as American Depositary Receipts, financial futures, Exchange Traded Funds, and the movement of the certain indexes of securities based on a statistical analysis of the historical relationship and that are categorized in level 2. Preferred stock and other equities traded on inactive markets or valued by reference to similar instruments are also categorized in level 2.

Corporate bonds. The fair value of corporate bonds is estimated using various techniques, which may consider recently executed transactions in securities of the issuer or comparable issuers, market price quotations (when observable), bond spreads, fundamental data relating to the issuer, and credit default swap spreads adjusted for any basis difference between cash and derivative instruments. Although most corporate bonds are categorized in level 2 of the fair value hierarchy, in instances when lower relative weight is placed on transaction prices, quotations, or similar observable inputs, they are categorized in level 3.

Asset-backed securities. The fair value of asset-backed securities is estimated based on models that consider the estimated cash flows of each tranche of the entity, establishes a benchmark yield, and develops an estimated tranche-specific spread to the benchmark yield based on the unique attributes of the tranche. To the extent that the inputs are observable and timely, the values would be categorized in level 2 of the fair value hierarchy; otherwise, they would be categorized as level 3.

Short term notes. Short term notes are valued using amortized cost, which approximates fair value. To the extent that the inputs are observable and timely, the values would be categorized in level 2 of the fair value hierarchy.

U.S. government securities. U.S. government securities are normally valued using a model that incorporates market observable data, such as reported sales of similar securities, broker quotes, yields, bids, offers, and reference data. Certain securities are valued principally using dealer quotations. U.S. government securities are categorized in level 1 or level 2 of the fair value hierarchy, depending on the inputs used and market activity levels for specific securities.

U.S. agency securities. U.S. agency securities comprise two main categories consisting of agency-issued debt and mortgage pass-throughs. Agency-issued debt securities are generally valued in a manner similar to U.S. government securities. Mortgage pass-throughs include to-be-announced (TBA) securities

AAG-INV 7.184

and mortgage pass-through certificates. TBA securities and mortgage pass-throughs are generally valued using dealer quotations. Depending on market activity levels and whether quotations or other data are used, these securities are typically categorized in level 1 or level 2 of the fair value hierarchy.

Restricted securities (equity and debt). Restricted securities for which quotations are not readily available are valued at fair value, as determined by the board of directors. Restricted securities issued by publicly traded companies are generally valued at a discount to similar publicly traded securities. Restricted securities issued by nonpublic entities may be valued by reference to comparable public entities or fundamental data relating to the issuer, or both. Depending on the relative significance of valuation inputs, these instruments may be classified in either level 2 or level 3 of the fair value hierarchy.

Derivative instruments. Listed derivatives that are actively traded are valued based on quoted prices from the exchange and categorized in level 1 of the fair value hierarchy. Over-the-counter (OTC) derivative contracts include forward, swap, and option contracts related to interest rates; foreign currencies; credit standing of reference entities; equity prices; or commodity prices, and warrants on exchange-traded securities. Depending on the product and terms of the transaction, the fair value of the OTC derivative products can be modeled taking into account the counterparties' creditworthiness and using a series of techniques, including simulation models. Many pricing models do not entail material subjectivity because the methodologies employed do not necessitate significant judgments, and the pricing inputs are observed from actively quoted markets, as is the case of interest rate swap and option contracts. A substantial majority of OTC derivative products valued by the company using pricing models fall into this category and are categorized within level 2 of the fair value hierarchy.

Financial Statements of Investment Companies

The following table summarizes the inputs used to value the company's assets and liabilities measured at fair value as of December 31, 20X8.[78]

Assets

	Level 1	Level 2	Level 3	Total
Common stocks—*Consumer durable goods*	$1,086,000	—	—	$1,086,000
Common stocks—*Consumer nondurable goods*	155,000	—	3,280,000	3,435,00
Common stocks—*Service industries*	869,000	—	—	869,000
Common stocks—*Other industries*	921,000	—	—	921,000
Convertible bonds	—	5,400,000	—	5,400,000
Indexed securities	—	—	2,100,000	2,100,000
Mortgage-backed securities	—	2,710,000	—	2,710,000
U.S. governmental obligations	—	3,475,000	—	3,475,000
Short term notes	—	1,225,000	—	1,225,000
Repurchase agreements	—	500,000	—	500,000
Derivative instruments*	—	419,000	—	419,000
Total	$3,031,000	$13,729,000	$5,380,000	$22,140,000

Liabilities

	Level 1	Level 2	Level 3	Total
Common stocks	$(1,673,000)	—	—	$(1,673,000)
Derivative Instruments*	(280,000)	(129,000)	—	$(409,000)
Total	$(1,953,000)	$(129,000)		$(2,082,000)

---

* Derivative instruments include call options written, foreign currency forward contracts, credit default swap contracts, and cumulative loss on futures contracts open at December 31, 20X8.

There were no transfers between level 1 and level 2 during the year.

---

[78] The classification of various financial instruments in this table is for illustrative purposes only and should not be construed as recommended practice for any particular financial instrument or class of financial instruments.

AAG-INV 7.184

The following is a reconciliation of assets for which level 3 inputs were used in determining value.

	Common Stock	Indexed Securities	Total
Beginning balance	$ 2,000,000	—	$ 2,000,000
Total realized gain (loss)	(500,000)	—	(500,000)
Change in unrealized appreciation (depreciation)	780,000	(300,000)	480,000
Cost of purchases	—	2,400,000	2,400,000
Proceeds from sales	1,000,000	—	1,000,000
Accrued interest	—	—	—
Transfers into level 3	—	—	—
Transfers out of level 3	—	—	—
Ending balance	$3,280,000	$2,100,000	$5,380,000

The total change in unrealized appreciation (depreciation) included in the statement of operations attributable to level 3 investments still held at December 31, 20X8 includes

| | $880,000 | $(300,000) | $580,000 |

3. Derivatives Transactions[79]

As of December 31, 20X8, portfolio securities valued at $634,500 were held in escrow by the custodian as cover for call options written by the company.

Transactions in options written during the year ended December 31, 20X8, were as follows:

	Number of Contracts	Premiums Received
Options outstanding at December 31, 20X7	100	$ 100,000
Options written	500	500,000
Options terminated in closing purchase transactions	(150)	(190,000)
Options expired	(80)	(150,000)
Options exercised	(150)	(150,000)
Options outstanding at December 31, 20X8	220	$ 110,000

As of December 31, 20X8, the company sold 10 financial futures contracts on 10 year U.S. Treasury notes for delivery in March 20X9. The company has recorded an unrealized loss of $50,000 as of December 31, 20X8, related to these contracts. The company has additionally recorded a liability of $10,000 as of December 31, 20X8, related to the current day's variation margin related to these contracts.

---

[79] Practitioners should consider all the disclosure requirements of FASB ASC 815, which may not be necessarily reflected in these financial statements and notes to the financial statements.

Financial Statements of Investment Companies

At December 31, 20X8, the company sold the following foreign currency forward exchange contracts:

	Unrealized Gains	Unrealized Loss
1,407,900,000 Japanese yen vs. $14,588,000 for settlement January 25, 20X9	$419,000	
14,394,000 Euro vs. $13,206,000 for settlement March 7, 20X9	—	($108,000)
	$419,000	($108,000)

Additionally, the company had entered into a credit default swap with American Trust Company as counterparty under which it had agreed to sell protection, expiring June 30, 20Y1, against $500,000 (par) of Baker Industries, Inc. 6 percent bonds due 20X9 for an annual premium of 1.75 percent. At December 31, 20X8, this contract had a fair value of $(21,000). The current credit rating of Baker Industries, as determined by major credit rating agencies, is BB/Ba. The unrealized depreciation in the contract at December 31, 20X8, indicates that the market's evaluation of a default has increased since the contract's inception but not to the extent that default is considered imminent.

The locations on the statement of assets and liabilities of the company's derivative positions by type of exposure, none of which are accounted for as hedging instruments under FASB ASC 815, *Derivatives and Hedging*, is as follows:

	Location	Fair Value of Asset Derivatives	Location	Fair Value of Liability Derivatives
Interest rate contracts			*	($50,000)
Foreign exchange contracts	Unrealized gain on foreign currency contract	$419,000	Unrealized loss on foreign currency contract	($108,000)
Credit contracts			Unrealized loss on swap contract	($21,000)
Equity contracts	Investments in securities**	$4,000	Call options written	($230,000)
Other contracts				
Total		$423,000		($409,000)

---

* Includes cumulative appreciation or depreciation of futures contracts described previously. Only current day's variation margin is reported within the statement of assets and liabilities.

** Includes value of the warrants that are considered derivatives under FASB ASC 815 guidance.

AAG-INV 7.184

Realized and unrealized gains and losses on derivatives contracts entered into during the year ended December 31, 20X8, by the company are recorded in the following locations in the statement of operations:

	Location	Realized Gain/Loss	Locations	Unrealized Gain/Loss
Interest rate contracts	Realized gain/loss—investments	$73,000	Unrealized gain/loss—investments	($50,000)
Foreign exchange contracts	Realized gain/loss—foreign currency transactions	18,000	Unrealized gain/loss—translation	311,000
Credit contracts		—	Unrealized gain/loss—investments	($120,000)
Equity contracts	Realized gain/loss—investments	($89,000)	Unrealized gain/loss—investments	($120,000)*
Other contracts		—		—
Total		$2,000		$120,000

* Includes value of the warrants that are considered derivatives under FASB ASC 815 guidance.

For nonexchange-traded derivatives (swaps and forward foreign currency contracts), under standard derivatives agreements, the company may be required to post collateral on derivatives if the company is in a net liability position with the counterparty exceeding certain amounts. Additionally, counterparties may immediately terminate derivatives contracts if the company fails to maintain sufficient asset coverage for its contracts, or its net assets decline by stated percentages.

4. Income Taxes

The tax character of distributions paid during 20X8 and 20X7 was as follows:

	20X8	20X7
Distributions paid from:		
Ordinary income	$ 755,000	$ 550,000
Long term capital gain	1,120,000	800,000
	1,875,000	1,350,000
Return of capital	—	66,000
	$1,875,000	$1,416,000

As of December 31, 20X8, the components of distributable earnings on a tax basis were as follows:

Undistributed ordinary income	$1,304,000
Undistributed long term gain	1,145,000
Unrealized appreciation	1,540,000
	$3,989,000

The difference between book-basis and tax-basis unrealized appreciation is attributable primarily to the tax deferral of losses on wash sales and the realization for tax purposes of unrealized gains on certain forward foreign currency contracts and investments in passive foreign investment companies.

Permanent book- and tax-basis differences, if any, result in reclassifications to paid-in capital. These reclassifications have no effect on net assets or results of operations. Permanent book- and tax-basis differences are primarily attributable to derivatives transactions.

The U.S. federal income tax basis of the company's investments at December 31, 20X8, was $19,321,000, and net unrealized appreciation for U.S. federal income tax purposes was $1,780,000 (gross unrealized appreciation $2,380,000; gross unrealized depreciation $600,000).

The company recognizes the tax benefits of uncertain tax positions only when the position is more likely than not to be sustained, assuming examination by tax authorities. Management has analyzed the company's tax positions and concluded that no liability for unrecognized tax benefits should be recorded related to uncertain tax positions taken on returns filed for open tax years (20X5–X8) or expected to be taken in the company's 20X9 tax returns. The company identifies its major tax jurisdictions as U.S. federal, New York State, and foreign jurisdictions where the company makes significant investments; however, the company is not aware of any tax positions for which it is reasonably possible that the total amounts of unrecognized tax benefits will change materially in the next 12 months.

5. Bank Loans

The company has an unsecured $3,000,000 bank line of credit; borrowings under this arrangement bear interest at 110 percent of the bank's prime rate. As of December 31, 20X8, the company was paying weighted average interest at 8 percent per year on its outstanding borrowings. No compensating balances are required. For the year ended December 31, 20X8, the average borrowings and interest rate under the line of credit were $1,700,000 and 6.50 percent, respectively. The December 31, 20X8, balance of $2,000,000 was the maximum borrowing during the year.

6. Capital Share Transactions

As of December 31, 20X8, 25,000,000 shares of $0.50 par value capital stock were authorized.

Transactions in capital stock were as follows:

	Shares 20X8	Shares 20X7	Amount 20X8	Amount 20X7
Shares sold	452,000	329,000	$ 2,186,000	$1,440,000
Shares issued in reinvestment of distributions	222,000	207,000	1,000,000	845,000
	674,000	536,000	3,186,000	2,285,000
Shares redeemed	104,000	121,000	456,000	530,000
Net increase	570,000	415,000	$2,730,000	$1,755,000

AAG-INV 7.184

On January 3, 20X9, a distribution of $0.20 per share was declared from net investment income. The dividend was paid on January 20, 20X9, to shareholders of record on January 10, 20X9.

7. Investment Transactions

Purchases and sales of investment securities (excluding short term securities and U.S. government obligations) were $23,420,000 and $24,030,000, respectively.

8. Portfolio Securities Loaned

As of December 31, 20X8, the company loaned common stocks having a fair value of approximately $570,000 and received $620,000 of cash collateral for the loan. This cash was invested in U.S. Treasury bills with maturities ranging from January to April 20X9.

9. Investment Advisory Fees and Other Transactions With Affiliates

The company receives investment management and advisory services under a management agreement (agreement) that provides for fees to be paid at an annual rate of 0.65 percent of the company's average daily net assets. Certain officers and directors of the company are also officers and directors of the investment adviser. The agreement provides for an expense reimbursement from the investment adviser if the company's total expenses, exclusive of taxes, interest on borrowings, dividends on securities sold short, brokerage commissions, and extraordinary expenses, exceed 1.5 percent of the company's average daily net assets for any full fiscal year. During the year ended December 31, 20X8, the investment adviser voluntarily waived $45,000 of its fee.

The investment adviser also received $5,000 in 20X8 from brokerage fees on executions of purchases and sales of the company's portfolio investments.

During 20X8, the company incurred legal fees of $7,000 to Brown and Smith, counsel for the company. A partner of the firm is a director of the company.

MNO Service Company (MNO), an affiliate of the investment adviser, is the distributor of the company's shares and received $10,000 in 20X8 from commissions earned on sales of the company's capital stock. The company has entered into a distribution agreement and plan of distribution pursuant to which the company pays MNO a fee, accrued daily and payable monthly, at an annual rate of 0.75 percent of average daily net assets of the company. During the year ended December 31, 20X8, MNO received contingent deferred sales charges of $18,000 from redeeming shareholders. Also, the amount of distribution expenses incurred by MNO and not yet reimbursed was approximately $187,000. This amount may be recovered from future payments under the plan or contingent deferred sales charges.

Included in the statement of operations under the caption "Custodian and transfer agent fees" are expense offsets of $4,000 arising from credits on cash balances maintained on deposit.

7.185

Financial Highlights

	20X8	20X7	20X6	20X5	20X4[80]
Per Share Operating Performance (for a share of capital stock outstanding throughout the period):					
Net asset value, beginning of period	$ 4.88	$ 4.46	$ 4.16	$ 4.81	$ 4.53
Income from investment operations:					
Net investment income	0.21	0.15	0.19	0.17	0.15
Net realized and unrealized gain (loss) on investment transactions	(0.04)	0.76	0.52	(0.42)	0.48
Total from investment operations	0.17	0.91	0.71	(0.25)	0.63
Less distributions	(0.50)	(0.47)	(0.41)	(0.40)	(0.35)
Tax return of capital distribution	—	(0.02)	—	—	—
Total distributions	(0.50)	(0.49)	(0.41)	(0.40)	(0.35)
Net asset value, end of period	$ 4.55	$ 4.88	$ 4.46	$ 4.16	$ 4.81
Total Return: [81]	3.48%	20.40%	17.07%	(5.02)%	3.91%
Supplemental Data:					
Net assets, end of period (000)	$19,173	$17,792	$14,410	$15,000	$14,000
Ratio to average net assets:					
Expenses[82]	1.33%[83]	1.31%	.99%	.82%	84%
Net investment income[84,85]	4.56%[86]	2.82%	4.22%	5.42%	5.10%
Portfolio turnover rate	92%	80%	108%	75%	62%

The accompanying notes are an integral part of these financial statements.

---

[80] Period from March 1, 20X4 (inception) to December 31, 20X4.
[81] Not annualized for periods less than one year.
[82] Annualized for periods less than one year.
[83] Such percentages are after advisory fee waivers and expense subsidies. The adviser voluntarily waived a portion of its investment advisory fee (equal to 0.22 percent of average net assets) in 20X8 and subsidized certain operating expenses (equal to 0.21 percent of average net assets) in 20X8.
[84] See footnote 82.
[85] The net investment income (loss) ratio excludes the effect of the incentive allocation.
[86] See footnote 83.

Illustrations of Calculations and Disclosures When Reporting Expense and Net Investment Income Ratios

7.186. The following are illustrations of average net assets computations related to determining expense and net investment income ratios in which there are various capital flows, assuming a single class of investment interest. Other average net assets computation methods (for example, summing and averaging monthly net assets, including the beginning and ending net assets for the year, or a method that also weights ending net assets) are also appropriate if the result is reasonable and consistently applied.

Example 1: Computation of average net assets in a nonregistered investment partnership that allows quarterly contributions and distributions and has quarterly accounting periods (that is, capital can flow in and out only at these times):

Net assets at the beginning of the period:	$100,000,000 × 3/12 =	$ 25,000,000
Valuation adjustment of $10 million and capital contribution of $25 million at April 1, 20X9:	$135,000,000 × 3/12 =	$ 33,750,000
Valuation adjustment of $(5) million, capital contribution of $10 million, and capital withdrawals of $30 million at July 1, 20X9:	$110,000,000 × 3/12 =	$ 27,500,000
Valuation adjustment of $20 million, capital contribution of $15 million, and capital withdrawals of $25 million at October 1, 20X9:	$120,000,000 × 3/12 =	$ 30,000,000
Average net assets		$116,250,000

Example 2: Computation of average net assets in a nonregistered investment partnership that does not have predetermined accounting periods (that is, capital can be called and distributed at any time), with significant write-up in fair value during the year:

Net assets at the beginning of the period:	$100,000,000 × 2/12 =	$ 16,666,667
$25m capital call at February 28, 20X9:	$125,000,000 × 1/12 =	$ 10,416,667
$20m write-up at March 31, 20X9:	$145,000,000 × 6/12 =	$ 72,500,000
$55m capital call at September 30, 20X9:	$200,000,000 × 1/12 =	$ 16,666,667
$25m distribution at October 31, 20X9:	$175,000,000 × 2/12 =	$ 29,166,667
Average net assets		$145,416,668

Financial Statements of Investment Companies

Disclosure for Incentive and Allocation Fees

For incentive fee:	
Operating (and interest/short dividends) expense	2.25%
Incentive fee	7.35%
Total expenses	9.60%
For incentive allocations:	
Operating (and interest/short dividends) expense	2.25%
Incentive allocation	7.35%
Total expenses and incentive allocation	9.60%

The expense ratio (expense and incentive allocation ratio) is calculated for each common class taken as a whole. The computation of such ratios based on the amount of expenses and incentive fee or incentive allocation assessed to an individual investor's capital may vary from these ratios based on different management fee and incentive arrangements (as applicable) and the timing of capital transactions.

Illustration of Calculation and Disclosure When Reporting the Internal Rate of Return

7.187 The following is an illustration of how to compute IRR for nonregistered investment partnerships that meet the criteria described in paragraph 7.159(c). Other nonregistered investment partnerships generally should calculate a total rate of return as described in paragraph 7.159(b) and illustrated in paragraph 7.188.

The following illustrates how an IRR is computed by a limited-life nonregistered investment partnership, from the perspective of the investor, at the end of its first and second years of operations. The formula used to compute the IRR is $0 = CF0 + (CF1/(1+IRR)) + (CF2/(1+IRR)2) +...+ (CFT/(1+IRR)T)$.

Assume that year 1 activity includes an initial investment (capital contribution) on January 1 of $1,000,000; $50,000 of appreciation (profit) reported on March 31; an additional capital contribution of $1,000,000 on April 1; additional appreciation of $80,000 reported on June 30; a distribution of $500,000 on July 1; and depreciation (loss) of $30,000 reported on December 31, resulting in a residual value on December 31, 01, of $1,600,000. The residual value, the ending net assets at the end of the period and considered a theoretical distribution, is calculated as follows: $1,000,000 (initial capital contribution) plus $1,000,000 (additional capital contribution) minus $500,000 (cash distribution) plus the net gain of $100,000 (50,000 + 80,000 – 30,000) equals $1,600,000.

Assume that year 2 activity includes $150,000 of appreciation (profit) reported on March 31; a capital contribution of $500,000 on April 1; $350,000 of additional appreciation (profit) reported on June 30; $150,000 of additional appreciation (profit) reported on September 30; a distribution of $300,000 on December 14; and $150,000 of depreciation (loss) reported on December 31, resulting in a residual value

AAG-INV 7.187

on December 31, 02, of $2,300,000 (calculated the same way as year 01).

					IRR Cash Flows	
Date	Description	Capital Call	Cash Distribution	Residual Value	Through 12/31/01	Through 12/31/02
1-Jan-01	Initial contribution	1,000,000			(1,000,000)	(1,000,000)
1-Apr-01	Additional capital contribution	1,000,000			(1,000,000)	(1,000,000)
1-Jul-01	Cash distribution		500,000		500,000	500,000
31-Dec-01	Residual value			1,600,000	1,600,000	N/A
1-Apr-02	Additional capital contribution	500,000				(500,000)
14-Dec-02	Distribution		300,000			300,000
31-Dec-02	Residual value			2,300,000		2,300,000
		IRR through December 31, '01			6.69%	
		IRR through December 31, '02				16.68%

The following illustrates the note disclosure of the IRR by the limited-life nonregistered investment partnership at the end of the second year of operations based on the assumptions outlined.

Note X—Financial Highlights

The internal rate of return since inception (IRR) of the limited partners, net of all fees and profit allocations (carried interest) to the manager (general partner), is 6.69 percent through December 31, year 01, and 16.68 percent through December 31, year 02.

The IRR was computed based on the actual dates of the cash inflows (capital contributions), outflows (cash and stock distributions), and the ending net assets at the end of the period (residual value) of the limited partners' capital account as of each measurement date.

Illustration of Calculation and Disclosure When Reporting the Total Return Ratio

7.188 The following are illustrations of how to compute the total return ratio for nonregistered investment partnerships, as discussed in paragraph 7.159(*b*):

Example 1: The following are illustrations of how a geometrically linked cash flow is computed assuming a beginning equity of $1,000,000; a capital contribution of $1,000,000 on April 1; and a capital withdrawal of $500,000 on July 1:

					Percent Return		
Period	Cash Flows	Beginning Equity	Period Return	Ending Equity	Period	Year to Date	Year to Date Formula
1/1–3/31		1,000,000	50,000	1,050,000	5.00%	5.00%	(1+.05)-1
4/1–6/30	1,000,000	2,050,000	80,000	2,130,000	3.90%	9.10%	[(1+0.05)*(1+0.0390)]-1
7/1–12/31	(500,000)	1,630,000	(30,000)	1,600,000	(1.84)%	7.09%	[(1+0.0910)*(1-0.0184)]-1

AAG-INV 7.188

Financial Statements of Investment Companies

Example 2: The following is an illustration of a presentation of total return considering an incentive allocation or fee:

	Limited Partner or Common Class
Total return before incentive allocation/fee	7.09%
Incentive allocation/fee	(1.60%)
Total return after incentive allocation/fee	5.49%

Total return is calculated for each common class taken as a whole. An individual investor's return may vary from these returns based on participation in new issues, private investments, different management fee and incentive arrangements (as applicable), and the timing of capital transactions.

Condensed Schedule of Investments

7.189 The following is an illustration of a condensed schedule of investments. Net assets are assumed to be $50,000,000.

Condensed Schedule of Investments[87]
December 31, 20XX

Principal Amount, Shares, or No. of Contracts	Description	Fair Value
	COMMON STOCKS (54.9%)	
	United States (33.7%)	
	Airlines (7.2%)	
53,125	Flight Airlines, Inc.	$1,811,297
	Other (3.6%)	1,819,074
		3,630,371
	Banks (1.9%)	937,099
	Financial services (2.9%)	1,433,210
	Foods (7.1%)	
106,607	Andrews Midlands Co.	2,825,078
	Other (1.4%)	702,824
		3,527,902
	Hospital supplies and services (5.6%)	
100,404	Chelsea Clinics, Inc.	2,811,297
	Technology (4.1%)	2,039,578
	Utilities (4.9%)	2,480,556
	Total United States (cost: $16,850,954)	16,860,013

(continued)

---

[87] This schedule does not include the disclosures relative to the investment objective and restrictions on redemption, as discussed in paragraph 7.33g of this guide because it is presumed that those disclosures are presented in the notes to the financial statements.

Investment Companies

Principal Amount, Shares or No. of Contracts	Description	Fair Value
	Hong Kong (5.8%)	
	Drugs (0.7%)	330,741
	Retail (4.0%)	1,984,445
	Utility telephone (1.1%)	552,235
	Total Hong Kong (cost: $2,756,959)	2,867,421
	Italy (5.6%)	
	Airlines (0.2%)	110,247
	Financial services (1.8%)	881,975
	Leisure related (3.5%)	1,763,951
	Office supplies (0.1%)	55,123
	Total Italy (cost: $2,912,465)	2,811,296
	Spain (5.4%)	
	Banks (2.4%)	1,212,716
	Oil (1.7%)	826,852
	Railroads (1.3%)	661,482
	Total Spain (cost: $2,643,197)	2,701,050
	United Kingdom (4.4%)	
	Financial services (2.3%)	1,157,593
	Technology (2.1%)	1,047,346
	Total United Kingdom (cost: $2,145,246)	2,204,939
	TOTAL COMMON STOCKS (cost: $27,308,821)	27,444,719
	DEBT SECURITIES (41.3%)	
	United States (21.4%)	
	Airlines (2.0%)	
$1,000,000	Flight Airlines Inc. 12%, 7/15/X5	1,000,000
	Government (19.4%)	
$3,000,000	U.S. Treasury bond, 4.50%, 11/15/X7	3,031,791
	U.S. Treasury bonds, 3.00%–4.75%, 1/30/X5–7/15/X7	6,686,175
		9,717,966
	Total United States (cost: $15,015,200)	10,717,966
	Mexico (19.9%)	
	Government	
$11,000,000	United Mexican States, 8.625%–9.125% 3/12/08–12/7/X9 (cost: $10,000,000)	9,922,224

AAG-INV 7.189

Principal Amount, Shares or No. of Contracts	Description	Fair Value
	TOTAL DEBT SECURITIES (cost: $25,015,200)	20,640,190
	LONG PUT AND CALL OPTIONS (2.4%)	
	United States	
	Telecommunications (cost: $1,225,800)	1,212,716
	INTEREST IN INVESTMENT PARTNERSHIP (10.0%)	
	(cost $4,000,000)	5,000,000
	XYZ Hedge Fund LP (35% owned) (XYZ Hedge Fund LP owns 6,000 shares valued $9,000,000 of Leisure Cruises Inc., which is a United States company in the travel industry. The partnership's share of this investment is valued at $3,150,000 as of December 31, 20XX.)	
	TOTAL INVESTMENTS (108.6%) (COST: $57,549,821)	$54,297,625
	SECURITIES SOLD SHORT (9.6%)	
	COMMON STOCKS (5.7%)	
	United States	
	Energy	
100,000	ABC Resources Co. (proceeds: $2,715,000)	$2,825,078
	DEBT SECURITIES (3.7%)	
	Canada (3.7%)	
	Telecommunication (proceeds: $1,950,000)	1,867,000
	WRITTEN OPTIONS (0.2%)	
	United States (0.2%)	
	Manufacturing (proceeds: $130,000)	127,309
	TOTAL SECURITIES SOLD SHORT (proceeds: $4,795,000)	$4,819,387

AAG-INV 7.189

Description	Fair Value	Expiration Dates	No. of Contracts
FUTURES CONTRACTS (12.5%)			
Financial (5.2%)			
Eurodollar (5.2%)	$2,611,825	Feb–Apr 20YX	122
Indexes (5.6%)			
S&P 500 (5.6%)	2,788,000	Mar–May 20YX	89
Metals (1.7%)	840,000		
TOTAL FUTURES CONTRACTS	$6,239,825		
FORWARDS (11.5%)			
Argentinian Peso (5.8%)	$2,910,000	Oct–Nov 20YX	
Other currencies (5.7%)	2,876,315		
TOTAL FORWARDS	$5,786,315		
SWAPS (13.4%)			
Interest rate swaps (5.7%)	$2,875,000		
Currency swaps (7.7%)			
Yen/U.S. dollar swaps (6.0%)	2,999,016	Jan–Feb 20YX	
Other (1.7%)	868,000		
TOTAL SWAPS	$6,742,016		

The accompanying notes are an integral part of these financial statements.

Illustrations of Nonregistered Investment Partnerships Schedule of Investments

7.190 The following are illustrative examples from TIS section 6910.18 on how to apply the disclosure guidelines of FASB ASC 946-210-50-6 in the condensed schedule of investments for nonregistered investment partnerships. This guidance is discussed in paragraph 7.37.

Example 1:

- U.S. Treasury Bond (long)—4 percent of net assets
- U.S. Treasury Bond (short)—(1 percent) of net assets
- U.S. Treasury Bond futures contract—Appreciation equals 2 percent of net assets

In the preceding example, the investment company should present separately the long bond and the futures contract in the condensed schedule of investments because, in aggregate, the gross asset position for this issuer exceeds 5 percent of net assets. The short bond position, which represents the only liability position associated with the issuer, is not required to be disclosed separately because the gross liability position is not more than 5 percent of net assets. This assessment for derivatives is made regardless of whether the exposure to the underlying is long or short. Assessments are based solely on the value of the derivative contract (that is, either a long or short position with depreciation or a negative fair value would be considered a liability and aggregated with other liabilities for the purpose of this test). The preparer may consider whether disclosure of all positions, including those 5 percent or less, would be appropriate or meaningful to the reader in the circumstances.

Example 2:

- Various bonds of X company (long)—4 percent of net assets
- Stock of X company (short)—(3 percent) of net assets
- Long exposure equity swap (X company is the underlying)—Fair value equals 2 percent of net assets
- Short exposure equity swap (X company is the underlying)—Fair value equals (1 percent) of net assets

The guidance in paragraph 6(e)–6(f) of FASB ASC 946-210-50 relates to 5 percent disclosures for any derivative position. That guidance states, "In applying the 5-percent test, total long and total short positions in any one issuer shall be considered separately." This guidance contemplates situations such as the preceding example 2 in which an investment company holds both a long and short exposure to the same derivative without closing out either derivative position. In such cases, the long and short exposure to the same derivative should be considered separately and should not be netted for the purpose of the 5 percent issuer exposure calculation. This is consistent with the approach for boxed security positions.

In the preceding example 2, the investment company should present separately the various long bond positions and the long exposure equity swap contract in the condensed schedule of investments because, in aggregate, the gross asset position for this issuer exceeds 5 percent of net assets. Because none of the long bond positions is individually more than 5 percent of net assets, FASB ASC 946-210-50-6(c)(2) permits the reporting of all the long bond positions of that issuer in the aggregate (that is, naming the issuer but showing a range of maturities, interest rates, and other applicable bond disclosures as opposed to individually listing out the details of each of the long bond positions), although the preparer may consider whether disclosure of individual positions provides more meaningful information to the reader of the financial statements. The short stock position and the short exposure equity swap contract are not required to be disclosed separately because the gross liability position is, in aggregate, not more than 5 percent of net assets. Again, the investment company is not precluded from disclosing separately the short stock position and the short exposure equity swap position if the disclosure of such positions is deemed to provide more meaningful information to the reader. The preparer should consider both the long exposure and short exposure in the equity swaps separately and should not net them for the purpose of the 5 percent exposure calculation if both equity swap contracts have not been closed out.

Example 3:

- Bond of X company (long)—3 percent of net assets
- Stock of X company (short)—(1 percent) of net assets
- Swap (X company is the underlying)—Fair value equals (2 percent) of net assets

In the preceding example 3, the investment company would not be required to present separately any of the positions in the condensed schedule of investments because the gross asset position of the issuer (represented by the bond) is not more than 5 percent of net assets, and the gross liability position (represented by the combined total values of the short stock position and the swap) is also not more than 5 percent of net assets.

Example 4:

- Bond of X company (long)—4 percent of net assets
- Stock of X company (short)—(2 percent) of net assets
- Swap (X company is the underlying)—Fair value equals 2 percent of net assets
- Swap (X company is the underlying)—Fair value equals (4 percent) of net assets

In the preceding example 4, the investment company should present separately each of the positions in the condensed schedule of investments because the gross asset position of the issuer (represented by the combined total values of the bond and the appreciated swap) and the gross liability position of the issuer (represented by the combined total values of the short stock position and the depreciated swap) are both greater than 5 percent of net assets.

Presentation of Fully Benefit-Responsive Investment Contracts

7.191 The following is an illustration from FASB ASC 946-210-55-2 of the presentation of fully benefit-responsive investment contracts in the statement of assets and liabilities and related footnote disclosure, as discussed in paragraphs 7.32 and 7.169.

Presentation for the Statement of Assets and Liabilities

Investments (at fair value)	$8,800,000
Wrapper contracts (at fair value)	100,000
Total assets	8,900,000
Total liabilities	200,000
Net assets reflecting all investments at fair value	$8,700,000
Adjustment from fair value to contract value for fully benefit-responsive investment contracts	1,100,000
Net assets	$9,800,000

Related Footnote Disclosure

	Major Credit Ratings	Investments at Fair Value	Wrapper Contracts at Fair Value	Adjustments to Contract Value
Traditional guaranteed investment contract A	AAA/Aaa	$1,600,000	—	$400,000
Bank ABC stable value fund I	N/A	1,800,000	—	200,000

Financial Statements of Investment Companies

	Major Credit Ratings	Investments at Fair Value	Wrapper Contracts at Fair Value	Adjustments to Contract Value
Wrapped portfolio A:				
Bond #1		850,000	—	—
Bond #2		910,000	—	—
Wrapper			40,000	—
Total wrapped portfolio A	AAA/Aa2	1,760,000	40,000	200,000
Wrapped portfolio B:				
Bond #3		850,000	—	—
Bond fund #1		860,000	—	—
Bond #4		930,000	—	—
Wrapper		—	60,000	—
Total wrapped portfolio B	AA-/Aa3	2,640,000	60,000	300,000
Short-term investments	AAA/Aaa	1,000,000		
Total		$8,800,000	$100,000	$1,100,000

Illustration of Deferred Fees

7.192 The following is an illustration of a deferred incentive fee presentation in the financial statements and the related disclosures, as discussed in paragraphs 7.74, 7.113, and 7.163:

Statement of Assets and Liabilities

Assets
Cash and cash equivalents	$206,000
Investments at fair value	166,585,000
Total assets	$166,791,000

Liabilities
Management fee payable	$400,000
Redemptions payable	1,000,000
Accrued expenses	100,000
Deferred incentive fees payable	4,800,000
Total liabilities	6,300,000
Net assets	$160,491,000

Statement of Operations

Investment income
Interest income	$5,576,000
Dividend income	1,766,000
Total investment income	$7,342,000

AAG-INV 7.192

Statement of Operations—continued

Expenses

Incentive fee	$2,680,000
Management fee	1,831,000
Change in net appreciation on deferred incentive fees	650,000
Administration fee	60,000
Professional fees and other	75,000
Total expenses	5,296,000
Net investment income	$2,046,000

Realized and unrealized gains (losses) from investment activities

Net realized gain on securities	$2,773,000
Net realized gain on swap and forward contracts	509,000
Net change in unrealized appreciation on securities	1,515,000
Net change in unrealized appreciation on swap and forward contracts	852,000
Net realized and unrealized gain from investment activities	$5,649,000
Net increase in net assets resulting from operations	$7,695,000

Notes to Financial Statements

Note X—Investment Management and Incentive Fees

Pursuant to an investment advisory agreement, the fund pays to the adviser a quarterly management fee of $1/4$ of 1 percent (1 percent per annum) of the net assets of the fund on the last day of each quarter. The adviser also is entitled to an annual incentive fee equal to 20 percent of the net profits attributable to each series of common shares, subject to a loss carryforward. If there is a net loss for the year, the incentive fee will not apply to future years until such net loss has been recovered, adjusted for redemptions.

The adviser may elect to defer receipt of all or a portion of the management or incentive fees earned for a particular fiscal year, and such amounts will be indexed to the fund's return. In the event of liquidation of the fund, any deferred amount, as adjusted for the appreciation or depreciation resulting from indexing, the deferred fee to the fund's return has a priority claim over the interests of the equity holders of the fund.

For the [year/period] ended December 31, 20XX, payment of 50 percent of the incentive fee incurred by the fund was deferred for X years. Cumulative deferred incentive fees as of December 31, 20XX totaled $3,850,000, and cumulative net appreciation on such amounts totaled $950,000. The net change in appreciation or depreciation of deferred incentive fees is recorded on a separate line item under "Expenses" within the statement of operations. Distributions of 20XX and prior year deferred incentive fees are scheduled for the period from [date range]. During the year ended December 31, 20XX, the distribution of previously deferred incentive fees amounted to $500,000.

The following is an example disclosure of a rollforward of deferred incentive fees payable, which is a best practice disclosure.

The deferred incentive fees payable balance as of December 31, 20XX, comprises the following:

Deferred incentive fees payable at January 1, 20XX	$3,310,000
Appreciation on deferred incentive fees for the year ended December 31, 20XX	650,000
Incentive fees deferred for the year ended December 31, 20XX	1,340,000
Deferred incentive fees paid for the year ended December 31, 20XX	(500,000)
Deferred incentive fees payable at December 31, 20XX	$4,800,000

Note X—Financial Highlights

The following represents the per share information, ratios to average net assets, and other supplemental information for the year ended December 31, 20XX:

	Class A Initial Series	Class B Initial Series
Per share operating performance:		
Beginning net asset value	$1,130.35	$1,123.80
Income from investment operations:		
Net investment income	11.01	6.76
Net realized and unrealized gain from investment activities	141.50	145.64
Total income from operations	152.51	152.40
Ending net asset value	$1,282.86	$1,276.20
Ratios to average net assets:		
Expenses other than incentive fee	1.43%	1.46%
Incentive fee	1.46	1.49
Total expenses	2.89	2.95
Change in net appreciation on deferred incentive fees	(0.40)	(0.43)
Total expense excluding change in net appreciation on deferred incentive fees	2.49%	2.52%
Net investment income	1.12%	1.09%
Total return prior to incentive fee	17.07%	16.93%
Incentive fee	(3.58)	(3.37)
Total return after incentive fee	13.49%	13.56%

The per share operating performance and total return are calculated for the initial series of each share class. The ratios to average net assets are calculated for each class taken as a whole. An individual investor's per share operating performance, total return, and ratios to average net assets may vary from these per share amounts and ratios based on participation in new issues and different

AAG-INV 7.192

Disclosure—Fair Value Measurements of Investments in Certain Entities That Calculate Net Asset Value per Share (or its Equivalent)

> **⊚ Update 7-6 *Accounting and Reporting*: Fair Value**
>
> ASU No. 2011-04, issued in May 2011, is effective for public entities during interim and annual periods beginning after December 15, 2011. It is effective for nonpublic entities for annual periods beginning after December 15, 2011. Early application is not permitted for public entities. Nonpublic entities may early implement during interim periods beginning after December 15, 2011. The guidance should be applied prospectively.
>
> Refer to section A.02 in appendix A for more information on this ASU if applicable to your reporting period.

7.193 As described in FASB ASC 820-10-50-6A and paragraph 7.83, for investments that are within the scope of paragraphs 4–5 of FASB ASC 820-10-15 measured at fair value on a recurring or nonrecurring basis during the period (regardless of whether the practical expedient has been applied), in addition to the required disclosures of paragraphs 1–2 and 5 of FASB ASC 820-10-50, FASB ASC 820-10 requires disclosure of information that enables users of its financial statements to understand the nature and risks of the investments and whether the investments are probable of being sold at amounts different from net asset value per share (or its equivalent, such as member units or an ownership interest in partners' capital to which a proportionate share of net assets is attributed). FASB ASC 820-10-55-64A provides the following example of how that information may be presented (note that the classes presented are examples only and not intended to be treated as a template; the classes should be tailored to the nature and risks of the reporting entity's investments).

	Fair Value (in millions)	*Unfunded Commitments*	*Redemption Frequency (If Currently Eligible)*	*Redemption Notice Period*
Equity long/short hedge funds[a]	$55	—	quarterly	30–60 days
Event driven hedge funds[b]	45	—	quarterly, annually	30–60 days
Global opportunities hedge funds[c]	35	—	quarterly	30–45 days
Multi-strategy hedge funds[d]	40	—	quarterly	30–60 days

Financial Statements of Investment Companies

	Fair Value (in millions)	Unfunded Commitments	Redemption Frequency (If Currently Eligible)	Redemption Notice Period
Real estate funds[e]	47	$20		
Private equity funds—international[f]	43	15		
Total	$265	$35		

[a] This class includes investments in hedge funds that invest both long and short primarily in U.S. common stocks. Management of the hedge funds has the ability to shift investments from value to growth strategies, from small to large capitalization stocks, and from a net long position to a net short position. The fair values of the investments in this class have been estimated using the net asset value per share of the investments. Investments representing approximately 22 percent of the value of the investments in this class cannot be redeemed because the investments include restrictions that do not allow for redemption in the first 12–18 months after acquisition. The remaining restriction period for these investments ranged from 3 to 7 months at December 31, 20X3.

[b] This class includes investments in hedge funds that invest in approximately 60 percent equities and 40 percent bonds to profit from economic, political, and government driven events. A majority of the investments are targeted at economic policy decisions. The fair values of the investments in this class have been estimated using the net asset value per share of the investments.

[c] This class includes investments in hedge funds that hold approximately 80 percent of the funds' investments in non-U.S. common stocks in the health care, energy, information technology, utilities, and telecommunications sectors and approximately 20 percent of the funds' investments in diversified currencies. The fair values of the investments in this class have been estimated using the net asset value per share of the investments. For one investment, valued at $8.75 million, a gate has been imposed by the hedge fund manager and no redemptions are currently permitted. This redemption restriction has been in place for 6 months and the time at which the redemption restriction might lapse cannot be estimated.

[d] This class invests in hedge funds that pursue multiple strategies to diversify risks and reduce volatility. The hedge funds' composite portfolio for this class includes investments in approximately 50 percent U.S. common stocks, 30 percent global real estate projects, and 20 percent arbitrage investments. The fair values of the investments in this class have been estimated using the net asset value per share of the investments. Investments representing approximately 15 percent of the value of the investments in this class cannot be redeemed because the investments include restrictions that do not allow for redemption in the first year after acquisition. The remaining restriction period for these investments ranged from 4 to 6 months at December 31, 20X3.

AAG-INV 7.193

(e) This class includes several real estate funds that invest primarily in U.S. commercial real estate. The fair values of the investments in this class have been estimated using the net asset value of the Company's ownership interest in the partners' capital. These investments can never be redeemed with the funds. Distributions from each fund will be received as the underlying investments of the funds are liquidated. It is estimated that the underlying assets of the fund will be liquidated over the next 7–10 years. Twenty percent of the total investments in this class is planned to be sold. However, the individual investments that will be sold have not yet been determined. Because it is not probable that an individual investment will be sold, the fair value of each individual investment has been estimated using the net asset value of the Company's ownership interest in partners' capital. Once it has been determined which investments will be sold and whether those investments will be sold individually or in a group, the investments will be sold in an auction process. The investee fund's management must approve of the buyer before the sale of the investments can be completed.

(f) This class includes several private equity funds that invest primarily in foreign technology companies. These investments can never be redeemed with the funds. Instead, the nature of the investments in this class is that distributions are received through the liquidation of the underlying assets of the fund. If these investments were held, it is estimated that the underlying assets of the fund would be liquidated over 5 to 8 years. However, as of December 31, 20X3, it is probable that all of the investments in this class will be sold at an amount different from the net asset value of the Company's ownership interest in partners' capital. Therefore, the fair values of the investments in this class have been estimated using recent observable transaction information for similar investments and nonbinding bids received from potential buyers of the investments. As of December 31, 20X3, a buyer (or buyers) for these investments has not yet been identified. Once a buyer has been identified, the investee fund's management must approve of the buyer before the sale of the investments can be completed.

Illustration of Reporting Financial Highlights, Net Asset Value Per Share, Shares Outstanding, and Share Transactions When Investors in Unitized Nonregistered Funds Are Issued Individual Classes or Series of Shares

7.194 The following is an illustration of the presentation in the financial statements and the related disclosures when investors in unitized nonregistered funds are issued individual classes or series of shares, as discussed in paragraphs 7.132 and 7.164:

> A fund issues class A and class B nonvoting shares to investors, and within each class, a separate series of shares is issued to each individual investor. Class A shares have a 1 percent management fee and a 20 percent incentive fee; class B shares are issued to related-party investors and, therefore, are not charged a management fee or an incentive fee. Class C voting shares are management shares and do not participate in the profits or losses of the fund. As of December 31, 20X7, there are 15,100 total shares outstanding totaling $1,517,600. The following shows such amounts outstanding as of December 31, 20X7, by class and series and the net asset values:
>
> > Class A Series 1—5,000 shares outstanding, NAV $500,000
> >
> > Class A Series 2—7,500 shares outstanding, NAV $765,000
> >
> > Class B Series 1—2,500 shares outstanding, NAV $252,500
> >
> > Class C—100 shares outstanding, NAV $100
>
> In the prior year, as of December 31, 20X6, there were 10,100 total shares outstanding, totaling $970,100. The following shows such amounts outstanding as of December 31, 20X6, by class and series and the NAVs:
>
> > Class A Series 1—6,000 shares outstanding, NAV $588,000
> >
> > Class B Series 1—3,000 shares outstanding, NAV $288,000
> >
> > Class B Series 2—1,000 shares outstanding, NAV $94,000
> >
> > Class C—100 shares outstanding, NAV $100

AAG-INV 7.194

Example Statement of Assets and Liabilities
Statement of Assets and Liabilities
December 31, 20X7

Assets

Cash and cash equivalents	$100,100
Investments at fair value	1,550,000
Total assets	$1,650,100

Liabilities

Redemptions payable	94,000
Management fees payable	4,000
Incentive fee payable	3,000
Accrued expenses	31,500
Total liabilities	132,500
Net assets (based on 12,500 class A shares; 2,500 class B shares; and 100 class C shares outstanding)	$1,517,600

Example Note Disclosures
Capital Share Transactions

As of December 31, 20X7, 5,000,000 shares of capital stock were authorized. Class A and class B shares have $0.01 par value, and class C shares have $1.00 par value. Transactions in capital stock were as follows:

Class A

	Shares		Amount	
	20X7	20X6	20X7	20X6
Shares sold	7,500	6,000	$750,000	$600,000
Shares redeemed	(1,000)	—	$(99,500)	—
Net increase	6,500	6,000	$650,500	$600,000

Class B

	Shares		Amount	
	20X7	20X6	20X7	20X6
Shares sold	—	4,000	—	$400,000
Shares redeemed	(1,500)	—	($148,750)	—
Net increase	(1,500)	4,000	($148,750)	$400,000

Class C

	Shares		Amount	
	20X7	20X6	20X7	20X6
Shares sold	—	100	—	$100
Shares redeemed	—	—	—	—
Net increase	—	100	—	$100

AAG-INV 7.194

Financial Highlights

The ratios to average net assets and total return are presented in the following table for each class taken as a whole, excluding managing shareholder interests, for the year ended December 31, 20X7. The ratios and total return are not annualized. The computation of similar financial information for other participating shareholders may vary based on the timing of their respective capital transactions.

Annual ratios to average net assets and total return for the year ended December 31, 20X7, are as follows:

	Class A	Class B
Ratios to average net assets:		
Expenses other than incentive fee	2.26%	1.26%
Incentive fee	0.31%	0.00%
Total expenses	2.57%	1.26%
Net investment income	0.93%	1.93%
Total return prior to incentive fee	3.48%	5.02%
Incentive fee	(0.40)%	(0.00)%
Total return after incentive fee	3.08%	5.02%

AAG-INV 7.194

Chapter 8
Other Accounts and Considerations

Investment Advisory (Management) Fee

8.01 As discussed in chapter 1, "The Investment Company Industry," of this guide, an investment company usually engages an investment adviser for a fee, which is the largest expense incurred by the investment company. This fee is usually reflected in the daily net asset value calculation at rates established by the investment advisory agreement. Certain agreements may provide for performance fee adjustments based on a comparison of the investment company's performance against an index specified in the agreement.

8.02 As stated in Financial Accounting Standards Board (FASB) *Accounting Standards Codification* (ASC) 946-20-25-10, performance fees by an investment adviser under an advisory agreement should be accrued at interim dates based on actual performance through the accrual date.[1] As discussed in paragraph 7.109 of this guide, Technical Questions and Answers (TIS) section 6910.29, "Allocation of Unrealized Gain (Loss), Recognition of Carried Interest, and Clawback Obligations" (AICPA, *Technical Practice Aids*), addresses when governing documents contain provisions that do not require the recognition of performance fees until a specified date or time.

8.03 However, according to the Securities and Exchange Commission's (SEC's) policy, interim payments to the adviser should be based on the minimum fee provided in the agreement because if performance for the year yields a fee that is lower than the interim payments, the excess may represent a loan to the adviser. Performance fees based on a rolling or moving period are discussed in Release No. 7113 of the Investment Company Act of 1940 (the 1940 Act).

Expenses

8.04 The investment company's expenses should be reviewed for compliance with the provisions of the investment advisory contract, the prospectus, and other relevant agreements. The investment company estimates its other expenses for the year and the period within which it will incur them and allocates them, usually daily, in computing net asset value. Estimated annual expenses should be reviewed continually and accruals adjusted as necessary. Typically, asset-based fees are recalculated by the auditor for reasonableness, and other expense items are reviewed by analytical procedures.

8.05 Some investment company prospectuses, offering memorandums, or agreements between the adviser or other servicer (such as an administrator)

---

[1] The joint Revenue Recognition project of the Financial Accounting Standards Board (FASB) and the International Accounting Standards Board is intended to clarify the principles for recognizing revenue and develop a common revenue standard for U.S. generally accepted accounting principles and International Financial Reporting Standards. Under the proposed revenue recognition model, investment advisers (particularly for hedge funds and private equity funds) would face new challenges to meet the requirements to recognize management and performance fees. Further, the exposure draft contains guidance that would supersede the guidance in FASB *Accounting Standards Codification* (ASC) 946-605 relating to distributor transfer of rights to certain future distribution fees, distribution fees and costs for mutual funds with no front-end sales fee, and recognition of all selling and marketing costs. Readers should remain alert for developments on this accounting guidance, which can be accessed from the Technical Plan and Project Updates page at www.fasb.org.

AAG-INV 8.05

and the fund may require the servicer to waive its fee and reimburse or assume certain expenses that exceed stated limitations. If so, the auditor should review the calculations for agreement with the governing document.

8.06 Expense limitation arrangements help new funds with lower asset levels maintain lower expense ratios, which results in a benefit to the shareholder. Typically, one condition attached to these arrangements is that the investment company agrees to repay the service provider (without interest) if, and to the extent that, the investment company's net assets increase sufficiently to permit such payments without exceeding the stated percentage expense limitation. Also, typically, these agreements (*a*) are terminable on short notice by either party without a penalty, (*b*) have a fixed expiration date, and (*c*) give the service provider no claim against the investment company for any amounts not reimbursed upon termination or expiration. The economic result of these agreements is to defer payment of the expenses until the investment company is financially able to bear them or, upon termination or expiration, to eliminate them entirely.

8.07 As explained in FASB ASC 946-20-05-8, some expense limitation agreements may provide that reimbursements by the fund adviser of expenses incurred by the fund in excess of the maximum permitted by the prospectus or offering document will be carried over to a future period and reimbursed to the fund adviser when, and to the extent that, the total expense ratio falls below the permitted maximum. Such agreements may also provide that reimbursement of excess expenses to the fund adviser is not required after a specified date or upon conclusion of a specified period from the time the fund initially incurred, or the adviser initially reimbursed, the expenses, such as three years.

8.08 According to FASB ASC 946-20-25-4, a liability for such excess expenses should be recognized if, and to the extent that, the expense limitation agreement's established terms for repayment of the excess expenses to the adviser by the fund and the attendant circumstances meet criteria (*a*), (*b*), and (*c*) of paragraph 36 of FASB Concepts Statement No. 6, *Elements of Financial Statements—a replacement of FASB Concepts Statement No. 3 (incorporating an amendment of FASB Concepts Statement No. 2)*, and the criteria in FASB ASC 450-20-25-2.[2] In most instances, a liability will not be recorded because it is not likely that excess expenses under such plans will meet the criteria in those paragraphs before amounts are actually due to the adviser under the reimbursement agreement. If an assessment of the specific circumstances (such as an agreement to reimburse for either an unlimited period or a period substantially greater than that necessary for the fund to demonstrate its economic

---

[2] Paragraph 36 of FASB Concepts Statement No. 6, *Elements of Financial Statements—a replacement of FASB Concepts Statement No. 3 (incorporating an amendment of FASB Concepts Statement No. 2)*, includes the following criteria:
    a. A present duty or responsibility to one or more other entities that entails settlement by a probable future transfer or use of assets (criterion [a])
    b. A duty or responsibility obligat[ing] . . . [the] entity, leaving it little or no discretion to avoid the future sacrifice (criterion [b])
    c. The transaction or other event obligating the entity has already happened (criterion [c])

FASB ASC 450-20-25-2 includes the following criteria:
    a. Information available prior to issuance of the financial statements indicates that it is probable that an asset had been impaired or a liability had been incurred at the date of the financial statements (criterion [a])
    b. The amount of the loss can be reasonably estimated (criterion [b])

viability, or an obligation to reimburse the servicer remains even after the cancellation of the fund's contract with the servicer) indicates that the preceding criteria are met, a liability should be recorded. FASB ASC 946-20-50-6 states that the existence of reimbursement agreements and the carryover of excess expenses potentially reimbursable to the adviser but not recorded as a liability should be disclosed in the notes to the financial statements.

8.09 FASB ASC 946-20-05-8 also explains that, under most excess expense plans, a fund is obligated to repay a servicer for expenses incurred previously only if, during a defined period, the fund retains the service provider and can reduce its expense ratio to a low enough level to permit payment, and the fund maintains that ratio at a sufficiently low level thereafter. Many substantive conditions could cause the fund to have no obligation to the servicer, including failure to attract assets, significant redemptions of shares by investors, market depreciation, and significant increases in other expenses, all of which could drive expenses up to or beyond the maximum under which payment would otherwise be made.

8.10 The Financial Reporting Executive Committee (FinREC) observed that even actual reimbursement of some expenses does not establish the appropriateness of accrual of additional unreimbursed amounts because these conditions must continually be met for the fund to be further obligated to the servicer.

Distribution Expenses

8.11 As discussed in FASB ASC 946-20-05-4, open-end investment companies, also known as funds, are permitted to finance the distribution of their shares under a plan pursuant to Rule 12b-1 (Rule 12b-1 is one of the regulations implementing the 1940 Act). Under Rule 12b-1, a fund's board of directors or trustees is required to perform an annual review of the plan and determine whether to continue or terminate it. Under a traditional 12b-1 plan, a fund's distributor may be compensated or reimbursed for its distribution costs or efforts through any of the following methods:

- A 12b-1 fee, payable by the fund, based on an annual percentage of the fund's average net assets (a *compensation plan*) or based on an annual percentage of the fund's average net assets limited to actual costs incurred, after deducting contingent deferred sales loads (CDSLs) received by the distributor (a *reimbursement plan*). Therefore, a compensation plan differs from a reimbursement plan only in that the latter provides for annual or cumulative limits, or both, on fees paid. Fees for both kinds of plans are treated as expenses in a fund's statement of operations.

- A front-end load, which is assessed on purchasing shareholders at the time fund shares are sold.

- A CDSL imposed directly on redeeming shareholders. The CDSL usually is expressed as a percentage, which declines with the passage of time, of the lesser of redemption proceeds or original cost. The CDSL normally ranges from 4 percent to 6 percent and typically is reduced by 1 percent per year (for example, from 6 percent to 5 percent) until the sales charge reaches 0 percent.

8.12 Financial Industry Regulatory Authority (FINRA) rules construe 12b-1 fees to be either *asset based sales charges* or *service fees*. These rules (section 2830 of the National Association of Securities Dealers Rules of Fair Practice, incorporated into the FINRA manual) limit the amount of asset-based sales charges that may be charged in any year to specified percentages of average net assets and provide aggregate limitations on the total amounts of sales charges received through front-end sales loads, deferred sales charges, and asset-based sales charges.

8.13 As noted in FASB ASC 946-20-05-5, Rule 12b-1 plans historically have provided that a fund's board of directors or trustees may terminate the plan with no penalty to the fund. (Termination of the plan does not necessitate termination of the fund.) Redeeming shareholders still would be subject to the CDSL, which would be paid to the distributor that sold the shares to those shareholders. However, with a traditional 12b-1 plan, the 12b-1 fees normally would be discontinued on plan termination. Some traditional reimbursement 12b-1 plans provide that, when the plan is terminated, the fund's board of directors or trustees has the option, but not the requirement, to pay the distributor for any costs incurred in excess of the cumulative CDSLs and 12b-1 fees that the distributor has received. Such a plan is referred to as a board-contingent plan. Under traditional reimbursement 12b-1 plans, including board-contingent plans, CDSL payments by shareholders continue to be remitted to the distributor until excess costs are fully recovered, after which the CDSL payments usually are remitted to the fund instead of the distributor. As stated in FASB ASC 946-20-50-4, if a 12b-1 distribution reimbursement plan provides for the carryover of unreimbursed costs to subsequent periods, the terms of reimbursement and the unreimbursed amount should be disclosed.

8.14 Reimbursement to the fund of expenses incurred under such plan (12b-1 expense reimbursement) should be shown as a negative amount and deducted from current 12b-1 expenses. Distribution expenses paid with an investment company's assets are accounted for as operating expenses. Under 12b-1 plans, including board-contingent plans, CDSL payments by shareholders are remitted to the distributor until aggregate regulatory limitations on sales charges to be received are met.

8.15 As explained in FASB ASC 946-20-05-6, with an enhanced 12b-1 plan, the fund is required to continue paying the 12b-1 fee after termination of the plan to the extent that the distributor has excess costs. CDSL payments by shareholders would continue to be remitted to the distributor to further offset excess costs. Thus, the major distinction between traditional and enhanced 12b-1 plans is the requirement for the fund to continue such payments upon plan termination.

8.16 The following table from FASB ASC 946-20-05-7 summarizes the 12b-1 plan attributes enumerated previously:

	Compensation	*Traditional Reimbursement* Nonboard-contingent	*Traditional Reimbursement* Board-contingent	*Enhanced*
Annual review and approval of plan by board, with ability to terminate plan	X	X	X	X

Other Accounts and Considerations

	Traditional Compensation	Traditional Reimbursement Nonboard-contingent	Traditional Reimbursement Board-contingent	Enhanced
Fund Payment Terms[3]				
Payment based on average net assets	X	X	X	X
Annual or cumulative limitation, or both, based on actual distribution costs		X	X	X
Upon termination of 12b-1 plan, board has option, but not obligation, to pay excess costs			X	
Upon termination of 12b-1 plan, fund is required to continue paying 12b-1 fee to the extent the distributor has excess costs				X

8.17 FASB ASC 946-20-25-3 states that a liability, with a corresponding charge to expense, should be recognized by a fund with an enhanced 12b-1 plan for excess costs. FASB ASC 946-20-30-3 explains that the initial amount of the liability and expense should equal the cumulative distribution costs incurred by the distributor less the sum of cumulative 12b-1 fees paid; cumulative CDSL payments; and future cumulative CDSL payments by current shareholders, if reasonably estimable. Paragraphs 3–4 of FASB ASC 946-20-35 note that any future cumulative CDSL payments should be based on (*a*) current net asset value per share, (*b*) the number of shares currently outstanding and the number of years that they have been outstanding, and (*c*) estimated shareholder persistency based on historical fund data or, if historical fund data are not available, group or industry data for a similar class of shares. Changes in the liability should be recognized in the statement of operations as an expense or a reduction of expense.

8.18 Paragraphs 4–5 of FASB ASC 946-20-30 note that the liability and expense should be measured at its present value, calculated using an appropriate current interest rate, if both (*a*) the amount and timing of cash flows are reliably determinable and (*b*) the distribution costs are not subject to a reasonable interest charge. If these conditions are not met, the liability should be calculated without discounting to present value.

8.19 FASB ASC 946-20-25-3 states that a liability for excess costs, computed in the same way as for an enhanced 12b-1 plan, should be recorded by a fund with a board-contingent plan when the fund's board commits to pay such costs.

8.20 As explained in FASB ASC 946-20-50-3, for both traditional and enhanced 12b-1 plans, funds should disclose in their interim and annual financial statements the principal terms of such plans and any plan provisions permitting or requiring payments of excess costs after plan termination. For

---

[3] Excludes front-end and contingent deferred sales load payments, which are made by shareholders and not the fund.

board-contingent and enhanced 12b-1 plans, the aggregate amount of distribution costs subject to recovery through future payments by the fund pursuant to the plan and through future CDSL payments by current shareholders should be disclosed. For enhanced 12b-1 plans, funds should disclose the methodology used to estimate future CDSL payments by current shareholders.

8.21 As stated in FASB ASC 946-20-45-2, an excess of cumulative 12b-1 fees and CDSL payments to date and future CDSL payments by current shareholders over the cumulative costs incurred by the distributor should not be reported as an asset.

Minutes

8.22 In reviewing the board of directors' or trustees' minutes, the auditor should note such significant items as dividend declarations, capital changes, and amendments to and continuation of contracts and agreements with such entities as the adviser, distributor, transfer agent, custodian, and underwriter. The auditor should note changes in fee structures or expense limitations for reference in auditing expenses.

Organization and Offering Costs

8.23 The provisions of FASB ASC 915, *Development Stage Entities*, apply to financial statements issued by investment companies in the development stage, as defined by the FASB ASC glossary. A *development stage entity* is an entity devoting substantially all its efforts to establishing a new business and for which either of the following conditions exists: (*a*) planned principal operations have not commenced, or (*b*) planned principal operations have commenced, but there has been no significant revenue therefrom.

8.24 A newly formed investment company incurs organization costs unless a sponsoring management company agrees to absorb such costs (see paragraph 8.05). Organization costs consist of costs incurred to establish the company and enable it legally to do business. A newly established series of a previously established investment company may also incur organization costs. In a master-feeder arrangement, these costs may be incurred at the master level, feeder level, or both. Organization costs for an investment company include, among other things, the following:

- Incorporation fees
- Legal services pertaining to the organization and incorporation of the business; drafting of bylaws, administration, custody and transfer agent agreements; and performing research and consultation services in connection with the initial meeting of directors or trustees
- Audit fees relating to the initial registration statement and auditing the initial seed capital statement of assets and liabilities

8.25 An open-end investment company organized to offer shares of capital stock to the public continuously and invest the proceeds from the sale of such capital stock, generally should not be considered organized until the company has registered securities with the SEC. Legal fees for preparing the initial registration statement are an offering cost. The SEC requires all organization costs incurred by the investment company to be presented as a liability in the

Other Accounts and Considerations

investment company's seed capital statement of assets and liabilities, which is included in the investment company's initial registration statement.

8.26 In accordance with FASB ASC 720-15-25-1, organization costs should be charged to expense as they are incurred.

8.27 The following chart summarizes those costs that are, or are not, generally treated as organization and offering costs and the accounting required under FASB ASC 720-15 or other U.S. generally accepted accounting principles (GAAP):

Cost	Accounting Treatment
Incorporation fees	Expense
Audit fees related to initial registration and seed capital audit	Expense
Legal fees related to	
• organization and incorporation of the business	Expense
• drafting bylaws	Expense
• drafting administration, custody, and transfer agent agreements	Expense
• performing research and consultation services in connection with the initial meeting of directors or trustees	Expense
• preparing the initial registration statement	Offering cost—see paragraph 8.30
Licensing fees	Amortize over term of license
Typesetting and printing prospectus	Offering cost—see paragraph 8.30
Registration fees	Offering cost—see paragraph 8.30
Tax opinion costs related to offering of shares	Offering cost—see paragraph 8.30

8.28 Once an investment company has been organized to do business, it usually engages immediately in its planned principal operations (that is, the sale of capital stock and investment of funds). Employee training, development of markets for the sale of capital stock, and similar activities are usually performed by the investment adviser or other agent, and the costs of these activities are not borne directly by the investment company. However, an investment company, particularly one not engaging an agent to manage its portfolio and perform other essential functions, may engage in such activities and bear those costs directly during its development stage.

8.29 *Offering costs*, as defined by the FASB ASC glossary, include the following:

- Legal fees pertaining to the investment company's shares offered for sale
- SEC and state registration fees

AAG-INV 8.29

- Underwriting and other similar costs
- Costs of printing prospectuses for sales purposes
- Initial fees paid to be listed on an exchange
- Tax opinion costs related to offering of shares
- Initial agency fees of securing the rating for bonds or preferred stock issued by closed-end funds

8.30 As discussed in paragraphs 5–6 of FASB ASC 946-20-25 and 946-20-35-5, offering costs of closed-end funds and investment partnerships should be charged to paid-in capital upon sale of the shares or units. Offering costs of open-end investment companies and closed-end funds with a continuous offering period should be accounted for as a deferred charge until operations begin and thereafter be amortized to expense over 12 months on a straight-line basis.

8.31 Other kinds of offering costs, such as front-end sales charges and deferred sales charges, are deducted from the proceeds received from shareholders or redemption proceeds paid to shareholders; are not paid by the fund; and are, therefore, outside the scope of offering costs, as defined herein.

8.32 Some closed-end funds and business development companies offer stock through shelf registration statements. According to TIS section 4110.10, "Costs Incurred in Shelf Registration" (AICPA, *Technical Practice Aids*), legal and other fees incurred for a stock issue under a shelf registration should be capitalized as a prepaid expense. When securities are taken off the shelf and sold, a portion of the costs attributable to the securities sold should be charged against paid-in-capital. Any subsequent costs incurred to keep the filing "alive" should be charged to expense as incurred. If the filing is withdrawn, the related capitalized costs should be charged to expense.

8.33 According to TIS section 6910.23, "Accounting Treatment of Offering Costs Incurred by Investment Partnerships" (AICPA, *Technical Practice Aids*), an investment partnership that continually offers its interests should defer offering costs incurred prior to the commencement of operations and then amortize them to expense over the period that it continually offers its interests, up to a maximum of 12 months. The straight-line method of amortization should generally be used. If the offering period terminates earlier than expected, the remaining deferred balance should be charged to expense. TIS section 6910.24, "Meaning of 'Continually Offer Interests'" (AICPA, *Technical Practice Aids*), provides a definition of *continually offer interests*, which explains that an investment partnership is deemed to continually offer its interests if an eligible, new investor may enter into an agreement to purchase an interest in the partnership on any business day or on a series of specified business days over a continuous period of time. For this purpose, a new investor is one that does not already own any interest in the investment partnership at the time of purchase. Some investment partnerships may offer their interests at a single point in time and require new investors to commit to providing capital contributions over a period of time. In this scenario, because the interests are not available for purchase over a continuous period, such investment partnerships would not be deemed to have a continuous offering period.

8.34 This treatment of offering costs by closed-end funds and investment partnerships results in such costs being borne by the initial shareholders or partners of the closed-end fund or partnership. The treatment of capitalizing offering costs by open-end investment companies is consistent with their continuous issuances and redemptions of shares.

8.35 Unit investment trusts (UITs) have characteristics that are similar to both open-end and closed-end investment companies. Some UITs offer shares only at a particular time, but others provide for ongoing sales over a longer offering period. FinREC recognized that requiring a UIT to charge its offering costs to paid-in capital at the commencement of its offering or immediately after its units or shares are sold to the underwriters would require the underwriters, not the shareholders, to bear those costs. The treatment of these offering costs is discussed in the following paragraph and matches those costs with the proceeds received from the sale of the units or shares. FinREC also considered whether these offering costs should be deferred until these units or shares are sold by the underwriters to the public. FinREC concluded that the capital-raising effort of the UIT is completed upon the sale of the units or shares to the underwriters; therefore, support for further deferral does not exist.

8.36 As explained in FASB ASC 946-20-35-6 and 946-20-40-1, offering costs of UITs should be treated as follows:

- Offering costs should be charged to paid-in capital on a pro rata basis as the units or shares are issued or sold by the trust (when the units are purchased by the underwriters). Units sold to underwriters on a firm basis are considered sold by the trust, and the offering costs associated with those units should be charged to paid-in capital when the units are purchased by the underwriters. Offering costs that remain unamortized at the end of the year should be reviewed for impairment.

- Offering costs that have not yet been charged to paid-in capital should be written off when it is no longer probable that the shares to which the offering costs relate will be issued in the future. It is presumed that those costs will not have a future benefit one year from the initial offering.

Unusual Income Items

8.37 Unusual income items, such as amounts recovered from the settlement of litigation, are usually recognized in the financial statements when the investment company acquires an enforceable right, in accordance with the gain contingency provisions of FASB ASC 450-30. For items considered payment in lieu of settlement, refer to paragraph 7.122 of this guide. Before an unusual item is collected, it should be valued by the board of directors or trustees, and subsequent changes in the fair value should be recorded. Items relating to specific portfolio securities are typically recorded as an adjustment to realized or unrealized gains or losses. Otherwise, the item and a subsequent revaluation should be presented as other income, if any, or a separate income item. If the item is sufficiently material in relation to net investment income, it should be presented as a line item immediately before net investment income, unless the item is clearly identifiable with realized or unrealized gains or losses.

Form N-SAR [4]

8.38 Form N-SAR is a semiannual and annual report filed with the SEC by all registered investment companies, small business investment companies, and UITs.

8.39 Form N-SAR contains numerous items and, as stated by Rule 30b1-1 of the 1940 Act, must be filed with the SEC within 60 days of the end of the semiannual or annual reporting period, as applicable. As stated by Rule 30a-1 of the 1940 Act, UITs are required to file annual reports only. The investment company's auditors are not required to audit, and report on, items contained in Form N-SAR.

8.40 Form N-SAR requires a management investment company to provide an auditor's report on the investment company's internal controls.[5] Form N-SAR states that the report should be

> based on the review, study and evaluation of the accounting system, internal accounting controls, and procedures for safeguarding securities made during the audit of the financial statements. The report should disclose material weaknesses in the accounting system, system of internal accounting control and procedures for safeguarding securities which exist as of the end of the registrant's fiscal year. Disclosure of a material weakness should include an indication of any corrective action taken or proposed.

The auditor's report should be presented as an exhibit to Form N-SAR filed for the investment company's fiscal year and should be addressed to the investment company's shareholders and board of directors or trustees, dated, and signed manually. It should also indicate the city and state where issued.

8.41 The SEC has indicated that it will not regard the fact that the auditor's report is attached to Form N-SAR as acknowledgment that the auditor has reviewed the form. The auditor is not deemed to be associated with Form N-SAR and, accordingly, has no responsibility to read it.

8.42 Small business investment companies or other investment companies not required by either the 1940 Act or other federal or state laws, or rules or regulations thereunder, to have audits of their financial statements are exempt from the provisions regarding auditors' reports on internal control.

Business Combinations

8.43 According to TIS section 6910.33, "Certain Financial Reporting, Disclosure, Regulatory, and Tax Considerations When Preparing Financial Statements of Investment Companies Involved in a Business Combination" (AICPA, *Technical Practice Aids*), most mergers of registered investment companies

---

[4] A registered investment company files its annual and semi-annual shareholder reports together with the certifications of principal executive and financial officers, as required by Rule 30a-2 of the Investment Company Act of 1940, on Form N-CSR. The form also provides for disclosure of other information relating to the investment company's code of ethics, audit committee, principal accountant fees and services, internal control over financial reporting, and (for closed-end funds) proxy-voting policies.

[5] Paragraph 11.32 of this guide illustrates an independent registered public accounting firm's report on a registered investment company's internal control based on the results of procedures performed in obtaining an understanding of internal control over financial reporting and assessing control risks in connection with the audit of the investment company's financial statements.

Other Accounts and Considerations

are structured as tax-free reorganizations in which shares of one company typically are exchanged for substantially all the shares or assets of another company (or companies). Following a business combination, portfolios of investment companies are often realigned, subject to tax limitations, to fit the objectives, strategies, and goals of the surviving company. Typically, shares of the acquiring fund are issued at an exchange ratio determined on the acquisition date, essentially equivalent to the acquiring fund's net asset value per share divided by the net asset value per share of the fund being acquired, both as calculated on the acquisition date. Adjusting the carrying amounts of assets and liabilities is usually unnecessary because virtually all assets of the combining investment companies (investments) are stated at fair value, in accordance with FASB ASC 820, *Fair Value Measurement*, and liabilities are generally short term so that their carrying values approximate their fair values.[6,7] However, conforming adjustments may be necessary when funds have different valuation policies (for example, valuing securities at the bid price versus the mean of the bid and asked price) in order to ensure that the exchange ratio is equitable to shareholders of both funds.

8.44 TIS section 6910.33 also explains that only one of the combining companies can be the legal survivor. In certain instances, it may not be clear which of the two funds constitutes the acquirer for financial reporting purposes. Although the legal survivor would normally be considered the acquirer, continuity and dominance in one or more of the following areas might lead to a determination that the fund legally dissolved should be considered the acquirer for financial reporting purposes:

- Portfolio management
- Portfolio composition
- Investment objectives, policies, and restrictions
- Expense structures and expense ratios
- Asset size

8.45 As stated in TIS section 6910.33, a registration statement on Form N-14 is often filed in connection with a merger of management investment companies registered under the 1940 Act, or of *business development companies*, as defined by Section 2(a)(48) of the 1940 Act. Form N-14 is both a proxy statement, in that it solicits a vote from the (legally) acquired fund's shareholders to approve the transaction, and a prospectus, in that it registers the (legally) acquiring fund's shares that will be issued in the transaction. Form N-14 frequently requires the inclusion of pro forma financial statements reflecting the effect of the merger.

8.46 TIS section 6910.33 also states that tax implications must be considered and monitored carefully in the planning, execution, and postmerger

---

[6] If the carrying value of the acquired investment company's liabilities differs materially from fair value on the acquisition date, refer to FASB ASC 805-30-30-8 for guidance on the recognition of the liabilities by the surviving entity.

[7] In May 2010, FASB issued the proposed Accounting Standards Update *Accounting for Financial Instruments and Revisions to the Accounting for Derivative Instruments and Hedging Activities—Financial Instruments (Topic 825) and Derivatives and Hedging (Topic 815)*. Entities that follow specialized industry guidance in FASB ASC 946, *Financial Services—Investment Companies*, would continue to initially measure their financial instruments at transaction price. Readers should remain alert for developments on this topic, which can be accessed from the Technical Plan and Project Updates page at www.fasb.org.

AAG-INV 8.46

stages of a business combination. The tax rules that must be considered include those related to the determination that the transaction is tax-free to the funds involved and their shareholders,[8] the qualification tests affecting regulated investment companies (RICs),[9] and the accounting for tax attributes of specific accounts such as earnings and profits,[10] capital loss carryforwards, and methods of tax accounting.[11] Management may consider obtaining a private letter ruling from the IRS or an opinion of counsel on the tax-free treatment. Upon completion of the acquisition, the portfolio securities obtained from the acquiree generally should be monitored because substantial turnover of the acquiree's portfolio securities may jeopardize the tax-free status of the reorganization. There are important differences in the tax rules affecting business combinations of RICs and nonregulated investment companies.

8.47 As further stated by TIS section 6910.33, merger-related expenses (mainly legal, audit, proxy solicitation, and mailing costs) are addressed in the plan of reorganization and often paid by the fund incurring the expense, although the adviser may waive or reimburse certain merger-related expenses. Numerous factors and circumstances should be considered in determining which entity bears merger-related expenses.

8.48 FASB ASC 805-10-25-23 notes that *acquisition-related costs* are costs that the acquirer incurs to effect a business combination. Acquisition-related costs include finder's fees; advisory, legal, accounting, valuation, and other professional or consulting fees; general administrative costs, including the costs of maintaining an internal acquisitions department; and costs of registering and issuing debt and equity securities. The acquirer should account for acquisition-related costs as expenses in the periods in which the costs are incurred and the services are received. The only exception to this is for costs relating to issuance of debt or equity securities, which should be recognized in accordance with other applicable GAAP.

8.49 TIS section 6910.33 goes on to state that if the combination is a taxable reorganization, the fair value of the assets acquired on the date of the combination becomes the assets' new cost basis. For financial reporting purposes, assets acquired in a tax-free reorganization may be accounted for in the same manner as a taxable reorganization. However, investment companies carry substantially all their assets at fair value as an ongoing reporting practice, and cost basis is principally used and presented solely for purposes of determining realized and unrealized gain and loss. Accordingly, an investment company, which is an acquirer in a business combination structured as a tax-free exchange of shares, may make an accounting policy election to carry forward the historical cost basis of the acquiree's investment securities for purposes of measuring realized and unrealized gain or loss for statement of operations presentation in order to more closely align the subsequent reporting of realized gains by the combined entity with tax-basis gains distributable to shareholders. The basis for such policy election should be disclosed in the notes to the financial statements, if material.

8.50 TIS section 6910.33 explains that the instructions to Forms N-1A and N-2 state that, for registered investment companies, costs of purchases

---

[8] Internal Revenue Code (IRC) Section 368(a) and IRS Notice 88-19.
[9] IRC Section 851.
[10] Section 1.852–12(b) of Title 26, *Internal Revenue*, of U.S. *Code of Federal Regulations*.
[11] IRC Section 381.

Other Accounts and Considerations

and proceeds from sales of portfolio securities that occurred in the effort to realign a combined fund's portfolio after a merger should be excluded in the portfolio turnover calculation. The amount of excluded purchases and sales should be disclosed in a note.[12]

8.51 FASB ASC 805-10-50-1 states that disclosures to enable users of the financial statements to evaluate the nature and effect of a business combination are required when business combinations occur during the reporting period or after the reporting date but before the financial statements are issued or available to be issued. "Pending Content" in FASB ASC 805-10-50-2 explains that disclosures for all business combinations should include the name and description of the acquiree, the acquisition date, the percentage of voting equity interests acquired, and the primary reasons for the business combination and a description of how the acquirer obtained control of the acquiree. Transactions that are recognized separately from the acquisition of assets and assumptions of liabilities in the business combination require additional disclosures. Business combinations achieved in stages also require additional disclosures.

8.52 In addition, "Pending Content" in FASB ASC 805-10-50-2 also states that if the acquirer is a public business entity, these additional disclosures are required:

- The amounts of revenue and earnings of the acquiree since the acquisition date included in the consolidated income statement for the reporting period
- If comparative financial statements are not presented, the revenue and earnings of the combined entity for the current reporting period as though the acquisition date for all business combinations that occurred during the year had been as of the beginning of the annual reporting period.
- If comparative financial statements are presented, the revenue and earnings of the combined entity as though the business combination(s) that occurred during the current year had occurred as of the beginning of the comparable prior annual reporting period (supplemental pro forma information).
- The nature and amount of any material, nonrecurring pro forma adjustments directly attributable to the business combination(s) included in the reported pro forma revenue and earnings (supplemental pro forma information).

If providing the public entity acquirer disclosures will not be practicable, that fact, along with an explanation of why the disclosure is impracticable, should be disclosed. In this context, *impracticable* is defined by any of the following conditions existing:

- After making every reasonable attempt to do so, the entity is unable to apply the requirement.
- Retrospective application requires assumptions about management's intent in a prior period that cannot be independently substantiated.

---

[12] See instructions 4(d)(iii) of item 13 of Form N-1A and instruction 17(c) of item 4 of Form N-2.

- Retrospective application requires significant estimates of amounts, and it is impossible to objectively distinguish information about those estimates that both

    — provides evidence of circumstances that existed on the date(s) at which those amounts would be recognized, measured, or disclosed under retrospective application and

    — would have been available when the financial statements for that prior period were issued.

8.53 TIS section 6910.33 notes that because of the importance of investment company taxation to amounts distributable to shareholders, certain additional disclosures are recommended for combinations of investment companies, including the tax status and attributes of the merger. Additionally, if the merger is a tax-free exchange, separate disclosures of the amount of unrealized appreciation or depreciation and the amount of undistributed investment company income of the acquiree at the date of acquisition, if significant, may provide meaningful information about amounts transferred from the acquiree, which may be distributable by the combined fund in future periods. See appendix F, "Illustrative Financial Statement Presentation for Tax-Free Business Combinations of Investment Companies," of this guide for an example of the calculation of an exchange ratio in an investment company merger, as well as merger-related financial statement disclosures.

Diversification of Assets

8.54 An investment company may use a worksheet to determine and document that it has complied with the diversification requirements stated in its registration statement. The auditor may review that worksheet to become satisfied about the fund's representations of the diversification of its assets. Those diversification requirements may differ from the requirements under Internal Revenue Code Subchapter M, discussed in chapter 6, "Taxes," of this guide.

Auditor's Responsibility for Other Information in Documents Containing Audited Financial Statements [13]

8.55 An entity may publish various documents that contain information in addition to audited financial statements (for example, annual reports and proxies). Other information in a document may be relevant to an audit performed by an independent auditor or the continuing propriety of the auditor's report.

8.56 Paragraph .01 of AU section 550, *Other Information in Documents Containing Audited Financial Statements* (AICPA, *Professional Standards*), states that in the absence of any separate requirement in the particular circumstances of the engagement, the auditor's opinion on the financial statements

---

[13] This guide primarily discusses auditing guidance issued by the Auditing Standards Board, which applies to nonissuers. *Issuers* are defined by Section 3 of the Securities Exchange Act of 1934 and include registered investment companies. Audits of issuers are required to be performed under Public Company Accounting Oversight Board standards. Users should evaluate their audit engagements to determine which auditing standards are applicable.

Other Accounts and Considerations

does not cover other information, and the auditor has no responsibility for determining whether such information is properly stated. AU section 550 requires the auditor to read the other information of which the auditor is aware because the credibility of the audited financial statements may be undermined by material inconsistencies between the audited financial statements and other information. If the auditor identifies a material inconsistency, the auditor should determine whether the audited financial statements or the other information needs to be revised. If the material inconsistency is identified prior to the report release date requires revision to the audited financial statements, and management refuses to make the revision, the auditor should modify the auditor's opinion. If the material inconsistency is identified prior to the report release date requires revision of the other information and management refuses to make the revision, the auditor should communicate this matter to those charged with governance and: include an explanatory paragraph in the auditor's report, withhold the auditor's report, or withdraw from the engagement (if possible under applicable law or regulation).

8.57 Paragraph .A3 of AU section 550 explains that other information may comprise the following: a report by management or those charged with governance on operations, financial summaries or highlights, financial ratios, names of officers and directors, and selected quarterly data. For purposes of GAAS, other information does not encompass, for example, the following: a press release or similar memorandum, information contained in analyst briefings, and information contained on the entity's website.

8.58 AU section 551, *Supplementary Information in Relation to the Financial Statements as a Whole* (AICPA, *Professional Standards*), states that the objective of the auditor, when engaged to report on supplementary information in relation to the financial statements as a whole, is to evaluate the presentation of the supplementary information in relation to the financial statements as a whole, and to report on whether the supplementary information is fairly stated, in all material respects, in relation to the financial statements as whole. *Supplementary information* (for purposes of GAAS) is defined as information presented outside the basic financial statements, excluding required supplementary information that is not considered necessary for the financial statements to be fairly presented in accordance with the applicable financial reporting framework. Paragraphs .A7–.A8 of AU section 551 explain that supplementary information includes additional details or explanations of items in or related to the basic financial statement, consolidating information, historical summaries of items extracted from the basic financial statements, statistical data, and other material, some of which may be from sources outside the accounting system or outside the entity. Supplementary information may be prepared in accordance with an applicable financial reporting framework, by regulatory or contractual requirements, in accordance with management's criteria, or in accordance with other requirements. The auditor may report on such information using the guidance in paragraphs .09–.13 of AU section 551.

Chapter 9

Unit Investment Trusts

9.01 A *unit investment trust* (UIT) is defined by Section 4(2) of the Investment Company Act of 1940 (the 1940 Act) as an investment company organized under a trust indenture, contract of custodianship or agency, or similar instrument. It has no board of directors or trustees, and it issues only redeemable securities, each representing an undivided interest in a unit of specified securities, but does not include a voting trust. Units remain outstanding until a unit holder tenders them to the trustee or sponsor for redemption or until the trust is terminated. The trusts typically have a limited life, ranging from 12 months to 30 years. Trust agreements usually require periodic pro rata distribution to the unit holders of the trust's entire net investment income and net realized capital gains, if any, and distribution of the proceeds of redemptions, maturities, or sales of securities in the trust, unless the proceeds are used to pay for units to be redeemed. A distinguishing feature of UITs from mutual funds is that the portfolio is intended to be relatively fixed; neither the sponsor nor the trustee has power to manage the portfolio. In general, securities may be sold only for limited purposes (for example, to generate proceeds to pay a redeeming unit holder).

9.02 *Distinguishing Characteristics of UITs.* The following table presents distinguishing characteristics of UITs from mutual funds.

Characteristic	UIT	Mutual Fund
Portfolio Management	Static portfolio: portfolio trades only in limited circumstances	Securities or instruments may be traded every day
Structure	Must use trust format	May be structured as a corporation or a business trust
Governance	Supervised by trustee	Actively governed by board of directors or trustees
Redeemability	Units are redeemable every day at net asset value (most sponsors maintain a secondary market in units as an alternative to redemption)	Shares are redeemable every day at net asset value (minus deferred sales charge and redemption fee, if any)
Term	Generally fixed life of 1–30 years or more	Generally no term limit
Tax Treatment	Pass-through pursuant to the grantor trust provisions of §671 of the IRC or as a "regulated investment company" ("RIC") under Internal Revenue Code (IRC) Sub-chapter M	Flow-through distributions pursuant to its qualification as a "RIC" under IRC Sub-chapter M

(continued)

Characteristic	UIT	Mutual Fund
Distribution	Typically sold in a single "firm commitment" offering of a fixed size through a syndicate of underwriters and dealers	Typically sold continuously through a distributor
Expenses/Fees	Generally includes a sales charge and minimal ongoing trustees' and sponsor's fees	Generally includes management fees, custody fees, transfer agency fees and other shareholder servicing fees and may include sales charges and/or ongoing distribution fees (12b-1 fees)
Registration Forms	Required Form S-6 under the 1933 Act and Form N-8B-2 under the 1940 Act	Required Form N-1A under the 1933 Act

9.03 A UIT is one of the three basic kinds of investment companies defined by the 1940 Act. The UIT structure is used primarily as an investment vehicle to hold (*a*) a portfolio of tax-exempt bonds, corporate bonds, government bonds, and/or common or preferred stocks or other kinds of securities or (*b*) the shares of a particular management investment company being accumulated under a contractual plan. (See chapter 10, "Variable Contracts—Insurance Entities," of this guide for a discussion of unit trusts as a funding medium for variable annuity contracts.) The form and content of financial statements of UITs are prescribed by Article 6 of Regulation S-X, and Rules 6-10(d) and 12-12 of Regulation S-X prescribe the form and content of financial schedules.

9.04 The discussion in this chapter covers two common types of UITs, fixed-income and equity UITs. The accounting and auditing procedures for UITs are similar to those for other investment companies described in this guide.[1] (See chapter 8, "Other Accounts and Considerations," of this guide for a discussion of accounting for offering costs of UITs.)

Fixed-Income and Equity UITs

9.05 Units in UITs representing self-liquidating pools of tax-exempt or taxable bonds or other taxable fixed-income securities held in custody by a corporate trustee were first offered to the investing public in the early 1960s. Trusts investing entirely or in part in equity securities became increasingly common in the 1990s.

9.06 The principal objective of most fixed-income UITs is to generate a consistent income stream that may be taxable or tax exempt by investing in a diversified portfolio of securities. The principal objectives of most equity UITs are to generate dividend income and achieve the potential for capital appreciation through investment in a fixed portfolio of stocks.

---

[1] This guide primarily discusses auditing guidance issued by the Auditing Standards Board that applies to nonissuers. Issuers are defined by Section 3 of the Securities Exchange Act of 1934 and include registered investment companies. Audits of issuers are required to be performed under Public Company Accounting Oversight Board standards. Users should evaluate their audit engagements to determine which auditing standards are applicable.

9.07 A sponsoring organization, such as an investment banking firm or a broker-dealer, initiates a UIT by accumulating a group of securities of a kind specified in the trust indenture. Portfolios may range in fair value from a few million dollars to $100 million or more and may consist of many individual securities. However, equity portfolios are typically seeded with approximately $150,000. Trusts with fixed income portfolios are typically established based on the anticipated number of units to be sold, but they may have additional subsequent deposits. A tax-exempt bond portfolio may be diversified by economic activity (such as education, health care, and housing) or geographic area, or it may be concentrated in a particular state to provide investors with income exempt from federal, state, or local income taxes or any combination thereof. The portfolio may be accumulated by the sponsor over a period ranging from a few days to several weeks or longer. At the deposit date, the portfolio of securities or contracts to purchase securities is conveyed to a corporate trustee at prices defined in the trust agreement. For fixed-income UITs, these prices are usually based on offering prices, rather than bid prices, as determined by an independent evaluator retained by the sponsor. For equity UITs, these prices are usually based on the trustee's or evaluator's evaluation of the fair value of the securities in the portfolio as of the deposit date. Cash or an irrevocable letter of credit issued by a commercial bank is delivered to the corporate trustee to cover the cost and accrued interest to settlement dates or expected dates of delivery, if any, of portfolio securities. Securities offered on a when-issued basis, delayed deliveries, or the normal settlement process may cause delayed deposits. An audit of a UIT is usually performed as of the opening of business on the initial date of deposit. As discussed subsequently, annual update audits would also be required if the sponsor continues to offer the UITs to the public.

9.08 The sponsoring company, underwriters, and other participants sell units of undivided interest at their public offering price, which is equal to the fair value[2] of the underlying securities owned by the trust plus principal cash, divided by the number of units outstanding plus a sales charge (the "principal net asset value"). The sales charge is a percentage of principal net asset value of the trust unit, and may be reduced on a graduated scale for large purchases. The purchaser of the units also pays the undistributed net income per unit which is the net income (investment income less expense) earned since the previous distribution divided by the number of units outstanding. Upon the formation of the trust, the sponsor may realize a profit or loss on the sale of the underlying securities in the portfolio to the trust equal to the difference between the aggregate cost of the portfolio to the sponsor and the aggregate valuation on the date of deposit. A note to the initial schedule of investments should disclose the aggregate cost of the securities and the related net gain or loss to the sponsor.

9.09 A UIT may be expandable. At the initial date of deposit, a limited amount of securities is placed in the trust, and a limited number of units are issued. However, the trust agreement may provide for expanding the trust in size and number of units through additional deposits of securities in the trust, usually for a period of 90 to 180 days. According to Section 26 of the

---

[2] *Fair value*, as defined by the Financial Accounting Standards Board (FASB) *Accounting Standards Codification* (ASC) glossary, is the price that would be received to sell an asset or paid to transfer a liability in an orderly transaction between market participants at the measurement date. For further information on fair value, see FASB ASC 820, *Fair Value Measurement*, as well as chapters 1, "The Investment Company Industry," and 2, "Investment Accounts," of this guide.

AAG-INV 9.09

9.10 A UIT generally does not offer units of participation continuously. However, the sponsor may maintain a secondary market by repurchasing units from unit holders at net asset value based on the aggregate bid price of the underlying securities and reoffering them at net asset value based on the aggregate bid or offering prices of the underlying securities plus a sales charge. If the sponsor does not maintain a secondary market or choose to purchase the units, a unit holder can redeem his or her units at net asset value that is usually based on the aggregate bid price of the underlying securities. Some UITs allow unit holders to exchange units of the trust for other kinds of UITs offered by the sponsors, based on relative net asset values, at a reduced sales charge.

9.11 After the initial deposit by the sponsoring entity, all accounting, recordkeeping, and income and principal distribution services are performed by the trustee. The trustee distributes the accumulated income to unit holders periodically, usually monthly or quarterly, but sometimes semiannually or annually. Usually, as securities are redeemed or mature, the proceeds are distributed to unit holders. Investors may have the option of reinvesting the proceeds from income or principal distributions into additional units of the trust or other investment vehicles of the sponsor.

9.12 The trustee generally reports to unit holders periodically on the fair values of the underlying securities and certain other financial information relating to the trust, as generally required by the trust agreement. The valuation policies are similar to those used by other investment companies. Audited financial statements[3] are usually not distributed to unit holders; however, unaudited calendar year-end distribution information is supplied by the sponsor or trustee. The trust agreement specifies the reporting of tax and other information.

9.13 Some or all of the debt securities owned by certain trusts are covered by insurance obtained by the issuer or trust to guarantee principal and interest payments when due. The treatment of the cost of an insurance policy on an insured portfolio is discussed in chapter 3, "Financial Instruments," of this guide. More recently, as part of the Dodd Frank Wall Street Reform and Consumer Protection Act, enacted on July 21, 2010, the assignment of ratings in a public document is considered to be expert advice; accordingly, UITs can no longer include bond ratings without the consent of the rating agency.

Taxes

9.14 Most UITs elect to qualify as regulated investment companies (RICs) under Internal Revenue Code Subchapter M by complying with the applicable requirements (see chapter 6, "Taxes," of this guide). They usually distribute all their taxable income and gains from sales of securities and are, therefore, not subject to federal income or excise taxes. Certain UITs may be organized as

---

[3] On Form N-CSR, a registered investment company files its audited annual and unaudited semi-annual shareholder reports together with the certifications of principal executive and financial officers required by Rule 30a-2 of the Investment Company Act of 1940. Unit investment trusts are exempt from the requirements of Form N-CSR. Instead, the audited financial statements of a unit investment trust (UIT) are filed as part of the prospectus update (485BPOS) if the sponsor wants to maintain a secondary market for the units.

grantor trusts. The tax requirements for a grantor trust structure are different from a RIC. A grantor trust is formed to facilitate the direct investment of its assets, and ownership of the trust represents undivided beneficial interests in the assets of the trust. If multiple classes of ownership exist, they must be incidental to the purpose of facilitating direct ownership (for example, certain senior or subordinated rights). The trustee does not have the power to vary investments. Unlike a RIC, a grantor trust does not have income and asset qualification tests. Also, the taxable income flows through to the participant as it is earned by the trust, so income recognition to the grantor or beneficiary does not depend on distributions from the trust. UITs structured as grantor trusts pass through principal and interest payments to the grantor or beneficiary, but the cash flows may not fully correlate with the taxable income reported. Under Widely Held Fixed Investment Trust rules, a grantor trust UIT may qualify for simplified reporting on Form 1099 of income, security sales, redemption proceeds, and certain other items. To qualify, at least one interest in the grantor trust UIT must be held by a "middleman" (for example, a custodian, broker, or nominee).[4]

9.15 If a UIT is a RIC and more than 50 percent of its total assets consist of securities on which interest is exempt from federal income taxes under existing law when received by a trust, the tax-exempt character of the interest is retained when distributed (net of the trust's expenses) to unit holders. Amounts realized from capital gains and paid to unit holders by the trust are taxable to the unit holder. (Chapter 6 discusses taxes in more detail.)

Illustrative Financial Statements

9.16 The financial statements of UITs are similar to those of management investment companies. When a trust is formed, the financial statements filed with the SEC on Form S-6[5] typically include a statement of condition, schedule of investments, and related notes (see illustrative statements in paragraphs 9.18–.22). Subsequently, if the sponsor repurchases and reoffers trust units in the secondary market, a posteffective amendment to Form S-6 must be filed during the relevant period with the SEC. The financial statements included in the posteffective amendment, which are prepared in accordance with Regulation S-X, include a statement of assets and liabilities, a schedule of investments, and statements of operations and changes in net assets (see illustrative statements in paragraphs 9.18–.22). Audited financial statements are provided to prospective investors in the prospectus. Form S-6 requires that both the statement of operations and statement of changes in net assets cover a three-year period. Financial highlights are required to cover a five-year period.[6]

9.17 Certain disclosures required of registered investment companies for compliance with SEC rules and regulations are not presented in the illustrative financial statements that follow because they are not otherwise required by

---

[4] See Treasury Reg. 1.671-5.

[5] See paragraph 1.27 of this guide.

[6] Form S-6, the registration statement for UITs under the Securities Act of 1933, contains specific requirements for exhibits UITs must file, including financial statements, for nonregistered investees that comprise greater than 25 percent of the trust property underlying any class of securities being registered. In accordance with Rule 4-01(a)(1) of Regulation S-X, financial statements for such nonregistered investees that are filed with the Commission must be prepared in accordance with generally accepted accounting principles and must comply with Regulation S-X.

U.S. generally accepted accounting principles. Such compliance disclosures include the following:

    a. The aggregate cost, for federal income tax purposes, of the portfolio of investments according to Rule 12-12 (note 8) of Regulation S-X

    b. The gross unrealized appreciation or depreciation for all securities, on a tax basis, according to Rule 12-12 (note 8) of Regulation S-X

Note: The illustrative financial statements and note disclosures included in this guide have been updated to reflect the Financial Accounting Standards Board (FASB) *Accounting Standards Codification*™ (ASC). However, FASB's notice to constituents suggests the use of plain English in financial statement note disclosures to describe broad FASB ASC topic references. FASB suggests a reference similar to "as required by the Derivatives and Hedging Topic of the FASB *Accounting Standards Codification*." Entities might consider revising their financial statement references to reflect this plain English referencing, rather than the use of specific FASB ASC references. The AICPA has provided these detailed references as a resource for its users.

9.18

Anytown Income Trust
First Intermediate Series
Statement of Assets and Liabilities
August 31, 20X8

Assets

Assets

Investments in securities at fair value (cost: $14,591,035) (note 1 and schedule 1)	$13,878,788
Interest receivable	339,174
Cash	166,489
Total assets	14,384,451

Liabilities and Net Assets

Liabilities

Trustee and evaluator fees payable	47
Accrued other expenses	475
Total liabilities	522

Net assets

Balance applicable to 15,500 units of fractional undivided interest outstanding (notes 1 and 3)	
Cost to original investors	15,475,560
Less initial underwriting commission	(619,022)
	14,856,538
Accumulated losses	(232,610)
Principal distributions to unit holders of proceeds from investment transactions	(239,999)
Net assets	14,383,929
Total liabilities and net assets	$14,384,451
Net asset value per unit (15,500 units)	$927,995

The accompanying notes are an integral part of these financial statements.

9.19

Schedule 1
Anytown Income Trust
First Intermediate Series
Portfolio of Investments
August 31, 20X8

Name of Issuer and Title of Issue	Coupon Rate (%)	Date of Maturity or Final Sinking Fund Payment	Principal Amount or Par Value	Fair Value	
Corporate debt obligations:					
Air transport					
Flying Tiger Lines Incorporated equipment trust certificates	9.000	10/01/Y1	$ 931,000	$ 912,380	
Total air transport (Percentage of net asset value)				912,380	(6.4%)
Banking					
Dominion Bankshares notes	9.500	4/01/Y3	1,000,000	1,022,500	
First Maryland Bancorp notes	9.750	11/01/Y3	250,000	252,500	
Southeast Banking Corporation notes	10.000	5/01/Y3	218,000	224,267	
Total banking (percentage of net asset value)				1,499,267	(10.4%)
Utilities					
Utah Power & Light Company first mortgage bonds	4.500	6/01/Y2	12,100,000	11,467,141	
Total utilities (percentage of net asset value)				11,467,141	(79.7%)
Total debt obligations (percentage of net asset value)				$13,878,788	(96.5%)

The accompanying notes are an integral part of these financial statements.

9.20

Anytown Income Trust
First Intermediate Series
Statements of Operations

	For the Year Ended August 31, 20X8	*From March 23, 20X7 (Date of Deposit) Through August 31, 20X7*
Investment income		
Interest income	$1,258,975	$554,509
Expenses (note 1)		
Trustee's fee	14,063	5,411
Evaluator's fee	1,350	375
Other	1,083	351
Total expenses	16,496	6,137
Net investment income	1,242,479	548,372
Realized and unrealized gain (loss) on investments (note 1)		
Net realized losses from investment transactions	(12,738)	(12,765)
Net change in unrealized appreciation (depreciation) of investments	(738,828)	26,581
Net gain (loss) on investments	(751,566)	13,816
Net increase in net assets resulting from operations	$ 490,913	$ 562,188

The accompanying notes are an integral part of these financial statements.

9.21

Anytown Income Trust
First Intermediate Series
Statements of Changes in Net Assets

	For the Year Ended August 31, 20X8	From March 23, 20X7 (Date of Deposit) Through August 31, 20X7
Increase (decrease) in net assets resulting from operations		
Net investment income	$1,242,479	$548,372
Net realized losses from investment transactions	(12,738)	(12,765)
Net change in unrealized appreciation (depreciation) of investments	(738,828)	26,581
Net increase in net assets resulting from operations	490,913	562,188
Distributions to unit holders (note 2)		
Accrued income as of the date of deposit	5,182	360,787
Net investment income	1,231,408	54,303
Proceeds from investment transactions	129,000	110,999
Total distributions	1,365,590	526,089
Increase (decrease) in net assets	(874,677)	36,099
Net assets		
Beginning of period	15,258,606	15,222,507
End of period	$14,383,929	$15,258,606

The accompanying notes are an integral part of these financial statements

9.22

Anytown Income Trust
First Intermediate Series
Notes to Financial Statements

1. Summary of Significant Accounting Policies

The trust was organized on March 23, 20X7, under the laws of the Commonwealth of Massachusetts by a trust indenture and agreement, and is registered as a unit investment trust under the Investment Company Act of 1940. The significant accounting policies of the trust include the following:

Basis of presentation. The financial statements are presented on the accrual basis of accounting.

Investments in securities at fair value. Security transactions are recorded on a trade-date basis. Investments in securities owned are carried at fair value, which is the closing bid price on the last day of trading during the period. The difference between cost and fair value is reflected as unrealized appreciation (depreciation) of investments. Realized gains (losses) from securities transactions are determined for federal income tax and financial reporting purposes on the identified cost basis.

FASB ASC 820-10-35 establishes a hierarchy that prioritizes inputs to fair value measurements. The three levels of inputs are as follows:

- *Level 1.* Unadjusted quoted prices in active markets that the trust has the ability to access for identical assets or liabilities
- *Level 2.* Inputs other than quoted prices included in level 1 that are observable for the asset or liability either directly or indirectly. These inputs may include quoted prices for the identical instrument in an inactive market, prices for similar instruments, interest rates, prepayment speeds, credit risk, yield curves, default rates, and similar data.
- *Level 3.* Unobservable inputs for the asset or liability to the extent observable inputs are not available, representing the trust's own assumptions about the assumptions that a market participant would use in valuing the asset or liability, and that would be based on the best information available.

The following table summarizes the inputs used to value the trust's assets and liabilities measured at fair value as of August 31, 20X8.[7]

Valuation Inputs	Investments in Securities
Level 1	—
Level 2	$13,878,888
Level 3	—
Total	$13,878,888

There were no transfers between level 1, level 2, and level 3 during the year.

---

[7] The classification of various financial instruments in this table is for illustrative purposes only and should not be construed as recommended practice for any particular financial instrument or class of financial instruments.

Income taxes. No provision for federal income taxes has been made in the accompanying financial statements because the trust has elected and intends to continue to qualify for the tax treatment applicable to regulated investment companies under the Internal Revenue Code. Under existing law, if the trust so qualifies, it will not be subject to federal income tax on net investment income and capital gains distributed to unit holders. Distributions to unit holders of the trust's net investment income will be taxable as ordinary income to unit holders. Capital gains distributions will be taxable as capital gains to unit holders.

Management has analyzed the trust's tax positions and concluded that no liability for unrecognized tax benefits should be recorded related to uncertain tax positions taken on returns filed for 20X7 or expected to be taken in the trust's 20X8 tax returns. The trust is not aware of any tax positions for which it is reasonably possible that the total amounts of unrecognized tax benefits will change materially in the next 12 months.

Investment expenses. The trust pays a fee for trustee services to XYZ Bank that is based on $0.75 per $1,000 of outstanding investment principal. In addition, a fixed fee of $35 is paid to a service bureau for portfolio valuation at least weekly and more often at the discretion of the trustee.

2. Distributions of Income and Redemption of Units

The trust agreement requires that the net investment income and net realized capital gains (if any) of the trust and, also, the proceeds from the sale, redemption, or maturity of securities (to the extent that the proceeds are not used to redeem units) be distributed to unit holders monthly.

The agreement also requires the trust to redeem units tendered for redemption, to the extent that such units are not purchased by the sponsor, at a price determined based on bid prices of the securities of the trust.

As of August 31, 20X8, the components of distributable earnings on a tax basis were as follows:

Undistributed ordinary income		$ 505,140
Unrealized depreciation of investments	(712,247)	
Accumulated net realized loss from investment transactions	(25,503)	(737,750)
		$(232,610)

3. Original Cost to Unit Holders

The original cost to investors[8] represents the aggregate initial offering price as of the date of deposit exclusive of accrued interest. The initial underwriting commission and investors' original cost of units, as shown on the statement of assets and liabilities, are based upon the assumption that the maximum sales commission was charged for each initial purchase of units.

---

[8] This information is required by Regulation S-X and is not otherwise required by U.S. generally accepted accounting principles.

4. Financial Highlights[9]

	8/31/X8	8/31/X7[10]
Per Share Operating Performance:		
Net asset value, beginning of period	$984.43	$982.10
Income from investment operations		
Net investment income	80.16	35.38
Net realized and unrealized gain (loss) on investment transactions	(48.49)	0.89
Total from investment operations	31.67	36.27
Less distributions	(88.10)	(33.94)
Net asset value, end of period	$928.00	$984.43
Total Return:	3.22%	3.51%
Ratios as a Percentage of Average Net Assets:		
Expenses[11]	0.11%	0.09%
Net investment income[12]	8.38%	8.21%

---

[9] Since the trust was organized in 20X7, only two years of financial highlights are shown versus the five years that are required.

[10] Date of deposit was March 23, 20X7.

[11] Percentages annualized for periods less than one year.

[12] See footnote 11.

AAG-INV 9.22

Chapter 10
Variable Contracts—Insurance Entities

Separate Accounts

10.01 This chapter discusses separate accounts of life insurance entities. Separate accounts, also known as variable accounts, are used to support variable annuity contracts and variable life insurance policies (hereinafter referred to together as *variable contracts*). Separate accounts are often registered investment companies under the Investment Company Act of 1940 (the 1940 Act).[1] A variable contract is both a security registered under the Securities Act of 1933 (the 1933 Act) and an insurance policy filed with, and approved and regulated by, state insurance departments.

10.02 A *variable annuity* or *life insurance contract*[2] is a contractual arrangement that combines some features of an investment company (the contract holder assumes the risk of investment gain or loss) with certain traditional insurance features (the insurance company assumes the risk of mortality and administrative expenses). A significant difference between a traditional or fixed annuity and a variable annuity is that, in sponsoring a fixed annuity, the insurance company assumes the risk of investment gain or loss and guarantees the contract holder a specified interest rate. In a variable annuity, the contract holder assumes the risk of investment gain or loss because the value of the contract holder's account varies with the investment experience of the specific portfolio of securities (that is, the securities held in the separate account). In both fixed and variable annuities, the insurance company (rather than the separate account) assumes the mortality risk and administrative expenses for a contractually fixed fee or fees. Certain other nontraditional annuity products have emerged in recent years, such as equity indexed annuities. Equity indexed annuities represent, in effect, a combination of a fixed annuity with a derivative so that the investor is exposed to investment risk without investing in a specific portfolio of securities. Fixed and equity indexed annuities are not further discussed in this guide. Variable contracts are funded by and issued through separate accounts of insurance entities. A registered separate account is either an open-end investment company or a unit investment trust (UIT).

10.03 A *separate account*, as defined by the Financial Accounting Standards Board (FASB) *Accounting Standards Codification* (ASC) glossary, is a separate investment account established and maintained by an insurance company under relevant state insurance law to which funds have been allocated for certain contracts of the insurance company or similar accounts used for foreign-originated products. It is established solely for the purpose of investing the assets of one or more plans. Funds in a separate account are not commingled with other assets of the insurance company for investment purposes.

---

[1] This chapter does not apply to separate accounts that are established as investment vehicles for pension plans, such as those described in the AICPA Audit and Accounting Guide *Employee Benefit Plans*. The financial statements of those separate accounts should be prepared in accordance with the practices discussed by chapter 7, "Financial Statements of Investment Companies," of this guide for investment companies.

[2] Hereinafter, references to variable annuity contracts also refer to variable life insurance contracts, unless otherwise indicated.

It includes separate accounts and subaccounts or investment divisions of separate accounts.

10.04 A separate account is not a legal entity but an accounting entity with accounting records for variable contract assets, liabilities, income, and expenses segregated as a discrete operation within the insurance entity. The insurance company's other separate accounts and its general account do not affect the results of a particular variable contract separate account. State insurance regulatory authorities require combined separate accounts to file an annual statement. The separate account is not taxed separately for federal and state tax purposes; it is included with the operations of the insurance entity. However, under federal regulation, variable annuity and variable life products are securities. For purposes of the 1940 Act, a separate account is an independent entity, separate from the insurance company, and it cannot rely on the act's exemption for insurance companies.

10.05 The following approaches are used to invest the underlying assets of variable contracts:

   a. Direct investment by the separate account in individual securities (the separate account is an open-end investment company)

   b. Investment in a registered investment company formed to receive proceeds from such contract holders (the separate account is a UIT)

   c. Investment in a registered investment company that sells shares to the public (the separate account is a UIT), an approach available only for tax-qualified variable annuities

10.06 Similar to an open-end investment company organized as a series fund, separate accounts are frequently structured with multiple subaccounts. Each subaccount has a unique investment strategy, and in the case of a separate account organized as a UIT, individual subaccounts will invest in different underlying investment companies. This structure allows contract holders to allocate their amount invested among various investment choices. Financial position and results of operations are maintained separately for each subaccount within the separate account.

History

10.07 In 1959, the Supreme Court ruled that variable annuities constitute securities subject to registration with the Securities and Exchange Commission (SEC). In 1964, the U.S. Court of Appeals for the Third Circuit ruled that separate accounts funding variable annuities are investment funds that are separable from the insurance entity and, therefore, not exempted from the 1940 Act. Variable annuities became increasingly popular in the late 1960s after federal legislation encouraged self-employed individuals to establish pension accounts.

10.08 The insurance industry introduced investment annuities in the mid-1960s as a further variation of variable annuities. Investment annuities allowed individual contract holders to select specific investment vehicles. Custodian accounts were established with a third party, usually a bank, in which contract holders deposited cash or other assets. The insurer received an annual fee, usually based on a percentage of the invested assets. Although the account's assets were owned by the insurer, they were segregated for the benefit of contract holders, who directed their investments and could sell or exchange them at any time. Further, it was possible to fully or partially redeem investment annuities before the annuity payout period began by paying the insurer a penalty. Assets remaining in an account at the contract holder's death accrued to the insurer as a terminal premium. Investment annuities are no longer treated as annuities for federal income tax purposes.[3]

10.09 The first variable annuity wrapped using mutual fund shares as its underlying investment vehicle (a wraparound annuity) was developed in 1972. A wraparound annuity differs from other variable annuities because it is based on shares of an underlying investment vehicle, not on a pro rata share of individual stocks, bonds, and other investments owned by a separate account. The wraparound annuity separate account's assets typically are invested in a fixed income fund, an equity fund, a liquid assets fund, or some combination of these funds. The contract holder may allocate all or a portion of each payment among those investments.

10.10 Variable life insurance was first offered for sale in the United States in 1976, after having been successful for several years in the Netherlands, the United Kingdom, and Canada. Early variable life insurance policies were fixed premium contracts providing coverage for the whole of life. Death benefits and cash values varied in relation to the investment experience of a separate pool of assets. Today, most variable life insurance policies are of the variable universal life design. These newer variable life policies allow the policy owner to vary the amount of premium paid and, depending on premiums and investment experience, may expire with or without value.

Product Design

10.11 A significant objective of a variable annuity contract is to provide an investment that is responsive to changes in the cost of living and that can be used to accumulate investment funds before retirement and to pay benefits after retirement. Before retirement, the accumulated value of the individual account varies with investment performance and may be withdrawn by the contract holder in whole or part with possible surrender charges, tax liabilities, or both, including possible tax penalties. A contract holder may elect to receive the accumulated value of the individual account at retirement in a lump sum, in periodic payments that are fixed or variable, or in a combination of both (depending on the options available under the particular contract). Periodic payments also may extend for various durations (for example, over the life of the annuity holder, over a defined period, or over the combined lives of the annuity holder and a designated beneficiary, (a joint and survivor annuity).

10.12 If a lump sum is elected, the contract owner receives the account value at the payment date. If a fixed payment is chosen, the contract owner will receive (*a*) a fixed periodic payment that is based upon the account value at the date of conversion to payout and (*b*) actuarial considerations. See paragraphs 10.18–.19 for a discussion of the methodology typically used when a variable benefit option is selected. More recent innovations permit contract owners to obtain a lump-sum commutation of a portion of the contract even after payments commence, guarantees of minimum account or payment values, or periodic payments adjusted for inflation.

---

[3] Revenue Ruling 80-274.

10.13 The provisions of a variable annuity contracts may require periodic payments to the sponsoring insurance entity by contract holders. Alternatively, the contract could call for a single premium payment or provide for other methods of payment. Products typically are designed as front-end loaded or back-end loaded, as specified in the prospectus. Products with a front-end load deduct sales charges from the contract holder's purchase payments, whereas back-end loaded products reduce the surrender value by contractually specified charges, if any. The net payment is used to buy accumulation units of the separate account. The value of the separate account at any time is allocated among contract holders based on the number and value of their accumulation units representing their interest in the separate account. The concept of the accumulation unit and the unit value are analogous to fund shares and net asset value per share. The total value of the contract holder's accumulation units is the amount available to the contract holder at any time.

10.14 If a contract holder dies during the accumulation period, the death benefit varies, depending on the terms of the contract. The value of the death benefit is determined as of the valuation date and paid according to the applicable laws and regulations governing the payment of death benefits. Death benefits may be based upon the contract value at the time of death, contract value as of a stated anniversary date, or total premiums paid. If a contract holder dies after the annuity commencement date, the death benefit is the amount specified in the annuity option selected by the contract holder (under certain options, the death benefit can be zero).

10.15 Typically, the insurance entity charges the separate account a specified amount for investment management services (if the separate account is organized as an open-end investment company), an amount for administrative expenses, and fees for mortality and expense risks assumed. Certain of these charges (for example, administrative charges) may be recovered through an annual contract charge, affected through a redemption of units. The insurance entity assumes the risk that the annuitant's mortality will be less favorable (that is, he or she will live longer) than the rates assumed (mortality risk) and that administration and investment expenses will exceed the fee charged (expense risk). The mortality risk charge also covers the risk that the account value at death will be insufficient to fund the minimum benefit.

10.16 The insurance entity also assumes the mortality risk by incorporating annuity rates into the contract, which cannot be changed. Variable annuity payments are computed based on contractually specified mortality tables. The insurance entity retains the longevity risk, regardless of the method of payout that the contract holders elect, and may be obligated to continue payments, although contract holders or their beneficiaries, depending on the payment options selected, may live longer than anticipated. The insurance entity may bear additional mortality risk if it offers a guaranteed minimum death benefit under which a minimum payment is made to a beneficiary if the annuity holder dies before the payout period commences. To compensate the insurance entity for assuming this mortality risk, a *mortality risk premium*, which is an amount usually computed as a percentage of the daily net asset value of the separate account, is deducted from the separate account. If the mortality risk premium is insufficient to compensate the insurance entity for its costs, the loss is assumed by the insurance entity. Conversely, if the mortality risk premium is greater than its costs, the excess is the insurance entity's gain.

10.17 The insurance entity undertakes to pay the expenses of the separate account and may or may not charge the account a direct fee for the services rendered. Regardless of whether any fees are charged for specific services, the insurance entity charges an expense risk premium to the separate account. This charge is to compensate the insurance entity for accepting the risk that expense charges will be insufficient to cover the entity's cost of providing administrative and other services, including payments to third parties, to the separate account. The annuity contract usually provides that this expense risk charge may vary but sets a maximum.

10.18 The amount of the first annuity payment of a variable annuity is determined by applying a factor in the applicable annuity table to the contract value as of the date on which annuity payments begin, in accordance with the annuity option specified in the application. The first payment is divided by the value of an *annuity unit*, a unit of measure used to calculate variable annuity payments and establish the number of annuity units for each monthly payment. The number of annuity units for a particular annuitant, determined on the annuity commencement date, remains fixed during the annuity payment period.

10.19 Under a variable benefit option, the amounts of the second and subsequent payments are determined by multiplying the fixed number of annuity units by the annuity unit value on the date on which the payments are due. Thus, subsequent payments vary in accordance with the underlying investment performance of the separate account and the resulting annuity unit value.

10.20 Variable life insurance policies have many of the same variable features as variable annuities. The premium for a variable life policy, less an expense or sales load and mortality charge, is invested in a separate account. The policy owner may specify, within limits, where this cash value is to be invested. Several options may be available, including various kinds of money market, fixed income, and equity funds.

10.21 The policy's death benefit and cash value vary directly with the performance of the fund(s) selected. However, a guaranteed minimum death benefit is available, providing a floor of protection regardless of the investment performance of the fund(s). Investment risk in excess of any guaranteed minimum death benefit is borne by the policy owner. The insurance entity retains only expense and mortality risk, as well as the risk of paying guaranteed minimum death benefits in excess of the value of the fund(s) in which the policyholder invested.

10.22 In all other respects, a variable life insurance policy works like a traditional whole life policy, and a variable universal life policy works like a common universal life policy. All the normal riders and attachments are typically available on variable products. Further information on life insurance contracts can be found in the AICPA Audit and Accounting Guide *Life and Health Insurance Entities*.

Contracts in the Payout (Annuitization) Period

10.23 As stated previously, a variable annuity payment option provides an annuity with payment amounts that are not predetermined but vary according to the results of the underlying investment. The payout (annuitization) period begins when amounts accumulated under the contract (the contract value) are applied under the method-of-payment option selected by the contract holder. At each financial reporting date, the separate account financial statements include an aggregate amount of net assets allocated to future contract benefits for the contracts in the payout (annuitization) period.

10.24 The *net assets allocated to future contract benefits*, sometimes referred to as the annuity reserve account, is the total of an actuarial computation of the discounted amount of the expected annuity payments for each contract or group of contracts based principally on the annuity payments at the current annuity unit value multiplied by the individuals' expected mortality rates based upon an annuity table.

10.25 For variable life contracts, the insurance entity charges the separate account for the cost of fixed premium variable life insurance coverage based on traditional methodology, which can be calculated using standard techniques. The charge for variable universal life insurance policies is usually determined in accordance with the National Association of Insurance Commissioners Universal Life Insurance Model Regulation.

SEC Registration

10.26 A separate account is established by resolution of the insurance entity's board of directors or trustees in accordance with the insurance laws of the state of domicile. It is subject to policy-form approval and other requirements in each state in which the entity offers the contract. Courts have determined that variable contracts and separate accounts are subject to registration and regulation under the 1933 Act and the 1940 Act, respectively. The registrant is the separate account.

10.27 In addition to accumulation units and net assets allocated to future annuity contract benefits established at the separate account level, as described previously, certain separate accounts withhold the mortality and expense payments from the insurance entity. Instead of paying the charges to the insurance entity in cash, the separate account may apply accumulation units or net assets to the insurance entity's own account. This may occur either at the discretion of the sponsoring insurance entity to build investible assets or at the requirement of the state insurance commission. (Under insurance regulations of certain states certain separate accounts have been required to withhold payments to the insurance entity.) The purpose of this holdback is to protect contract holders against adverse mortality in the event that the insurance entity is unable to fulfill its responsibilities to insulate the separate account from mortality risk. If the holdback is maintained in the form of accumulation units or otherwise participates in the investment experience of the separate account, it should be reported in net assets by the separate account under the caption "Retained in variable account by insurance entity." If the holdback does not participate in the investment experience of the separate account (that is, it is fixed in amount), it should be reported by the separate account as a liability.

10.28 Initially, variable contract issuers registered as management investment companies because they invested their assets directly in securities and, therefore, resembled typical mutual funds in their investment objectives. The 1940 Act has many technical requirements for a management investment company, including requirements for an elected board of directors or trustees and proxy statements. The requirements for a board of directors or trustees

Variable Contracts—Insurance Entities

and proxy statements in certain circumstances, among others, are inconsistent with the legal status of the separate account, which is not a legal entity existing apart from the insurance entity.

10.29 Most separate accounts have registered under the 1940 Act as UITs to avoid some technical requirements for entities registered as management investment companies under that act. Further, the form of a UIT satisfies the need for separate accounting for the performance of specific pools of assets of group annuity contracts, personal contracts, and annuity contracts subject to different tax rules. The UIT form may also accommodate lower expense charges and more flexibility in adding new products and changing the features (for example, expenses) of current products. (Changes to fund-level expenses can be achieved through contract owner approval but without the need to amend the contracts.)

10.30 There are two registration forms for use by separate accounts offering variable annuity contracts that register under the 1933 Act and the 1940 Act. Form N-3 is the registration form for separate accounts registered as management investment companies. Form N-4 is the registration form for UITs.

10.31 Variable life separate accounts, as UITs, register under the 1940 Act and register their securities under the 1933 Act on Form N-6. This form is tailored directly to variable life products.

Auditing Considerations[4]

10.32 Because most features of a variable annuity and variable life contract are similar to those of a mutual fund, the auditing guidance in other chapters of this guide also applies to these variable contracts. However, major differences exist between variable annuities and mutual funds in accounting for contracts in the payout period and in the calculation of the net assets allocated to contracts in the payout period (annuity reserve account). In addition, when a separate account organizes as a UIT investing in a mutual fund, other audit issues can arise. Finally, the auditor should consider various issues arising due to unique aspects of the taxation of insurance entities.

10.33 Mortality and interest rate assumptions (based on the annuity option selected by the contract holder, the contract holder's age at issue, and the date of issue of the annuity) are the two most significant factors in determining the annuity reserve account. The auditor should become satisfied with the annuity reserve account by consulting published tables for the appropriate factors and testing that those factors have been appropriately applied to the master file containing all outstanding contracts in the payout period. Similarly, the auditor should become satisfied with the determination of amounts receivable from or payable to the insurance entity based on its mortality experience on contracts in the payout period (see paragraph 10.35). A broad outline of procedures to be followed in auditing actuarial computations is described in the AICPA Audit and Accounting Guide *Life and Health Insurance Entities*.

---

[4] This guide primarily discusses auditing guidance issued by the Auditing Standards Board that applies to nonissuers. *Issuers* are defined by Section 3 of the Securities Exchange Act of 1934 and include registered investment companies. Audits of issuers are required to be performed under Public Company Accounting Oversight Board standards. Users should evaluate their audit engagements to determine which auditing standards are applicable.

10.34 For variable life contracts, the net assets maintained by the separate account (excluding any amounts held for the account of the insurance entity) are analogous to the cash value of the underlying insurance policies. The liability for death benefits is held by the insurance entity.

10.35 As stated previously, the insurance entity assumes certain risks in issuing variable annuities and variable life contracts. If mortality experience on annuity contracts in the payout period runs favorably or unfavorably to the insurer's estimate (see paragraphs 10.23–.25), it does not affect the separate account but creates an amount payable to or receivable from the insurance entity, respectively. Among the factors that may be evaluated in examining the financial statements of a separate account funding a variable annuity is the insurance entity's ability to perform if the variable annuity's assets are insufficient to meet the variable annuity's obligations.

10.36 When the separate account is organized as a UIT, certain considerations can arise due to the relationship between the separate account and underlying investment company. If the auditor of the separate account is not the auditor of the fund, the separate account auditor may evaluate the effect, if any, that this has on the audit. The fiscal year-ends of the separate account and underlying investment company are often the same. In most cases, the underlying investment company is registered under the 1940 Act such that the audited financial statements of the fund will usually be available to the separate account auditor from public sources as audit evidence with respect to the fund's value. If the underlying investment company is not registered under the 1940 Act, the separate account auditor might consider what communications with the fund auditor are appropriate and, in general, may consider what other steps are appropriate, including those steps described in paragraphs 5.69–.94 of this guide, to rely on the work of another auditor or perform other procedures.

10.37 If the underlying fund and separate account have different year-ends, questions may arise regarding auditing investment valuation. As noted in the preceding paragraph, the auditor of the separate account usually has available audited financial statements to provide audit evidence with respect to the value of the investment in the fund. When the fund is not audited at the separate account year-end date, the auditor should consider what other audit procedures might be appropriate to substantiate the separate account's valuation, including, for investments in investment companies not registered under the 1940 Act, the procedures discussed in paragraphs 5.89–.94 of this guide. Audit procedures for investments in investment companies registered under the 1940 Act might include confirmation of shares outstanding and period-end net asset values with the investment company's transfer agent and review of the most recent interim (quarterly or semiannual) filing of the investment company containing portfolio information.

10.38 The auditor's report is typically addressed to the board of directors or trustees of the sponsoring insurance entity and the contract holders of the separate account.

Taxation of Variable Contracts

10.39 Variable annuity contracts are designed for use primarily by individuals for personal savings or retirement plans, which, under the provisions of the Internal Revenue Code (IRC), may be qualified or nonqualified plans. Variable life contracts are designed for individuals to provide market-sensitive

Variable Contracts—Insurance Entities

cash surrender values and death benefits. The ultimate effect of federal income taxes on the contract value, annuity payments, cash values, death benefits, and economic benefit to the contract owner, annuitant, or beneficiary depends on the separate account's tax status, the purpose for which the contract is purchased, and the individual's tax and employment status. The discussion in this section is general and not intended to be an all-inclusive and comprehensive treatise on the current tax status of variable annuities.

10.40 If an annuity contract qualifies as such under the IRC, a contract holder is generally not taxed on increases in the value of the contract until he or she receives payment in a lump sum or as an annuity under the settlement option elected, nor is he or she taxed upon the investment buildup in cash values. Although the assets and liabilities of the separate account are segregated from the sponsoring life insurance entity's regular business, it is not considered a separate taxable entity. The tax treatment of the separate account depends upon the character of the contracts held by the separate account. If the contracts qualify as variable contracts that are adequately diversified (see paragraphs 10.50–.52), then IRC Section 817 dictates the taxation of the separate account. If the contracts do not qualify as variable or are not adequately diversified, then the activity of the separate account will be governed by the tax rules applicable to life insurance entities under IRC Subchapter L. The separate account is not subject to the tax rules applicable to regulated investment companies (RICs) under IRC Subchapter M.

10.41 Under IRC Section 817, reinvested investment income is applied to increase insurance entity reserves under the contracts, and the increase in reserves is deductible from income. Usually a provision for federal income taxes on investment income or gains is not necessary; therefore, a provision is not made in the variable annuity separate account financial statements.

10.42 IRC Section 817(g) provides that a variable annuity contract will be taxed in the same manner as a traditional or fixed annuity if the payments under the variable contract are computed based on recognized mortality tables and the investment return of the individual segregated account.

10.43 When the UIT approach was developed using mutual funds as the underlying investment, insurers relied on several tax rulings as the basis for treating mutual fund wraparounds similarly to traditional variable annuities.

10.44 In Revenue Ruling 80-274, the IRS concluded that the position of a contract holder of an annuity wrapped around a savings account is as if the investment had been maintained or established directly with a savings and loan association. Thus, the contract holder is taxed on a current basis on the separate account income.

10.45 Revenue Ruling 81-225 states that, for federal income tax purposes, the insurance entity, not the contract holder, will be considered the owner of mutual fund shares underlying investments for an annuity contract, provided that such shares are unavailable to the public. Accordingly, under that ruling, if the mutual fund shares are not available to the public, the contract holder is not treated as the owner of the shares, and dividends applicable to such shares are not currently includable in the contract holder's gross income.

10.46 On August 18, 2003, the IRS published Revenue Rulings 2003-91 and 2003-92. The IRS described Revenue Ruling 2003-91 as a safe harbor from which taxpayers may operate and referred to Revenue Ruling 2003-92 as having clarified and amplified Revenue Ruling 81-225.

10.47 Revenue Ruling 2003-91 described a situation in which a separate account used for funding variable contracts was divided into various subaccounts. The contracts and subaccounts were issued under the following conditions:

- The contract holder could not select or direct a particular investment to be made by the separate account or subaccounts; all investment decisions are made by the insurance entity or separate account in their absolute discretion.
- Investment strategies of the subaccounts are sufficiently broad to prevent a contract holder from making particular investment decisions through investing in a subaccount.
- Only the insurance entity could add or substitute subaccounts or investment strategies and the insurance entity does not communicate or consult with any contract holder regarding investment selection or strategy.
- Investments in the subaccounts are only available through the purchase of variable contracts and are not otherwise publicly available.

10.48 The IRS concluded that such an account did not provide the contract holder direct or indirect control over the separate account or any subaccount asset; thus, the holder would not be considered the tax owner of the underlying assets. The IRS also observed that the ability to allocate premiums or transfer funds between subaccounts did not indicate sufficient control for the contract holder to be treated as the owner, for tax purposes, of the underlying assets.

10.49 Conversely, Revenue Ruling 2003-92 addressed a situation in which an insurance entity proposed to offer deferred variable contracts under which certain qualified purchasers could invest in a limited number of subaccounts, each of which represented an interest in a specific investment partnership that is not publicly traded. If interests in the partnership were also available for purchase by the general public (that is, outside the variable contract structure), the IRS held that the qualified purchaser contract holder, not the insurance entity, would be the owner, for tax purposes, of the partnership interest. However, if interests in the partnership were only available for purchase within variable contract structures, the insurance entity would be considered the owner of the partnership interest.

10.50 IRC Section 817(h) and the regulations thereunder require the investments of a separate account (or the underlying mutual fund, if the separate account is a UIT) to be adequately diversified to qualify as an annuity contract under IRC Section 72 (qualification under IRC Section 72 is necessary to avoid current taxation of both current and built-up earnings of the contract). In order for the separate account to be adequately diversified, the fair value of the largest holding may not exceed 55 percent of the fair value of total assets, the 2 largest holdings may not exceed 70 percent, the 3 largest holdings may not exceed 80 percent, and the 4 largest holdings may not exceed 90 percent (measured on a quarterly basis). Regulation 1.817-5(b)(1) describes what assets must be included in the calculation and what assets may be excluded.

10.51 U.S. government securities are subject to IRC Section 817(h) diversification rules. The treatment of U.S. government securities for purposes of determining separate account diversification is different from that applied to RICs. Under IRC Section 817(h), each government agency or instrumentality is treated as a separate issuer for purposes of diversification testing.

10.52 As an alternative to the general diversification standards described previously, IRC Section 817(h)(2) provides safe harbor diversification standards that are similar to those for RICs and often easier to administer. However, the safe harbor diversification rules differ from those of RICs in that the total assets of the separate account represented by cash, cash items (including receivables), U.S. government securities, or securities of other RICs may not exceed 55 percent of the value of total assets in the account. Regulation 1.817-5(b)(3) provides special rules that apply to a segregated asset account with respect to variable life insurance contracts.

10.53 IRC Section 72(s) provides that a contract should not be treated as an annuity for tax purposes unless it provides for certain required distributions in the event of the contract holder's death.

10.54 IRC Section 72(q) imposes certain penalties on early withdrawals from annuity contracts.

10.55 The federal excise tax rules governing the timing and amounts of distributions do not apply to insurance-related mutual funds if no taxable investors are present. Further, in organizing the separate account, the sponsoring insurance entity may invest taxable seed money of up to $250,000 without subjecting the fund to the excise tax rules (IRC Section 4982).

10.56 Dividends and distributions from the fund to the separate account are usually reinvested. As a result, some insurance funds do not actually pay any dividends or distributions. Rather, they satisfy their fund-level tax qualification tests by using a procedure known as consent dividends (IRC Section 565). Under this procedure, with annual written consent from each investor (that is, the separate accounts), distributions are deemed to be passed through from the fund to the investors. This is manageable operationally because, in practice, the number of separate accounts invested in a single fund is limited.

Illustrative Financial Statements

10.57 The financial statements illustrated in this chapter are for variable annuity separate accounts registered as UITs. For separate accounts with multiple subaccounts, the financial position and results of operations generally should be presented separately for each subaccount. This kind of arrangement is presented with individual columns for each subaccount. The total information for the separate account as a whole is not meaningful. Accordingly, a subaccount that is similar to a series mutual fund is the reporting entity, and the auditor's report could be modified to cover the individual subaccounts (see paragraph 11.17 of this guide). The financial statements of a subaccount may also be presented as if the subaccount were a separate entity. Variable annuity separate accounts registered as management investment companies would prepare financial statements that conform to those presented in chapter 7, "Financial Statements of Investment Companies," of this guide, although certain financial statement notes that follow would also apply. Under the requirements of SEC Form N-4, variable annuity separate accounts registered as UITs present a period-end statement of assets and liabilities, a statement of operations for the most recent year, and a statement of changes in net assets for the most recent two years in the same manner as a registered investment company. This format is illustrated in the exhibit. Variable life separate accounts registered as UITs on Form N-6 also would follow the form of the exhibit. Certain contract charges (for example, cost of insurance) would be shown on the statement of changes in net assets, which is similar to the presentation of annuity contract charges.

10.58 Certain disclosures required of registered investment companies for compliance with SEC rules and regulations are not presented in the following illustrative financial statements because they are not otherwise required by U.S. generally accepted accounting principles. In addition, certain disclosures are impractical due to the characteristics of the separate account. These disclosures include the following:

- The total cost, for federal income tax purposes, of the portfolio of investments according to Rules 12-12 and 12-12C[5] of Regulation S-X.
- The components of net assets presented as a separate schedule or in the notes to the financial statements according to Rule 6-05.5 of Regulation S-X. However, the net asset value per unit at the beginning and end of each period and the total net assets at the end of the period are to be provided for the most recent five years.

10.59 As stated in FASB ASC 946-205-50-31, separate accounts with more than two levels of contract charges or net unit values per subaccount may elect to present the required financial highlights for contract expense levels that had units issued or outstanding during the reporting period (including number of units, unit fair value, net assets, expense ratio, investment income ratio, and total return) for either

 a. each contract expense level that results in a distinct net unit value and for which units were issued or outstanding during each reporting period or

 b. the range of the lowest and highest level of expense ratio and the related total return and unit fair values during each reporting period.

The calculation of the ranges for the total return ratio and unit fair values should correspond to the groupings that produced the lowest and highest expense ratios.

10.60 Paragraphs 32–33 of FASB ASC 946-205-50 explain that the financial highlights table in the separate account's financial statements should state clearly that the expense ratio considers only the expenses borne directly by the separate account and excludes expenses incurred directly by the underlying funds or charged through the redemption of units. If the ranges of expense ratios, total returns, and unit fair values are presented, the insurance enterprise should disclose instances in which individual contract values do not fall

---

[5] Amendments to Article 12 of Regulation S-X permit a registered investment company to include a summary portfolio schedule in its reports to shareholders. Refer to chapter 7 of this guide for further discussion of U.S. generally accepted accounting principles applicable for the preparation of financial statements of investment companies.

within the ranges presented (for example, if a new product is introduced late in a reporting period and the total return does not fall within the range). The expense disclosure should also include ranges of all fees that are charged by the separate account and a description of those fees, including whether they are assessed as direct reductions in unit values or through the redemption of units for all policies contained within the separate account.

> *Note:* The illustrative financial statements and note disclosures included in this guide have been updated to reflect FASB ASC. However, in FASB's notice to constituents, it suggests the use of plain English in financial statement note disclosures to describe broad FASB ASC topic references. FASB suggests a reference similar to "as required by the Derivatives and Hedging Topic of the FASB *Accounting Standards Codification*." Entities might consider revising their financial statement references to reflect this plain English referencing, rather than the use of specific FASB ASC references. The AICPA has provided these detailed references as a resource for its users.

10.61

ABC Variable Annuity Separate Account I
of ABC Life Insurance Company
Statement of Assets and Liabilities
December 31, 20X8

	Money Market	Equity Index
Assets:		
ABC Investment Fund		
Investments at fair value:		
Money Market Portfolio, 57,231,590 shares (cost: $57,231,590)	$57,231,590	$—
Equity Index Portfolio, 23,961,595 shares (cost: $325,054,036)	—	350,797,752
Total assets	57,231,590	350,797,752
Liabilities:		
Payable to ABC Life Insurance Company	—	46,109
	$57,231,590	$350,751,643
Net assets:		
Accumulation units	$57,231,590	$349,750,644
Contracts in payout (annuitization) period	—	610,108
Retained in Separate Account I by ABC Life Insurance Company	—	390,891
Total net assets	$57,231,590	$350,751,643
Units outstanding	4,136,795	19,674,291
Unit value (accumulation)	$13.83	$17.83

The accompanying notes are an integral part of these financial statements.

10.62

ABC Variable Annuity Separate Account I
of ABC Life Insurance Company
Statement of Operations
for the Year Ended December 31, 20X8

	Money Market	Equity Index
Income:		
Dividends	$4,602,399	$6,450,878
Expenses:		
Mortality and expense risk	548,224	1,753,874
Administrative charges[6]	182,741	584,624
Net investment income	3,871,434	4,112,380
Realized gains (losses) on investments		
Realized gain on sale of fund shares	—	4,050,008
Realized gain distributions	—	400,900
Realized gain	—	4,450,908
Change in unrealized appreciation during the year	—	20,728,111
Net increase in net assets from operations	$3,871,434	$29,291,399

The accompanying notes are an integral part of these financial statements.

---

[6] If, under the annuity contract, the administrative charge is levied as a direct charge to the contract holders' accounts, rather than against the separate account, this would be included as an item separate from contract transactions in the statement of changes in net assets. In such cases, the exclusion of the direct charges from the expense ratios appearing in the financial highlights should be noted. If the charge is applied uniformly to all accounts based on the value of the contract holder's account, consideration should be given to indicating the effect of the charge on contract holder costs (expressed as a percentage of net assets) in the note.

AAG-INV 10.62

10.63

ABC Variable Annuity Separate Account I
of ABC Life Insurance Company
Statement of Changes in Net Assets
for the Years Ended December 31, 20X8 and 20X7

	Money Market		*Equity Index*	
	20X8	20X7	20X8	20X7
Increase in net assets from operations:				
Net investment income	$3,871,434	$3,534,624	$4,112,380	$1,100,710
Realized gains	—	—	4,450,908	462,877
Unrealized appreciation during the year	—	—	20,728,111	22,480,579
Net increase in net assets from operations	3,871,434	3,534,624	29,291,399	24,044,166
Contract transactions:				
Payments received from contract owners	14,367,366	17,444,822	37,527,318	11,075,691
Transfers between subaccounts (including fixed account), net	(15,063,795)	(18,267,246)	155,175,016	59,808,957
Transfers for contract benefits and terminations	(11,945,485)	(10,017,075)	(4,238,812)	(1,639,933)
Contract maintenance charges	(40,061)	(51,366)	(210,505)	(65,202)
Adjustments to net assets allocated to contracts in payout period	—	—	6,500	—
Net increase (decrease) in net assets from contract transactions	(12,681,975)	(10,890,865)	188,259,517	69,179,513
Increase (decrease) in amounts retained in Variable Annuity Account I, net	—	—	90,967	(122,904)
Total increase (decrease) in net assets	(8,810,541)	(7,356,241)	217,641,883	93,100,775
Net assets at beginning of period	66,042,131	73,398,372	133,109,760	40,008,985
Net assets at end of period	$57,231,590	$66,042,131	$350,751,643	$133,109,760

The accompanying notes are an integral part of these financial statements.

10.64

ABC Variable Annuity Separate Account I
of ABC Life Insurance Company
Notes to Financial Statements

1. Organization

The ABC Variable Annuity Separate Account I (Separate Account I), a unit investment trust registered under the Investment Company Act of 1940, as amended, was established by ABC Life Insurance Company (ABC) on April 1, 20XX, and exists in accordance with the regulations of the New York Insurance Department. Separate Account I is a funding vehicle for individual variable annuity contracts. Separate Account I currently consists of two investment divisions: Money Market and Equity Index, each of which is treated as an individual separate account. Each investment division invests all its investible assets in the corresponding portfolio of ABC Investment Fund, Inc.

Under applicable insurance law, the assets and liabilities of Separate Account I are clearly identified and distinguished from ABC's other assets and liabilities. The portion of Separate Account I's assets applicable to the variable annuity contracts is not chargeable with liabilities arising out of any other business ABC may conduct.

2. Significant Accounting Policies

Investments are made in the portfolios of ABC Investment Fund and valued at fair value based on the reported net asset values of such portfolios, which in turn value their investment securities at fair value. Transactions are recorded on a trade date basis. Dividend income and realized gain distributions are recorded on the ex-distribution date.

Realized gains and losses on the sales of investments are computed on the basis of the identified cost of the investment sold.

Net assets allocated to contracts in the payout period are computed according to the 1983a Individual Annuitant Mortality Table. The assumed investment return is 3.5 percent unless the annuitant elects otherwise, in which case the rate may vary from 3.5 percent to 7 percent, as regulated by the laws of the respective states. The mortality risk is fully borne by ABC and may result in additional amounts being transferred into the variable annuity account by ABC to cover greater longevity of annuitants than expected. Conversely, if amounts allocated exceed amounts required, transfers may be made to the insurance entity.

The operations of Separate Account I are included in the federal income tax return of ABC, which is taxed as a life insurance entity under the provisions of the Internal Revenue Code (IRC). Under the current provisions of the IRC, ABC does not expect to incur federal income taxes on the earnings of Separate Account I to the extent that the earnings are credited under the contracts. Based on this, no charge is being made currently to Separate Account I for federal income taxes. ABC will review periodically the status of this policy in the event of changes in the tax law. A charge may be made in future years for any federal income taxes that would be attributable to the contracts.

The preparation of financial statements in accordance with U.S. generally accepted accounting principles (GAAP) requires management to make estimates and assumptions that affect amounts reported therein. Actual results could differ from these estimates.

AAG-INV 10.64

3. Investments

As described in note 2, Separate Account I measures the fair value of its investment in ABC Investment Fund on a recurring basis. GAAP establishes a hierarchy that prioritizes inputs to valuation methods. The three levels of inputs are as follows:

- *Level 1.* Unadjusted quoted prices in active markets for identical assets or liabilities that Separate Account I has the ability to access.
- *Level 2.* Observable inputs other than quoted prices included in level 1 that are observable for the asset or liability either directly or indirectly. These inputs may include quoted prices for the identical instrument on an inactive market, prices for similar instruments, interest rates, prepayment speeds, credit risk, yield curves, default rates, and similar data.
- *Level 3.* Unobservable inputs for the asset or liability, to the extent observable inputs are not available, representing Separate Account I's own assumptions about the assumptions that a market participant would use in valuing the asset or liability, and that would be based on the best information available.

The following table summarizes the inputs used to value Separate Account I's assets measured at fair value as of December 31, 20X8.[7]

Valuation Inputs	Money Market	Equity Index
Level 1	$57,231,590	$350,797,752
Level 2	—	—
Level 3	—	—
Total	$57,231,590	$350,797,752

There were no transfers between level 1 and level 2 during the year.

The cost of purchases and proceeds from sales of investments for the year ended December 31, 20X8 were as follows:

	Purchases	Sales
Money Market Subaccount	$ 13,855,466	$22,666,007
Equity Index Subaccount	245,503,854	37,232,105

4. Expenses and Related-Party Transactions

ABC deducts a daily charge from the net assets of Separate Account I equivalent to an effective annual rate of 0.25 percent for administrative expenses and 0.75 percent for the assumption of mortality and expense risks. ABC also deducts an annual maintenance charge of $35 for each contract from the ABC Retirement Reserves Contract value. The maintenance charge, which is recorded as a redemption in the accompanying statement of changes in net assets, is waived on certain contracts.

Additionally, during the year ended December 31, 20X8, management fees were paid indirectly to ABC Management Company, an affiliate of ABC in its

---

[7] The classification of various financial instruments in this table is for illustrative purposes only and should not be construed as recommended practice for any particular financial instrument or class of financial instruments.

capacity as adviser to ABC Investment Fund. The fund's advisory agreement provides for a fee at the annual rate of 0.15 percent of the average net assets of the Money Market Fund and 0.45 percent of the average net assets of the Equity Index Fund.

[Other: Consider disclosures of other fees to affiliates not otherwise disclosed, such as sales load charges retained by the insurance entity.]

5. Changes in Units Outstanding

The changes in units outstanding for the years ended December 31, 20X8 and 20X7 were as follows:

	Money Market		Equity Index	
	20X8	20X7	20X8	20X7
Units issued	1,075,828	1,346,281	11,530,377	5,387,478
Units redeemed	(1,967,393)	(2,191,438)	(268,220)	(115,368)
Net increase (decrease)	(891,565)	(845,157)	11,262,157	5,272,110

6. Unit Values

A summary of unit values and units outstanding for variable annuity contracts, net investment income ratios, and expense ratios, excluding expenses of the underlying funds, for each of the five years in the period ended December 31, 20X8, follows:

> a. The following format should be presented if the insurance enterprise chooses to disclose each contract expense level that results in a distinct net unit value and for which units were issued or outstanding during each of the five years ended December 31, 20X8.

AAG-INV 10.64

Investment Companies

		Net Assets		Investment Income Ratio[8]	Expense Ratio[9]	Total Return[10]
Units	Unit Value	(000s)				

Money Market Investment Division

December 31

20X8						
4,136,795	$13.83	$57,232	5.25%	1.00%	5.30%
20X7						
5,028,360	13.13	66,042	5.02	1.00	5.07
20X6						
5,873,517	12.50	73,398	8.46	1.00	8.54
20X5						
2,058,353	11.52	23,705	8.23	1.00	8.31
20X4						
967,550	10.63	10,291	6.24	1.00	6.30
7/1/X3						
500,000	10.00	5,000			

---

[8] These amounts represent the dividends, excluding distributions of capital gains, received by the subaccount from the underlying mutual fund, net of management fees assessed by the fund investment adviser, divided by the average net assets. These ratios exclude those expenses, such as mortality and expense charges, that are assessed against contract owner accounts either through reductions in the unit values or the redemption of units. The recognition of investment income by the subaccount is affected by the timing of the declaration of dividends by the underlying fund in which the subaccount invests.

[9] These amounts represent the annualized contract expenses of the separate account, consisting primarily of mortality and expense charges, for each period indicated. These ratios include only those expenses that result in a direct reduction to unit values. Charges made directly to contract owner accounts through the redemption of units and expenses of the underlying fund have been excluded.

[10] These amounts represent the total return for the periods indicated, including changes in the value of the underlying fund, and expenses assessed through the reduction of unit values. These ratios do not include any expenses assessed through the redemption of units. Investment options with a date notation indicate the effective date of that investment option in the variable account. The total return is calculated for each period indicated or from the effective date through the end of the reporting period.

AAG-INV 10.64

Variable Contracts—Insurance Entities

Units	Net Assets Unit Value	Net Assets (000s)	Investment Income Ratio[11]	Expense Ratio[12]	Total Return[13]
Equity Index Division					
December 31					
20X8					
19,674,291	$17.83	$350,752	2.23%	1.00%	12.68%
20X7					
8,412,134	15.82	133,110	2.35	1.00	24.16
20X6					
3,140,024	12.74	40,009	3.12	1.00	(9.50)
20X5					
3,879,972	14.08	54,630	3.24	1.00	11.94
20X4					
2,162,080	12.58	27,195	3.98	1.00	6.20

b. The following format should be presented if the insurance enterprise chooses to present the range of the lowest to highest level of expense ratio and the related total return and unit fair values during each of the five years ended December 31, 20X8. Certain of the information is presented as a range of minimum to maximum values based on the product grouping representing the minimum and maximum expense ratio amounts.

	Units (000s)	At December 31 Unit Fair Value Lowest to Highest	Net Assets (000s)	For the Year Ended December 31 Investment[14] Income Ratio	Expense Ratio[15] Lowest to Highest	Total Return[16] Lowest to Highest
Money Market Investment Division						
20X8	4,137	$10.51–$14.06	$57,232	5.25%	1.00%–2.65%	4.10%–5.30%
20X7	5,028	10.00–13.20	66,042	5.02	1.00–2.60	4.01–5.07
20X6	5,874	9.37–13.21	73,398	8.46	1.00–2.60	7.45–8.54
20X5	2,058	8.72–12.23	23,705	8.23	1.00–2.55	5.65–8.31
20X4	968	8.25–12.50	10,291	6.24	1.00–2.45	5.25–6.30

---

[11] See footnote 8.
[12] See footnote 9.
[13] See footnote 10.
[14] See footnote 8.
[15] See footnote 9.
[16] These amounts represent the total return for the periods indicated, including changes in the value of the underlying fund, and expenses assessed through the reduction of unit values. These ratios do not include any expenses assessed through the redemption of units. Investment options with a date notation indicate the effective date of that investment option in the variable account. The total return is calculated for each period indicated or from the effective date through the end of the reporting period. As the total return is presented as a range of minimum to maximum values, based on the product grouping representing the minimum and maximum expense ratio amounts, some individual contract total returns are not within the ranges presented.

AAG-INV 10.64

		At December 31			For the Year Ended December 31	
	Units (000s)	Unit Fair Value Lowest to Highest	Net Assets (000s)	Investment Income Ratio	Expense Ratio Lowest to Highest	Total Return Lowest to Highest
Equity Index Division						
20X8	19,674	$10.51–$19.06	$350,752	2.23%	1.00%–2.65%	5.10%–12.18%
20X7	8,412	10.00–20.20	133,110	2.35	1.00–2.60	6.80–24.16
20X6	3,140	9.37–14.21	40,009	3.12	1.00–2.60	(9.50)–9.10
20X5	3,880	8.72–15.23	54,630	3.24	1.00–2.55	5.65–11.94
20X4	2,162	8.25–13.50	27,195	3.98	1.00–2.45	5.25–6.20

  c. An insurance enterprise may choose to present all expenses that are charged by the separate account in either a table or narrative format. The disclosure should list all fees that are charged by the separate account and a description of those fees, including whether they are assessed as direct reductions in unit values or through the redemption of units for all policies contained within the separate account. For this example, expenses disclosed are based on the ranges of all products within the separate account; the expenses may also be listed in more detail (for example, individual charges broken out by products within the separate account) in either table or narrative format.

ABC Variable Annuity Separate Account I

Mortality and Expense Charge
Basic charges are assessed through reduction of unit values.   1.00%–1.70%

Death Benefit Options
The options are assessed through reduction in unit values:

- Ratchet Option—Equal to the highest account balance among prior specified anniversary dates adjusted for deposits less partial withdrawals since the specified anniversary date   0.15%–0.20%

- Roll-Up Option—Equal to the total of deposits made to the contract less an adjustment for partial withdrawals, accumulated at a specified interest rate   0.20%–0.40%

Guaranteed Minimum Income Benefits
These benefits are assessed through a reduction in unit values and provide that the periodic annuity benefits will

- not fall below a contractually specified level.   0.20%–0.55%

- be based on the higher of actual account values at the date that the policy owner elects to annuitize or a contractually specified amount.   0.30%–0.40%

Administrative Charge
This charge is assessed through the redemption of units.   Years 1–5: $30
   Years 6+: $10

Alternatively, the expense ratio represents the annualized contract expenses of ABC Variable Annuity Separate Account I for the period indicated and includes only those expenses that are charged through a reduction of the unit value. Included in this category are mortality and expense charges and the cost of any riders that the policyholder has elected. These fees range between 1.00 percent and 2.65 percent, depending on the product and options selected. Expenses of the underlying fund portfolios and charges made directly to contract owner accounts through the redemption of units are excluded. For this separate account, charges made through the redemption of units ranged from $10 to $30 per policy annually.

Chapter 11

Independent Auditor's Reports and Client Representations

> **Ⓞ Update 11-1 *Audit*: Clarified Auditing Standards**
>
> With the issuance of Statement on Auditing Standards (SAS) Nos. 122–125 (AICPA, *Professional Standards*) in 2011, the Auditing Standards Board (ASB) achieved a major milestone in its Clarity Project, which was designed to make generally accepted auditing standards (GAAS) easier to read, understand, and apply. These clarified SASs are effective for audits of financial statements for periods ending on or after December 15, 2012.
>
> The auditing guidance in this guide will be conformed to reflect the guidance in SAS Nos. 122–125 in the next edition, when these clarified SASs are effective. Although extensive, the revisions to GAAS resulting from SAS Nos. 122–125 do not change many of the requirements found in the existing auditing standards that they supersede.
>
> This chapter contains numerous references to the auditing interpretations of AU section 508, *Reports on Audited Financial Statements* (AICPA, *Professional Standards*). All auditing interpretations corresponding to an AU section have been considered in the development of the clarified auditing standard and have either been incorporated accordingly and withdrawn by the ASB, or retained and revised to reflect the issuance of the AU-C section. The interpretations of AU section 508 referred to in this chapter were incorporated into the respective clarified standards, with the exception of Interpretation No. 16, "Effect on Auditor's Report of Omission of Schedule of Investments by Investment Partnerships That Are Exempt From Securities and Exchange Commission Registration Under the Investment Company Act of 1940," of AU section 508 (AICPA, *Professional Standards*, AU sec. 9508 par. .76–.84), which was withdrawn as a part of the Clarity Project. See further discussion of Interpretation No. 16 of AU section 508 in update 11-2.
>
> To assist auditors and financial reporting professionals in making the transition, this guide includes the following appendixes:
>
> - Appendix B, "Guidance Updates—Clarified Auditing Standards," identifies the changes, either substantive or primarily clarifying in nature, that may affect an auditor's practice or methodology relative to the applicable sections of SAS Nos. 122–125.
> - Appendix C, "Mapping and Summarization of Changes—Clarified Auditing Standards," provides a cross reference of the sections in the superseded auditing standards to the applicable sections in the clarified auditing standards. It also summarizes the changes resulting from the requirements of SAS Nos. 122–125.
>
> The preface of this guide, and the Financial Reporting Center on www.aicpa.org, provide more information on the Clarity Project. Visit www.aicpa.org/sasclarity.

AAG-INV

11.01 The following auditor's reports[1] on financial statements illustrate pertinent items discussed in this guide, but they do not cover all the diverse circumstances that may occur in practice. It is essential, therefore, that the auditor's report reflects the requirements of the particular circumstances. Financial reporting for publicly registered investment companies is governed by the rules of the Securities and Exchange Commission (SEC) (for example, Regulation S-X), and there may be differences between this guide and SEC rules.

Considerations for Audits Performed in Accordance With Public Company Accounting Oversight Board (PCAOB) Standards

Auditing Standard No. 1, *References in Auditors' Reports to the Standards of the Public Company Accounting Oversight Board* (AICPA, *PCAOB Standards and Related Rules*, Auditing Standards), as approved by the SEC and among other matters, requires registered public accounting firms to include in their reports on engagements performed pursuant to the PCAOB's auditing and related professional practice standards a reference to the standards of the PCAOB (United States). PCAOB Auditing Standard No. 1 replaces in auditors' reports the sentence "We conducted our audits in accordance with auditing standards generally accepted in the United States of America," with the following sentence: "We conducted our audits in accordance with the standards of the Public Company Accounting Oversight Board (United States)." The SEC is required to approve all PCAOB auditing standards. Since Auditing Standard No. 1 has been approved, the SEC has also approved PCAOB standards relating to performing an integrated audit, audit documentation, reporting on whether a previously reported material weakness continues to exist, evaluating consistency of financial statements, and engagement quality review.

Reports on Financial Statements of Nonregistered Investment Companies

11.02 The following form of the auditor's report may be used to express an unqualified opinion on the financial statements of a nonregistered investment company:[2]

Independent Auditor's Report

To the Shareholders and
Board of Directors/Trustees of
XYZ Investment Company

We have audited the accompanying statement of assets and liabilities of XYZ Investment Company (the Company), including the schedule

---

[1] This guide primarily discusses auditing guidance issued by the Auditing Standards Board that applies to nonissuers. *Issuers* are defined by Section 3 of the Securities Exchange Act of 1934 and include registered investment companies. Audits of issuers are required to be performed under Public Company Accounting Oversight Board (PCAOB) standards. Users should evaluate their audit engagements to determine which auditing standards are applicable.

[2] This form of report is prescribed by paragraph .08 of AU section 508, *Reports on Audited Financial Statements* (AICPA, *Professional Standards*). Registered public accounting firms must comply with the standards of the PCAOB in connection with the preparation or issuance of any audit report on the financial statements of an issuer, as discussed in paragraph 11.01. Readers should understand the provisions of the Sarbanes-Oxley Act of 2002, the Securities and Exchange Commission (SEC) regulations implementing the Sarbanes-Oxley Act of 2002, and the rules and standards of the PCAOB, as applicable to their circumstances, to determine if the standards of the PCAOB should be applied.

AAG-INV 11.01

of investments, as of December 31, 20X8, and the related statements of operations, cash flows[3] and changes in net assets for the year then ended.[4] These financial statements are the responsibility of the Company's management. Our responsibility is to express an opinion on these financial statements based on our audit.

We conducted our audit in accordance with auditing standards generally accepted in the United States of America.[5] Those standards require that we plan and perform the audit to obtain reasonable assurance about whether the financial statements are free of material misstatement. An audit includes examining, on a test basis, evidence supporting the amounts and disclosures in the financial statements. An audit also includes assessing the accounting principles used and significant estimates made by management, as well as evaluating the overall financial statement presentation. We believe that our audit provides a reasonable basis for our opinion.

In our opinion, the financial statements referred to above present fairly, in all material respects, the financial position of XYZ Investment Company as of December 31, 20X8, the results of its operations, its cash flows[6] and changes in its net assets for the year then ended, in conformity with accounting principles generally accepted in the United States of America.[7]

Independent Auditor
Anytown, USA
February 21, 20X9

---

[3] Financial Accounting Standards Board (FASB) *Accounting Standards Codification* (ASC) 230-10-15-4 exempts highly liquid companies that meet specified conditions from the requirements to provide a statement of cash flows. See chapter 7, "Financial Statements of Investment Companies," of this guide for further discussion.

[4] If the financial highlights are presented in a separate schedule (as opposed to in a footnote), the schedule of financial highlights should be mentioned, along with the financial statements, throughout the independent auditor's report.

[5] AU section 508 states that a basic element of the auditor's report is a statement that the audit was conducted in accordance with generally accepted auditing standards and an identification of the United States of America as the country of origin of those standards. Interpretation No. 14, "Reporting on Audits Conducted in Accordance With Auditing Standards Generally Accepted in the United States of America and in Accordance With International Standards on Auditing," of AU section 508 (AICPA, *Professional Standards*, AU sec. 9508 par. .56–.59), states that if the audit also was conducted in accordance with International Standards on Auditing in their entirety, the auditor may so indicate that fact in the auditor's report. This can be done by modifying this sentence as follows (new language is shown in italics):

We conducted our audit in accordance with auditing standards generally accepted in the United States of America *and in accordance with International Standards on Auditing*.

[6] See footnote 3.

[7] Interpretation No. 19, "Financial Statements Prepared in Conformity With International Financial Reporting Standards as Issued by the International Accounting Standards Board," of AU section 508 (AICPA, *Professional Standards*, AU sec. 9508 par. .93–.97), states that the auditor may report on general purpose financial statements presented in conformity with International Financial Reporting Standards (IFRSs), as issued by the International Accounting Standards Board. In that scenario, in the auditor's report, the auditor would refer to IFRSs, rather than U.S. generally accepted accounting principles. An example opinion paragraph would be as follows (new language is shown in italics):

In our opinion, the financial statements referred to above present fairly, in all material respects, the financial position of XYZ Investment Company as of December 31, 20X8, the results of its operations, its cash flows, and changes in its net assets for the year then ended, in conformity with *International Financial Reporting Standards as issued by the International Accounting Standards Board*.

AAG-INV 11.02

> **⊙ Update 11-2 *Audit*: Clarified Auditing Standards**
> Concurrent with the effective date of the ASB's SAS Nos. 122–125 (see update 11-1), Interpretation No. 16 of AU section 508 will be withdrawn. However, the auditing guidance in the interpretation remains relevant and will continue to be included in this guide in this and subsequent editions.

11.03 In accordance with paragraph .41 of AU section 508 and as discussed in Interpretation No. 16 of AU section 508, if financial statements of an investment partnership that is exempt from SEC registration do not include the U.S. generally accepted accounting principles (GAAP) required schedule of investments[8] disclosures that are discussed in paragraph 7.33 of this guide, the auditor should express a qualified or an adverse opinion in the report. If it is practicable for the auditor to determine the disclosures or any portion thereof, the auditor should include the information in the audit report expressing the qualified or adverse opinion (unless its omission from the auditor's report is recognized as appropriate by a specific SAS).

11.04 Interpretation No. 16 of AU section 508 discusses the example provided in paragraph .42 of AU section 508 of a report qualified for inadequate disclosure (assuming that the auditor has concluded that it is not practicable to present the required information and the effects are such that the auditor has concluded an adverse opinion is not appropriate), as follows:

Independent Auditor's Report

[Same first and second paragraphs as the standard report.]

The Company's financial statements do not disclose *[describe the nature of the omitted information that is not practicable to present in the auditor's report]*. In our opinion, disclosure of this information is required by accounting principles generally accepted in the United States of America.

In our opinion, except for the omission of the information discussed in the preceding paragraph, ...

11.05 Interpretation No. 16 of AU section 508 explains that Financial Accounting Standards Board (FASB) *Accounting Standards Codification* (ASC) 946, *Financial Services–Investment Companies*, does not make it clear how the guidance in paragraphs .41–.42 of AU section 508 should be applied to reports on financial statements of investment partnerships that are exempt from SEC registration and that do not include all the investment information required in the schedule of investments as required by FASB ASC 946. For example, if the financial statements did not disclose each of the required items for each investment, the guidance in AU section 508 paragraph .41 indicates the auditor should, if practicable, include the missing information (for example, the schedule of investments or information about individual investments) in the auditor's report. However, the example in AU section 508 paragraph .42 provides that the auditor would disclose the nature of the missing information,

---

[8] Additional financial statement presentation and disclosure requirements, of which exclusion may also result in a qualified or an adverse opinion, for investment partnerships that are exempt from SEC registration under the Investment Company Act of 1940 (the 1940 Act) can be found in FASB ASC 946, *Financial Services–Investment Companies*.

Independent Auditor's Reports and Client Representations

rather than the actual information, in the auditor's report. In applying AU section 508 paragraphs .41–.42 to an auditor's report on financial statements of an investment partnership that is exempt from SEC registration and that does not include the required schedule of investments information required by FASB ASC 946-210-50-6, it is not sufficient for the auditor to describe "the nature of the omitted disclosures" in his or her report expressing a qualified (or adverse) opinion. The example in AU section 508 paragraph .42 does not change the requirement in AU section 508 paragraph .41 for the auditor to issue a qualified or adverse opinion and also to provide the missing information, if practicable. If the investment disclosures required by FASB ASC 946 are not included in the financial statements and it is practicable for the auditor to determine them or any portion thereof, the auditor should include the information in his or her report expressing the qualified or adverse opinion.

11.06 Footnote 15 of AU section 508 indicates that it is practicable to provide the missing information if "the information is reasonably obtainable from management's accounts and records and . . . providing the information in the report does not require the auditor to assume the position of a preparer of financial information." Ordinarily, it would be practicable for the auditor to obtain and present the information about investments constituting more than 5 percent of net assets called for by the disclosure requirement described in paragraph 7.33(b) of this guide. However, the auditor might be in the position of preparer of financial information due to the need to categorize the investments for the purpose of preparing the schedule called for by the disclosure requirement described in paragraph 7.33(a) of this guide and, therefore, would not include the schedule in his or her report. In rare cases, the schedule of investments information may be so limited that the auditor may conclude that disclosure of the entire schedule is practicable.

11.07 As discussed in Interpretation No. 16 of AU section 508, and consistent with paragraph .42 of AU section 508, following is an illustration of a report that expresses a qualified opinion because the schedule of investments fails to disclose investments constituting more than 5 percent of net assets but, in all other respects, conforms to the requirements of GAAP:

Independent Auditor's Report

[Same first and second paragraphs as the standard report.]

The Schedule of Investments included in the Partnership's financial statements does not disclose required information about the following investments, each constituting more than 5 percent of the Partnership's total net assets, at December 31, 20X8:

- Amalgamated Buggy Whips, Inc., 10,000 shares of common stock-fair value $3,280,000 (Consumer nondurable goods)
- Paper Airplane Corp., 6.25 percent Cv. Deb. due 20YX, $4.5 million par value-fair value $4,875,000 (Aviation)

In our opinion, disclosure of this information is required by accounting principles generally accepted in the United States of America.

In our opinion, except for the omission of the information discussed in the preceding paragraph, the financial statements[9] referred to above present fairly, ...

11.08 An illustration of an adverse opinion relating to failure to present the entire schedule of investments and all the related required information follows, as shown in Interpretation No. 16 of AU section 508.[10] Paragraph .58 of AU section 508 requires the auditor to express an adverse opinion when, in the auditor's judgment, the financial statements as a whole are not presented fairly, in accordance with GAAP. When the auditor expresses an adverse opinion, the opinion paragraph should include a direct reference to a separate paragraph that discloses the basis for the adverse opinion. In the following illustration, the auditor has concluded that an adverse opinion is necessary due to inadequate disclosure and that presenting all the required information is not practicable:[11]

Independent Auditor's Report

[Same first and second paragraphs as the standard report.]

The Partnership has declined to prepare and present a Schedule of Investments and the related information as of December 31, 20X8. Accounting principles generally accepted in the United States of America require presentation of this Schedule and the related information. Presentation of this Schedule would have disclosed required information about the following investments, each constituting more than 5 percent of the Partnership's total net assets, at December 31, 20X8:

- Amalgamated Buggy Whips, Inc., 10,000 shares of common stock-fair value $3,280,000 (Consumer nondurable goods)[12]
- Paper Airplane Corp., 6.25 percent Cv. Deb. due 20YX, $4.5 million par value-fair value $4,875,000 (Aviation)

In addition, presentation of the Schedule of Investments would have disclosed *[describe the nature of the information that it is not practicable to present in the auditor's report]*.

In our opinion, because the omission of a Schedule of Investments results in an incomplete presentation as explained in the preceding paragraph, the financial statements[13] referred to above do not present fairly, ...

11.09 When the financial statements contain securities whose fair values were estimated by the board of directors or trustees in the absence of readily

---

[9] See footnote 4.

[10] Paragraph .36 of AU section 508 discusses the factors that the auditor considers in deciding whether to issue a qualified or an adverse opinion.

[11] See footnote 2 to paragraph 11.02.

[12] In the absence of a schedule of investments containing categorizations by type, country or geographic region, and industry, such categorizations should be provided only if readily ascertainable from management's accounts and records. The auditor should not assign such categorizations if management has not done so.

[13] See footnote 4.

Independent Auditor's Reports and Client Representations

ascertainable fair values,[14] and the auditor concludes that the valuation procedures are inadequate or unreasonable or that the underlying documentation does not support the valuation, the auditor should express a qualified opinion in a manner similar to the following:[15]

Independent Auditor's Report

To the Shareholders and
Board of Directors/Trustees of
XYZ Investment Company

[*Same first and second paragraphs as in the report illustrated in paragraph 11.02.*]

As explained in Note 2, the financial statements include securities valued at $_____ (_____ percent of net assets), whose fair values have been estimated by the Board of Directors/Trustees in the absence of readily ascertainable fair values. We have reviewed the procedures used by the Board of Directors/Trustees in arriving at its estimate of fair value of such securities and have inspected underlying documentation. In our opinion, those procedures are not reasonable, and the documentation is not appropriate to determine the securities' estimated fair values. The effect on the financial statements of not applying adequate valuation procedures is not readily determinable.

In our opinion, except for the effects on the financial statements[16] of the valuation of investment securities determined by the Board of Directors/Trustees, as described in the preceding paragraph, the financial statements referred to above present fairly, in all material respects, the financial position of XYZ Investment Company as of December 31, 20X8, the results of its operations, its cash flows,[17] and changes in its net assets for the year then ended, in conformity with accounting principles generally accepted in the United States of America.

Independent Auditor
Anytown, USA
January 21, 20X9

When the deficiencies in procedures and documentation are sufficiently serious or pervasive to suggest that the financial statements as a whole do not present the financial position and results of operations in accordance with GAAP, an adverse opinion may be more appropriate than a qualified opinion.

11.10 Interpretation No. 17, "Clarification in the Audit Report of the Extent of Testing of Internal Control Over Financial Reporting in Accordance with

---

[14] AU section 328, *Auditing Fair Value Measurements and Disclosures* (AICPA, *Professional Standards*), contains expanded guidance on the audit procedures for fair value measurements and disclosures. Under AU section 328, the auditor's substantive tests of fair value measurements involve (*a*) testing management's significant assumptions, the valuation model, and the underlying data; (*b*) developing independent fair value estimates for corroborative purposes; or (*c*) examining subsequent events and transactions that confirm or disconfirm the estimate.

[15] This form of report is prescribed by AU section 508. Registered public accounting firms must comply with the standards of the PCAOB in connection with the preparation or issuance of any audit report on the financial statements of an issuer, as discussed in paragraph 11.01. Readers should understand the provisions of the Sarbanes-Oxley Act of 2002, the SEC regulations implementing the Sarbanes-Oxley Act of 2002, and the rules and standards of the PCAOB, as applicable to their circumstances, to determine if the standards of the PCAOB should be applied. Any opinion other than an unqualified opinion does not satisfy a registrant's filing obligation.

[16] See footnote 4.

[17] See footnote 3.

AAG-INV 11.10

Generally Accepted Auditing Standards," of AU section 508 (AICPA, *Professional Standards*, AU sec. 9508 par. .85–.88), provides for audits of nonissuers an example of additional language that may be added to an auditor's standard report to explain that an audit includes consideration of internal control over financial reporting as a basis for designing audit procedures but not for the purpose of expressing an opinion on the effectiveness of internal control over financial reporting.

The following illustrates the optional wording that may be added to reports, in accordance with Interpretation No. 17 of AU section 508:

Independent Auditor's Report

To the Shareholders and
Board of Directors/Trustees of
XYZ Investment Company

[Same first paragraph as in the report illustrated in paragraph 11.02.]

We conducted our audit in accordance with auditing standards generally accepted in the United States of America.[18] Those standards require that we plan and perform the audit to obtain reasonable assurance about whether the financial statements[19] are free of material misstatement. An audit includes consideration of internal control over financial reporting as a basis for designing audit procedures that are appropriate in the circumstances, but not for the purpose of expressing an opinion on the effectiveness of the Company's internal control over financial reporting. Accordingly, we express no such opinion. An audit also includes examining, on a test basis, evidence supporting the amounts and disclosures in the financial statements, assessing the accounting principles used and significant estimates made by management, as well as evaluating the overall financial statement presentation. We believe that our audit provides a reasonable basis for our opinion.

[Same third paragraph as in the report illustrated in paragraph 11.02.]

Independent Auditor
Anytown, USA
February 21, 20X9

11.11

Considerations for Audits Performed in Accordance With PCAOB Standards

Interpretation No. 18, "Reference to PCAOB Standards in an Audit Report on a Nonissuer," of AU section 508 (AICPA, *Professional Standards*, AU sec. 9508 par. .89–.92), provides guidance on the appropriate referencing of PCAOB auditing standards in audit reports for those auditors who are engaged to perform an audit in accordance with PCAOB standards when auditing nonissuers.

11.12 The following form of report is used in connection with a review of semiannual financial statements of a nonregistered investment company:

---

[18] See footnote 5.
[19] See footnote 4.

Report Prepared in Accordance With Standards Established by the American Institute of Certified Public Accountants[20]

Independent Accountant's Review Report

To the Shareholders and
Board of Directors/Trustees of
XYZ Investment Company

We have reviewed the accompanying statement of assets and liabilities of XYZ Investment Company (the Company), including the schedule of investments, as of June 30, 20X8, and the related statements of operations and changes in net assets[21] for the six-month period ended June 30, 20X8. This financial information is the responsibility of the Company's management.

We conducted our review in accordance with standards established by the American Institute of Certified Public Accountants. A review of interim financial information consists principally of applying analytical procedures and making inquiries of persons responsible for financial and accounting matters. It is substantially less in scope than an audit conducted in accordance with auditing standards generally accepted in the United States, the objective of which is the expression of an opinion regarding the financial statements taken as a whole. Accordingly, we do not express such an opinion.

Based on our review, we are not aware of any material modifications that should be made to the accompanying interim financial information for it to be in conformity with accounting principles generally accepted in the United States of America.

Independent Accountant
Anytown, USA
August 7, 20X8

Reports on Financial Statements of Registered Investment Companies

11.13 Under the Investment Company Act of 1940 (the 1940 Act), the auditor's report on the audit of a registered investment company's financial statements must state specifically that securities have been confirmed or physically examined to substantiate their existence.[22] Auditors must address their reports on financial statements of a registered investment company to the company's shareholders and board of directors.[23,24]

---

[20] AU section 722, *Interim Financial Information* (AICPA, *Professional Standards*), provides additional guidance on performing reviews of interim financial information. The term *interim financial information* means financial information or statements covering a period less than 1 full year or a 12-month period ending on a date other than the entity's fiscal year-end. Interim financial information may be condensed or in the form of a complete set of financial statements. Further, users should consult paragraph .39 of AU section 722 for report modifications if comparative financial information is presented.

[21] See footnote 4.

[22] Section 30(g) of the 1940 Act and section 404.03a of the SEC's *Codification of Financial Reporting Policies*.

[23] Section 32(a) of the 1940 Act.

[24] Refer to SEC Guidance for BDC Auditors at www.sec.gov/divisions/investment/issues-of-interest.shtml. Under section 30(g) of the 1940 Act and the Commission's Accounting Series Release

(continued)

11.14 The following form of auditor's report may be used to express an unqualified opinion on the financial statements of a registered investment company:[25]

Report of Independent Registered Public Accounting Firm

To the Shareholders and
Board of Directors of
XYZ Investment Company

We have audited the accompanying statement of assets and liabilities of XYZ Investment Company (the Company), including the schedule of investments, as of December 31, 20X8, and the related statements of operations and cash flows[26] for the year then ended, the statements of changes in net assets for each of the two years in the period then ended, and the financial highlights for each of the five years in the period then ended.[27] These financial statements and financial highlights are the responsibility of the Company's management. Our responsibility is to express an opinion on these financial statements and financial highlights based on our audits.

We conducted our audits in accordance with the standards of the Public Company Accounting Oversight Board (United States). Those standards require that we plan and perform the audit to obtain reasonable assurance about whether the financial statements and financial highlights are free of material misstatement. An audit includes examining, on a test basis, evidence supporting the amounts and disclosures in the financial statements. Our procedures included confirmation of securities owned as of December 31, 20X8, by correspondence with the custodian and brokers. An audit also includes assessing the accounting principles used and significant estimates made by management, as well as evaluating the overall financial statement presentation. We believe that our audits provide a reasonable basis for our opinion.

In our opinion, the financial statements and financial highlights referred to above present fairly, in all material respects, the financial position of XYZ Investment Company as of December 31, 20X8, the results of its operations and its cash flows[28] for the year then ended, the changes in its net assets for each of the two years in the period then ended, and the financial highlights for each of the five years in the

---

(footnote continued)

No. 118 (Dec. 23, 1970), the certificate of independent public accountants ("auditor") contained in the financial statements of investment companies registered under the 1940 Act must include a statement "that such independent public accountants have verified securities owned, either by actual examination, or by receipt of a certificate from the custodian." Although section 59 of the 1940 Act does not make section 30(g) applicable to business development companies (BDCs), a BDC's auditor plays an important role under the 1940 Act in preventing a BDC's assets from being lost, misused or misappropriated. Therefore, the staff believes that it is a best practice for a BDC to have its auditor verify all of the securities owned by the BDC, either by actual examination or by receipt of a certificate from the custodian, and affirmatively state in the audit opinion whether the auditor has confirmed the existence of all such securities.

[25] See footnote 2.

[26] See footnote 3.

[27] In accordance with Item 13 of Form N1-A, in an open-end fund's registration statement, an auditor must opine on all five years of financial highlights required to be presented in the open-end fund's prospectus or, if shorter, the period of the fund's operations.

[28] See footnote 3.

Independent Auditor's Reports and Client Representations

period then ended, in conformity with accounting principles generally accepted in the United States of America.

Independent Auditor
Anytown, USA
January 21, 20X9

11.15 The reference to *and brokers* in the fourth sentence of the scope paragraph is not normally necessary if the investment company's financial statements do not show an amount payable for securities purchased. When broker confirmations are not received, and alternative procedures are performed, the sentence may be modified to read "and brokers or by other appropriate auditing procedures where replies from brokers were not received." Also, if securities were physically inspected or subject to other extended procedures for purposes of the audit, the report should be modified to state that those procedures were performed.

11.16 Auditors may expand their audit reports to explain that they considered internal control over financial reporting as a basis for designing audit procedures but not for the purpose of expressing an opinion on the effectiveness of internal control over financial reporting. Following is an illustration of a report that may be used to make this clarification. The audit report is similar to the illustration in paragraph 11.14, but it also includes additional language that clarifies that the auditor is not required to audit the registered investment company's internal control over financial reporting.

Considerations for Audits Performed in Accordance With PCAOB Standards

The additional language is pertinent because, although the auditor is required to follow the standards of the PCAOB in conducting the financial statement audit of a registered investment company that is an issuer, the auditor is not required to conduct an audit of internal control over financial reporting for an investment company registered under Section 8 of the 1940 Act. Business development companies, however, are required to include a report of management on the company's internal control over financial reporting. Auditing Standard No. 5, *An Audit of Internal Control Over Financial Reporting That Is Integrated with An Audit of Financial Statements* (AICPA, *PCAOB Standards and Related Rules*, Auditing Standards), provides guidance that applies when an auditor is engaged to perform an audit of management's assessment of the effectiveness of internal control over financial reporting that is integrated with an audit of the financial statements.

Report of Independent Registered Public Accounting Firm

To the Shareholders and
Board of Directors of
XYZ Investment Company

[*Same first paragraph as in the report illustrated in paragraph 11.14.*]

We conducted our audits in accordance with the standards of the Public Company Accounting Oversight Board (United States). Those standards require that we plan and perform the audit to obtain reasonable assurance about whether the financial statements and financial highlights are free of material misstatement. The Company is not required to have, nor were we engaged to perform, an audit of its internal control over financial reporting. Our audits included consideration of internal control over financial reporting as a basis for designing audit procedures that are appropriate in the circumstances, but not for the purpose of expressing an opinion on the effectiveness of the Company's internal control over financial reporting. Accordingly, we express no such opinion. An audit also includes examining, on a test basis, evidence supporting the amounts and disclosures in the financial statements, assessing the accounting principles used and significant estimates made by management, as well as evaluating the overall financial statement presentation. Our procedures included confirmation of securities owned as of December 31, 20X8, by correspondence with the custodian and brokers. We believe that our audits provide a reasonable basis for our opinion.

[*Same third paragraph as in the report illustrated in paragraph 11.14.*]

Independent Auditor
Anytown, USA
January 21, 20X9

11.17 The auditor's report needs to be modified for a fund referred to as a series fund because of the uniqueness of the financial statements that have evolved to present its financial position, results of operations, and cash flows. The financial position, results of operations, and cash flows of some or all the portfolios or other entities constituting the series are frequently presented in separate columns. The financial statements of the series may also be presented as if the series were a separate entity. In both cases, the scope of the audit must be sufficient to enable the auditor to report on the individual financial statements of each series constituting the fund.

11.18 The following illustration is for a multi-columnar presentation of all the portfolios constituting the series:[29]

Report of Independent Registered Public Accounting Firm

To the Shareholders and
Board of Directors of
XYZ Series Investment Company

We have audited the statements of assets and liabilities, including the schedules of investments, of XYZ Series Investment Company (the Company) comprising the Foreign, Domestic Common Stock, Long-Term Bond, and Convertible Preferred Portfolios as of December 31, 20X8, and the related statements of operations and cash flows,[30] for the year then ended, the statements of changes in net assets for each of the two years in the period then ended, and the financial highlights for each of the five years in the period then ended. These financial statements and financial highlights are the responsibility of the Company's management. Our responsibility is to express an opinion on these financial statements and financial highlights based on our audits.

[*Same second paragraph as in the report illustrated in paragraph 11.14.*]

In our opinion, the financial statements and financial highlights referred to above present fairly, in all material respects, the financial

---

[29] See footnote 2.
[30] See footnote 3.

Independent Auditor's Reports and Client Representations

position of each of the portfolios constituting the XYZ Series Investment Company, as of December 31, 20X8, the results of their operations and cash flows[31] for the year then ended, the changes in their net assets for each of the two years in the period then ended, and their financial highlights for each of the five years in the period then ended, in conformity with accounting principles generally accepted in the United States of America.

Independent Auditor
Anytown, USA
January 21, 20X9

11.19 The following illustration is for a presentation of one of the portfolios or entities constituting the series:[32]

Report of Independent Registered Public Accounting Firm

To the Shareholders and
Board of Directors of
XYZ Series Investment Company

We have audited the accompanying statement of assets and liabilities, including the schedule of investments, of the Convertible Preferred Portfolio (one of the portfolios constituting the XYZ Series Investment Company [the Company]) as of December 31, 20X8, and the related statements of operations and cash flows[33] for the year then ended, the statement of changes in net assets for each of the two years in the period then ended, and the financial highlights for each of the five years in the period then ended. These financial statements and financial highlights are the responsibility of the Company's management. Our responsibility is to express an opinion on these financial statements and financial highlights based on our audits.

[Same second paragraph as in the report illustrated in paragraph 11.14.]

In our opinion, the financial statements and financial highlights referred to above present fairly, in all material respects, the financial position of the Convertible Preferred Portfolio of the XYZ Series Investment Company as of December 31, 20X8, and the results of its operations and its cash flows[34] for the year then ended, the changes in its net assets for each of the two years in the period then ended, and the financial highlights for each of the five years in the period then ended, in conformity with accounting principles generally accepted in the United States of America.

Independent Auditor
Anytown, USA
January 21, 20X9

---

[31] See footnote 3.
[32] See footnote 2.
[33] See footnote 3.
[34] See footnote 3.

AAG-INV 11.19

Reports for a Registered Investment Company That Issues a Condensed Schedule of Investments in the Financial Statements Provided to Shareholders

11.20 The SEC permits a registered investment company to include a summary schedule of investments in securities of unaffiliated issuers in its reports to shareholders. If this presentation is elected, the full schedule of investments in securities of unaffiliated issuers is filed with the SEC on Form N-CSR, Item 6 (see further discussion about these amendments in footnote 2 to paragraph 7.01 of this guide). According to SEC regulations, the full schedule of investments of unaffiliated issuers must be audited and accompanied by an independent auditor's report for the year-end date only, in conjunction with the annual audit. The following forms of report may be used for an annual audit of the financial statements of a registered investment company that presents a summary schedule of investments in securities of unaffiliated issuers in its reports to shareholders and files the full schedule of investments in securities of unaffiliated issuers at year-end on Form N-CSR, Item 6.[35]

Example 1-A: Full Auditor's Report on Financial Statements of a Registered Investment Company for Inclusion in Form N-CSR—Stand-Alone Fund—(Shareholder Report Includes Condensed Schedule of Investments and Supplemental Detailed Schedule of Investments Included in the Form N-CSR Filing)

Report of Independent Registered Public Accounting Firm

To the Shareholders and
Board of Directors of
XYZ Investment Company

We have audited the accompanying statement of assets and liabilities of XYZ Investment Company (the Company), including the schedule of investments, as of December 31, 20X8, and the related statements of operations and cash flows[36] for the year then ended, the statements of changes in net assets for each of the two years in the period then ended, and the financial highlights for each of the five years in the period then ended. These financial statements and financial highlights are the responsibility of the Company's management. Our responsibility is to express an opinion on these financial statements and financial highlights based on our audits.

We conducted our audits in accordance with the standards of the Public Company Accounting Oversight Board (United States). Those standards require that we plan and perform the audit to obtain reasonable assurance about whether the financial statements and financial highlights are free of material misstatement. An audit includes examining, on a test basis, evidence supporting the amounts and disclosures in

---

[35] Registered public accounting firms must comply with the standards of the PCAOB in connection with the preparation or issuance of any audit report on the financial statements of an issuer, as discussed in paragraph 11.01. Readers should understand the provisions of the Sarbanes-Oxley Act of 2002, the SEC regulations implementing the Sarbanes-Oxley Act of 2002, and the rules and standards of the PCAOB, as applicable to their circumstances, to determine if the standards of the PCAOB should be applied. Readers should consult the standards of the PCAOB and related interpretive guidance when preparing or issuing any audit report in accordance with the standards of the PCAOB.

[36] See footnote 3.

Independent Auditor's Reports and Client Representations

the financial statements. Our procedures included confirmation of securities owned as of December 31, 20X8, by correspondence with the custodian and brokers.[37] An audit also includes assessing the accounting principles used and significant estimates made by management, as well as evaluating the overall financial statement presentation. We believe that our audits provide a reasonable basis for our opinion.

In our opinion, the financial statements and financial highlights referred to above present fairly, in all material respects, the financial position of XYZ Investment Company as of December 31, 20X8, the results of its operations and its cash flows[38] for the year then ended, the changes in its net assets for each of the two years in the period then ended, and the financial highlights for each of the five years in the period then ended, in conformity with accounting principles generally accepted in the United States of America.

Our audits were conducted for the purpose of forming an opinion on the basic financial statements taken as a whole. The schedule of investments in securities as of December 31, 20X8 appearing in Item 6 of this Form N-CSR is presented for the purpose of additional analysis and is not a required part of the basic financial statements. This additional information is the responsibility of the Company's management. Such information has been subjected to the auditing procedures applied in our audit of the basic financial statements and, in our opinion, is fairly stated in all material respects in relation to the basic financial statements taken as a whole.

Independent Auditor
Anytown, USA
January 21, 20X9

Example 1-B: Separate Opinion on the Supplemental Detailed Schedule of Investments Included in the Form N-CSR Filing—Stand-Alone Fund—(Shareholder Report Includes Condensed Schedule of Investments and Supplemental Detailed Schedule of Investments Included in the Form N-CSR Filing)

Report of Independent Registered Public Accounting Firm

To the Shareholders and
Board of Directors of
XYZ Investment Company

We have audited the financial statements of XYZ Investment Company (the Company) as of December 31, 20X8, and for the year then ended and have issued our unqualified report thereon dated January 21, 20X9 (which report and financial statements are included in Item 1 of this Certified Shareholder Report on Form N-CSR). We conducted our audit in accordance with the standards of the Public Company Accounting Oversight Board (United States). Our audit included an audit of XYZ Investment Company's schedule of investments in securities (the Schedule) as of December 31, 20X8 appearing in Item 6 of this Form N-CSR. This Schedule is the responsibility of the Company's management. Our responsibility is to express an opinion on this Schedule based on our audit.

---

[37] See paragraph 11.15.
[38] See footnote 3.

In our opinion, the Schedule referred to above, when read in conjunction with the financial statements of the Company referred to above, presents fairly, in all material respects, the information set forth therein.

Independent Auditor
Anytown, USA
January 21, 20X9

11.21 The following form of report is used in connection with a review of semiannual financial statements of a registered investment company:

Report Prepared in Accordance With PCAOB Standards[39]

Report of Independent Registered Public Accounting Firm

To the Shareholders and
Board of Directors of
XYZ Investment Company

We have reviewed the accompanying statement of assets and liabilities of XYZ Investment Company (the Company), including the schedule of investments, as of June 30, 20X8, and the related statements of operations, changes in net assets, and financial highlights for the six-month period ended June 30, 20X8. These financial statements and financial highlights are the responsibility of the Company's management.

We conducted our review in accordance with the standards of the Public Company Accounting Oversight Board (United States). A review of interim financial information consists principally of applying analytical procedures and making inquiries of persons responsible for financial and accounting matters. It is substantially less in scope than an audit conducted in accordance with the standards of the Public Company Accounting Oversight Board, the objective of which is the expression of an opinion regarding the financial statements taken as a whole. Accordingly, we do not express such an opinion.

Based on our review, we are not aware of any material modifications that should be made to the accompanying financial statements and financial highlights for them to be in conformity with accounting principles generally accepted in the United States of America.

We have previously audited, in accordance with the standards of the Public Company Accounting Oversight Board, the statement of changes in net assets for the year ended December 31, 20X7, and financial highlights for each of the five years in the period ended December 31, 20X7; and in our report dated January 21, 20X8, we expressed

---

[39] AU section 722 provides additional guidance on performing reviews of interim financial information in accordance with PCAOB standards. The term *interim financial information* means financial information or statements covering a period less than 1 full year or a 12-month period ending on a date other than the entity's fiscal year-end. Registered public accounting firms must comply with the standards of the PCAOB in connection with the preparation or issuance of any report on reviews of interim financial information of an issuer, as discussed in paragraph 11.01. Readers should understand the provisions of the Sarbanes-Oxley Act of 2002, the SEC regulations implementing the Sarbanes-Oxley Act of 2002, and the rules and standards of the PCAOB, as applicable to their circumstances, to determine if the standards of the PCAOB should be applied. Readers should consult the standards of the PCAOB and related interpretive guidance when preparing or issuing any report on reviews of interim financial information in accordance with the standards of the PCAOB.

Independent Auditor's Reports and Client Representations **363**

an unqualified opinion on such statement of changes in net assets and financial highlights.

Independent Accountant
Anytown, USA
August 7, 20X8

Report on Examinations of Securities Pursuant to Rules 17f-1 and 17f-2 Under the 1940 Act

11.22 The following form of report is used for examinations of securities conducted pursuant to Rules 17f-1 and 17f-2 of the 1940 Act.[40] Paragraph (b)(4) of Rule 17f-1 requires that all registered investment companies whose securities are maintained in the custody of a member of a national securities exchange have an independent public accountant conduct an examination of such securities three times per year (at each of the annual and semiannual period-ends and at one other date, chosen by the accountant, during the fiscal year). Rule 17f-2(f) requires that all registered investment companies that maintain custody of their own securities, as defined in the rule, have an independent public accountant conduct an examination of such securities three times per fiscal year, at least two of which shall be chosen by the accountant without prior notice to the investment company. The SEC staff requires that the examination be conducted to the first level of nonaffiliation (that is, confirmations of security holdings may be relied upon to verify existence and ownership only if they are received from a nonaffiliate, such as the Depository Trust Company or the Federal Reserve's book entry system). If a portion of an investment company's portfolio is not maintained in the custody of a member of a national securities exchange or held by the investment company, the provisions of Rules 17f-1 and 17f-2 do not apply to those securities. This report follows the examination engagement provisions of AT section 601, *Compliance Attestation* (AICPA, *Professional Standards*), and Auditing Standard No. 1 and is illustrated in the following paragraph for an examination pursuant to Rule 17f-2.

This illustrative report should be used when a practitioner expresses an opinion on management's assertion about compliance with the requirements of Rule 17f-2(b)–(c) under the 1940 Act. AT section 601 enables true direct reporting on subject matter.[41]

Report of Independent Registered Public Accounting Firm

To the Board of Directors
XYZ Investment Company

We have examined management's assertion, included in the accompanying Management Statement Regarding Compliance With Certain Provisions of the Investment Company Act of 1940, that XYZ Investment Company (the Company) complied with the requirements of subsections (b) and (c) of Rule 17f-2[42] under the Investment Company Act

---

[40] Section 404.01a of the SEC's *Codification of Financial Reporting Policies* describes the nature of the examination to be made and the content of the auditor's report.

[41] Readers should consult the standards of the PCAOB and related interpretive guidance when preparing or issuing report in accordance with the standards of the PCAOB. Readers should understand the provisions of the Sarbanes-Oxley Act of 2002, the SEC regulations implementing the Sarbanes-Oxley Act of 2002, and the rules and standards of the PCAOB, as applicable to their circumstances, to determine if the standards of the PCAOB should be applied.

[42] Subsections (b)(l) and (b)(6) of Rule 17f-1.

AAG-INV 11.22

of 1940 as of August 31, 20X8. Management is responsible for the Company's compliance with those requirements. Our responsibility is to express an opinion on management's assertion about the Company's compliance based on our examination.

Our examination was conducted in accordance with the standards of the Public Company Accounting Oversight Board (United States) and, accordingly, included examining, on a test basis, evidence about the Company's compliance with those requirements and performing such other procedures as we considered necessary in the circumstances. Included among our procedures were the following tests performed as of August 31, 20X8, and with respect to agreement of security purchases and sales, for the period from April 30, 20X8 (the date of our last examination), through August 31, 20X8 [*itemize all that apply*]:

- Count and inspection of all securities located in the vault of [*Custodian*] in [*location*] without prior notice to management[43]
- Confirmation of all securities held by institutions in book entry form [*specify each institution, that is, the Federal Reserve Bank of (City), The Depository Trust Company, and so on*]
- Confirmation of all securities hypothecated, pledged, placed in escrow, or out for transfer with brokers, pledgees, or transfer agents
- Reconciliation of all such securities to the books and records of the Company and the Custodian
- Confirmation of all repurchase agreements with brokers/banks and agreement of underlying collateral with [*Custodian*] records
- Agreement of [*insert number*] security purchases and [*insert number*] security sales or maturities since our last report from the books and records of the Company to broker confirmations

We believe that our examination provides a reasonable basis for our opinion. Our examination does not provide a legal determination on the Company's compliance with specified requirements.

In our opinion, management's assertion that XYZ Investment Company complied with the requirements of subsections (b) and (c) of Rule 17f-2 of the Investment Company Act of 1940 as of August 31, 20X8, with respect to securities reflected in the investment account of the Company is fairly stated, in all material respects.

This report is intended solely for the information and use of management and the Board of Directors of XYZ Investment Company and the Securities and Exchange Commission and is not intended to be and should not be used by anyone other than these specified parties.

Independent Accountant
Anytown, USA
October 21, 20X8

---

[43] The phrase *without prior notice to management* should be deleted if the procedures were not performed on a surprise basis.

Management Statement Regarding Compliance With Certain Provisions of the Investment Company Act of 1940[44]

> We, as members of management of XYZ Investment Company (the Company), are responsible for complying with the requirements of subsections (b) and (c) of Rule 17f-2, "Custody of Investments by Registered Management Investment Companies," of the Investment Company Act of 1940. We are also responsible for establishing and maintaining effective internal controls over compliance with those requirements. We have performed an evaluation of the Company's compliance with the requirements of subsections (b) and (c) of Rule 17f-2 as of August 31, 20X8, and from [*last examination date*] through August 31, 20X8.
>
> Based on this evaluation, we assert that the Company was in compliance with the requirements of subsections (b) and (c) of Rule 17f-2 of the Investment Company Act of 1940 as of August 31, 20X8, and from [*last examination date*], through August 31, 20X8, with respect to securities reflected in the investment account of the Company.
>
> XYZ Investment Company
>
> By:
>
> [*Signature*]
>
> _____
>
> [*Name and title of appropriate operating official—CEO/COO*]

Report on Examinations of Securities Pursuant to Rule 206(4)-2 Under the Investment Advisers Act of 1940

11.23 In December 2009, the SEC adopted rules designed to substantially increase the protections for investor funds and securities of which an investment adviser registered with the SEC has custody. Depending on the investment adviser's custody arrangement, the rules would require the adviser to be subject to a surprise examination and, in some cases, a custody controls examination, which were generally not required under the previous rules. The effective date of the amendment is March 12, 2010, subject to certain exceptions. Readers are encouraged to review the full text of Rule Release No. IA-2968, *Custody of Funds or Securities of Clients by Investment Advisers*. Additionally, both the SEC and the AICPA have released frequently asked questions that are periodically updated about the custody rule and can be accessed from the Division of Investment Management page of the SEC's website and from the Investment Companies Expert Panel page under the Financial Reporting Center on the AICPA's website, respectively.

11.24 An examination of funds and securities must be conducted pursuant to Rule 206(4)-2(a)(4) under the Investment Advisers Act of 1940. This rule requires that all registered investment advisers (or an investment adviser required to register) who have custody of client funds or securities, as defined, have an independent public accountant conduct an examination on a surprise

---

[44] Alternatively, management's assertion may be included in a representation letter. Accordingly, the auditor's report should be modified to reflect this alternative, in accordance with AT section 601, *Compliance Attestation* (AICPA, *Professional Standards*). AT section 601 enables true direct reporting on the subject matter.

basis once every calendar year. The independent public accountant must also file a certificate on Form ADV-E with the SEC within 120 days of the time chosen by the independent public accountant stating that he or she has examined the funds and securities and describing the nature and extent of the examination.[45] This surprise examination report follows the provisions of AT section 601. AT section 601 enables true direct reporting on the subject matter. The rule also requires that a qualified custodian maintain client funds and securities in a separate account for each client under that client's name or in accounts that contain only the clients' funds and securities under the adviser's name as agent or trustee for the clients. Notice to clients must be provided when an account is opened (and following any changes) with a qualified custodian on their behalf, which details the qualified custodian's name and address and the manner in which the funds or securities are maintained. The investment adviser must also have a reasonable basis, after due inquiry, for believing that the qualified custodian sends an account statement, at least quarterly, to each of the investment advisers' clients for which it maintains funds or securities.[46]

11.25 Advisers to pooled investment vehicles may be deemed to comply with the surprise examination requirements of the rule by obtaining an audit of the pool and delivering the audited financial statements to pool investors within 120 days of the pool's fiscal year-end.[47] That audit must be conducted by an accounting firm registered with, and subject to regular inspection by, the PCAOB. Lastly, the advisers to pools complying with the rule by distributing audited financial statements to investors must obtain an audit upon liquidation of the pool when the liquidation occurs prior to the pool's fiscal year-end. If the pooled investment vehicle does not distribute audited financial statements to its investors, the adviser must obtain an annual surprise examination and have a reasonable basis, after due inquiry, for believing that the qualified custodian sends an account statement of the pooled investment vehicle to its investors in order to comply with the custody rule. For a pool that is not relying on the audit provision to satisfy the custody rule, the rule requires privately offered securities held by the pool to be placed with a qualified custodian (as defined in

---

[45] Frequently asked questions on Form ADV-E can be accessed through the Division of Investment Management page, "IARD: Electronic Filing for Advisers" on the SEC's website at www.sec.gov. The independent accountant, upon finding any material discrepancies during the course of the examination, should notify the SEC within one business day of the finding by means of a facsimile transmission or e-mail, followed by first class mail, directed to the attention of the Director of the Office of Compliance Inspections and Examinations. See Rule 206(4)-2(a)(4)(ii) under the 1940 Act. For purposes of the examination, a *material discrepancy* is material noncompliance with the provisions of either Rule 206(4)-2 or Rule 204-2(b) under the Investment Advisers Act of 1940. Instructions from the SEC for sending independent accountant notification of material discrepancies found during annual surprise examination can be found within those FAQs.

[46] See Rule 206(4)-2(b) under the 1940 Act for exceptions to these requirements for shares of mutual funds, certain privately offered securities, fee deductions, limited partnerships subject to annual audit, registered investment companies, and certain related persons.

[47] In 2006, the SEC issued a letter indicating that it would not recommend enforcement action under this rule against an adviser of a fund of funds relying on the annual audit provision of Rule 206(4)-2 if the audited financial statements of the fund of funds are distributed to investors in the fund of funds within 180 days of the end of its fiscal year. See the August 10, 2006, SEC staff letter *ABA Committee on Private Investment Entities*. The amendments to the custody rule do not affect the views of the staff expressed in that letter. In 2011, the SEC issued an FAQ indicating that when an adviser's client is a "top tier" pooled investment vehicle that invests in one or more funds of funds, and such top tier pool invests 10 percent or more of its total assets in one or more funds of funds, as defined in the ABA Letter, that are not, and are not advised by, a related person of the top tier pool, its general partner, or its adviser. the Division would not recommend enforcement action to the Commission under rule 206(4)-2 if the audited financial statements of the top tier pool are distributed to pool investors within 260 days of the end of the top tier pool's fiscal year.

AAG-INV 11.25

Independent Auditor's Reports and Client Representations

a subsequent paragraph), and it requires the accounting firm performing the surprise examination to verify these privately offered securities, along with other funds and securities.

11.26 If the investment adviser or its related person maintains client funds or securities as a qualified custodian in connection with advisory services provided to clients, additional requirements exist, in accordance with Rule 206(4)-2(a)(6). Such investment adviser must at least once each calendar year obtain or receive from its related person a written internal control report related to its or its affiliates' custodial services, including the safeguarding of funds and securities, which includes an opinion from an independent public accountant that is registered with, and subject to, regular inspection by the PCAOB. Regardless of whether an adviser to a pooled investment vehicle obtains a surprise examination or satisfies that requirement by obtaining an audit and distributing the audited financial statements to pool investors within 120 days of the end of the pooled investment vehicle's fiscal year,[48] if the pooled investment vehicle's assets are maintained with a qualified custodian that is either the adviser to the pool or a related person of the adviser, the adviser to the pool would have to obtain or receive from the related person an internal control report. This requirement could be satisfied with a type 2 Service Organization Control (SOC) 1 report (formerly known as a type 2 SAS No. 70 report) or an examination on internal control conducted in accordance with AT section 601. As explained in question XIII.3 of the SEC's *Staff Responses to Questions About the Custody Rule*, in addition to the two types of reports mentioned previously and Release IA-2969, all of which satisfy the requirements for an internal control report, a report under AT section 101, *Attest Engagements* (AICPA, *Professional Standards*), would also be acceptable. This internal control report must include an opinion about whether controls have been placed in operation as of a specific date and are suitably designed and operating effectively to meet control objectives relating to custodial services, including the safeguarding of funds and securities held by either the investment adviser or its related person on behalf of the advisory clients during the year. The accountant must also verify that the funds and securities are reconciled to a custodian other than the investment adviser or its related person (for example, the Depository Trust Corporation). The accountant's tests of the custodian's reconciliation should include either direct confirmation, on a test basis, with unaffiliated custodians or other procedures designed to verify that the data used in the reconciliations performed by the qualified custodian is obtained from unaffiliated custodians and unaltered.

11.27 A *qualified custodian* is defined by the rule as (*a*) a bank, as defined in Section 202(a)(2) of the Investment Advisers Act of 1940, or a savings association, as defined in Section 3(b)(1) of the Federal Deposit Insurance Act of 1950, that has deposits insured by the Federal Deposit Insurance Corporation under the Federal Deposit Insurance Act of 1950; (*b*) a broker-dealer registered under Section 15(b)(1) of the Securities Exchange Act of 1934 (the 1934 Act) holding the client assets in customer accounts; (*c*) a futures commission merchant registered under Section 4f(a) of the Commodity Exchange Act holding the client assets in customer accounts, but only with respect to clients' funds and security futures, or other securities incidental to transactions in contracts for the purchase or sale of a commodity for future delivery and options thereon; and (*d*) a foreign financial institution that customarily holds financial assets

---

[48] See footnote 47.

for its customers, provided that the foreign financial institution keeps the advisory clients' assets in customer accounts segregated from its proprietary assets. Additionally, *related person* is defined in the rule as any person, directly or indirectly, controlling or controlled by the investment adviser and any person who is under common control with the investment adviser.

11.28 The rule defines *custody* to mean an investment adviser or its related person holding, directly or indirectly, client funds or securities or having any authority to obtain possession of them. Custody includes the following:

- Possession of client funds or securities (but not checks drawn by clients and made payable to third parties) unless the investment adviser receives them inadvertently and returns them to the sender promptly but in any case within three business days of receiving them

- Any arrangement (including a general power of attorney) under which the investment adviser is authorized or permitted to withdraw client funds or securities maintained with a custodian upon the investment adviser's instruction to the custodian

- Any capacity (such as general partner of a limited partnership, managing member of a limited liability company or a comparable position for another type of pooled investment vehicle, or trustee of a trust) that gives the investment adviser or his or her supervised person legal ownership of, or access to, client funds or securities

Therefore, custody does not equate to serving as a qualified custodian under the rule.

11.29 When the investment adviser or its related person maintains the client funds and securities as a qualified custodian in connection with advisory services provided to clients, the independent public accountant engaged to perform the surprise examination must be registered with, and subject to regular inspection by, the PCAOB.

11.30 These illustrative reports should be used when a practitioner expresses an opinion on management's assertion about compliance with Rule 204-2(b) and certain provisions of Rule 206(4)-2 of the Investment Advisers Act of 1940 and when the practitioner expresses an opinion on the company's compliance with Rule 204-2(b) and certain provisions of Rule 206(4)-2 of the Investment Advisers Act of 1940, respectively. Paragraph .54 of AT section 601 states that the practitioner may examine and report directly on an entity's compliance, or he or she may examine and report on the responsible party's written assertion, except when the examination discloses noncompliance with the applicable requirements that the practitioner believes have a material effect on the entity's compliance (in that case, the practitioner should opine on the entity's specified compliance requirements, not the responsible party's assertion).

Independent Auditor's Reports and Client Representations **369**

Illustrative Report of Independent Accountant on Examinations of Securities Pursuant to Rule 206(4)-2 (Report on Management's Assertion) and Management's Assertion

Report of Independent Accountant

[To the Board of Directors[49] of
XYZ Investment Advisers, Inc.]

We have examined management's assertion, included in the accompanying Management Statement Regarding Compliance with Certain Provisions of the Investment Advisers Act of 1940, that [*XYZ Investment Advisers, Inc.*] (the "Company") complied with paragraph (a)(1) of Rule 206(4)-2 of the Investment Advisers Act of 1940 (the "Act") as of [*examination date*] and complied with Rule 204-2(b) of the Act during the period from [*prior examination date*][50] to [*examination date*].[51] Management is responsible for the Company's compliance with those requirements. Our responsibility is to express an opinion on management's assertion about the Company's compliance based on our examination.

Our examination was conducted in accordance with attestation standards established by the American Institute of Certified Public Accountants and, accordingly, included examining, on a test basis, evidence about the Company's compliance with those requirements and performing such other procedures as we considered necessary in the circumstances. Included among our procedures were the following tests which were performed for a sample of client accounts as of [*examination date*], which is a date we selected without prior notice to management: [*provide a brief description and itemize all that apply*]

- Reading contract provisions with qualified custodians;[52]
- Count and inspection of securities located in the vault of the Company in [*location*] or in [*location*] of [*persons associated with the Company*];
- Confirmation of cash and securities held by qualified custodians either under the client's name or in the name of the Company as agent or trustee for clients;
- [*Where a qualified custodian is either the adviser or a person related to the adviser*] For those client funds and securities maintained by the Company [*or a related person*] as a qualified custodian, obtaining and considering the most recent internal control report required to be obtained by the Company under Rule 206(4)-2(a)(6);

---

[49] If no board of directors exists, identify the equivalent body with oversight responsibility.

[50] In accordance with Question IV.5 of *Staff Responses to Questions About the Custody Rule*, when the investment adviser becomes subject to the surprise examination requirement for the first time, the accountant should report on the investment adviser's compliance with Rule 204-2(b) for a period beginning no later than the date that the adviser became subject to the surprise examination requirement through the examination date.

[51] This date should be the same as-of date as in the accompanying Management Statement Regarding Compliance.

[52] The practitioner should assess the need for this procedure based on the extent of the relationship between the investment adviser and qualified custodian or whether other procedures provide sufficient evidence to express an opinion on management's assertion about compliance with paragraph (a)(1) of Rule 206(4)-2.

AAG-INV 11.30

- Confirmation of privately offered securities, as defined in Rule 206(4)-2(b)(2), held directly by the Company with the issuer of or counterparty to the security [*or, where replies were not received, alternative procedures*];
- Reconciliation of cash and securities counted or confirmed to the books and records of client accounts maintained by the Company;
- Confirmation with clients[53] of the detail of cash and securities held as of the date of examination by the Company on behalf of such clients and contributions and withdrawals of cash and securities to and from the account [*or for those confirmations not received, alternative procedures*],[54] and reconciliation of confirmations received [*and other evidence obtained*] to the Company's books and records;
- Confirmation with clients of accounts that were closed or for which funds were returned to the clients;
- Confirmation with clients of accounts having a zero balance as of the date of the examination.

We believe that our examination provides a reasonable basis for our opinion. Our examination does not provide a legal determination on the Company's compliance with specified requirements, including the Company's identification of "securities" as defined by Section 202(a)(18) of the Act and its determination of "custody" as defined by Rule 206(4)-2(d)(2) under the Act. It is the responsibility of [*XYZ Investment Advisers, Inc.*] to determine its investment advisory clients under the Act.

In our opinion, management's assertion that [*XYZ Investment Advisers, Inc.*] was in compliance with the requirements of paragraph (a)(1) of Rule 206(4)-2 of the Investment Advisers Act of 1940 as of [*examination date*], and has complied with Rule 204-2(b) of the Act for the period from [*prior examination date*] through [*examination date*], is fairly stated, in all material respects.

This report is intended solely for the information and use of management and the Board of Directors of [*XYZ Investment Advisers, Inc.*] and the Securities and Exchange Commission[55] and is not intended to be and should not be used by anyone other than these specified parties.

[Independent Accountant (signed)]
[Anytown, USA]
[Date]

---

[53] When performing a surprise examination for an adviser to a pooled investment vehicle or vehicles, the practitioner should add *and investors in pooled investment vehicles*.

[54] The report should delineate procedures performed for (*a*) confirmation replies received with exception and (*b*) confirmation requests for which replies were not received. The presentation of procedures performed should be sufficiently specific for the reader to understand the nature and extent of the procedures performed.

[55] If applicable, also specify state securities administrators with which the report is required to be filed.

Management Statement Regarding Compliance With Certain Provisions of the Investment Advisers Act of 1940[56]

We, as members of management of [XYZ Investment Advisers, Inc.] (the "Company") are responsible for complying with the requirements of Rule 204-2(b), "Books and Records to be Maintained by Investment Advisers," and Rule 206(4)-2, "Custody of Funds or Securities of Clients by Investment Advisers," of the Investment Advisers Act of 1940 (the "Act"). We are also responsible for establishing and maintaining effective internal controls over compliance with the requirements of Rule 204-2(b) and Rule 206(4)-2. We have performed an evaluation of the Company's compliance with paragraph (a)(1) of Rule 206(4)-2 of the Act as of [*examination date*] and compliance with Rule 204-2(b) of the Act during the period from [*prior examination date*] to [*examination date*]. Based on this evaluation, we assert that the Company was in compliance with the Act as described below:

Rule 204-2(b) under the Act requires that an investment adviser who has custody or possession of funds and/or securities of any client must record all transactions for such clients in a journal and in separate ledger accounts for each client and must maintain copies of confirmations of all transactions in such accounts and a position record for each security in which a client has an interest. In addition, paragraph (1) of Rule 206(4)-2(a) provides, in general, that it shall constitute a fraudulent, deceptive, or manipulative act or practice for any investment adviser to have custody of client funds or securities unless a qualified custodian maintains those funds and securities (i) in a separate account for each client under that client's name; or (ii) in accounts that contain only clients' funds and securities, under the investment adviser's name as agent or trustee for the clients.

[*If applicable: Paragraph (a)(6) of Rule 206(4)-2 provides, in general, that an investment adviser that maintains, or has custody because a related person maintains, client funds or securities pursuant to Rule 206(4)-2 as a qualified custodian in connection with advisory services provided to clients must obtain, or receive from its related person, no less frequently than once each calendar year, a written internal control report prepared by an independent public accountant. The internal control report must include an opinion of an independent public accountant as to whether controls have been placed in operation as of a specific date, and are suitably designed and are operating effectively to meet control objectives relating to custodial services, including the safeguarding of funds and securities held by either the adviser or a related person on behalf of the advisory clients, during the year. Also, as part of the internal control report, the independent public accountant must verify that the funds and securities are reconciled to a custodian other than the adviser or the adviser's related person.*]

For purposes of this assertion, "security" has the meaning ascribed to it by Section 202(a)(18) of the Act, and "custody" has the meaning ascribed by Rule 206(4)-2(d)(2) under the Act. It is our responsibility to determine our investment advisory clients under the Act. The clients,

---

[56] Alternatively, management's assertion may be included in a representation letter. Accordingly, the auditor's report should be modified to reflect this alternative, in accordance with AT section 601.

and client funds and securities, to which this assertion applies, have been determined in a manner consistent with the manner in which we report clients for which custody of funds and securities exists under Items 9A(2) and 9B(2) of Form ADV, if the responses to those Items were prepared as of the date of this assertion.

[XYZ Investment Advisers, Inc.]

By:

_____

[Name]
Chief Financial Officer

_____

[Date]

Illustrative Report of Independent Accountant on Examinations of Securities Pursuant to Rule 206(4)-2 (Direct Report on Management's Compliance)

Report of Independent Accountant

[To the Board of Directors[57] of
XYZ Investment Advisers, Inc.]

We have examined the compliance of [*XYZ Investment Advisers, Inc.*] (the "Company") with paragraph (a)(1) of Rule 206(4)-2 of the Investment Advisers Act of 1940 (the "Act") as of [*examination date*] and with Rule 204-2(b) of the Act during the period from [*prior examination date*][58] to [*examination date*]. Management is responsible for the Company's compliance with those requirements. Our responsibility is to express an opinion on the Company's compliance based on our examination.

Our examination was conducted in accordance with attestation standards established by the American Institute of Certified Public Accountants and, accordingly, included examining, on a test basis, evidence about the Company's compliance with those requirements and performing such other procedures as we considered necessary in the circumstances. Included among our procedures were the following tests which were performed for a sample of client accounts as of [*examination date*], which is a date we selected without prior notice to management: [*provide a brief description and itemize all that apply*]

- Reading contract provisions with qualified custodians;[59]
- Count and inspection of securities located in the vault of the Company in [*location*], or in [*location*] of [*persons associated with the Company*];

---

[57] If no board of directors exists, identify the equivalent body with oversight responsibility.

[58] In accordance with Question IV.5 of "*Staff Responses to Questions About the Custody Rule*", when the investment adviser becomes subject to the surprise examination requirement for the first time, the accountant should report on the investment adviser's compliance with Rule 204-2(b) for a period beginning no later than the date that the adviser became subject to the surprise examination requirement through the examination date.

[59] The practitioner should assess the need for this procedure based on the extent of the relationship between the investment adviser and qualified custodian or whether other procedures provide sufficient evidence to express an opinion on compliance with paragraph (a)(1) of Rule 206(4)-2.

Independent Auditor's Reports and Client Representations

- Confirmation of cash and securities held by qualified custodians either under the client's name or in the name of the Company as agent or trustee for clients;
- [*Where a qualified custodian is either the adviser or a person related to the adviser*] For those client funds and securities maintained by the Company [*or a related person*] as a qualified custodian, obtaining and considering the most recent internal control report required to be obtained by the Company under Rule 206(4)-2(a)(6);
- Confirmation of privately offered securities, as defined in Rule 206(4)-2(b)(2), held directly by the Company with the issuer of or counterparty to the security [*or, where replies were not received, alternative procedures*];
- Reconciliation of cash and securities counted or confirmed to the books and records of client accounts maintained by the Company;
- Confirmation with clients[60] of the detail of cash and securities held as of the date of examination by the Company on behalf of such clients and contributions and withdrawals of cash and securities to and from the account [*or for those confirmations not received, alternative procedures*][61] and reconciliation of confirmations received [*and other evidence obtained*] to the Company's books and records;
- Confirmation with clients of accounts that were closed or for which funds were returned to the clients;
- Confirmation with clients of accounts having a zero balance as of the date of the examination.

We believe that our examination provides a reasonable basis for our opinion. Our examination does not provide a legal determination on the Company's compliance with specified requirements, including the Company's identification of "securities" as defined by Section 202(a)(18) of the Act and its determination of "custody" as defined by Rule 206(4)-2(d)(2) under the Act. It is the responsibility of [*XYZ Investment Advisers, Inc.*] to determine its investment advisory clients under the Act.

In our opinion, [*XYZ Investment Advisers, Inc.*] was in compliance, in all material respects, with the requirements of paragraph (a)(1) of Rule 206(4)-2 under the Investment Advisers Act of 1940 as of [*examination date*] and has complied with Rule 204-2(b) under the Act for the period from [*prior examination date*] through [*examination date*].

---

[60] When performing a surprise examination for an adviser to a pooled investment vehicle or vehicles, the practitioner should add "*and investors in pooled investment vehicles.*"

[61] The report should delineate procedures performed for (*a*) confirmation replies received with exception, and (*b*) confirmation requests for which replies were not received. The presentation of procedures performed should be sufficiently specific for the reader to understand the nature and extent of the procedures performed.

AAG-INV 11.30

This report is intended solely for the information and use of management and the Board of Directors of [*XYZ Investment Advisers, Inc.*] and the Securities and Exchange Commission[62] and is not intended to be and should not be used by anyone other than these specified parties.

[Independent Accountant (signed)]
[Anytown, USA]
[Date]

11.31 The following illustrative report should be used when the investment adviser or its related person maintains client funds or securities as a qualified custodian in connection with advisory services provided to clients. In this illustrative report, an independent public accountant that is registered with, and subject to regular inspection by, the PCAOB expresses an opinion on the investment adviser's or related person's controls relating to custody of client assets.

Illustrative Report of Independent Registered Public Accounting Firm on Management's Assertion Regarding Controls at a Custodian Pursuant to Rule 206(4)-2 and Release No. IA-2969 Under the Investment Advisors Act of 1940

Report of Independent Registered Public Accounting Firm

To the Board of Directors of
XYZ Investment Custodian, Inc.[63]

[*Introductory paragraph*]

We have examined the assertion made by the management of XYZ Custodian, Inc. (XYZ Custodian), pertaining to its controls over the custody of client funds and securities for registered investment advisers that are related persons, as that term is defined in Rule 206(4)-2 under the Investment Advisers Act of 1940 (related persons). Management's assertion is presented in the accompanying document titled, "Management's Assertion Regarding XYZ Custodian's Controls Over Custody Pursuant to Rule 206(4)-2 Under the Investment Advisers Act of 1940 (the Act)." Management has established certain control objectives (specified control objectives) and related controls pertaining to custody services, including the safeguarding of client funds and securities, pursuant to Rule 206(4)-2 and Release No. IA-2969 under the Act. XYZ Custodian's specified control objectives and the related controls are included in the accompanying document, "Description of XYZ Custodian's Controls and Control Objectives Pursuant to Rule 206(4)-2 and Release No. IA-2969 under the Act" (management's description), which is incorporated by reference in management's assertion.

[*The following paragraph should be added to the report if certain control objectives, or parts thereof, are addressed in a report on a subservice provider's controls or in another (other) report(s) on the custodian's controls and are excluded from management's assertion and description.*]

---

[62] If applicable, also specify state securities administrators with which the report is required to be filed.

[63] If no board of directors exists, identify the equivalent body with oversight responsibility.

Independent Auditor's Reports and Client Representations

As indicated in management's assertion and description, XYZ Custodian uses [*name or type of subservice provider(s)*] to perform [*function performed by the subservice provider*]. Management's description indicates that the specified control objective(s)[64] related to [*specify the subject matter of the control objective(s), or parts thereof, addressed in the report on the subservice provider's controls*] are addressed in an examination report on the subservice provider's controls issued by an independent registered public accounting firm.[65] In addition, management's description indicates that XYZ Custodian's specified control objectives[66] related to [*specify the subject matter of the control objective(s), or parts thereof, addressed in a another report on the custodian's controls*] are addressed in another examination report issued by an independent registered public accounting firm. Because [parts of] these control objectives are excluded from management's assertion and description, the scope of our work did not include examining the design, implementation, or operating effectiveness of controls to achieve [those parts of] the control objectives and we do not express an opinion thereon.

Management's assertion states that

- the controls described in management's description were suitably designed and implemented throughout the period January 1, 20X1, to December 31, 20X1, to provide reasonable assurance that the specified control objectives set forth therein would be achieved, if those controls were complied with satisfactorily [*and related persons applied the complementary user entity controls contemplated in the design of XYZ Custodian's controls throughout the period January 1, 20X1, to December 31, 20X1*] and

- the controls set forth in management's description were operating with sufficient effectiveness to provide reasonable assurance that the specified control objectives included in the description were achieved throughout the period January 1, 20X1, to December 31, 20X1 [*if related persons applied the complementary user entity controls contemplated in the design of XYZ Custodian's controls throughout the period January 1, 20X1, to December 31, 20X1*].

Management of XYZ Custodian is responsible for its assertion. Our responsibility is to express an opinion on management's assertion based on our examination.

[*Scope paragraph*]

Our examination was conducted in accordance with attestation standards established by the American Institute of Certified Public Accountants. Those standards require that we plan and perform the

---

[64] If only certain controls within a control objective are addressed in the examination report, state "certain controls to meet the specified control objective(s)."

[65] The report on controls would cover the suitability of the design, implementation, and operating effectiveness of the controls.

[66] If only certain controls within a control objective are addressed in the examination report, state "certain controls to meet XYZ Custodian's specified control objective(s)."

AAG-INV 11.31

examination to obtain reasonable assurance about whether management's assertion is fairly stated in all material respects. Our examination included obtaining an understanding of and evaluating the suitability of the design, implementation, and operating effectiveness of the controls intended to achieve the specified control objectives and examining, on a test basis, evidence supporting management's assertion and performing such other procedures as we considered necessary in the circumstances. Included among our procedures were [*provide a brief description of the procedures performed, including the nature, timing, extent, and results thereof, to verify that funds and securities are reconciled to depositories and unaffiliated custodians, such as confirming and reconciling a sample of security positions with unaffiliated custodians and depositories and / or alternative procedures used to verify that the data used in reconciliations is unaltered*] as of [*identify date(s) selected for testing*]. We believe that our examination provides a reasonable basis for our opinion.

Our examination was limited to examining, for the purposes described above, management's assertion about the specified control objectives and related controls included in management's description and did not consider any other control objectives or controls that may be relevant to XYZ Custodian's or the related persons' internal control over the custody of securities and funds for any specific client or clients of XYZ Custodian. Further, the relative effectiveness and significance of specific controls at XYZ Custodian, and their effect on related persons' internal control over custody of securities and funds, are dependent on their interaction with the controls and other factors present at individual related persons. We have performed no procedures to evaluate the effectiveness of such controls or such other factors at individual related persons.

The control objectives and related controls set forth in management's description have been provided to assist the related persons that use XYZ Custodian's services with their compliance with the requirements of Securities and Exchange Commission (SEC) Rule 206(4)-2 under the Investment Advisers Act of 1940.

[*Inherent limitations paragraph*]

Management's description covers the period January 1, 20X1, to December 31, 20X1. Any projection of such information to the future is subject to the risk that, because of change, the description may no longer portray the controls in existence. The potential effectiveness of controls to achieve the specified control objectives is subject to inherent limitations and, accordingly, errors or fraud may occur and not be detected. Furthermore, the projection of any evaluations, based on our findings, to future periods is subject to the risk that controls may become inadequate because of changes in conditions; that the degree of compliance with such controls may deteriorate; or that changes made to the system or controls, or the failure to make needed changes to the system or controls, may alter the validity of such evaluations.

[*Opinion paragraph*]

In our opinion, management's assertion referred to above is fairly stated, in all material respects, based on the specified control objectives set forth in management's description.

[Restricted use paragraph]

This report is intended solely for the information and use of XYZ Custodian; related persons that used XYZ Custodian's services during some or all of the period [January 1, 20X1, to December 31, 20X1]; the independent registered public accounting firms of such related persons; and the SEC and is not intended to be and should not be used by anyone other than these specified parties.

[Signature of Independent Registered Public Accountant]
[Date]

Illustrative Management Assertion[67] Regarding XYZ Custodian's Controls Over Custody Pursuant to Rule 206(4)-2 Under the Investment Advisers Act of 1940

XYZ Custodian provides custody services to registered investment advisers that are related persons, as that term is defined in Rule 206(4)-2 under the Investment Advisers Act of 1940 (related persons). Management has established certain control objectives (specified control objectives) and related controls pertaining to its custody services, including the safeguarding of client funds and securities, pursuant to Rule 206(4)-2 and Release No. IA-2969 under the Act. These specified control objectives and related controls are the responsibility of XYZ Custodian and are presented in the accompanying document, "Description of XYZ Custodian's Controls and Control Objectives Pursuant to Rule 206(4)-2 and Release No. IA-2969 Under the Act" (description), which is incorporated by reference in this assertion. We, as members of management of XYZ Custodian, are responsible for the description;[68] for establishing the specified control objectives and related controls; and for the suitability of the design, implementation, and operating effectiveness of the controls.

The description is provided to enable related persons, when performing their annual evaluation of compliance with Rule 206(4)-2 under the Act, to consider such information, along with information about their own controls over the custody of client funds and securities.

[The following paragraph should be added to the assertion if certain control objectives, or parts thereof, are excluded from the description and are addressed in a report on the subservice provider's controls or in another report on the custodian's controls. Management's description should include an appendix that identifies the control objectives that are excluded from the description and identifies the internal control report(s) in which those controls are addressed.]

The appendix to the description identifies the control objectives, or parts thereof, that are excluded from the description and addressed in

---

[67] In the event that management identifies a material misstatement or deviation from the criteria, the practitioner should follow the guidance in paragraph .66 of AT section 101, *Attest Engagements* (AICPA *Professional Standards*), and report directly on the subject matter, not the assertion.

[68] The description should identify the nature of any subservice providers used, the functions they perform, and whether the relevant control objectives and related controls of the subservice provider are excluded from the description. If the subservice provider's controls are excluded from the description, the description would, however, include relevant user entity controls and monitoring controls over the subservice provider. Control objectives and related controls that are excluded from the description should be the subject of an examination of design, implementation, and operating effectiveness by a registered public accounting firm.

reports on the subservice provider's controls or in another report on XYZ Custodian's controls.

We have evaluated whether XYZ Custodian's controls were suitably designed, implemented, and operating effectively to achieve the specified control objectives throughout the period January 1, 20X1, to December 31, 20X1. The criteria against which the controls were evaluated are the specified control objectives included in the description. Based on our evaluation, we assert that

- the controls included in the description were suitably designed and implemented throughout the period January 1, 20X1, to December 31, 20X1, to provide reasonable assurance that the specified control objectives[69] would be achieved, if those controls were complied with satisfactorily [*and related persons applied the complementary user entity controls contemplated in the design of XYZ Custodian's controls throughout the period from January 1, 20X1, to December 31, 20X1*[70]] and
- the controls set forth in the description were operating with sufficient effectiveness to provide reasonable assurance that the specified control objectives included in our description were achieved throughout the period January 1, 20X1, to December 31, 20X1 [*if related persons applied the complementary user entity controls contemplated in the design of XYZ Custodian's controls throughout the period from January 1, 20X1, to December 31, 20X1*].

By: _____

[*Signature, name, and title of appropriate official*]

By: _____

[*Signature, name, and title of appropriate official*]

---

[69] The control objectives and related controls included in the description (unless covered in another report on the service organization's controls or a report on controls at a subservice provider) address the areas of client account setup and maintenance, authorization and processing of client transactions, security maintenance and setup, processing of income and corporate action transactions, reconciliation of funds and securities to depositories and other unaffiliated custodians, and client reporting. Relevant general computer controls should also be included in the description when automated controls or reliance on computer-generated information are material elements of addressing control objectives.

[70] Refer to complementary user entity controls only in situations in which the application of controls by the registered investment adviser is necessary to achieve the specified control objectives. Otherwise, omit the reference.

AAG-INV 11.31

Independent Auditor's Reports and Client Representations **379**

Illustrative Description of XYZ Custodian's Controls and Control Objectives Pursuant to Rule 206(4)-2 and Release No. IA-2969 Under the Act

[*In instances where the service organization uses any subservice providers, include in this section a description of the nature and functions they perform, and whether the relevant control objectives and related controls of the subservice provider are excluded from the description. If control objectives and/or related controls are so excluded from the description, include the relevant service organization controls, including monitoring controls over the subservice provider, under "Control Activities" in the control matrix below.*]

XYZ Custodian's Control Objectives Pursuant to Rule 206(4)-2 and Release No. IA-2969 Under the Act[71]	Control Activities[72]	Related-Person Investment Adviser Considerations, if Necessary[73]
Controls provide reasonable assurance that documentation for the opening and modification of client accounts is received, authenticated, and established completely, accurately, and timely on the applicable system.	• A new account setup specialist compares the details of new accounts in the system with the source documentation and evidences this procedure with a signature after the review is complete. Any discrepancies are forwarded to the individual who set up the account for reprocessing.	• The related-person investment adviser is responsible for submitting accurate, complete, and authorized account in-formation in a timely manner. • The related-person investment adviser is responsible for coordinating the account funding and providing instructions for the delivery of assets.

(continued)

---

[71] If there are substantive differences between XYZ Custodian's control objectives and those in Interpretive Release No. IA-2969, *Commission Guidance Regarding Independent Public Accountant Engagements Performed Pursuant to Rule 206(4)-2 Under the Investment Advisers Act of 1940*, of Rule 206(4)-2 of the Investment Advisers Act of 1940, those differences should be explained in the appendix.

[72] The control activities and related person considerations shown for the initial objective are intended to be illustrative and should be tailored to the circumstances of the entity that is the subject of the report. They are not intended to represent required or recommended controls.

[73] See footnote 47.

AAG-INV 11.31

XYZ Custodian's Control Objectives Pursuant to Rule 206(4)-2 and Release No. IA-2969 Under the Act	Control Activities	Related-Person Investment Adviser Considerations, if Necessary
Controls provide reasonable assurance that client transactions, including contributions and withdrawals, are authorized and processed in a complete, accurate, and timely manner.		
Controls provide reasonable assurance that trades are properly authorized, settled, and recorded completely, accurately, and timely in the client account.		
Controls provide reasonable assurance that new securities and changes to securities are authorized and established in a complete, accurate, and timely manner.		
Controls provide reasonable assurance that securities income and corporate action transactions are processed to client accounts in a complete, accurate, and timely manner.		
Controls provide reasonable assurance that physical securities are safeguarded from loss or misappropriation.		
Controls provide reasonable assurance that cash and security positions are reconciled completely, accurately, and on a timely basis between the custodian and depositories.		

AAG-INV 11.31

XYZ Custodian's Control Objectives Pursuant to Rule 206(4)-2 and Release No. IA-2969 Under the Act	Control Activities	Related-Person Investment Adviser Considerations, if Necessary
Controls provide reasonable assurance that account statements reflecting cash and security positions are provided to clients in a complete, accurate, and timely manner.		

Investment Companies

Relevant General Computer Control Objectives[74]	Control Activities	Related-Person Investment Adviser Considerations, if Necessary
Controls provide reasonable assurance that logical access to programs, data, and computer resources is restricted to authorized and appropriate users.		
Controls provide reasonable assurance that physical access to computer and other resources is restricted to authorized and appropriate personnel.		
Controls provide reasonable assurance that changes to application programs and related data management systems are authorized, tested, documented, approved, and implemented to result in the complete, accurate, and timely processing and reporting of transactions and balances.		
Controls provide reasonable assurance that network infrastructure is configured as authorized to support the effective functioning of application controls to result in valid, complete, accurate, and timely processing and reporting of transactions and balances and protect data from unauthorized changes.		
Controls provide reasonable assurance that application and system processing are authorized and executed in a complete, accurate, and timely manner and deviations, problems, and errors are identified, tracked, recorded, and resolved in a complete, accurate, and timely manner.		

---

[74] These relevant general computer control objectives are included for illustrative purposes only. They are consistent with the illustrative general computer control objectives in the AICPA Guide *Service Organizations: Applying SSAE No. 16, Reporting on Controls at a Service Organization (SOC 1)*. They may be included in the description when automated controls or reliance on computer-generated information is important to the achievement of the control objectives.

AAG-INV 11.31

Relevant General Computer Control Objectives	Control Activities	Related-Person Investment Adviser Considerations, if Necessary
Controls provide reasonable assurance that data transmissions between the service organization and its user entities and other outside entities are from authorized sources and are complete, accurate, secure, and timely.		

AAG-INV 11.31

Appendix[75]

Illustrative Mapping of Control Objectives Pursuant to Rule 206(4)-2 and Release No. IA-2969 Under the Act to Independent Registered Public Accounting Reports on Controls

Control Objectives Pursuant to Rule 206(4)-2 and Release No. IA-2969 Under the Act	Report on XYZ Custodian's Controls Over Custody Pursuant to Rule 206(4)-2 Under the Investment Advisers Act of 1940	Service Auditor's Type 2 Report on ABC Trust Services for the Period January 1, 201X, to June 30, 201X	Service Auditor's Type 2 Report on DEF Subservice Organization's Controls Over Its Subcustodian's Services for the Period January 1, 201X, to June 30, 201X
Controls provide reasonable assurance that documentation for the opening and modification of client accounts is received, authenticated, and established completely, accurately, and timely on the applicable system.			
Controls provide reasonable assurance that client transactions, including contributions and withdrawals, are authorized and processed in a complete, accurate, and timely manner.			

---

[75] When control objectives or parts thereof are excluded from the description and covered in another report on the service organization's controls or a report on a subservice provider's controls, this mapping should be included as an appendix to management's description. The appendix should include a column for each report identifying the control objective(s) from Release No. IA-2969 covered by that report. When all the control objectives are fully covered in the description, this mapping is not necessary. In completing the mapping, checkmarks, explanations of particular facts and circumstances, or a combination of both, may be used to indicate the applicability of the report to the specific control objective(s).

AAG-INV 11.31

Independent Auditor's Reports and Client Representations   **385**

Control Objectives Pursuant to Rule 206(4)-2 and Release No. IA-2969 Under the Act	Report on XYZ Custodian's Controls Over Custody Pursuant to Rule 206(4)-2 Under the Investment Advisers Act of 1940	Service Auditor's Type 2 Report on ABC Trust Services for the Period January 1, 201X, to June 30, 201X	Service Auditor's Type 2 Report on DEF Subservice Organization's Controls Over Its Subcustodian's Services for the Period January 1, 201X, to June 30, 201X
Controls provide reasonable assurance that trades are properly authorized, settled, and recorded completely, accurately, and timely in the client account.			
Controls provide reasonable assurance that new securities and changes to securities are authorized and established in a complete, accurate, and timely manner.			
Controls provide reasonable assurance that securities income and corporate action transactions are processed to client accounts in a complete, accurate, and timely manner.			
Controls provide reasonable assurance that physical securities are safeguarded from loss or misappropriation.			

(continued)

AAG-INV 11.31

Control Objectives Pursuant to Rule 206(4)-2 and Release No. IA-2969 Under the Act	Report on XYZ Custodian's Controls Over Custody Pursuant to Rule 206(4)-2 Under the Investment Advisers Act of 1940	Service Auditor's Type 2 Report on ABC Trust Services for the Period January 1, 201X, to June 30, 201X	Service Auditor's Type 2 Report on DEF Subservice Organization's Controls Over Its Subcustodian's Services for the Period January 1, 201X, to June 30, 201X
Controls provide reasonable assurance that cash and security positions are reconciled completely, accurately, and on a timely basis between the custodian and depositories.			
Controls provide reasonable assurance that account statements reflecting cash and security positions are provided to clients in a complete, accurate, and timely manner.			

AAG-INV 11.31

Report on Internal Control Required by the SEC Under Form N-SAR

11.32 The following is an illustration of the independent registered public accounting firm's report on a registered investment company's internal control based on the results of procedures performed in obtaining an understanding of internal control over financial reporting and assessing control risk in connection with the audit of the investment company's financial statements. Under PCAOB standards, the auditor should obtain an understanding of internal control sufficient to plan the audit by performing procedures to understand the design of controls relevant to an audit of financial statements and determining whether they have been placed in operation.[76] The instructions to Form N-SAR further note that the internal control report is to be based on review, study, and evaluation of the financial reporting information system and internal control over financial reporting, including control activities for safeguarding securities. This report should reflect any material weaknesses identified as of the fiscal year-end date.

Report of Independent Registered Public Accounting Firm

To the Shareholders and
Board of Directors of
XYZ Investment Company

In planning and performing our audit of the financial statements of XYZ Investment Company ("the Company") as of and for the year ended December 31, 20X8, in accordance with the standards of the Public Company Accounting Oversight Board (United States), we considered the Company's internal control over financial reporting, including controls over safeguarding securities, as a basis for designing our auditing procedures for the purpose of expressing our opinion on the financial statements and to comply with the requirements of Form N-SAR, but not for the purpose of expressing an opinion on the effectiveness of the Company's internal control over financial reporting. Accordingly, we express no such opinion.

The management of the Company is responsible for establishing and maintaining effective internal control over financial reporting. In fulfilling this responsibility, estimates and judgments by management are required to assess the expected benefits and related costs of controls. A company's internal control over financial reporting is a process designed to provide reasonable assurance regarding the reliability of financial reporting and the preparation of financial statements for external purposes in accordance with generally accepted accounting principles (GAAP). A company's internal control over financial reporting includes those policies and procedures that (1) pertain to the maintenance of records that, in reasonable detail, accurately and fairly reflect the transactions and dispositions of the assets of the company; (2) provide reasonable assurance that transactions are recorded as necessary to permit preparation of financial statements in accordance with GAAP, and that receipts and expenditures of the company are being made only in accordance with authorizations of management and directors of the company; and (3) provide reasonable assurance

---

[76] See footnote 41.

regarding prevention or timely detection of unauthorized acquisition, use or disposition of a company's assets that could have a material effect on the financial statements.

Because of its inherent limitations, internal control over financial reporting may not prevent or detect misstatements. Also, projections of any evaluation of effectiveness to future periods are subject to the risk that controls may become inadequate because of changes in conditions, or that the degree of compliance with the policies or procedures may deteriorate.

A deficiency in internal control over financial reporting exists when the design or operation of a control does not allow management or employees, in the normal course of performing their assigned functions, to prevent or detect misstatements on a timely basis. A material weakness is a deficiency, or combination of deficiencies, in internal control over financial reporting, such that there is a reasonable possibility that a material misstatement of the Company's annual or interim financial statements will not be prevented or detected on a timely basis.

Our consideration of the Company's internal control over financial reporting was for the limited purpose described in the first paragraph and would not necessarily disclose all deficiencies in internal control that might be material weaknesses under standards established by the Public Company Accounting Oversight Board (United States). However, we noted no deficiencies in the Company's internal control over financial reporting and its operation, including controls over safeguarding securities, that we consider to be a material weakness as defined above as of December 31, 20X8.

This report is intended solely for the information and use of management and the Board of Directors of XYZ Investment Company and the Securities and Exchange Commission and is not intended to be and should not be used by anyone other than these specified parties.

Independent Registered Public Accounting Firm
Anytown, USA
February 14, 20X9

Report for a Closed-End Fund Security Agency Rating

11.33 The following is an example of an agreed-upon procedures report to be issued to a closed-end fund in connection with maintaining a security agency rating. This report is in accordance with AT section 201, *Agreed-Upon Procedures Engagements* (AICPA, *Professional Standards*). Trust indentures or articles supplementary of the relevant security often provide information to understand the necessary procedures. Because such procedures may be included in the documents, it is often advisable for the auditor to be involved in the drafting stage to prevent the inclusion of inappropriate procedures. The auditor should obtain evidence that users have accepted responsibility for, and have a clear understanding of, the procedures to be performed by obtaining an engagement letter; a written acknowledgment; or other similar evidence, such as discussing the nature of management's assertion and the procedures with the users.

Independent Accountant's Report on Applying Agreed-Upon Procedures

To the Board of Directors/Trustees of
XYZ Closed-End Fund
and
(Rating Agency [Agencies],
Bond Trustee [Remarketing Agents],
and other parties as required by governing document)

We have performed the procedures enumerated, which were agreed to by [*list specified parties—see above salutation*], solely to assist you in evaluating the accompanying Portfolio Valuation Reports (the Reports) of XYZ Closed-End Fund (the Fund) as of March 31, 20X8, as specified in section [*number*] of the [*governing document*] dated as of February 15, 20X8. The Fund's management is responsible for the portfolio valuation reports. This agreed-upon procedures engagement was conducted in accordance with attestation standards established by the American Institute of Certified Public Accountants. The sufficiency of these procedures is solely the responsibility of those parties specified in this report. Consequently, we make no representation regarding the sufficiency of the procedures described either for the purpose for which this report has been requested or for any other purpose. In performing the procedures enumerated, we have relied on information provided by sources external to the Fund without further investigation.

The procedures and associated findings are as follows:

1. We recalculated the discounted eligible portfolio fair value and eligible portfolio fair value calculations with respect to issue size, issuer diversification, and industry diversification and found such calculations to be mathematically correct. We have made no independent verification of management's classification of portfolio securities by issuer or industry.

2. We compared the basic maintenance amount calculation with the definition of the basic maintenance amount in the [*governing document*], noting agreement. We recalculated the basic maintenance amount and found it to be mathematically correct. We have made no independent verification of management's estimate of projected expenses as required to compute the basic maintenance amount.

3. We recalculated the excess discounted funds for the basic maintenance amount by deducting the basic maintenance amount from the total discounted value of the fund and found the results to be mathematically correct within $1.

4. We compared [*indicate test basis, if applicable*] the [*Rating Agency's*] ratings issuer name, issue size, and coupon rate listed in the Reports to the March 20X8 [*Rating Agency's*] Bond guide and found them to be in agreement.

5. We compared the prices for each issue used in calculating the fair value of investment securities in the Reports to the lower of the two bid prices on a report provided by [*Custodian Bank*] and found them to be in agreement. We

AAG-INV 11.33

understand that the Fund provides the price to the Custodian, and the Custodian receives confirmation of these prices from brokers. We have made no independent verification of the fair value of the investment securities listed in the Reports.

6. We compared each security included in the Reports with the definition of eligible portfolio property, as described in the [*governing document*], and found them to be in agreement. We have made no independent verification of the accuracy of the description of the investment securities listed in the Reports.

We were not engaged to and did not conduct an examination, the objective of which would be the expression of an opinion on the accompanying Portfolio Valuation Reports of the XYZ Closed-End Fund. Accordingly, we do not express such an opinion. Had we performed additional procedures, other matters might have come to our attention that would have been reported to you. Our procedures do not provide a legal determination on XYZ Closed-End Fund's compliance with the requirements of the [*governing document*].

This report is intended solely for the information and use of [*list or refer to specified parties—see above salutation*], and is not intended to be and should not be used by anyone other than these specified parties.

Independent Accountant
Anytown, USA
April 30, 20X8

Reports on Processing of Transactions by a Transfer Agent[77]

11.34 The following illustrates a report to be issued on a description of a transfer agent's system and the suitability of the design and operating effectiveness of controls. This form of report is prescribed by paragraph .A68 of AT section 801, *Reporting on Controls at a Service Organization*,[78] (AICPA, *Professional Standards*).

---

[77] Pursuant to the New York Stock Exchange requirement under rule 906.02, "Transfer Agent Registrar Agreement—Type A," when a transfer agent also acts as registrar for a single security issue (such as the case for closed-end funds), the transfer agent's independent public accountant is required to issue a report regarding the segregation of duties between the transfer agent and registrar functions. Such a report typically covers a period of time, rather than being stated as of a specific date.

[78] Paragraph .42 of AT section 801, *Reporting on Controls at a Service Organization* (AICPA, *Professional Standards*), requires a service auditor to inquire whether management is aware of any events subsequent to the period covered by management's description of the service organization's system up to the date of the service auditor's report that could have a significant effect on management's assertion. The AICPA Guide *Service Organizations: Applying Service Organizations: Applying SSAE No. 16, Reporting on Controls at a Service Organization Guide (SOC 1)* contains information for CPAs reporting on controls at a service organization that affect user entities' internal control over financial reporting. Also, the AICPA Guide *Reporting on Controls at a Service Organization Relevant to Security, Availability, Processing Integrity, Confidentiality, or Privacy (SOC 2)* summarizes the three new service organization controls (SOC) engagements and provides detailed guidance on planning, performing, and reporting on SOC 2 engagements.

AAG-INV 11.34

Independent Auditor's Reports and Client Representations **391**

Independent Accountant's Report

To ABC Service Corp.

Scope

We have examined ABC Service Corp.'s description of its transfer agent controls throughout the period July 1, 20X7, to June 30, 20X8, and the suitability of the design and operating effectiveness of controls to achieve the related control objectives stated in the description. The description indicates that certain control objectives specified in the description can be achieved only if complementary user entity controls contemplated in the design of ABC Service Corp.'s controls are suitably designed and operating effectively, along with related controls at the transfer agent. We have not evaluated the suitability of the design or operating effectiveness of such complementary user entity controls.[79]

Service organization's responsibilities

On page [XX] of the description, ABC Service Corp. has provided an assertion about the fairness of the presentation and the suitability of the design and operating effectiveness of the controls to achieve the related control objectives stated in the description. ABC Service Corp. is responsible for preparing the description and for the assertion, including the completeness, accuracy, and method of presentation of the description and the assertion, providing the services covered by the description, specifying the control objectives and stating them in the description, identifying the risks that threaten the achievement of the control objectives, selecting the criteria, and designing, implementing, and documenting controls to achieve the related control objectives stated in the description.

Service auditor's responsibilities

Our responsibility is to express an opinion on the fairness of the presentation of the description and on the suitability of the design and operating effectiveness of the controls to achieve the related control objectives stated in the description, based on our examination. We conducted our examination in accordance with attestation standards established by the American Institute of Certified Public Accountants. Those standards require that we plan and perform our examination to obtain reasonable assurance about whether, in all material respects, the description is fairly presented and the controls were suitably designed and operating effectively to achieve the related control objectives stated in the description throughout the period July 1, 20X7, to June 30, 20X8.

An examination of a description of a transfer agent's system and the suitability of the design and operating effectiveness of the transfer agent's controls to achieve the related control objectives stated in the description involves performing procedures to obtain evidence about the fairness of the presentation of the description and the suitability of the design and operating effectiveness of those controls to achieve the

---

[79] This illustrative report, in accordance with paragraph .A68 of AT section 801, includes modifications in the scope and opinion paragraphs because the application of complementary user entity controls is necessary to achieve the related control objectives stated in the description of the transfer agent's controls.

AAG-INV 11.34

related control objectives stated in the description. Our procedures included assessing the risks that the description is not fairly presented and that the controls were not suitably designed or operating effectively to achieve the related control objectives stated in the description. Our procedures also included testing the operating effectiveness of those controls that we consider necessary to provide reasonable assurance that the related control objectives stated in the description were achieved. An examination engagement of this type also includes evaluating the overall presentation of the description and the suitability of the control objectives stated therein, and the suitability of the criteria specified by the transfer agent and described at page [aa]. We believe that the evidence we obtained is sufficient and appropriate to provide a reasonable basis for our opinion.

Inherent limitations

Because of their nature, controls at a transfer agent may not prevent, or detect and correct, all errors or omissions. Also, the projection to the future of any evaluation of the fairness of the presentation of the description, or conclusions about the suitability of the design or operating effectiveness of the controls to achieve the related control objectives is subject to the risk that controls at a transfer agent may become inadequate or fail.

Opinion

In our opinion, in all material respects, based on the criteria described in ABC Service Corp.'s assertion on page [aa],

   a. the description fairly presents the transfer agent controls that were designed and implemented throughout the period July 1, 20X7, to June 30, 20X8.
   b. the controls related to the control objectives stated in the description were suitably designed to provide reasonable assurance that the control objectives would be achieved if the controls operated effectively throughout the period July 1, 20X7, to June 30, 20X8 and user entities applied the complementary user entity controls contemplated in the design of ABC Service Corp.'s controls throughout the period July 1, 20X7, to June 30, 20X8.
   c. the controls tested, which together with the complementary user entity controls referred to in the scope paragraph of this report, if operating effectively, were those necessary to provide reasonable assurance that the control objectives stated in the description were achieved, operated effectively throughout the period July 1, 20X7, to June 30, 20X8.

Description of tests of controls

The specific controls tested and the nature, timing, and results of those tests are listed on pages [yy–zz].

Restricted use

This report, including the description of tests of controls and results thereof on pages [yy–zz], is intended solely for the information and use of ABC Service Corp., user entities of ABC Service Corp.'s transfer

Independent Auditor's Reports and Client Representations **393**

agent controls during some or all of the period July 1, 20X7, to June 30, 20X8, and the independent auditors of such user entities, who have a sufficient understanding to consider it, along with other information including information about controls implemented by user entities themselves, when assessing the risks of material misstatements of user entities' financial statements. This report is not intended to be and should not be used by anyone other than these specified parties.

Independent Auditor
Anytown, USA
July 31, 20X8

11.35 The following is an example of a report to be issued on the annual study and evaluation of a transfer agent's internal control, as required to be filed with the SEC pursuant to Rule 17Ad-13 of the 1934 Act. Such engagements are performed in accordance with AT section 101.

This illustrative report (example 2 in appendix A, "Examination Reports," of AT section 101, with additional language related to the restriction on the use of the report) should be used when a practitioner expresses an opinion on management's assertion about the effectiveness of an entity's internal control. If a practitioner examines and reports directly on an entity's effectiveness of internal control (versus the responsible party's written assertion), the practitioner must consider example 3 in appendix A of AT section 101 for an example of the report to be used.

Considerations for Audits Performed in Accordance With PCAOB Standards

An understanding of the provisions of the Sarbanes-Oxley Act of 2002, the SEC regulations implementing the Sarbanes-Oxley Act of 2002, and the rules and standards of the PCAOB, as applicable to their circumstances, is important in order for readers to determine if the standards of the PCAOB should be applied (see paragraph 11.01 for further discussion). Auditing Standard No. 1 replaces the sentence "Our examination was conducted in accordance with the attestation standards established by the American Institute of Certified Public Accountants and, accordingly, included examining, on a test basis, evidence supporting management's assertion and performing such other procedures as we considered necessary in the circumstances to evaluate internal control over the transfer agent and registrar functions, using the objectives set forth in Rule 17Ad-13(a)(3) of the Securities Exchange Act of 1934," with the sentence "Our examination was conducted in accordance with the standards of the Public Company Accounting Oversight Board (United States) and, accordingly, included examining, on a test basis, evidence supporting management's assertion and performing such other procedures as we considered necessary in the circumstances to evaluate internal control over the transfer agent and registrar functions, using the objectives set forth in Rule 17Ad-13(a)(3) of the Securities Exchange Act of 1934." The illustrative report for an issuer would also replace the title "Independent Accountant's Report" with "Report of Independent Registered Public Accounting Firm."

Independent Accountant's Report

To the Board of Directors
of ABC Service Corp.

We have examined management's assertion, included in its representation letter dated December 15, 20X8, that ABC Service Corp. maintained effective internal control, including the appropriate segregation of responsibilities and duties, over the transfer agent and registrar[80] functions, as of October 31, 20X8, and that no material inadequacies as defined by Rule 17Ad-13(a)(3) of the Securities Exchange Act of 1934 existed at such date. ABC Service Corp.'s management is responsible for maintaining effective internal control over transfer agent and registrar functions. Our responsibility is to express an opinion on management's assertion based on our examination.

Our examination was conducted in accordance with the attestation standards established by the American Institute of Certified Public Accountants and, accordingly, included examining, on a test basis, evidence supporting management's assertion and performing such other procedures as we considered necessary in the circumstances to evaluate internal control over the transfer agent and registrar functions, using the objectives set forth in Rule 17Ad-13(a)(3) of the Securities Exchange Act of 1934. We believe that our examination provides a reasonable basis for our opinion.

In our opinion, management's assertion that ABC Service Corp. maintained effective internal control, including the appropriate segregation of responsibilities and duties, over the transfer agent and registrar functions, and that no material inadequacies existed as defined by Rule 17Ad-13(a)(3) of the Securities Exchange Act of 1934 as of October 31, 20X8, is fairly stated, in all material respects, based on the criteria established by Rule 17Ad-13(a)(3) of the Securities Exchange Act of 1934.

This report is intended solely for the information and use of management and the Board of Directors of ABC Service Corp. and the Securities and Exchange Commission and is not intended to be and should not be used by anyone other than these specified parties.

Independent Accountant
Anytown, USA
December 15, 20X8

11.36 Interpretation No. 8, "Including a Description of Tests of Controls or Other Procedures, and the Results Thereof, in an Examination Report," of AT section 101 (AICPA, *Professional Standards*, AT sec. 9101 par. .70–.72), discusses whether, during an examination engagement under AT section 101, a practitioner's examination report may include in a separate section a description of tests of controls or other procedures performed in support of the practitioner's opinion. Although AT section 101 does not preclude a practitioner from including a separate section of the report that contains a description of tests of controls or other procedures performed and the results thereof, consideration should be given to whether this description may overshadow the overall opinion or would cause report users to misunderstand the opinion. Therefore,

---

[80] The words *and registrar* should be omitted throughout this report if the function does not exist within the transfer agent's operations.

Independent Auditor's Reports and Client Representations **395**

this determination requires judgment based on the circumstances of the particular engagement. The addition of a description of tests of controls or other procedures performed and the results thereof in a separate section of an examination report may increase the need for the use of the report to be restricted to specified parties. In determining whether to include such a description, the following conditions are relevant:

- Whether there has been a request for such information and whether the specified parties making the request have an appropriate business need or reasonable basis for requesting the information
- Whether the specified parties have an understanding of the nature and subject matter of the engagement and experience in using the information in such reports
- Whether including such a description in the examination report is likely to cause report users to misunderstand the opinion
- Whether the practitioner's tests of controls or other procedures performed directly relate to the subject matter of the engagement

Reporting Pursuant to the Global Investment Performance Standards

Note: The guidance presented in this section of the guide, including the example reports, reflects the guidance in Statement of Position (SOP) 06-1, *Reporting Pursuant to the Global Investment Performance Standards* (AICPA, *Technical Practice Aids*, AUD sec. 14,420).

11.37 The CFA Institute (formerly known as the Association for Investment Management and Research [AIMR]) developed the AIMR Performance Presentation Standards (AIMR-PPS) and the Global Investment Performance Standards (GIPS)[81] (collectively, the performance standards). Although compliance with the performance standards is voluntary, an investment management firm's claim of compliance with the performance standards is widely regarded as providing a competitive advantage. As of January 1, 2006, AIMR-PPS converged with GIPS, and AIMR-PPS no longer exists as a separate set of standards.[82] SOP 06-1 provides guidance to practitioners for engagements to examine and report on aspects of a firm's compliance with GIPS (a verification engagement) and engagements to examine and report on the performance presentation of specific composites (a performance examination). Such examination engagements should be performed pursuant to AT section 101. AT section 101 permits the practitioner to report either on the assertions or directly on the subject matter to which the assertions relate.

11.38 In January 2010, the CFA Institute released the revised GIPS. The significant changes to the GIPS include: the requirement of assets to be valued

---

[81] For information on the appropriate use of the AIMR-PPS or GIPS, or both, registered trademark, see the CFA Institute website at www.cfainstitute.org. All the following references to GIPS in this chapter refer to GIPS revised as of January 2010.

[82] All firms that previously claimed compliance with AIMR-PPS are granted reciprocity for GIPS compliance for periods prior to January 1, 2006.

AAG-INV 11.38

using a fair value methodology when no market value is available, the requirement to present the standard deviation (widely accepted as a common measure of portfolio risk) of the monthly returns of both the composite and the benchmark, the requirement for the firms to disclose their verification status (that is, whether they have been verified), and required prescribed language describing what is and is not covered by verification. The effective date for the 2010 edition of the GIPS is January 1, 2011. Compliant presentations that include performance for periods that begin on or after that date must be prepared in accordance with the 2010 edition of the GIPS. See www.gipsstandards.org/ for more information.

11.39 The following are examples of illustrative attest reports for a verification. These reports are presented in appendix C, "Illustrative Attest Reports: Verification," of SOP 06-1. The reports also illustrate how the reference to a verification may be incorporated into the attest report.

Example 1: Reporting Directly on the Subject Matter

Independent Accountant's Report

Atlas Asset Management
10 Main Street
Anytown, USA

We have examined Atlas Asset Management's (the Company) (1) compliance with all the composite construction requirements of the Global Investment Performance Standards (GIPS® standards) on a firm-wide basis for the 10-year period ended December 31, 20Y0, and (2) design of its processes and procedures to calculate and present performance results in compliance with the GIPS standards as of December 31, 20Y0. The Company's management is responsible for compliance with the GIPS standards and the design of its processes and procedures. Our responsibility is to express an opinion based on our examination.

Our examination was conducted in accordance with attestation standards established by the American Institute of Certified Public Accountants and, accordingly, included examining, on a test basis, evidence about the Company's compliance with the above-mentioned requirements, evaluating the design of the Company's processes and procedures referred to above, and performing the procedures for a verification set forth by the GIPS standards and such other procedures as we considered necessary in the circumstances. We believe that our examination provides a reasonable basis for our opinion.

In our opinion, Atlas Asset Management has, in all material respects:

- Complied with all the composite construction requirements of the GIPS standards on a firm-wide basis for the 10-year period ended December 31, 20Y0; and
- Designed its processes and procedures to calculate and present performance results in compliance with the GIPS standards as of December 31, 20Y0.

We did not examine the performance results of the Company's composites for any period through December 31, 20Y0, including any performance presentations that may accompany this report and, accordingly, we express no opinion on any such performance results.[83]

[*Signature*]

September 1, 20Y1

Example 2: Reporting on Management's Assertions—Assertions Included in Practitioner's Report

Independent Accountant's Report

Atlas Asset Management
10 Main Street
Anytown, USA

We have examined management's assertions that Atlas Asset Management (the Company) (1) complied with all the composite construction requirements of the Global Investment Performance Standards (GIPS® standards) on a firm-wide basis for the 10-year period ended December 31, 20Y0, and (2) designed its processes and procedures to calculate and present performance results in compliance with the GIPS standards as of December 31, 20Y0. These assertions are the responsibility of the Company's management. Our responsibility is to express an opinion on these assertions based on our examination.

Our examination was conducted in accordance with attestation standards established by the American Institute of Certified Public Accountants and, accordingly, included examining, on a test basis, evidence supporting management's assertions and performing the procedures for a verification set forth by the GIPS standards and such other procedures as we considered necessary in the circumstances. We believe that our examination provides a reasonable basis for our opinion.

In our opinion, management's assertions referred to above are fairly stated, in all material respects, based on the GIPS standards.

We did not examine the performance results of the Company's composites for any period through December 31, 20Y0, including any performance presentations that may accompany this report and, accordingly, we express no opinion on any such performance results.[84]

[*Signature*]

September 1, 20Y1

Example 3: Reporting on Management's Assertions—Assertions Accompany Practitioner's Report

Independent Accountant's Report

Atlas Asset Management
10 Main Street
Anytown, USA

We have examined the accompanying management assertions of Atlas Asset Management (the Company) regarding compliance with all the

---

[83] If the verifier has issued a separate performance examination report concurrently, it may insert the following instead: "This report does not relate to any composite presentation of the Company that may accompany this report, and accordingly, we express no opinion on any such performance results."

[84] See footnote 83.

composite construction requirements of the Global Investment Performance Standards (GIPS® standards) for the 10-year period ended December 31, 20Y0, and the design of its processes and procedures for complying with the GIPS standards as of December 31, 20Y0. These assertions are the responsibility of the Company's management. Our responsibility is to express an opinion on these assertions based on our examination.

Our examination was conducted in accordance with attestation standards established by the American Institute of Certified Public Accountants and, accordingly, included examining, on a test basis, evidence supporting management's assertions and performing the procedures for a verification set forth by the GIPS standards and such other procedures as we considered necessary in the circumstances. We believe that our examination provides a reasonable basis for our opinion.

In our opinion, management's assertions referred to above are fairly stated, in all material respects, based on the GIPS standards.

We did not examine the performance results of the Company's composites for any period through December 31, 20Y0, including any performance presentations that may accompany this report and, accordingly, we express no opinion on any such performance results.[85]

[*Signature*]

September 1, 20Y1

Example 3A: Illustrative Management's Assertions for Report Example 3

Atlas Asset Management
10 Main Street
Anytown, USA

We assert that (1) Atlas Asset Management (the Company) has complied with all the composite construction requirements of the Global Investment Performance Standards (GIPS® standards) on a firm-wide basis for the 10-year period ended December 31, 20Y0, and (2) the Company's processes and procedures are designed to calculate and present performance results in compliance with the GIPS standards as of December 31, 20Y0.

[*Signature*]

John Q. Smith
Chief Executive Officer
Atlas Asset Management

11.40 The following are examples of illustrative attest reports for a verification and performance examination. These reports are presented in appendix D, "Illustrative Attest Reports: Verification and Performance Examination," of SOP 06-1. The reports also illustrate how the reference to a verification or performance examination may be incorporated into the attest report.

---

[85] See footnote 83.

Example 1: Reporting Directly on the Subject Matter (Verification and Performance Examination Report)

Independent Accountant's Report

Atlas Asset Management
10 Main Street
Anytown, USA

We have examined Atlas Asset Management's (the Company) (1) compliance with all the composite construction requirements of the GIPS® standards on a firm-wide basis for the 10-year period ended December 31, 20Y0, and (2) design of its processes and procedures to calculate and present performance results in compliance with the GIPS standards as of December 31, 20Y0. We have also examined the accompanying [*refer to accompanying composite performance presentation*] of the Company's XYZ Composite for the periods from January 1, 20X1, through December 31, 20Y0. The Company's management is responsible for compliance with the GIPS standards and the design of its processes and procedures and for the [*refer to accompanying composite performance presentation*]. Our responsibility is to express an opinion based on our examination.

Our examination was conducted in accordance with attestation standards established by the American Institute of Certified Public Accountants and, accordingly, included examining, on a test basis, evidence about the Company's compliance with the above-mentioned requirements; evaluating the design of the Company's processes and procedures referred to above; examining, on a test basis, evidence supporting the accompanying composite performance presentation; and performing the procedures for a verification and a performance examination set forth by the GIPS standards and such other procedures as we considered necessary in the circumstances. We believe that our examination provides a reasonable basis for our opinion.

In our opinion, Atlas Asset Management has, in all material respects:

- Complied with all the composite construction requirements of the GIPS standards on a firm-wide basis for the 10-year period ended December 31, 20Y0; and
- Designed its processes and procedures to calculate and present performance results in compliance with the GIPS standards as of December 31, 20Y0.

Also, in our opinion, [*refer to accompanying composite performance presentation*] of the Company's XYZ Composite for the periods from January 1, 20X1 through December 31, 20Y0, is presented, in all material respects, in conformity with the GIPS standards.

This report does not relate to any composite presentation of the Company other than the Company's XYZ Composite.

[*Signature*]

September 1, 20Y1

Example 1A appears in its original form in SOP 06-1 and former editions of this guide. However this example has been updated to reflect the new disclosure requirement of verification status as required under the 2010 edition of the GIPS.

Example 1A: Illustrative GIPS—Compliant Presentation for Report Example

Atlas Asset Management
XYZ Composite
January 1, 20X1 through December 31, 20Y0

Year	Gross-of-Fees Return (Percent)	Net-of-Fees Return (Percent)	Benchmark Return (Percent)	Number of Portfolios	Internal Dispersion (Percent)	Total Composite Assets (US$ Million)	Total Firm Assets (US$ Million)
20X1	16.0	15.0	14.1	26	4.5	165	236
20X2	2.2	1.3	1.8	32	2.0	235	346
20X3	22.4	21.5	24.1	38	5.7	344	529
20X4	7.1	6.2	6.0	45	2.8	445	695
20X5	8.5	7.5	8.0	48	3.1	520	839
20X6	−8.0	−8.9	−8.4	49	2.8	505	1014
20X7	−5.9	−6.8	−6.2	52	2.9	499	995
20X8	2.4	1.6	2.2	58	3.1	525	1125
20X9	6.7	5.9	6.8	55	3.5	549	1225
20Y0	9.4	8.6	9.1	59	2.5	575	1290

Atlas Asset Management has prepared and presented this report in compliance with the Global Investment Performance Standards (GIPS® standards). Atlas Asset Management has been independently verified for the periods January 1, 20X1 to December 31, 20Y0. The verification report is available upon request. Verification assesses whether (1) the firm has complied with all the composite construction requirements of the GIPS standards on a firm-wide basis and (2) the firm's policies and procedures are designed to calculate and present performance in compliance with the GIPS standards. Verification does not ensure the accuracy of any specific composite presentation.

Notes:

1. Atlas Asset Management (the Company) is a balanced portfolio investment adviser that invests solely in U.S. securities. The Company is defined as an independent investment management firm that is not affiliated with any parent organization. For the period from 20X1 through 20Y0, the Company has been verified by Verification Services LLP. A copy of the verification report is available upon request. Additional information regarding the firm's policies and procedures for calculating and reporting performance results is available upon request.

2. The composite includes all nontaxable balanced portfolios with an asset allocation of 30 percent S&P 500® and 70 percent Large-Cap Growth Bond Index Fund, which allow up to a 10 percent deviation in asset allocation.

3. The benchmark: 30 percent S&P 500®; 70 percent Large-Cap Growth Bond Index Fund rebalanced monthly.

4. Valuations are computed and performance reported in U.S. dollars.

5. Gross-of-fees performance returns are presented before management and custodial fees but after all trading expenses. Returns are presented net of non-reclaimable withholding taxes. Net-of-fees performance returns are calculated by deducting the highest fee of 0.25 percent from the quarterly gross composite return. The management fee schedule is as follows: 1.00 percent on the first $25,000,000; 0.60 percent thereafter.

6. This composite was created in February 20X1. A complete list and description of firm composites is available upon request.

7. Internal dispersion is calculated using the equal-weighted standard deviation of all portfolios that were included in the composite for the entire year.

Example 2: Reporting Directly on the Subject Matter (Performance Examination Report With a Reference to a Separate Report on Verification)

Independent Accountant's Report

Atlas Asset Management
10 Main Street
Anytown, USA

We have examined the accompanying[86] [*refer to accompanying composite performance presentations*] of Atlas Asset Management's (the Company) ABC and XYZ Composites for the periods from January 1, 20X1, through December 31, 20Y0. The Company's management is responsible for these performance presentations. Our responsibility is to express an opinion based on our examination. We previously conducted an examination (also referred to as a verification) of the Company's (1) compliance with all the composite construction requirements of the Global Investment Performance Standards (GIPS® standards) on a firm-wide basis for the 10-year period ended December 31, 20Y0, and (2) design of its processes and procedures to calculate and present performance results in compliance with the GIPS standards as of December 31, 20Y0; our report dated August 7, 20Y1, with respect thereto is attached.

Our examination was conducted in accordance with attestation standards established by the American Institute of Certified Public Accountants and, accordingly, included examining, on a test basis, evidence supporting the accompanying composite performance presentations, and performing the procedures for a performance examination set forth by the GIPS standards and such other procedures as we considered necessary in the circumstances. We believe that our examination provides a reasonable basis for our opinion.

In our opinion, [*refer to accompanying composite performance presentations*] of the Company's ABC and XYZ Composites for the periods

---

[86] See example 1A for an illustrative composite performance presentation that would accompany the report.

from January 1, 20X1, through December 31, 20Y0, are presented, in all material respects, in conformity with the GIPS standards.

This report does not relate to any composite presentation of the Company other than the Company's ABC and XYZ Composites.

[*Signature*]

September 1, 20Y1

Example 3: Reporting on Management's Assertions; Assertions Accompany Practitioner's Report

Independent Accountant's Report

Atlas Asset Management
10 Main Street
Anytown, USA

We have examined the accompanying management assertions of Atlas Asset Management (the Company) regarding compliance with the composite construction requirements of the Global Investment Performance Standards (GIPS® standards) for the 10-year period ended December 31, 20Y0, and the design of its processes and procedures for complying with the GIPS standards as of December 31, 20Y0. We have also examined management's assertion relating to the presentation of the Company's ABC and XYZ Composites for the periods from January 1, 20X1, through December 31, 20Y0.[87] These assertions are the responsibility of the Company's management. Our responsibility is to express an opinion on these assertions based on our examination.

Our examination was conducted in accordance with attestation standards established by the American Institute of Certified Public Accountants and, accordingly, included examining, on a test basis, evidence supporting management's assertions and performing the procedures for a verification and a performance examination set forth by the GIPS standards and such other procedures we considered necessary in the circumstances. We believe that our examination provides a reasonable basis for our opinion.

In our opinion, management's assertions referred to above are fairly stated, in all material respects, based on the GIPS standards.

This report does not relate to any composite presentation of the Company other than the Company's accompanying ABC and XYZ Composites.

[*Signature*]

September 1, 20Y1

Example 3A: Illustrative Management's Assertions for Report Example 3

Atlas Asset Management
10 Main Street
Anytown, USA

We assert that (1) Atlas Asset Management (the Company) has complied with all the composite construction requirements of the Global Investment Performance Standards (GIPS® standards) on a firm-wide

---

[87] If management's assertions do not accompany the report, this sentence and the preceding sentence would be modified to include management's complete assertions.

Independent Auditor's Reports and Client Representations

basis for the 10-year period ended December 31, 20Y0, and (2) the Company's processes and procedures are designed to calculate and present performance results in compliance with the GIPS® standards as of December 31, 20Y0.

We also assert that the accompanying composite performance presentations for the ABC and XYZ Composites for the periods from January 1, 20X1, through December 31, 20Y0, are presented in conformity with the GIPS standards.[88]

[*Signature*]

John Q. Jones
Chief Executive Officer,
Atlas Asset Management Company

Illustrative Representation Letter—XYZ Investment Company

11.41 Following is an illustrative management representation letter for an audit of investment company financial statements.[89] The auditor should consider obtaining representation on additional items, including, when applicable, an investment adviser's intentions to continue waiving fees and the amount and terms of unreimbursed distribution costs carried forward.[90]

January 21, 20X9

To [*Independent Auditor*]

We are providing this letter in connection with your audit of the statement of assets and liabilities, including the schedule of investments (or statement of net assets), of XYZ Investment Company (the Company) as of December 31, 20X8, and the related statements of operations (and cash flows, if applicable), for the year then ended, changes in net assets for the two years then ended, and the financial highlights for the five years then ended, for the purpose of expressing an opinion as to whether the financial statements present fairly, in all material respects, the financial position, results of operations (and cash flows, if applicable), changes in net assets, and financial highlights of XYZ Investment Company in conformity with accounting principles generally accepted in the United States of America. We confirm that we are responsible for the fair presentation in the financial statements of financial position, results of operations, changes in net assets, (cash

---

[88] See footnote 86.

[89] Under the final clarified standard *Written Representations*, an additional representation to include would be the following: "We have provided you unrestricted access to those persons within the Company from whom you determined it necessary to obtain audit evidence." The clarified auditing standards are effective for audits of financial statements for periods ending on or after December 15, 2012. However, nothing precludes an auditor from implementing aspects of the clarified SASs before their effective date, as long as the auditor continues to comply with the current standards. For additional details on clarified standards, please see the preface and appendix B, "Guidance Updates–Clarified Auditing Standards."

[90] See paragraphs 75–82 of Auditing Standard No. 5, *An Audit of Internal Control Over Financial Reporting That Is Integrated with An Audit of Financial Statements* (AICPA, *PCAOB Standards and Related Rules*, Auditing Standards), for additional written representations required from management when performing an integrated audit of financial statements and internal control over financial reporting or an audit of the financial statements in accordance with PCAOB standards.

AAG-INV 11.41

flows, if applicable), and financial highlights in conformity with generally accepted accounting principles.

Certain representations in this letter are described as being limited to matters that are material. Items are considered material, regardless of size, if they involve an omission or misstatement of accounting information that, in light of surrounding circumstances, makes it probable that the judgment of a reasonable person relying on the information would be changed or influenced by the omission or misstatement.

We confirm, to the best of our knowledge and belief as of [*date of auditor's report*], the following representations made to you during your audit:

1. The financial statements referred to above are fairly presented in conformity with accounting principles generally accepted in the United States of America.
2. We have made available to you all—
    a. Financial records and related data.
    b. Minutes of the meetings of stockholders, directors or trustees, and committees of directors or trustees, or summaries of actions of recent meetings for which minutes have not yet been prepared.
    c. Information relating to all statutes, laws, or regulations that have a direct effect on our financial statements.
    d. Information relating to contracts with and results of work by specialists, including those engaged to review investments (including investment valuations), systems, processes, operations, or compliance programs having a material effect on the financial statements or internal control over financial reporting of the Company.
3. There have been no communications from regulatory agencies, such as the SEC or the Internal Revenue Service, concerning noncompliance with or deficiencies in financial reporting practices.
4. There are no material transactions that have not been properly recorded in the accounting records underlying the financial statements.
5. We acknowledge our responsibility for the design and implementation of programs and controls to prevent and detect fraud.
6. We have no knowledge of any fraud or suspected fraud affecting the Company involving—
    a. Management,
    b. Employees who have significant roles in internal control, or
    c. Others where the fraud could have a material effect on the financial statements.

Independent Auditor's Reports and Client Representations

7. We have no knowledge of any allegations of fraud or suspected fraud affecting the Company received in communications from employees, former employees, analysts, regulators, short sellers, or others.

8. There are no significant deficiencies, including material weaknesses, in the design or operation of internal control over financial reporting that are reasonably likely to adversely affect the Company's ability to record, process, summarize and report financial information.

   a. (If applicable) The effects of the uncorrected financial statement misstatements summarized in the accompanying schedule are immaterial, both individually and in the aggregate, to the financial statements taken as a whole.

9. The Company has no plans or intentions that may materially affect the carrying amounts or classification of assets and liabilities.

10. The following have been properly recorded or disclosed in the financial statements:

    a. Related-party transactions and other transactions with affiliates, including fees, commissions, purchases, and sales

    b. Guarantees, whether written or oral, under which the Company is contingently liable

    c. Significant estimates and material concentrations known to management that are required to be disclosed in accordance with the Financial Accounting Standards Board (FASB) *Accounting Standards Codification* (ASC) 275-10 [*Significant estimates are estimates at the balance sheet date that could change materially within the next year. Concentrations refer to volumes of business, revenues, available sources of supply, or markets or geographic areas for which events could occur that would significantly disrupt normal finances within the next year.*]

    d. Arrangements with financial institutions involving compensating balances, or other arrangements involving restrictions on cash balances and lines of credit or similar arrangements [*Note: If this is not applicable, refer to item 9.*]

    e. Capital stock repurchase options or agreements, or capital stock reserved for options, warrants, or other requirements (possibly applicable to closed-end companies)

    f. All financial instruments, including those with off-balance-sheet risk (such as swaps, forwards, and futures), as required under accounting principles generally accepted in the United States of America.[91]

g. Each significant concentration of credit risk arising from all financial instruments whether from an individual counterparty or group of counterparties in accordance with FASB ASC 825-10-50.

11. There are no—

a. Violations or possible violations of laws or regulations whose effects should be considered for disclosure in the financial statements or as a basis for recording a loss contingency.

b. Unasserted claims or assessments that our lawyer has advised us are probable of assertion and must be disclosed in accordance FASB ASC 450, *Contingencies*.[92]

c. Other liabilities or gain or loss contingencies that are required to be accrued or disclosed by FASB ASC 450.

12. The financial statements include all assets and liabilities of which we are aware as of December 31, 20X8. The Company has satisfactory title to all owned assets, and there are no liens or encumbrances on such assets nor has any asset been pledged as collateral. All portfolio securities are marketable, except as disclosed in the financial statements.

13. The Company has complied with all aspects of contractual agreements that would have a material effect on the financial statements in the event of noncompliance.

14. We also advise you that, to the best of our knowledge and belief—

a. Portfolio securities are stated at fair value as determined in accordance with the valuation methods set forth in the current prospectus. All Company investments during the period were made

---

[91] Under the final clarified standard *Written Representations*, this representation would be as follows:
> The following information about financial instruments with off-balance-sheet risk and financial instruments with concentrations of credit risk:
> - The extent, nature, and terms of financial instruments with off-balance-sheet risk
> - The amount of credit risk of financial instruments with off-balance-sheet risk and information about the collateral supporting such financial instruments
> - Significant concentrations of credit risk arising from all financial instruments and information about the collateral supporting such financial instruments

The clarified auditing standards are effective for audits of financial statements for periods ending on or after December 15, 2012. However, nothing precludes an auditor from implementing aspects of the clarified SASs before their effective date, as long as the auditor continues to comply with the current standards. For additional information on the clarified auditing standards, please see the preface and appendix B.

[92] If the client has not consulted a lawyer, the auditor normally would rely on the review of internally available information, and this representation might be worded as follows:
> We are not aware of any pending or threatened litigation, claims, or assessments or unasserted claims or assessments that are required to be accrued or disclosed in the financial statements, in accordance with FASB ASC 450, *Contingencies*, and we have not consulted a lawyer concerning litigation, claims, or assessments.

Independent Auditor's Reports and Client Representations 407

in accordance with the investment policies stated in the current prospectus. [(*For those funds that have significant investments stated at fair value as determined by management or the board of directors or trustees to address the appropriateness of the valuation methodology and fair values assigned, the following sentence should be added:* "For securities whose fair values have been estimated by management [the Board of Directors or trustees], the valuation principles used are appropriate and have been consistently applied and the fair values are reasonable and supported by the documentation.")][93,94]

b. [*Nonregistered investment companies*] Interests in the Company have been offered for sale in accordance with its offering document and by no other means. No offer or solicitation of the Company's interests has been made in any jurisdiction in which such offer or solicitation would be unlawful. [*Registered investment companies*] The Company complied with the provisions of the Investment Company Act of 1940, as amended, and the rules and regulations thereunder, and with the provisions of its prospectus and the requirements of the various Blue Sky laws under which the Company operates.

c. The Company's shares have been issued and redeemed during the period in accordance with its offering document ([*registered investment companies*] registration statement) and applicable regulation. The daily net asset value has been properly computed throughout the year ([*registered investment companies*] for open-end funds in accordance with Rule 2a-4 of the act ([or Rule 2a-7

---

[93] AU section 328 contains expanded guidance on the audit procedures for fair value measurements and disclosures. Among other things, AU section 328 lists several representations about fair value measurements and disclosures contained in the financial statements that the auditor may consider obtaining from management. AU section 328 provides that, depending on the nature, materiality, and complexity of fair values, management representations about fair value measurements and disclosures contained in the financial statements also may include representations about the following:

- The appropriateness of the measurement methods, including related assumptions, used by management in determining fair value and the consistency in the application of the methods
- The completeness and adequacy of disclosures related to estimated fair value information
- Subsequent events requiring adjustment to the estimated fair value measurements and disclosures

[94] Under the final clarified standard *Written Representations*, for those funds that have significant investments stated at fair value, as determined by management or the board of directors to address the appropriateness of the valuation methodology and fair values assigned, the following sentence would be added to the letter of representations: "For securities whose fair values have been estimated by management [the board of directors], the valuation principles and significant assumptions used result in a measure of fair value appropriate for financial statement measurement and disclosure purposes."

The clarified auditing standards are effective for audits of financial statements for periods ending on or after December 15, 2012.

AAG-INV 11.41

for money market funds]) and was correctly applied in the computation of sales and redemption transactions.

d. The Company did not make any commitments during the year as underwriter, nor did it engage in any transactions made on margin, in joint trading or in a joint investment account.[95]

e. [*Nonregistered investment companies*] For U. S. federal income tax purposes, the Company is taxed as a [*describe*] and has incurred no material tax liabilities under the provisions of FASB ASC 740, *Income Taxes*. [*Registered investment companies*] The Company has complied with the requirements of subchapter M of the Internal Revenue Code of 1986, as amended, through the date of this letter, and intends to continue to so comply. The Company intends to distribute substantially all of its net investment income and capital gains to shareholders; accordingly, no federal income tax liability has been recorded in the financial statements. [*All investment companies*] The Company has filed all required tax forms in the jurisdictions in which it invests or does business by the applicable deadlines in which noncompliance or failure to file would have a material effect on the Company's financial statements, and, for required tax filings not yet completed, we plan to file, and to make timely payment for any unpaid taxes due and payable, by the applicable deadlines. We have provided you with all information and our assessment related to uncertain tax positions that we have taken, or expect to take, of which we are aware. We have made you aware of and have disclosed any significant tax positions for which it is reasonably possible the amount of unrecognized tax benefit will either increase or decrease within the next 12 months.

f. The Company, except to the extent indicated in its financial statements, does not own any securities of persons who are directly affiliated as defined in Section 2(a)(3) of the act.[96]

g. The Company has complied with the provisions of its code of ethics.

To the best of our knowledge and belief, no events or transactions have occurred subsequent to the balance sheet date and through the date

---

[95] These representations are required for SEC purposes and, therefore, should not be included in the representation letter for a nonpublic entity.

[96] See footnote 95.

Independent Auditor's Reports and Client Representations

of this letter that would require adjustment to or disclosure in the aforementioned financial statements.

_____
[Name of President or Chief Executive Officer and Title]

_____
[Name of Treasurer or Chief Financial Officer and Title]

11.42 For registered investment companies that include certifications of the principal executive officer and principal financial officer in filings on Form N-CSR, the individuals certifying in those capacities should also sign the representation letter in order to directly confirm and document the communications to auditors described in their certifications (see paragraph 2.170 of this guide). Other officers who provide material representations during the audit should also be considered for inclusion as signers.

Appendix A
Guidance Updates

> This appendix contains additional information on applicable guidance updates presented throughout the chapters of this guide, specifically guidance issued through the "as of" date of this guide that is not yet effective but will be for the next edition of this guide, and incorporated therein. Readers should consider this information for the reporting period to which it applies.
>
> For guidance updates related to clarified auditing standards, see appendix B, "Guidance Updates—Clarified Auditing Standards."

Accounting and Reporting Updates

A.01 ASU No. 2011-03 [Updates 2-2, 7-2]

Financial Accounting Standards Board (FASB) Accounting Standards Update (ASU) No. 2011-03, *Transfers and Servicing (Topic 860): Reconsideration of Effective Control for Repurchase Agreements*, issued in April 2011, is effective for the first interim or annual period beginning on or after December 15, 2011, and should be applied prospectively to transactions or modifications of existing transactions that occur on or after that date. Early adoption is not permitted.

Accounting and Reporting: Reconsideration of Effective Control [Update 2-2]

The paragraphs that follow replace paragraphs 2.124–.126 upon the effective date of ASU No. 2011-03.

> Investment companies may lend securities (principally to broker-dealers). Such transactions are documented as loans of securities in which the borrower of securities generally is required to provide collateral to the lender, commonly cash but sometimes other securities or standby letters of credit, with a value slightly higher than that of the securities borrowed. If the collateral is cash, the lender of securities normally earns a return by investing that cash, typically in short-term, high-quality debt instruments, at rates higher than the rate paid or rebated to the borrower. Investment of cash collateral is subject to the investment company's investment restrictions. If the collateral is other than cash, the lender of securities typically receives a fee. The investment company, as lender, receives amounts from the borrower equivalent to dividends and interest on the securities loaned. As with other extensions of credit, there are risks of delay in recovery or even loss of rights in the collateral should the borrower of the securities fail financially.
>
> As discussed in FASB ASC 860-30-25-7, many securities lending transactions are accompanied by an agreement that both entitles and obligates the transferor to repurchase or redeem the transferred financial assets before their maturity. FASB ASC 860-10-40-24 states that an agreement that both entitles and obligates the transferor to repurchase or redeem transferred financial assets from the transferee

maintains the transferor's effective control over those assets, as described in FASB ASC 860-10-40-5(c)(1), if all of the conditions in "Pending Content" in FASB ASC 860-10-40-24 are met (the financial assets to be repurchased or redeemed are the same or substantially the same as those transferred, the agreement is to repurchase or redeem them before maturity at a fixed or determinable price, and the agreement is entered into contemporaneously with, or in contemplation of, the transfer.) Those transactions should be accounted for as secured borrowings in which either cash or securities that the holder is permitted by contract or custom to sell or repledge received as collateral are considered the amount borrowed, the securities loaned are considered pledged as collateral against the cash borrowed and reclassified as set forth in FASB ASC 860-30-25-5(a), and any rebate paid to the transferee of securities is interest on the cash that the transferor is considered to have borrowed.

Paragraphs 4–5 of FASB ASC 860-30-25 explain that the accounting for noncash collateral by the debtor (or obligor) and the secured party depends on whether the secured party has the right to sell or repledge the collateral and whether the debtor has defaulted. Cash collateral should be derecognized by the payer and recognized by the recipient not as collateral but, rather, as proceeds of either a sale or borrowing.

Accounting and Reporting: Reconsideration of Effective Control [Update 7-2]

The paragraph that follows replaces paragraph 7.77 upon the effective date of ASU No. 2011-03.

FASB ASC 860-30-25-5 describes the accounting for noncash collateral by the debtor (obligor) and secured party, which depends on whether the secured party has the right to sell or repledge the collateral and whether the debtor has defaulted. FASB ASC 860-30-25-4 explains that cash collateral used in securities lending transactions should be derecognized by the debtor and recognized by the secured party, not as collateral, but, rather, as proceeds of either a sale or borrowing. FASB ASC 860-30-25-7 explains that many securities lending transactions (including those of many investment companies) often both entitle and obligate the transferor to repurchase or redeem the transferred financial assets before their maturity, and the transferor, accordingly, maintains effective control over those assets. Those transactions should be accounted for as secured borrowings if all the conditions in "Pending Content" in FASB ASC 860-10-40-24 are met (the financial assets to be repurchased or redeemed are the same or substantially the same as those transferred, the agreement is to repurchase or redeem them before maturity at a fixed or determinable price, and the agreement is entered into contemporaneously with, or in contemplation of, the transfer.) Transactions in which: (*a*) cash (or other securities that the holder is permitted by contract or custom to sell or repledge) received as collateral is considered the amount borrowed, (*b*) the securities loaned are considered pledged as collateral against the cash borrowed and reclassified as set forth in FASB ASC 860-30-25-5(a), and (*c*) any rebate paid to the transferee of securities is interest on the cash that the transferor is considered to have borrowed should be accounted for as secured borrowings.

Guidance Updates 413

A.02 ASU No. 2011-04 [Updates 2-1, 7-3, 7-6]

ASU No. 2011-04, *Fair Value Measurement (Topic 820): Amendments to Achieve Common Fair Value Measurement and Disclosure Requirements in U.S. GAAP and IFRSs*, issued in May 2011, is effective for public entities during interim and annual periods beginning after December 15, 2011. It is effective for nonpublic entities for annual periods beginning after December 15, 2011. Early application is not permitted for public entities. Nonpublic entities may early implement during interim periods beginning after December 15, 2011. The guidance should be applied prospectively.

Accounting and Reporting: Fair Value [Update 2-1]

The paragraphs that follow replace the existing paragraphs 2.32–.89 upon the effective date of ASU No. 2011-04.

Valuing Investments

Values and changes in values of investments held by investment companies are as important to investors as the investment income earned. FASB ASC 946-10-15-2 states that investment companies are required to report their investment assets (for example, securities and derivatives) at *fair value*, which is defined by the FASB ASC glossary as the price that would be received to sell an asset or paid to transfer a liability in an orderly transaction between market participants at the measurement date.[17] As discussed in "Pending Content" in FASB ASC 820-10-35-41, quoted market prices in active markets are the best evidence of the fair value of a financial instrument, except as explained in FASB ASC 820-10-35-41C.[18] An *active market* is defined in "Pending Content" in the FASB ASC glossary as a market in which transactions for the asset or liability take place with sufficient frequency and volume to provide pricing information on an ongoing basis.

Registered investment companies are also governed by the definition of *value* found in Section 2(a)(41) of the 1940 Act and further interpreted in section 404.03 of the SEC's *Codification of Financial Reporting Policies*. Section 2(a)(41) states that value is defined, with respect to securities for which market quotations are readily available, the market value of such securities and, with respect to other securities and assets, fair value, as determined in good faith by the board of directors. This is also described in Accounting Series Release No. 118.[19]

---

[17] In May 2010, FASB issued the proposed ASU *Accounting for Financial Instruments and Revisions to the Accounting for Derivative Instruments and Hedging Activities—Financial Instruments (Topic 825) and Derivatives and Hedging (Topic 815)*. Entities that follow specialized industry guidance in FASB ASC 946, *Financial Services—Investment Companies*, would continue to initially measure their financial instruments at transaction price. Readers should remain alert for developments on this topic, which can be accessed from the Technical Plan and Project Updates page at www.fasb.org.

[18] FASB's Valuation Resource Group provides FASB and FASB staff with information on existing implementation issues related to fair value measurements used for financial statement reporting purposes and the alternative viewpoints associated with those implementation issues. Readers should remain aware of developments from this group and use the information and minutes posted from these meetings under the Advisory Groups tab on the FASB website as a resource.

[19] The SEC has established a bibliography of regulatory guidance relating to the valuation of investments in accordance with the 1940 Act, including references to applicable laws, regulations, releases, selected staff guidance, and enforcement actions. The bibliography is accessible in the Division of Investment Management section of the SEC website.

AAG-INV APP A

Many financial instruments are traded publicly in active markets; therefore, end-of-day market quotations are readily available. However, if quoted market prices in active markets are not available, fair value may be estimated in a variety of ways, depending on the nature of the instrument and the manner in which it is traded.[20] Management's best estimate in good faith (under the oversight of the board of directors or trustees) of fair value should be based on the consistent application of a variety of factors, in accordance with the valuation policy followed by the fund, with the objective being to determine the exit price or amount at which the investment could be exchanged in a current transaction between willing parties, other than in a forced or liquidation sale. The fair value reported for investments is not reduced by transaction costs such as estimated brokerage commissions and other costs that would be incurred in selling the investments.

"Pending Content" in FASB ASC 820-10-35 establishes a fair value hierarchy that prioritizes the inputs to valuation techniques used to measure fair value into three broad levels. The fair value hierarchy gives the highest priority to quoted prices (unadjusted) in active markets for identical assets or liabilities (level 1) and the lowest priority to unobservable inputs (level 3). FASB ASC 820, *Fair Value Measurement*, also clarifies that fair value is market based, as opposed to an entity-specific measure.

An investment company's registration statement or offering circular describes the methods used to value its investments.[21] Section 404.03 of the SEC's *Codification of Financial Reporting Policies* describes various methods for estimating fair value.

As discussed in paragraphs 2–3 of FASB ASC 946-320-35, valuing securities listed and traded on one or more securities exchanges or unlisted securities traded regularly in over-the-counter (OTC) markets (for example, U.S. Treasury bonds, notes, and bills or stocks quoted on the OTC Bulletin Board or Pink OTC Markets) ordinarily is not difficult because quotations of completed transactions are published daily, or price quotations are readily obtainable from financial reporting services or individual broker-dealers. A security traded in an active market on the valuation date is valued at the last quoted sales price.

A security listed on more than one national securities exchange should be valued at the last quoted sales price at the time of valuation on the exchange on which the security is principally traded; securities traded both on a national exchange and in the OTC market should be valued based on the price in the market in which the security is principally traded. If the security was not traded in the principal market on the valuation date, the security should be valued at the last quoted sales price on the next most active market if management determines that price to be representative of fair value. If the price is determined not to be representative of fair value, the security should be valued based on quotations readily available from principal-to-principal markets, financial publications, or recognized pricing services, or a good-faith estimate of fair value should be made.

---

[20] Section 2(a)(41) of the 1940 Act.
[21] Items 11 and 23 of Form N-1A.

AAG-INV APP A

Guidance Updates

"Pending Content" in FASB ASC 820-10-35-6C and 820-10-30-2 provide that even when there is no observable market to provide pricing information, a fair value measurement should assume that a transaction takes place at that date, considered from the perspective of a market participant that holds the asset or owes the liability. The objective of a fair value measurement focuses on the price that would be received to sell the asset or paid to transfer the liability (an *exit price*), not the price that would be paid to acquire the asset or received to assume the liability in an exchange transaction (an *entry price*). However, "Pending Content" in FASB ASC 820-10-30-3 explains that, in many cases, the transaction price will equal the fair value (for example, that might be the case when on the transaction date the transaction to buy an asset takes place in the market in which the asset would be sold).

"Pending Content" in paragraphs 5–6 of FASB ASC 820-10-35 states that the transaction to sell the asset or transfer the liability takes place in the principal market for the asset or liability or, in the absence of a principal market, the most advantageous market for the asset or liability. As defined by "Pending Content" in the FASB ASC glossary, the *principal market* is the market with the greatest volume and level of activity for the asset or liability. Also, as defined by "Pending Content" in the FASB ASC glossary, the *most advantageous market* is the market which maximizes the amount that would be received to sell the asset or minimizes the amount that would be paid to transfer the liability, after taking into account transaction costs and transportation costs. A reporting entity need not undertake an exhaustive search of all possible markets to identify the principal market or the most advantageous market, but it should take into account all information that is reasonably available. If there is a principal market for the asset or liability, the fair value measurement should represent the price in that market (whether that price is directly observable or estimated using another valuation technique), even if the price in a different market is potentially more advantageous at the measurement date. The reporting entity must have access to the principal (or most advantageous) market at the measurement date. Because different entities (and businesses within those entities) with different activities may have access to different markets, the principal (or most advantageous) market for the same asset or liability might be different for different entities (and businesses within those entities). Therefore, the principal (or most advantageous) market (and thus, market participants) should be considered from the perspective of the reporting entity, thereby allowing for differences between and among entities with different activities.

As explained in "Pending Content" in FASB ASC 820-10-35-9B, the price in the principal (or most advantageous) market used to measure the fair value of the asset or liability should not be adjusted for transaction costs, which should be accounted for in accordance with the provisions of other accounting guidance. As defined by the FASB ASC glossary, *transaction costs* are the costs to sell an asset or transfer a liability in the principal (or most advantageous) market for the asset or liability that are directly attributable to the disposal of the asset or the transfer of the liability. Transaction costs meet both of

AAG-INV APP A

the following criteria: they result directly from and are essential to that transaction, and they would not have been incurred by the entity had the decision to sell the asset or transfer the liability not been made.

Securities markets, financial publications, and recognized pricing services frequently provide quotations of bid price and asked price. Those quotations may be used if a principal-to-principal market is the primary market for the security on the valuation date or, in the absence of trading, on the valuation date of the security normally traded primarily on an exchange. Some investment companies use the bid price to value all securities, some use the mean between the bid and asked prices, and some use a valuation within the range between the bid and asked prices that is considered to best represent fair value in the circumstances. If price quotations are obtained from individual broker-dealers making a market in the security, some investment companies will estimate fair value as the mean of the quoted prices obtained. Each of those policies is acceptable if applied consistently and in accordance with the investment company's established pricing policy. Neither use of the asked price alone to value investments nor use of the bid price alone to value short sales or short positions is acceptable. If only a bid price or an asked price is available for a security on the valuation date, or the spread between the bid and asked price on that date is substantial, quotations for several days could be, for example, reviewed in determining whether the last quoted price is representative of fair value.

Many funds utilize pricing services to obtain security valuations. Those pricing services may include quotations on listed securities and OTC securities, as described in the preceding paragraphs. Also, particularly for debt securities, pricing services may provide valuations determined by other pricing techniques. Methods generally recognized in the valuation of financial instruments include comparison to reliable quotations of similar financial instruments, pricing models, matrix pricing, or other formula-based pricing methods. Those methodologies incorporate factors for which published market data may be available. For instance, the mathematical technique known as matrix pricing may be used to determine fair value based on market data available with respect to the issue and similar issues without exclusive reliance on issuer-specific quoted market prices.

Fair Value Determination When the Volume or Level of Activity Has Significantly Decreased

Situations may arise when quoted market prices are not readily available or when market quotations are available, but it is questionable whether they represent fair value. Examples include the following instances:

- Market quotations and transactions are infrequent, and the most recent quotations and transactions occurred substantially prior to the valuation date.
- The market for the security is "thin" (that is, there are few transactions or market-makers in the security, the spread between the bid and asked prices is large, and price quotations vary substantially either over time or among individual market-makers).

Guidance Updates 417

- The last quoted market prices for foreign securities are as of the close of a market that precedes the fund's normal time for valuation, and certain events have taken place since the close of that foreign market that provide evidence that the market prices of those securities would be substantially different at the fund's normal time for valuation if such foreign market were open at that time. Such matters are referred to by the SEC staff as an example of a significant event.[22]
- Trading in a market or for a specific security had been suspended during a trading day and had not reopened by the fund's normal time for valuation for such reasons as the declaration of a market emergency by a regulatory body, the imposition of daily price change limits or "circuit-breakers," or the intended release of information by an issuer was expected to have a material effect on a security's value.

Similar circumstances may also affect the appropriateness of valuations supplied by pricing services. Situations such as the preceding are expected to be rare but may occur. In those cases, an investment company may establish a policy to substitute a good-faith estimate of fair value for the quoted market price or pricing service valuation. Any policy adopted should be consistently applied in all situations when significant pricing differences are determined to exist.

"Pending Content" in paragraphs 54C–54M of FASB ASC 820-10-35 clarify the application of FASB ASC 820 in determining fair value when the volume and level of activity for an asset or liability has significantly decreased. Guidance is also included in identifying transactions that are not orderly. In addition, paragraphs 90–98 of FASB ASC 820-10-55 include illustrations on the application of this guidance.

The definition of *fair value* states that it is the price obtained in an orderly transaction. The "Pending Content" in the FASB ASC glossary defines an *orderly transaction* as a transaction that assumes exposure to the market for a period before the measurement date to allow for marketing activities that are usual and customary for transactions involving such assets and liabilities; it is not a forced transaction (for example, a forced liquidation or distress sale).

Consistent with "Pending Content" in FASB ASC 820-10-35-54G, even when there has been a significant decrease in the volume or level of activity for the asset or liability, the objective of a fair value measurement remains the same. "Pending Content" in FASB ASC 820-10-35-54C lists a number of factors a reporting entity should evaluate the significance and relevance of to determine whether, on the basis of the evidence available, there has been a significant decrease in the volume or level of activity. According to "Pending Content" in FASB ASC 820-10-35-54D, if, after evaluating the factors, the conclusion is reached that there has been a significant decrease in the volume or

---

[22] April 30, 2001, letter from the SEC Division of Investment Management to the Investment Company Institute regarding valuation issues. The letter further states that significant fluctuations in domestic markets may constitute a significant event.

AAG-INV APP A

level of activity for the asset or liability in relation to normal market conditions, further analysis of the transactions or quoted prices is needed. A decrease in the volume or level of activity on its own may not indicate that a transaction price or quoted price does not represent fair value or that a transaction in that market is not orderly. However, if a reporting entity determines that a transaction or quoted price does not represent fair value (for example, there may be transactions that are not orderly), an adjustment to the transactions or quoted prices will be necessary if the reporting entity uses those prices as a basis for measuring fair value and that adjustment may be significant to the fair value measurement in its entirety. According to "Pending Content" in FASB ASC 820-10-35-54F, the objective is to determine the point within the range of fair value measurements that is most representative of fair value under the current market conditions. A wide range of fair value measurements may be an indication that further analysis is needed.

"Pending Content" in FASB ASC 820-10-35-54H states that estimating the price at which market participants would be willing to enter into a transaction at the measurement date under current market conditions if there has been a significant decrease in the volume or level of activity for the asset or liability depends on the facts and circumstances at the measurement date and requires judgment. A reporting entity's intention to hold the asset or to settle or otherwise fulfill the liability is not relevant, however, because fair value is a market-based measurement, not an entity-specific measurement.

According to "Pending Content" in FASB ASC 820-10-35-54I, a reporting entity should evaluate the circumstances to determine whether, on the weight of the evidence available, the transaction is orderly. When there has been a significant decrease in the volume or level of activity for the asset or liability, it is not appropriate to conclude that all transactions are not orderly (that is, distressed or forced). Circumstances that may indicate that a transaction is not orderly include the following:

- There was not adequate exposure to the market for a period before the measurement date to allow for marketing activities that are usual and customary for transactions involving such assets or liabilities under current market conditions.
- There was a usual and customary marketing period, but the seller marketed the asset or liability to a single market participant.
- The seller is in or near bankruptcy or receivership (that is, the seller is distressed).
- The seller was required to sell to meet regulatory or legal requirements (that is, the seller was forced).
- The transaction price is an outlier when compared with other recent transactions for the same or a similar asset or liability.

The determination of whether a transaction is orderly or is not orderly is more difficult if there has been a significant decrease in the volume or level of activity for the asset or liability in relation to normal market activity for the asset or liability (or similar assets or liabilities).

"Pending Content" in FASB ASC 820-10-35-54J states that a reporting entity should consider all of the following when measuring fair value or estimating market risk premiums:

- If the evidence indicates that the transaction is not orderly, a reporting entity should place little, if any, weight (compared with other indications of fair value) on that transaction price.
- If the evidence indicates that a transaction is orderly, a reporting entity should take into account that transaction price. The amount of weight placed on that transaction price when compared with other indications of fair value will depend on the facts and circumstances, such as the volume of the transaction, the comparability of the transaction to the asset or liability being measured, and the proximity of the transaction to the measurement date.
- If a reporting entity does not have sufficient information to conclude whether a transaction is orderly, it should take into account the transaction price. However, that transaction price may not represent fair value (that is, the transaction price is not necessarily the sole or primary basis for measuring fair value or estimating market risk premiums). When a reporting entity does not have sufficient information to conclude whether particular transactions are orderly, the reporting entity should place less weight on those transactions when compared with other transactions that are known to be orderly.

In making the determination regarding whether a transaction is orderly, a reporting entity does not need to undertake exhaustive efforts, but should not ignore information that is reasonably available. When a reporting entity is a party to a transaction, it is presumed to have sufficient information to conclude whether the transaction is orderly. Refer to FASB ASC 820 for more information.

Valuation Techniques

Rule 38a-1 under the 1940 Act requires registered investment companies and business development companies (referred to in the adopting release as funds) to adopt policies and procedures reasonably designed to prevent the violation of federal securities laws. In the adopting release, the SEC stated that Rule 38a-1

> requires funds to adopt policies and procedures that require the fund to monitor for circumstances that may necessitate the use of fair value prices; establish criteria for determining when market quotations are no longer reliable for a particular portfolio security; provide a methodology or methodologies by which the fund determines the current fair value of the portfolio security; and regularly review the appropriateness

420 Investment Companies

and accuracy of the method used in valuing securities, and make any necessary adjustments. [footnotes omitted][23]

Investment companies offering their shares on Forms N-1A and N-3 are also required by the SEC to provide a brief explanation in their prospectuses of the circumstances under which they will use fair value prices and the effects of using fair value pricing.[24]

The SEC's *Codification of Financial Reporting Policies* provides guidance on the factors to be considered in, and the responsibilities for and methods used for, the valuation of securities for which market quotations are not readily available.[25] The following paragraphs regarding securities valued in good faith are consistent with those SEC policies and are intended to summarize and provide guidance on this topic.

The objective of the estimating procedures is to state the securities at the amount at which they could be exchanged in a current transaction between willing parties, other than in a forced or liquidation sale. The term *current transaction* means realization in an orderly disposition over a reasonable period. All relevant factors generally should be considered in selecting the method of estimating in good faith the fair value of each kind of security.

In estimating in good faith the fair value of a particular financial instrument, the board or its designee (the valuation committee) generally should, to the extent necessary, take into consideration all indications of fair value that are available. This guide does not purport to delineate all factors that may be considered; however, the following is a list of some of the factors to be considered:[26]

- Financial standing of the issuer
- Business and financial plan of the issuer and comparison of actual results with the plan
- Cost at the date of purchase
- Size of the position held and the liquidity of the market
- Contractual restrictions on the disposition
- Pending public offering with respect to the financial instrument
- Pending reorganization activity affecting the financial instrument (such as merger proposals, tender offers, debt restructurings, and conversions)
- Reported prices and the extent of public trading in similar financial instruments of the issuer or comparable entities
- Ability of the issuer to obtain the needed financing
- Changes in the economic conditions affecting the issuer

---

[23] SEC Final Rule Release No. IC-26299, *Compliance Programs of Investment Companies and Investment Advisers*, under the 1940 Act.

[24] SEC Final Rule Release No. IC-26418, *Disclosure Regarding Market Timing and Selective Disclosure of Portfolio Holdings*, under the 1940 Act.

[25] Sections 404.03–.94 of the SEC's *Codification of Financial Reporting Policies*.

[26] The SEC's *Codification of Financial Reporting Policies* provides guidance on the factors to be considered and the methods used to value securities for which market quotations are not readily available.

AAG-INV APP A

Guidance Updates 421

- A recent purchase or sale of a security of the entity
- Pricing by other dealers in similar securities
- Financial statements of the investees

No single method exists for estimating fair value in good faith because fair value depends on the facts and circumstances of each individual case. Valuation methods may be based on a multiple of earnings or a discount or premium from a market of a similar, freely traded security of the same issuer; on a yield to maturity with respect to debt issues; or on a combination of these and other methods. In addition, with respect to derivative products, other factors (such as volatility, interest and foreign exchange rates, and term to maturity) should be considered. The board of directors or trustees should be satisfied, however, that the method used to estimate fair value in good faith is reasonable and appropriate and that the resulting valuation is representative of fair value.

According to sections 404.03–.04 of the SEC's Codification of Financial Reporting Policies, the information considered and the basis for the valuation decision should be documented, and the supporting data should be retained. The board may appoint individuals to assist it in the estimation process and to make the necessary calculations. The rationale for the use of a good-faith estimate of fair value that is different from market quotations or pricing service valuations ordinarily should be documented. If material, the circumstances surrounding the substitution of good-faith estimates of fair value for market quotations or pricing service valuations should be disclosed in the notes to the financial statements.

"Pending Content" in paragraphs 24–27 of FASB ASC 820-10-35 describe the valuation techniques that should be used to measure fair value. The objective of using a valuation technique is to estimate the price at which an orderly transaction to sell the asset or to transfer the liability would take place between market participants at the measurement date under current market conditions. Three widely used valuation techniques are the market approach, cost approach, and income approach. These approaches are described in "Pending Content" in paragraphs 3A–3G of FASB ASC 820-10-55, as follows:

- The market approach uses prices and other relevant information generated by market transactions involving identical or comparable assets, liabilities, or a group of assets and liabilities, such as a business. Valuation techniques consistent with the market approach include matrix pricing and often use market multiples derived from a set of comparables.
- The cost approach reflects the amount that would be required currently to replace the service capacity of an asset (often referred to as current replacement cost).
- The income approach converts future amounts (for example, cash flows or income and expenses) to a single current (that is, discounted) amount. When the income approach is used, the fair value measurement reflects current market expectations about those future amounts. Valuation

AAG-INV APP A

techniques consistent with the income approach include present value techniques, option-pricing models, and the multiperiod excess earnings method.

"Pending Content" in FASB ASC 820-10-35-24 states that valuation techniques that are appropriate in the circumstances and for which sufficient data are available to measure fair value, maximizing the use of relevant observable inputs and minimizing the use of unobservable inputs should be used by a reporting entity. "Pending Content" in FASB ASC 820-10-35-24B explains that in some cases, a single valuation technique will be appropriate (for example, when valuing an asset or a liability using quoted prices in an active market for identical assets or liabilities). In other cases, multiple valuation techniques will be appropriate (for example that might be the case when valuing a reporting unit). If multiple valuation techniques are used to measure fair value, the results (that is, respective indications of fair value) should be evaluated, considering the reasonableness of the range of values indicated by those results. "Pending Content" in FASB ASC 820-10-55-35 illustrates the use of multiple valuation techniques. A fair value measurement is the point within that range that is most representative of fair value in the circumstances.

As explained in "Pending Content" in paragraphs 25–26 of FASB ASC 820-10-35, valuation techniques used to measure fair value should be applied consistently. However, a change in a valuation technique or its application is appropriate if the change results in a measurement that is equally or more representative of fair value in the circumstances. Such a change would be accounted for as a change in accounting estimate, in accordance with the provisions of FASB ASC 250, *Accounting Changes and Error Corrections*.

Present Value Techniques

"Pending Content" in paragraphs 5–20 of FASB ASC 820-10-55 describe the use of present value techniques to measure fair value. Those paragraphs neither prescribe the use of a single specific present value technique nor limit the use of present value techniques to measure fair value to the techniques discussed therein. A fair value measurement of an asset or a liability using a present value technique captures all of the following elements from the perspective of market participants at the measurement date: an estimate of future cash flows; expectations about possible variations in the amount and timing of the cash flows; the time value of money; the price for bearing the uncertainty inherent in the cash flows (that is, a risk premium); other factors that market participants would take into account in the circumstances; and for a liability, the nonperformance risk relating to that liability, including the reporting entity's (that is, the obligor's) own credit risk.

"Pending Content" in FASB ASC 820-10-55-6 provides the general principles that govern any present value technique used to measure fair value, as follows:

- Cash flows and discount rates should reflect assumptions that market participants would use when pricing the asset or liability.

Guidance Updates

- Cash flows and discount rates should take into account only the factors attributable to the asset or liability being measured.
- To avoid double counting or omitting the effects of risk factors, discount rates should reflect assumptions that are consistent with those inherent in the cash flows. For example, a discount rate that reflects the uncertainty in expectations about future defaults is appropriate if using the contractual cash flows of a loan (that is, a discount rate adjustment technique), but is not appropriate if using expected (that is, probability-weighted) cash flows (that is, an expected present value technique) because the expected cash flows already reflect assumptions about the uncertainty in future defaults.
- Assumptions about cash flows and discount rates should be internally consistent. For example, nominal cash flows, which include the effects of inflation, should be discounted at a rate that includes the effects of inflation.
- Discount rates should be consistent with the underlying economic factors of the currency in which the cash flows are denominated.

FASB ASC 820-10-55-9 describes how present value techniques differ in how they adjust for risk and in the type of cash flows they use. For example, the discount rate adjustment technique (also called the traditional present value technique) uses a risk-adjusted discount rate and contractual, promised, or most likely cash flows. In contrast, method 1 of the expected present value technique uses risk-adjusted expected cash flows and a risk-free rate. Method 2 of the expected present value technique uses expected cash flows that are not risk adjusted and a discount rate adjusted to include the risk premium that market participants require. That rate is different from the rate used in the discount rate adjustment technique. "Pending Content" in FASB ASC 820-10-55-13 notes that, in the expected present value technique, the probability-weighted average of all possible future cash flows is referred to as the expected cash flows. The traditional present value technique and two methods of expected present value techniques are discussed more fully in FASB ASC 820-10-55.

The Fair Value Hierarchy

Because fair value is a market-based measurement, as stated in "Pending Content" in FASB ASC 820-10-35-9, fair value should be measured using the assumptions that market participants would use in pricing the asset or liability (referred to as inputs), assuming that market participants act in their economic best interest. "Pending Content" in the FASB ASC glossary defines *inputs* as assumptions that market participants would use when pricing the asset or liability, including assumptions about risk, such as the risk inherent in a particular valuation technique used to measure fair value (such as a pricing model) or the risk inherent in the inputs to the valuation technique. Inputs may be observable or unobservable (both as defined by "Pending Content" in the FASB ASC glossary):

- *Observable inputs* are developed using market data, such as publicly available information about actual events or transactions, and that reflect the assumptions that market participants would use when pricing the asset or liability.
- *Unobservable inputs* are inputs for which market data are not available and that are developed using the best information available about the assumptions that market participants would use when pricing the asset or liability.

"Pending Content" in paragraphs 37–54B of FASB ASC 820-10-35 establishes a fair value hierarchy that distinguishes between observable and unobservable inputs. "Pending Content" in FASB ASC 820-10-05-1C states that when a price for an identical asset or liability is not observable, a reporting entity measures fair value using another valuation technique that maximizes the use of relevant observable inputs and minimizes the use of unobservable inputs.

The fair value hierarchy in "Pending Content" in FASB ASC 820-10-35 prioritizes the inputs to valuation techniques used to measure fair value into three broad levels. The three levels are discussed in

- paragraphs 40–46 of FASB ASC 820-10-35, which states that level 1 inputs are quoted prices (unadjusted) in active markets for identical assets or liabilities that the reporting entity can access at the measurement date. FASB ASC 820-10-35-44 affirms the requirement that the fair value of a position in a single asset or liability (including a position comprising a large number of identical assets or liabilities, such as a holding of financial instruments) that trades in an active market should be measured within level 1 as the product of the quoted price for the individual asset or liability and the quantity held by the reporting entity. That is the case, even if a market's normal daily trading volume is not sufficient to absorb the quantity held, and placing orders to sell the position in a single transaction might affect the quoted price.
- paragraphs 47–51 of FASB ASC 820-10-35, which state that level 2 inputs are inputs other than quoted prices included within level 1 that are observable for the asset or liability, either directly or indirectly. If the asset or liability has a specified (contractual) term, a level 2 input must be observable for substantially the full term of the asset or liability. Adjustments to level 2 inputs will vary depending on factors specific to the asset or liability. Those factors include the condition or location of the asset, the extent to which inputs relate to items that are comparable to the asset (including those factors described in FASB ASC 820-10-35-16D), and the volume or level of activity in the markets within which the inputs are observed. An adjustment to a level 2 input that is significant to the entire measurement might result in a fair value measurement categorized within level 3 of the fair value hierarchy if the

Guidance Updates

adjustment uses significant unobservable inputs. Level 2 inputs include the following:

— Quoted prices for similar assets or liabilities in active markets

— Quoted prices for identical or similar assets or liabilities in markets that are not active

— Inputs other than quoted prices that are observable for the asset or liability (for example, interest rates and yield curves observable at commonly quoted intervals, implied volatilities, and credit spreads)

— Inputs that are derived principally from, or corroborated by, observable market data by correlation or other means (market-corroborated inputs)

- paragraphs 52–54A of FASB ASC 820-10-35, which state that level 3 inputs are unobservable inputs for the asset or liability. Unobservable inputs should be used to measure fair value to the extent that relevant observable inputs are not available, thereby allowing for situations in which there is little, if any, market activity for the asset or liability at the measurement date. A reporting entity should develop unobservable inputs using the best information available in the circumstances, which might include the entity's own data. In developing unobservable inputs, a reporting entity may begin with its own data, but it should adjust those data if reasonably available information indicates that other market participants would use different data or there is something particular to the reporting entity that is not available to other market participants (for example, an entity-specific synergy). A reporting entity need not undertake exhaustive efforts to obtain information about market participant assumptions. Unobservable inputs should reflect the assumptions that market participants would use when pricing the asset or liability, including assumptions about risk. Assumptions about risk include the risk inherent in a particular valuation technique and the risk inherent in the inputs to the valuation technique. A measurement that does not include an adjustment for risk would not represent a fair value measurement if market participants would include one when pricing the asset or liability. The reporting entity should take into account all information about market participant assumptions that is reasonably available.

As explained in "Pending Content" in FASB ASC 820-10-35-37A, in some cases, the inputs used to measure the fair value of an asset or a liability might be categorized within different levels of the fair value hierarchy. In those cases, the fair value measurement is categorized in its entirety in the same level of the fair value hierarchy as the lowest level input that is significant to the entire measurement. Adjustments to arrive at measurements based on fair value, such as costs to sell when measuring fair value less costs to sell, should not be taken into account when determining the level of the fair value hierarchy within which a fair value measurement is categorized.

As discussed in "Pending Content" in FASB ASC 820-10-35-38, the availability of relevant inputs and their relative subjectivity might affect the selection of appropriate valuation techniques. However, the fair value hierarchy prioritizes the inputs to valuation techniques, not the valuation techniques used to measure fair value. For example, a fair value measurement developed using a present value technique might be categorized within level 2 or level 3, depending on the inputs that are significant to the entire measurement and the level of the fair value hierarchy within which those inputs are categorized.

As stated in "Pending Content" in FASB ASC 820-10-35-2C, the effect on the measurement arising from a particular characteristic will differ depending on how that characteristic would be taken into account by market participants. FASB ASC 820-10-55-51 illustrates a restriction's effect on fair value measurement.

Application of Fair Value Measurements

"Pending Content" in FASB ASC 820-10-35-10A provides that a fair value measurement of a nonfinancial asset takes into account a market participant's ability to generate economic benefits by using the asset in its highest and best use or by selling it to another market participant that would use the asset in its highest and best use. The "Pending Content" in the FASB ASC glossary defines highest and best use as the use of a nonfinancial asset by market participants that would maximize the value of the asset or the group of assets and liabilities (for example, a business) within which the asset would be used. Further, "Pending Content" in FASB ASC 820-10-35-11A states that the fair value measurement of a nonfinancial asset assumes that the asset is sold consistent with the unit of account (which may be an individual asset). That is the case even when that fair value measurement assumes that the highest and best use of the asset is to use it in combination with other assets or with other assets and liabilities because a fair value measurement assumes that the market participant already holds the complementary assets and associate liabilities.[27]

According to "Pending Content" in paragraphs 16–16A of FASB ASC 820-10-35, a fair value measurement assumes that a financial or nonfinancial liability or an instrument classified in a reporting entity's shareholders' equity is transferred to a market participant at the measurement date. The transfer of a liability or an instrument classified in a reporting entity's shareholders' equity assumes the following: (a) a liability would remain outstanding and the market participant transferee would be required to fulfill the obligation; (b) an instrument classified in a reporting entity's shareholders' equity would remain outstanding and the market participant transferee would take

---

[27] "Pending Content" in FASB ASC 820-10-35 limits the application of the "highest and best use" concept to nonfinancial assets. ASU No. 2011-04, *Fair Value Measurement (Topic 820): Amendments to Achieve Common Fair Value Measurement and Disclosure Requirements in U.S. GAAP and IFRSs*, specifies that the highest and best use and valuation premise are relevant only when measuring the fair value of nonfinancial assets and are not relevant when measuring the fair value of financial assets or liabilities.

on the rights and responsibilities associated with the instrument. It is also assumed the liability or instrument would not be settled with the counterparty, cancelled, or otherwise extinguished on the measurement date. Even when there is no observable market to provide pricing information about the transfer of a liability or an instrument classified in a reporting entity's shareholders' equity (for example, because contractual or other legal restrictions prevent the transfer of such items), there might be an observable market for such items if they are held by other parties as assets (for example, a corporate bond or a call option on a reporting entity's shares).

"Pending Content" in paragraphs 16B–16BB of FASB ASC 820-10-35 state that when a quoted price for the transfer of an identical or a similar liability or instrument classified in a reporting entity's shareholders' equity is not available, and the identical item is held by another party as an asset, a reporting entity should measure the fair value from the perspective of a market participant that holds the identical item as an asset at the measurement date. In such cases, a reporting entity should measure the fair value of the liability or equity instrument as follows:

 a. using the quoted price in an active market for the identical item held by another party as an asset, if that price is available
 b. if that price is not available, using other observable inputs, such as the quoted price in a market that is not active for the identical item held by another party as an asset
 c. if the observable prices in (a) and (b) are not available, using another valuation technique, such as:
    1. an income approach
    2. a market approach

According to "Pending Content" in FASB ASC 820-10-35-16D, a reporting entity should adjust the quoted price of a liability or an instrument classified in a reporting entity's shareholders' equity held by another party as an asset only if there are factors specific to the asset that are not applicable to the fair value measurement of the liability or equity instrument. A reporting entity should ensure that the price of the asset does not reflect the effect of a restriction preventing the sale of that asset. Some factors that may indicate that the quoted price of the asset should be adjusted including the following: the quoted price for the asset relates to a similar, but not identical, liability or equity instrument held by another party as an asset, or the unit of account for the asset is not be the same as for the liability or equity instrument.

"Pending Content" in FASB ASC 820-10-35-16H explains that when a quoted price for the transfer of an identical or a similar liability or instrument classified in a reporting entity's shareholders' equity is not available and the identical item is not held by another party as an asset, a reporting entity should measure the fair value of the liability or equity instrument using a valuation technique from the perspective of a market participant that owes the liability or has issued the claim on equity.

When measuring the fair value of a liability or an instrument classified in a reporting entity's shareholders' equity, "Pending Content" in FASB ASC 820-10-35-18B states that a reporting entity should not include a separate input or an adjustment to other inputs relating to the existence of a restriction that prevents the transfer of the item because the effect of that restriction is either implicitly or explicitly included in the other inputs to the fair value measurement.

"Pending Content" in paragraphs 17–18 of FASB ASC 820-10-35 provide that the fair value of a liability should reflect the effect of nonperformance risk (which includes, but is not limited to, a reporting entity's own credit risk). Nonperformance risk is assumed to be the same before and after the transfer of the liability. When measuring the fair value of a liability, a reporting entity should take into account the effect of its credit risk (credit standing) and any other factors that might influence the likelihood that the obligation will or will not be fulfilled.

Offsetting Positions in Market Risks or Counterparty Credit Risk

As stated by "Pending Content" in FASB ASC 820-10-35-18D, a reporting entity that holds a group of financial assets and financial liabilities is exposed to market risks (that is, interest rate risk, currency risk, or other price risk) and to the credit risk of each of the counterparties. If the reporting entity manages that group of financial assets and financial liabilities on the basis of its net exposure to either market risks or credit risk, the reporting entity is permitted to apply an exception to FASB ASC 820 for measuring fair value. That exception permits a reporting entity to measure the fair value of a group of financial assets and financial liabilities on the basis of the price that would be received to sell a net long position (that is, an asset) for a particular risk exposure or to transfer a net short position (that is, a liability) for a particular risk exposure in an orderly transaction between market participants at the measurement date under current market conditions. Accordingly, a reporting entity should measure the fair value of the group of financial assets and financial liabilities consistently with how market participants would price the net risk exposure at the measurement date. "Pending Content" in paragraphs 18E–18L of FASB ASC 820-10-35 provides further details on this exception.

Investments in Entities That Calculate Net Asset Value per Share

"Pending Content" in paragraphs 54B and 59–62 of FASB ASC 820-10-35 contains guidance for permitting the use of a practical expedient, with appropriate disclosures, when measuring the fair value of an alternative investment that does not have a readily determinable fair value if certain criteria are met. A reporting entity is permitted, as a practical expedient, to estimate the fair value of an investment within the scope of "Pending Content" in paragraphs 4–5 of FASB ASC 820-10-15 using the net asset value per share (or its equivalent, such as member units or an ownership interest in partners' capital to which a proportionate share of net assets is attributed) of the investment, if the net asset value per share of the investment (or its equivalent) is calculated in a manner consistent with the measurement principles of FASB ASC 946, *Financial Services—Investment Companies*, of the reporting entity's measurement date. "Pending Content" in FASB ASC 820-10-15-4 explains that this guidance applies only to an investment

Guidance Updates

that meets both of the following criteria as of the reporting entity's measurement date:

    a. The investment does not have a readily determinable fair value.[28]

    b. The investment is in an entity that has all the attributes specified in FASB ASC 946-10-15-2 (investment activity, unit ownership, pooling of funds, and reporting entity) or, if one or more of the attributes specified in FASB ASC 946-10-15-2 are not present, is in an entity for which it is industry practice to issue financial statements using guidance that is consistent with the measurement principles in FASB ASC 946.

Certain attributes of the investment (such as restrictions on redemption) and transaction prices from principal-to-principal or brokered transactions will not be considered in measuring the fair value of the investment if the practical expedient is used. The practical expedient reduces complexity and improves consistency and comparability in the application of FASB ASC 820 while reducing the costs of applying FASB ASC 820. This guidance also improves transparency by requiring additional disclosures about investments within its scope to enable users of financial statements to understand the nature and risks of investments and whether the sale of the investments is probable at amounts different from net asset value per share.

As discussed in Technical Questions and Answers (TIS) section 2220.18, "Applicability of Practical Expedient" (AICPA, *Technical Practice Aids*), these investments, typically referred to as alternative investments, include interests in hedge funds, private equity funds, real estate funds, venture capital funds, offshore fund vehicles, commodity funds, and funds of funds. Further, TIS section 2220.19, "Unit of Account" (AICPA, *Technical Practice Aids*), states that, for interests in alternative investments, the appropriate unit of account is the interest in the investee fund itself, not the underlying investments within the investee fund; this is because the reporting entity owns an undivided interest in the whole of the investee fund portfolio and typically lacks the ability to dispose of individual assets and liabilities in the investee fund portfolio.

FASB ASC 820-10-35-60 notes that, if the net asset value obtained from the investee is not as of the reporting entity's measurement date or is not calculated in a manner consistent with the measurement principles of FASB ASC 946, the reporting entity should consider whether an adjustment to the most recent net asset value is necessary. The objective of this adjustment would be to estimate a net asset value

---

[28] "Pending Content" in FASB ASC 820-10-15-5 notes that the definition of readily determinable fair value indicates that an equity security would have a readily determinable fair value if any one of three conditions is met. One of those conditions is that sales prices or bid-and-asked quotations are currently available on a securities exchange registered with the SEC or in the over-the-counter (OTC) market, provided that those prices or quotations for the OTC market are publicly reported by the National Association of Securities Dealers Automated Quotations System or Pink Sheets LLC. The definition notes that restricted stock meets that definition if the restriction expires within one year. If an investment otherwise would have a readily determinable fair value, except that the investment has a restriction expiring in more than one year, the reporting entity should not apply paragraphs 59–62 of FASB ASC 820-10-35 and FASB ASC 820-10-50-6A to the investment.

AAG-INV APP A

per share that is consistent with the aforementioned measurement principles.

TIS section 2220.20, "Determining Whether NAV Is Calculated Consistent With FASB ASC 946, *Financial Services—Investment Companies*" (AICPA, *Technical Practice Aids*), provides guidance to assist management of the reporting entity in determining whether net asset value is calculated consistent with FASB ASC 946. As part of this determination, a reporting entity should independently evaluate the fair value measurement process utilized by the investee fund manager to calculate the net asset value. This evaluation is a matter of professional judgment and includes determining that the investee fund manager has an effective process and related internal controls in place to estimate the fair value of its investments that are included in the net asset value calculation. The reporting entity's controls used to evaluate the process of the investee fund manager may include initial due diligence, ongoing monitoring, and financial reporting controls. Only after considering all relevant factors can the reporting entity reach a conclusion about whether the reported net asset value is calculated consistent with the measurement principles of FASB ASC 946. The reporting entity may consider the following key factors relating to the valuation received from the investee fund manager:

- The investee fund's fair value estimation processes and control environment and any changes to those processes or control environment
- The investee's fund policies and procedures for estimating fair value of the underlying investments and any changes to those policies or procedures
- The use of independent third-party valuation experts to augment and validate the investee fund's procedures for estimating fair value
- The portion of the underlying securities held by the investee fund that are traded on active markets
- The professional reputation and standing of the investee fund's auditor (this is not intended to suggest that the auditor is an element of the investee fund's internal control system but as a general risk factor in evaluating the integrity of the data obtained from the investee fund manager)
- Qualifications, if any, of the auditor's report on the investee fund's financial statements
- Whether there is a history of significant adjustments to the net asset value reported by the investee fund manager as a result of the annual financial statement audit or otherwise
- Findings in the investee fund's adviser or administrator's type 2 Service Organization Control (SOC) 1 report, if any
- Whether net asset value has been appropriately adjusted for items such as carried interest and clawbacks
- Comparison of historical realizations to the last reported fair value

Guidance Updates

TIS section 2220.20 goes on to discuss the scenario in which a reporting entity invests in a fund of funds. That reporting entity could conclude on the consistency of the net asset value calculation with FASB ASC 946 by assessing (a) whether the fund-of-funds manager has a process that considers the aforementioned key factors in the calculation of the net asset value reported by the fund of funds and (b) if the fund-of-funds manager has obtained or estimated the net asset value from underlying fund managers in a manner consistent with paragraphs 59–62 of FASB ASC 820-10-35 as of the measurement date. The reporting entity is not required to look through the fund-of-funds interest to underlying fund investments if the reporting entity has concluded that the fund-of-funds manager reports net asset value consistent with FASB ASC 946 for the fund-of-funds interest.

TIS section 2220.22, "Adjusting NAV When It Is Not as of the Reporting Entity's Measurement Date" (AICPA, *Technical Practice Aids*), illustrates how the reporting entity should estimate an adjustment when net asset value is calculated consistently with FASB ASC 946 but not as of the reporting entity's measurement date. One option is for the reporting entity to request the investee fund manager to provide a supplemental net asset value calculation consistent with the measurement principles of FASB ASC 946 as of the reporting entity's measurement date. Alternatively, it may be necessary to adjust or roll forward (or roll back) the reported net asset value for factors that could cause it to differ from the net asset value at the measurement date. When the reporting entity's measurement date is prior to the net asset value calculation date, it may be more appropriate to use that net asset value and perform a rollback, rather than using a reported net asset value calculated prior to the entity's measurement date. TIS section 2220.22 lists factors that may necessitate an adjustment to the reported net asset value when it is not calculated as of the reporting entity's measurement date and contains an example rollforward net asset value calculation.

TIS section 2220.23, "Adjusting NAV When It Is Not Calculated Consistent With FASB ASC 946" (AICPA, *Technical Practice Aids*), illustrates how a reporting entity may estimate the adjustment when a reported net asset value is not calculated consistently with the measurement principles of FASB ASC 946. In this situation, the reporting entity should consider and understand the reasons why net asset value has not been based upon fair value, whether a fair value based net asset value can be obtained from the investee manager, and whether the specific data needed to adjust the reported net asset value can be obtained and properly utilized to estimate a fair value based net asset value. Some examples of circumstances in which the reporting entity may be able to obtain data to estimate an adjustment include, but are not limited to, the reported net asset value is on a cash basis, the reported net asset value utilizes blockage discounts taken on securities valued using level 1 inputs (which is inconsistent with FASB ASC 820), and the reported net asset value has not been adjusted for the impact of unrealized carried interest or incentive fees. Consequently, if the reporting entity finds that it is not practicable to calculate an adjusted net asset value, then the practical expedient is not available. The reporting entity may also elect not to utilize the practical

AAG-INV APP A

expedient. In those cases, the reporting entity should apply the general measurement principles of FASB ASC 820 instead.

"Pending Content" in FASB ASC 820-10-35-61 states that a reporting entity should decide on an investment-by-investment basis whether to apply the practical expedient and should apply that practical expedient consistently to the fair value measurement of the reporting entity's entire position in a particular investment, unless it is probable at the measurement date that the reporting entity will sell a portion of an investment at an amount different from net asset value per share (or its equivalent), as described in FASB ASC 820-10-35-62. In those situations, the reporting entity should account for the portion of the investment that is being sold in accordance with other provisions in FASB ASC 820 and should not apply the practical expedient discussed in "Pending Content" in FASB ASC 820-10-35-59.

According to FASB ASC 820-10-35-62, a reporting entity is not permitted to estimate the fair value of an investment within the scope of paragraphs 4–5 of FASB ASC 820-10-15 using the net asset value per share of the investment (or its equivalent) as a practical expedient if it is probable at the measurement date that a reporting entity will sell a portion of the investment at an amount different from the net asset value per share (or its equivalent). A sale is considered probable only if all of the following criteria are met as of the reporting entity's measurement date:

- Management, having the authority to approve the action, commits to a plan to sell the investment.
- An active program to locate a buyer and other actions required to complete the plan to sell the investment have been initiated.
- The investment is available for immediate sale subject only to terms that are usual and customary for sales of such investments.
- Actions required to complete the plan indicate that it is unlikely that significant changes to the plan will be made or that the plan will be withdrawn.

TIS section 2220.27, "Determining Fair Value of Investments When the Practical Expedient Is Not Used or Is Not Available" (AICPA, *Technical Practice Aids*), discusses what inputs or investment features should be considered in estimating fair value for entities that do not elect to use net asset value as a practical expedient or are unable to adjust the most recently reported net asset value to estimate a net asset value that is calculated in a manner consistent with the measurement principles of FASB ASC 946 as of the reporting entity's measurement date. In this situation, examples of factors that could be used when estimating fair value (depending on the valuation technique[s] and facts and circumstances) are as follows:

- Net asset value (as one valuation factor)
- Transactions in principal-to-principal or brokered markets (external markets) and overall market conditions
- Features of the alternative investment

Guidance Updates

- Expected future cash flows appropriately discounted
- Factors used to determine whether there has been a significant decrease in the volume and level of activity for the asset when compared with normal market activity for the asset ("Pending Content" in FASB ASC 820-10-35-54C)

TIS section 2220.27 also discusses investment features of alternative investments, such as lockup periods and the ability of the fund to identify and make acceptable investments, which a reporting entity may consider in determining fair value when the practical expedient is unavailable or not elected.

"Pending Content" in FASB ASC 820-10-35-54B states that categorization within the fair value hierarchy of a fair value measurement of an investment that is measured at net asset value per share requires judgment. This guidance provides the following considerations:

- If a reporting entity has the ability to redeem its investment with the investee at net asset value per share (or its equivalent) at the measurement date, the fair value measurement of the investment should be categorized within level 2 of the fair value hierarchy.
- If a reporting entity will never have the ability to redeem its investment with the investee at net asset value per share (or its equivalent), the fair value measurement of the investment should be categorized within level 3 of the fair value hierarchy.
- If a reporting entity cannot redeem its investment with the investee at net asset value per share (or its equivalent) at the measurement date, but the investment may be redeemable with the investee at a future date (for example, investments subject to a lockup or gate or investments whose redemption period does not coincide with the measurement date), the reporting entity should take into account the length of time until the investment will become redeemable in determining whether the fair value measurement of the investment should be categorized within level 2 or level 3 of the fair value hierarchy. For example, if the reporting entity does not know when it will have the ability to redeem the investment, or it does not have the ability to redeem the investment in the near term at net asset value per share (or its equivalent), the fair value measurement should be categorized within level 3 of the fair value hierarchy[29]

---

[29] Refer to the May 12, 2011 AICPA Expert Panel Meeting Highlights. Expert panel (EP) members discussed situations where an investment company holds investments in multiple classes of an investee fund. For instance, a fund of funds holds $3,000,000 in Class A of the investee, and $500,000 in Class S (a side pocket class) of the investee. For the purposes of leveling in the ASC 820 hierarchy, a question arises whether the investment should be bifurcated if the investment into Class A meets the criteria for level 2, but the investment into Class S is illiquid, and, therefore, a level 3 investment. The EP discussed industry practice in leveling such investments and noted that the EP members generally believe that in the situation of a unitized fund as described above, there could be multiple units of account for an interest in an investee fund, and that a similar analogy would apply to investments in partnerships where a portion of the investment is locked up or has other varying liquidity characteristics.

AAG-INV APP A

TIS section 2220.24, "Disclosures—Ability to Redeem Versus Actual Redemption Request" (AICPA, *Technical Practice Aids*), discusses redemptions from alternative funds. In most cases, redemptions at net asset value are only permitted with advance notice, ranging from 30 to 120 days. Even if the reporting entity has not submitted a redemption request effective on the measurement date, as long as the reporting entity has the ability to redeem at net asset value in the near term (for example, it has the contractual and practical ability to redeem) at the measurement date, then, consistent with "Pending Content" in FASB ASC 820-10-35-54B(a), the investment may be classified as level 2. TIS section 2220.25, "Impact of 'Near Term' on Classification Within Fair Value Hierarchy" (AICPA, *Technical Practice Aids*), explains that what is viewed as near term is a matter of professional judgment and depends on the specific facts and circumstances. A redemption period of 90 days or less generally would be considered near term because any potential discount relative to the time value of money to the next redemption date would be unlikely to be considered a significant unobservable input, in accordance with FASB ASC 820. However, other factors, such as the likelihood or actual imposition of gates, may influence the determination of whether the investment will be redeemable in the near term.

Money market funds.[30] As set forth in Rule 2a-7 under the 1940 Act, a money market fund may value securities using the amortized cost or penny-rounding method,[31] subject to certain determinations by its board of directors or trustees. Rule 2a-7 requires, among other things, in the case of a money market fund using the amortized cost method, that the fund's board of directors or trustees "establish written procedures reasonably designed ... to stabilize the money market fund's net asset value per share, as computed for the purpose of distribution, redemption and repurchase at a single value." Rule 2a-7 sets forth procedures that must be adopted by the board of directors or trustees when using the amortized cost or penny-rounding method of valuation. Additionally, for funds using the amortized cost method, the board of directors or trustees should perform a periodic review of both the monitoring of and the extent of any deviation from fair value and the methods used to calculate the deviations.

Accounting and Reporting: Fair Value [Update 7-3]

The paragraphs that follow replace existing paragraphs 7.80–.84 upon the effective date of ASU No. 2011-04.

Fair Value Disclosures

FASB ASC 820-10-50 discusses the disclosures required for assets and liabilities measured at fair value. "Pending Content" in FASB ASC 820-10-50-1 explains that for assets and liabilities that are measured at fair value on a recurring or nonrecurring basis in the statement of financial position after initial recognition, a reporting entity is required

---

[30] See footnote 17.

[31] A money market fund using either method (*a*) may not acquire any instrument with a remaining maturity (as the term is defined in Rule 2a-7) of greater than 397 calendar days; (*b*) must maintain a dollar-weighted average portfolio maturity of 60 days or less; or (*c*) must maintain a dollar-weighted average portfolio maturity of 120 calendar days, determined without reference to the exceptions regarding interest rate readjustments.

Guidance Updates

to disclose information that helps users of its financial statements assess the valuation techniques and inputs used to develop those measurements. For recurring fair value measurements using significant unobservable inputs (level 3), the reporting entity is required to disclose information to help users assess the effect of the measurements on earnings (or changes in net assets) or other comprehensive income for the period.

To meet that objective, "Pending Content" in FASB ASC 820-10-50-2 requires a reporting entity to disclose, at minimum, the following information for each class of assets and liabilities measured at fair value in the statement of financial position after initial recognition:

  a. For recurring and nonrecurring fair value measurements, the fair value measurement at the end of the reporting period, and for nonrecurring fair value measurements, the reasons for the measurement.

  b. For recurring and nonrecurring fair value measurements, the level of the fair value hierarchy within which the fair value measurements are categorized in their entirety (level 1, 2, or 3).

  c. For assets and liabilities held at the end of the reporting period that are measured at fair value on a recurring basis, the amounts of any transfers between level 1 and level 2 of the fair value hierarchy, the reasons for those transfers, and the reporting entity's policy for determining when transfers between levels are deemed to have occurred. Transfers into each level should be disclosed and discussed separately from transfers out of each level. "Pending Content" in FASB ASC 820-10-50-2C explains that a reporting entity should disclose and consistently follow its policy for determining when transfers between levels of the fair value hierarchy are deemed to have occurred. The policy about the timing of recognizing transfers should be the same for transfers into the levels as for transfers out of the levels. Examples of policies for determining the timing of transfers include the following: the date of the event or change in circumstances that caused the transfer, the beginning of the reporting period, and the end of the reporting period.

  d. For recurring and nonrecurring fair value measurements categorized within level 2 and level 3 of the fair value hierarchy, a description of the valuation technique(s) and the inputs used in the fair value measurement. If there has been a change in valuation technique, the reporting entity should disclose that change and the reason(s) for making it. For fair value measurements categorized within level 3 of the fair value hierarchy, a reporting entity should provide quantitative information about the significant unobservable inputs used in the fair value measurement.

  e. For recurring fair value measurements categorized within level 3 of the fair value hierarchy, a reconciliation from the opening balances to the closing balances, disclosing

AAG-INV APP A

separately changes during the period attributable to the following:

    i. Total gains or losses for the period recognized in earnings (or changes in net assets), and the line item(s) in the statement of income (or activities) in which those gains or losses are recognized.

    ii. Total gains or losses for the period recognized in other comprehensive income, and the line item(s) in other comprehensive income in which those gains or losses are recognized.

    iii. Purchases, sales, issues, and settlements (each of those types of changes disclosed separately).

    iv. The amounts of any transfers into or out of level 3 of the fair value hierarchy, the reasons for those transfers, and the reporting entity's policy for determining when transfers between levels are deemed to have occurred. Transfers into level 3 should be disclosed and discussed separately from transfers out of level 3.

f. For recurring fair value measurements categorized within level 3 of the fair value hierarchy, the amount of the total gains or losses for the period in $d(i)$ included in earnings (or changes in net assets) that is attributable to the change in unrealized gains or losses relating to those assets and liabilities held at end of the reporting period, and the line item(s) in the statement of income (or activities) in which those unrealized gains or losses are recognized.

g. For recurring and nonrecurring fair value measurements categorized within level 3 of the fair value hierarchy, a description of the valuation processes used by the reporting entity (including, for example, how an entity decides its valuation policies and procedures and analyzes changes in fair value measurements from period to period).

h. For recurring fair value measurements categorized within level 3 of the fair value hierarchy, a narrative description of the sensitivity of the fair value measurement to changes in unobservable inputs if a change in those inputs to a different amount might result in a significantly higher or lower fair value measurement. If there are interrelationships between those inputs and other unobservable inputs used in the fair value measurement, a reporting entity should also provide a description of those interrelationships and how they magnify or mitigate the effect of changes in the unobservable inputs on the fair value measurement. To comply with that disclosure requirement, the narrative description of the sensitivity to changes in unobservable inputs should include, at a minimum, the unobservable inputs disclosed when complying with d.

i. For recurring and nonrecurring fair value measurements, if the highest and best use of a nonfinancial asset differs from its current use, a reporting entity should disclose

Guidance Updates 437

that fact and why the nonfinancial asset is being used in a manner that differs from its highest and best use.

"Pending Content" in FASB ASC 820-10-50-2F states that a nonpublic entity is not required to disclose the information discussed in *c* and *g*.

"Pending Content" in FASB ASC 820-10-50-2B explains that a reporting entity should determine appropriate classes of assets and liabilities on the basis of: the nature, characteristics, and risks of the asset or liability; and the level of the fair value hierarchy within which the fair value measurement is categorized. Further, the number of classes may need to be greater for fair value measurements within level 3 of the fair value hierarchy because those measurements have a greater degree of uncertainty and subjectivity. A class of assets and liabilities will often require greater disaggregation than the line items presented in the statement of financial position.

"Pending Content" in FASB ASC 820-10-50-3 states that, for derivative assets and liabilities, the reporting entity should present both the fair value disclosures discussed in paragraph 7.81*a–c* on a gross basis and the reconciliation disclosures discussed in paragraph 7.81*d–e* on a gross or net basis.

"Pending Content" in FASB ASC 820-10-50-6A requires disclosures for investments that are within the scope of paragraphs 4–5 of FASB ASC 820-10-15 and measured at fair value on a recurring or nonrecurring basis during the period and that help users of financial statements to understand the nature and risks of the investments and whether the investments are probable of being sold at amounts different from net asset value per share (or its equivalent). These disclosures are required, regardless of whether the practical expedient has been applied. These disclosures, to the extent applicable, are required for each class of investment. The required disclosures, at a minimum, are as follows:

a. The fair value measurement (as determined by applying paragraphs 59–62 of FASB ASC 820-10-35) of the investments in the class at the reporting date and a description of the significant investment strategies of the investee(s) in the class.

b. For each class of investment that includes investments that can never be redeemed with the investees, but the reporting entity receives distributions through the liquidation of the underlying assets of the investees, the reporting entity's estimate of the period of time over which the underlying assets are expected to be liquidated by the investees.

c. The amount of the reporting entity's unfunded commitments related to investments in the class.

d. A general description of the terms and conditions upon which the investor may redeem investments in the class (for example, quarterly redemption with 60 days' notice).

e. The circumstances in which an otherwise redeemable investment in the class (or a portion thereof) might not be redeemable (for example, investments subject to a lockup

AAG-INV APP A

or gate). Also, for those otherwise redeemable investments that are restricted from redemption as of the reporting entity's measurement date, the reporting entity should disclose its estimate of when the restriction from redemption might lapse. If an estimate cannot be made, the reporting entity should disclose that fact and how long the restriction has been in effect.

  f. Any other significant restriction on the ability to sell investments in the class at the measurement date.

  g. If a reporting entity determines that it is probable that it will sell an investment or investments for an amount different from net asset value per share (or its equivalent), as described in FASB ASC 820-10-35-62, the reporting entity should disclose the total fair value of all investments that meet the criteria in FASB ASC 820-10-35-62 and any remaining actions required to complete the sale.

  h. If a group of investments would otherwise meet the criteria in FASB ASC 820-10-35-62, but the individual investments to be sold have not been identified (for example, if a reporting entity decides to sell 20 percent of its investments in private equity funds, but the individual investments to be sold have not been identified), so the investments continue to qualify for the practical expedient in FASB ASC 820-10-35-59, the reporting entity should disclose its plans to sell and any remaining actions required to complete the sale(s).

Paragraph 7.193, from "Pending Content" in FASB ASC 820-10-55-107, provides an example of the disclosures required by "Pending Content" in FASB ASC 820-10-50-6A.

TIS section 2220.26, "Categorization of Investments for Disclosure Purposes" (AICPA, *Technical Practice Aids*), explains that certain entities that specialize in one particular investment category or have a significant investment in one such category should categorize investments and tailor disclosures to address the concentrations of risk that are specifically attributable to the investments. For example, a private equity fund of funds should not simply categorize its investments as "private equity" because this categorization is not specific enough to address the nature and risks of the investee funds. More specific categorization, perhaps relating to industry; geography; vintage year; or the strategy of the investees (venture, buyout, mezzanine), may be more appropriate and useful to the reader.

Accounting and Reporting: Fair Value [Update 7-6]

The paragraphs that follow replace existing paragraph 7.193 upon the effective date of ASU No. 2011-04.

As described in "Pending Content" in FASB ASC 820-10-50-6A and paragraph 7.83, for investments that are within the scope of paragraphs 4–5 of FASB ASC 820-10-15 measured at fair value on a recurring or nonrecurring basis during the period (regardless of whether the practical expedient has been applied), disclosure of information that helps users to understand the nature, characteristics, and risks

Guidance Updates

of the investments by class and whether the investments are probable of being sold at amounts different from net asset value per share (or its equivalent, such as member units or an ownership interest in partners' capital to which a proportionate share of net assets is attributed) are required. "Pending Content" in FASB ASC 820-10-55-107 provides the following example of how that information may be presented (note that the classes presented are examples only and not intended to be treated as a template; the classes should be tailored to the nature, characteristics, and risks of the reporting entity's investments).

	Fair Value (in millions)	Unfunded Commitments	Redemption Frequency (If Currently Eligible)	Redemption Notice Period
Equity long/short hedge funds[a]	$55	—	quarterly	30–60 days
Event driven hedge funds[b]	45	—	quarterly, annually	30–60 days
Global opportunities hedge funds[c]	35	—	quarterly	30–45 days
Multi-strategy hedge funds[d]	40	—	quarterly	30–60 days
Real estate funds[e]	47	$20		
Private equity funds—international[f]	43	15		
Total	$265	$35		

[a] This class includes investments in hedge funds that invest both long and short primarily in U.S. common stocks. Management of the hedge funds has the ability to shift investments from value to growth strategies, from small to large capitalization stocks, and from a net long position to a net short position. The fair values of the investments in this class have been estimated using the net asset value per share of the investments. Investments representing approximately 22 percent of the value of the investments in this class cannot be redeemed because the investments include restrictions that do not allow for redemption in the first 12–18 months after acquisition. The remaining restriction period for these investments ranged from 3 to 7 months at December 31, 20X3.

[b] This class includes investments in hedge funds that invest in approximately 60 percent equities and 40 percent bonds to profit from economic, political, and government driven events. A majority of the investments are targeted at economic policy decisions. The fair values of the investments in this class have been estimated using the net asset value per share of the investments.

[c] This class includes investments in hedge funds that hold approximately 80 percent of the funds' investments in non-U.S. common stocks in the health care, energy, information technology, utilities, and telecommunications

AAG-INV APP A

sectors and approximately 20 percent of the funds' investments in diversified currencies. The fair values of the investments in this class have been estimated using the net asset value per share of the investments. For one investment, valued at $8.75 million, a gate has been imposed by the hedge fund manager and no redemptions are currently permitted. This redemption restriction has been in place for 6 months and the time at which the redemption restriction might lapse cannot be estimated.

(d) This class invests in hedge funds that pursue multiple strategies to diversify risks and reduce volatility. The hedge funds' composite portfolio for this class includes investments in approximately 50 percent U.S. common stocks, 30 percent global real estate projects, and 20 percent arbitrage investments. The fair values of the investments in this class have been estimated using the net asset value per share of the investments. Investments representing approximately 15 percent of the value of the investments in this class cannot be redeemed because the investments include restrictions that do not allow for redemption in the first year after acquisition. The remaining restriction period for these investments ranged from 4 to 6 months at December 31, 20X3.

(e) This class includes several real estate funds that invest primarily in U.S. commercial real estate. The fair values of the investments in this class have been estimated using the net asset value of the Company's ownership interest in the partners' capital. These investments can never be redeemed with the funds. Distributions from each fund will be received as the underlying investments of the funds are liquidated. It is estimated that the underlying assets of the fund will be liquidated over the next 7–10 years. Twenty percent of the total investments in this class is planned to be sold. However, the individual investments that will be sold have not yet been determined. Because it is not probable that an individual investment will be sold, the fair value of each individual investment has been estimated using the net asset value of the Company's ownership interest in partners' capital. Once it has been determined which investments will be sold and whether those investments will be sold individually or in a group, the investments will be sold in an auction process. The investee fund's management must approve of the buyer before the sale of the investments can be completed.

(f) This class includes several private equity funds that invest primarily in foreign technology companies. These investments can never be redeemed with the funds. Instead, the nature of the investments in this class is that distributions are received through the liquidation of the underlying assets of the fund. If these investments were held, it is estimated that the underlying assets of the fund would be liquidated over 5 to 8 years. However, as of December 31, 20X3, it is probable that all of the investments in this class will be sold at an amount different from the net asset value of the Company's ownership interest in partners' capital. Therefore, the fair values of the investments in this class have been estimated using recent observable transaction information for similar investments and nonbinding bids received from potential buyers of the investments. As of December 31, 20X3, a buyer (or buyers) for these investments has not yet been identified. Once a buyer has been identified, the investee fund's management must approve of the buyer before the sale of the investments can be completed.

Audit Updates

A.03 SAS No. 121

Audit: Interim Financial Information [Update 7-4]

The paragraphs that follow replace the existing paragraph 7.173 upon the effective date of SAS No. 121, Revised Applicability of Statement on Auditing Standards No. 100, *Interim Financial Information (AICPA,* Professional Standards*).*

AU section 722[54] establishes standards and provides guidance on the nature, timing, and extent of the procedures to be performed by an independent accountant when conducting a review of interim financial information if the following conditions are satisfied:

a. The entity's latest annual financial statements have been audited by the accountant or a predecessor.

b. The accountant has been engaged to audit the entity's current year financial statements, or audited the entity's latest annual financial statements and, when it is expected that the current year financial statements will be audited, the appointment of another accountant to audit the current year financial statements is not effective prior to the beginning of the period covered by the review.

c. The entity prepares its interim financial information in accordance with the same financial reporting framework as that used to prepare the annual financial statements.

d. When the interim financial information is condensed information, all of the following conditions are met:

   i. The condensed interim financial information purports to conform with an appropriate financial reporting framework, which includes appropriate form and content of interim financial statements (for example, FASB ASC 270, *Interim Reporting*).

   ii. The condensed interim financial information includes a note that the financial information does not represent complete financial statements and should be read in conjunction with the entity's latest annual audited financial statements.

   iii. The condensed interim financial information accompanies the entity's latest audited annual financial statements or such audited annual financial statements are made readily available by the entity. The financial statements are deemed to be readily available if a third-party user can obtain the financial statements without any further action by the entity (for example, financial

---

[54] This guide primarily discusses auditing guidance issued by the ASB that applies to nonissuers. Issuers are defined by Section 3 of the Securities Exchange Act of 1934 and include registered investment companies. Audits of issuers are required to be performed under Public Company Accounting Oversight Board (PCAOB) standards. Users should evaluate their audit engagements to determine which auditing standards are applicable.

statements on an entity's website may be considered readily available, but being available upon request is not considered readily available).

The term interim *financial information* means financial information or statements covering a period less than 1 full year or for a 12-month period ending on a date other than the entity's fiscal year-end. Interim financial information may be condensed or in the form of a complete set of financial statements.

Considerations for Audits Performed in Accordance With Public Company Accounting Oversight Board (PCAOB) Standards

Registered public accounting firms must comply with the standards of the PCAOB in connection with the preparation or issuance of any report on reviews of interim financial information of an issuer, as defined by the Sarbanes-Oxley Act of 2002, and other entities, when prescribed by the rules of the SEC (collectively referred to as issuers). Auditing Standard No. 5, *An Audit of Internal Control Over Financial Reporting That Is Integrated with An Audit of Financial Statements* (AICPA, *PCAOB Standards and Related Rules*, Auditing Standards), provides direction regarding the auditor's evaluation responsibilities related to (*a*) management's quarterly certifications on internal control over financial reporting when performing an integrated audit of financial statements and (*b*) internal control over financial reporting. (See the preface of this guide for more information about management's assessment of the effectiveness of internal control.)

# Appendix B

Guidance Updates—Clarified Auditing Standards

> This appendix includes information about how the clarified Statement on Auditing Standards (SAS) Nos. 122–125 may affect an auditor's practice or methodology. These clarified standards are effective for audits of financial statements for periods ending on or after December 15, 2012. The auditing guidance in this guide will be conformed to reflect the guidance in SAS Nos. 122–125 in the next edition, which is when these clarified SASs are effective.
>
> As a result of the Auditing Standards Board's (ASB's) Clarity Project, all extant[1] AU sections have been modified. In some cases, individual AU sections have been revised into individual clarified standards. In other cases, some AU sections have been grouped together and revised as one or more clarified standards. In addition, the ASB revised the AU section number order established by SAS No. 1, *Responsibilities and Functions of the Independent Auditor* (AICPA, *Professional Standards*, AU sec. 110), to follow the same number order used in International Standards on Auditing (ISAs) for all clarified AU sections for which there are comparable ISAs.
>
> Although the Clarity Project was not intended to create additional requirements, some revisions have resulted in substantive changes (primarily clarifying changes) that may require auditors to make adjustments in their practices. When the guide chapters include guidance updates (in shaded text) alerting the reader to these changes and directing the reader to this appendix, the corresponding guidance updates are noted at the applicable AU-C sections included in this appendix. Guidance update numbers consist of the chapter number followed by the sequentially numbered guidance update number within any given chapter (for example, update 3-1 would be the first guidance update in chapter 3). Readers should consider this information for the reporting period to which it applies.
>
> ## Substantive Changes
>
> Substantive changes are considered likely to affect the firms' audit methodology and engagements because they contain *substantive* or *other changes*, defined as having one or both of the following characteristics:
>
> - A change or changes to an audit methodology that may require effort to implement
> - A number of small changes that, although not individually significant, may affect audit engagements

(continued)

---

[1] The term *extant* is used throughout this appendix in reference to the standards that are superseded by the clarified standards.

AAG-INV APP B

> **Primarily Clarifying Changes**
>
> Primarily clarifying changes are intended to explicitly state what may have been implicit in the extant standards, which, over time, resulted in diversity in practice.
>
> The preface of this guide and the Financial Reporting Center at www.aicpa.org/FRC provide more information about the Clarity Project. You can also visit www.aicpa.org/SASClarity.

Audit Updates—Clarified Auditing Standards

Part I: Substantive Changes

The AU-C sections in this part are considered likely to affect the firms' audit methodology and engagements because they contain *substantive* or *other changes*, defined as having one or both of the following characteristics:

- A change or changes to an audit methodology that may require effort to implement
- A number of small changes that, although not individually significant, may affect audit engagements

The auditor may need to address the changes in these AU-C sections early in the audit process. Some of the requirements may affect decisions to accept an engagement, and some will need to be communicated early in the planning process. The clarified standards are effective for audits of financial statements for periods ending on or after December 15, 2012, and may require the auditor to apply certain of the substantive changes as early as the planning stage for 2012 year-end audits. The auditor needs to review these AU-C sections to identify areas that apply to his or her practice.

B.01 Consideration of Laws and Regulations

AU-C section 250, *Consideration of Laws and Regulations in an Audit of Financial Statements* (AICPA, *Professional Standards*), requires the performance of procedures to identify instances of noncompliance with those laws and regulations that may have a material effect on the financial statements. Specifically, it requires the auditor to inspect correspondence, if any, with the relevant licensing or regulatory authorities. Because the extant standard did not require the auditor to perform procedures to identify such instances of noncompliance, unless specific information concerning possible illegal acts came to the auditor's attention, this requirement is expected to affect current practice.

Additionally, AU-C section 250 makes explicit several requirements for the auditor that were implicit in the extant standard and, accordingly, are not expected to change current practice, including the following:

- Obtain an understanding of the legal and regulatory framework.
- Obtain an understanding of how the entity is complying with that framework.
- Determine whether the auditor has a responsibility to report suspected noncompliance to parties outside the entity.

Guidance Updates—Clarified Auditing Standards

- Document identified or suspected noncompliance, including the results of any discussions about such items.

AU-C section 250 states that because of the inherent limitations of an audit, some material misstatements in the financial statements may not be detected, even though the audit is properly planned and performed in accordance with generally accepted auditing standards (GAAS). The concept described as "inherent limitations of an audit" is different from the concept of "no assurance" in the extant standard, which, in relation to indirect illegal acts, states that an audit performed in accordance with GAAS provides no assurance that noncompliance with laws and regulations will be detected or that any contingent liabilities that may result will be disclosed. The differing descriptions of these concepts are not expected to affect current practice.

The requirement in the extant standard to obtain a written representation from management concerning the absence of noncompliance with laws or regulations is included in AU-C section 580, *Written Representations* (AICPA, *Professional Standards*).

AU-C section 250 supersedes AU section 317, *Illegal Acts by Clients* (AICPA, *Professional Standards*).

B.02 Communicating Internal Control Related Matters [Update 2-3]

AU-C section 265, *Communicating Internal Control Related Matters Identified in an Audit* (AICPA, *Professional Standards*), adds two new requirements for communication of internal control matters and makes explicit two requirements that were implicit in the extant standards.

AU-C section 265 adds the following two new requirements:

- It requires the auditor to communicate in writing or orally, only to management, other deficiencies in internal control identified during the audit that have not been communicated to management by other parties and that, in the auditor's professional judgment, are of sufficient importance to merit management's attention. The ASB does not view this new requirement as a difference from the extant standard because auditor judgment is the sole determinant regarding whether a deficiency, other than a material weakness or significant deficiency, is of sufficient importance to communicate to management. Likewise, the extant standard does not preclude the auditor from communicating other internal control matters to management if the auditor believes that it is important to do so.

- It requires the auditor to include in the written communication an explanation of the potential effects of the significant deficiencies and material weaknesses identified. The ASB believes that management and those charged with governance need this information to enable them to take appropriate remedial action. Further, the ASB does not believe that this requires additional effort by the auditor because the potential effects would have been considered as part of the evaluation of the severity of the deficiency. The potential effects of this requirement do not need to be quantified.

For audits in which the auditor was engaged to report on the effectiveness of an entity's internal control over financial reporting under AT section 501, *An Examination of an Entity's Internal Control Over Financial Reporting That Is Integrated With an Audit of Its Financial Statements* (AICPA, *Professional*

Standards), the preceding items are not required because they are already included within the examination requirements.

AU-C section 265 also makes explicit two requirements that were implicit in the extant standards and, accordingly, are not expected to change current practice:

- It requires the auditor to determine whether, on the basis of the audit work performed, the auditor has identified one or more deficiencies in internal control.
- It requires the auditor to include specific matters in the optional written communication stating that no material weaknesses were identified during the audit. The new language is similar to that used in the written communication of significant deficiencies and material weaknesses presented in an illustrative example in the extant standard but not explicitly required.

AU-C section 265 supersedes AU section 325, *Communicating Internal Control Related Matters Identified in an Audit* (AICPA, *Professional Standards*).

B.03 Related Parties

AU-C section 550, *Related Parties* (AICPA, *Professional Standards*), shifts the focus of the audit to looking at the risk of material misstatements from related parties, regardless of which financial reporting framework is used. The shift to a risk-based approach to auditing-related parties may be significant for audits of financial statements prepared in accordance with an other comprehensive basis of accounting (OCBOA). AU-C section 550 is framework neutral, encompassing financial reporting frameworks, in addition to accounting principles generally accepted in the United States of America (GAAP), such as International Financial Reporting Standards, as promulgated by the International Accounting Standards Board, as well as special purpose frameworks described in AU-C section 800, *Special Considerations—Audits of Financial Statements Prepared in Accordance With Special Purpose Frameworks* (AICPA, *Professional Standards*). Note that the objectives, requirements, and definitions in AU-C section 550 are applicable irrespective of whether the applicable financial reporting framework establishes requirements for related-party disclosures.

AU-C section 550 supersedes AU section 334, *Related Parties* (AICPA, *Professional Standards*). The extant standard focuses on auditing the amounts and disclosures pursuant to GAAP and centers on the provisions of Financial Accounting Standards Board *Accounting Standards Codification* 850, *Related Party Disclosures*.

B.04 Group Audits

AU-C section 600, *Special Considerations—Audits of Group Financial Statements (Including the Work of Component Auditors)* (AICPA, *Professional Standards*), specifically articulates the procedures necessary for a group engagement team to perform when auditing group financial statements. The requirements of AU-C section 600 may affect a firm's decision whether to accept or continue an engagement. In addition, a major area of change addresses effective communication with, and supervision of, the component auditor.

The clarified standard identifies a *group audit* as the audit of group financial statements (that is, financial statements that include the financial information of more than one component). A group audit exists, for example, when management prepares financial information that is included in the group financial

Guidance Updates—Clarified Auditing Standards   **447**

statements related to a function, process, product or service, or geographical location (subsidiary in a foreign country). Group audits usually, but not always, include the work of component auditors. A component auditor performs work on financial information related to a component of the group that the group engagement team will use for the group audit and can be an auditor within the same audit firm (member office firm in another city or country) or a different audit firm. A component auditor would include, for example, another auditor or an audit team from another office that performs inventory testing in remote locations for the group auditor.

AU-C section 600 is significantly broader in scope than the extant standard. It shifts the focus of the audit from how to conduct an audit that involves other auditors to how to conduct an effective audit of group financial statements (see the subsequent section, "Terminology"). AU-C section 600 includes requirements of GAAS established in other standards that are applied in audits of group financial statements. AU-C section 600 strengthens existing standards by making it easier for auditors to understand and apply the requirements of GAAS, such as those contained in the risk assessment standards, in the context of an audit of group financial statements. The extant standard was written in 1972 and, thus, does not take into consideration the risk assessment standards.

Differences in Focus and Approach

Because AU-C section 600 is based on ISA 600, *Special Considerations—Audits of Group Financial Statements (Including the Work of Component Auditors)*, the scope of AU-C section 600, including its objective, requirements, and guidance, has been significantly expanded from the scope of the extant standard. AU-C section 600 specifically articulates the procedures necessary for the group engagement team to perform in order to be involved with component auditors to the extent necessary for an effective audit and, compared with the extant standard, better articulates the degree of involvement required when reference is made to component auditors in the auditor's report.

The requirements of AU-C section 600 address the following:

- Acceptance and continuance considerations
- The group engagement team's process to assess risk
- The determination of materiality to be used to audit the group financial statements
- The determination of materiality to be used to audit components
- The selection of components and account balances for audit testing
- Communications between the group engagement team and component auditors
- Assessing the adequacy and appropriateness of audit evidence by the group engagement team in forming an opinion on the financial statements

In situations when the group engagement partner does not make reference to a component auditor in the auditor's report on the group financial statements, all the requirements of AU-C section 600 apply, when relevant, in the context of the specific group audit engagement. Highlights of the requirements, particularly those that represent a change from existing standards, follow.

In situations when the group engagement partner decides to make reference to a component auditor in the audit report on the group financial statements,

AAG-INV APP B

certain of the requirements of AU-C section 600 do not apply. Note that, although AU-C section 600 is based on ISA 600, ISA 600 does not permit reference to a component auditor in the auditor's report on the group financial statements. This is the most significant area of divergence between the clarified standards and the ISAs.

Terminology

As previously mentioned, AU-C section 600 includes several new terms, as well as certain revised terms, from the extant standard. The term *group* is introduced, which is defined as "all the components whose financial information is included in the group financial statements. A group always has more than one component." *Component* is defined as "an entity or business activity for which group or component management prepares financial information that is required by the applicable financial reporting framework to be included in the group financial statements." *Group financial statements* are defined as "financial statements that include the financial information of more than one component."

The term *principal auditor*, which is used in the extant standard, is not used in AU-C section 600 and has been replaced by the terms *group engagement partner, group engagement team,* or *auditor of the group financial statements*.

The definition of *group engagement partner* is aligned with the definition of *engagement partner* provided in AU-C section 220, *Quality Control for an Engagement Conducted in Accordance With Generally Accepted Auditing Standards* (AICPA, *Professional Standards*), as follows: "The partner or other person in the firm who is responsible for the group audit engagement and its performance and for the auditor's report on the group financial statements that is issued on behalf of the firm."

The group engagement partner is the individual responsible for

- the direction, supervision, and performance of the group audit engagement in compliance with professional standards and regulatory and legal requirements and
- determining whether the auditor's report that is issued is appropriate in the circumstances.

However, the group engagement partner may be assisted in fulfilling his or her responsibilities by the group engagement team or, as appropriate in the circumstances, by the firm. To help distinguish when such assistance is permitted, AU-C section 600 uses the terms *group engagement partner, group engagement team,* and *auditor of the group financial statements*.

Requirements to be undertaken by the group engagement partner are addressed to the group engagement partner. When the group engagement team may assist the group engagement partner in fulfilling a requirement, the requirement is addressed to the group engagement team. When it may be appropriate in the circumstances for the firm to fulfill a requirement, the requirement is addressed to the auditor of the group financial statements.

Group engagement team is defined as "partners, including the group engagement partner, and staff who establish the overall group audit strategy, communicate with component auditors, perform work on the consolidation process, and evaluate the conclusions drawn from the audit evidence as the basis for forming an opinion on the group financial statements." Note that auditors who do not meet the definition of a *member of the group engagement team* are considered to be component auditors. Thus, a component auditor may work for a network firm of the group engagement partner's firm or may even work for a different office of the same firm.

Acceptance and Continuance

An overall difference between AU-C section 600 and the extant standard is the change in focus when determining whether to accept or continue the engagement. AU-C section 600 bases that determination on whether the auditor believes that he or she will be able to obtain sufficient appropriate audit evidence over the group financial statements, including whether the group engagement team will have appropriate access to information. The extant standard bases that determination on whether the auditor would be able to sufficiently participate in the group audit in order to be the principal auditor.

Note that this approach means a change in the mindset of the group engagement partner from considering the group engagement team's coverage of the principal amounts and reliance on other (component) auditors to considering the sufficiency of the group engagement team's involvement in the performance of the audit, including involvement in the work of the component auditors.

Link to the Risk Assessment Standards

In aligning with ISA 600, AU-C section 600 focuses on the application of the risk assessment standards to the performance of the group audit, including references and discussion of their specific application in group audit situations.

Involvement With, and Understanding of, Component Auditors

The clarified standard requires the group engagement team to gain an understanding of the component auditor. This understanding includes certain aspects that are already covered by the extant standard, such as competence and independence, as well as additional areas, such as a determination of the extent to which the group engagement team will be able to be involved in the work of the component auditor.

Once an understanding of the component auditor has been gained, the group engagement partner may choose to either

- assume responsibility for, and, thus, be required to be involved in, the work of component auditors, insofar as that work relates to the expression of an opinion on the group financial statements or
- not assume responsibility for, and, accordingly, make reference to, the audit of a component auditor in the auditor's report on the group financial statements.

Involvement in the work performed by a component auditor will involve the group engagement team undertaking the following actions:

- Establishing component materiality to be used by the component auditor.
- Performing risk assessment procedures and participating in the assessment of risks of material misstatement and the planned audit response. These may be performed together with the component auditor or by the group engagement team.

Materiality

The clarified standard requires the group engagement team to determine materiality and performance materiality for the group as a whole, as well as component materiality (that is, the materiality to be used to audit the financial information of a component for purposes of the group audit). The extant standard does not provide guidance on the application of materiality in the audit of group financial statements. Component materiality is determined by the group engagement team, regardless of whether the group engagement partner is making reference to the audit of a component auditor. For purposes of the group audit, component materiality is required to be lower than group materiality in order to reduce the risk that the aggregate of detected and undetected misstatements in the group financial statements exceeds the materiality for the group financial statements as a whole.

Responding to Assessed Risks

AU-C section 600 builds on the principle in the extant standard that, in order to achieve a proper review of matters affecting the consolidating or combining of accounts in the financial statements, the principal auditor should adopt appropriate measures to assure the coordination of activities with those of the other auditor. AU-C section 600 includes requirements and guidance relating to work to be performed on all components for which the group engagement partner is assuming responsibility for the work of the component auditor, regardless of whether that work is performed by the group engagement team or component auditors. It includes requirements and guidance specifying the nature, timing, and extent of the group engagement team's involvement in the work of the component auditors, particularly when performing work on significant components.

A *significant component* is defined in AU-C section 600 as "a component identified by the group engagement team that

- is of individual financial significance to the group or
- due to its specific nature or circumstances, is likely to include significant risks of material misstatement of the group financial statements."

For components that are financially significant, an audit of the component's financial information is performed. For components considered significant due to their likelihood of including significant risks of material misstatements, an audit or other audit procedures are performed. For components that are not significant, the group engagement team performs analytical procedures at the group level.

AU-C section 600 also includes requirements and guidance related to the group wide internal controls, the consolidation process, and subsequent events.

Communication With Others and Documentation

The clarified standard requires the group engagement team to communicate specific items to the component auditor and to request that the component auditor also communicate with the group engagement team about certain matters. Specific items are also required to be communicated to group management or those charged with governance of the group, or both.

AAG-INV APP B

Guidance Updates—Clarified Auditing Standards 451

The clarified standard also requires explicit documentation, including an analysis of the group's components indicating the significant components and type of work performed on the components.

Other Changes

In order for reference to the component auditor to be made in the auditor's report on the group financial statements, the component financial statements need to be prepared using the same financial reporting framework as the group financial statements, and the component auditor has to have performed an audit on the financial statements of the component in accordance with GAAS or, when required by law or regulation, auditing standards promulgated by the Public Company Accounting Oversight Board. The ASB believes that this requirement makes explicit what is implicit in the extant standard.

The AICPA is developing an Audit Risk Alert, *Group Audits*, which will be available in 2012 and will provide additional guidance for implementing this standard.

AU-C section 600 supersedes AU section 543, *Part of Audit Performed by Other Independent Auditors* (AICPA, *Professional Standards*).

B.05 Auditor's Reports

The following clarified standards include auditor report changes describing management's responsibility; the use of headings; and the introduction of the two new terms *emphasis-of-matter* and *other-matter paragraphs*, replacing the term *explanatory paragraph*:

- AU-C section 700, *Forming an Opinion and Reporting on Financial Statements* (AICPA, *Professional Standards*)
- AU-C section 705, *Modifications to the Opinion in the Independent Auditor's Report* (AICPA, *Professional Standards*)
- AU-C section 706, *Emphasis-of-Matter Paragraphs and Other-Matter Paragraphs in the Independent Auditor's Report* (AICPA, *Professional Standards*)

These clarified standards include close integration with AU-C sections 210, *Terms of Engagement* (AICPA, *Professional Standards*) and 580. AU-C section 700 includes a requirement to describe management's responsibility for the preparation and fair presentation of the financial statements in more detail than what was required in the extant standards. The description includes an explanation that management is responsible for the preparation and fair presentation of the financial statements in accordance with the applicable financial reporting framework and that this responsibility includes the design, implementation, and maintenance of internal control relevant to the preparation and fair presentation of financial statements that are free from material misstatement, whether due to fraud or error. This clarified standard also includes the use of headings throughout the auditor's report to clearly distinguish each section of the report.

AU-C section 706 introduces and describes

- an *emphasis-of-matter* as a paragraph included in the auditor's report that refers to a matter appropriately presented or disclosed in the financial statements. An emphasis-of-matter paragraph would refer to any paragraph added to the auditor's report that relates to a matter that is appropriately presented or disclosed in

AAG-INV APP B

the financial statements. Some of these paragraphs are required by certain standards, whereas others are added at the discretion of the auditor, consistent with current practice. However, all such paragraphs are to be considered emphasis-of-matter paragraphs because they are intended to draw the users' attention to a particular matter.

- an *other-matter* as a paragraph included in the auditor's report that refers to a matter other than those presented or disclosed in the financial statements that, in the auditor's judgment, is relevant to the users' understanding of the audit, the auditor's responsibilities, or the auditor's report.

Accordingly, the term *explanatory paragraph* is no longer to be included in GAAS. Instead, additional communications in the auditor's report are labeled as either emphasis-of-matter or other-matter paragraphs. AU-C section 706 requires an emphasis-of-matter or other-matter paragraph to always follow the opinion paragraph and to be included in a separate section of the auditor's report under the heading "Emphasis of Matter" or "Other Matter."

AU-C section 705 has no significant changes from the extant standard.[2]

AU-C section 700, 705, and 706 supersede AU section 410, *Adherence to Generally Accepted Accounting Principles* (AICPA, *Professional Standards*); paragraphs .01–.02 of AU section 530, *Dating of the Independent Auditor's Report* (AICPA, *Professional Standards*); and paragraphs .01–.11, .14–.15, .19–.32, .35–.52, .58–.70, and .74–.76 of AU section 508, *Reports on Audited Financial Statements* (AICPA, *Professional Standards*).

Part II: Primarily Clarifying Changes

The AU-C sections discussed in this part have primarily clarifying changes that are intended to explicitly state what may have been implicit in the extant standards, which, over time, resulted in diversity in practice. Certain of these clarified standards address management responsibilities that may need to be communicated to clients early in the planning stage. Some of these requirements may already be performed in practice, although not explicitly required by the extant standards. Most notably, certain of the new requirements shift the timing of certain requirements from the reporting stage of an audit to the planning stage. The new requirements in this section may not have a substantial impact but may result in adjustments to the timing and responsibilities of the auditor and his or her clients and will need to be reviewed by the auditor to ensure that all requirements have been properly addressed.

B.06 Terms of Engagement

AU-C section 210 requires the auditor to establish an understanding regarding services to be performed for each engagement (new and continuing) and to document that understanding through a written communication with the client.

---

[2] Although AU-C section 705, *Modifications to the Opinion in the Independent Auditor's Report* (AICPA, *Professional Standards*), is discussed here with the other AU-C section 700, *Forming an Opinion and Reporting on Financial Statements* (AICPA, *Professional Standards*), reporting sections, it primarily contains formatting changes and, thus, if separately categorized, would not be included in part I.

Financial Reporting Framework

The clarified standard requires the auditor to determine whether the financial reporting framework to be applied in the preparation of the financial statements is acceptable. The auditor's responsibility for determining the acceptability of the applicable financial reporting framework, which is necessary in order to express an opinion on the financial statements, has been implicit in GAAS. It is appropriate that this determination be performed in conjunction with accepting the engagement.

The clarified standard requires the auditor to obtain management's agreement that it acknowledges and understands its responsibility for selecting the appropriate financial reporting framework, establishing and maintaining internal control, and providing access and information to the auditor. The extant standard requires the auditor to establish an understanding with management that includes management's responsibilities, including the selection and application of financial reporting, establishing and maintaining internal control, and making all financial records and related information available to the auditor as matters that may be included in the understanding established with the client. Thus, a level of detail that is suggested in the extant standard is now a requirement. The ASB believes that it is appropriate to require that management's responsibilities be explicit in the engagement letter because there is no point in starting an audit if management won't acknowledge its responsibilities.

Imposed Limitation on the Scope

If management or those charged with governance of an entity that is not required by law or regulation to have an audit impose a limitation on the scope of the auditor's work in the terms of a proposed audit engagement such that the auditor believes that the limitation will result in the auditor disclaiming an opinion on the financial statements as a whole, the auditor should not accept such a limited engagement as an audit engagement unless the audit is required by law or regulation. AU-C section 210 requires that, unless required by law or regulation to do so, the auditor should not accept the engagement if the auditor has determined that the applicable financial reporting framework is not acceptable or if the agreement with management that it acknowledges and understands its responsibility for selecting the appropriate financial reporting framework has not been obtained. Existing GAAS does not contain these requirements. Thus, these changes in requirements will affect current practice.

Recurring Audits

For recurring audits, the clarified standard requires the auditor to assess whether circumstances require the terms of the audit engagement to be revised. If the auditor concludes that the terms of the engagement need not be revised, the auditor should remind the entity of the terms of the engagement by means of a new engagement letter or a reminder, either written or oral, that the responsibilities in the previous terms of engagement still apply. The extant standard requires that the auditor should establish an understanding with the client for each engagement, which, in practice, may not result in a reminder each year for recurring audits. AU-C section 210 also requires that the reminder, which may be written or oral, should be documented. These requirements may affect current practice, depending on how the extant standard has been interpreted.

AAG-INV APP B

Changing Level of Assurance

AU-C section 210 addresses situations in which the auditor is requested to change the audit engagement to an engagement that conveys a lower level of assurance. These situations are addressed in Statements on Standards for Accounting and Review Services; thus, including these requirements in GAAS will not affect current practice.

Legal or Regulatory Requirements to the Auditor's Report

Additionally, AU-C section 210 addresses situations in which the law or regulations prescribe the layout or wording of the auditor's report in a form or in terms that are significantly different from the requirements of GAAS. Extant standards require that, in such circumstances, the auditor reword the prescribed form or attach a separate report. AU-C section 210 includes the explicit requirement that if the auditor determines that rewording the prescribed form or attaching a separate report would not be permitted or would not mitigate the risk of users misunderstanding the auditor's report, the auditor should not accept the engagement. Thus, this change in requirement may affect current practice.

AU-C section 210 supersedes paragraphs .05–.10 of AU section 311, *Planning and Supervision* (AICPA, *Professional Standards*), and paragraphs .03, .05–.10, and .14 of AU section 315, *Communications Between Predecessor and Successor Auditors* (AICPA, *Professional Standards*).

B.07 Quality Control for Audit Engagements

AU-C section 220 contains requirements and application material that address specific responsibilities of the auditor regarding quality control procedures for an audit of financial statements. This clarified standard strengthens the requirements of the extant standard by making it easier for auditors to understand and apply those quality control procedures that apply to an audit of financial statements (the extant standards do not contain explicit requirements regarding quality control procedures). However, because these procedures are required by Statement on Quality Control Standards (SQCS) No. 7, *A Firm's System of Quality Control*, they should not affect current practice. SQCS No. 8, *A Firm's System of Quality Control (Redrafted)* (AICPA, *Professional Standards*, QC sec. 10A), superseded SQCS No. 7 on January 1, 2012, and no substantive differences exist between the two standards. One perceived change that may affect many firms is that SQCS No. 8 makes clear that monitoring has to include review of complete engagements; it cannot all come from preissuance reviews.

Quality control systems, policies, and procedures are the responsibility of the audit firm. AU-C section 220 specifies quality control procedures at the engagement level that assist the auditor in achieving the objectives of the quality control standards and addresses requirements for supervision in an audit that are included in the extant standard but have not been included in AU-C section 300, *Planning an Audit* (AICPA, *Professional Standards*).

AU-C section 220 supersedes AU section 161, *The Relationship of Generally Accepted Auditing Standards to Quality Control Standards* (AICPA, *Professional Standards*).

B.08 Using a Service Organization [Updates 2-4, 2-6, and 4-1]

AU-C section 402, *Audit Considerations Relating to an Entity Using a Service Organization* (AICPA, *Professional Standards*), makes certain changes to the auditor's report, adds new requirements for the auditor to conduct communications with client management about the service organization, and requires the auditor to evaluate the impact of certain matters to his or her audit procedures.

AU-C section 402 changes the extant standard in the following ways:

- A user organization is now known as a user *entity*.
- A user auditor is permitted to make reference to the work of a service auditor in the user auditor's report to explain a modification of the user auditor's opinion. In such circumstances, AU-C section 402 requires the user auditor's report to indicate that such reference does not diminish the user auditor's responsibility for that opinion. (As in the extant standard, the user auditor is prohibited from making reference to the work of a service auditor in a user auditor's report containing an unmodified opinion.)
- AU-C section 402 requires a user auditor to inquire of management of the user entity about whether the service organization has reported to the user entity any fraud, noncompliance with laws and regulations, or uncorrected misstatements. If so, it requires the user auditor to evaluate how such matters affect the nature, timing, and extent of the user auditor's further audit procedures.
- In determining the sufficiency and appropriateness of the audit evidence provided by a service auditor's report, the user auditor should be satisfied regarding the adequacy of the standards under which the service auditor's report was issued.

AU-C section 402 contains guidance only for user auditors. Guidance for service auditors is contained in Statement on Standards for Attestation Engagements No. 16, *Reporting on Controls at a Service Organization* (AICPA, *Professional Standards*, AT sec. 801).

AU-C section 402 supersedes AU section 324, *Service Organizations* (AICPA, *Professional Standards*).

B.09 Audit Evidence-Specific Considerations

AU-C section 501, *Audit Evidence—Specific Considerations for Selected Items* (AICPA, *Professional Standards*), combines the requirements and guidance from extant AU sections 331, *Inventories*; 332, *Auditing Derivative Instruments, Hedging Activities, and Investments in Securities*; and 337, *Inquiry of a Client's Lawyer Concerning Litigation, Claims, and Assessments* (AICPA, *Professional Standards*).[3]

---

[3] Many of the requirements of extant AU section 332, *Auditing Derivative Instruments, Hedging Activities and Investments in Securities* (AICPA, *Professional Standards*), are essentially the same as requirements in other clarified standards, primarily AU-C section 540, *Auditing Accounting Estimates, Including Fair Value Accounting Estimates, and Related Disclosures* (AICPA, *Professional Standards*), and the suite of standards known as the risk assessment standards, which includes AU-C sections 501, *Audit Evidence—Specific Considerations for Selected Items*; 320, *Materiality in Planning and Performing an Audit*; 450, *Evaluation of Misstatements Identified During the Audit*; 300, *Planning an Audit*; 315, *Understanding the Entity and Its Environment and Assessing the Risks of Material Misstatement*; and 330, *Performing Audit Procedures in Response to Assessed Risks and Evaluating the Audit Evidence Obtained* (AICPA, *Professional Standards*).

(continued)

AU-C section 501 takes a more principles-based approach to determining whether to seek direct communication with the entity's lawyers than the extant standard. It requires the auditor to seek direct communication with the entity's external legal counsel (through a letter of inquiry) only if the auditor assesses a risk of material misstatement regarding litigation or claims or when audit procedures performed indicate that material litigation or claims may exist. (Extant AU section 337 states, in part, that "the auditor should request the client's management to send a letter of inquiry to those lawyers with whom management consulted concerning litigation, claims, and assessments.") AU-C section 501 requires the auditor to document the basis for any determination not to seek direct communication with the entity's legal counsel.

Requirements and guidance addressing auditing investments accounted for using the equity method have been excluded from AU-C section 501 because the auditing of equity investees is addressed more broadly by AU-C section 600.

AU-C section 501 supersedes AU sections 331; 332; 337; 337A, *Appendix—Illustrative Audit Inquiry Letter to Legal Counsel*; and 337C, *Exhibit II—American Bar Association Statement of Policy Regarding Lawyers' Responses to Auditors' Requests for Information* (AICPA, *Professional Standards*), and rescinds AU sections 337B, *Exhibit I—Excerpts From Financial Accounting Standards Board* Accounting Standards Codification 450, *Contingencies*, and 901, *Public Warehouses—Controls and Auditing Procedures for Goods Held* (AICPA, *Professional Standards*).

B.10 External Confirmations [Update 2-5]

AU-C section 505, *External Confirmations* (AICPA, *Professional Standards*), provides additional application material regarding the use of oral responses to confirmation requests as audit evidence. The extant standard notes that an oral confirmation should be documented, implying that it is acceptable to have an oral confirmation. AU-C section 505 requires the auditor to obtain written confirmations; additional audit procedures may be necessary in order to meet this requirement. For example, the auditor may need to send additional confirmation follow-ups to avoid additional audit work.

Although AU-C section 505 provides guidance regarding the use of oral responses to confirmation requests as audit evidence, it specifically clarifies that the receipt of an oral response to a confirmation request does not meet the definition of an *external confirmation*. It provides guidance on how the response may be considered part of alternative procedures performed in order to obtain sufficient appropriate audit evidence.

AU-C section 505 also addresses the responsibilities of the auditor when management refuses to allow the auditor to send a confirmation request. These responsibilities include communicating with those charged with governance if the auditor concludes that management's refusal is unreasonable or if the

---

(footnote continued)

The Auditing Standards Board concluded that the application of those requirements in the other clarified standards to the subject matter addressed by the extant standard is most appropriately addressed as interpretive guidance in the Audit Guide *Auditing Derivative Instruments, Hedging Activities, and Investments in Securities.* Consideration of these requirements and related application guidance will be a specific focus in updating the Audit Guide.

Guidance Updates—Clarified Auditing Standards **457**

auditor is unable to obtain relevant and reliable audit evidence from alternative audit procedures. These procedures are not required by the extant standard.

In AU-C section 505, the definition of *external confirmation* includes audit evidence obtained by electronic or other medium (for example, through the auditor's direct access to information held by a third party). AU-C section 505 also clarifies the following in regard to such:

- Access to the information must come from the third party.
- Access provided by management to the auditor does not meet the definition of an *external confirmation*.
- Even when audit evidence is received from external sources, the auditor must consider the risk that the electronic confirmation process is not secure or is improperly controlled.

The presumptively mandatory requirement in the extant standard to confirm accounts receivable is included in AU-C section 330, *Performing Audit Procedures in Response to Assessed Risks and Evaluating the Audit Evidence Obtained* (AICPA, *Professional Standards*). The requirement is placed in that clarified standard because it is part of the process of determining the appropriate audit procedures to perform. AU-C section 505 presumes that the auditor has already determined that an external confirmation is the appropriate audit procedure.

AU-C section 505 supersedes AU section 330, *The Confirmation Process* (AICPA, *Professional Standards*).

B.11 Opening Balances on Initial and Reaudit Engagements

AU-C section 510, *Opening Balances—Initial Audit Engagements, Including Reaudit Engagements* (AICPA, *Professional Standards*), strengthens existing standards by making clear that reviewing a predecessor auditor's audit documentation cannot be the only procedure performed to obtain sufficient appropriate audit evidence regarding opening balances, and it clarifies that initial audit engagements include reaudits.

Although the extant standards do not explicitly state that reviewing a predecessor auditor's audit documentation is all that needs to be performed to obtain sufficient appropriate audit evidence regarding opening balances, the ASB felt that this clarification needed to be made because the perception of many auditors is that this procedure alone is sufficient.

AU-C section 510 incorporates guidance from ISA 510, *Initial Audit Engagements—Opening Balances*, which requires the auditor to obtain sufficient appropriate audit evidence about whether

 a. opening balances contain misstatements that materially affect the current period's financial statements, and
 b. accounting policies reflected in the opening balances have been consistently applied in the current period's financial statements and whether changes in the accounting policies have been properly accounted for and adequately presented and disclosed in accordance with the applicable financial reporting framework.

AU-C section 510 supersedes paragraphs .01–.02, .04, .11–.13, and .15–.23 of AU section 315.

B.12 Using the Work of An Auditor's Specialist [Update 2-6]

AU-C section 620, *Using the Work of an Auditor's Specialist* (AICPA, *Professional Standards*), is expected to affect current practice because it creates incremental documentation requirements. The extant standard on this topic specifically scopes out from the standard the use of specialists employed by the firm who participate in the audit; however, the clarified standard encompasses these in-house firm specialists.

The extant standard also provides requirements and guidance addressing the use of management's specialist. They have now been included in AU-C section 501 under the view that audit evidence produced by management's experts (internal or external) needs to be evaluated by the auditor for relevance and reliability like any other audit evidence.

AU-C section 620 supersedes AU section 336, *Using the Work of a Specialist* (AICPA, *Professional Standards*).

B.13 Consistency of Financial Statements

AU-C section 708, *Consistency of Financial Statements* (AICPA, *Professional Standards*), requires the auditor to compare and evaluate changes and material reclassifications of prior year financial statements to possible changes in accounting principle or adjustment to correct an error in previously issued financial statements. It also requires the auditor to evaluate a material change in financial statement classification and the related disclosure to determine whether such a change is also either a change in accounting principle or an adjustment to correct a material misstatement in previously issued financial statements. If so, the requirements in the clarified standard apply.

AU-C section 708 also recognizes that the applicable financial reporting framework usually sets forth the method of accounting for accounting changes; therefore, the references to accounting guidance previously included in the extant standard have not been included.

Furthermore, to reflect a more principles-based approach to standard setting, certain requirements that are duplicative of broader requirements in the extant standard are included in the "Application and Other Explanatory Material" section in AU-C section 708.

AU-C section 708 supersedes AU section 420, *Consistency of Application of Generally Accepted Accounting Principles* (AICPA, *Professional Standards*).

B.14 Special Purpose Frameworks

AU-C section 800 replaces *OCBOA* with *special purpose framework* and provides additional requirements for the auditor in addressing special considerations in the application of the standards to an audit of financial statements prepared in accordance with a special purpose framework.

Special purpose frameworks are limited to cash, tax, regulatory, or contractual bases of accounting, commonly referred to as OCBOAs. The term *OCBOA* is replaced with the term *special purpose framework*, which no longer includes a definite set of criteria having substantial support that is applied to all material items appearing in financial statements.

The clarified standard requires

- the auditor to obtain an understanding of the purpose for which the financial statements are prepared, the intended users, and the steps taken by management to determine that the special purpose framework is acceptable in the circumstances.

- the auditor to obtain management's agreement that it acknowledges and understands its responsibility to include all informative disclosures that are appropriate for the special purpose framework used to prepare the financial statements, including, but not limited to, additional disclosures beyond those required by the applicable financial reporting framework that may be necessary to achieve fair presentation, and to evaluate whether such disclosures are necessary.

- the auditor, in the case of special purpose financial statements prepared in accordance with a contractual basis of accounting, to obtain an understanding of any significant interpretations of the contract that management made in the preparation of those financial statements and to evaluate whether the financial statements adequately describe such interpretations.

- the auditor to provide the explanation of management's responsibility for the financial statements in the auditor's report and to make reference to management's responsibility for determining that the applicable financial reporting framework is acceptable in the circumstances when management has a choice of financial reporting frameworks in the preparation of the financial statements.

- the auditor's report, in the case of financial statements prepared in accordance with a regulatory or contractual basis of accounting, to describe the purpose for which the financial statements are prepared or to refer to a note in the special purpose financial statements that contains that information.

- the auditor's report to include an emphasis-of-matter paragraph under an appropriate heading that, among other things, states that the special purpose framework is a basis of accounting other than GAAP.

- the auditor's report to include specific elements if the auditor is required by law or regulation to use a specific layout, form, or wording of the auditor's report.

AU-C section 800 supersedes AU section 544, *Lack of Conformity With Generally Accepted Accounting Principles* (AICPA, *Professional Standards*), and AU section 623, *Special Reports* (AICPA, *Professional Standards*), except paragraphs .19–.21.

B.15 Single Financial Statements and Specific Elements, Accounts, or Items

AU-C section 805, *Special Considerations—Audits of Single Financial Statements and Specific Elements, Accounts, or Items of a Financial Statement* (AICPA, *Professional Standards*), changes certain implicit requirements from the extant standards to explicit requirements, such as determining whether the audit is practicable and whether the auditor is able to perform procedures on interrelated items. It also provides certain new requirements for standalone statements regarding the type of opinion permitted in regard to the opinion issued on the complete set of financial statements.

460 Investment Companies

AU-C section 805 addresses special considerations in the application of GAAS to an audit of a single financial statement or of a specific element, account, or item of a financial statement. It does not apply to a component auditor's report issued as a result of work performed on the financial information of a component at the request of a group engagement team for purposes of an audit of group financial statements. It explains that a single financial statement and specific element include the related notes, which ordinarily comprise a summary of significant accounting policies and other relevant explanatory information.

The clarified standard

- requires the auditor, if the auditor is not also engaged to audit the entity's complete set of financial statements, to determine whether the audit of a single financial statement or specific element is practicable and to determine whether the auditor will be able to perform procedures on interrelated items. In the case of an audit of a specific element that is, or is based upon, the entity's stockholders' equity or net income (or the equivalents thereto), it requires the auditor to perform procedures necessary to obtain sufficient appropriate audit evidence about the financial position or results of operations, respectively.

- requires the auditor to obtain an understanding of the purpose for which the single financial statement or specific element is prepared, the intended users, and the steps taken by management to determine that the application of the applicable financial reporting framework is acceptable in the circumstances.

- requires the auditor to determine the acceptability of the financial reporting framework, including whether its application will result in a presentation that provides adequate disclosures to enable the intended users to understand the information conveyed and the effect of material transactions and events on such information.

- requires the auditor, if the auditor undertakes an engagement to audit a single financial statement or specific element in conjunction with an engagement to audit the complete set of financial statements, to issue a separate auditor's report and express a separate opinion for each engagement.

- requires the auditor, in the report on a specific element, to indicate the date of the auditor's report on the complete set of financial statements and, under an appropriate heading, the nature of the opinion expressed.

- permits, except as otherwise indicated, an audited single financial statement or a specific element to be published together with the audited complete set of financial statements, provided that the presentation of the single financial statement or specific element is sufficiently differentiated from the complete set of financial statements.

- requires the auditor, if the opinion in the auditor's report on the complete set of financial statements is modified, to determine the effect that this may have on the auditor's opinion on a single financial statement or specific element. In the case of an audit of a specific element, if the modified opinion is relevant to the audit of the specific element, it requires the auditor to

AAG-INV APP B

Guidance Updates—Clarified Auditing Standards 461

— express an adverse opinion on the specific element when the modification on the complete set of financial statements arises from a material misstatement.

— disclaim an opinion on the specific element when the modification on the complete set of financial statements arises from an inability to obtain sufficient appropriate audit evidence.

- permits the auditor, when it is necessary to express an adverse opinion or disclaim an opinion on the complete set of financial statements as a whole, but in the context of a separate audit of a specific element, the auditor, nevertheless, considers it appropriate to express an unmodified opinion on that element, to express or disclaim such an opinion only if

— that opinion is expressed in an auditor's report that is neither published together with, nor otherwise accompanies, the auditor's report containing the adverse opinion or disclaimer of opinion, and

— the specific element does not constitute a major portion of the complete set of financial statements, or the specific element is not, or is not based upon, the entity's stockholders' equity or net income or the equivalent.

- prohibits the auditor from expressing an unmodified opinion on a single financial statement if the auditor expressed an adverse opinion or disclaimed an opinion on the complete set of financial statements as a whole.

- requires the auditor, if the auditor's report on the complete set of financial statements includes an emphasis-of-matter or other-matter paragraph that is relevant to the audit of the single financial statement or specific element, to include a similar emphasis-of-matter paragraph or other-matter paragraph in the auditor's report on the single financial statement or specific element.

- permits the auditor to report on an incomplete presentation but one that is otherwise in accordance with GAAP by including an emphasis-of-matter paragraph in the auditor's report that states the purpose for which the presentation is prepared; refers to the note that describes the basis of presentation; and indicates that the presentation is not intended to be a complete presentation of the entity's assets, liabilities, revenues, or expenses.

AU-C section 805 supersedes paragraphs .33–.34 of AU section 508 and paragraphs .11–.18 of AU section 623.

B.16 Summary Financial Statements

AU-C section 810, *Engagements to Report on Summary Financial Statements* (AICPA, *Professional Standards*), addresses the auditor's responsibilities when reporting on summary financial statements derived from financial statements audited by that same auditor. This clarified standard puts certain restrictions on auditors for reporting on summary financial statements, including new requirements for the auditor in relation to the use of information issued by other auditors, the use of information provided by management, and obtaining

AAG-INV APP B

certain representations from management. Additionally, an auditor cannot report on summary financial statements that the auditor has not audited.

AU-C section 810

- eliminates reporting on selected financial data.
- introduces the notion of criteria for preparing summary financial statements and requires the auditor to determine whether the criteria applied by management in the preparation of the summary financial statements are acceptable.
- requires the auditor to obtain management's agreement that it acknowledges and understands its responsibilities for the summary financial statements, including its responsibility to make the audited financial statements readily available to the intended users of the summary financial statements.
- establishes that being available upon request is not considered readily available.
- establishes specific procedures to be performed as the basis for the auditor's opinion on the summary financial statements.
- establishes specific elements of the auditor's report, including management's responsibility and a description of the auditor's procedures.
- requires the auditor to request management to provide, in the form of a representation letter addressed to the auditor, written representations relating to the summary financial statements.
- requires the auditor's opinion to state that the summary financial statements are consistent, in all material respects, with the audited financial statements from which they have been derived, in accordance with the applied criteria, when the auditor has concluded that an unmodified opinion on the summary financial statements is appropriate. The extant standard requires the auditor's opinion to state whether the information set forth in the summary financial statements is fairly presented, in all material respects, in relation to the complete set of financial statements from which it has been derived.
- requires the auditor to withdraw from the engagement, when withdrawal is possible under applicable law or regulation, when the auditor's report on the audited financial statements contains an adverse opinion or a disclaimer of opinion. Otherwise, AU-C section 810 requires the auditor to state in the report that it is inappropriate to express, and the auditor does not express, an opinion on the summary financial statements.
- clarifies the auditor's responsibilities related to subsequent events and subsequently discovered facts when the date of the auditor's report on the summary financial statements is later than the date of the auditor's report on the audited financial statements.
- includes specific requirements relating to comparatives, unaudited information presented with summary financial statements, and other information included in a document containing the summary financial statements and related auditor's report.

- addresses the auditor's responsibilities as they relate to the auditor's association with summary financial statements.

AU-C section 810 supersedes AU section 552, *Reporting on Condensed Financial Statements and Selected Financial Data* (AICPA, *Professional Standards*).

B.17 Restricted-Use Alert

AU-C section 905, *Alert That Restricts the Use of the Auditor's Written Communication* (AICPA, *Professional Standards*), applies to auditor's reports and other written communications (hereinafter referred to as *written communications*) issued in connection with an engagement conducted in accordance with GAAS.

It establishes an umbrella requirement to include an alert that restricts the use of the auditor's written communication when the subject matter of that communication is based on

- measurement or disclosure criteria that are determined by the auditor to be suitable only for a limited number of users who can be presumed to have an adequate understanding of the criteria,
- measurement or disclosure criteria that are available only to the specified parties, or
- matters identified or communicated by the auditor during the course of the engagement that are not the primary objective of the engagement (commonly referred to as a *by-product of the audit*).

The appendix to AU-C section 905 lists other standards that contain requirements for such an alert in accordance with the aforementioned umbrella requirements.

The alert language in AU-C section 905, which indicates that the communication is solely for the information and use of the specified parties, is consistent with the extant standard, except when the engagement is also performed in accordance with *Government Auditing Standards*, and the written communication pursuant to that engagement is required by law or regulation to be made publicly available. In this circumstance, the alert language describes the purpose of the communication and states that the communication is not intended to be and should not be used for any other purpose. No specified parties are identified in this type of alert.

AU-C section 905 also modifies the guidance pertaining to single combined reports covering both communications that are required to include an alert regarding the intended use and communications that are for general use, which do not ordinarily include such an alert. The extant standard states that if an auditor issues a single combined report, the use of a single combined report should be restricted to the specified parties. AU-C section 905, however, indicates that the alert regarding the intended use pertains only to the communications required to include such an alert. Accordingly, the intended use of the communications that are for general use is not affected by this alert.

AU-C section 905 does not include a requirement, as required by the extant standard, for the auditor to consider informing his or her client that restricted-use reports are not intended for distribution to nonspecified parties, and it makes clear that an auditor is not responsible for controlling the distribution of the written communication. The alert required by AU-C section 905 is designed to avoid misunderstandings related to the use of the written communication, particularly when taken out of the context in which it is intended to be used. An auditor may consider informing the entity that the written communication is not intended for distribution to parties other than those specified in the written communication.

AU-C section 905 supersedes AU section 532, *Restricting the Use of an Auditor's Report* (AICPA, *Professional Standards*).

B.18 Financial Reporting Framework Accepted in Another Country

AU-C section 910, *Financial Statements Prepared in Accordance With a Financial Reporting Framework Generally Accepted in Another Country* (AICPA, *Professional Standards*), requires the auditor to obtain an understanding of a relevant financial reporting framework generally accepted in another country and relevant auditing standards other than GAAS. The extant standard indicates that the auditor should consider consulting with persons having expertise in auditing and accounting standards of another country. The ASB believes that the consideration of consulting with persons having expertise in auditing and accounting standards should not be a requirement; therefore, this extant standard requirement has been converted to application material in the clarified standard.

AU-C section 910 eliminates the concept of limited use and, in instances when a report that is to be used in the United States is prepared in accordance with a financial reporting framework generally accepted in another country, requires the auditor to include an emphasis-of-matter paragraph highlighting the foreign financial reporting framework and permits the auditor to express an unqualified opinion. The extant standard requires the auditor to report using the U.S. form of report, modified as appropriate (qualified or adverse), because of departures from U.S. GAAP, if financial statements prepared in accordance with a financial reporting framework generally accepted in another country would have more than limited use in the United States. The extant standard further requires that when the financial statements would not have more than limited use in the United States, the auditor's report may include, as appropriate, an opinion only with respect to the financial reporting framework generally accepted in the other country (and no opinion relative to U.S. GAAP).

AU-C section 910 supersedes AU section 534, *Reporting on Financial Statements Prepared for Use in Other Countries* (AICPA, *Professional Standards*).

Appendix C

Mapping and Summarization of Changes — Clarified Auditing Standards

This appendix maps the extant[1] AU sections to the clarified AU-C sections. As a result of the Auditing Standards Board's (ASB's) Clarity Project, all extant AU sections have been modified. In some cases, individual AU sections have been revised into individual clarified standards. In other cases, some AU sections have been grouped together and revised as one or more clarified standards. In addition, the ASB revised the AU section number order established by Statement on Auditing Standards No. 1, *Responsibilities and Functions of the Independent Auditor* (AICPA, *Professional Standards*, AU sec. 110), to follow the same number order used in International Standards on Auditing (ISAs) for all clarified AU sections for which there are comparable ISAs. The clarified standards are effective for periods ending on or after December 15, 2012. Early adoption is not permitted.

Although the Clarity Project was not intended to create additional requirements, some revisions have resulted in changes that may require auditors to make adjustments in their practices. To assist auditors in the transition process, these changes have been organized into the following four types:

- Substantive changes
- Primarily clarifying changes
- Primarily formatting changes
- Standards not yet issued in the Clarity Project

This appendix identifies those AU-C sections associated with these four types of changes.

Substantive Changes

Substantive changes are considered likely to affect the firms' audit methodology and engagements because they contain *substantive* or *other changes*, defined as having one or both of the following characteristics:

- A change or changes to an audit methodology that may require effort to implement
- A number of small changes that, although not individually significant, may affect audit engagements

Primarily Clarifying Changes

Primarily clarifying changes are intended to explicitly state what may have been implicit in the extant standards, which, over time, resulted in diversity in practice.

(continued)

---

[1] The term *extant* is used throughout this appendix in reference to the standards that are superseded by the clarified standards.

AAG-INV APP C

Primarily Formatting Changes

Primarily formatting changes from the extant standards do not contain changes that expand the extant sections in any significant way and may not require adjustments to current practice.

Standards Not Yet Issued in the Clarity Project

Standards not yet issued in the Clarity Project contain the remaining sections that are in exposure or have not yet been reworked.

The preface of this guide and the Financial Reporting Center at www.aicpa.org/FRC provide more information about the Clarity Project. You can also visit www.aicpa.org/SASClarity.

Extant AU Sections Mapped to the Clarified AU-C Sections

Extant AU Section		AU Section Superseded	New AU-C Section		Type of Change
110	Responsibilities and Functions of the Independent Auditor	All	200	Overall Objectives of the Independent Auditor and the Conduct of an Audit in Accordance With Generally Accepted Auditing Standards [1]	Primarily formatting changes
120	Defining Professional Requirements in Statements on Auditing Standards	All			
150	Generally Accepted Auditing Standards	All			
161	The Relationship of Generally Accepted Auditing Standards to Quality Control Standards	All	220	Quality Control for an Engagement Conducted in Accordance With Generally Accepted Auditing Standards	Primarily clarifying changes
201	Nature of the General Standards	All	200	Overall Objectives of the Independent Auditor and the Conduct of an Audit in Accordance With Generally Accepted Auditing Standards [1]	Primarily formatting changes
210	Training and Proficiency of the Independent Auditor	All			
220	Independence	All			
230	Due Professional Care in the Performance of Work	All			
311	Planning and Supervision	All except paragraphs .08–.10	300	Planning an Audit	Primarily formatting changes
		Paragraphs .08–.10	210	Terms of Engagement	Primarily clarifying changes

(continued)

Extant AU Sections Mapped to the Clarified AU-C Sections—*continued*

Extant AU Section		AU Section Superseded	New AU-C Section		Type of Change
312	Audit Risk and Materiality in Conducting an Audit	All	320	Materiality in Planning and Performing an Audit	Primarily formatting changes
			450	Evaluation of Misstatements Identified During the Audit	Primarily formatting changes
314	Understanding the Entity and Its Environment and Assessing the Risks of Material Misstatement	All	315	Understanding the Entity and Its Environment and Assessing the Risks of Material Misstatement	Primarily formatting changes
315	Communications Between Predecessor and Successor Auditors	All except paragraphs .03–.10 and .14	510	Opening Balances— Initial Audit Engagements, Including Reaudit Engagements	Primarily clarifying changes
		Paragraphs .03–.10 and .14	210	Terms of Engagement	Primarily clarifying changes
316	Consideration of Fraud in a Financial Statement Audit	All	240	Consideration of Fraud in a Financial Statement Audit	Primarily formatting changes
317	Illegal Acts by Clients	All	250	Consideration of Laws and Regulations in an Audit of Financial Statements	Substantive changes
318	Performing Audit Procedures in Response to Assessed Risks and Evaluating the Audit Evidence Obtained	All	330	Performing Audit Procedures in Response to Assessed Risks and Evaluating the Audit Evidence Obtained	Primarily formatting changes

Mapping and Summarization of Changes **469**

Extant AU Sections Mapped to the Clarified AU-C Sections—*continued*

Extant AU Section		AU Section Superseded	New AU-C Section		Type of Change
322	The Auditor's Consideration of the Internal Audit Function in an Audit of Financial Statements	All	Planned to be issued as AU-C section 610	The Auditor's Consideration of the Internal Audit Function in an Audit of Financial Statements	Standards not yet issued in the Clarity Project
324	Service Organizations	All	402	Audit Considerations Relating to an Entity Using a Service Organization	Primarily clarifying changes
325	Communicating Internal Control Related Matters Identified in an Audit	All	265	Communicating Internal Control Related Matters Identified in an Audit	Substantive changes
326	Audit Evidence	All	500	Audit Evidence	Primarily formatting changes
328	Auditing Fair Value Measurements and Disclosures	All	540	Auditing Accounting Estimates, Including Fair Value Accounting Estimates, and Related Disclosures [2]	Primarily formatting changes
329	Analytical Procedures	All	520	Analytical Procedures	Primarily formatting changes
330	The Confirmation Process	All	505	External Confirmations	Primarily clarifying changes
331	Inventories	All	501	Audit Evidence— Specific Considerations for Selected Items [3]	Primarily clarifying changes
332	Auditing Derivative Instruments, Hedging Activities, and Investments in Securities	All	501	Audit Evidence— Specific Considerations for Selected Items [3]	Primarily clarifying changes

(continued)

AAG-INV APP C

Extant AU Sections Mapped to the Clarified AU-C Sections—*continued*

Extant AU Section		AU Section Superseded	New AU-C Section		Type of Change
333	Management Representations	All	580	Written Representations	Primarily formatting changes
334	Related Parties	All	550	Related Parties	Substantive changes
336	Using the Work of a Specialist	All	620	Using the Work of an Auditor's Specialist	Primarily Clarifying Changes
337	Inquiry of a Client's Lawyer Concerning Litigation, Claims, and Assessments	All	501	Audit Evidence—Specific Considerations for Selected Items [3]	Primarily clarifying changes
339	Audit Documentation	All	230	Audit Documentation	Primarily formatting changes
341	The Auditor's Consideration of an Entity's Ability to Continue as a Going Concern	All	Planned to be issued as AU-C section 570	Going Concern (in exposure)	Standards not yet issued in the Clarity Project
342	Auditing Accounting Estimates	All	540	Auditing Accounting Estimates, Including Fair Value Accounting Estimates, and Related Disclosures [2]	Primarily formatting changes
350	Audit Sampling	All	530	Audit Sampling	Primarily formatting changes
380	The Auditor's Communication With Those Charged With Governance	All	260	The Auditor's Communication With Those Charged With Governance	Primarily formatting changes
390	Consideration of Omitted Procedures After the Report Date	All	585	Consideration of Omitted Procedures After the Report Release Date	Primarily formatting changes

Extant AU Sections Mapped to the Clarified AU-C Sections—*continued*

Extant AU Section		AU Section Super-seded	New AU-C Section		Type of Change
410	Adherence to Generally Accepted Accounting Principles	All	700	Forming an Opinion and Reporting on Financial Statements [4]	Substantive changes
420	Consistency of Application of Generally Accepted Accounting Principles	All	708	Consistency of Financial Statements	Primarily clarifying changes
431	Adequacy of Disclosure in Financial Statements	All	705	Modifications to the Opinion in the Independent Auditor's Report [5]	Primarily formatting changes
504	Association With Financial Statements	All	N/A	Withdrawn	

(continued)

AAG-INV APP C

Extant AU Sections Mapped to the Clarified AU-C Sections—*continued*

Extant AU Section		AU Section Superseded	New AU-C Section		Type of Change
508	Reports on Audited Financial Statements	Paragraphs .01–.11, .14–.15, .19–.32, .35–.52, .58–.70, and .74–.76	700	Forming an Opinion and Reporting on Financial Statements [4]	Substantive changes
			705	Modifications to the Opinion in the Independent Auditor's Report [5]	Primarily formatting changes
			706	Emphasis-of-Matter Paragraphs and Other-Matter Paragraphs in the Independent Auditor's Report [6]	Substantive changes
		Paragraphs .12–.13	600	Special Considerations—Audits of Group Financial Statements (Including the Work of Component Auditors)	Substantive changes
		Paragraphs .16–.18 and .53–.57	708	Consistency of Financial Statements	Primarily clarifying changes
		Paragraphs .33–.34	805	Special Considerations—Audits of Single Financial Statements and Specific Elements, Accounts, or Items of a Financial Statement	Primarily clarifying changes
		Paragraphs .71–.73	560	Subsequent Events and Subsequently Discovered Facts [7]	Primarily formatting changes

Extant AU Sections Mapped to the Clarified AU-C Sections—*continued*

Extant AU Section		AU Section Superseded	New AU-C Section		Type of Change
530	Dating of the Independent Auditor's Report	Paragraphs .01–.02	700	Forming an Opinion and Reporting on Financial Statements [4]	Substantive changes
		Paragraphs .03–.08	560	Subsequent Events and Subsequently Discovered Facts [7]	Primarily formatting changes
532	Restricting the Use of an Auditor's Report	All	905	Alert That Restricts the Use of the Auditor's Written Communication	Primarily clarifying changes
534	Reporting on Financial Statements Prepared for Use in Other Countries	All	910	Financial Statements Prepared in Accordance With a Financial Reporting Framework Generally Accepted in Another Country	Primarily clarifying changes
543	Part of Audit Performed by Other Independent Auditors	All	600	Special Considerations—Audits of Group Financial Statements (Including the Work of Component Auditors)	Substantive changes
544	Lack of Conformity With Generally Accepted Accounting Principles	All	800	Special Considerations—Audits of Financial Statements Prepared in Accordance With Special Purpose Frameworks [8]	Primarily clarifying changes
550	Other Information in Documents Containing Audited Financial Statements	All	720	Other Information in Documents Containing Audited Financial Statements	Primarily formatting changes

(continued)

AAG-INV APP C

Extant AU Sections Mapped to the Clarified AU-C Sections—*continued*

Extant AU Section		AU Section Super-seded	New AU-C Section		Type of Change
551	Supplementary Information in Relation to the Financial Statements as a Whole	All	725	Supplementary Information in Relation to the Financial Statements as a Whole	Primarily formatting changes
552	Reporting on Condensed Financial Statements and Selected Financial Data	All	810	Engagements to Report on Summary Financial Statements	Primarily clarifying changes
558	Required Supplementary Information	All	730	Required Supplementary Information	Primarily formatting changes
560	Subsequent Events	All	560	Subsequent Events and Subsequently Discovered Facts [7]	Primarily formatting changes
561	Subsequent Discovery of Facts Existing at the Date of the Auditor's Report	All			

AAG-INV APP C

Mapping and Summarization of Changes

Extant AU Sections Mapped to the Clarified AU-C Sections—*continued*

Extant AU Section		AU Section Superseded		New AU-C Section	Type of Change
623	Special Reports	Paragraphs .19–.21	806	Reporting on Compliance With Aspects of Contractual Agreements or Regulatory Requirements in Connection With Audited Financial Statements	Primarily formatting changes
		Paragraphs .01–.10 and .22–.34	800	Special Considerations— Audits of Financial Statements Prepared in Accordance With Special Purpose Frameworks [8]	Primarily clarifying changes
		Paragraphs .11–.18	805	Special Considerations— Audits of Single Financial Statements and Specific Elements, Accounts, or Items of a Financial Statement	Primarily clarifying changes
625	Reports on the Application of Accounting Principles	All	915	Reports on Application of Requirements of an Applicable Financial Reporting Framework	Primarily formatting changes
634	Letters for Underwriters and Certain Other Requesting Parties	All	920	Letters for Underwriters and Certain Other Requesting Parties	Primarily formatting changes
711	Filings Under Federal Securities Statutes	All	925	Filings With the U.S. Securities and Exchange Commission Under the Securities Act of 1933	Primarily formatting changes

(continued)

AAG-INV APP C

Extant AU Sections Mapped to the Clarified AU-C Sections—*continued*

Extant AU Section		AU Section Superseded	New AU-C Section		Type of Change
722	Interim Financial Information	All	930	Interim Financial Information	Primarily formatting changes
801	Compliance Audits	All	935	Compliance Audits	Primarily formatting changes
901	Public Warehouses—Controls and Auditing Procedures for Goods Held	All	501	Audit Evidence—Specific Considerations for Selected Items [3]	Primarily clarifying changes

Legend:

[n] Bracketed number indicates a clarity standard that supersedes more than one extant AU section.

The AICPA has developed an Audit Risk Alert to assist auditors and members in practice prepare for the transition to the clarified standards. It has been organized to give you the background information on the development of the clarified standards and to identify the new requirements and changes from the extant standards. Check out the Audit Risk Alert *Understanding the Clarified Auditing Standards* (product no. ARACLA12P), which is available in the AICPA store on www.cpa2biz.com.

Appendix D

Venture Capital, Business Development Companies, and Small Business Investment Companies

As described by Financial Accounting Standards Board (FASB) *Accounting Standards Codification* (ASC) 946-10-05-6, venture capital investment companies, including most small business investment companies (SBICs), and business development companies differ in operating method from other types of investment companies. The usual open-end or closed-end company is a passive investor, whereas the venture capital investment company is more actively involved with its investees. In addition to providing funds, whether in the form of loans or equity, the venture capital investment company often provides technical and management assistance to its investees as needed and requested. The portfolio of a venture capital investment company may be illiquid by the very nature of the investments, which typically have no public market. Often, any gains on those investments are realized over a relatively long holding period. The nature of the investments, therefore, requires valuation procedures that differ markedly from those used by the typical investment company that is covered in this guide.

Venture capital investment companies may also incur liabilities not generally found in other investment companies, including certain debts or loans and might be able to use leverage more extensively.

Leverage opportunities available to the owners of SBICs are not available to open-end companies. SBICs, by statute, may borrow from the Small Business Administration (SBA), often at advantageous rates, up to two or three times their paid-in capital.

As stated by FASB ASC 946-20-45-7, although all venture capital investment companies should prepare their financial statements in conformity with U.S. generally accepted accounting principles (GAAP), the statement presentation of some venture capital investment companies may need to be tailored to present the information in a manner most meaningful to their particular group of investors. For example, if debt is a significant item, a conventional balance sheet might be more appropriate than a statement of net assets.

Also, different regulatory requirements may apply to these entities. Publicly owned SBICs are subject to the provisions of Article 5 of Regulation S-X, whereas other publicly owned venture capital investment companies are subject to Article 6.

As noted by FASB ASC 946-20-45-6, the unique features (primarily the existence of significant debt) of SBICs often make it desirable that their financial statements be presented in a conventional balance sheet format.

SBICs are regulated by the SBA and, accordingly, are required to comply with Part 107 of the SBA rules and regulations. Part 107 deals with specific aspects of SBA regulation, such as the relevant audit procedures and reporting requirements (for example, on Form 468) of the SBA for SBICs; the system of account classification; and guidance on proper techniques and standards to be followed in valuing portfolios. SBA guidelines on valuing portfolio investments may not be in accordance with FASB ASC 820, *Fair Value Measurement*.

478 Investment Companies

The auditor of an SBIC should be familiar with the relevant publications and aware of changes in SBA regulations.[1]

The format for reporting the results of SBIC operations varies from that presented in this guide for other types of investment companies because the financial statements for SBICs are presented based on regulations promulgated by the SBA, which is a comprehensive basis of accounting other than GAAP. SBICs may consider maintaining separate accounting records for GAAP and SBA reporting purposes.

---

[1] This guide primarily discusses auditing guidance issued by the Auditing Standards Board that applies to nonissuers. Issuers are defined by Section 3 of the Securities Exchange Act of 1934 and include registered investment companies. Audits of issuers are required to be performed under Public Company Accounting Oversight Board standards. Users should evaluate their audit engagements to determine which auditing standards are applicable.

AAG-INV APP D

Appendix E

Computation of Tax Amortization of Original Issue Discount, Market Discount, and Premium

Table 1
Amortization of Original Issue Discount

	Method of Amortization	Reporting of Amortization — On a Daily Basis	Reporting of Amortization — At Disposition	Characterization of Amortization — Capital Gain	Characterization of Amortization — Interest Income
Taxable obligations:					
Short term corporate obligations[1]	SL[2]	X			X
Long term corporate obligations					
Issued before 5/28/69	SL		X		X
Issued 5/28/69 – 7/1/82	SL	X			X
Issued after 7/1/82	YTM	X[3]			X
Short term government obligations[1]	SL[2]	X			X
Long term government obligations					
Issued before 7/2/82	SL		X		X
Issued after 7/1/82	YTM	X[3]			X
Tax-exempt obligations:					
Short term obligations[1]	SL[2]	X			X[4]
Long term obligations					
Issued prior to 9/4/82 and acquired prior to 3/2/84	SL	X			X[4]
All other acquisitions	YTM	X			X[4]

SL = Straight line (ratable)
YTM = Yield to maturity

[1] *Short term* is defined as having a maturity of not more than one year after the date of issue.

[2] An election may be made to use the yield-to-maturity method.

[3] The accrual period with respect to which the original issue discount is computed and compounded is a one-year period for obligations issued before January 1, 1985, and is a six month period for obligations issued after December 31, 1984.

[4] The amortization is characterized as tax-exempt interest.

AAG-INV APP E

Table 2
Amortization of Market Discount

	Method of Amortization	Reporting of Amortization — On a Daily Basis	Reporting of Amortization — At Disposition	Characterization of Amortization — Capital Gain	Characterization of Amortization — Interest Income
Taxable obligations:					
Short term obligations[1]					
Government obligations	SL[2]	X			X
Corporate obligations	YTM[3]	X			X
Long term obligations					
Issued after 7/18/84	SL[2]	[4]	X		X[5]
Issued before 7/19/84	N/A		X	X	
Tax-exempt obligations:					
Acquired on or before 4/30/93					
Long term	N/A				
Short term	N/A				
Acquired after 4/30/93					
Long term	SL[2]	[4]	X[6]		X[6]
Short term	N/A				

SL = Straight line (ratable)
YTM = Yield to maturity
N/A = Not applicable

[1] *Short term* is defined as having a maturity of not more than one year after the date of issue.

[2] An election may be made to use the yield-to-maturity method.

[3] An election may be made to use the straight-line method.

[4] An election may be made to report amortization currently as interest. The election would apply to all market discount bonds acquired on or after the first day of the taxable year in which the election is made.

[5] The amortization of the accrued discount is treated as interest income to the extent of the realized gain on disposition.

[6] Market discount amortization represents taxable income.

Table 3
Amortization of Premium

	Method of Amortization	Reporting of Amortization — On a Daily Basis	Reporting of Amortization — At Disposition	Characterization of Amortization — Nondeductible Expense	Characterization of Amortization — Offset to Interest Income
Taxable obligations:					
Obligations issued after 9/27/85					
If election is made to amortize	YTM	[1]			
If no election is made to amortize	N/A[5]				
Obligations issued before 9/28/85	[3]	[1]	X		X[2]
Tax-exempt obligations:					
Obligations issued after 9/27/85	YTM[4]	X			X
Obligations issued before 9/28/85	[3]	X		X	

YTM = Yield to maturity
N/A = Not applicable; no amortization needed

[1] An election is made to report amortization currently. Such will apply to all bonds held by the taxpayer at the beginning of the taxable year and to all bonds thereafter acquired by the taxpayer.

[2] For bonds acquired between October 23, 1986, and January 1, 1988, premium amortization is treated as interest expense.

[3] Any reasonable method of amortization may be used.

[4] The amortization should be computed by taking into account call dates and call prices.

[5] Premium is part of the tax basis of security and affects tax gain or loss on the disposition or maturity of the obligation.

Appendix F

Illustrative Financial Statement Presentation for Tax-Free Business Combinations of Investment Companies

The following financial statements and disclosures illustrate a tax-free business combination of investment companies (discussed in chapter 8, "Other Accounts and Considerations," of this guide), as illustrated in Technical Questions and Answers section 6910.33, "Certain Financial Reporting, Disclosure, Regulatory, and Tax Considerations When Preparing Financial Statements of Investment Companies Involved in a Business Combination" (AICPA, *Technical Practice Aids*). The illustrative notes are unique to a business combination. The exhibits assume that fund B merges into fund A as of the close of business on December 31, 20X4, and that both fund A and fund B have a January 31 fiscal year-end. Exhibit 1 presents the financial position of each fund immediately before the acquisition and the combined fund immediately after the acquisition. Exhibit 2 presents the results of operations and changes in net assets of each fund for the 11 month fiscal period immediately before the acquisition and the results of operations and summary changes in net assets information for the combined fund for the 1 month period subsequent to the acquisition. Exhibit 3 presents the statement of operations, statement of changes in net assets, and appropriate notes of the combined entity immediately after the acquisition. (The January 31, 20X5, statement of net assets of the combined entity is not presented because it will be identical in form to the December 31, 20X4, statement.)

Note: The illustrative financial statements and note disclosures included in this guide have been updated to reflect Financial Accounting Standards Board (FASB) *Accounting Standards Codification*™ (ASC). However, in FASB's notice to constituents, it suggests the use of plain English in financial statement note disclosures to describe broad FASB ASC topic references. FASB suggests a reference similar to "as required by the Derivatives and Hedging Topic of the FASB *Accounting Standards Codification*." Entities might consider revising their financial statement references to reflect this plain English referencing, rather than the use of specific FASB ASC references. We have provided these detailed references as a resource for our users.

Exhibit 1

Financial Position of Each Fund Immediately Before Acquisition

Statement of Net Assets
December 31, 20X4

	Fund A	Fund B
Investments in securities at fair value (Cost: Fund A—$18,000,000 Fund B—$9,000,000)	$20,000,000	$10,000,000
Other assets	1,000,000	500,000
	21,000,000	10,500,000
Liabilities	1,000,000	500,000
Net assets	$20,000,000	$10,000,000
Shares outstanding	2,000,000	1,000,000
Net asset value per share	$10.00	$10.00

Calculation of Exchange Ratio

Net assets of fund B	$10,000,000
Divided by fund A net asset value per share	10.00
Fund A shares issuable	**1,000,000**
Fund B shares outstanding	1,000,000
Exchange ratio (fund A shares issuable/fund B shares outstanding)	**1 for 1**

Financial Position of Combined Entity Immediately After Acquisition

Statement of Net Assets
December 31, 20X4

Investments in securities at fair value (Cost—$27,000,000)	$30,000,000
Other assets	1,500,000
	31,500,000
Liabilities	1,500,000
Net assets	$30,000,000
Shares outstanding	3,000,000
Net asset value per share	$10.00

Note: The individual components of net assets (paid-in capital, undistributed income and capital gains, and unrealized appreciation and depreciation) are not presented in this example but are similarly combined.

Exhibit 2

Statement of Operations
Eleven Months Ended December 31, 20X4

	Fund A	Fund B
Dividend and interest income	$3,200,000	$1,600,000
Management fee	100,000	50,000
Transfer agent fee	50,000	25,000
Other expenses	50,000	25,000
	200,000	100,000
Investment income—net	3,000,000	1,500,000
Realized and unrealized gain on investments		
Net realized gain on investments	1,000,000	500,000
Change in unrealized appreciation	1,000,000	500,000
Net realized and unrealized gain on investments	2,000,000	1,000,000
Net increase in net assets resulting from operations	$5,000,000	$2,500,000

Statement of Changes in Net Assets
Eleven Months Ended December 31, 20X4

	Fund A	Fund B
Increase (decrease) in net assets		
Operations		
Investment income—net	$3,000,000	$1,500,000
Net realized gain on investments	1,000,000	500,000
Change in unrealized appreciation	1,000,000	500,000
	5,000,000	2,500,000
Dividends to shareholders from		
Investment income—net	(3,000,000)	(1,500,000)
Net realized gain on investments	(1,000,000)	(500,000)
Capital share transactions	2,000,000	250,000
Total increase	3,000,000	750,000
Net assets		
Beginning of year	17,000,000	9,250,000
End of year	$20,000,000	$10,000,000

AAG-INV APP F

Exhibit 2—(continued)

Statement of Operations of Combined Entity
Month Ended January 31, 20X5

Dividend and interest income	$400,000
Management fee	15,000
Transfer agent fee	5,000
Other expenses	5,000
	25,000
Investment income—net	$375,000
Realized and unrealized gain on investments	
Net realized gain on investments	100,000
Change in unrealized appreciation	100,000
Net gain on investments	200,000
Net increase in net assets resulting from operations	$575,000

Other Changes in Net Assets Information
Month Ended January 31, 20X5

a. No dividends were paid during the month.
b. Capital shares transactions were as follows:

	Shares	Amount
Shares sold	20,000	$200,000
Shares redeemed	(10,000)	($100,000)
	10,000	$100,000

Exhibit 3

Statements of Operations and Changes in Net Assets of the Combined Entity Immediately After Acquisition

Fund A
Statement of Operations
Year Ended January 31, 20X5

Dividend and interest income ($3,200,000 + $400,000)		$3,600,000
Management fee ($100,000 + $15,000)	$115,000	
Transfer agent fee ($50,000 + $5,000)	55,000	
Other expenses ($50,000 + $5,000)	55,000	
		225,000
Investment income—net		3,375,000
Realized and unrealized gain on investments		
Net realized gain on investments ($1,000,000 + $100,000)	1,100,000	
Change in unrealized appreciation ($1,000,000 + $100,000)	1,100,000	
Net gain on investments		2,200,000
Net increase in net assets resulting from operations		$5,575,000

Fund A
Statement of Changes in Net Assets
Year Ended January 31, 20X5

	20X5	20X4
Increase (decrease) in net assets		
Operations		
Investment income—net	$ 3,375,000	$ 2,400,000
Net realized gain on investments	1,100,000	700,000
Change in unrealized appreciation	1,100,000	300,000
	5,575,000	3,400,000
Dividends to shareholders from		
Investment income—net	(3,000,000)	(2,400,000)
Net realized gain on investments	(1,000,000)	(700,000)
Capital share transactions (notes 6–7)	12,100,000	1,100,000
Total increase	13,675,000	1,400,000
Net assets		
Beginning of year	17,000,000	15,600,000
End of year	$30,675,000	$17,000,000

Exhibit 3—(continued)

Notes to Financial Statements of the Combined Entity Immediately After Acquisition

Note 6—Acquisition of Fund B[1]

On December 31, 20X4, fund A acquired all the net assets of fund B, an open-end investment company, pursuant to a plan of reorganization approved by fund B shareholders on December 26, 20X4. The purpose of the transaction was to combine two funds managed by Investment Adviser C with comparable investment objectives and strategies. The acquisition was accomplished by a tax-free exchange of 1 million shares of fund A, valued at $10 million, for 1 million shares of fund B outstanding on December 31, 20X4. The investment portfolio of fund B, with a fair value of $10 million and identified cost of $9 million at December 31, 20X4, was the principal asset acquired by fund A. For financial reporting purposes, assets received and shares issued by fund A were recorded at fair value; however, the cost basis of the investments received from fund B was carried forward to align ongoing reporting of fund A's realized and unrealized gains and losses with amounts distributable to shareholders for tax purposes.[2] Immediately prior to the merger, the net assets of fund A were $20 million.

Note: The following paragraph is only required for *public business entities*, as defined in the FASB ASC glossary. For purposes of this disclosure and consistent with "Pending Content" in FASB ASC 805-10-50-2(h), assume that, had the acquisition occurred on February 1, 20X4—the beginning of fund A's fiscal year—$10,000 of the transfer agent fee and $15,000 of other expenses—a total of $25,000—would have been eliminated.

---

[1] Financial Accounting Standards Board (FASB) *Accounting Standards Codification* (ASC) 805-10-50-2(h)(4) states that if the acquirer is a public business entity, the nature and amount of any material, nonrecurring pro forma adjustments directly attributable to the business combination(s) included in the reported pro forma revenue and earnings (supplemental pro forma information) should be disclosed. This additional disclosure requirement is a result of Accounting Standards Update No. 2010-29, *Business Combinations (Topic 805): Disclosure of Supplementary Pro Forma Information for Business Combinations (a consensus of the FASB Emerging Issues Task Force)*. The illustration provided does not include any material, nonrecurring pro forma adjustments; and thus, the additional disclosure is not required herein. However, readers should be aware such a disclosure would be necessary if a business combination did have material, nonrecurring pro forma adjustments.

[2] If material amounts of undistributed net investment income or undistributed realized gains are transferred to the acquirer, which the acquirer will be required to distribute, those amounts should also be disclosed. Material acquired loss carryovers should also be disclosed or cross referenced to related income tax disclosures.

Illustrative Financial Statement Presentation

Assuming the acquisition had been completed on February 1, 20X4, the beginning of the annual reporting period of fund A, fund A's pro forma results of operations for the year ended January 31, 20X5,[3] are as follows:

Net investment income	$4,900,000[4]
Net gain (loss) on investments	$3,200,000[5]
Net increase (decrease) in net assets resulting from operations	$8,100,000

Because the combined investment portfolios have been managed as a single integrated portfolio since the acquisition was completed, it is not practicable to separate the amounts of revenue and earnings of fund B that have been included in fund A's statement of operations since December 31, 20X4.

Note 7—Capital Share Transactions

As of January 31, 20X5, 100 million shares of $1 par value capital stock were authorized. Transactions in capital stock were as follows:

	Shares		Amount	
	20X5	*20X4*	*20X5*	*20X4*
Shares sold	520,000	300,000	$5,000,000	$3,000,000
Shares issued in connection with the acquisition of fund B	1,000,000		10,000,000	
Shares issued in the reinvestment of dividends	300,000	250,000	3,000,000	2,400,000
	1,820,000	550,000	18,000,000	5,400,000
Shares redeemed	610,000	450,000	5,900,000	4,300,000
Net increase	1,210,000	100,000	$12,100,000	$1,100,000

---

[3] "Pending Content" in FASB ASC 805-10-50-2 states that if the acquirer is a public business entity, and comparative financial statements are presented, supplemental pro forma information should be presented as if the business combination that occurred during the current year had occurred as of the beginning of the comparable prior annual reporting period. Investment companies should base the application of this provision on whether they are required to present comparative statements of operations in their financial statements. Typically, business development companies registered with the Securities and Exchange Commission are required to present comparative statements of operations, but other registered open-end and closed-end investment companies are not required to do so.

[4] As reported, $3,375,000 plus $1,500,000 fund B premerger plus $25,000 of pro-forma eliminated expenses.

[5] As reported, $2,200,000 plus $1,000,000 fund B premerger.

AAG-INV APP F

Appendix G

Illustrations for Separately Calculating and Disclosing the Foreign Currency Element of Realized and Unrealized Gains and Losses

Illustrations A and B apply if separate disclosures of the foreign currency elements of unrealized and realized gains and losses on investments are chosen by the reporting entity.

A. Purchases and Sales

ABC Fund uses US$ as its functional currency.

ABC buys 1,000 shares of XYZ @ £15.00 with a spot exchange rate of $1.75 = £1.00.

Foreign currency (FC) cost basis = £15.00 X 1,000 = £15,000

Functional currency cost basis = £15,000 X 1.75 = $26,250

Market gain/loss = (FC sale proceeds − FC cost) X foreign exchange (FX) rate on day of sale

Currency gain/loss = FC cost X (FX rate day of sale − FX rate day of purchase)

Assume a sale of 1,000 XYZ @ £12.00 and $1.50 = £1.00:

FC proceeds	= £12.00 X 1,000	= £12,000
Functional currency proceeds	= £12,000 X 1.50	= $18,000
Market loss	= (£12,000 − £15,000) X 1.50	= $(4,500)
Currency loss	= (£15,000 X 1.50 − 1.75)	= $(3,750)
Total loss		$(8,250)

Proof

Functional currency proceeds	$18,000
Functional currency cost	$(26,250)
	$(8,250)

B. Securities—Mark to Market

Day 1: *1,000 XYZ marked to market @ £16.00; spot rate: $1.85 = £1.00.*

Market gain/loss = (FC current market value − FC cost) X current FX rate

Currency gain/loss = FC cost X (current FX rate − FX rate on day of purchase)

Market gain	= (£16,000 − £15,000) X 1.85	= $1,850
Currency gain	= £15,000 X (1.85 − 1.75)	= $1,500
Total gain in functional currency		$3,350

Total gain − (£16,000 X 1.85) − (£15,000 X 1.75) = $29,600 − $26,250 = $3,350

Mark-to-Market Journal Entries

[Average rates may be used if fluctuations in exchange rates aren't significant]

Day 2: *1,000 XYZ marked to market @ £17.00; spot rate: $1.80 = £1.00.*

Market gain	= (£17,000 − £15,000) X 1.80	=	$3,600
Currency gain	= £15,000 X (1.80 − 1.75)	=	$ 750
Total functional currency gain			$4,350

Daily Journal Entries

Market gain/loss	= $3,600 − $1,850	=	$1,750
Currency gain/loss	= $750 − $1,500	=	($750)
Day 2 gain ($4,350 − $3,350)		=	$1,000

C. Other Assets/Liabilities—FX Mark to Market

Sale of 1,000 XYZ @ £ 12.00 = £12,000 receivable @ $1.50 = £1.00 = $18,000

Day 1: *Spot rate moves to $1.55 = £1.00.*
Currency gain = £12,000 X (1.55 − 1.50).05 = $600

Day 2: *Spot rate moves to $1.58 = £1.00.*
Currency gain = £12,000 X (1.58 − 1.50).08 = $960

	Day 1	Day 2
Currency gain		
Daily Journal Entry	$600	$360

D. Changes Between Trade and Settlement Dates[1]

Trade Date
Purchase 1,000 XYZ @ £15.00; exchange rate: $1.75 = £1.00.

Cost basis:	$26,250 or	£15,000
DR: sterling securities at cost	$26,250	
CR: payables for securities purchased		$26,250

Settlement Date
Spot rate: $1.80 = £1.00; £15,000 is purchased at the spot rate for $27,000.

DR: payables for securities purchased	$26,250	
DR realized currency gain/loss	$750	
CR: cash		$27,000

---

[1] The payable should be valued between the trade and settlement date such that the balance at the settlement date would equal the amount due at the foreign exchange price. There would also be unrealized gain or loss that would be converted to realized gain or loss upon settlement. It should not be assumed, based on this example, that the calculation of foreign currency gain or loss is only recognized on the settlement date.

E. Settlement Against Foreign Currency Cash Balances

£20,000 balance is available in London.

Lot a: £10,000 purchased @ $1.65 per £1.00
$US cost basis: $16,500

Lot b: £10,000 purchased @ $1.85 per £1.00
$US cost basis: $18,500

Assume lot b will be liquidated first at $1.80 per £1.00.
Lot b:
DR: cash	$18,000	
DR: realized currency gain/loss	$ 500	
CR: sterling cash at cost		$18,500

Assume one half of lot a will be liquidated at $1.80 per £1.00.
Lot a:
DR: cash	$9,000	
CR: sterling cash at cost		$ 8,250
CR: realized currency gain/loss		$ 750

Realized FX gain on payable remains the same.

Between Purchase Settlement and Sale Trade Dates
Mark the holding to market, based on both local market price and daily spot rate.

F. Sale of XYZ—Trade Date

Sell 1,000 XYZ @ £18.00; exchange rate: $1.90 = £1.00
Total proceeds: $34,200 or £18,000
FX gain is recognized on the sale trade date based on the holding period.
Receivable is booked at the spot rate on sale trade date.

DR: receivable for securities sold	$34,200		
CR: sterling securities at cost (£15,000 X £1.75)		=	$26,250
CR: realized market gain/loss (£18,000 − £15,000) X 1.90		=	$5,700[2]
CR: realized currency gain/loss (15,000 X 1.90) − 26,250		=	$2,250[3]

Maintain local currency basis (£18,000) on the receivable record.

Between Sale Trade Date and Settlement Date
Mark the receivable to market based on the prevailing spot rate.

(continued)

---

[2] If separate disclosures of the foreign currency elements of unrealized and realized gains and losses on investments are chosen by the entity.

[3] See footnote 2.

Sale Settlement Date
Spot rate: $1.85 = £1.00
£18,000 is converted at the spot rate to $33,300.
FX loss is recognized upon the receipt (settlement) of the receivable.
DR: cash $33,300
DR: realized currency gain/loss $ 900
CR: receivables from securities sold $34,200

If foreign currency cash received is to be kept as local currency:
Purchase: £18,000 @ $1.85 = £1.00
Cost basis: $33,300
DR: sterling cash at cost $33,300
CR: cash $33,300

Appendix H
References to AICPA Technical Practice Aids

The following nonauthoritative questions and answers, commonly referred to as Technical Questions and Answers (TIS), have been prepared by the AICPA staff and are included in AICPA *Technical Practice Aids*. The questions and answers have not been approved, disapproved, or otherwise acted upon by the Financial Reporting Executive Committee or any other senior technical committee of the AICPA. They are not sources of established accounting principles, as described in Financial Accounting Standards Board (FASB) *Accounting Standards Codification* (ASC) 105, *Generally Accepted Accounting Principles*, nor are they sources of authoritative generally accepted auditing standards. The AICPA staff believes that the questions and answers listed here may be useful and relevant for users of this guide. Other questions and answers may also be useful and relevant to users of this guide, depending on the facts and circumstances.

TIS Section No.	Title
6910.16	Presentation of Boxed Investment Positions in the Condensed Schedule of Investments of Nonregistered Investment Partnerships
6910.17	Disclosure of Long and Short Positions
6910.18	Disclosure of an Investment in an Issuer When One or More Securities or One or More Derivative Contracts are Held—Nonregistered Investment Partnerships
6910.19	Information Required to Be Disclosed in Financial Statements When Comparative Financial Statements of Nonregistered Investment Partnerships Are Presented
6910.20	Presentation of Purchases and Sales/Maturities of Investments in the Statement of Cash Flows
6910.21	Recognition of Premium/Discount on Short Positions in Fixed-Income Securities
6910.22	Presentation of Reverse Repurchase Agreements
6910.23	Accounting Treatment of Offering Costs Incurred by Investment Partnerships
6910.24	Meaning of "Continually Offer Interests"
6910.25	Considerations in Evaluating Whether Certain Liabilities Constitute "Debt" for Purposes of Assessing Whether an Investment Company Must Present a Statement of Cash Flows
6910.26	Additional Guidance on Determinants of Net Versus Gross Presentation of Security Purchases and Sales/Maturities in the Statement of Cash Flows of a Nonregistered Investment Company

(continued)

TIS Section No.	Title
6910.27	Treatment of Deferred Fees
6910.28	Reporting Financial Highlights, Net Asset Value (NAV) Per Share, Shares Outstanding, and Share Transactions When Investors in Unitized Nonregistered Funds Are Issued Individual Classes or Series of Shares
6910.29	Allocation of Unrealized Gain (Loss), Recognition of Carried Interest, and Clawback Obligations
6910.30	Disclosure Requirements of Investments for Nonregistered Investment Partnerships When Their Interest in an Investee Fund Constitutes Less Than 5 Percent of the Nonregistered Investment Partnership's Net Assets
6910.31	The Nonregistered Investment Partnership's Method for Calculating Its Proportional Share of Any Investments Owned by an Investee Fund in Applying the "5 Percent Test" Described in TIS Section 6910.30
6910.32	Additional Financial Statement Disclosures for Nonregistered Investment Partnerships When the Partnership Has Provided Guarantees Related to the Investee Fund's Debt
6910.33	Certain Financial Reporting, Disclosure, Regulatory, and Tax Considerations When Preparing Financial Statements of Investment Companies Involved in a Business Combination
2220.18	Applicability of Practical Expedient
2220.19	Unit of Account
2220.20	Determining Whether NAV Is Calculated Consistent With FASB ASC 946, *Financial Services—Investment Companies*
2220.21	Determining Whether an Adjustment to NAV Is Necessary
2220.22	Adjusting NAV When It Is Not as of the Reporting Entity's Measurement Date
2220.23	Adjusting NAV When It Is Not Calculated Consistent With FASB ASC 946
2220.24	Disclosures—Ability to Redeem Versus Actual Redemption Request
2220.25	Impact of "Near Term" on Classification Within Fair Value Hierarchy
2220.26	Categorization of Investments for Disclosure Purposes
2220.27	Determining Fair Value of Investments When the Practical Expedient Is Not Used or Is Not Available

AAG-INV APP H

Appendix I
International Financial Reporting Standards

> *Note:* The following content may include certain changes made since the original print version of the guide.

Introduction

The following information provides a brief overview of the ongoing globalization of accounting standards, International Financial Reporting Standards (IFRSs) as a body of accounting literature, the status of convergence with IFRSs in the United States, and the related issues that accounting professionals need to consider today.

Globalization of Accounting Standards

As the business world becomes more globally connected, regulators, investors, audit firms, and public and private companies of all sizes are expressing an increased interest in having common accounting standards among participants in capital markets and trading partners around the world. Proponents of convergence with, or adoption of, IFRSs for financial reporting in the United States believe that one set of financial reporting standards would improve the quality and comparability of investor information and promote fair, orderly, and efficient markets.

Many critics, however, believe that accounting principles generally accepted in the United States of America (U.S. GAAP) are the superior standards and question whether the use of IFRSs will result in more useful financial statements in the long term and whether the cost of implementing IFRSs will outweigh the benefits. Implementing IFRSs will require a staggering effort by management, auditors, and financial statement users, not to mention educators.

The increasing acceptance of IFRSs, both in the United States and around the world, means that now is the time to become knowledgeable about these changes. The discussion that follows explains the underpinnings of the international support for a common set of high quality global standards and many of the challenges and potential opportunities associated with such a fundamental shift in financial accounting and reporting.

The international standard setting process began several decades ago as an effort by industrialized nations to create standards that could be used by developing and smaller nations. However, as cross-border transactions and globalization increased, other nations began to take interest, and the global reach of IFRSs expanded. More than 100 nations and reporting jurisdictions permit or require IFRSs for domestic listed companies and most have fully conformed to IFRSs as promulgated by the International Accounting Standards Board (IASB) and include a statement acknowledging such conformity in audit reports. Several countries, including Argentina and Canada, adopted IFRSs on January 1, 2011, and many other countries have plans to converge (or eliminate significant differences between) their national standards and IFRSs in 2012.

For many years, the United States has been a strong leader in international efforts to develop globally accepted standards. Among other actions in support of IFRSs, the U.S. Securities and Exchange Commission (SEC) removed the requirement for foreign private issuers registered in the United States to reconcile their financial reports with U.S. GAAP if their accounts complied with IFRSs as issued by the IASB. In addition, the SEC continues to analyze and evaluate appropriate steps toward, and challenges related to, incorporating IFRSs into the U.S. financial reporting system, as subsequently described.

In addition to the support received from certain U.S. based entities, financial and economic leaders from various organizations have announced their support for global accounting standards. Most notably, in 2009, the Group of Twenty Finance Ministers and Central Bank Governors (G20), a group from 20 of the world's industrialized and developing economies (with the 20th member being the European Union, collectively), called for standard setters to redouble their efforts to complete convergence in global accounting standards.

Acceptance of a single set of high quality accounting standards may present many significant opportunities, including the improvement in financial reporting to global investors, the facilitation of cross-border investments, and the integration of capital markets. Further, U.S. entities with international operations could realize significant cost savings from the use of a single set of financial reporting standards. For example, U.S. issuers raising capital outside the United States are required to comply with the domestic reporting standards of the foreign country and U.S. GAAP. As a result, additional costs arise from the duplication and translation of financial reporting information.

Many multinational companies support the use of common accounting standards to increase comparability of financial results among reporting entities from different countries. They believe common standards will help investors better understand the entities' business activities and financial position. Large public companies with subsidiaries in multiple jurisdictions would be able to use one accounting language company-wide and present their financial statements in the same language as their competitors. In addition, some believe that in a truly global economy, financial professionals, including CPAs, will be more mobile, and companies will more easily be able to respond to the human capital needs of their subsidiaries around the world.

Although certain cost reductions are expected, the initial cost of convergence with IFRSs is expected to be one of the largest obstacles for many entities, including accounting firms and educational institutions. Substantial internal costs for U.S. corporations in the areas of employee training, IT conversions, and general ledger software have been predicted. In addition, the time and effort required from various external functions, including the education of auditors, investors, lenders, and other financial statement users, will be significant factors for consideration.

Although the likelihood of acceptance of IFRSs may lack clarity for the time being, U.S. companies should consider preparing for the costly transition to new or converged standards, which likely will include higher costs in the areas of training and software compliance.

Who is the IASB?

The IASB is the independent standard setting body of the IFRS Foundation, formerly, the International Accounting Standards Committee Foundation. As a private sector organization, the IFRS Foundation has no authority to impose funding regimes on countries. However, a levy system and national contributions through regulatory and standard-setting authorities or stock exchanges have been introduced in a number of countries to fund the organization. Although the AICPA was a founding member of the International Accounting Standards Committee, the IASB's predecessor organization, it is not affiliated with the IASB.

The IASB, founded on April 1, 2001, in London, England, is responsible for developing IFRSs and promoting the use and application of these standards. In pursuit of this objective, the IASB cooperates with national accounting standard setters to achieve convergence in accounting standards around the world.

The structure includes the following primary groups: (*a*) the IFRS Foundation, an independent organization having two main bodies: the IFRS Foundation trustees and the IASB; (*b*) the IFRS Advisory Council; and (*c*) the IFRS Interpretations Committee, formerly the International Financial Reporting Interpretations Committee (IFRIC). The trustees appoint the IASB members, exercise oversight, and raise the funds needed, but the IASB itself has responsibility for establishing IFRSs.

The IFRS Foundation is linked to a monitoring board of public authorities, including committees of the International Organization of Securities Commissions, the European Commission, and the SEC. The monitoring board's main responsibilities are to ensure that the trustees continue to discharge their duties as defined by the IFRS Foundation Constitution, as well as approving the appointment or reappointment of trustees. In addition, through the monitoring board, capital markets authorities that allow or require the use of IFRSs in their jurisdictions will be able to more effectively carry out their mandates regarding investor protection, market integrity, and capital formation.

The IASB board members are selected chiefly upon their professional competence and practical experience. The trustees are required to select members so that the IASB will comprise the best available combination of technical expertise and international business and market experience and to ensure that the IASB is not dominated by any particular geographical interest or constituency. The IASB has members from several different countries, including the United States. The members are responsible for the development and publication of IFRSs, including *International Financial Reporting Standard for Small- and Medium-sized Entities (IFRS for SMEs)*, and for approving the interpretations of IFRSs as developed by the IFRS Interpretations Committee.

The IFRS Interpretations Committee, founded in March 2002, is the successor of the previous interpretations committee, the Standing Interpretations Committee (SIC), and is the interpretative body of the IASB. The role of the IFRS Interpretations Committee is to provide timely guidance on newly identified financial reporting issues not specifically addressed in IFRSs or issues in which interpretations are not sufficient.

IFRSs are developed through a formal system of due process and broad international consultation, similar to the development of U.S. GAAP.

Readers are encouraged to become involved in the standard-setting process by responding to open calls from the standard setting organizations.

What Are IFRSs?

The term *IFRSs* has both a narrow and broad meaning. Narrowly, IFRSs refers to the numbered series of pronouncements issued by the IASB, collectively called *standards*. More broadly, however, IFRSs refer to the entire body of authoritative IASB literature, including the following:

1. Standards, whether labeled IFRSs or International Accounting Standards (IASs)[1]
2. Interpretations, whether labeled IFRIC (the former name of the interpretive body) or SIC (the predecessor to IFRIC)[2]

The preface to the IFRS *2011 Bound Volume* states that IFRSs are designed to apply to the general purpose financial statements and other financial reporting of all profit-oriented entities, including commercial, industrial, and financial entities, regardless of legal form or organization. IFRSs are not designed to apply to not-for-profit entities or those in the public sector,[3] but these entities may find IFRSs appropriate in accounting for their activities.

The IASB's *Conceptual Framework for Financial Reporting* (conceptual framework) establishes the concepts that underlie the preparation and presentation of financial statements for external users. The IASB is guided by the conceptual framework in the development of future standards and in its review of existing standards. The conceptual framework is not an IFRS, and when there is a conflict between the conceptual framework and any IFRS, the standard will prevail. The conceptual framework is an overall statement of guidance for those interpreting financial statements, whereas IFRSs are issue and subject specific.

When an IFRS specifically applies to a transaction, other event, or condition, the accounting policy or policies applied to that item shall be determined by applying the IFRS and considering any relevant implementation guidance issued by the IASB for the IFRS.

Further, if an IFRS does not address a specific transaction, event, or condition explicitly, IAS 8, *Accounting Policies, Changes in Accounting Estimates and Errors*, states that management should use its judgment in developing and applying an accounting policy that results in information that is relevant and reliable. With respect to the reliability of financial statements, IAS 8 states that the financial statements (*a*) represent faithfully the financial position, financial performance, and cash flows of the entity; (*b*) reflect the economic substance of transactions, other events, and conditions; (*c*) are neutral; (*d*) are prudent; and (*e*) are complete in all material respects. When making this type of judgment, management should refer to, and consider the applicability of, the following in descending order:

---

[1] See www.ifrs.org for a current listing of International Financial Reporting Standards (IFRSs) and International Accounting Standards (IASs).

[2] See www.ifrs.org for a current listing of International Financial Reporting Interpretations Committee and Standing Interpretations Committee interpretations.

[3] Generally speaking, *public* means government-owned entities, and *private* means nongovernment-owned entities.

International Financial Reporting Standards   **501**

1. The requirements and guidance in IFRSs dealing with similar and related issues
2. The definitions, recognition criteria, and measurement concepts for assets, liabilities, income, and expenses in the IASB Framework

Management may also consider the most recent pronouncements of other standard setting bodies that use a similar conceptual framework (for example, U.S. GAAP), other accounting literature, and accepted industry practices to the extent that these do not conflict with IFRSs.

IFRS for SMEs

IFRS for SMEs is a modification and simplification of full IFRSs aimed at meeting the needs of private company financial reporting users and easing the financial reporting burden on private companies through a cost-benefit approach. *IFRS for SMEs* is a self-contained, global accounting and financial reporting standard applicable to the general purpose financial statements of entities that, in many countries, are known as small- and medium-sized entities (SMEs). Full IFRSs and *IFRS for SMEs* are promulgated by the IASB.

SMEs are entities that publish general purpose financial statements for external users and do not have public accountability. An entity has public accountability under the IASB's definition if it files its financial statements with a securities commission or other regulatory organization or it holds assets in a fiduciary capacity (for example, banks, insurance companies, brokers and dealers in securities, pension funds, and mutual funds). It is not the IASB's intention to exclude entities that hold assets in a fiduciary capacity for reasons incidental to their primary business (for example, travel agents, schools, and utilities) from utilizing *IFRS for SMEs*.

The needs of users of SME financial statements often are different from the needs of users of public company financial statements and other entities that likely would use full IFRSs. Whereas full IFRSs were designed specifically to meet the needs of equity investors in the public capital markets, *IFRS for SMEs* was developed with the needs of a wide range of users in mind. Users of the financial statements of SMEs may be more focused on shorter-term cash flows, liquidity, balance sheet strength, interest coverage, and solvency issues. Full IFRSs may impose a burden on SME preparers in that full IFRSs contain topics and detailed implementation guidance that generally are not relevant to SMEs. This burden has been growing as IFRSs have become more detailed. As such, a significant need existed for an accounting and financial reporting standard for SMEs that would meet the needs of their financial statement users while balancing the costs and benefits from a preparer perspective.

Practically speaking, *IFRS for SMEs* is viewed as an accounting framework for entities that do not have the capacity or resources to use full IFRSs. In the United States, the term SME would encompass many private companies.

In May 2008, the AICPA Governing Council voted to recognize the IASB as an accounting body for purposes of establishing international financial accounting and reporting principles and amended appendix A, "Council Resolution Designating Bodies to Promulgate Technical Standards," of Rule 202, *Compliance With Standards* (AICPA, *Professional Standards*, ET sec. 202 par. .01), and Rule 203, *Accounting Principles* (AICPA, *Professional Standards*, ET sec. 203 par. .01). This amendment gives AICPA members the option to use IFRSs as an alternative to U.S. GAAP. Accordingly, IFRSs are not considered to be an

AAG-INV APP I

other comprehensive basis of accounting. Rather, they are a source of generally accepted accounting principles.

As such, a key professional barrier to using IFRSs and, therefore, *IFRS for SMEs*, has been removed. Any remaining barriers may come in the form of unwillingness by a private company's financial statement users to accept financial statements prepared under *IFRS for SMEs* and a private company's expenditure of money, time, and effort to convert to *IFRS for SMEs*.[4]

The AICPA has developed a resource that compares *IFRS for SMEs* with corresponding requirements of U.S. GAAP. This resource is available in a Wiki format, which allows AICPA members and others to contribute to its development. To learn more about the resource, view available sections, and contribute to its content, visit the Wiki at http://wiki.ifrs.com/.

The Financial Accounting Standards Board and IASB Convergence Efforts[5]

To address significant differences between IFRSs and U.S. GAAP, the Financial Accounting Standards Board (FASB) and the IASB agreed to a "Memorandum of Understanding" (MoU), which was originally issued in 2006 and subsequently updated. Readers are encouraged to monitor the FASB and IASB websites for additional developments regarding the convergence efforts, such as discussion papers, exposure drafts, and requests for comments.

Comparison of U.S. GAAP and IFRSs

One of the major differences between U.S. GAAP and IFRSs lies in the conceptual approach: U.S. GAAP is based on principles, with heavy use of rules to illustrate the principles; however, IFRSs are principles based, without heavy use of rules.

In general, a principles-based set of accounting standards, such as IFRSs, is broad in scope. The standards are concise, written in plain language, and provide for limited exceptions and bright lines. Principles-based standards typically require a higher level of professional judgment, which may facilitate an enhanced focus on the economic purpose of a company's transactions and how the transactions are reflected in its financial reporting.

A noticeable result of these differences is that IFRSs provide much less overall detail. In developing an IFRS, the IASB expects preparers to rely on core principles and limited application guidance with fewer prescriptive rules. In contrast, FASB often leans more toward providing extensive prescriptive guidance and detailed rules. The guidance provided in IFRSs regarding revenue recognition, for example, is significantly less extensive than U.S. GAAP. IFRSs also contain relatively little industry-specific guidance.

---

[4] CPAs are encouraged to consult their state boards of accountancy to determine the status of reporting on financial statements prepared in accordance with *International Financial Reporting Standard for Small- and Medium-sized Entities* within their individual state.

[5] Because the convergence projects discussed are active and subject to change, updates will be posted periodically to www.journalofaccountancy.com. Readers also are encouraged to monitor the progress of these projects at the respective boards' websites: www.ifrs.org and www.fasb.org.

International Financial Reporting Standards

An inherent issue in a principles-based system is the potential for different interpretations of similar transactions across jurisdictions and entities, which may affect the relative comparability of financial reporting.

Because of long-standing convergence projects between the IASB and FASB, the extent of the specific differences between IFRSs and U.S. GAAP is decreasing. Yet, significant differences remain, which could result in significantly different reported results, depending on a company's industry and individual facts and circumstances. For example, some differences include the following:

- IFRSs do not permit last in, first out (LIFO) inventory accounting.
- IFRSs allow for the revaluation of assets in certain circumstances.
- IFRSs use a single-step method for impairment write-downs rather than the two-step method used in U.S. GAAP, making write-downs more likely.
- IFRSs have a different probability threshold and measurement objective for contingencies.
- IFRSs generally do not allow net presentation for derivatives.

U.S. GAAP also addresses some specific transactions not currently addressed in IFRSs, such as accounting for reorganizations, including quasi reorganizations; troubled debt restructuring; spin-offs; and reverse spin-offs. In addition, U.S. GAAP is designed to apply to all nongovernmental entities, including not-for-profit entities, and includes specific guidance for not-for-profit entities, development stage entities, limited liability entities, and personal financial statements.

The difference in the amount of industry-specific guidance also illustrates the different approaches. Currently, IFRSs include only several standards (for example, IAS 41, *Agriculture*)[6] that might be regarded as primarily industry-specific guidance. However, the scope of these standards includes all entities to which the scope of IFRSs applies. In contrast, U.S. GAAP has considerable guidance for entities within specific industries. For example, on liability recognition and measurement alone, U.S. GAAP contains specific guidance for entities in the following industries, which is not found in IFRSs:

- Health care
- Contractors and construction
- Contractors and the federal government
- Entertainment, with separate guidance for casinos, films, and music
- Financial services, with separate guidance for brokers and dealers and depository and lending, insurance, and investment companies

For nonmonetary transactions, U.S. GAAP provides specific guidance for the airline, software, and entertainment industries.

---

[6] In addition to IAS 41, *Agriculture*, the other IFRSs that address issues specific to certain industries are IFRS 4, *Insurance Contracts*, and IFRS 6, *Exploration for and Evaluation of Mineral Resources*.

SEC Work Plan

The SEC continues to affirm its support for a single set of high-quality, globally accepted accounting standards and for the convergence of U.S. GAAP and IFRSs. In May 2011, the SEC staff produced a work plan outlining how such a transition might happen. Many of the panelists from a July 2011 roundtable discussion favored the "condorsement" approach that was included in the work plan. Under this approach, FASB would endorse IFRS into U.S. GAAP over a defined period of time, instead of following a "big bang" approach. Among other things, the work plan addresses some of the comments and concerns received regarding future convergence, including the following:

- Sufficient development and application of IFRSs for the U.S. reporting system
- The independence of standard setting for the benefit of investors
- Investor understanding and education regarding IFRSs
- Examination of the U.S. regulatory environment that would be affected by a change in accounting standards
- The impact on issuers, both large and small, including changes to accounting systems, changes to contractual arrangements, corporate governance considerations, and litigation contingencies
- Human capital readiness

The work plan is included as an appendix at the end of the SEC's release, which is located on the SEC's website at www.sec.gov.

In November 2011, the SEC released a staff paper that summarizes the current status of convergence projects, which are grouped by both short-term and long-term, as well as by level of priority (greater priority versus lower priority). Currently, the three projects that are of greater priority are financial instruments, revenue recognition, and leases. Refer to www.sec.gov for the full-version of the staff paper.

Although the SEC has not yet made a decision on whether or not to approve the use of IFRSs, a decision is expected to be made during the first half of 2012.

AICPA

In response to an SEC staff paper issued in May 2011, the AICPA issued a comment letter in August 2011, recommending that U.S. public companies be allowed the option of adopting use of IFRSs as the commission weighs a possible future framework for incorporating IFRSs into the U.S. financial reporting system. The letter states that the adoption option would be another important step towards achieving the goal of incorporating IFRSs into the U.S. financial reporting system and that the number of companies that would choose such an option would not be such that system-wide readiness would become an issue. The comment letter further states AICPA's agreement with the SEC in that FASB should continue to have an active role in the international financial reporting arena to ensure that U.S. interests are suitably addressed in the development of IFRSs. Results from an IFRS Readiness Survey conducted by the AICPA in September 2011 show that a majority of CPAs support optional adoption of IFRSs. This would allow publicly traded U.S. companies to use IFRS while the SEC decides whether to incorporate the standards into U.S. reporting requirements.

Additional Resources

Website	URL
AICPA	www.aicpa.org
AICPA International Financial Reporting Standards Resources	www.ifrs.com
International Accounting Standards Board and IFRS Foundation	www.ifrs.org
Comparison Wiki of *International Financial Reporting Standard for Small- and Medium-sized Entities* and U.S. generally accepted accounting principles	http://wiki.ifrs.com
Financial Accounting Standards Board	www.fasb.org

Appendix J

Schedule of Changes Made to the Text From the Previous Edition

As of May 1, 2012

This schedule of changes identifies areas in the text and footnotes of this guide that have that have changed since the previous edition. Entries in the table of this appendix reflect current numbering, lettering (including that in appendix names), and character designations that resulted from the renumbering or reordering that occurred in the updating of this guide.

Reference	Change
General	Information related to standards issued but not yet effective on or before the "as of" date of this guide has been placed in shaded "Guidance Update" boxes, with a reference to appendix A, "Guidance Updates." See appendix A for more information.
General	Information related to clarified auditing standards issued but not yet effective on or before the "as of" date of this guide has been placed in shaded "Guidance Update" boxes, with a reference to appendix B, "Guidance Updates—Clarified Auditing Standards." See appendix B for more information.
General	The use of footnotes denoted with a symbol instead of a number (referred to as "temporary" footnotes) has been discontinued. All content in such footnotes has been added to chapter text, converted to a numbered footnote, or deleted.
Preface	Updated.
Paragraph 1.14	Revised for clarification.
Former footnote 8 in paragraph 1.27	Deleted; see paragraph 1.27.
Paragraphs 1.27 and 1.33	Revised for clarification.
Footnote 14 in paragraph 1.34	Added to reflect the issuance of Financial Accounting Standards Board's (FASB's) proposed Accounting Standards Update (ASU) *Technical Corrections*.

(continued)

Reference	Change
Paragraphs 1.40–.41	Revised for clarification.
Paragraphs 2.32 and 2.64	Revised for clarification.
Former paragraph 2.80	Deleted; see paragraph 2.77.
Paragraph 2.80	Revised to reflect Statement on Standards for Attestation Engagements (SSAE) No. 16, *Reporting on Controls at a Service Organization* (AICPA, *Professional Standards*, AT sec. 801).
Footnote 28 in paragraph 2.87	Added for clarification.
Paragraph 2.127	Revised for clarification.
Paragraph 2.128	Added for clarification.
Paragraph 2.165	Added to reflect Public Company Accounting Oversight Board (PCAOB) Auditing Standard Nos. 8–15 (AICPA, *PCAOB Standards and Related Rules*, Auditing Standards).
Former paragraph 2.165 and former preceding heading	Moved to paragraph 2.215.
Former paragraph 2.166	Deleted for clarification.
Former paragraphs 2.167–.178	Moved to paragraphs 2.216–.230.
Paragraph 2.178 and footnote 39	Revised to reflect SSAE No. 16.
Former paragraphs 2.179–.181	Moved to paragraphs 2.231–.233.
Footnote 43 to paragraph 2.181	Added for clarification.
Former paragraphs 2.182–.204	Moved to paragraphs 2.234–.258.
Paragraph 2.215	Moved from former paragraph 2.165; revised for clarification.
Paragraphs 2.216–.218	Moved from former paragraphs 2.167–.169.
Paragraph 2.219	Added to reflect PCAOB Auditing Standard No. 12, *Identifying and Assessing Risks of Material Misstatement* (AICPA, *PCAOB Standards and Related Rules*, Auditing Standards).
Paragraph 2.220	Moved from former paragraph 2.170; Revised to reflect SSAE No. 16.
Paragraph 2.221	Moved from former paragraph 2.171.
Paragraph 2.222	Added to reflect PCAOB Auditing Standard No. 12.

AAG-INV APP J

Schedule of Changes

Reference	Change
Paragraphs 2.223–.226	Moved from former paragraphs 2.172–.175; paragraph 2.223 revised for clarification.
Paragraph 2.227	Added to reflect PCAOB Auditing Standard No. 12.
Paragraphs 2.228–.249	Moved from former paragraphs 2.176–.197; paragraph 2.236 revised for clarification.
Paragraph 2.250	Added to reflect PCAOB Auditing Standard No. 13, *The Auditor's Responses to the Risks of Material Misstatement* (AICPA, *PCAOB Standards and Related Rules*, Auditing Standards).
Paragraphs 2.251–.255	Moved from former paragraphs 2.198–.202.
Paragraph 2.256	Added to reflect PCAOB Auditing Standard No. 14, *Evaluating Audit Results* (AICPA, *PCAOB Standards and Related Rules*, Auditing Standards).
Paragraphs 2.257–.258	Moved from former paragraphs 2.203–.204.
Paragraph 3.05	Revised for clarification.
Paragraphs 3.13–.17 and preceding heading	Added for clarification.
Former paragraph 3.32, former paragraphs 3.34–.35, and former preceding heading	Deleted for clarification.
Paragraphs 3.38–.39 and preceding heading and paragraphs 3.40–.41 and preceding heading	Added for clarification.
Footnote 7 in paragraph 3.43	Revised to reflect Commodity Futures Trading Commission (CFTC) revisions to Part 4 Regulations.
Footnote 8 in paragraph 3.43	Revised for clarification.
Former paragraphs 3.45–.46 and former preceding heading	Moved to follow paragraph 3.57.
Paragraph 3.52	Revised for clarification.
Paragraphs 3.56–.57 and preceding heading	Added for clarification.

(continued)

Reference	Change
Paragraphs 3.58–.59 and preceding heading	Moved from former paragraphs 3.45–.46; paragraph 3.59 revised for clarification.
Paragraphs 3.60–.61	Added for clarification.
Paragraphs 3.63 and 3.67	Revised for clarification.
Paragraph 4.21	Revised for clarification; revised to reflect SSAE No. 16; footnote 7 revised to reflect SSAE No. 16.
Paragraphs 4.22 and 4.31	Revised for clarification.
Paragraph 4.32	Revised to reflect PCAOB Auditing Standard No. 12.
Footnote 14 in paragraph 4.45	Revised to reflect the Auditing Standards Board's (ASB's) Clarity Project.
Footnote 15 in paragraph 4.45	Added to reflect PCAOB proposed Auditing Standard *Confirmations*.
Paragraphs 5.11, 5.17, 5.19, and 5.41–.42	Revised for clarification.
Footnote 2 in paragraph 5.54	Added for clarification.
Paragraphs 5.85–.86 and exhibit 5-3	Revised for clarification.
Footnote 10 in exhibit 5-3, footnote 21 in exhibit 5-4, and footnote 34 in exhibit 5-6	Added for clarification.
Exhibit 5-6	Revised for clarification.
Text box before paragraph 6.03	Deleted.
Heading before paragraph 6.13	Revised for clarification.
Paragraphs 6.20, 6.22, and 6.24	Revised to reflect the Regulated Investment Company (RIC) Modernization Act of 2010.
Paragraph 6.27	Revised for clarification.
Paragraphs 6.30 and 6.33	Revised to reflect the RIC Modernization Act of 2010.
Paragraph 6.46	Revised for clarification.
Paragraphs 6.55, 6.67, 6.77–.78, 6.81–.82, 6.85, 6.88, and 6.91	Revised to reflect the RIC Modernization Act of 2010; former footnotes 72–74 deleted to reflect the RIC Modernization Act.
Paragraph 6.101	Revised for clarification; former footnote 100 deleted for clarification.
Footnote 5 in paragraph 7.01	Added to reflect the issuance of FASB's proposed ASU *Technical Corrections*.

AAG-INV APP J

Schedule of Changes 511

Reference	Change
Footnote 17 in paragraph 7.12	Added to reflect FASB's proposed ASU *Consolidation (Topic 810): Parent's Accounting for the Cumulative Translation Adjustment upon the Sale or Transfer of a Group of Assets That Is a Nonprofit Activity or a Business within a Consolidated Foreign Entity (a consensus of the FASB Emerging Issues Task Force)*.
Paragraph 7.15	Revised for clarification.
Footnote 21 in paragraph 7.29	Added for clarification.
Footnote 27 in paragraph 7.31	Revised for clarification.
Footnote 28 in paragraph 7.33	Added for clarification.
Paragraph 7.48	Revised for clarification.
Paragraph 7.81	Revised to reflect ASU No. 2010-06, *Fair Value Measurements and Disclosures (Topic 820): Improving Disclosures about Fair Value Measurements*.
Footnote 47 in paragraph 7.142	Added to reflect the issuance of FASB's proposed ASU *Technical Corrections*.
Paragraphs 7.173, 7.177, 7.180, and 7.183–.184	Revised for clarification; footnote 57 in paragraph 7.176, footnote 61 in paragraph 7.177, footnotes 66 and 69 in paragraph 7.180, and footnote 79 in paragraph 7.185 added for clarification.
Paragraph 7.193	Revised to reflect ASU No. 2010-06.
Former footnote 1 in paragraph 8.02	Content added to paragraph 8.02.
Footnote 1 in paragraph 8.02	Added to reflect FASB's proposed ASU *Revenue Recognition (Topic 605): Revenue from Contracts with Customers*.
Paragraph 8.52	Revised to reflect ASU No. 2010-29, *Business Combinations (Topic 805): Disclosure of Supplementary Pro Forma Information for Business Combinations (a consensus of the FASB Emerging Issues Task Force)*.
Paragraph 8.54	Revised for clarification.
Paragraph 8.56	Revised to reflect SAS No. 118, *Other Information in Documents Containing Audited Financial Statements* (AICPA, *Professional Standards*, AU sec. 550).

(continued)

AAG-INV APP J

Reference	Change
Paragraph 8.57	Added to reflect SAS No. 118.
Paragraph 8.58	Revised to reflect SAS No. 119, *Supplementary Information in Relation to the Financial Statements as a Whole* (AICPA, *Professional Standards*, AU sec. 551).
Paragraphs 9.01, 9.07–.10, 9.12, and 9.14 and footnote 3 in paragraph 9.12	Revised for clarification; footnote 4 in paragraph 9.14 added for clarification.
Paragraph 9.02	Added for clarification.
Former paragraph 9.15	Deleted for clarification.
Paragraphs 9.16, 9.18, and 9.21–.22	Revised for clarification; footnotes 6 and 10–11 in paragraph 9.22 added for clarification.
Paragraphs 10.01–.02, 10.04, 10.09–.10, 10.13, 10.16, 10.20, 10.49, and 10.56	Revised for clarification.
Paragraph 11.02	Revised for clarification.
Paragraph 11.03	Revised for Interpretation No. 16, "Effect on Auditor's Report of Omission of Schedule of Investments by Investment Partnerships That Are Exempt From Securities and Exchange Commission Registration Under the Investment Company Act of 1940," of AU section 508, *Reports on Audited Financial Statements* (AICPA, *Professional Standards*, AU sec. 9508 par. .76–.84).
Footnote 8 in paragraph 11.03	Added for clarification.
Paragraphs 11.04–.05	Added to reflect Interpretation No. 16 of AU section 508.
Paragraph 11.06	Moved from paragraph 11.03.
Paragraphs 11.07–.08	Revised for Interpretation No. 16 of AU section 508.
Paragraphs 11.09–.10 and 11.12	Revised for clarification.
Footnote 24 in paragraph 11.13	Added for clarification.
Footnote 47 in paragraph 11.25	Revised for clarification.
Paragraph 11.26	Revised for SSAE No. 16.
Paragraph 11.30	Revised for clarification.
Paragraph 11.31	Revised for SSAE No. 16.

AAG-INV APP J

Schedule of Changes

Reference	Change
Paragraph 11.33	Revised for clarification.
Paragraph 11.34 and footnote 78	Revised for SSAE No. 16; former footnotes 77–79 deleted for SSAE No. 16; footnote 79 in paragraph 11.34 added for SSAE No. 16.
Footnote 81 in paragraph 11.37, paragraph 11.40	Revised to reflect revised Global Investment Performance Standards (GIPS).
Paragraph 11.38	Added to reflect revised GIPS.
Footnotes 89, 91, and 93–94 in paragraph 11.41	Revised for the ASB's clarity project.
Appendixes A, B, and C	Added.
Former Appendixes C and D.	Deleted for clarification.
Appendix D	Revised for clarification.
Appendix E	Table 2 revised for clarification.
Appendix F	Exhibit 3 revised to reflect ASU No. 2010-29.
Appendix I	Revised for the passage of time.
Glossary	Updated.

AAG-INV APP J

Glossary

The following terms can be found in the Financial Accounting Standards Board (FASB) *Accounting Standards Codification* (ASC) glossary:

actual-income-available method. A method to calculate distributions to shareholders from net investment income in which actual net investment income that has been allocated to each class (as recorded on the books) is divided by the record date shares for each class to derive the dividend payable per share.

amortization. The process of reducing a recognized liability systematically by recognizing revenues or reducing a recognized asset systematically by recognizing expenses or costs.

amortized cost. The sum of the initial investment less cash collected less write-downs plus yield accreted to date.

annuity contract. A contract in which an insurance entity unconditionally undertakes a legal obligation to provide specified pension benefits to specific individuals in return for a fixed consideration or premium. An annuity contract is irrevocable and involves the transfer of significant risk from the employer to the insurance entity. Annuity contracts are also called allocated contracts.

board-contingent plan. A reimbursement 12b-1 plan that provides that, on the plan's termination, a fund's board of directors or trustees has the option, but not requirement, to pay the distributor for any excess costs incurred by the distributor.

callable obligation. An obligation is callable at a given date if the creditor has the right at that date to demand, or to give notice of its intention to demand, repayment of the obligation owed to it by the debtor [further industry-specific information is provided in the second section of this glossary under the term **callable**].

call option. A contract that allows the holder to buy a specified quantity of stock from the writer of the contract at a fixed price for a given period [further industry-specific information is provided in the second section of this glossary].

capital infusions. Expenditures made directly to the issuer to ensure that operations are completed, thereby allowing the issuer to generate cash flows to service the debt. Such expenditures are usually nonrecurring. In certain cases, bondholders may receive additional promissory notes, or the original bond instrument may be amended to provide for repayment of the capital infusions.

closed-end funds. Closed-end funds are investment companies that issue a fixed number of shares (that generally trade on an open market) to raise capital, similar to the way in which an entity sells stock in an initial public offering [further industry-specific information is provided in the second section of this glossary].

compensation plan. A plan that provides for a 12b-1 fee, payable by the fund, based on a percentage of the fund's average net assets. The 12b-1 fee may be more or less than the costs incurred by the distributor.

conduit debt securities. Certain limited-obligation revenue bonds, certificates of participation, or similar debt instruments issued by a state or local governmental entity for the express purpose of providing financing for a specific third party (the conduit bond obligor) that is not a part of the state or local government's financial reporting entity. Although conduit debt securities bear the name of the governmental entity that issues them, the governmental entity often has no obligation for such debt beyond the resources provided by a lease or loan agreement with the third party on whose behalf the securities are issued. Further, the conduit bond obligor is responsible for any future financial reporting requirements.

contingent deferred sales load [CDSL]. A sales charge imposed directly on redeeming shareholders based on a percentage of the lesser of the redemption proceeds or original cost. The percentage may decrease or be eliminated based on the duration of share ownership (frequently decreases by 1 percent a year). Also referred to as a back-end load [further industry-specific information is provided in the second section of this glossary under the term **contingent deferred sales charge (CDSC)**].

control. The direct or indirect ability to determine the direction of management and policies through ownership, contract, or otherwise [further industry-specific information is provided in the second section of this glossary].

convertible security. A security that is convertible into another security based on a conversion rate. For example, convertible preferred stock that is convertible into common stock on a two-for-one basis (two shares of common for each share of preferred).

distributor. Usually the principal underwriter who sells the fund's capital shares by acting as an agent (intermediary between the fund and an independent dealer or the public) or as a principal, buying capital shares from the fund at net asset value and selling shares through dealers or to the public (see definition of *underwriter* in Section 2(a)(40) of the Investment Company Act of 1940 [the 1940 Act]).

dividends. Dividends paid or payable in cash, other assets, or another class of stock and does not include stock dividends or stock splits (further industry specific information provided in the second section of this glossary).

enhanced 12b-1 plan. A reimbursement 12b-1 plan that provides that, on termination of the plan, the fund is required to continue paying the 12b-1 fee to the extent the distributor has excess costs.

equity security. Any security representing an ownership interest in an entity (for example, common, preferred, or other capital stock) or the right to acquire (for example, warrants, rights, and call options) or dispose of (for example, put options) an ownership interest in an entity at fixed or determinable prices. However, the term does not include convertible debt or preferred stock that by its terms either must be redeemed by the issuing entity or is redeemable at the option of the investor.

exchange market. An active exchange market is a market in which closing prices are both readily available and generally representative of fair value. An example of such a market is the New York Stock Exchange [further industry-specific information is provided in the second section of this glossary under the term **exchange**].

fail-to-deliver. A fail-to-deliver is a securities sale to another broker-dealer that has not been delivered to the buying broker-dealer by the close of business on the settlement date.

fail-to-receive. A fail-to-receive is a securities purchase from another broker-dealer not received from the selling broker-dealer by the close of business on the settlement date.

fair value. The price that would be received to sell an asset or paid to transfer a liability in an orderly transaction between market participants at the measurement date.

forward exchange contract. A forward exchange contract is an agreement between two parties to exchange different currencies at a specified exchange rate at an agreed-upon future date.

futures contract. A standard and transferable form of contract that binds the seller to deliver to the bearer a standard amount and grade of a commodity to a specific location at a specified time. It usually includes a schedule of premiums and discounts for quality variation.

high-yield debt securities. Corporate and municipal debt securities having a lower-than-investment-grade credit rating (BB+ or lower by Standard & Poor's, or Ba or lower by Moody's). Because high-yield debt securities typically are used when lower-cost capital is not available, they have interest rates several percentage points higher than investment-grade debt and often have shorter maturities. These high-yielding corporate and municipal debt obligations are frequently referred to as junk bonds [further industry-specific information is provided in the second section of this glossary under the term **junk bonds**].

interest method. The method used to arrive at a periodic interest cost (including amortization) that will represent a level effective rate on the sum of the face amount of the debt and (plus or minus) the unamortized premium or discount and expense at the beginning of each period.

liquidity. An asset's or liability's nearness to cash [further industry specific information is provided in the second section of this glossary].

mortgage-backed securities. Securities issued by a governmental agency or corporation (for example, Government National Mortgage Association [GNMA] or Federal Home Loan Mortgage Corporation [FHLMC]) or by private issuers (for example, Federal National Mortgage Association [FNMA], banks, and mortgage banking entities). Mortgage-backed securities generally are referred to as mortgage participation certificates or pass-through certificates. A participation certificate represents an undivided interest in a pool of specific mortgage loans. Periodic payments on GNMA participation certificates are backed by the U.S. government. Periodic payments on FHLMC and FNMA certificates are guaranteed by those corporations, but are not backed by the U.S. government.

net asset value per share. Net asset value per share is the amount of net assets attributable to each share of capital stock (other than senior equity securities, that is, preferred stock) outstanding at the close of the period. It excludes the effects of assuming conversion of outstanding convertible securities, whether or not their conversion would have a diluting effect [further industry-specific information is provided in the second section of this glossary].

nonregistered investment partnerships—financial highlights. Nonregistered investment partnerships, when disclosing financial highlights, shall interpret the terms classes, units, and theoretical investments as follows:

- a. Classes. Nonregistered investment funds typically have one of the following two classes of ownership interest, with one class being the management interest in the fund and the other being the investment interest:

    1. For unitized funds (that is, funds with units specifically called for in the governing underlying legal or offering documents), the management interest usually is a voting class and the investment interest is a nonvoting class. Temporary series of shares (that is, shares that are intended at the time of issuance to be consolidated at a later date with another specified series of shares that remains outstanding indefinitely) are not considered separate classes. Permanent series of a class of share shall be the basis for which that share's financial highlights are determined and presented.

    2. For nonunitized funds, the management interest usually is the general partner class and the investment interest usually is the limited partner class. Generally, a class has certain rights as governed by underlying legal documents or offering documents and local law. Rights to certain investments that do not otherwise affect the rights available under the underlying legal documents and local law do not ordinarily represent a separate share class. For example, rights to income and gains from a specific investment attributed solely to investors at the date the investment is made (side-pocket investments) are not considered to give rise to a share class. Similarly, a temporary series of shares is not considered a share class.

- b. Units. Only funds with units specifically called for in the governing underlying legal or offering documents shall be considered unitized. Some funds may employ units for convenience in making allocations to investors for internal accounting or bookkeeping purposes, but the units are not required or specified by legal or offering documents, and for all other purposes operate like nonunitized investment partnerships. For per-share operating performance, those funds are not considered unitized.

- c. Theoretical investment. The term theoretical investment in FASB ASC 946-205–50-20 shall be considered as the actual aggregate amount of capital invested by each reporting class of investor as of the beginning of the fiscal reporting period, adjusted for cash flows related to capital contributions or withdrawals during the period.

offering costs. Offering costs include all of the following:

- a. Legal fees pertaining to the investment company's shares offered for sale
- b. Securities and Exchange Commission (SEC) and state registration fees

Glossary

    c. Underwriting and other similar costs
    d. Costs of printing prospectuses for sales purposes
    e. Initial fees paid to be listed on an exchange
    f. Tax opinion costs related to offering of shares
    g. Initial agency fees of securing the rating for bonds or preferred stock issued by closed-end funds.

payment-in-kind bonds. Bonds in which the issuer has the option at each interest payment date of making interest payments in cash or in additional debt securities. Those additional debt securities are referred to as baby or bunny bonds. Baby bonds generally have the same terms, including maturity dates and interest rates, as the original bonds (parent payment-in-kind bonds). Interest on baby bonds may also be paid in cash or in additional like-kind debt securities at the option of the issuer.

put option. A contract that allows the holder to sell a specified quantity of stock to the writer of the contract at a fixed price during a given period [further industry-specific information is provided in the second section of this glossary].

record-share method. A method to calculate distributions to shareholders from net investment income in which the sum of net investment income available for all classes after deducting allocated expenses, but before consideration of class-specific expenses, is divided by the total outstanding shares on the dividend record date for all classes to arrive at a gross dividend rate for all shares. From this gross rate, an amount per share for each class (the amount of incremental expenses accrued during the period divided by the record date shares outstanding for the class) is subtracted. The result is the per-share dividend available for each class.

reimbursement plan. A plan that provides for a 12b-1 fee, payable by the fund, that may not exceed the lesser of an annual percentage of the fund's average net assets or actual costs incurred by the distributor net of CDSL received by the distributor.

return of capital. Distributions by investment companies in excess of tax-basis earnings and profits.

separate account. A special account established by an insurance entity solely for the purpose of investing the assets of one or more plans. Funds in a separate account are not commingled with other assets of the insurance entity for investment purposes [further industry-specific information is provided in the second section of this glossary].

simultaneous-equations method. A method to calculate distributions to shareholders from net investment income that seeks to ensure, by using simultaneous equations, that the distribution rates will differ among the classes by the anticipated differential in expense ratios.

step bonds. Bonds that involve a combination of deferred-interest payment dates and increasing interest payment amounts over the bond lives and, thus, bear some similarity to zero-coupon bonds and to traditional debentures.

stock dividend. An issuance by a corporation of its own common shares to its common shareholders without consideration and under conditions indicating that such action is prompted mainly by a desire to give the recipient shareholders some ostensibly separate evidence of a part of their respective interests in accumulated corporate earnings without distribution of cash or other property that the board of directors or trustees deems necessary or desirable to retain in the business. A stock dividend takes nothing from the property of the corporation and adds nothing to the interests of the stockholders; that is, the corporation's property is not diminished and the interests of the stockholders are not increased. The proportional interest of each shareholder remains the same.

stock split. An issuance by a corporation of its own common shares to its common shareholders without consideration and under conditions indicating that such action is prompted mainly by a desire to increase the number of outstanding shares for the purpose of effecting a reduction in their unit market price and, thereby, of obtaining wider distribution and improved marketability of the shares. Sometimes called a stock split-up.

structured note. A debt instrument whose cash flows are linked to the movement in one or more indexes, interest rates, foreign exchange rates, commodities prices, prepayment rates, or other market variables. Structured notes are issued by U.S. government-sponsored enterprises, multilateral development banks, municipalities, and private entities. The notes typically contain embedded (but not separable or detachable) forward components or option components such as caps, calls, and floors. Contractual cash flows for principal, interest, or both can vary in amount and timing throughout the life of the note based on nontraditional indexes or nontraditional uses of traditional interest rates or indexes.

traditional 12b-1 plan. A compensation or reimbursement plan pursuant to Rule 12b-1 that permits the use of a fund's assets to pay distribution-related expenses under certain conditions. The 12b-1 fees under traditional 12b-1 plans are normally discontinued upon plan termination, but may continue to be paid after plan termination under a board-contingent plan.

transfer. The conveyance of a noncash financial asset by and to someone other than the issuer of that financial asset. A transfer includes the following

    a. Selling a receivable

    b. Putting a receivable into a securitization trust

    c. Posting a receivable as collateral.

A transfer excludes the following

    a. The origination of a receivable

    b. Settlement of a receivable

    c. The restructuring of a receivable into a security in a troubled debt restructuring [further industry-specific information is provided in the second section of this glossary].

variable annuity contract. An annuity in which the amount of payments to be made are specified in units, rather than in dollars. When payment is due, the amount is determined based on the value of the investments in the annuity fund [further industry-specific information is provided in the second section of this glossary under the term **variable annuity**].

warrant. A security that gives the holder the right to purchase shares of common stock in accordance with the terms of the instrument, usually

Glossary

upon payment of a specified amount [further industry-specific information is provided in the second section of this glossary].

workout expenditures. Professional fees (legal, accounting, appraisal) paid to entities unaffiliated with the investment company's advisor or sponsor in connection with any of the following:

    a. Capital infusions

    b. Restructurings or plans of reorganization

    c. Ongoing efforts to protect or enhance an investment

    d. The pursuit of other claims or legal actions.

The following is a list of additional terms that have been used in this guide and further information on select terms defined in the FASB ASC glossary:

401(k) plan. A plan by which an employee may elect, as an alternative to receiving taxable cash as compensation or a bonus, to contribute pretax dollars to a qualified tax-deferred retirement plan.

accumulation unit. The basic valuation unit of a deferred variable annuity. Such units are valued daily to reflect investment performance and the prorated daily deduction for expenses.

adjustable rate mortgage. A mortgage loan whose interest is reset periodically to reflect market rate changes.

adviser. See **investment adviser**.

advisory and service fee (contract). The fee charged to an investment company by its investment adviser under a contract approved by vote of a majority of the company's shares. The fee is usually computed as a percentage of the average net assets and may also provide for an additional bonus or penalty based on performance (see **incentive fee**).

affiliated company. Under Sections 2(a)(2) and 2(a)(3) of the 1940 Act, an *affiliated company* means a company that is an affiliated person. An *affiliated person of another person* means (*a*) any person directly or indirectly owning, controlling, or holding, with power to vote, 5 percent or more of the outstanding voting securities of such other person; (*b*) any person 5 percent or more of whose outstanding voting securities are directly or indirectly owned, controlled, or held, with power to vote, by such other person; (*c*) any person directly or indirectly controlling, controlled by, or under common control with such other person; (*d*) any officer, director, partner, copartner, or employees of such other person; (*e*) if such other person is an investment company, any investment adviser thereof or any member of an advisory board thereof; and (*f*) if such other person is an unincorporated investment company not having a board of directors, the depositor thereof (see **controlled company**).

against the box. Short sale by the holder of a long position in the same stock.

American depository receipt (ADR). A certificate issued by an American bank to evidence ownership of original foreign shares. The certificate is transferable and can be traded. The original foreign stock certificate is deposited with a foreign branch or correspondent bank of the issuing American bank.

as-of transaction. A transaction recorded on the books of an investment company after the date on which the transactions should have been recorded. This term relates to shareholder purchases and redemptions and also portfolio security purchases and sales.

asked price. The lowest price that a dealer is willing to accept to sell a security at a particular time (also known as the offer price).

asset allocation. Apportioning of investment funds among categories of assets, such as cash equivalents, stocks, and fixed income instruments.

baby bond. A bond having a par value of less than $1,000, usually $25–$500. Also refers to the distribution of additional bonds instead of cash payments in connection with interest payable on a payment-in-kind bond or similar security (also known as bunny bonds).

banker's acceptance. A time or sight draft drawn on a commercial bank by a borrower, usually in connection with a commercial transaction. The borrower is liable as is the bank, which is the primary obligor, to pay the draft at its face amount on the maturity date.

basis point. A measurement of changes in price or yields for fixed-income securities. One basis point equals 0.01 percent, or 10 cents per $1,000 per annum.

bid price. The highest price that a dealer is willing to pay to purchase a security at a particular time.

bifurcation. When applied to securities traded in foreign currencies, the separation of underlying factors relating to a transaction initially measured in one currency and reported in a second currency. Any difference between originally recorded amounts and currently consummated or measured amounts can be split into changes in the foreign exchange rate and changes in foreign currency-denominated fair value.

Blue Sky laws. State laws governing the sale of securities, including mutual fund shares, and activities of brokers and dealers within the particular state and applicable also in interstate transactions having some substantial connection with the state.

bond discount. The difference between the face amount of a bond and the lower price paid by a buyer.

bond premium. The difference between the face amount of a bond and the higher price paid by a buyer.

book entry shares. Share ownership evidenced by records maintained by a transfer agent, rather than by physical stock certificates.

break point. A quantity of securities purchased at which a lower sales charge takes effect. Also, an aggregate amount of investment company assets in excess of which a lower rate of investment advisory fee is chargeable.

broker. Any person engaged in the business of effecting transactions in securities for the account of others (with certain exceptions). This does not include any person solely by reason of the fact that such person is an underwriter for one or more investment companies (see Section 2[a][6] of the 1940 Act).

Glossary

business development company (BDC). A company defined in Section 2(a)(48) of the 1940 Act as a closed-end investment company that chooses to be treated as a BDC under the act and is operated to make investments in eligible portfolio companies, follow-on investments in former eligible portfolio companies acquired by the company when the investee was an eligible portfolio company, and investments in certain bankrupt or insolvent companies.

CBOE. Abbreviation for the Chicago Board Options Exchange, a national securities exchange based in Chicago that provides a continuous market for trading in put and call options.

CFTC. Abbreviation for the Commodity Futures Trading Commission, an agency established by Congress to regulate U.S. commodity futures markets and futures commission merchants. Among other things, this agency establishes rules governing the minimum financial, reporting, and audit requirements of its members. Its function is similar to that performed by the SEC in regulating broker-dealers in securities and various securities markets.

CUSIP (number). A means of uniformly describing and identifying specific security issues in numeric form. Developed by the Committee on Uniform Security Identification Procedure.

callable. Redeemable by the issuer before the scheduled maturity. The issuer may pay the holders a premium price if such a security is retired early. Such securities are usually called when interest rates fall so significantly that the issuer can save money by floating new bonds at lower rates (defined in the FASB ASC glossary, as presented in the first section of this glossary under the term **callable obligation**).

call option. A contract that entitles the holder to buy (call), at his or her option, a specified number of underlying units of a particular security at a specified price (strike price) either on (European style) or at any time until (American style) the stated expiration date of the contract. The option, which may be transferable, is bought in the expectation of a price rise above the strike price. If the price rises, the buyer exercises or sells the option. If the price does not rise, the buyer lets the option expire and loses only the cost of the option. There is a listed and also an over-the-counter (OTC) market in options. During the existence of an option, the exercise price and number of underlying units are adjusted on the ex-dividend date for cash dividends, rights, and stock dividends or splits. (Defined in the FASB ASC glossary, as presented in the first section of this glossary.)

capital gain dividend. Under Internal Revenue Code (IRC) Section 852 (and as used in chapter 6, "Taxes," of this guide), any dividend or part thereof that is reported by the company as a capital gain dividend in written statements furnished to its shareholders, except in the case of excess reported amounts. If the aggregate reported amount with respect to the company for any taxable year exceeds the net capital gain of the company for such taxable year, a capital gain dividend is the excess of the reported capital gain dividend amount over the excess reported amount that is allocable to such reported capital gain dividend amount. In nontax contexts, however, this term is used interchangeably with capital gains distribution.

capital gain or loss. A profit or loss realized from the sale of capital assets, such as *portfolio securities*, as defined in IRC Section 1221.

capital gains distribution. A dividend paid to investment company shareholders from net capital gains realized by a regulated investment company on the disposition of portfolio securities (see Section 19[b] and Rules 19a-1 and 19b-1 of the 1940 Act).

certificates of deposit. Short-term, interest-bearing certificates issued by commercial banks or savings and loan associations against funds deposited in the issuing institution.

classes of shares. Securities offered by an investment company with different shareholder requirements and commitments. For example, class A shares may be sold with a front-end load, but class B shares may be sold with a 12b-1 asset-based charge and a contingent deferred sales charge.

clearing agency. A central location at which security transactions of members are matched to determine the quantities to be received or delivered.

closed-end fund. An investment company having a fixed number of shares outstanding, which it does not stand ready to redeem. Its shares are traded similarly to those of other public corporations. See Section 5(a) of the 1940 Act. (Defined in the FASB ASC glossary, as presented in the first section of this glossary.)

collateralized mortgage obligation (CMO). A mortgage-backed bond that separates mortgage pools into different maturity classes called tranches. Each tranche is then sold separately.

commercial paper. Short-term, unsecured promissory notes issued by corporations. Commercial paper is usually sold on a discount basis (see Section 3[a][3] of the Securities Act of 1933 [the 1933 Act] and Section 3[a][10] of the Securities Exchange Act of 1934 [the 1934 Act]).

common (collective) trust fund. An account maintained by the trust department of a bank or trust company for the pooling of investment funds of its own trust account customers. It is exempt from the 1940 Act under Section 3(c)(3) or 3(c)(11).

contingent deferred sales charge (CDSC). A charge related to an issuer's payments for distribution pursuant to a Rule 12b-1 plan. It is imposed only on redemption and may be reduced or eliminated as the duration of ownership continues. Also known as a CDSL (defined in the FASB ASC glossary, as presented in the first section of this glossary).

contractual plan. A type of accumulation plan under which the total intended investment is specified with provisions for periodic payments over a stated period. Such plans are sometimes called front-end load plans because a substantial portion of the sales charge applicable to the total investment is usually deducted from early payments (see Sections 2[a][27] and 27 of the 1940 Act concerning periodic purchase plans).

control. Defined by Section 2(a)(9) of the 1940 Act as the power to exercise (regardless of whether exercised) a controlling influence over the management or policies of a company, unless that power results solely from an official position with the company (defined in the FASB ASC glossary, as presented in the first section of this glossary).

Glossary

controlled company. Defined by the 1940 Act as a direct or an indirect ownership of more than 25 percent of the outstanding voting securities of a company (see **affiliated company**).

corporate actions. An action by a company's board of directors or trustees, including dividend declarations, reorganizations, mergers, and acquisitions.

corporate bonds. Debt instruments issued by private corporations as distinct from those issued by government agencies or municipalities. Corporate bonds have three distinguishing features: they are taxable; they normally have a par value of $1,000; and they normally have a term maturity.

custodian. A bank; trust company; or, less frequently, a member of a national securities exchange responsible for receiving delivery and the safekeeping of an investment company's cash and securities (see Section 17[f] of the 1940 Act).

DTC. Acronym for the Depository Trust Company. A depository for eligible securities that facilitates clearance between member organizations and banks without the necessity of receiving or delivering actual certificates.

DVP. Abbreviation for delivery versus payment, under which physical possession and ownership are transferred only upon cash payment.

daily limits. Limits established by exchanges on fluctuations in prices of futures contracts (other than the current month's delivery contracts) during a trading session.

dealer. Any person engaged in the business of buying and selling securities for such person's own account through a broker or otherwise (does not include an insurance or investment company). Mutual fund shares are frequently sold through dealers (see Section 3[a][5] of the 1934 Act and Section 2[a][11] of the 1940 Act).

declaration date. The day on which the board of directors or trustees or, if so authorized, a committee of the board announces a distribution of cash or other specified assets to be paid at a specified future time to shareholders of record on a specified record date. The amount of distribution is usually specified on a per share basis, although investment company distributions are occasionally specified in an aggregate amount to assure the desired federal income tax consequence.

deemed dividend. A dividend not paid in cash or other consideration. For a regulated investment company, the term is used in connection with net realized long-term capital gains that are retained undistributed, in whole or part, by the regulated investment company and on which it pays the federal income tax on behalf of shareholders as a whole. Each shareholder reports his or her share of the deemed dividend as a long-term capital gain and receives (*a*) a credit against his or her federal income tax liability for his or her share of the tax paid by the regulated investment company and also (*b*) an increase in basis of those shares. (See **designated capital gain**.)

deficiency dividend. A special dividend attributable to the underdistribution of taxable income paid by a regulated investment company to protect its special tax status.

AAG-INV GLO

delayed delivery contract. A transaction involving deferral of the settlement date beyond normal terms to some point further in the future, as agreed upon by both buyer and seller.

depositor. A person other than the trustee or custodian who is primarily responsible for the organization of a unit investment trust (UIT) that deposits the portfolio with (that is, sells the portfolio to) the trustee and who has certain continuing responsibilities in administering the affairs of that trust (see Sections 17(a)(1)(C) and 26 of the 1940 Act).

designated capital gain. A term used by a regulated investment company to refer to its election to retain long-term capital gains realized during the year (see **deemed dividend**).

distributions. Dividends paid from net investment income and realized capital gains (see **capital gains distribution**).

diversification. Investment of a portfolio in securities that have different kinds of investment risk in order to moderate the portfolio's overall risk of loss. Most commonly refers to diversification by a securities issuer but can also be used in reference to industry exposure; creditworthiness or quality of security issuers taken as a whole; or, in international portfolios, exposure to national (or regional) economies. Sometimes, the term may be used in reference to security kinds (for example, fixed income versus equity securities).

diversified investment company. A management investment company having at least 75 percent of its total assets in cash and cash items (including receivables), government securities, securities of other investment companies, and other securities limited to not more than 5 percent of its total assets in any one issuer and not more than 10 percent of the voting securities of any one issuer, in accordance with Section 5(b)(1) of the 1940 Act.

dividends. Pro rata payments to shareholders, typically from earnings. In the context of investment companies, applied to payments derived from net investment income and realized capital gains (see **distributions**). (Defined in the FASB ASC glossary, as presented in the first section of this glossary.)

dollar roll. A series of securities transactions in which an investment company purchases a mortgage-backed security (such as terms to be announced) and concurrently sells that security for settlement at a future date.

eligible portfolio company. Defined by Section 2(a)(46) of the 1940 Act of 1940 as any issuer that (*a*) is organized under the laws of, and has its principal place of business in, any state or states; (*b*) is neither an investment company (other than a small business investment company [SBIC] that is licensed by the Small Business Administration [SBA] to operate under the Small Business Investment Act of 1958 and that is a wholly-owned subsidiary of the BDC) nor a company that would be an investment company, except for the exclusion from the definition of *investment company* in Section 3(c); and (*c*) satisfies one of the following: (i) does not have a class of securities registered on a national securities exchange or eligible for margin purchase under Federal Reserve Board rules; (ii) is actively controlled by a BDC, either alone or as part of a group acting together, and has an affiliate of the BDC on its board of directors; (iii) has total assets of not more than $4 million and capital and surplus (shareholders' equity less retained earnings) of not less than $2 million; (iv) meets such other criteria as the SEC may, by rule, establish as consistent with the public interest, the protection of investors, and the purposes fairly intended by the policy and provisions of the 1940 Act. In most instances, it must be a company to which the BDC extends significant managerial assistance, either through the exercise of control or through an arrangement whereby the BDC, acting through its directors, officers, and employees, provides significant guidance and counsel concerning the management, operations, or business objectives and policies of the company.

equalization. An accounting method used to prevent a dilution of the continuing shareholders' per share equity in undistributed net investment income caused by the continuous sales and redemptions of capital shares.

eurodollars. U.S. dollars deposited in banks outside the United States.

evaluator. One who determines the daily or periodic value per unit for UITs.

exchange. An organized forum for the trading of securities or commodities by members for their own accounts or the accounts of their customers. The most active U. S. securities exchange is the New York Stock Exchange (NYSE); the most active domestic commodities exchanges are the CBOE and the Chicago Mercantile Exchange. (Defined in the FASB ASC glossary, as presented in the first section of this glossary, under the term **exchange market**.)

exchange privilege. The ability of a shareholder to redeem shares of an open-end fund and simultaneously purchase shares of another open-end fund within the same family of investment companies, often at no or reduced fees. When applied to variable annuities and variable life insurance contracts, refers to the ability of an investor to exchange shares of one fund owned indirectly through the contract for another fund offered as an investment option within that contract.

exchange traded fund (ETF). A form of open-end investment company (or, less frequently, a UIT), the shares of which are traded on a stock exchange. An ETF also permits subscriptions or redemptions daily but only through the in-kind receipt or delivery of specified quantities of specific securities in exchange for a minimum number of ETF shares (referred to as a creation unit).

excise tax. A 4 percent tax imposed if a regulated investment company (RIC) fails to make minimum distributions to shareholders each calendar year. The required distribution is the sum of 98 percent of net investment income for the calendar year and 98.2 percent of capital gain net income for the 12 months ended October 31. The difference between actual distributions and the required distribution is subject to the tax. If the RIC distributed less than 100 percent of income in a prior year, the shortfall increases the current-year required distribution.

ex-dividend or ex-distribution date. Synonym for shares being traded without dividend or capital gains distribution. The buyer of a stock selling ex-dividend does not acquire a right to receive a previously declared but not-yet-paid dividend. Dividends are payable on a fixed date to shareholders recorded on the stock transfer books of the disbursing company as of a previous date of record (see **record date**). For example, a dividend may be declared as payable to holders of record on the books of the disbursing company on a given Friday. Because three business days are allowed for delivery of the security in regular-way transactions, the stock is declared ex-dividend as of the opening of the market on the preceding Wednesday (or on one business day earlier for each intervening nontrading day). Therefore, anyone buying the stock on and after Wednesday is not entitled to the dividend. For nontraded shares of mutual funds, the ex-dividend date is the same as the record date.

expense limitation. An agreement between an investment company and its investment adviser in which the adviser agrees to limit its advisory fee or the total expenses of the company to an amount that is usually based on a stipulated relationship between total expenses and average net assets. Limitations may be either contractual or voluntary.

ex-rights. Similar to ex-dividend. The buyer of a stock selling ex-rights is not entitled to a rights distribution.

ex-warrants. Stocks or bonds trading without attached warrants, entitling holders to subscribe to additional shares within specified periods and at specified prices.

FINRA. Financial Industry Regulatory Authority, formed by the combination of the regulatory functions of the National Association of Securities Dealers, Inc. (NASD) and the NYSE.

face amount certificate company. As defined by Section 28 of the 1940 Act, an investment company that issues *installment-type certificates*, as defined by Section 2(a)(15) of the act.

fixed income security. A preferred stock or debt security with a stated percentage or dollar income return.

flat. A method of trading in certain kinds of bonds, usually income bonds that do not pay interest unless it has been earned and declared payable, or bonds on which the issuer has defaulted in paying interest. The seller of a bond trading flat is not entitled to receive the interest that has accrued since the date of the last interest payment and delivers the bond with all unpaid coupons attached or a due bill authorizing the buyer to collect interest, if any, which may be paid by the issuer in the future.

forward placement commitment contract. An OTC contract for delayed delivery of securities in which the buyer agrees to buy, and the seller agrees to deliver, a specified security at a specified price at a specified future date.

forward pricing. The pricing of mutual fund shares for sale, repurchase, or redemption at a price next computed after an order has been received. Mutual fund shares are usually priced once or twice per day.

guaranteed investment contract. Nontradeable contract that guarantees the return of principal and a specific minimum rate of return on invested capital over the life of the contract. Many contracts also provide for withdrawals of principal at par at specified dates or upon specified conditions before maturity, or both. Most frequently used by pension and retirement plans in which withdrawals are permitted to fund retirement benefits, payments to employees leaving the company, or transfers of benefits among investment options (see also FASB ASC 946-210-45 and 946-210-50).

Glossary

hedge fund. An investment company seeking to minimize market risks or maximize returns by holding securities believed likely to increase in value and simultaneously being short in securities believed likely to decrease in value. The only objective is capital appreciation. Hedge funds also may use leverage techniques.

hedging. A means of risk protection against loss, typically reducing market price risk, market interest rate risk, foreign exchange risk, or credit risk.

hypothecate. To pledge securities to brokers as collateral for loans made to purchase securities or cover short sales.

illiquid. Not readily convertible into cash, such as a stock, bond, or commodity that is not actively traded and would be difficult to sell in a current sale. Not more than 15 percent of the net assets of an open-end investment company registered under the 1940 Act (5 percent for money market funds) may be invested in illiquid securities.

inadvertent investment company. An industrial or service company deemed to be an investment company because it inadvertently meets the criteria of Section 3(a) of the 1940 Act and must register under that act and comply with its provisions. Under the 1940 Act, also known as a transient investment company.

incentive allocation. A partnership allocation based upon the fund's performance reallocating profits from the capital account of a limited partner to the capital account of a general partner. The incentive may be an absolute percentage of the fund's performance or a percentage of performance in excess of a specified benchmark.

incentive fee. A fee paid to an investment adviser based upon the fund's performance for the period. The incentive may be an absolute share of the fund's performance or a share of performance in excess of a specified benchmark. For registered investment companies offered to the general public, any performance fee must be based on a comparison of performance to a specified index and must provide for an equivalent penalty if the performance fails to match the index return.

index. A statistical composite that measures changes in the economy or financial markets.

index option. Calls or puts on indexes of stock, or less frequently, other securities.

indexed security. A security whose value is based on the absolute or relative value, over a period of time or at a point in time, of a financial indicator, such as a measure of interest rates, exchange rates, commodity prices, or stock prices.

indexing. Constructing a portfolio to match the composition or performance of a broad-based index.

initial margin deposit. A commodity transaction term meaning the amount of money or its equivalent specified by the commodity exchange under which the contract is traded, held as a good faith deposit to make sure that the customer meets the variation margin requirement. Maintenance margin refers to additional deposits. (See **margin**, a securities transaction term.)

interested person. Under Section 2(a)(19) of the 1940 Act, a person affiliated with an investment company, a member of his or her *immediate family* (as defined), a person affiliated with the company's investment adviser or principal underwriter, an investment company's legal counsel, any broker or dealer or its affiliated persons, and any other person as so determined administratively by the SEC based on relationships.

interval fund. A form of closed-end fund registered using Form N-2 under the 1933 Act and the 1940 Act, which may sell shares to investors on a regular basis (as frequently as daily) but only repurchases shares at specified intervals (for example, monthly or quarterly).

inverse floater. A floating rate note in which the rate paid increases (decreases) at a multiple of declines (rises) in the floating market rate.

investment adviser (manager). Under Section 2(a)(20) of the 1940 Act, any person who, pursuant to contract with an investment company, regularly furnishes advice with respect to the desirability of investing in, purchasing or selling securities or other property, or is empowered to determine what securities or other property shall be purchased or sold.

Investment Advisers Act of 1940. Provides for the registration and regulation of most persons who render investment advice to individuals or institutions, including investment companies, for compensation.

investment advisory agreement. An agreement between an investment company and investment manager engaging the investment manager to provide investment advice to the investment company for a fee (see Sections 15[a], 15[c], and 36[b] of the 1940 Act).

investment company. An entity that pools shareholders' funds to provide the shareholders with professional investment management.

Investment Company Act of 1940. Provides for the registration and regulation of investment companies.

investment company trade associations. Such associations as the Investment Company Institute, the National Investment Company Service Association, the Mutual Fund Education Alliance, the National Association of Small Business Investment Companies, the Mutual Fund Directors Forum, the Independent Directors Council, and the Closed-End Fund Association.

investment grade bonds. Bonds rated by a rating service in one of its top four categories (AAA to BBB/Baa).

investment partnership. A partnership, usually a limited partnership, organized under state law to invest and trade in securities.

junk bonds. Bonds with a rating of BB+/Ba or lower issued by a company without a long record of sales and earnings or with questionable credit strength, which often include step-interest and payment-in-kind bonds. (Also known as high-yield bonds and defined in the FASB ASC glossary, as presented in the first section of this glossary, under the term **high-yield debt securities**.)

LIBOR (London Interbank Offered Rate). The rate of interest that the most creditworthy international banks dealing in eurodollars charge each other for large loans. Various instruments' rates are tied to LIBOR.

letter of intent. An agreement by which a shareholder agrees to buy a specified dollar amount of mutual fund shares, usually over 13 months, in return for a reduction in the sales charge applicable to a comparable lump-sum purchase.

leverage. Borrowing to enhance return. Buying securities on margin is an example of leverage.

liquidity. A measure of the ease with which a security trades in large blocks without a substantial drop in price (defined in the FASB ASC glossary, as presented in the first section of this glossary).

listed security. A security listed and traded on a stock exchange.

long. Denotes ownership or right to possession of securities.

management fee. An amount charged by an investment adviser under a contract approved by the holders of a majority of a registered investment company's outstanding shares. The fee may gradually decline as a fixed or reducing percentage of the average net assets and may also provide for an additional bonus (or penalty) based on performance. (See **incentive fee**.)

management investment company. Under Section 4(3) of the 1940 Act, a management company (often referred to as a management investment company) is defined as any investment company other than a face amount certificate company (as defined in Section 4[1]) or a UIT (as defined in Section 4[2]). The term *management company* is sometimes used to refer to the investment adviser of an investment company.

margin. A securities transaction term meaning the amount of money or its equivalent, specified by the Board of Governors of the Federal Reserve System, that a customer must deposit with a broker in a securities transaction on margin (see **initial margin deposit**, a commodity transaction term).

margin account. A means of leveraging offered by security brokers or dealers to permit their customers to buy securities, in part, with borrowed funds. The difference between the price of a security and funds provided by the customer is loaned by the broker or dealer to the customer.

market price. Usually the last reported price at which a security has been sold or, if the security was not traded or trading prices are not reported, a price arrived at based on recent bid and asked prices.

mark-to-market. A procedure to adjust the carrying value of a security, an option, or a futures contract to fair value.

matrix pricing. A mathematical technique used to value normal institutional-sized trading units of debt securities without relying exclusively on quoted prices of the specific security. Factors such as the issue's coupon or stated interest rate, maturity, rating, and quoted prices of similar issues are considered in developing the issue's current market yield.

money market fund. A mutual fund whose investments are primarily or exclusively in short-term debt securities designed to maximize current income with liquidity and capital preservation, usually maintaining per share net asset value at a constant amount, such as $1.

money market investments. Short-term government obligations, commercial paper, bankers' acceptances, and certificates of deposit, of high credit standing and typically with remaining terms to maturity of one year or less.

municipal bond fund. An investment company whose shares represent holdings solely or largely of securities on which interest is exempt from federal income taxes.

municipal notes and bonds. Securities that are issued by states, cities, and other local government authorities to fund public projects. The interest on these bonds is often exempt from federal taxes and, under certain conditions, is exempt from state and local taxes. Municipal notes usually mature in less than three years.

mutual fund. The popular name for an open-end management investment company (see **open-end investment company**).

NASDAQ. Abbreviation for the NASDAQ Stock Market, an electronic stock market (formerly known as the National Association of Securities Dealers Automated Quotation System).

NASD. Acronym for the National Association of Securities Dealers, Inc. Formerly an association of broker-dealers doing business in the OTC market. Prior to its incorporation into FINRA, NASD supervised and regulated the trading conduct and sales practices of its members.

NSCC. Abbreviation of the National Securities Clearing Corporation, a subsidiary of the Depository Trust & Clearing Corporation that provides trade processing, clearance, delivery, and settlement services to its members. It deals with brokers, dealers, and banks in the United States and Canada.

NYSE. Acronym for the New York Stock Exchange. It is the largest securities exchange in the United States. The NYSE also furnishes facilities for its members, allied members, member firms, and member corporations to aid them in conducting securities business.

net assets. The term used by an investment company to designate the excess of the fair value of securities owned, cash, receivables, and other assets over the liabilities of the company.

net asset value per share. The value per share of outstanding capital stock of an investment company computed (usually daily by mutual funds) by dividing net assets by the total number of shares outstanding. (See Rule 2a-4 of the 1940 Act; defined in the FASB ASC glossary, as presented in the first section of this glossary).

no-action letter. A letter issued to an investment adviser or investment company (registrant) by the staff of the SEC in response to a request filed by the registrant describing a proposed business activity that may or may not conform to SEC rules and regulations. In a no-action letter, the SEC staff indicates whether, based on the facts presented by the registrant, the SEC staff will recommend no action be taken against the registrant for engaging in the proposed activity. A no-action letter does not have the force of law; however, it represents an interpretation of the SEC staff that may be applied in a situation in which the registrant is engaging in an activity not addressed by existing SEC rules and regulations.

no-load fund. A mutual fund selling and redeeming its shares at net asset value without adding sales charges, although some such funds have Rule 12b-1 plans permitting payment of distribution expenses with fund assets. A mutual fund may not call itself no load if a 12b-1 fee is levied exceeding 0.25 percent of fund assets per year. Investors deal directly with the fund, not through an investment dealer or broker.

nondiversified investment company. A management investment company other than a *diversified company*, as defined in Section 5(b) of the 1940 Act.

offering price. The price at which mutual fund shares or investment trust units can be bought, often equaling net asset value plus a sales load.

offset. A closing transaction involving the purchase or sale of an option or futures contract having the same features as one already held. This could be a hedge, such as a short sale of a stock, to protect capital gain or the purchase of a futures contract to protect a commodity price or a straddle representing the purchase of offsetting put and call options on a security.

offshore fund. An investment company organized outside the United States.

open contract. An unperformed or unsettled contract. May be used in referring to new issues traded when, as, and if issued or in referring to commodity futures trading. The term is used to designate contracts bought or sold and still outstanding.

open-end investment company. A mutual fund that is ready to redeem its shares at any time and that usually offers its shares for sale to the public continuously (see Section 5[a][1] of the 1940 Act).

original issue discount. A federal income tax term for interest to the holder of a bond that represents the difference between the face amount of a bond and its original sales price.

over-the-counter (OTC). A securities trading market made up of broker-dealers that may or may not be members of a securities exchange. Securities are traded in the OTC market between broker-dealers acting either as principals (dealers) or agents for customers (brokers). The OTC market is the principal market for U.S. government bonds, corporate bonds, and municipal securities, and a substantial number of U.S. equity securities are traded on an OTC basis.

passive foreign investment company (PFIC). A foreign corporation is a PFIC if either 75 percent of its gross income is passive, or 50 percent or more of the average value of its assets, computed quarterly, produce or could produce *passive income*, as defined in the IRC.

payable date. The date on which a dividend is payable to holders of record on some previous record date.

penny-rounding method. A method permitted by Rule 2a-7 of the 1940 Act under which the net asset value per share of a money market fund is computed based on the fair values of all investments and then rounded to the nearest 1 percent.

performance fee. See **incentive fee**.

AAG-INV GLO

periodic payment plan. See **accumulation unit** and Sections 2(a)(27) and 27 of the 1940 Act.

personal holding company. An income tax term defined as a corporation of which 60 percent of adjusted ordinary gross income is *personal holding company income,* as defined in the IRC, and 5 or fewer individuals own more than 50 percent in value of its outstanding stock during the last half of the taxable year.

point. A rise or decline of $1 per share used to refer to the purchase or sale of stocks. If used for the purchase or sale of bonds, the term means a rise or decline of $10 per $1,000 principal amount.

portfolio. Securities owned by an investment company or other investor in securities.

portfolio turnover rate. A measure of portfolio activity calculated for an investment company by dividing the lesser of purchases or sales of securities, excluding securities having maturity dates at acquisition of one year or less, by the average value of the portfolio securities held during the period (see Form N-SAR instructions to item 71, Form N-1A Item 13 Instruction 4(d), and Form N-2 Item 4 Instruction 17).

premium on redemptions (repurchases). See **redemption (repurchase) fee (or charge)**.

price make-up sheet. A detailed computation of the net asset value of a mutual fund.

principal. A person, especially a dealer, who buys or sells securities for his or her own account. Also refers to the face amount of a security without accrued interest.

principal underwriter. See **distributor**, defined in the FASB ASC glossary, as presented in the first section of this glossary, and the definition of *underwriter* in Section 2(a)(40) of the 1940 Act.

private placement. The direct sale of a block of securities of a new or secondary issue to a single investor or group of investors. The sale or placement is usually made through an investment banker, and the securities' public resale is restricted if they are not registered under the 1933 Act. (See **restricted security**.)

prospectus. A circular required by the 1933 Act describing securities being offered for sale to the public (see Section 2[a][31] of the 1940 Act).

proxy. A person authorized to vote the shares of an absent shareholder at a meeting of shareholders. Also refers to the written authorization given to that person. (See Section 20[a] of the 1940 Act.)

proxy statement. A publication sent to stockholders by a board of directors or trustees or its adversaries or others usually containing financial reports (for merger and other financial proposals), stockholders' meeting notices, and voting information on certain matters to solicit proxies from the holders (see Rule 20a-1 under the 1940 Act and Regulation 14A under the 1934 Act).

put option. A contract that entitles the holder to sell (put), at his or her option, a specified number of underlying units of a particular security at a specified price (strike price) either on (European-style) or at any time until (American-style) the contract's stated expiration date. The option, which may be transferable, is bought in the expectation that the price will decline below the strike price. If the price declines below the strike price, the buyer exercises or sells the option. If the price does not decline below the strike price, the buyer lets the option expire and loses only the cost of the option. There are both listed and OTC markets in options. During the existence of an option, the exercise price and number of underlying units are adjusted on the ex-dividend date for cash dividends, rights, and stock dividends or splits (defined in the FASB ASC glossary, as presented in the first section of this glossary).

real estate mortgage investment conduit (REMIC). An investment vehicle created to hold pools of mortgages and to issue two classes of interest in the REMIC: regular interest and residual interests. The vehicle is not subject to taxation and may be used to protect investors in mortgage-related instruments from double taxation.

realized gain or loss. See **capital gain or loss**.

record date. The date on which an owner of a share of stock must be registered on the books of a company as a shareholder to receive a declared dividend or, among other things, to vote on company affairs.

recordkeeping agent. An outside service bureau, bank, or other agency engaged by an investment company to maintain records of purchases and sales of investments, sales and redemptions of fund shares, and shareholders' account statements.

redemption. A stockholder's tender of investment company shares to the company or person designated by the company, requiring liquidation of such shares in exchange for proceeds, usually in cash, representing the net asset value of the shares tendered, occasionally less a redemption fee (see Section 2[a][32] of the 1940 Act).

redemption in kind. Redemption of investment company shares by payment in portfolio securities, not cash. Permissible in certain circumstances for many mutual funds and tax-free exchange funds. (see Rule 18f-1 under the 1940 Act).

redemption or repurchase price. The price, net asset value less a redemption fee, at which a share of a mutual fund is redeemed or repurchased (see Section 2[a][32] of the 1940 Act).

redemption (repurchase) fee (or charge.) A percentage of net asset value that may be charged to the investor on redemptions or repurchases of an open-end investment company's shares (see Section 10[d][4] of the 1940 Act).

registered investment company. An investment company that has filed a registration statement with the SEC as an investment company, in accordance with the requirements of the 1940 Act. The *investment company*, as defined in Section 3(a) of the act, primarily invests, reinvests, or trades in securities; issues face-amount certificates; or engages in investing and owning investment securities, other than government securities, that have a value exceeding 40 percent of the company's total assets (Section 3[a][1]), with some exceptions to the latter (stated in Section 3[b]).

AAG-INV GLO

registrar. Usually a trust company or bank responsible for preventing the issuance of more stock than authorized by the issuing company (see **transfer agent**).

regulated investment company (RIC). An investment company that qualifies for the special tax treatment provided for by IRC subchapter M.

Regulation S-X. Accounting rules for the form and content of financial statements and schedules required under the 1933 Act, the 1934 Act, and the Energy Policy and Conservation Act of 1975. Article 6 applies to financial statements for, and specified rules in article 12 apply to financial schedules of, registered investment companies.

reinvestment. The automatic purchase of additional shares using the proceeds of dividends and capital gain distributions.

repurchase. Liquidation of investment company shares through a principal underwriter or a broker-dealer on behalf of shareholders, sometimes for a purchase or service charge or brokerage commission.

repurchase agreement. An agreement under which an investment company pays for and receives (purchases) securities from a seller who agrees to repurchase them within a specified time at a specified price. A repurchase agreement is known on the side of a selling broker-dealer or other seller as a reverse repurchase agreement.

restricted security. A portfolio security that may be sold privately but that is required to be registered with the SEC or exempted from such registration before it may be sold in a public distribution. A private placement stock is frequently referred to as letter stock.

return. See **yield**.

reverse repurchase agreement. An agreement under which the investment company transfers (sells) securities for cash to another party (purchaser), usually a broker, and agrees to repurchase them within a specified time at a specified price. A reverse repurchase agreement is known in the broker-dealer industry as a repurchase agreement.

right. A privilege offered by a corporation to its shareholders pro rata to subscribe to a certain security at a specified price, often for a short period. Rights may or may not be transferable.

right of accumulation. A method permitting aggregation of mutual fund shares being acquired with shares previously acquired and currently owned to qualify for a quantity discount that reduces the sales charge on a single purchase.

Rule 2a-7. A rule under the 1940 Act that permits money market funds to value investments at amortized cost or through the use of the penny-rounding method.

Rule 12b-1. A rule under Section 12 of the 1940 Act that permits the use of a fund's assets to pay distribution-related expenses under conditions prescribed therein (see **board-contingent plan** and **enhanced 12b-1 plan** defined in the FASB ASC glossary, as presented in the first section of this glossary).

Rule 144A. A rule under the 1933 Act that provides a safe harbor exemption from the registration requirements for resales of restricted securities to qualified institutional buyers.

SBA. Acronym for the Small Business Administration, an agency established by Congress to administer the Small Business Investment Company Act of 1958.

SBIC. Acronym for a small business investment company, an investment company registered under the Small Business Investment Company Act of 1958 and established to provide capital to small business enterprises.

SEC. Acronym for the Securities and Exchange Commission, an agency established by Congress to administer federal securities laws.

sale against the box. Similar to a short sale, except that the seller already owns the stock being sold but keeps possession of it and, therefore, has to borrow the equivalent stock to deliver to the purchaser.

sales charge. An amount providing for the underwriter's and dealer's commission that is added to the net asset value of an open-end investment company's shares in computing the offering price and stated as a percentage of the offering price. A sales charge can also be imposed on redemption.

Section 4(2). A section of the 1933 Act that exempts transactions by an issuer not involving a public offering from registration under that act.

Securities Act of 1933 (1933 Act). Principal federal law regulating the public offering of corporate securities. Among other things, it regulates the contents of prospectuses and similar documents and is intended to ensure that potential investors receive adequate information to make reasonably informed investment decisions.

Securities Exchange Act of 1934 (1934 Act). Regulates securities brokers and dealers, stock exchanges, transfer agents, and the trading of securities in the securities markets. Also, among other things, establishes requirements for periodic reporting by registrants.

Securities Investor Protection Corporation (SIPC). A federal corporation established for the purpose of protecting customers of broker-dealers in financial difficulty.

securities lending. The practice of lending portfolio securities, usually for delivery against a short sale. The loan is usually collateralized by cash or government securities.

seed money. An initial amount of capital contributed to a company at its inception (see Section 14[a] of the 1940 Act).

senior security. Under Section 18 of the 1940 Act, any obligation constituting a security (as defined) and evidencing indebtedness and any class of equity security having priority over any other class with respect to distribution of assets and payment of dividends.

separate account. An account established and maintained by an insurance company that holds particular assets allocated to that account and is credited or charged with income, gains, or losses from these assets separately from income, gains, or losses of the insurance company's general accounts.

Sometimes referred to as a variable account, a separate account funds variable annuities or variable life insurance policies. Although it is not an entity but is only an account within the insurance company, it may be an *investment company* within the meaning of the 1940 Act. (See Section 2[a][37] of the act; defined in the FASB ASC glossary, as presented in the first section of this glossary.)

series fund. An investment company that offers multiple segregated portfolios of common stock (see Rule 6-03[j] of Regulation S-X).

settlement date. The date on which security transactions are settled by delivering or receiving securities and receiving or paying cash pursuant to an earlier agreement of purchase and sale called a trade (see **trade date**).

short. A stock record position representing the physical location of a security (such as box, transfer, and so forth) or meaning that the security is due from others (such as failed to receive or owed to the brokerage concern by a customer due to a short sale).

short sale. A sale of securities that requires borrowing equivalent securities to make delivery to the purchaser.

Small Business Investment Incentive Act of 1980. Amended the 1940 Act by, among other things, allowing closed-end companies to elect to be regulated as BDCs under Section 2(a)(48) and Sections 54–65 of the 1940 Act (see **business development company [BDC]**).

Small Business Investment Company Act of 1958. Authorizes the SBA to provide government funds to small business investment companies licensed under that act.

spread. A combination of put and call options at different prices—one below and the other above the current market price—for the same quantity of a security. Also refers to the difference between the bid and asked prices of a security and to the dealer's commission on a security offering.

standby commitment contract. An agreement to accept future delivery of a security at a guaranteed price or fixed yield on exercise of an option held by the other party to the agreement.

straddle. A combination of one put and one call option, identical with respect to the security issue, number of shares, exercise price, and expiration date.

stripping. The brokerage practice of separating a fixed income security into its corpus and coupons, which are then sold separately.

synthetic floaters. A structured instrument that uses the principal of, and a portion of the interest payments from, long-term municipal bonds, (in some cases combined with interest rate swaps), to create an investment that pays a floating short-term interest rate. Often issued in tandem with inverse floaters. Many synthetic floaters are known as "tender option bonds", as they include the right to put the instruments to the issuer or a third party at regular intervals, or upon the occurrence of certain events, at a stated price (usually par).

TBA. Abbreviation for to be announced future government-sponsored enterprises' pools that are bought and sold for future settlement. TBA refers to the announcement of the specific pools to be delivered or received.

tender offer. A public offer to buy from all current holders not less than a specified amount of an issuer's securities at a fixed price.

total return. A periodic measure of a fund's overall change in value that assumes the reinvestment of dividends and capital gain distributions. (Total return is a standardized method prescribed by the SEC, as described in item 26 of Form N-1A.)

trade. An agreement of purchase and sale in a securities market to be settled or performed by payment and delivery on a later settlement date.

trade date. The date that a security transaction is actually entered into to be settled on a later settlement date.

transfer. A change of ownership of registered securities on the books of the issuer (defined in the FASB ASC glossary, as presented in the first section of this glossary).

transfer agent. An agent for a securities issuer who keeps records of the names of the issuer's registered shareholders, their addresses, and the number of shares that they own. The agent must be sure that certificates presented to the office for transfer are canceled and that new certificates are issued in the name of the transferee. (See **registrar**.)

turnover. The frequency at which securities are purchased and sold by an investment company.

undertaking. An agreement between a registrant and the SEC staff in connection with the filing of a registration statement whereby the registrant agrees to take a future action requested by the staff but not otherwise necessarily or expressly required by the securities' statutes but (in a federal registration) that may be required by SEC rules or SEC forms that have the same legal status as the rules by which they were adopted.

underwriting. The act of distributing a new issue of securities (primary offering) or a large block of previously issued securities (secondary offering). A firm-commitment underwriting obligates the underwriter to purchase the underwritten securities, regardless of whether they can be resold. A best-efforts underwriting only obligates the underwriter to buy from the issuer only those securities that it is able to sell to purchasers.

unit investment trust (UIT). An investment company organized under a trust indenture that issues only redeemable securities, each of which represents an undivided interest in a unit of specified (usually unmanaged) securities (see Section 26 of the 1940 Act).

unlisted security. A security that is not listed on a securities exchange (see **over-the-counter [OTC]**).

unrealized appreciation or depreciation. The excess (appreciation) or deficiency (depreciation) of the fair value of securities over (under) their cost.

unregistered securities. Securities that are not registered under the 1933 Act.

variable annuity. An annuity having a provision for the accumulation of an account value, benefit payments, or both that vary according to the investment experience of the separate account to which the amounts paid for the annuity are allocated (defined in the FASB ASC glossary, as presented in the first section of this glossary, under the term **variable annuity contract**).

variation margin. A term used in commodity operations. Refers to last-day point fluctuation—a difference between the settling price of the day before and the last day's settling price—on net positions long and short.

venture capital investment company. A closed-end investment company whose primary investment objective is capital growth and whose capital is usually invested wholly or largely in restricted securities in negotiated transactions to form or develop companies with new ideas, products, or processes.

warrant. A type of option to purchase additional securities from the issuer. Commonly affixed to the certificates for other securities at the time when the combined securities units are originally issued and usually separable, sometimes, on and after a subsequent date. Also, a document evidencing options to purchase shares. (Defined in the FASB ASC glossary, as presented in the first section of this glossary.)

wash sale. A sale of stock or other securities in which a taxpayer has acquired or entered a contract or option to acquire substantially identical stock or other securities within a period beginning 30 days before and ending 30 days after the date of the sale (a 61-day period). A loss resulting from such a sale is not deductible for federal income tax purposes, but a gain is taxable. (See IRC Section 1091.)

when-issued. A short form designation for when, as, and if issued. The term indicates a conditional transaction in a security authorized for issuance but not yet actually issued. All such transactions are settled if and when the actual security is issued.

yield. The return on investment that an investor receives from dividends or interest expressed as a percentage of the current market price of the security or, if the investor already owns the security, the price paid. Yield also may refer to the SEC yield, a standardized yield calculation method prescribed by the SEC based upon interest and dividend income of the fund (see item 26 of the instructions to Form N-1A).

yield to maturity. The rate of return on a debt security held to maturity, giving effect to the stated interest rate, accrual of discount, and amortization of premium.

zero coupon bond. A type of debt instrument that makes no periodic interest payment but is issued at a deep discount from its face value. The holder derives his or her return from the gradual appreciation in the value of the security, which redeems at face value at a specified maturity date.

AICPA® Online Professional Library

Powerful Online Research Tools

The AICPA Online Professional Library offers the most current access to comprehensive accounting and auditing literature, as well business and practice management information, combined with the power and speed of the Web. Through your online subscription, you'll get:

- Cross-references within and between titles — smart links give you quick access to related information and relevant materials
- First available updates — no other research tool offers access to new AICPA standards and conforming changes more quickly, guaranteeing that you are always current with all of the authoritative guidance!
- Robust search engine — helps you narrow down your research to find your results quickly
- And much more...

Choose from two comprehensive libraries or select only the titles you need!

With the *Essential A&A Research Collection*, you gain access to the following:
- AICPA Professional Standards
- AICPA Technical Practice Aids
- PCAOB Standards & Related Rules
- Accounting Trends & Techniques
- All current AICPA Audit and Accounting Guides
- All current Audit Risk Alerts

One-year individual online subscription
Item # ORS-XX

OR

***Premium A&A Research Collection* and get everything from the *Essential A&A Research Collection* plus:**
- AICPA Audit & Accounting Manual
- All current Checklists & Illustrative Financial Statements
- eXacct: Financial Reporting Tools & Techniques
- IFRS Accounting Trends & Techniques

One-year individual online subscription
Item # WAL-BY

You can also add the FASB *Accounting Standards Codification*™ and the GASB Library to either collection.

Take advantage of a 30-day free trial!
See for yourself how these powerful online libraries can improve your productivity and simplify your accounting research.

Visit **cpa2biz.com/library** for details or to subscribe.